Transport Economics

Transport Economics
4th Edition

Kenneth Button

University Professor, Schar School of Policy and Government, George Mason University, USA

EE Edward Elgar
PUBLISHING

Cheltenham, UK • Northampton, MA, USA

Published by
Edward Elgar Publishing Limited
The Lypiatts
15 Lansdown Road
Cheltenham
Glos GL50 2JA
UK

Edward Elgar Publishing, Inc.
William Pratt House
9 Dewey Court
Northampton
Massachusetts 01060
USA

A catalogue record for this book
is available from the British Library

Library of Congress Control Number: 2022931653

ISBN 978 1 78643 566 8 (cased)
ISBN 978 1 78643 568 2 (paperback)
ISBN 978 1 78643 567 5 (eBook)

Typeset by Cheshire Typesetting Ltd, Cuddington, Cheshire

Printed and bound in Great Britain by TJ Books Ltd, Padstow, Cornwall

Contents

Preface

The first edition of *Transport Economics* appeared in 1982. This, the fourth edition, provides an update of the subject together with current data, case studies, and examples.

A lot has changed in the study of transport economics over the past 40 years, and changes continue. Many of these are the result of a better understanding of economics in general. Others are more transport-specific and reflect social, technical, and political developments. An updating of *Transport Economics* is seen as necessary to reflect both of these broad categories of change.

Improved and more complete data, greater use of mathematics and advanced econometrics, the emergence of experimental economics, and advances in computer technology have seen more technical rigor introduced into economics. And the changes have been part of the way transport economics has changed. This revised edition of *Transport Economics* reflects some of these developments. But these are refinements rather than revolutions. Much of our core understanding of transport economics remains intact. The increased recognition of the role of behavioral economics which allows relaxation of some traditional assumptions regarding human behavior is, for example, still seen by most as a refinement rather than a major paradigm shift.

Although conforming to general economic rules, transport is also very contextual and contexts change. There have been, for example, major technology changes, even over the decade since the appearance of the last edition of this book. New forms of local transport have emerged including transportation network companies like Uber and Lyft and micromobility modes such as electric-scooters. The development of the smartphone, and in particular Apple's iPhone in 2007, has led to almost universal access to global positioning systems and, with this, real-time information for route guidance and tracking. This has affected both the ways individuals plan and adjust their travel as well as the ways in which freight-supply chains are designed and operated. These, and other technology shifts, influence the specifics of individual markets and are considered in this new edition.

Additionally, much of the drafting of this edition took place during the Covid-19 pandemic. The impact of this, and the associated policy actions to reduce its spread, had immediate and obvious implications for transport at all levels of aggregation. In many cases, such as commuting, shopping, and tourism it reduced individual travel greatly. In other cases, as with the transport of medication and the home delivery of food and other supplies, it increased the movement of goods is specific types of markets. Supply-chain economics has taken on new dimensions in our lives. These are certainly matters of the moment and require the immediate attention of politicians and practitioners as well as filling the media. But their longer-term effects are less certain.

While, at the time of writing, there has been evidence of a movement back to something like what may be considered 'the norm' that prevailed before 2020, the precise details of how the post-pandemic world will look are still unclear. What is assumed here is that the fundamentals of transport economics essentially remain intact even if the qualitative and quantitative parameters change post-Covid. In other words, the theories and methodologies underpinning transport economics remain valid, even though the magnitudes of individual parameters in specific markets may have changed. The basic principles of supply and demand still hold: if the price of gasoline rises, less will still be demanded even if the effect is quantitively different to past experiences.

The book retains the 14-chapter format of recent past editions. This broadly conforms to a chapter a week per semester. The chapters, although following a particular path, can also be used independently as free-standing modules.

To assist in pedagogy, 20 or so free-standing 'Exhibits' now provide a variety of case studies and narratives to supplement the text. These are designed to add greater flesh to the economic theory. More up-to-date examples and illustrations also make the understanding of economic principles easier and assist in the assimilation of economic concepts.

Additionally, there are changes to the referencing style compared to the three previous editions. I adopt the Harvard Manual (author–date citation) style in place of the Chicago (footnote) style. This is more in line with usage in modern economic writing. The referencing is still light and focuses on material useful when following up ideas and events. The book remains a mixture of prose, tables, figures, graphs, and equations, the aim being to help understanding rather than to overpower or impress the reader with advanced technique.

As in the past, I hope that teachers, students, and other readers will find the new edition of *Transport Economics* interesting and useful.

Finally, a large word of thanks for the comments on previous editions that I have received over the years from students, academics, practitioners, and others. I may not have taken them all on board, but they have all been tremendously helpful in the production of this work.

Kenneth Button

Acronyms

AVI	automatic vehicle identification
BAH	British Airports Holdings
BAC	blood alcohol concentration
BART	Bay Area Rapid Transit (United States)
BOOT	build, own, operate, and transfer
BTC	British Transport Commission
BTU	British thermal unit
CAA	Civil Aviation Authority (United Kingdom)
CAB	Civil Aeronautics Board (United States)
CAFC	company average fuel consumption (Canada)
CAFE	corporate average fuel economy (United States)
CBA	cost–benefit analysis
CBD	central business district
CBSA	core-based statistical area
CFC	chlorofluorocarbon
CIF	cost, insurance, and freight
CO	carbon monoxide
CO_2	carbon dioxide
CORSIA	Carbon Offsetting and Reduction Scheme for International Aviation
Covid	coronavirus disease
CRS	computer reservation system
CTP	Common Transport Policy (European Union)
C-TPAT	Customs–Trade Partnership Against Terrorism
dB	decibel
DBF	design, build, and finance
DBFM	design, build, finance, and maintain
DBFOM	design, build, finance, operate, and maintain
DEA	data envelopment analysis
DICE	dynamic integrated climate change
EPA	Environmental Protection Agency (United States)
EU	European Union
EUAA	European Union Aviation Allowances
EU ETS	European Union Emissions Trading System
FAA	Federal Aviation Administration (United States)
FAMS	Federal Air Marshal Service
FFDO	Federal Flight Deck Officer
FHWA	Federal Highways Administration (United States)

FOB	free on board
FOC	flight operating cost
FUND	framework for uncertainty, negotiation, and distribution
GATT	General Agreement on Tariffs and Trade
GDP	gross domestic product
GNP	gross national product
GPS	global positioning systems
HATS	household activities travel simulator
HC	hydrocarbons
HGV	heavy goods vehicle
HOV	high-occupancy vehicle
HSR	high-speed rail
IAM	integrated assessment model
IATA	International Air Transport Association
ICAO	International Civil Aviation Organization
ICC	Interstate Commerce Commission (United States)
IPSB	installation of physical secondary barriers
ITS	intelligent transport system
LRMC	long-run marginal cost
MAC	marginal abatement costs
Maglev	magnetic levitation rail system
MIDAS	Motorway Incident Detection and Automatic Signalling (United Kingdom)
mpg	miles per gallon
MSA	metropolitan statistical area
NAFTA	North American Free Trade Agreement
NATA	New Approach to Appraisal
NATS	National Air Traffic Services (United Kingdom)
NEF	noise exposure forecast
NHS	National Highway System (United States)
NHTSA	National Highway Traffic Safety Administration (United States)
NNI	Noise and Numbers Index
NO_X	nitrogen oxides
NTT	new trade theory
OECD	Organisation for Economic Co-operation and Development
OPEC	Organization of the Petroleum Exporting Countries
O_3	ozone
PAGE	policy analysis of the greenhouse effect
PAYD	pay-as-you-drive
Pb	lead
PBS	planning balance sheet
pcu	passenger car unit
PNdB	perceived noise decibel
PPP	public–private partnership
PSV	public service vehicles

PTA	passenger transport authority
PZEV	partial zero emission vehicle
RHTM	regional highway traffic model (United Kingdom)
RRL	Road Research Laboratory
RTA	regional trade area
SCC	social cost of carbon
SELNEC	South-east Lancashire, North-east Cheshire (United Kingdom)
SO$_2$	sulfur dioxide
SRMC	short-run marginal cost
SUV	sports utility vehicle
TEN	Trans-European Network
TEU	twenty-foot equivalent unit
TFP	total factor productivity
TGV	*Train à Grande Vitesse* (France)
TNC	transportation network company
TPP	Transport Policy and Programme
UPTPS	Urban Public Transport Planning System
US DOT	United States Department of Transportation
USMCA	United States–Mexico–Canada Agreement
UNCTAD	United Nations Conference on Trade and Development
VOC	volatile organic compound
WTO	World Trade Organization
ZEV	zero emission vehicle

1   Transport, Economics, and Economists

1.1   Some Background

Clifford Winston (2013) begins his assessment of the state of United States transport by summarizing exactly what transport[1] is:

> Transportation is a friction – a cost in both money and time – that must be incurred
> by individuals and firms to complete almost any market transaction. An efficient and
> extensive transportation system greatly enriches the standard of living in modern
> society by reducing the cost of nearly everything in the economy; expanding indi-
> viduals' access to and choices of employers and employers' choices of workers; ena-
> bling firms and urban residents to benefit from the spatial concentration of economic
> activities, referred to as agglomeration economies; reducing trade costs and allowing
> firms to realize efficiency gains from specialization, comparative advantage, and
> increasing returns; and limiting firms' ability to obtain market power by locating in
> geographically isolated markets with no competition.

In 1982 I opened the first edition of *Transport Economics* with a quote taken
from an address to the United Kingdom's Chartered Institute of Transport by
K.J.W. Alexander (1975). He made the rather sober point that despite the importance of transport in the economy:

> the number of academic economists who specialize exclusively in transport could
> probably be counted on two hands. If one adds to these economists the applied
> economists employed in the transport business and the specialist consultants working
> exclusively in that field I would be surprised if the total number exceeded sixty or
> seventy.

In other words, while transport is, as Winston highlighted nearly 40 years
later, a crucial part of any successful economy, the number of active transport
economists is relatively small. There are certainly more than 60 or 70 today, but
transport still tends to be dominated by engineers, and more recently by those
engaged in supply-chain management.

This paucity of transport economists is rather strange given the fascina-
tion that transport has held for very eminent economists. Indeed, John Maynard
Keynes, perhaps the most eminent and disruptive economist in the twentieth century, once confessed that when young, 'I find economics increasingly

---

[1] The English term 'transport' is used throughout as opposed to the more common
American term 'transportation' to avoid any confusion with the penal sentences given
in the past to British criminals. Proper nouns are exempted.

satisfactory, and I think I am rather good at it. I want to manage a railway, or organize a trust or at least swindle the investing public'.

We also find that some of the more contemporary economists began their academic careers delving into transport-related questions. The Nobel Prize awardee James Buchanan, for example, was early in his career interested in road finance and indeed wrote his Master's dissertation on 'Gasoline tax sharing among local units of government in Tennessee'. Another laureate, Vernon Smith, had an interest in aircraft landing slot pricing, and yet another, William Vickrey, in road congestion and public transport supply. Maurice Allais, the 1988 laureate, gave his name to the European Economic Community's 1965 report, 'Choice of pricing policy for transport', perhaps a somewhat unexpected exercise for a physicist turned theoretical economist. Drifting to the extreme periphery of transport-related work, Richard Thaler, the 2017 recipient of the award, made significant advances in behavioral economics by, among other things, studying the use of male urinal pans at Amsterdam Airport!

The situation as seen by Alexander in the mid-1970s largely continued in the 1990s when the second edition of *Transport Economics* was published. There were more transport economists in the public sector generally assisting in engineering activities and investment appraisal, but still their number was not large. Most academic transport economists were likewise linked to civil engineering departments, with a few in business schools. In the United States, it was often taught as part of a public utilities program.

By the time the third edition of *Transport Economics* went into proofs in 2009 there were certainly more, but still relatively few economists specializing in the subject. But there was one significant change. The field of transport logistics had developed considerably and was making extensive use of economics. One reason for this was the widespread deregulation of transport markets throughout the world from the 1980s. This had resulted in suppliers of transport services being subjected much more to market forces. They were less restricted by government-imposed constraints and essentially had to think for themselves. They needed to maximize efficiency to survive in competitive conditions. Put simply, transport economists could help a company's bottom line by highlighting opportunity costs.

Of course, the world had also moved on in other ways. Logistics involving the planning, implementing, and controlling procedures for efficient and effective transport and storage of goods, including services and related information, from the point of origin to the point of consumption, had increased in importance. The world economy had also become more global both in terms of person and goods movement and inevitably this threw up a variety of new transport challenges. There were now mega global supply chains and manufacturers dominating the value of trade. Economics offers a portfolio of models to tackle some of these issues arising in the new world. It has become a core component of professionally oriented degrees in managerial science.

A second important change by 2009 was that people had become seriously concerned with the state of the environment, and notions such as sustainable development had taken center-stage. Transport imposes a variety of environment costs on society, ranging from the very local problem of urban traffic noise to emitting huge amounts of gases that contribute to global warming. Economics provides ways of assessing the potential costs and benefits of policies designed to contain, if not always remove, the adverse environmental costs of transport.

In subsequent editions of this book, I therefore saw little reason to drop Alexander's quote, and, although there had been something of a minor upsurge in interest in transport economics, the subject still forms a small branch of the economic discipline.

Moving into the 2020s, the important role of transport logistics and the issues surrounding sustainable transport remain, and while the growth in world trade has been temporarily slowed by the Covid-19 pandemic, transport economics seems to have become more important. Accompanying this, the information systems required to ensure networks work smoothly have grown in sophistication and created their own economic challenges. Individuals, for example, use global positioning systems (GPS) to plan and track their own movements and businesses, whether public or private, make extensive use of information systems in tracking, controlling, and managing the transport of their own goods, or in the case of passenger modes, their 'human cargoes'. Network and information economics now inevitably interfaces and overlaps with transport economics.

We also have new technologies and transport systems. While these often involve greater mass movement by mega mode – for example, super jumbo-jets and larger container ships – they also entail innovations at the local level with the emergence of transport network companies such as Uber, and micromobility as offered by electric-scooters (commonly known as 'e-scooters'). The managerial and operational models for some of these latter modes, and perhaps especially ride-hail companies, have been developed with considerable input from the economist, while in other cases there have been economic interests on the regulatory side (Button, 2020).

The Covid-19 pandemic of 2020–22, the spread of which was in part due to the ease of mobility we now enjoy, brought about, at least in the short term, a sea change in transport policy. It led to many forms of transport coming to a standstill, or at least a crawl, as social distancing and quarantining became almost universal. Economists were aware of the potential effects that ease of mobility and contact can have on the spread of disease. Indeed, another Nobel economist, Robert Shiller (2017), had already dwelt on the Kermack–McKendrick theory of disease epidemics and their similarity to economic bubbles when giving his Presidential Address to the American Economic Association in 2015.

Nevertheless, Alexander's statement also highlighted the fact that many transport economic issues have traditionally been under-researched and often poorly understood by non-economists. This situation has, however, improved somewhat since the mid-1970s. One indicator is the increase over the years in the number of serious academic journals that regularly publish papers on transport economics. Most notable of these are the specialist *Journal of Transport Economics and Policy*, which first appeared in 1967, the *International Journal of Transport Economics*, which came a little later, and more recently *Research in Transport Economics*. But there are also publications such as the *Journal of Urban Economics, Journal of Regional Science, Journal of Transportation, Journal of Transport Reviews, Journal of Urban Economics*, and the *Transportation Research* series of journals that often carry transport economics articles. In addition, more mode-specific journals have emerged, such as *Maritime Economics and Logistics* and the *Journal of Air Transport Management*, which often carry material focusing on economic issues. But, nevertheless, compared to many areas of economic study, transport remains remarkably neglected.

Everything is also relative, and there have been some surges of interest in certain aspects of transport economics. One example of this occurred in the mid-1980s, when Clifford Winston (1985), in examining developments in transport economics, was able to comment on 'a current intensity [of interest in the field] not witnessed for more than fifty years', this surge being mainly related to the analysis of the impacts of more liberal or, to use the American term, 'deregulated' transport markets that were emerging. More recently, the role of transport as a facilitator of economic growth has attracted attention both at the microeconomic level and at the macro. Matters of transport security and the financing of transport networks were themes attracting considerable attention during the early part of the twenty-first century, as was the role of transport in international trade.

This relative lack of contemporary academic interest in transport economics is surprising because transport problems have in the more distant past stimulated major developments in general economic theory. This includes the development of the notion of consumer surplus by French economist engineers, such as Jules Dupuit, in the 1840s, the refinement of cost allocation models by John Bates Clark, Frank Taussig, and others in the early part of the twentieth century, the examination of the marginal cost pricing principle to improve the charging of rail services, and work on congestion and the environment by Arthur Pigou in the 1920s.

More recently, the advent of computers has encouraged work on applied econometrics (for example, the development of discrete choice models in consumer theory by Dan McFadden, and refinements to flexible-form cost functions) and on mathematical programming (including the use of data-envelopment analysis to assess the relative efficiency of different transport suppliers) using transport case studies as a basis for analysis. The advent of 'big data' sets has more recently provided fertile inputs for the empirical analysis of transport economic issues (Milne and Watling, 2019). Nevertheless, full-time transport economists in universities remain thin on the ground, and their numbers in businesses and government are not much larger.

In the past, the relatively small number of clearly identifiable specialist transport economists may have been attributable to the diverse nature of the industries involved in their work that range from taxi-cabs and bicycles to oil-tankers and jumbo-jets with their various institutional and technical peculiarities. Non-economists – lawyers, management scientists, and engineers – often have specialist knowledge of the industry concerned with a secondary background in some key aspects of economics needed in their work. At the applied level, numerous small firms that do not have the resources to employ full-time specialist transport economists does not mean they do not have individuals that fulfil some economic role in the organization.

The paucity of professional transport economists may also be explained by a tendency for physical planners and transport engineers to dominate substantive investment and policy decision-making within the sector. Where economics is used in this context it is often within the engineering framework and carried through by engineers: so-called 'engineering economics'. This situation has only gradually been changing with innovations in management and planning, and in the way that political institutions have evolved. Transport is now seen in a much wider context. But this still leaves the questions: What is modern transport economics? How did it evolve and what are the intellectual and practical driving forces underlying it?

1.2 A Brief History of Transport Economics

As with most academic 'disciplines', economics has never been easy to define. Not too seriously, the Chicago economist Jacob Viner is meant to have said, 'Economics is what economists do'. This is not exactly helpful to the non-transport economists' world. But it is generally agreed that economics is about human behavior and resource allocation, and about the allocation of scarce resources. It focuses a lot on the role of markets in doing this, but not exclusively so. Various aspects of it border on a variety of other disciplines such as law, sociology, and engineering, often making boundaries vague. It may also be essentially descriptive in the sense of it approaching a value-neutral science (it tells us that in most conditions the quantity demanded of something will fall if its price rises), but it can also contain elements of prescription (it is a good thing for social welfare if prices are low), the latter often being called political economy. All these elements, and some others, become important when studying the economics of transport.

What was called *Modern Transport Economics* by Michael Thomson (1974) began slowly to take shape in the late 1960s and early 1970s. Up until that time, as Rakowski (1976) points out, 'the field had essentially been in a state of semi-dormancy since the 1920s', and while considerable institutional studies had been conducted, very little analytical work as we would understand it today had been attempted. Indeed, the two standard American textbooks on transport economics in the late 1960s were D.F. Pegrum's *Transportation: Economics and Public Policy* and Phillip Locklin's *Economics of Transportation*, both of which went to numerous editions. These texts were highly institutional in approach and, as an indicator of their divergence from textbooks of the 2020s, contained only five or so line drawings between them and no equations.

If one is looking for a watershed in the history of modern transport economics it would probably be the publication of John Meyer et al.'s *Economics of Competition in the Transportation Industries* in 1959, which provided a state-of-the-art review of resource allocation problems in the sector, coupled with rigorous statistical analysis. There had been several seminal economic works relating to transport that appeared prior to this, including James Buchanan's re-examination of congestion and Beckmann et al.'s set of studies from 1956, but Meyer's book really set the tone for the way transport topics are analysed.

Interest in transport matters expanded throughout the 1960s with, for example, William Vickey's analysis of road charging and the role of public transit subsidies, Ian Little and James Mirrlees' development of tools for investment appraisal and especially of cost–benefit analysis (CBA), Quandt and Baumol's improvements in methods of transport demand modeling based on McFadden's work and the ideas of Kelvin Lancaster, Moses and Williamson's development of innovative methods of travel time evaluation, and so on. All these are topics we shall return to later, albeit in their more modern manifestations, and in many cases with some real-world examples of applications.

The changes were not all academic. This period also saw public policy-makers become more interested in the role of economics in improving decision-making across the board. In many countries specialist departments were established in national, state, or municipal government to examine the economic implications of various transport policy options.

The 1960s and early 1970s saw a slew of official reports appear. In the United Kingdom these included 'Road track costs', the Smeed Report on 'The economics of road pricing', the Beeching report on 'The reshaping of British railways', and the report of the Roskill Commission on the Third London Airport. The last set out the framework for the way economics can help in mega-project investment appraisal. The European Union, then just established as the European Economic Community, produced reports and plans in the early 1960s for integrating and coordinating economic approaches to transport provision across much of Europe including the Allais Report on 'Choice of pricing policy in transport'. In the United States this was the period of the large land-use transport studies including the Chicago Area Transportation Study from the late 1950s, the Puget Sound Regional Transportation Study, and the Detroit Regional Transportation and Land-use Study. These were largely engineering studies seeking to deal with mounting congestion problems, but economic analysis was part of the assessment process, although not always well applied (Meyer and Gómez-Ibáñez, 1983).

While it is seldom easy to explain the timing of change, the reasons for the renewed research interest in the 1960s, especially in the United States, Rakowski (1976) attributes to 'the problems of physical distribution and the development of a new field which has come to be called business logistics', 'expanded interest in all phases of urban transportation', and 'a great deal of research in the areas of transport in the developing countries'. Kenneth Gwilliam (1980) echoes these themes but places emphasis on the growing problems of urban transport in the 1960s and the recognition that land-use and transport needed to be considered together, and usually simultaneously, if the problems were to be successfully tackled. As a result of this, he argues, 'the boundaries between transport economics and urban and regional planning were obscured'.

While the broad underlying intellectual thrust of modern transport has not significantly changed since the 1970s and early 1970s, namely the use of economic theory to enhance transport efficiency in the broadest sense, the topics of focus have shifted to some extent and the economic tools used have been improved and fine-tuned. The late 1970s saw concern in many parts of the world with the macroeconomic problems associated with 'stagflation': the simultaneous occurrence of high levels of unemployment and poor economic growth accompanied by inflation. The economics that arose placed emphasis on improving industrial efficiency, including that of transport. The failure of a large part of the United States railroad industry became a catalyst for some of the major changes in transport. The adoption of 'Reaganomics' in the United States and Thatcherism in the United Kingdom, involving similar approaches towards what became known as 'supply-side economics', led to a homing-in on reducing costs in heavily regulated industries such as transport.

The empirical analysis of researchers such as William Jordan and Michael Levine provided evidence of excess costs associated with regulation, the theories of Baumol and others on contestable market structures offered a new way of looking at competitive forces, and Harold Demsetz's work provided a basis for enhancing the efficiency with which transport infrastructure is provided and maintained. Work by a variety of Chicago economists, including George Stigler and Sam Peltzman, began to focus on the motivations of those responsible for framing and administrating regulatory regimes, arguing that they seldom served the public interest. The outcome was what some have called the 'age of regulatory reform' (Button and Swann, 1989), which focused on removing distorting regulations and allowing greater market flexibility.

More recently public concern, combined with academic curiosity, has led to economists switching more of their attention to matters pertaining to the environmental implications of transport supply, the role that economics can play in enhancing the transport logistics supply chain, and the financing of infrastructure. Transport, as we will see, can impose considerable strains on the environment and, although this has long been recognized, the scale and nature of transport has changed, as has scientific knowledge on the implications of these strains – and especially so in the context of global impacts.

Frances Cairncross' term the 'death of distance' also came to the fore in the early 2020s. While many aspects of this are associated with the rise of information technology and the speed of information dissemination, transport also played a significant interactive role. Globalization, internationalization, and domestic economic growth within many countries have been, in part, the result of improved logistics, including just-in-time supply-chain management. Although often not appreciated, many of these improvements in logistics are the result of the application of basic economic principles.

Finally, modern transport requires an extensive infrastructure of roads, rail tracks, ports, air traffic control systems, bridges, and so on. The construction and the maintenance of this infrastructure must be paid for. While in the past transport economics has focused primarily on deciding which elements to build or repair, with the tax-payer bearing much of the financial burden, there is now concern with the methods of finance to use and the overall amount of national resources that is being devoted to various types of infrastructure. This issue is increasingly important in many mature economies as old infrastructure becomes obsolete or needs maintenance, but is perhaps more critical in lower-income nations lacking many key transport networks.

When considering this background, it is important to emphasize that transport economics is not distinct from all other branches of economics. Indeed, many of the seminal papers on the subject have appeared in the general economics literature and have often been produced by individuals with a broad interest in economics rather than being transport specialists. Nevertheless, as in most areas of study, as our knowledge has increased, it has become difficult, if not impossible, for economists to follow developments in all branches of their discipline. The Renaissance woman or man of economics is in the past. There has been an inevitable increase in specialization. Transport economics has in general terms a long history, but, as Rakowski and others suggest, it was only in the 1970s or so that it became a major field of academic study within universities, and only subsequently did a body of specialists emerge. So the modern transport economist is a relatively new beast. But what is it that he or she studies?

1.3   The Subject Matter of Transport Economics

The scope of each of the various subdisciplines of economics (for example, agricultural economics, development economics, and public sector economics) is determined not so much by 'schools of thought' or philosophies, but rather by the type of subject matter examined and the problems tackled. Transport economists are interested in the economic problems of moving goods and people; they are not normally so concerned with either the industries producing the vehicles and infrastructure (aircraft manufacturing, road construction companies, ship building, etc.) or with some of the very wide implications of transport policy (for example, on the balance of payments), although matters to do with the environment certainly attract increasing amounts of their attention. Of course, this does not mean that transport issues are viewed in complete isolation from their wider context but it does mean that the main emphasis and thrust of analysis is directed towards the more immediate transport implications.

While much of the economic analysis of transport issues is at the micro level (for example, looking at the decisions of individuals or firms) or at the meso level (focusing on transport industries or the importance of transport on a specific region), there is also some interest in the macroeconomic impacts of transport, for example on its effects on national productivity, globalization of trade, or labor force migration.

This book seeks to give adequate coverage to all levels of aggregation. Initially, however, we step back a little and spend time considering the economic institutions within which transport services are supplied and on individuals and firms seeking its services. Much of the theoretical economics that we encounter is rather abstract and largely assumes away the role of economic institutions, although this is now changing gradually. Institutional structures are important. Elementary economics, for example, talks about things like perfect competition, but such markets could not exist without laws giving property rights to suppliers or without contracts between sellers and buyers. As the Nobel Prize-winning economist Ronald Coase (1992) said in the context of economic reforms in the former USSR countries, '[t]hese ex-communist countries are advised to move to a market economy, and their leaders wish to do so, but without the appropriate institutions no market economy of any significance is possible'.

Traditionally, however, within economics, institutions have largely been treated as exogenous, a factor that is to be taken as given, and forming part of the *ceteris paribus* assumptions of the economic analysis. Few economists spent time studying it, and those who did, such as Thorsen Veblen and Kenneth Galbraith, were treated in their day as rather marginal to mainstream economics – some even considering them 'sociologists'! However, this view is changing, and as Oliver Williamson (2000) observed, '[w]e are still very ignorant about institutions. ... Chief among the causes of ignorance is that institutions are very complex. That neoclassical economics was dismissive of institutions and that much of organization theory lacked scientific ambitions have also been contributing factors'.

The so-called 'new institutional economics' has moved the economic study of institutions away from being a largely descriptive, legalistic, and traditional historical way of viewing the world to one that offers microanalysis of such issues as to why economic institutions have emerged in the way they have. It has also moved away from a largely negative way of looking at neoclassical economics to one with its own theoretical constructs and tools of analysis. This approach importantly sets the neoclassical economics that underlies most of the work in transport economics up until the 1990s within a larger context. Figure 1.1 is a simplified diagram that sets out four levels of social analysis. It is self-explanatory except that the solid arrows show constraints that come down from higher levels of analysis, while the dotted arrows indicate the direction of feedbacks. The data offered in the figure represent the rough frequency in years over which change takes place.

Long-term issues tend to receive less attention in transport economics the further one moves from narrow resource-allocation matters. Their importance cannot be neglected, however. There have been, perhaps, two major societal changes that have impacted on culture in the broadest sense since the end of the Second World War, and have had important ramifications for transport.

First, there was the demise of the Soviet Union and the move away from centralized planning, together with the gradual uptake of capitalism in China. These, and similar developments elsewhere, represent major shifts in the embedded attitudes of these countries and with this has come new ways of thinking about the role of transport in society and the ways in which it should be provided.

Second, there have been changing attitudes towards free trade, and with these have come internationalization and globalization. The resultant approach

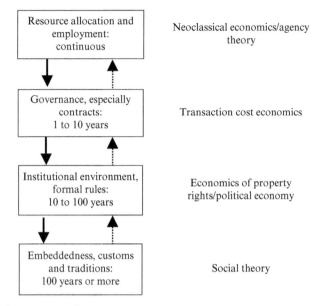

Figure 1.1 *Institutions and economics*

to tariffs and other barriers to international economic policies have had profound effects on shipping, air transport, and many forms of surface transport. The establishment of the League of Nations in 1920 laid the way for this, and it has extended since the end of the Second World War. It is not just a matter of global institutions such as the World Bank, the International Maritime Organization, and the International Civil Aviation Organization being formed, but rather that there is now a belief that they have a durable role to play in society. This forms a basis for new economic systems and an embedded global view on how business, including transport, can be conducted.

The institutional environment box in Figure 1.1 involves formal laws, regulations, and rules, and at a higher level, 'constitution'. It is also concerned with the instruments of law – legislatures and bureaucracies – and mechanisms of enforcement. For example, it relates to legal reforms such as the 1978 Air Transportation Act that liberalized domestic aviation in the United States, or the Single European Market Act that came into force in Europe in 1987 and led to a phased deregulation of transport and other markets within the European Union. But it also importantly includes the issue of property rights and their enforcement. So-called 'Pigouvian externalities', such as pollution, and 'club good' problems of traffic congestion are the most obvious areas of interest for transport economists in this regard. From an economics-of-transport perspective, the question becomes one of getting the rules right to meet societal demands.

Governance – basically the way business is done – is important and here the economic emphasis is on notions of contracts. Strictly, it is about crafting order, and thereby mitigates conflict and realizes mutual gains. There are many factors – cultural, structural, cognitive, and political – that influence the way these formal and informal institutions develop. If we take shipping as a case study, governance embodies such things as the evolving structure of coordination of shipping activities that began with conferences – essentially cartels – in the 1970s and has developed through consortia into strategic alliances, whereby changes occur discretely rather than continuously. These, like their brethren in the airline industry, can involve agreements on such things as schedules and rates, with flexibility over which vessels carry any individual assignment.

There are also contractual issues within the larger integrated supply chains that, for example, tie, to varying degrees, shipping with other elements in the logistics system, most immediately ports but extending beyond this. Governance is different from government in the sense that governance involves informal agreements within a legal structure. As an example, the United States deregulated its domestic airline industry by an act of congress, whereas the United Kingdom essentially got the same result because the Civil Aviation Authority reinterpreted the existing set of laws. Because of high transactions costs – legal costs and the like – the recent trend has seen a considerable amount of contract management and dispute settlement action be dealt with directly by the parties involved, in other words, within market frameworks rather than by legal actions.

Finally, there are the ongoing processes involving the day-to-day activities that take place involving transport. This is essentially the traditional bread-and-butter of micro- and mesoeconomic analysis taking into account the specific nuances of transport. Resource-allocation issues have, since the days of Adam Smith and more especially Alfred Marshall in the late 1890s, centered on getting the marginal conditions right. To assess how this might be achieved in theory, and how it materialized in practice, requires some notion of nature of the relevant cost and demand conditions – the guts of most introductory economics courses. The basic principles, although the nuances are still being refined, are pretty well understood and much of the recent attention in transport economics has therefore been on quantification and, in particular, quantification of networks.

Historically, however, this has not always been the case. Much of the early analysis of market structures in transport, for example, paid scant heed to the network nature of the industry and *ipso facto* to network externalities. Much of the interest until the 1980s or so, as we have hinted at previously, had been on traditional economic parameters such as market-concentration ratios, the degrees of product differentiation, and the levels of vertical integration. While all can be important instruments in the economist's toolkit, the network nature of the transport, and the service nature of its outputs, received much less direct attention in the analysis. Much of the early work on transport demand modeling was also either devoid of any of these network features, or embraced them in a mechanical fashion. But network features are important, although they often inconveniently add complexity to useful analysis.

All network service industries have essentially identical economic characteristics. Their output is non-durable, although they normally require significant amounts of infrastructure. There are also often very significant external benefits that, tied with various forms of scale effects, produce network economies. From the consumers' perspective, these external economies are related to the fact that the larger the number of links in a network, the greater the degree of connectivity, and with this the larger the choice set available to them – often called economies of market presence. On the cost-savings side, the ability, where this is most effi-cient, to channel traffic through hubs, rather than carry traffic directly between origins and destinations, creates economies of scope (cost savings by combining traffic) and of density (the more intensive use of the mode). But complex net-works can also create costs, and most especially when congestion develops on link roads or flight paths, or at hubs such as sea- and airports.

So, what does all this mean regarding the day-to-day work of transport economists? In summary, an understanding of economic institutions is now generally seen as important for analysing broad transport issues, nevertheless the main 'tools' of the transport economist are still taken directly from the toolkit of standard micro- and mesoeconomic theory, although one should add that the actual implements used have changed significantly over the years. The pre- and immediate post-Second World War emphasis centered on the transport indus-tries (that is, the railways, road haulage, shipping, etc.) and on ways in which the transport supply could be improved within largely regulated structure so that maximum benefit would be derived from public and private transport operations. The situation was summarized by one geographer who felt that transport eco-nomics at that time was concerned almost entirely with 'matters of organization, competition and charging, rather than with the effects of transport facilities on economic activities' (O'Connor, 1965).

To some extent, and especially in relation to international transport and, to a lesser extent, inter-urban transport, this interest has remained. It has, however, more recently been supplemented by concern with the wider welfare and spatial implications of transport. Greater emphasis is now placed on the environmental and distributional effects of the transport system and, in some cases, market efficiency is seen as an undesirably narrow criterion upon which to base major decisions. As Alexander argued, in the speech cited at the beginning of this chapter, one of the most important roles for economists is to make clear the overall resource costs of transport rather than just the accounting costs. It is no accident, perhaps, that much of the early work in CBA was in the transport field.

Transport economics has, like virtually all other branches of economics, become more mathematical and quantitative in recent years. At the theoretical level, it now often seeks to develop a sequence of formalized models that try to express a complicated reality. The dominant pre-war idea that economics is con-cerned mainly with establishing broad principles (for example, that the quantity demanded rises, *ceteris paribus*, as price falls) has also given way, with the advent of econometric techniques and the computer age, together with improved data sources, to attempts at detailed measurement (that is, a rise of x tons in the quan-tity demanded will, *ceteris paribus*, follow from a $\$y$ fall in unit price). Transport economists are now heavily involved in trying to assess the precise quantitative effect of different policy options and with forecasting likely changes in transport demand.

At the public policy level, the increasing sophistication of transport opera-tions, combined with both the long lead times that are required for full policy implementation and the financial costs involved, place mounting strains upon economists to produce useful, quantified predictions of future trends. The increased appreciation of the commercial benefits of better forecasting and costing as part of the supply-chain management process has led to greater employment of numerate economists in the private sector as well as the public. The rise of public–private partnerships has added to this trend.

From the relatively small base of the 1960s, transport economists, although not abundant, have now become established in most areas of transport policy-making at all administrative levels. Their increased interest in the overall welfare consequences of different transport strategies, together with a willingness to attempt some form of quantitative assessment, has led to transport economists becoming closely involved in major transport planning exercises. They have an established role in advising on appropriate actions at the national policy for-mulation level, but this has also spread down to a more specific function at the local and, where relevant, state planning level. At the strategic level, transport economists, for example, have made a significant contribution to the urban transportation planning in industrial countries since the late 1960s, and have been involved in many detailed appraisals of traffic investment and management schemes in developed countries. Multi-lateral agencies, such as the World Bank and the African, Asian, and Inter-American Development Banks, play roles in the latter.

In line with this, the toolkits of transport economists have changed. The advances made in transport investment appraisal – most notably the development of CBA techniques – as practical instruments of analysis led to the adoption of economic criteria for the assessment of many large-scale investment projects in the 1960s and 1970s (for example, the Third London Airport scheme and Victoria Underground Line in the United Kingdom). Recent refinements have resulted in rather more uniform CBA procedures being employed as a standard method of small-scale transport project appraisal. As we see later, these include the COBA and NATA packages developed in the United Kingdom for trunk road invest-ment appraisal, and the procedures favored by the World Bank – most notably those created by Little and Mirrlees in the *Project Appraisal and Planning for Developing Countries* guide – for appraising transport schemes in low-income countries.

The dichotomy between the wealth of the industrial nations and the poverty of Third World countries has resulted in large-scale programs being initiated to stimulate the economic development of the latter. Much of this aid has been in the form of monies and resources to improve transport provision. Over 20 percent of World Bank lending, for example, goes on transport projects, as does about 15 percent of Bank assistance – grants, expertise, etc. Although it has not always been agreed that aid always stimulates growth (Baur, 1971), or that if it does, transport investments are the most suitable projects to finance, it is nevertheless important that within the narrow confines of transport efficiency these monies are spent wisely. Transport economists have become increasingly involved in the Third World in transport project appraisal work.

Large private transport businesses often employ economists but more often they, and smaller enterprises, make use of the many specialist consultancy companies offering expert advice. The growth in interest in supply-chain logistics, which spans all movement and storage of raw materials, work-in-process inventory, and finished goods from point of origin to point of consumption, and within that just-in-time management, has led to a much more implicit incorporation of economics into transport activities.

One way of looking at this is through the notion of 'value chain' initiated by Michael Porter (1985). A value chain is the additional value added as more inputs are incorporated into the production process for a specific final output. It describes the full chain of a business's activities in the creation of a product or service – from the initial reception of materials through its delivery to market, and everything in between. Products pass through all activities of the chain in order and at each activity the product gains some value. The combined interactive chain of activities gives the products more added value than the sum of the added values of individual activities. Capturing the value generated along the chain is the new approach taken by many management strategists. For example, a manufacturer might require its parts suppliers to be located near its assembly plant to minimize the cost of transport or it may require regular delivery of components to keep production going whilst holding minimum stocks of the component. By exploiting the upstream and downstream information flowing along the value chain, the firms seek to bypass intermediaries creating new business models, or in other ways create improvements in its value system.

Figure 1.2 provides a simplified generic value chain. The key point about it is the extensive number of linkages required through a production process from the initial extraction of raw materials to the final delivery of goods to a market and their subsequent servicing. Transport is, at various levels of aggregation and in different forms, important at all stages. Just-in-time management is, as we see in Chapter 9 when we look at the links between transport economics and transport logistics, important in ensuring that few resources are tied up in the process at any one time so that inventory holdings are optimized.

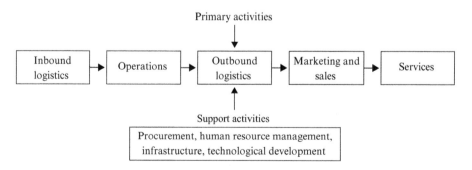

Figure 1.2 *The simple notion of the value chain*

The remainder of this introduction is concerned with setting the scene for the body of the book. Initially in these sections, some of the main economic features of the transport sector are discussed. The intention is, however, not to point to the uniqueness of transport but rather to highlight the characteristics of the sector that pose special problems for economists. Recent trends in transport are then reviewed and commented upon. To keep the subject matter manageable, much of the focus will be on the American and British situations, although experiences elsewhere will not be neglected. This is followed by a brief review of what appear to be some of the longer-term factors that are going to attract the attention of transport economists. Finally, a detailed contextual section explains the format of the book and outlines briefly the rationale for the structure adopted.

1.4   The Economic Characteristics of Transport

Possibly the most important characteristic of transport is that it is not normally wanted in its own right. As Denys Munby (1968) put it half a century ago, '[o]nly the psychologically disturbed or inadequate want transport for its own sake'. In other words, the desire for most transport is a derived one, but appropriate provision enables the benefits of a myriad of other, final benefits to be enjoyed. It is a major facilitator for enhancing personal welfare and for such things as economic development.

People wish, in general, to travel so that some benefit can be obtained at their destination. The trip itself is to be as short as possible. Of course, there are 'joy riders' and 'tourists', such as those who take cruises, and there are those at the extreme, like William Sidis, who are peridromophiles. But these people tend to be in the minority. Similarly, users of freight transport perceive transport as a cost in their overall production function and seek to minimize it wherever possible. The derived nature of the demand for transport is often forgotten in everyday debate but it underlies all economics of transport.

Just as the demand for transport exhibits specific if not unique features, certain aspects of supply are nearly unique to transport. More specifically, part of the plant is 'mobile' – almost by definition – and is entirely different in its characteristics to the fixed plant (for example, rail track, airports, etc.). The fixed component is usually extremely long-lived and expensive to replace. While most factories in the manufacturing sector may have a physical life expectancy of 100 years at most, we still use ports and roads constructed in Roman times. Further, few pieces of transport infrastructure have alternative uses: some former waterways have been turned into leisure areas and disused railway lines into cycle routes and footpaths, but these tend to be exceptions.

In contrast, most mobile plant is relatively short-lived and replacement usually occurs with physical obsolescence rather than technical obsolescence as with the fixed components. It is also cheap, with the prospect of alternative employment if demand declines in one market; for example, a bus can be transferred to another route or another form of service – in technical terms transport operators have few 'sunk costs'. Also, unlike fixed plant, the mobile components of transport are generally subject only to minimal scale economies. (Ships and aircraft may be exceptions to this in some cases.)

The fixed component, on the other hand, is normally subject to quite substantial economies of scale. Once a rail track is laid the marginal cost of using it falls until some maximum capacity is reached. This also generally means that there is a minimum practical size below which the provision of transport infrastructure is uneconomical. There are minimum traffic flows, for example, below which it is not economically practical to build highways or airports.

As Michael Thomson (1974) pointed out, it is these features of the fixed and mobile components of transport that have influenced the present institutional arrangements in the sector. The high cost of provision, longevity, and scale economies associated with the fixed components create tendencies towards monopoly control, while the ease of entry, flexibility, and lack of scale effects tend to stimulate competition in the mobile sector. In common with many other countries, with the notable exception of the United States, official reaction in Britain to this situation has in the past tended towards the nationalization and public ownership of transport infrastructure and the regulation of competition in the mobile sector. Nations differ in the degree to which fixed transport assets are publicly owned (there are private railways in some countries while several European states have privately operated motorways) and in the types of regulation imposed on mobile factors. The overall impression, however, is consistent.

While the rationale for the public provision of the fixed components of transport can be linked to the containment of any monopoly exploitation which may accompany private ownership (although British and American experiences in the nineteenth century suggests that control might equally well be enforced through price regulation), the need to regulate the mobile component stems from another aspect of transport operations. Transport generates considerable external effects (the most obvious of which are congestion and pollution); as Thomson said in the 1970s, it is an engineering industry carried on outside the factory. It is, therefore, felt to be important to at least contain the harmful effects of transport and at best to ameliorate them.

Coupled with this is the imperfect knowledge enjoyed by operators and their inability to foresee relatively short-term change in demand. Regulation is, therefore, often justified to ensure that excessive competition at times of depressed demand does not reduce the capacity of the transport system to an extent that it cannot meet higher demand during the upturn. This is clearly a matter of serious concern when a major crisis such as a pandemic affects society.

This also ties in with political-economy arguments that many types of transport should be seen as a service that should meet a 'need', in a broad sense, rather than be supplied under the market forces of supply and demand. Hence, traditional market forces need to be supplemented with government interventions to ensure that this wider, social criterion of transport operations is pursued rather than the simple profit motive. A clear example of this is to be seen in a major nineteenth-century Supreme Court ruling in the United States, *Munn v. Illinois*, when it was ruled that transport is 'affected with a public interest'.

1.5 This Book

The remainder of this book follows the general pattern set in previous editions. Economics is boringly static in that sense, and this book is concerned with the application of economic theory to the transport sector. Unlike other books, which often concentrate on specific modes of transport such as the railways or shipping, or specific sectors such as the nationalized transport industries, or have a geographical bent such as the transport policy of the European Union or urban transport problems, one of the main aims of this book is to show that many problems in transport are common to all modes (albeit with minor variations) and cover many different circumstances and spaces. Consequently, the approach is to show how economic theory may be applied to improve the overall efficiency of the transport sector; examples are, therefore, drawn from all forms of transport and many contexts.

Also, while it is unavoidable, not to say desirable, that official transport policy must be implicitly incorporated into the analysis, this is not a book explicitly about transport policy. Economic forces do not operate in a vacuum but within the context of laws and governance structures. Indeed, economists of the public-choice persuasion, such as James Buchanan and Gordon Tullock (1962), put emphasis on this political-economy dimension. But there are underlying 'laws' of economics that transcend circumstances. As said earlier, if prices go up, people want to buy less of that product.

It is felt useful, on occasions, to give brief details of institutional arrangements since they inevitably influence the relevant type of economic analysis to apply (for example, a thumbnail sketch of the historical and institutional framework of urban transport planning is included for this purpose), but, again, this is primarily for contextual reasons. The closing chapter is explicitly concerned with policy and institutions, and with the matter of the economic regulation of transport markets.

At the theoretical level, the discussion is couched largely in terms of verbal and diagrammatic analysis. Mathematical expressions are not shunned, but equations are included rather as reference points, permitting readers to look up practical working models should they subsequently wish to undertake their own empirical investigations. There are virtually no mathematical derivations, but important equations are 'talked around' and the reader, with a few exceptions, should find no difficulty in following the book even if his/her mathematical education has been neglected or forgotten.

Indeed, the philosophy of the approach adopted here is very much akin to that espoused by the great nineteenth-century economist, Alfred Marshall, in a letter to a colleague, A.L. Bowley, in 1906:

> But I know I had a growing feeling in the later years of my work at the subject that a good mathematical theorem dealing with economic hypotheses was very unlikely to be good economics: and I went more and more on the rules – (1) Use mathematics as a shorthand language, rather than as an engine of inquiry. (2) Keep to them until you have done. (3) Translate into English. (4) Then illustrate by examples that are important in real life. (5) Burn the mathematics. (6) If you can't succeed in (4), burn (3). This last I did often.

Although several Nobel Prize-winning economists, including Paul Samuelson, Jan Tinbergen, and Tjalling Koopmans, pointed out that much of economics deals with quantitative concepts – prices, output, income, and so on – and, therefore, inherently has a strong mathematic component (indeed, Samuelson was credited with saying 'mathematics is the language of economics'), even they accepted that there are limits to this.

Those interested in the mathematical extensions of the arguments on specific topics in the book are referred to the references cited. These often set out the underlying theory being discussed in more technical terms. The latter are also designed to direct readers to the more applied work in the field and the numerous challenges that economists encounter in trying to quantify various aspects of the transport system. An understanding of basic microeconomic theory is assumed and, while a knowledge of intermediate economic theory would be helpful, most of the theory does not go beyond that found in a standard introductory economics text.

For those new to economics, or in need of an *aide mémoire* to previous study, there are several introductory microeconomics books to be recommended, including those by Paul Samuelson and William Nordhaus (2009), Paul Krugman and Robin Wells (2018), William Baumol et al. (2019), and Gregory Mankiw (2020). In all cases the authors' experiences extend well beyond academia to bring a degree of reality to their writings.

Any divisions of written material are partly arbitrary and really designed to make things digestible for readers. Chapters forming this book are no exception. Where to put material on the economics of transport security? Under logistics (after all much of it is a business problem)? Why not externalities (since part of it affects the public at large)? Why not transport policy (since there is a large public policy element involved in delivering secure supply chains)? Decisions have been made, but inevitably the material could have been arranged in a variety of alternative ways. The important point is simply to remember that economics is a way of helping to understand problems.

The book begins in Chapter 2 by looking at the nature and scale of transport at the beginning of the twenty-first century, and its recent trends. It looks at it in global, national, and local economies. It moves on in Chapter 3 to look at its broad interactions with other sectors of the economy, especially the land market. Such interactions are often neglected in the explicit transport literature but are central to understanding the role of transport in society. This is followed by a related chapter concerned with the demand for transport services, the benefits derived from transport, and the methods of measuring these benefits, drawing largely upon the tools of welfare economics.

While Chapters 3 and 4 are essentially demand-orientated, the three following chapters are primarily concerned with cost and supply aspects (costs here being seen both in terms of conventional financial cost problems and, also, in terms of wider external costs). The accountancy costs of running transport are now recognized by policy-makers as offering too narrow a picture of the overall social costs associated with the movement of goods and persons. The wider costs are those that are imposed by transport users on each other, and that reduce the internal efficiency of the transport system, and the environmental costs that are inflicted on wider society.

The remaining chapters concentrate on optimizing the size and use made of the transport sector both in the short term and in the longer term. Methods of pricing by transport-supplying companies are reviewed in the context of the nature of their transport activities and markets being served, with, once again, emphasis being directed to the wider social dimension as well as to narrow commercial criteria. Chapter 8 looks at methods of optimizing the environmental effects of transport on society in general, and Chapter 9 focuses on the challenges of dealing with the problems of traffic congestion, not only on our streets but also at airports and seaports. The importance of transport in the supply chain and modern logistics management is reviewed in Chapter 10.

Longer-term planning and investment decisions are considered in some detail in Chapter 11. This is because of both the complexities of the issues involved and the scale of resources wastage if wrong decisions are made. The sheer costs involved can be enormous, and particularly so where major pieces of new infrastructure are under consideration – for example, an international airport or a Channel Tunnel. The inconvenience and disruption of construction to the existing transport networks is also often significant. The problems of financing and funding such undertakings are becoming more challenging and the respective roles and interactions of the government and private sectors are considered.

The long physical working life of many transport projects, let alone the lead time often needed before they become operational, means that it is important to be able to forecast the future demands likely to be placed on infrastructure, and consequently, in Chapter 12, space is devoted to economic demand forecasting techniques. The emphasis is, once again, focused on the economic assumptions involved rather than the econometric and estimation problems that may be encountered, although the latter are not entirely neglected.

The final chapters of the book take a much broader view of transport, considering in Chapter 13 the role that transport policy may play in general economic development both in the wealthier nations and in less developed countries. The question of appropriate regulations and the factors that have influenced transport policy over the years is explicitly examined in Chapter 14. The discussion is concerned with the relative merits of central coordination and direction of transport *vis-à-vis* the use of market mechanisms and competitive processes.

Each chapter is referenced to permit readers to follow up specific points in more detail should they wish. These references are light and are not intended to cover all the literature. They are directed to help students and newcomers to the field. The aim is that they should be references to material that is relatively accessible to most readers, rather than obscure reports, working papers, etc., which are often extremely difficult for those outside official circles or the academic sphere to obtain. Additionally, many of the references are to classic papers that can easily be found electronically. These are mainly linked to key ideas and concepts. There is also quite a lot of 'name-dropping'. For some people, including me, authors or other important figures act as 'hangers' to suspend their ideas from.

Experience suggests that students often feel in the information age that any article or book written more than five years or so ago is outdated. This is, of course, a folly of inexperience. Good studies that reveal universal principles are 'good studies' whatever their vintage. The lists of key references are also kept short so that the main items are immediately apparent to those interested. Many are to collections or surveys that go into greater depth on topics than we can in this short volume.

References

Alexander, K.J.W. (1975) Some economic problems of the transport industry, *Chartered Institute of Transport Journal*, 36, 306–308.

Baumol, W.J., Binder, A., and Solow, J. (2019) *Macroeconomics: Principles and Policy, 14th edition*, Centage Learning.

Baur, P. (1971) *Dissent on Development*, Weidenfeld and Nicolson.

Beckman, M., McGuire, C.B., and Winsten, C.B. (1956) *Studies in the Economics of Transportation*, Yale University Press.

Buchanan, J.M. and Tullock, G. (1962) *The Calculus of Consent: Logical Foundations of Constitutional Democracy*, University of Michigan Press.

Button, K.J. (2020) The 'Ubernomics' of ridesourcing: the myths and the reality, *Transport Reviews*, 40, 1–19.

Button K.J. and Swann, D. (eds) (1989) *The Age of Regulatory Reform*, Oxford University Press.

Coase, R.H. (1992) The institutional structure of production, *American Economic Review*, 82, 713–19.

Gwilliam, K.J. (1980) Review of 'Transport Economics', *Economic Journal*, 90, 677–8.

Krugman, P. and Wells, R. (2018) *Microeconomics, 5th edition*, Worth.

Mankiw, G.N. (2020) *Principles of Microeconomics, 9th edition*, Centage Learning.

Meyer, J. and Gómez-Ibáñez, J. (1983) *Autos, Transit and Cities*, Harvard University Press.

Meyer, J.R., Peck, M.J., Stenason, J., and Zwick, C. (1959) *The Economics of Competition in the Transportation Industries*, Harvard University Press.

Milne, D. and Watling, D. (2019) Big data and understanding change in the context of planning transport systems, *Journal of Transport Geography*, 76, 235–44.

Munby, D. (1968) *Transport*, Penguin.

O'Connor, A.M. (1965) *Railways and Development in Uganda*, Oxford University Press for the East African Institute of Social Research.

Porter, M.E. (1985) *Competitive Advantage: Creating and Sustaining Superior Performance*, Free Press.

Rakowski, J.P. (1976) *Transport Economics: A Guide to Information Sources*, Gale Research.

Samuelson, P.A. and Nordhaus, W.D. (2009) *Microeconomics, 19th edition*, McGraw-Hill.

Shiller, R.J. (2017) Narrative economics, *American Economic Review*, 107, 967–1007.

Thomson, M. (1974) *Modern Transport Economics*, Penguin.

Williamson, O. (2000) The new institutional economics: taking stock, looking ahead, *Journal of Economics Literature*, 38, 595–613.

Winston, C. (1985) Conceptual developments in the economics of transportation: an interpretive survey, *Journal of Economic Literature*, 23, 57–94.

Winston, C. (2013) On the performance of the U.S. transportation system: caution ahead, *Journal of Economic Literature*, 51, 773–82.

2 Transport and the Economy: Some Numbers

2.1 Introduction

Transport is important; some have described it as the blood of an economy. It is, in both physical and financial terms, a major global economic sector, an employer of large numbers of people, the consumer of vast quantities of raw materials, and it takes up a lot of personal time in its use. Whether it is now relatively more important than it was in the past is difficult to say. Certainly, the major civilizations of yesteryear put considerable emphasis on supporting their transport systems, and many, such as the Phoenicians, the Romans, the Chinese, and the Dutch, centered their economies around their quite distinctly different transport systems. The Chinese, for instance, have always been essentially a land power, whereas the Dutch and the Phoenicians were maritime traders.

To understand just why there is such considerable interest in transport and its efficiency, it would initially be useful to look at a few facts and figures on its role globally, regionally, and more locally. The descriptions here are far from complete. Many of the implications and effects of transport lie outside of the sector, including environmental effects and land-use interactions, and we shall deal with these more explicitly in separate chapters.

The present chapter is largely about the quantifiable, although it does provide some qualitative information regarding transport. But it is always helpful to remember words supposedly written by Albert Einstein on a blackboard: 'Not everything that counts can be counted, and not everything that can be counted counts'. Many aspects of transport affecting how, when, and why people travel, or why cargo consignees choose a specific shipper, are not easily quantified. Some of these factors are not easily encapsulated in some convenient metric, while in other cases they are subjective. Nevertheless, they may be highly significant when looking at how the transport system functions. This has been gradually recognized by transport economists who are showing increasing interest in behavioral economics.

In addition, we should also hold in the backs of our minds the words of the nineteenth-century British Prime Minister and novelist, Benjamin Disraeli, who allegedly cautioned that '[t]here are three kinds of lies: lies, damned lies, and statistics'. Basically, he was referring to the persuasive power of numbers, and the use of statistics to support weak arguments, and the tendency of people to disparage statistics that do not support their positions. We shall attempt to be as objective as possible in setting out some of the more insightful transport data. Some of the more qualitative and subjective aspects are considered in later discussions.

But even so, it is impossible to paint anything like a complete quantitative picture of the nature and importance of modern transport. One could approach the challenge by focusing on a single country or industry – say shipping or railroads – but this would inevitably be partial. Also looking at any single country's transport system can make it appear as if that country is special or unique. Certainly, in some ways any data will inevitably be context-specific, but there are broader trends and features that transcend physical boundaries, and many of the economic challenges that confront policy-makers are almost global in their incidence – traffic congestion being the most obvious case. Nevertheless, the examples offered in this chapter are fairly wide-ranging to illustrate more general patterns and features.

We begin by looking at the very large pictures, international trade in transport services, and then gradually move down the levels of aggregation, with a diversion at the end to consider some emerging trends and trend breaks. Because local transport parameters can vary quite considerably, and because we deal with many specific local matters in subsequent chapters, this part of the description is less complete. There is also a bias in that there is a disproportionate amount of American data and information provided, although this is supplemented in places with data from the United Kingdom and other countries.

In addition, it is important to remember that there can be quite large margins of error in transport data. Many statistics used are based on surveys that have inevitable statistical confidence intervals associated with them. Many surveys are also spasmodic and are not done often or at regular intervals. Questions asked often differ over time and there are issues of definitions when making comparisons across countries (for example, of high-speed rail services which are defined differently by the European Union and the International Union of Railways). These problems persist despite the efforts of the Organisation for Economic Co-operation and Development (OECD), Eurostat, the World Trade Organization (WTO), and other bodies to achieve greater standardization.

Much transport is provided by the private sector (including, in the case of car drivers, inputs of the travelers themselves), and the type and quality of such of data can be significantly different from that gathered by public agencies. Most of the private sector is commercially oriented and thus focuses on data that help in better business decision-making, rather than that needed for good public policy analysis. This often means, for example, that it is shorter-term. Commercial activities are largely interested in time frames involving cost recovery, and data are seldom gathered consistently, because private companies are generally concerned with projects of immediate interest to them. Additionally, most private firms operate in markets where a need for a degree of commercial confidentiality engenders a reluctance to reveal data.

Even when census data are used, this type of information is normally only collected every decade with extrapolations or samples used to fill in the intervening years. Added to this, most data that are collected on transport reflect physical characteristics of systems, and this is not always ideal for economic analysis. This latter problem has become more acute in recent years as transport industries have become less regulated and there have been privatizations. With these institutional changes, commercial considerations have mitigated incentives to provide public data and financial information.

2.2   The Global Picture

International trade has existed since the formation of nation states, and indeed was the *raison d'être* for the establishment of many. Classical economists, however, when trying to explain the intensity and patterns of international trade, paid little attention to the role of transport – it was largely 'assumed away'. Their focus was on the comparative advantages of the nations producing the commodities being traded. Recently the emergence of the 'new trade theory' (NTT), often associated with Paul Krugman (2009), has changed things. The NTT recognizes that a large part of trade is intra-industrial, involving countries both importing and exporting very similar goods (for example, Germany both imports cars from and exports cars to Japan). Transport costs can form an important, if seldom the main, element in explaining some of the current patterns of trade.

According to the WTO, global recorded merchandise trade in 2018 amounted to $19.67 trillion, and no doubt there was much more that fell out of the official statistics. While much of this involved the more traditional industrial regions of Europe (with Germany accounting for $1.56 trillion of the region's exports and $1.29 trillion of its imports), the United States ($1.66 trillion of its exports and $2.61 trillion of its imports), and Japan ($0.74 trillion of its exports and $0.75 trillion of its imports), the new mega-economies of China (with $2.49 trillion of its exports and $2.14 trillion of its imports) and India are also now major players. Table 2.1 offers details in terms of merchandise imports.

Both aggregate spatial and temporal patterns in world trade in merchandise are highly correlated with patterns and trends in national gross domestic product (GDP) – the production taking place within a country's borders. Figure 2.1 provides a graph of recent trends. Clear ups and downs are seen in the world economy as it has experienced trade cycles. Nevertheless, the correlation, if not the causality between GDP and merchandise exports, is clear.

While these financial trends are useful, and germane to many economic debates, they do not offer comprehensive insights into the physical nature of transport demands or the quantity of resources that are being used to meet it. For example, while international shipping carries some 90 percent of global trade measured by weight, air transport accounts for 35 percent of that moved by value despite only carrying 1 percent of the tonnage. The value of what is moved is often unrelated to its physical magnitude, and, in this case, air transport tends to move high-value, low-volume commodities where speed and reliability of delivery are at a premium. Table 2.2 provides some more general information concerning the growth of international air transport in the movement of people and freight. Again, a broad correlation is seen.

Table 2.1　*World merchandise imports by region and selected countries ($ billions at constant prices)*

	1983	1993	2003	2018
Value world ($ billions)	1,833	3,805	7,694	19,394
North America	18.5	21.3	22.4	18.4
United States	14.3	15.9	16.9	13.5
Mexico	0.7	1.8	2.3	2.5
Canada	3.4	3.7	3.2	2.4
South & Central America				
& the Caribbean	3.9	3.3	2.5	3.3
Brazil	0.9	0.7	0.7	1.0
Chile	0.2	0.3	0.3	0.4
Europe	44.1	44.5	45.0	36.9
Germany	8.1	9.0	7.9	6.6
United Kingdom	5.3	5.5	5.2	3.5
France	5.6	5.7	5.2	3.5
Netherlands	3.3	3.3	3.4	3.3
Commonwealth of				
Independent States	–	1.5	1.7	2.2
Africa	4.6	2.6	2.2	3.0
South Africa	0.8	0.5	0.5	0.6
Middle East	6.2	3.3	2.8	3.8
Asia	18.5	23.5	23.5	32.4
China	1.1	2.7	5.4	11.0
Japan	6.7	6.4	5.0	3.9
India	0.7	0.6	0.9	2.6
Australia & New Zealand	1.4	1.5	1.4	1.4

Source:　World Trade Organization.

Transport supply has grown to cater for the demands of the internationalization of supply chains and globalization. Since the development of unitization in the 1960s, container ships and trains have been a core input into the international movement of finished goods and components. For example, in 2019 there were 5,150 large container vessels engaged in that market. Added to this were 11,562 large bulk carriers and 7,444 crude-oil-tankers. Because of the finances needed to invest and operate modern shipping fleets, the emergence of large shipping companies has accompanied this. Table 2.3 details the major operators together with their relative market shares. Four companies dominate the market in container services, although that does not mean they operate the largest vessels; for example, ships like HMM's *Copenhagen*, *Le Havre*, and *Gdansk* can carry up to 23,964 TEUs.[1]

---

[1] The TEU is an inexact unit of cargo capacity used to describe the capacity of container ships and terminals. It is based on the volume of a 20-foot-long shipping container, a standard-sized metal box that can be easily transferred between different modes of transport, such as ships, trains, and trucks.

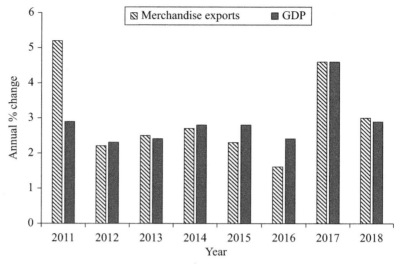

Source: World Trade Organization.

Figure 2.1   *The volume of world merchandise trade and GDP (2011–18)*

Table 2.2   *International and global revenue air traffic*

	Passengers (millions)	Passenger-km (millions)	Freight tonnes[a] (millions)	Freight tonne-km[a] (millions)
2009	2,488	4,561,413	40.0	155,819
2010	2,705	4,924,229	47.6	186,631
2011	2,870	5,248,140	48.7	187,191
2012	3,004	5,528,880	48.0	185,239
2013	3,138	5,832,564	49.1	185,975
2014	3,316	6,181,177	50.7	194,633
2015	3,556	6,644,666	51.0	197,131
2016	3,794	7,135,773	52.8	204,187
2017	4,062	7,707,118	56.6	222,996
2018	4,322	8,257,635	58.0	230,967

Note: a. Excludes mail.

Source: International Civil Aviation Organization.

Unlike shipping, the freight operations of air transport overlap quite considerably with passenger services. To meet the demand for air cargo services, for example, there were 1,870 dedicated freighter aircraft in 2018, representing about 42 percent of the 700 billion available tonne-kilometer air freight capacity, the remaining 58 percent being moved in the belly holds of passenger aircraft. But, just like shipping, both the supplying companies – passenger and freight – of international air services are huge undertakings. Although size can be measured in several ways, in terms of fleets for example, American Airlines in 2019 had 957 planes, Delta Air Lines had 880, and United Airlines had 777. But, as with

Table 2.3 *Leading container service operators (2020), based on the number of ships and TEUs*

Company	Headquarters	Ships	Total TEUs	Market share (%)
APM–Maersk	Denmark	676	4,051,436	16.90
Mediterranean Shipping	Switzerland	574	3,815,410	16.00
COSCO Group	China	488	2,978,334	12.50
CMA CGM Group	France	532	2,824,214	11.80
Hapag–Lloyd	Germany	241	1,726,578	7.20
ONE	Japan	211	1,548,426	6.50
Evergreen Marine	Taiwan	196	1,268,361	5.30
HMM	South Korea	69	651,884	2.70
Yang Ming Marine Transport Co.	Taiwan	91	608,072	2.50
PIL	Singapore	107	342,405	1.40
Zim Integrated Shipping Services	Israel	64	305,343	1.30
Wan Hai Lines	Taiwan	105	285,070	1.20
Zhonggu Logistics Corp.	China	115	168,581	0.70
Republic of Korea Marine Transport Co.	South Korea	68	162,276	0.70
IRISL Group	Iran	48	152,419	0.60

Source: Alphaliner.

shipping lines, the importance of single fleets of ships or planes does not reflect the market power they can exercise by combining their capacity and schedules. Something returned to later.

Transport requires infrastructure as well as vessels, planes, and vehicles, to move goods and people around the globe. This infrastructure is generally physically large, and inevitably expensive and immobile. It involves investments that seldom have uses beyond those for which they are designed – in economic terms, most infrastructure is a 'sunk cost'. This is a problem we see later when looking at technology improvements, or new regulations, which result in existing infrastructure becoming economically obsolete well before it is physically worn out.

To give an impression of the scale of some of the transport infrastructure in the world, Table 2.4 lists the largest seaports in terms of what they handled, together with changes in their rankings, between 2015 and 2018. The increased importance of China is seen in terms of the number of its ports and their movement up the table over time. Table 2.5 offers broadly comparable data on international passenger airports, in this case measured by the number of international passengers they handled.

It is more difficult to isolate international road and rail infrastructure, although land modes play a significant role in international trade not only as the trunk-haul carrier across land borders but also in providing feeder services to sea and air movements. Because the infrastructure of land modes is generally extensively shared with domestic transport, separating out the international component is not easy. Indicators of the scale of selected national major road networks, which are used for both domestic and international movements, are

Table 2.4 *The world's largest container seaports by million TEUs (ordered by size, 2018)*

Port	Country	2015	2016	2017	2018
Shanghai	China	36.54	37.13	40.23	42.01
Singapore	Singapore	30.92	30.90	33.67	36.60
Shenzhen	China	24.20	23.97	25.21	27.74
Ningbo-Zhoushan	China	20.63	21.60	24.61	26.35
Guangzhou Harbor	China	17.22	18.85	20.37	21.87
South Korea	South Korea	19.45	19.85	20.49	21.66
Hong Kong	Hong Kong	20.07	19.81	20.76	19.60
Qingdao	China	17.47	18.01	18.30	18.26
Tianjin	China	14.11	14.49	15.07	16.00
Jebel Ali	Dubai	15.60	15.73	15.37	14.95
Rotterdam	Netherlands	12.23	12.38	13.73	14.51
Port Klang	Malaysia	11.89	13.20	13.73	12.32
Antwerp	Belgium	9.65	10.04	10.45	11.10
Kaohsiung	Taiwan	10.26	10.46	10.27	10.45
Xiamen	China	9.18	9.61	10.38	10.13

Table 2.5 *Largest airports by international passenger numbers (2019)*

Airport	Location	Passengers
Dubai International Airport	Dubai	8,888,536,700
London Heathrow Airport	United Kingdom	7,530,693,900
Hong Kong International Airport	Hong Kong	7,436,097,600
Amsterdam Airport Schiphol	Netherlands	7,095,625,800
Incheon International Airport	South Korea	6,767,614,700
Charles de Gaulle International Airport	France	6,638,349,400
Singapore Changi Airport	Singapore	6,489,000,000
Frankfurt Airport	Germany	6,177,466,300
Suvarnabhumi Airport	Thailand	5,086,884,600
Ataturk International Airport	Turkey	4,897,877,000
Taiwan Taoyuan International Airport	Taiwan	4,615,216,400
Kuala Lumpur International Airport	Malaysia	4,353,174,100
Madrid Barajas International Airport	Spain	4,185,712,500
London Gatwick Airport	United Kingdom	4,147,685,800
Munich Airport	Germany	3,654,578,700
Barcelona–El Prat International Airport	Spain	3,654,578,700
Haneda International Airport	Japan	3,530,007,600
Hamad International Airport	Qatar	3,449,507,800
John F. Kennedy International Airport	United States	3,348,507,800
Lester Pearson International Airport	Canada	3,161,034,800

Note: There are larger airports that primarily handle domestic traffic – for example, Hartsfield–Jackson Atlanta International Airport handled 110.53 million passengers in 2019 and Beijing Capital International Airport some 110.01 million.

Source: Airports Council International.

Table 2.6 *Motorway (freeway) networks of higher-income countries (2018)*

Country	Total length 1,000 km	Kilometers per 10,000 km²
United States	263,932	268
Canada	17,000	17
Mexico	15,044	77
Spain	14,701	291
Germany	12,917	362
France	11,465	209
Italy	6,726	223
Korea	4,044	404
United Kingdom	3,686	151
Portugal	2,988	324
Netherlands	2,646	637
Turkey	2,155	28
Sweden	1,927	43
Belgium	1,763	577
Austria	1,719	205
Switzerland	1,419	344
Denmark	1,128	262
Finland	810	24
Slovenia	770	380
New Zealand	183	7

Source: Organisation of Economic Co-operation and Development.

seen in Table 2.6. The final column puts these data in the context of the differing sizes of countries. The road orientation of American society is well known, but only in absolute terms. Countries such as Korea, Germany, Belgium, and the Netherlands have more kilometers of road per unit of area.

A similar set of statistics for railroads, again listed in order of size, is seen in Table 2.7. Unlike roads that are almost universally used for the movement of both freight and people, railway networks are often more specialized. For example, the Canadian and the United States system, excepting Amtrak and some local services around larger cities, is primarily a freight system, whereas that of the United Kingdom, and many geographically smaller countries, are used mainly by passengers. Russia has a more mixed system. High-speed rail lines are almost entirely passenger systems. The concept of infrastructure and the way in which it is measured can thus be contextual, whether one is looking at its importance to the freight or the passenger sectors. As we see in Chapter 5, this can pose problems when trying to allocate costs of infrastructure to various transport user groups, and setting the fares and rates for using them.

Another and linked difficulty with this type of data is that of devising a common unit of measurement – for example, freight moved from an airport is measured in tons and containers from seaports in TEUs, whereas passengers are measured in terms of individuals. When studying something like fuel use, it is reasonable to reduce everything to tons carried. There is a high correlation between the two. But this is hardly appropriate when allocating the full costs of a flight

Table 2.7   *World's largest railway networks by kilometers*

Country	Kilometers	Year
United States	149,407	2017
China	146,300	2020
India	99,235	2015
Russia	85,600	2019
Canada	64,000	2017
Germany	40,626	2017
Argentina	36,966	2014
Australia	33,168	2017
Brazil	29,817	2014
France	29,273	2017
Japan	27,311	2015
Mexico	23,389	2020
South Africa	22,387	2017
Ukraine	20,952	2016
Poland	19,209	2017
Iran	16,998	2014
Italy	16,798	2016
Spain	16,355	2017
United Kingdom	16,320	2017
Kazakhstan	15,530	2018
Sweden	14,180	2020
Turkey	12,740	2010

on which goods and people are carried. The on-board facilities needed for people and cargo movement are entirely different.

Time-series comparisons can also be difficult. Output measures (for example, ton-miles or passenger-kilometers), although appearing to circumvent problems of comparability over broad categories of transport, in fact tend to be inadequate. Such measures ignore changes in the quality and costs of alternatives. For example, flying with a low-cost airline today is very different to flying with the full-service airlines of the 1970s. It is possible to count physical units (for example, the number of cars or planes), but lack of homogeneity again prevents meaningful, in-depth comparisons within individual modes. For example, an average car in the early 2000s was very different from the average car today. Despite these comments it is still possible to look at official statistics and obtain an overall feel for the transport situation evolving in a very general sense.

While international trade, and transport with it, has grown globally, trade between and within certain blocs of countries and regional trade areas (RTAs) has tended to expand even more rapidly because of their new institutional structures. Most notable has been the creation of the North American Free Trade Agreement (NAFTA), restructured since 2020 as the United States–Mexico–Canada Agreement (USMCA), and the continued widening and deepening of the European Union. (The latter is discussed in detail in Chapter 14.) Figure 2.2 shows just how important these trade blocs have become as markets in themselves.

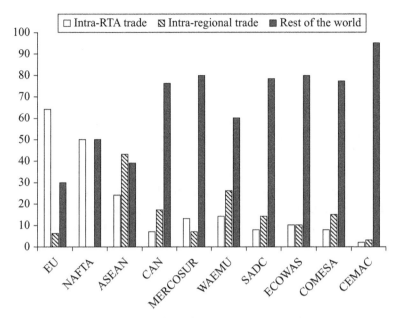

Source: World Trade Organization, *World Trade Statistical Review*, 2019; WTO, 2020.

Figure 2.2   *Value of trade involving regional trading blocs (2017)*

These relatively new institutional arrangements have both fostered greater demand for transport services as barriers to trade in goods and services as trade were diminished and made it easier to provide transport as cross-border regulations were relaxed. In some cases, as with the European Union, they also allow cabotage – the ability of a foreign transport operator to pick up and set down in another country – which increases transport flexibility and efficiency further (Button, 2011). For example, the creation of the European Single Internal Market in 1992 has been estimated to have led to a 4.5 to 7 percent rise in the European Union's gross national product (GNP), with an increase of 30 to 50 percent in trans-frontier lorry traffic.

As another example of open borders, the NAFTA, was a trilateral trade bloc in North America created by the governments of the United States, Canada, and Mexico, and was, in terms of the combined purchasing power and GDP of its members, the largest trade bloc in world and the second-largest by nominal GDP comparisons. From its creation in 1994, NAFTA provided a stimulus to trade between its member states, including that between Mexico and Canada transiting the United States. Table 2.8 provides some details of increases in the value of trade from the inception of the NAFTA free trade agreement until 2015.

2.3   Transport at the National Level

Transport forms a major component of the national output as well as accounting for a large part of national expenditure in most developed countries. For example,

Table 2.8   *NAFTA trade volumes by value ($ millions)*

	1993	2015	Real increase (%)ᵃ
United States–Canada	199.18	518.22	63.50
United States–Mexico	85.22	481.54	255.00
Mexico–Canada	4.05	34.34	432.50
Tri-lateral	288.46	1,034.10	125.20

Source: a. US Bureau of Labor Statistics, Consumer Price Index.

in 2014 expenditure on transport represented 18.7 percent of total national expenditure in the United States. In the United Kingdom it was 16.2 percent, and in Japan, 10.0 percent. A substantial part of this, as seen for the United States in Table 2.9, is taken up by final domestic demand, with private consumption being the dominant element of this.

It is also clear that within the United States and many other countries there is a strong reliance on the automobile in physical as well as financial terms. Air transport, however, is also important in the United States compared to other countries, mainly because of the high-income levels and the distances traveled in North America. These features are reflected in data offered in Table 2.10 for the United States and in Table 2.11 for England, although in the latter it is expressed in terms of the travel patterns of an average family rather than as an aggregate. The English data are included here because there is more complete

Table 2.9   *Final demand for United States transport ($ billions in 2009 prices)*

	2000	2008	2015
Gross domestic product	12,565	14,834	16,397
Personal consumption of transport	945	925	1,021
Motor vehicles & parts	346	341	419
Motor vehicle fuels, lubricants, & fluids	266	262	267
Transport services	333	321	298
Gross private domestic investment	213	167	335
Transport structures	9	10	12
Transport equipment	204	157	302
Exports (+)	218	269	321
Imports (−)	328	355	467
Government transport-related purchases	283	290	283
Federal purchases	25	38	n.a.
State & local purchases	246	233	n.a.
Defense-related purchases	12	20	n.a.
{Percent of GDP spent on transport}ᵃ	10.60%	8.70%	7.29%

Notes: a. Aggregate transport expenditure adjusted for the omission of some categories of transport expenditures and rounding.
n.a. = not available.

Source: US Bureau of Transportation Statistics.

Table 2.10 *United States passenger transport by mode (million passenger-kilometers)*

	2005	*2010*	*2015*	*2018*
Air	921,943	892,720	1,017,355	1,162,615
Highway	7,833,657	8,062,501	8,504,252	8,928,457
Transit	75,840	84,695	89,637	86,631
Inter-city/Amtrak	8,660	10,332	10,519	10,237
Walking	n.a.	n.a.	n.a.	n.a.
Cycling	n.a.	n.a.	n.a.	n.a.

Note: Passenger-kilometers in the number of trips taken by each mode multiplied by the
average length of those trips.
n.a. = not available.

Table 2.11 *Average number of household trips by main mode in England*

	2005	*2010*	*2015*	*2019*
Private:				
Walk	272	234	219	250
Walks of over a mile	74	65	68	65
Bicycle	15	15	17	16
Car/van driver	434	402	381	380
Car/van passenger	234	212	204	200
Motorcycle	4	3	3	2
Other private transport	8	7	7	7
Public:				
Bus in London	19	25	20	18
Other local bus	43	42	41	32
Non-local bus	1	1	1	–
London Underground	9	9	9	12
Surface Rail	16	19	20	21
Taxi-/mini-cab	11	9	10	11
Other public transport	3	2	3	3

information on cycling and walking than in the United States. We also see a discernably greater use of public modes in the United Kingdom than in the United States, a pattern for example repeated in most Continental European countries. More recent trends have also been for the car to continue to increase its modal share in most countries over time, although at a markedly slower rate in recent years for many of the highest-income nations as vehicle ownership approaches saturation – basically a situation where everyone able and permitted to drive has access to a car.

As shown later, the rise in private transport use is closely related to higher car ownership levels – although the question of cause and effect is a complex one (Chapter 4). What should be remembered, however, is that while the relative use of private transport is rising, the role of public transport, especially for commuter trips into large cities, is still very important when discussing transport, and is often rising in absolute terms and for specific journey purposes as urbanization increases. Air transport increasingly dominates longer trips even outside of the United States and, in particular, trips involving tourism.

What the tables do not show is the share of household expenditure by the different income groups that is spent on transport. What is found from this breakdown of expenditure data is that the proportion of outlays devoted to transport tends to rise with household income reflecting the 'superior good' nature of the activity. What official data also show is the use made by different income groups of the various modes. In the United Kingdom, for example, railways are used primarily by those in the higher-income groups, as is the private car. In contrast, bus transport is used disproportionately more by the poorer sectors of the community. We shall return to this when looking at urban transport trends.

Within countries there are also distinctions in terms of how freight is transported, and the trends these movements have been taking over time. As seen in Table 2.12, in terms of ton-miles of inland freight transport, trucking has the largest share in the United States although other modes, and especially railroads, have been gaining in importance. This is a pattern, however, that is not reflected in all higher-income nations. As shown in Table 2.13, the wider picture generally shows a steady decline in the relative, but not always absolute, role of freight railroads.

Table 2.12 also provides information on pipeline movements in the United States, an important but often neglected form of freight transport. Physical limits to the type of commodities which can be carried in this way – basically liquids, including sewage and slurry, and gas – are likely to prevent pipelines from ever becoming more than a minority mode of transport. Indeed, if society moves to a carbon neutral economy, then some of their roles will diminish as the importance of oil as an energy source declines.

This contrasts with the situation regarding trucking where the trend has been clearly upwards. The explanation for this lies partly in the increase in unitization of the goods shipped coupled with an uptake of just-in-time production and distribution. This has resulted in firms holding lower inventories, a subject dealt with

Table 2.12 *United States ton-miles of freight (millions)*

	2000	*2005*	*2015*	*2018*
Total ton-miles	5,065,648	5,379,424	5,110,527	5,250,670
Air	14,983	15,746	13,190	15,969
Truck	1,971,087	2,210,106	1,985,827	2,033,921
Railroad	1,465,960	1,696,425	1,738,283	1,729,638
Domestic water transport	645,799	591,447	490,627	491,800
Coastwise	283,872	263,580	175,604	173,600
Lakewise	57,879	51,976	46,436	46,900
Internal	302,558	274,366	267,447	270,200
Intraport	1,490	1,525	1,139	1,100
Pipeline	967,819	865,700	882,600	979,343

Source: US Bureau of Transportation Statistics.

Table 2.13   *Freight moved by mode by country (2000 and 2017, billion tonne-kilometers)*

	Road		Rail		Coastal shipping	
	2000	*2017*	*2000*	*2017*	*2000*	*2017*
United Kingdom	153.7	156.1	181.2	172.0	66.2	23.0
Austria	17.2	18.4	16.6	22.3	–	–
France	184.4	162.6	53.4	40.7	10.5	–
Germany	280.7	313.1	77.5	129.3	–	–
Italy	158.6	119.7	25.8	22.3	33.4	64.9
Spain	148.7	231.1	12.2	10.5	37.8	49.7
Sweden	31.4	40.7	20.1	21.8	8.1	6.5
Czech Republic	39.0	44.3	17.5	15.8	–	–
Poland	54.4	111.8	54.5	54.8	–	–
Switzerland	13.6	17.2	11.1	11.7	–	–
China	612.9	6,677.2	1,377.1	2,696.2	17.1	5,508.4
Japan	313.1	210.8	22.2	22.7	241.7	180.0
United States	3,396.7	2,954.2	2,257.6	2,523.4	414.4	250.7[a]

Note: a. 2016.

Source: Organisation for Economic Co-operation and Development.

in some depth in Chapter 10. To ensure that their stocks are adequate this means more deliveries with inventories essentially being held in the transport system rather than warehouses. Although rail and air transport have important roles in this business model, trucks combine the flexibility with the cost structure required for maximum efficiency over short and medium distances.

The public sector plays an important role in the direct provision of national transport services in most countries, although the scale and nature of that role differs. Table 2.14 shows the importance in a federal regime such as the United States of state as well as central government expenditures. It has been rising over time with respect to all modes. There are some caveats to be considered, however, when using these data. The figures likely hide some transport outlays, for example regarding the military as well as transport-related expenditures embodied in the accounts for such items as law and order, environmental services, and health functions of government. Additionally, public expenditure is subjected to cycles that reflect the state of a national economy and macroeconomic government policies. For example, following the attacks of September 11, 2001, the United States considerably increased its direct expenditure on transport security, and after the Covid-19 pandemic there began a phase of infrastructure expansion and renewal. An added problem in looking at this type of aggrege data in large, and especially federal, countries is that they can miss outlays at lower levels of government, for example by local or municipal authorities.

Transport is a major employer in most countries, for example Indian Railways' 1.254 million employees in 2020 make it the world's eighth-largest employer. Considerable inputs of labor extends through the transport infrastructure investment phase, construction of vehicles through to operations and

Table 2.14 *Government expenditure on transport in the United States (current $ millions)*

	2007	2011	2014	2017
Highways	174,808	193,649	207,118	223,429
Federal	36,981	45,536	47,290	47,170
State & local	137,827	148,113	159,827	176,258
Air	34,107	39,200	38,576	43,004
Federal	17,895	19,610	20,022	20,165
State & local	16,212	19,590	18,554	22,839
Transit	46,183	53,042	59,699	66,861
Federal	9,199	9,620	11,520	11,728
State & local	36,984	43,422	48,179	55,133
Water	11,301	13,919	14,296	14,921
Federal	6,543	8,871	8,394	8,622
State & local	4,758	5,048	5,902	6,299
Rail	1,477	2,426	2,812	3,108
Federal	1,477	2,426	2,812	3,108
State & local	0	0	0	0
Pipeline	76	101	110	89
Federal	76	101	110	40
State & local	0	0	0	49
General support	891	1,447	1,389	873
Federal	878	1,426	1,367	850
State & local	13	21	22	23
Total	*268,843*	*303,784*	*324,000*	*352,285*

maintenance. Some idea of the importance of transport employment in the United States economy is seen in Table 2.15 which provides time-series data from 2000 to 2019. (By way of comparison, using slightly different definitions, the European Union employed 11.3 million people in transport in 2016.) The table combines not simply those directly employed in transport but also embraces those engaged in related industries. Over the longer term, there has been a steady relative decline in employment in transport in the overall American labor force as people have switched from public transport to the automobile and as modes such as trucking, the railroads, and airlines have improved their labor efficiency.

In technical terms there has been considerable scope for factor substitutability in transport as technology has responded to the relatively high costs of labor in the sector that has allowed for capital to replace labor; for example, two-person cockpits on commercial aircraft, reduction of brakemen on railroads, and automated metro trains. Transport has been what is often called 'technologically progressive' (Baumol, 1967). This may come about through scale effects (for example, the use of larger ships with the same-size crew to carry more cargo) or the substitution of labor functions (for example, navigation on aircraft by automated systems or the loading of ships by robots). Given the massive increase in freight and passenger traffic over time that appears in the earlier tables, combined with the small overall rise, or even decline, in the number of transport and related workers, there has clearly been a very significant overall rise in labor productivity

Table 2.15   *Transport employment in the United States (thousands)*

	2000	2005	2010	2015	2019
United States labor force	132,011	134,034	130,345	141,825	150,939
Transport-related labor force	13,901	13,395	12,054	13,542	14,815
Transport & warehousing	4,401	4,348	4,179	4,859	5,618
Transport-related manufacturing	11,660	11,076	9,305	10,777	11,492
Postal service	880	774	659	597	607
Government employment	867	888	876	845	869

in the transport industries. The emergence of drones and autonomous taxis and trucks is strengthening this trend.

2.4   Local Transport

Local transport can roughly be divided into urban and rural, although suburban transport can have its own characteristics and has become a subject of specific interest. Almost by definition there are only limited common features across cities. Figure 2.3 gives an indication of the variations in the sizes of the largest. It is difficult to argue that they are a homogenous group.

Local transport conditions and use depend on, amongst other things, the geography of the area (for example, whether it is hilly, has waterways through it, or is close to another urban area), its history (for example, whether it has inherited a legacy of infrastructure more suited to a bygone era), its economic roles (for example, whether it is a political or commercial center, or has a large manufacturing base), and the political attitudes of local politicians (for example, whether they foster motor vehicle use or have a public transit bias). Similar factors influence transport in rural areas, including the nature of local agriculture or mineral extraction, the historical provision of infrastructure, the density of population, and the peculiarities of the area's geography.

Some very broad general patterns are identifiable in at least cities in the higher-income countries of the world, and to some extent in poorer nations. We have fewer data on rural areas in part because they tend to be less densely populated, especially in industrial nations, but also because traditional concerns of transport planners, most notably those involving traffic congestion, tend to be much less pronounced. Indeed, many rural areas suffer from depopulation.

Urban Transport

Increasing numbers of people are living in urban areas as agricultural efficiency improves and as industrialization spreads. The World Bank estimates that about 55 percent of the global population are now urban dwellers. Even in the long-industrialized countries there have been significant changes in land use and in urban form more generally as incomes have risen, as the service sector

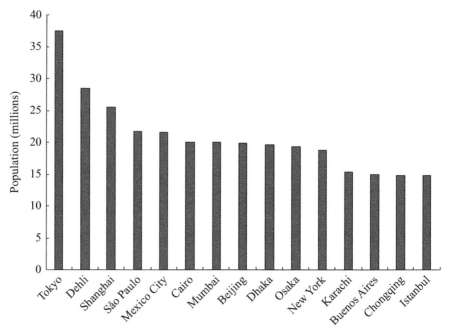

Source: United Nations.

Figure 2.3   *Fifteen largest cities by population*

has increased in importance, and as there have been demographic changes. Interventions by urban planners have brought about their own impacts, trends highlighted 60 years ago by Jane Jacobs (1961). There has been widespread urban sprawl from most cities as their populations have increased. This not only poses problems of a practical nature, such as the provision of public services and the delineation of appropriate areas for local government, but from a descriptive perspective, it means that data collected on old zoning systems can often obscure some of the newer trends in urban transport, such as long-distance commuting and reverse commuting. There have been some efforts to overcome this data problem in recent years. The United States, for example, has sought to partially resolve it by providing data on 'metropolitan statistical areas' (MSAs) and 'combined statistical areas'; for example, the former combines data from administrative units within a contiguous area of relatively high population density.

Even in suburban areas, transport trends found within traditional city areas are not replicated because of their lower densities of housing and population, dominated by single-family homes on small plots surrounded at close quarters by very similar dwellings. The planning authorities also tend to adopt zoning patterns that separate residential and commercial development, as well as different intensities and densities of development. At the simplest level this means that daily needs are not within walking distance of most homes and reliance on cars increases, and that over time the distance of the average commute rises.

To cope with some of these issues, 'edge cities' have emerged: concentrations of business, shopping, and entertainment outside a traditional urban area in what had recently been a residential suburb or semi-rural community (Garreau, 1991). Most edge cities develop at or near existing or planned freeway intersections and near major airports. They rarely include heavy industry. They are large geographically because they are built around automobile mobility.

As a very broad generalization, most major cities in the world now suffer from serious traffic congestion problems, and this sometimes can extend well beyond traditional notions of the 'rush hour'. This is, however, a subject we shall deal with in some depth in Chapters 6 and 9. Here we focus more on the general characteristics of urban transport, and simply highlight some of the major differences that exist between cities.

Figure 2.4 provides details of the relative use that is made of various passenger transport modes in several major cities across the globe. Very significant differences can immediately be seen in walking, cycling, and more locally offered services. There is also a general correlation, as one may anticipate, between the levels of car ownership (Table 2.16) in cities and the use made of the motor car, although this may be deceptive if part of the mileage driven is outside of the urban area. The higher-income countries also generally see less use of public transport modes. This is partly because of higher car ownership rates, but also reflects that public transport, and especially buses, are often seen as inferior

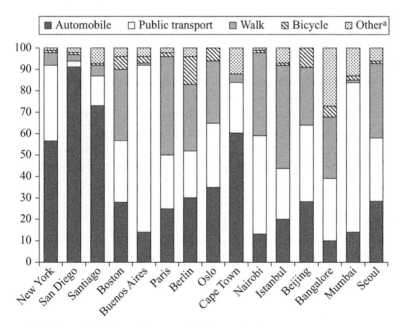

Note: a. Includes auto rickshaw, private two-wheelers, and taxis.

Source: Deloitte City Mobility Index, 2019.

Figure 2.4 *Mode split in a selection of major cities (2017)*

Table 2.16   *Car ownership per 1,000 population in selected countries (2017)*

Country	Cars/1,000	Country	Cars/1,000	Country	Cars/1,000
United States	838[g]	South Korea	475[h]	Colombia	116[g]
Malta	768[h]	United Kingdom	471	Cape Verde	101[a]
Australia	730[g]	Denmark	438	Senegal	44[e]
Poland	719[g]	Malaysia	433[c]	Angola	32[e]
Canada	685[g]	Bahrain	422	India	28[f]
Luxembourg	670	Slovakia	408	Pakistan	17[g]
Italy	655[h]	Bulgaria	393	Burkina Faso	16[e]
Japan	649[h]	Latvia	381[h]	Mozambique	14[d]
Spain	648	Hungary	355	Ethiopia	9
Slovenia	541	Argentina	316[e]	Niger	7[b]
Belgium	508	Israel	314[h]	Guinea	5[c]
Norway	514	Mexico	297[e]	Rwanda	5[c]
Greece	487	Uruguay	280[e]	Bangladesh	4[e]
Libya	483	China	188[i]	Somalia	3[b]
Netherlands	478	South Africa	174[h]		

Notes: a. 2007. b. 2009. c. 2012. d. 2014. e. 2015. f. 2016. g. 2018. h. 2019. i. 2020.

Source: United Nations.

goods for which the perception of the quantity of the service – sharing with others, wait time between services, walking to pick-up points, etc. – falls with rising incomes.

The data also do not tell us much about a topic that we shall devote time to later in the book. These are the economic policies that are being pursued in various cities to influence the amount of travel undertaken and the modes that are targeted. These are generally endogenous to the urban situation in that policy-makers in cities that have large volumes of car traffic for their size are, because of this, forced to encourage the use of alternative public transport modes. As Michael Anderson (2014) has shown, even if public transport carries only a small share of commuters in a city, it can have large effects on the overall transport system's efficiency and congestion levels. Road congestion does not rise linearly with traffic flow.

Rural Transport

While there has been a global movement towards urbanization, there is still a significant amount of movement outside of cities, which for convenience we call 'rural transport'. Much of this is transit traffic in the sense that it involves the movement of people and goods between urban areas and does not stop, except for breaks of various kinds, as part of this movement. Pure rural transport has its origins and destinations outside of urban areas, or involves movement between cities and non-city areas. Globally, much of this transport involves the move-ment of agricultural products, and those involved in their production, although it increasingly can involve tourism. Further, although we focus mainly on economically developed countries where urbanization is extensive, rural transport is often much more a subject of study in lower-income nations that still have a significant rural population.

Defining rural transport is not simple, and circumstances vary with countries and regions within countries (Hough and Taleqani, 2018). For these reasons, only one nation's rural transport situation is described. Looking at the United States, the Office of Management and Budget's definition of metropolitan areas (core counties with one or more central cities of at least 50,000 residents with a Census Bureau-defined urbanized area and a total metropolitan area population of over 100,000 or fringe counties that are economically associated with core counties) provides a residual of non-metropolitan counties located outside the areas that have no cities with 50,000 or more residents. This is taken as rural. About 61 million Americans live in rural areas, according to data from the American Community Survey. Figure 2.5 shows some of the key socioeconomic differences between the urban and rural populations of the United States.

In terms of transport, 95.8 percent of households in rural areas had access to a car in 2015, compared with 88.9 percent of urban households. The 'carless' rural communities were characterized by persistent poverty and had high concentrations of Black, Hispanic, or Native American residents. Rural residents without access to cars are often dependent on public transport, especially in high-poverty areas. This is also true of the percentage of people with a disability and the aged. Median age and the percentage of the population aged 65 or older has increased in both urban and rural areas since the year 2000, but the increase has been greatest among the rural population.

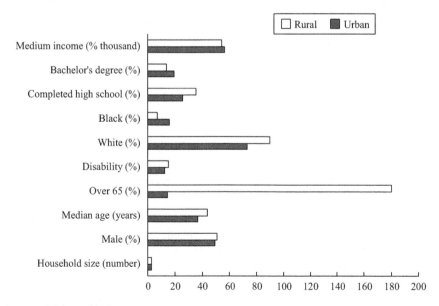

Source: Mattson (2017).

Figure 2.5 *Comparisons of the United States urban and rural populations (2015)*

During the 1990s, public transport services grew, with non-metropolitan providers offering 62 percent more passenger trips, 93 percent more miles traveled, and 60 percent more vehicles available. Public transport is available in 60 percent of rural counties, but with 28 percent of about 1,200 systems offering only a limited service. About two-thirds of rural systems operate in single counties or are city/town in scope; only one out of four rural transit providers operate in a multi-county area. About 60 percent of rural providers are public agencies, and roughly a third are non-profit groups; less than 5 percent are private companies or tribal entities.

The number of American rural communities served by long-distance bus services declined sharply in the years following bus deregulation in 1982. The inter-city bus industry now serves about 4,300 locations, down from over 15,000 prior to 1982, with many of the service discontinuations concentrated in rural communities. Still, 89 percent of the rural population is served by long-distance bus services; it is the dominant mode of scheduled inter-city passenger transport for most rural residents. One reason for this is that fewer than 200 non-metropolitan places in the United States are served by passenger rail services, and, following the terrorist attacks of 2001, the airline passenger industry suffered a downturn, with smaller communities especially hard hit. The number of flights to small, non-hub airports dropped 19 percent between 2000 and 2003. The outbreak of Covid-19 in 2020 led to a further decline in services.

Many rural roads in the United States are in need of repair. In 2020, 13 percent of America's rural roads were rated in poor condition and 21 percent in mediocre condition. Additionally, 8 percent of the nation's rural bridges were rated in poor/structurally deficient condition exhibiting significant deterioration to major components. These bridges were often posted for lower weight or closed to traffic, restricting or redirecting large vehicles, including agricultural equipment, commercial trucks, school buses, and emergency services vehicles.

The Micro-micro Level: Households

At the lowest level of aggregation, it is households and individuals that use a nation's transport system and ultimately pay for it. Travel budgets vary considerably between households, and across income categories. A plethora of factors influence this: household income, locations of home and work, age of the household members, physical capability of household members, priorities in leisure spending, climate, and so on. Added to this, the adoption of different definitions and data collection methods make international comparisons challenging but some general patterns emerge.

While there is much variability across households within any country, as well as between countries, it is generally true that household transport expenditure vies with housing and food as the largest item in households' budgets. From Table 2.17, which sets out details of the average British family's weekly

Table 2.17 *Weekly household expenditure out of net income in Great Britain (2018/19, in 2003 prices)*

	Average weekly expenditure (£)
Food & non-alcoholic drinks	61.90
Alcoholic drink, tobacco, & narcotics	8.00
Clothing & footwear	24.40
Housing, fuel, & power	79.40
Household goods & services	40.08
Health	8.00
Transport	80.20
Communication	21.30
Recreation & culture	76.90
Education	5.70
Restaurants & hotels	51.90
Miscellaneous goods & services	46.70
Other expenditure items	77.20
Total	*585.60*

Source: UK Family Expenditure Survey.

expenditure, transport is clearly one of the larger items accounting for about 14 percent of a household's budget. For comparison, and accepting the caveat that definitions can differ between countries, for the United States in 2018 (in 2003 prices), an average household with expenditures of $788.61 spent $259.47 of it on housing, $133.91 on transport (about 17 percent), and $99.00 on food. In Japan it was 10 percent. Data are sparser, but the same three items dominate household expenditure in poorer countries. In India, for example, in 2017 food accounted for 28 percent of household expenditure, housing and utilities 17 percent, and transport 16 percent; while in Brazil housing accounted for 36.6 percent of expenditure, transport 19.6 percent, and food 17.5 percent.

The pattern does seem to be changing slightly, or at least in some of the higher-income countries, with the outlays on transport declining as a proportion of household expenditure. In the United States, for example, it was about 19 percent in 1987. The explanation for this may in part be that real transport costs have fallen, and therefore the same or more transport may be obtained for a smaller outlay. There may be more substitutes for transport as information and communications systems have improved. The increased use of substitutes such as video conferencing, remote working, and online shopping being examples of this. But it may be that the demand for transport has moved towards a point of saturation as household members make nearly all the trips they want, and increases in income are directed elsewhere. Transport may be seen in economic terms as becoming an 'inferior good' in this case. In other words, the Engel curve, describing how the proportion of household income spent on a good like transport varies with income, has taken a negative gradient.

2.5 Emerging Trends

The world is not static and there are several emerging, as well as ongoing, trends that are beginning to influence the sorts of issues that transport economists address. Added to this, in the medium term, is the considerable uncertainty that will accompany the world economy and social systems as the longer-term effects of the Covid-19 pandemic begin to emerge. At the time of writing there is considerable uncertainty about the exact form and magnitude of the effects of the virus on markets and institutional structures. Here there is no attempt to join the debates that are taking place, but rather we assume that some of the broad changes that were being seen pre-Covid will have matured and will have implications for transport. We shall, however, add a few separate observations regarding Covid in Section 2.6. Here the focus is on trends apparent at the beginning of 2020.

First, in the established industrial world the long-term trend, despite periodic downturns in the business cycle (including recessions in many countries from 2007 to 2009) and periods of very rapid growth as in the late 1990s ('irrational exuberance', to quote Alan Greenspan), would seem to be for continued economic expansion. The recent past has already witnessed significant increases in traffic and vehicle ownership in these countries and there are reasons to expect this trend to continue in broad terms over the years. Globalization does not seem to have fully been completed, although the economic success of the Single Internal Market within the European Union and the NAFTA/USMCA are providing demonstration effects of the benefits of removing trade restrictions. The natural growth in trade accompanying these developments will create demand for more transport services, but this inevitably will take place in the context of limited infrastructure capacity. Even if there are major investment initiatives, it takes time to construct new ports, roads, and so on.

Looking to Europe, a lot has been written on impacts for transport of the creation of the Single European Market in 1992, and certainly the new situation with an enlarged membership has implications for transport not only within the member states but also for countries of the European Free Trade Area involved in the larger European Economic Space (see Chapter 14). The problem has been how to cater for such traffic growth in a fully, economically efficient manner, a fact recognized by the European Union in its transport policy statements.

Second, it is becoming clearer that the liberalization of Eastern Europe, coupled with the new political geography that has emerged, is posing problems as well as offering opportunities for the countries in the region. Liberalization meant that the overall 'transport market' in Europe expanded considerably in line with major new urban and industrial centers being brought within the market system. It means, therefore, that many major transport links are now part of Europe's transport future. In many ways this has proved advantageous for the long-term development of European transport because it creates something more akin to a natural market for transport services than existed previously, but there are problems with defining priorities and financing investments in the system.

Short-term problems also remain because of the attitude regarding transport that had grown up in Eastern and Central Europe since the early 1990s and the impact this has had on the physical transport infrastructure now in place. The transport systems of Eastern Europe were traditionally dominated by rail and suffered from low productivity and over-staffing compared to Western Europe. It had been developed from the late 1940s to meet the trading patterns of the members of the Council for Mutual Economic Assistance. There remain challenges in filling the voids in infrastructure linking the Eastern economies with the West that grew up in this period.

North America has begun, albeit slowly, to integrate its economies through free trade arrangements that are shifting patterns of production and, with this, the demands for transport services. Coupled with this, the general growth in importance of international trade for the United States has put increasing strains on its international border crossings, a situation worsened by the costs of meeting enhanced security arrangements. As with Europe, there are pressures for seeking innovative ways to finance new infrastructure, maintain and upgrade what is already in place, and to make better use of existing capacity (Transportation Research Board, 2003).

It is not only in the industrialized nations and in the post-communist states that new conditions are emerging. If there is to be economic development in the low-income countries of Africa, Asia, and South and Central America then transport will inevitably change. There is ample evidence from China, India, and some other economies that the economies of some of these states have expanded rapidly since 2020, although this is not so true of many of the lowest-income countries. Returning to Table 2.16, this shows very low levels of car ownership in the poorest countries. Additionally, these countries tend to have some of the least safe transport systems; Botswana, for example, has the highest road mortality rate on roads at 30 deaths per 100,000 population.

Economic expansion, however, especially if it results in significant growth in some larger countries, could lead to substantial demands for car ownership, more mobility, and the need for major new infrastructure initiatives, as well as imposing serious congestion and safety challenges. As can be seen from earlier discussions, the link between per capita income and vehicle ownership is a strongly positive one. It will also mean that there will be increasing strains put on the environment, both within these countries and in terms of global effects such as emissions of greenhouse gases.

A significant feature of most low-income countries in recent years has been the secular drift of population into urban areas. Historically, the growth of car ownership in the largest cities in Third World countries was already of the order of 7 to 15 percent in the decade 1960–70. Added to this, the actual cost of transport in these cities has risen significantly, with households spending over 5 percent of their income on transport, and in some cases 15 percent, and city governments spending 15 to 25 percent of their annual budgets on transport investments and operations.

Looking forward, the transport situation in the urban areas of the developing world is inevitably going to get worse in the short to medium term. The

Exhibit   *Response of air transport to a pandemic*

The 2020 Covid-19 pandemic seriously affected the demand for and supply of air transport. Passengers were reluctant to fly for fear of infection and official policies of quarantining and banning traffic from selected countries caused a catastrophic collapse in demand. For cargo, the accompanying global recession meant contraction of supply chains.

The suddenness of the pandemic resulted in the hub-and-spoke system simply evaporating, pushing down passenger load factors and pushing up costs. With no adjustment time, the industry quickly experienced a collapse in domestic and international air passenger demand that led to airlines having to park more than 17,000 passenger jets by May 2020. Two dozen airlines had collapsed by the summer of that year, despite measures by many governments to sustain at least a core network of services.

While air cargo rose 2 percent between February and July 2020 compared to the comparable period for 2019 as initially supplemental airlift was required to relocate medical equipment and supplies, later significant volumes of cargo relocated from passenger aircrafts' belly holds to dedicated cargo planes. The figure provides a clearer picture of trends in transported cargo volumes.

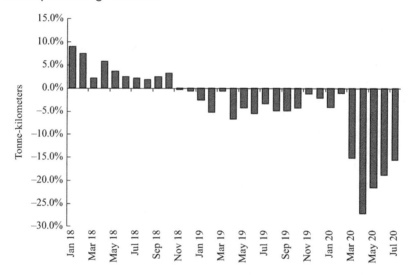

Covid-19 affected markets differently, requiring diverse responses by airlines. Lufthansa, for instance, advanced retirement of its A380 fleet, while many carriers reduced their fleets, put aircraft into 'long-term storage', or cancelled orders. In other cases, including Austrian, Swiss, and Icelandair, carriers reconfigured planes for cargo use. Others pulled out of mergers, for example the withdrawal of LOT's bid for Condor.

Governments sought to tide their carriers over. Some provided loans, for example Germany ($6.75 billion to Lufthansa) and Korea ($970 million to Korean Air via state-owned banks). Some, such as the United States, introduced payroll grants, while many provided easy credit facilities. Airlines, in turn, made concessions, for example giving up landing slots to competitors, withdrawing from short routes where high-speed rail was an alternative, and modifying membership of their boards.

Given their strategic role, the oversight bodies could do little besides offering advice and collating information as it became available. The International Civil Aviation Organization, for example, developed a 'COVID-19 Recovery Platform' offering guidance for airports, airlines, aircraft, crew, and cargo handlers on how to reduce the public health risk while strengthening confidence among the traveling public, the global supply chain, and governments.

See also: S. Albers and V. Rundshagen (2020) European airlines' strategic responses to the COVID-19 pandemic (January–May, 2020), *Journal of Air Transport Management*, 87, No 101863.

mid-1980s saw eight of the largest cities in the world with populations of over 10 million located in low-income countries. Predictions are that this number will have doubled by the end of the twenty-first century, while 18 further agglomerations in the developing world will have populations of between 5 and 10 million. A major difficulty is that the growth of urbanization and the level of motor car ownership and use are closely linked, While this is partly due to the concentration of wealth in the urban areas it is also entwined with the geographical spread which accompanies urbanization and the resultant increase in the average journey length.

Comparing Nairobi and Mexico City, for example, shows average trip lengths of between 1.5 and 2.8 miles for the former, while those for the latter, which is much larger, are between 3.5 and 6.0 miles. Public transport is much less efficient at serving a spatially dispersed market and hence the automobile is used more often. How to plan and cater for the inevitable expansion in traffic as urbanization continues in these countries will be a mounting problem for transport economists, as will be finding resources. Some indication of the resources that are currently being spent in China, for example, is that $4.25 billion was invested in Beijing's infrastructure in 2004, and another $22 billion leading up to the 2008 Olympics, to reduce the city's traffic congestion issues.

The emergence of the economies of China and India has seen further urbanization trends and with this has come new demands for consumer goods, including automobiles (see Table 2.18 for details of China). These countries combined account for about 37 percent of the world's population, and between 1980 and 2005 the real personal income of India more than doubled, and more than quadrupled in China (Pucher et al., 2007). The outcome has been a tripling of motor vehicles in India and a tenfold increase in China. The transport situation has been exacerbated by the urbanization resulting from these economic trends; the development area of Chinese cities, for example, tripled between 1985 and 2005 while the population only doubled, producing significant urban sprawl. A similar pattern emerges for India. There are different patterns of travel in urban areas between the two countries, however, with over half the trips in Chinese

Table 2.18   *Durable goods for 1,000 households (2006 or most recent prior year)*

	China		India		Total
	Urban	Rural	Urban	Rural	
Automobiles	4.3	–	4.0	0.7	1.7
Bicycles	117.6	98.4	51.9	57.2	55.7
Cameras	48.0	3.7	0.0	0.0	0.0
Computers	47.2	–	0.0	0.0	0.0
Microwave ovens	50.6	–	–	–	–
Motorcycles[a]	20.4	44.6	28.3	7.9	13.6
Refrigerators	91.8	22.5	30.8	4.8	12.1
Telephones	93.3	64.1	–	–	–
Mobile telephones	137.4	89.4	70.4	27.5	39.5
Televisions[b]	137.4	89.4	70.4	27.5	39.5
Video disc players[c]	70.2	–	8.2	1.7	3.6
Washing machines	96.8	43.0	12.5	0.9	4.1

Notes: a. Data for India include scooters. b. Data for China include color TVs; data for India include all TVs. c. Data for India include VCRs.

mega-cities being non-motorized compared to only 25 percent in India. In both cases, however, motorization is growing rapidly – especially in terms of motorized two-wheeled vehicles that, for instance, grew in number from 200,000 to over 50 million in China from 1981 to 2002.

But it is not only the local transport systems that are finding it difficult to cope with rising demands as incomes rise in many developing countries; other elements of transport infrastructure networks are also coming under increasing pressure. The amount and quality of infrastructure varies widely between developing countries. In many cases, the issue is simply that there is insufficient infrastructure for the needs of a country. This can be a major problem for landlocked, exporting countries which, in addition to moving their output over their own territories, have to also rely on the infrastructure of intermediate nations (Arvis et al., 2010). While this has been a long-standing problem for some countries, in other cases, there is simply a shortage of capacity to meet a sudden increase in demands for their products.

Countries like China, which have seen large increases in their international trade since 1990, find themselves with pressures on their airport and seaport capacities to meet the globalized patterns of activities they now engage in. Table 2.19, for example, shows the increase in Chinese freight movements by mode between 1980 and 2018, and Figure 2.6 shows the rapid growth in air cargo traffic at the country's main airports from 1990 to 2004. This pressure on capacity extends to national inter-urban transport systems as the domestic supply chain expands not just to feed the gateway ports but also as increased production itself puts pressure on the domestic freight networks.

In terms of surface transport, in 2005 China had a road network of more than 3.3 million kilometers, although about 1.47 million kilometers was 'village roads'; paved roads were 770,265 kilometers of the total in 2004; the

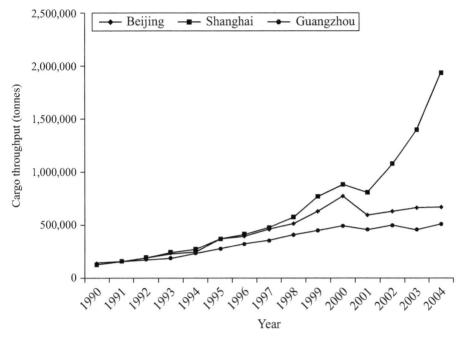

Figure 2.6   *Air cargo growth at China's main airports (1990 to 2004)*

Table 2.19   *Annual freight movement in China by mode (million tonnes)*

	1980	1990	2000	2010	2018
Rail	1,112.79	1,506.81	1,785.81	3,642.71	4,026.71
Road	3,820.48	7,240.40	10,388.13	24,480.52	39,568.71
Water	426.76	800.94	1,223.91	3,789.49	7,026.84
Air	0.09	0.37	1.97	5.65	7.70
Pipeline	105.25	157.50	187.00	499.72	898.07

remainder were gravel, improved earth standard, or merely earth tracks. In 2003 they moved nearly 11.6 billion tons of freight and provided 769.6 trillion passenger-kilometers. Highways (some 130,000 kilometers) have been critical to China's economic growth, as they worked to mitigate a poor distribution network. Massive new investments mean that all major cities are expected to be linked with a 55,000-kilometer inter-provincial expressway system by 2020. (By comparison, the United States' Interstate freeway system is about 47,000 miles.) The highway and road systems carried nearly 11.6 billion tons of freight and 769.6 trillion passenger-kilometers in 2003.

Both bi-lateral and multi-lateral aid, most notably through the World Bank and the United Nations, but also from blocs such as the European Union, has been used in the past to help less economically advanced countries improve their transport systems. Table 2.20, for example, shows the recent expenditures of the World Bank, and future commitments are of the same order of magnitude, although

Table 2.20   *Commitments by the World Bank for transport ($ billions)*

Mode	Commitments		Commitments	
	1996–2000	*Percent*	*2001–2006*	*Percent*
Roads	13.0	73	11.9	73
Railways	1.5	9	1.3	8
Ports	1.2	6	0.5	3
Aviation	0.1	0	0.5	3
General transport	2.2	12	2.2	13
Total	*18.0*	*100*	*16.4*	*100*

Source: The World Bank (2007).

with a somewhat broader focus in terms of how the monies will be spent. Most of these funds are committed to enhancing the transport infrastructure of recipient countries, but there is increasing interest in ensuring that environmental and safety considerations are brought to bear at the project decision-making level.

It seems unlikely that the poorer nations of the world will require less assistance to maintain their transport systems in the future, although there are now more efforts by the aid-giving agencies to ensure that the monies provided are used effectively. Added to this, there is increased encouragement for these countries to do more by way of self-help in terms of imposing user charges on infrastructure to at least recover some of the costs and to limit its use to activities contributing most to economic development.

2.6   Some Comments on the Short-term Effects of Covid-19 on Transport

The combined short-term market effects of Covid-19 in 2020 and the reactions of policy-makers regarding transport were unprecedented in peacetime. A few brief comments are provided with some data to highlight the scale and nature of the effects of the pandemic within the first 18 months of its arrival. The aim is not in any way to offer a full picture but rather to focus on several of the more pronounced patterns, as well as indicating some recovery trends.

At the global level, air transport and international rail services were impacted in two different ways. The demand for passenger services fell as international business and leisure declined as both individuals and businesses cut back on their mobility when confronted with the threat of catching the virus. Governments restricted access to their countries to contain the spread of Covid-19 in the public interest. Table 2.21 offers an insight into the magnitude of the impacts of Covid-19 on passenger seats being flown for major airline markets. A wide variation of initial adverse effects is clear. Globally, seats fell by nearly 40 percent between 2019 and 2020, while countries such as the United Kingdom, Singapore, Germany, and the United Arab Emirates saw losses of well over

Table 2.21 *Air seats June 2021, as a percentage of seats for comparable dates in 2019 and 2020*

	June 24, 2019 (%)	June 22, 2020 (%)
Australia	–36.2	336.3
Brazil	–43.6	242.6
China	–0.3	34.9
France	–54.1	196.7
Germany	–67.0	115.0
India	–49.1	79.3
Japan	–58.7	–23.2
Mexico	–15.3	122.2
Singapore	–82.9	209.7
South Africa	–47.7	465.9
South Korea	–46.8	16.6
Spain	–50.1	230.8
UAE	–59.4	156.7
United Kingdom	–77.7	43.3
United States	–18.8	137.4
Global	–37.9	81.4

Source: Official Airline Guide.

50 percent. The third column of the table shows the pick-up in 2021 with traffic up over 81 percent over 2020.

Regarding local transport, there were considerable variations on traffic flows across cities. Given the substitutability of physical movement and electronic communication, cities with larger service-sector employment saw larger falls in vehicular traffic as people worked from home and made more use of various delivery services. Some modes lost more traffic than others. As can be seen from Figure 2.7, while the temporal patterns of automobile and metro (in London, the Tube) are very similar between January 2020 and June 2021, the overall decline in public transport was significantly greater. This was almost certainly due to both concern with traveling with potentially affected strangers and the requirement to wear face masks on public transport.

While person and goods movements were rapidly and radically reduced with the onset of the pandemic, the movement of information was much less affected. This was because of the greater uptake of electronic communication and, in particular, of e-commerce and video meetings. This was certainly not a new phenomenon. Use of video conferencing and various other forms of electronic information exchange had been gradually growing since the emergence of the internet and world-wide web in association with hardware developments of such things as the smartphone. Considerable numbers of individuals were already working at home prior to the arrival of Covid-19 (Figure 2.8). But after the onset of the pandemic, video conferencing increased exponentially.

One indicator of these trends are the flows of revenues earned by the video conferencing companies. Zoom, for example, saw a 169 percent first-quarter increase in its year-on-year revenue for the financial year ending January 2021,

Source: UK Department for Transport.

Figure 2.7   *Daily London automobile (upper) and Tube passengers (lower), March 3, 2020 to June 21, 2021 compared with same dates in 2019*

which accelerated to 355, 367, and 369 percent in the second, third, and fourth quarters. In terms of e-commerce, online retail sales in the United States increased by 32.4 percent year-on-year in 2020 and were up 39 percent in the first quarter of 2021. While some of this was the result of the ongoing growth in electronic transfers, much came from reductions in physical interactions.

2.7   Where are the Numbers?

This chapter has made copious use of a wide range of data sources. Statistics of this kind, however, can rapidly become outdated. There have been long-standing concerns over the availability of timely economic data regarding transport, its limited coverage, and its quality (for example, see Head, 1980), although this may reflect the insatiable demand of economists as much as reality. The widespread use of the world-wide web makes it easy to update data and to add new sets. It

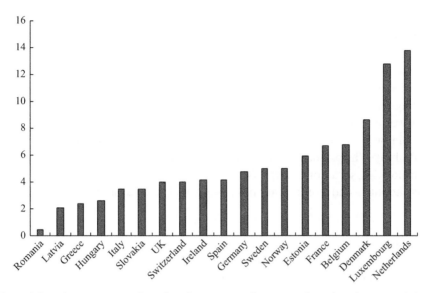

Figure 2.8   *The percentage of employed persons aged 15–64 working from home (2017)*

also allows readers to critique the relevance and accuracy of the quantitative information that is offered in this book. Here, a few words are offered as to the sorts of public data sources that are openly available as well as some information on the specific types of economic statistics that can be useful when looking at how transport systems function.

Data on transport are widely available but differ in their quality and the ways in which they are presented. The quote of Disraeli's cited earlier should not be forgotten. The units used, for example, need to be treated carefully; fuel use may be expressed in kilometers per liter or in miles per gallon (and of course a United States gallon is about 20 percent smaller than an imperial gallon to confuse things further). There may be a big difference, as already noted, between the importance of, say, various modes of transport when assessed in physical terms as opposed to value terms. Money values themselves can be at current values, with no allowance for inflation, or in constant prices set against a base year when they are adjusted for changes in the value of money.

Governments at all levels publish data, as do trade associations, transport undertakings, and research institutes. A few useful sites include the following. For the United States, national data are collected by the US Department of Transportation's Bureau of Transportation Statistics (http://www.bts.gov/); for the United Kingdom corresponding data are provided by the Department for Transport (http://www.dft.gov.uk/pgr/statistics/); Eurostat provides data for the European Union (http://epp.eurostat.ec.europa.eu); and for Canada a comparable site is https://tc.canada.ca/en/road-transportation/motor-vehicle-safety/statistics-data. The OECD's International Transport also offers compilations of international data (https://www.oecd-ilibrary.org/transport/data/itf-transport-statistics_trsprt-data-en). With modern search engines it is a relatively simple matter to seek out national data for other countries.

Internationally, the United Nations' International Civil Aviation Organization (http://www.icao.int/) and its International Maritime Organization (http://www.imo.org/) provide statistics on air transport and shipping respectively, and its World Tourism Organization (http://www.unwto.org/) covers the transport-intensive and growing tourism sector. The World Bank offers data and studies relating to the transport and related conditions in developing countries (http://www.worldbank.org/).

Major professional and trade organizations include the International Union of Railways (https://uic.org/support-activities/statistics/), the International Air Transport Association (https://www.iata.org/en/services/statistics/), and the International Road Confederation (https://www.irf.global/statistics/).

References

Anderson, M.L. (2014) Subway, strikes, and slowdowns: the impacts of public transit on traffic congestion, *American Economic Review*, 104, 15–33.

Arvis, J.-F., Raballand, G., and Marteau, J.-F. (2010) *The Cost of Being Landlocked: Logistics Costs and Supply Chain Reliability*, World Bank.

Baumol, W.J. (1967) Macroeconomics of unbalanced growth: the anatomy of urban crisis, *American Economic Review*, 57, 415–26.

Button, K.J. (2011) Transport policy, in A.M. El-Agraa (ed.), *The European Union: Economics and Policies*, 9th edn, Cambridge University Press.

Garreau, J. (1991) *Edge City: Life on the New Frontier*, Doubleday.

Head, J. (1980) Transport statistics: sources and limitations, *Transportation Journal*, 20, 33–46.

Hough, J. and Taleqani, A.R. (2018) Future of rural transit, *Journal of Public Transportation*, 21, 31–42.

Jacobs, J. (1961) *The Death and Life of Great American Cities*, Random House.

Krugman, P. (2009) The increasing returns revolution in trade and geography, *American Economic Review*, 99, 561–71.

Mattson, J. (2017) *Rural Transit Fact Book 2017*, Upper Great Plains Transportation Institute.

Pucher, J., Peng, Z., Mittal, N., Zhu, Y., and Korattyswaroopam, N. (2007) Urban transport trends and policies in China and India: impacts of rapid economic growth, *Transport Reviews*, 27, 379–410.

Transportation Research Board (2003) Freight capacity in the 21st century, TRB Special Report 271.

The World Bank (2007) *A Decade of Action in Transport: An Evaluation of World Bank Assistance to the Transport Sector, 1995–2005*, World Bank.

3   Transport and Location

3.1   The Desire for Movement and Mobility

The nineteenth-century Scottish novelist, Robert Louis Stevenson, once said, 'For my part, I travel not to anywhere, but to go. I travel for travel's sake. The great affair is to move' (Stevenson, 1879). As highlighted in the discussion in Chapter 1, Stevenson was very much in the minority. Few people travel for the sheer joy of it, although some modes of transport do arouse feelings of excitement, romance, or sentiment. But even here, there are fine lines to be drawn. Drifting down a Venetian Canal in a gondola, sipping a glass of prosecco as the sun sets with the right person sitting beside you can clearly provide utility, but is this really from the transport? There are also, of course, people who take touring holidays each year where sight-seeing from a bus or car is an integral part of the enjoyment, but, again, is it the transport *per se* that provides the utility?

Most individuals travel because they wish to benefit from the social, recreational, educational, employment, and other opportunities that become accessible with movement. Similarly, freight transport opens opportunities for greater efficiency in production, and it permits extensive geographical specialization with the accompanying benefits of an increased division of labor. Larger markets can be served. More simply, transport permits the spatial disadvantages of separation to be reduced. The concept was taken even further in 1997 with the publication of Frances Cairncross' *The Death of Distance*, which argued that the internet was becoming an enormously efficient way to transport digital data around the world. Put simply, that electronic communication was replacing the personal and physical transport in many activities.

Almost five decades ago, however, Michael Thomson (1974) provided a helpful and durable classification of seven main reasons why people in the modern world still desire to transport either themselves or their property:

- The heterogeneity of the earth's surface means that no one part of it can provide all the products people wish for. An acceptable bundle of such goods can only be obtained by either moving around collecting them, or having them brought to you.
- The continuation of modern society and the high levels of material well-being rely upon a degree of productive specialization. Industry requires a multiplicity of diverse inputs which must be collected from wide-ranging sources and, to permit the necessary level of specialization, extensive market areas must be tapped and served.

- In addition to specialization, high-quality transport permits the exploitation of other major economies of scale. There are essentially technical economies associated with high levels of output and which include automation, bulk handling, research and development activities, mass marketing, and purpose-built equipment.
- Transport has always served a political and military role. Internally, a country seeks good transport both to permit more effective defense of its borders and to improve the political cohesion of the nation. The Romans were certainly aware of this and most of their road building was to this end, as was the construction of trans-continental railroads in the United States and Canada. Externally, good transport permits a country to dominate any colonial or subservient provinces, while more aggressive states require transport to pursue their expansionist policies. Politically, the ownership of expensive, modern transport infrastructure (especially aircraft or mercantile marine) is also treated as a symbol of power and status. In most developed countries the scale of transport required to meet economic needs normally exceeds that required to meet political or military criteria, although individual components of a transport system (for example, specific roads or airports) may be provided explicitly for non-economic reasons.
- Without transport, social relationships and contacts can be very restricted. Transport permits social intercourse, and with it may come a greater understanding of the problems and attitudes of various geographically distant groups. In the developed world the enhancement of social understanding brought about by increased international travel is well recognized, but in many less developed countries the introduction of much more basic transport technology can have profound effects upon the social relationships between inhabitants of formerly isolated towns and villages which are, by 'Western standards', very close together.
- Modern transport has widened cultural opportunities, permitting people to examine the artistic treasures of other countries and to explore their own national heritage. It also allows for the staging of international exhibitions, sports spectaculars, concerts, parades, and fairs that stimulate new trends and innovations in the cultural and sporting spheres.
- Transport is desired to permit people to live and work apart; it permits the geographical separation of employment from leisure. It increases the life-style options open to people, giving them a choice among residential locations away from cities but involving a heavy commitment to travel, or ones much closer to the main employment center but involving short commuting journeys. Transport, quite simply, widens the location choices open to households.

What becomes apparent from Thomson's listing is the close link between location decisions (of both individuals and firms) and the transport system. Much of what he says is still valid but is becoming increasingly nuanced with new technologies, personal life-style, and new approaches to logistics. Here we look at both the more traditional economic models linking transport and economic decisions regarding location and consider some of the more recent implications for these models following the arrival of the information age. The latter topic is extended in Chapter 10, which deals with the development in logistics and its economic analysis.

3.2   Transport: the 'Chicken' or the 'Egg'?

If one takes very broad statistics, then there is unquestionably a link between mobility and affluence. This is, for example, clear from Table 3.1, which presents some of the findings contained in a classic study by Wilfred Owen (1987), regarding levels of per capita GDP across a range of countries and the transport mobility expressed as a combination of such things as passenger miles per annum of automobile, rail, and domestic air travel, miles of railway, and number of trucks, enjoyed by those living in these countries. While measures are not very sophisticated, a general correlation is apparent. What is less clear is the direction of causation. Does high income lead to or result from higher levels of mobility? Or to put it in more technical terms, is mobility a function of the supply of transport services? Or does the supply of transport services result from an inherent demand for mobility? The answers are not immediately apparent.

Table 3.1   *Mobility across countries*

	GNP per capita	Travel mobility	Freight mobility
Switzerland	139	104	81
Sweden	119	96	151
United States	106	160	260
Netherlands	101	83	42
France	100	100	100
Canada	95	114	374
Australia	91	107	335
Japan	87	96	94
United Kingdom	63	78	47
Italy	53	86	49
Spain	43	54	44
Venezuela	24	32	55
Yugoslavia	24	32	55
Brazil	18	18	23
Mexico	15	14	42
Colombia	11	6	47
Nigeria	6	5	5
Egypt	5	5	13
Pakistan	2	3	10
China	2	3	16
India	2	5	26
Bangladesh	1	2	3

At another level, in previous chapters it was suggested that one of the reasons for the increased interest in transport economics from the late 1960s was the recognition of the important link between transport and land-use patterns, and especially those relating to urban form and intra-urban location. The effects of changes in the transport system on land use tend to be long-term (they are often called 'activity shifts') but, given the longevity of much transport infrastructure, such interactions must to some extent concern current transport policy-makers. The changes that occur in land use will also, in turn, by altering the nature and size of the local residential population and industrial bases, exert an enormous influence on future transport demand. A major new suburban underground railway system, for example, will immediately attract some travelers away from other modes of transport in addition to encouraging trips to be made by former non-travelers. In the longer term, sites near the underground termini will become desirable while those further away will appear relatively less attractive. There will therefore be important implications for residential and employment location patterns. Additionally, changing location and trip-making patterns will alter such things as car ownership decisions.

While these interactions are now fully recognized, it is difficult to construct a comprehensive theory that fully reflects all the linkages. The problem is further compounded by the fact that transport and land-use changes are ongoing modifications to the spatial economy. There are continual cycles of cause and effect, and it is impossible to decide upon a point where it is sensible to break into this continuum of change. Consequently, from a pragmatic standpoint, there is need to make careful judgments as to whether land use is influenced by transport or vice versa. To some extent the final decision must rest with the questions being considered.

Urban and regional scientists tend to treat transport as the influential variable because their focus of attention is on the spatial dimension. Questions are posed, for example, in terms of why certain population densities occur or why specific urban economies interact. In contrast, transport economics usually accepts a given land-use pattern and looks at methods of providing efficient transport services within this constraint. Questions center, for instance, on problems of aligning routes or controlling traffic flows.

An example of this latter approach that reveals both the methodology of conventional transport economics, but also highlights some of the difficulties in the modeling of urban decision-making, was developed by John Kain (1964). His econometric study looking specifically at public transport subsidies and calibrated using information from a 1953 survey of 40,000 households in Detroit, adopts four steps in its argument:

- Workers initially select a residential density in which to live depending upon their income, their preference for a specific plot size, and the price of residential land.
- Once a location has been selected, the decision to purchase a car is treated as dependent upon the local residential density, family income, public transport availability, and the composition of the worker's family.

- The decision whether to use public transport for the journey to work, besides depending upon the previous decisions regarding location and car owner-ship, is thought to be influenced by the quality of local public transport, and the demands of non-working members of the household to make use of the car (if one is owned).
- The length of journeys is treated as dependent both on previous deci-sions of the worker and on the price of residential land adjacent to workplaces.

The implied chain of decision-making is, therefore, uni-directional (or 'recursive') and of the form seen in Figure 3.1.

While Kain was clearly aware of the feedbacks from transport to land use, for a variety of statistical and theoretical reasons he could not adequately reflect them in his model. Besides not allowing for the longer-term feedbacks from travel behavior to land use, the sequence takes no account of the influence of public transport quality on the car ownership decision, or the length of journeys on the longer-term provision of public transport. What the sequence does do, however, is to permit Kain to examine the case for subsidizing public transport within the current urban land-use framework. The assumptions of the sequential type of framework used by Kain are analogous to the standard *ceteris paribus* assump-tions of conventional partial equilibrium microeconomics. They also suffer from the same limitations but do provide boundaries within which useful analysis can be conducted.

Michael Wegener (2004) has suggested another way of looking at this issue involving a focus on feedback cycles (Figure 3.2) and the recognition that trip and location decisions co-determine each other. It is also very much the approach used in many engineering-based and human-geography-derived development theories. Essentially:

- The distribution of land uses, such as residential, industrial, or commercial, over the urban area determines the locations of human activities including living, working, shopping, education, and leisure.
- The distribution of human activities in space requires spatial interactions or trips in the transport system to overcome distance between the locations of activities.
- The distribution of infrastructure in the transport system creates opportu-nities for spatial interactions, and can be measured by accessibility.
- The distribution of accessibility in space co-determines location decisions and so results in changes in the land-use system.

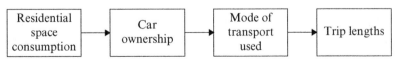

Figure 3.1 *Recursive view of location and travel*

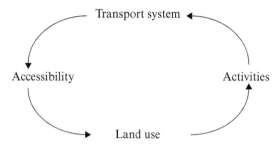

Figure 3.2   *The land-use transport feedback cycle*

Much of this book is concerned exclusively with the transport sector and with short-run travel decisions. In general, it therefore implicitly assumes that the causal link runs from land use to transport, and that land use is pre-determined. In a way this may be regarded as a short-term view, land use being less flexible than transport. It seems inappropriate, however, not to give some brief overview of the approach adopted by spatial scientists. Not to do so would in effect ignore the part played by transport in both shaping land-use patterns and determining the size of the market areas served by various industries. In the remainder of this chapter, therefore, we present a brief introductory outline of modern location theory, concentrating primarily on that aspect of theory that gives a central role to transport. The theory is supplemented by some discussion of the applied work that offers quantification of the important role played by transport in this field. Later in the book (in Chapter 13) the subject of transport and location interaction is touched upon again in the context of economic development.

3.3   Industrial Location and Transport

From the beginning, economic theories of industrial location argued that transport plays a key role in decisions concerning where industrial activities will be located. As we have seen, provision of good transport permits producers to be separated from both their sources of new materials and their eventual customers. Alfred Weber (1929) developed an early model for mobile plant with transport costs determining the location of manufacturing industry. In Figure 3.3 all potential customers are located at A_1 while the two raw materials required by the manufacturing industry are located respectively at A_2 and A_3. The 'd's represent distances between the points of raw material supply and final demand. It is assumed that all other factors of production are freely available at all potential production sites and that, topographically, all activities are located on a uniform plain.

Transport costs are assumed to be proportional with respect to both distances covered and weight of goods carried. The location of a manufacturing plant will therefore depend on the relative pulls of the various material locations and the market. The problem is then one of finding the site, Z, for manufacture which minimizes total costs, in other words the location which minimizes T where:

$$T = a_1 \mathbf{r}_{A_1} + a_2 \mathbf{r}_{A_2} + a_3 \mathbf{r}_{A_3} \tag{3.1}$$

where:

a_1 is the physical amount of the final goods consumed at A_1;

a_2 is the physical amount of the raw material available at A_2 required to produce a_1 of the final good;

a_3 is the physical amount of the raw material available at A_3 required to produce a_1 of the final good; and

$\mathbf{r}_{A_1}, \mathbf{r}_{A_2}$, and $\mathbf{r}_{A_3}$ are the respective distances from sites A_1, A_2, and A_3.

It is easily seen that if any two of a_1, a_2, and a_3 are exceeded by the third, then the location of production is determined at the site associated with this third variable. For example, if $a_2 > (a_1 + a_3)$, then production of the final commodity should be at site A_2. If no location is dominant, then graphical methods can be used to find the least-cost site. A second triangle is drawn with its sides ('d's) proportional to a_1, a_2, and a_3 and the three angles measured. We denote the angle opposite the a_1 as α_1, that opposite a_2 as α_2, and finally that opposite a_3 as α_3. These angles then form the basis for erecting similar triangles around the original location triangle (see Figure 3.3). Circles are drawn which touch the points of each triangle and the optimal production site Z is then found at the location where all three circles intersect. (If Z is found to be outside of the original location triangle, then it is simple to prove that one of the corner solutions, A_1, A_2, or A_3 is preferable.) This location minimizes transport costs, as defined in equation (3.1).

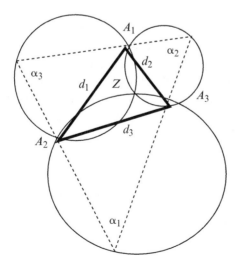

Figure 3.3 *Weber's model of industrial location*

This simple analysis implicitly assumes that transport costs are linearly related to distance, but there is ample evidence that there are often considerable diseconomies associated with short hauls and with partially full loads. While Weber originally suggested that one could adjust the sides of the location triangle to capture this, the situation requires rather more complicated modifications. The difficulty is that in these circumstances location and transport costs are co-determined; without knowledge of the final location (that is, Z), it is impossible to assess the magnitude, if any, of economies of long-haul transport. There is a suggestion, however, that, other things being equal, tapered transport rates (that is, when the rate per mile declines with distance) tend, in some circumstances, to draw industry to either the source of raw materials or the market for final products.

Suppose that only one raw material is needed to produce a final product, or that the range of raw materials required is located at a single point, and this is to be found at location A in Figure 3.4. Further, there is no loss of weight in the manufacturing process required to produce the final product that will eventually be sold at location M. Either the transport system offers a through service from A to M costing $10 per ton or alternatively there are services from A to the intermediate site B costing $6 per ton and one from B to M also costing $6 per ton. Since we assume no weight loss in production the cost-conscious manufacturer is clearly indifferent between A and M but would not select site B because $(AB + BA) > AM$ in cost terms.

To relax the assumption of no weight loss in manufacturing does not remove the disadvantage suffered by B relative to A which is now preferable to location M. (It is possible in this situation for B to be preferred to M if a location at A is impracticable for technical or planning reasons, but this would depend upon the relative importance of the taper *vis-à-vis* the weight loss in manufacture.) Weight loss will only influence the choice between A and M, and this may even be true if different rates are charged not simply by haul length but also by type of commodity.

Even if it is more expensive per ton to carry the final product it may still be preferable to locate production facilities at the material source rather than the final market. In the United States, for example, the meat-packing industry of the nineteenth century was gradually drawn westwards to the main source of beef (initially to Chicago and then to Omaha and Kansas City) even though rail rates per ton-mile favored transport of live animals rather than carcasses. The simple

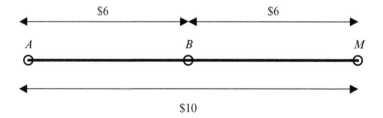

Figure 3.4   *The effects of tapered transport rates on industrial location*

fact was that the dressed meat of a steer weighs only 54 percent of the live animal weight; hence locations near the raw material were favored.

Of course, firms do not in general locate in isolation from one another; there are often agglomeration economies in locating near similar firms or suppliers. August Lösch demonstrated that with all firms facing identical production and transport cost schedules, and confronted by a spatially uniform total market, the market would be divided out so that each firm would serve a hexagonal market area. The equilibrium number of firms, and the area served by each, would be determined by transport costs. The existence of several different but interdependent product markets would, in the Löschian model, tend to encourage concentrations of firms at specific locations.

Discussion of the details of these location and other models is beyond the scope of this volume, but it should be becoming increasingly apparent that transport costs have increasingly been recognized to be only one of many factors which influence industrial location. The factors influencing location include (in addition to transport considerations) market structure, demand elasticities, external economies of geographical concentration, expectations of future market changes, and processing costs. Greenhutt (1963), for example, suggests that in practice transport costs only become of major importance if freight costs form a large proportion of total costs or differ significantly among potential locations.

While theoretical models of industrial location offer useful insights into the role transport plays, its actual relevance in the real world requires detailed empirical study. If Greenhutt's argument is followed, in many cases transport costs are such a small component of overall production costs that it appears to be more costly to acquire the information necessary to find the least-cost location than to suffer the inefficiencies of a suboptimal situation. For example, Cook's (1967) classic study of industrial location in the Midlands of England found that many firms were ignorant or only partially aware of their transport costs. One can attempt to isolate such transport cost-insensitive industries by looking at the relative importance of transport costs in their overall costs of production.

Table 3.2 offers some estimates of the percentage of the value of net output for a variety of United States and Japanese industries attributable to transport costs in the mid-1980s. There are clear differences between the countries, and between the various industries within them. It seems reasonable to conclude from this table that, *ceteris paribus*, industries producing primary products such as agriculture, petroleum, and wood products are going to be more influenced in their location choices by transport considerations than others such as machinery, furniture, and precision instruments. Production of raw materials represent nodal solutions in the Weberian triangle, with production at the raw material source. (In the United States it has often been suggested that Gary, Indiana, was originally chosen specifically by US Steel to minimize transport costs.)

Changes in industrial structure since the 1950s, and especially the movement away from basic industries to manufactures and services, suggests that transport is experiencing a diminishing influence over location decisions at least at the inter-regional level. Further, the existence of comprehensive transport and

Table 3.2   *Transport costs as a percentage of final consumer costs*

Producer	Transport costs (%)	
	United States	*Japan*
Agricultural products	7.85	2.43
Food products	1.59	2.16
Textiles	0.58	6.33
Apparel & leather products	0.22	0.69
Paper & wood products	1.91	3.37
Furniture	0.53	2.03
Publishing	1.46	1.16
Chemical products	1.38	0.59
Petroleum products	2.60	1.56
Rubber & plastic products	1.79	0.99
Glass, clay, & stone products	1.36	4.50
Primary metal products	2.54	1.34
Finished metal products	0.93	0.75
Machinery	0.47	0.64
Electrical equipment	1.08	0.71
Transport vehicles	2.56	0.88
Precision instruments	0.15	0.90
Other	0.69	1.13
Total	*1.70*	*1.83*

Source: Adapted from Pirog and Lancioni (1997).

communications networks in virtually all industrialized countries means that proximity to good transport is much easier to achieve now than in the past.

These factors, however, may not be as new as sometimes supposed. In early empirical work by Gudgin (1978) looking at the 1968 United Kingdom Census of Production, it was found 'that almost three-quarters of British industry incurs total transport costs at levels of less than three percent of the value of gross output. In 95 percent of industry, by value of production, the transport costs are less than 5 percent of total costs'. This finding was reaffirmed in Diamond and Spence (1989) in a study of 190 manufacturing and service industries, also in the United Kingdom, which found that most firms reported transport costs of between 3 and 6 percent of production costs. Interestingly, at 9.9 percent transport costs at the time represented a considerably higher proportion of costs in the service sector than for manufacturing firms (4.7 percent).

Cost statistics can, however, give a slightly distorted impression of the influence of transport. While transport costs may form only a relatively small proportion of output costs in many sectors they may, nevertheless, have significant influence on levels of net profits. Again, drawing on United Kingdom data, Chisholm (1971), for instance, suggests that transport costs may have represented as much as 25 percent of profits in the manufacturing industry during the 1960s. Additionally, while transport costs may, on average, be low for some industries they may vary considerably among areas. Edwards (1975) suggested that there existed a range of about 20 percent in transport costs of manufacturing industry by region in 1963.

It should also be remembered that simple cost estimates may disguise variations in other attributes of transport (speed, regularity, etc.) which can influence decision-makers. Reliable inter-urban transport, good international transport links, and high-quality local transport (necessary to retain scarce skilled labor) are, for instance, often very important for modern high-technology industry. In an analysis of the largest United States commercial airports, for example, Button et al. (1999) found they attract considerable amounts of high-technology employment, some 12,000 such jobs compared to cities without these facilities.

Survey evidence, questioning industrialists about the motivations underlying their location or relocation decisions also provides some guidance to the importance of transport considerations. There are obvious difficulties in using such results – for example, the sample may be unrepresentative, respondents offer answers which they hope may further their individual interests, while others offer *ex post* rationalizations of their actions – but some information may be gleaned from them.

The UK Trade and Industry Sub-committee of the House of Commons Expenditure Committee in 1973, for example, when seeking information about the effectiveness of regional economic policies, was told by five of the 17 major industrial firms interviewed that high transport costs were a specific disadvantage for locations in developed areas. While accepting this as an objective comment, it is important to note not simply the relatively small number of firms concerned but also their nature – for example, three were car manufacturers and one was a large steel tube mill. These were large firms engaged in the production of bulky products whose per unit transport costs were likely to be high.

The United Kingdom's Armitage Committee in its 1980 Inquiry into *Lorries, People and the Environment* supported this line and concluded that '[w]hen industry and commerce make decisions about the location of factories or their systems of distribution, it is often less important to reduce transport costs than to reduce other costs such as those of stockholding or to take advantage of the grants for setting up factories in assisted areas'. Such a view is consistent with that of Cameron and Clark (1966), who in their study of 71 firms which located in assisted areas found that accessibility to main markets was only ranked third as a location factor (behind the availability of trained labor and local authority cooperation), while local goods transport facilities were listed fifth and accessibility to main suppliers sixth.

One factor which emerges from these studies, and has limited support in econometric work, is that during the post-war phase of full employment and strengthened land-use controls, access to markets and raw material supplies was often overshadowed in location decisions by the availability of scarce skilled labor and factory space. Historically, international confirmation of this position was seen in West Germany where a survey of newly located plants found that accessibility to motorways ranked only fourth in the list of location criteria (Fischer, 1971).

More localized studies suggest that good passenger transport facilities may influence industrial location rather more than the quality of long-distance or freight transport. In retailing and some other activities this argument is further extended to embrace firms' desire to be accessible to customers. The importance of local transport is, for instance, seen in a study of factors affecting location choices of high-technology firms in Pennsylvania. Allen and Robertson (1983) found that while proximity to market, proximity to family, and commuting distance came first, second, and fourth respectively in terms of factors influencing firms, regional surface transport and proximity to an airport came only thirteenth and sixteenth respectively. This confirms the emphasis that has been placed upon the ready availability of trained workers.

It is certainly clear from a number of surveys – for example, Table 3.3 reports the results of one United States overview focusing on 162 studies – that the availability of suitable labor is a key factor in location choices of both high-technology and more traditional industries. There is also evidence that local transport can be influential in attracting or retaining labor, although the relationships can be complex and industry specific (Zandiatashbar and Hamidi, 2021).

Transport and transport-related considerations would seem, therefore, to still be very relevant in the location decisions of modern industries although the specific transport attributes of importance may have changed somewhat over the years.

In addition to the appreciation that transport is often not the dominant factor in location choice, there is now the increasing view amongst behavioral economists that notions of cost minimization do not always motivate firms. Hence, even if one can isolate the factors of interest to firms, it is not certain that they should be treated within a cost-minimizing framework. In many cases, provided a site offers, *ceteris paribus,* a location where transport costs are below some threshold, it is considered acceptable. In other cases, the first acceptable location encountered is adopted rather than a protracted search pursued. The influence of social setting and amenities on those who make the decisions about location,

Table 3.3   *Factors influencing the location of branch plants in the United States*

Rank	High-technology	Other plants
1	Labor	Labor
2	Transport availability	Market access
3	Quality of life	Transport availability
4	Market access	Materials access
5	Utilities	Utilities
6	Site characteristics	Regulatory practice
7	Communications characteristics	Quality of life
8	Business climate	Business climate
9	Taxes	Site characteristics
10	Development organizations	Taxes

Source: Adapted from Stafford (1985).

and on the staffs whose preferences they need to consider, were highlighted in this context many years ago by Eversley (1965). Firms often, therefore, adopt 'satisficing' policies in site selection rather than attempting to profit- or revenue-maximize or to cost-minimize. Under these conditions the exact role played by transport costs becomes almost impossible to define. It seems likely, though, that once a location has been chosen, a major rise in transport costs would be necessary to overcome the basic inertia that seems to accompany such a managerial objective.

3.4 Economic Gateways and Corridors

Economic activities clearly require the movement of resources: factors to points of production and goods and services to markets, and even in the information age, ideas and data from the generator to the user. The distances involved in this have historically been increasing, and the making of any final produce may now require many thousands of miles of transport input. Distance *per se*, however, is not always (and has perhaps seldom) been the crucial element that influences the relative success of competitive production sites; other things being constant, factors such as time, frequency, reliability, and security are often more important. In this context appropriate transport is relevant. This, because of the attributes of transport and the costs of delivering them, often leads to a channeling of movements through gateways and along corridors. This is not in itself the issue. The challenge concerns the nature and number of these gateways and corridors and their form.

As with any economic resource, transport services suffer from scarcity; they are not ubiquitous, and, indeed, allocating resources to them inevitably involves taking resources from elsewhere. In the past this scarcity, and with it an opportunity cost, was often neglected in trade theory and, by association, economic development theory. Classical Ricardian economics of the nineteenth century, for example, focused exclusively on the comparative advantages in production at different locations, while in classical spatial economics, albeit at a more local level, it was assumed there existed infinite radial transport links within a concentric economic geographical space (a topic we implicitly look at in Section 3.6). But transport supply is constrained by its characteristics.

Transport is a network industry and it is, therefore, natural to think in terms of the role that transport may play in stimulating economic development along links in transport networks and at various nodal points; normally towns and cities. Historians have long viewed the trade and migration passages that existed in prehistoric times as important for the spread of civilization as it emerged, and subsequent trade routes as facilitating economic progress and disseminating knowledge. Those living in early commercial cities benefitted from the flows passing through their areas when they could exercise control over them and charge for passage.

The much more recent opening-up of North America has attracted a lot of attention, in part one suspects because of the availability of written records.

Whebell (1969) explained the growth of southern Ontario, Canada, in terms of a five-stage corridor development process occurring over an extended period and embracing significant technical changes. In contrast Scholvin at al. (2019) focus on gateway cities, distinguishing between them and hubs and examining the ways in which they change over time. Gateways are explained in economic terms by considering threshold values of distance and levels of productivity.

Discussions of gateways and corridors, together with their role in economic development, are not new. They aroused interest in the 1980s and 1990s with the onset of the 'hi-tech boom'. Indeed, many high-technology concentrations were designated either explicitly or implicitly by their corridor geography – Silicon Valley, the Route 128 Corridor, and the Dulles Corridor in the US, the M4 Corridor in the UK, etc. – while others, such as the Research Triangle in the US, were visualized in terms of having a gateway role. These concentrations highlight the synergies between transport and certain types of capital investment, but are more local in their orientation than the macro-corridors and gateways that are seen as linking regions or countries to wider markets.

Gateways have tended gradually to move farther apart as it has become easier for traffic and individuals to both pass through them and as transport systems have evolved to traverse the distance between them. Figure 3.5 represents a traditional view of gateways. At the national level in most countries there are one or more major hub cities that are linked to their borders by corridors that end at gateway cities offering links to the international market. In spatial economic terms, the main distinction between the hub city and the gateway city is that, while the former fulfils the classic role of serving a concentric hinterland, the gateway city services a cone-shaped market extending away from the border and along the corridor.

Corridors are essentially links between major nodes; in some ways they can be treated as 'super-links' and this is seen as distinguishing them from spokes in a hub-and-spoke network, a standard pattern of transport supply discussed in

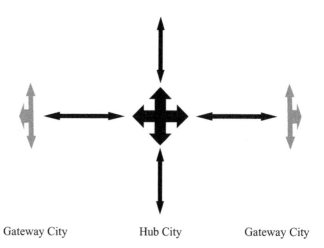

Gateway City   Hub City   Gateway City

Figure 3.5   *Notions of transport gateways, corridors, and hubs*

Chapter 6. A major difficulty, however, involves the level of aggregation that one is dealing with.

At the global-historic level, macro-macro level corridors are defined as routes that mankind used to populated the world – for example, the 'Bering land bridge' allowing migration from Europe to the American continent. But in the modern, high-technology, information age a corridor may be an electronic channel over which a piece of information is sent. The term suffers from almost infinite vagueness. This is not very helpful when it comes to in-depth analysis or forecasting but it does have its uses in general assessments of trends and can serve as a focal point of terminology when policy-makers want to coordinate actions, as for example in the creation of trade corridors.

It is also relatively easy to relate the picture seen in Figure 3.5 to specific contexts in more recent history. In the United States, for example, the two gateway cities were often seen in the mid-1800s as New York on one coast and San Francisco on the other. Once into the country, goods or migrants could move into the hinterland, often dispersing more broadly through a hub such as Chicago. Railroads largely facilitated this movement. The nature of international maritime and domestic railroad transport at the time, as well as institutional controls, led to this pattern of behavior. The gateways proved challenging barriers to cross and, while trade and migration was extensive, it was not easy and it was costly, and reverse migration and visits to family left behind proved almost impossible for the many individuals even if they did succeed in their new land.

The pattern of Canada's largest freight railroad, the Canadian National route network (Figure 3.6), provides a classic representation of the form that in theory a gateway/corridor structure looks like, and it is perhaps no accident that much of the early analytical writings on the subject came from Canada. The maritime gateways on the two coasts, and the inland crossing gateways to the United States funnel goods and, more in the past, individuals to and from the major hub cities of the country – Toronto, Montreal, etc. Similar patterns emerge for the more recent road network.

The world is changing, and transport has been both a cause of this change, but, mainly because of the derived nature of the demand for its services, has also had to react to it. These changes have implications for the demands that are placed on mobility of both people and goods. They have produced significant changes in the amount of geographical specialization and in both internal and external trade. The traditional barriers to trade, most obviously the physical geographical ones associated with oceans, mountains, rivers, and distance, but also the institutional ones tied to tariff and non-tariff barriers and fragmented financial markets, as well as the social ones of cultural and linguistic diversity, have had their potency reduced.

Transport costs for both passengers and freight have fallen considerably since the 1980s and 1990s. This is, in part, a function of technology improvements, including those found in complementary sectors such as telecommunications and warehousing, but it also stems from institutional developments and especially the liberalization of many transport markets. Economies of scale and

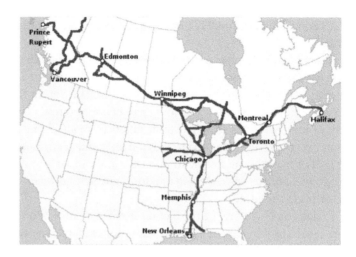

Figure 3.6 *Canadian National's railroad network*

scope have come with the freeing of international trade more generally, and the adoption of innovative methods of supplying logistics services of all types by the private sector.

The increased volume of trade, both within and between countries, and changes in its nature, have led to the emergence of new gateways and corridors to handle it. The development of the inter-modal terminal port at Prince Rupert in western Canada seen in Figure 3.6 is an example of this. The amount of competition between various gateway/corridor combinations, and their importance in economic development, even those involving existing combinations, have also changed for a variety of reasons. The full picture of what has happened is complex and is still not fully documented or agreed upon. It is a topic returned to in a slightly different way when the links between transport and development are discussed in Chapter 13.

3.5   Output, Market Areas, and Transport Costs

Transport costs are not only instrumental in influencing where firms locate, but they also play an important role in determining the market area served by each firm. Transport costs, given the place of industrial location, can determine the total quantity of goods sold and the price and the spatial distribution of this output. Lösch conducted much of the early work looking at market areas, but here we focus on a specific transport-orientated model that was devised by van Es and Ruijgrok (1974). The simple model treats transport demand as derived from the demand for the final product and assumes all supply and demand curves to be linear. For expositional ease, the relevant functions are treated in a manner running counter to economic convention; specifically, price is treated as dependent upon demand rather than vice versa. Initially our firm, which produces a homogeneous product, supplies a single customer who is located some distance from its pre-determined site. Hence, we have:

$$P^s = a_0 + a_1 Q^s + P^t \tag{3.2a}$$

$$P^d = b_0 - b_1 Q^d \tag{3.2b}$$

$$Q^d = Q^s \tag{3.2c}$$

$$P^s = P^d \tag{3.2d}$$

where:

P^s is the supply price of the commodity;
P^d is the demand price of the commodity;
Q^s is the quantity of the commodity supplied;
Q^d is the quantity of the commodity demanded; and
P^t is a constant transport cost per unit carried to the customer and treated as a cost borne by the supplier.

Manipulation and combination of these equations yields the profit-maximizing supply, Q^e, that is:

$$Q^e = \left(\frac{b_0 - a_o}{a_1 + b_1} \right) - \left(\frac{P^t}{a_1 + b_1} \right) \tag{3.3}$$

It is immediately clear that transport costs exert a negative influence on the quantity the profit-maximizing firm ought to supply, that is, if $P^t = 0$, then the equilibrium output would rise by $(P^t)/(b_1 + a_1)$. Further, we can derive the equilibrium price (P^e) that should be charged to the customer:

$$P^c = \left(\frac{a_1 b_0 - a_0 b_1}{a_1 + b_1} \right) + \left(\frac{b_1 P^t}{a_1 + b_1} \right) \tag{3.4}$$

Here we see that the transport cost component increases the equilibrium price by $[(b_1 P^t)/(a_1 + b_1)]$. The effects of this, together with the effects of transport costs on Q^e, are illustrated graphically in Figure 3.7. The vertical axis shows the final price per unit paid by the customer and the horizontal axis the quantity of goods sold. The introduction of the transport cost element to the diagram has the effect of pushing the supply curve up from $P^s(P^t = 0)$ to $P^s(P^t > 0)$. It is evident that transport cost rises will push up final prices and reduce the quantity sold. The exact impact depends not only upon the magnitude of P^t but also the elasticities of supply and demand – greater inelasticity increases the influence on price exerted by transport cost considerations.

To estimate the market area served when potential customers are spread evenly around the production site it is initially assumed that identical individuals

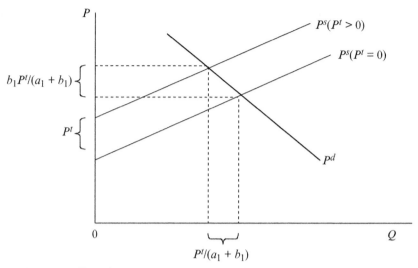

Figure 3.7   *The effect of transport costs on price and output*

are located at equal distances along a straight road from the site of the supplier. The customers will be confronted by prices that are composed of a fixed factory price reflecting production costs and a variable transport cost dependent upon the distance they live from the production site. Since each customer – by assumption – exhibits a similar demand response it is, therefore, the transport component that determines the amount each will buy. At the edge of the firm's market area, the amount supplied to the marginal customer vanishes to zero; this will be when $P^t = (b_0 - a_0)$. If j customers are served before this limit is reached, then from equation (3.3) we can see that the sales of the firm (Q^T) will amount to:

$$Q^T = \sum_j Q_j^e = j\left(\frac{b_0 - a_0}{a_1 + b_1}\right) - \left(\sum_j P_j^e\right)\left(\frac{1}{a_1 + b_1}\right) \tag{3.5}$$

where Q^e represents sales to customer j.

This approach can be extended to show the entire geographical area served by the firm. In Figure 3.8 the vertical axis represents the quantity supplied to each customer, on the assumption that the customers are evenly spread over the plane. The amount sold to a customer falls from very high levels $Q^e = [(b_0 - a_0)/(b_1 + a_1)]$ immediately adjacent to the site of supply – where transport costs are zero – and falls to zero when transport costs become excessive.

The amount sold can be measured by calculating the volume of the cone, that is:

$$D = b\pi \int_0^R (P + T)TdT \tag{3.6}$$

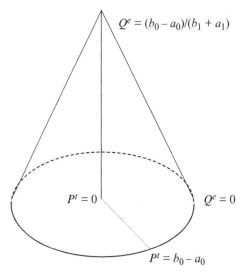

Figure 3.8 labels:
$$Q^e = (b_0 - a_0)/(b_1 + a_1)$$
$$P^t = 0$$
$$Q^e = 0$$
$$P^t = b_0 - a_0$$

Figure 3.8   *The influence of transport costs on market area*

where:

> D is demand as a function of the free on board (FOB) price net of mill price P;
> b is twice the population density of a square in which it costs one money unit to ship one unit of the commodity along one side;
> $d = f(P + T)$ is an individual demand as a function of the price of the commodity at the place of consumption;
> P is the FOB net mill price of the commodity;
> T is freight cost per unit from the factory to the consumer; and
> R is the maximum possible transport cost.

While this type of approach (relating the sales, prices, and market area of production to transport costs) is obvious theoretically, interestingly it does rely upon many abstractions from reality for its internal consistency. As with many theories, some of the assumptions associated with the model outline above may be relaxed: it is possible, for example, to allow for variations in population density, for heterogeneity in consumer tastes, and for non-perfectly elastic supply conditions – but this does tend to add complexity to the analysis. The general impression conveyed, however, is always the same, namely that transport costs are key in determining the size of the geographical market served by a firm and the total volume of its sales. Further, one situation where the effects of transport improvements may have a magnified effect on the market area is when the the producing industry is capable of exploiting manufacturing scale economies. This is not a novel idea and, indeed, it was recognized over two centuries ago by the classical economist Adam Smith in his *Wealth of Nations*.

3.6   Urban Transport and Land Values

The previous sections have been concerned with the interaction between transport and the physical, spatial economy, but little has been said regarding the way in which transport quality can affect land values. Location, to date, has tended to be viewed in terms of where a firm would locate and the area that would be served. Little has been said about the distribution of land among alternative uses either within one sector, such as manufacturing, or among sectors, notably between industrial and residential use. Very early work on this problem can be traced back to Johann von Thünen's century-old land-rent model which attempted to explain differences in agricultural land rent. He argued that concentric zones of crop specialization would develop around the central market, the key feature of the model being that land-rent differentials over homogeneous space are determined entirely by transport cost savings. While the nineteenth-century agrarian economy provided the inspiration for the 'bid-rent curve' (sometimes, 'bid–rent curve' is used) analysis, it is in the context of twentieth-century urban development that it has been most fully developed.

The Urban Bid-Rent Curve

Robert Haig in the 1920s was the first to apply von Thünen's argument in the urban context that:

> [s]ite rents and transportation costs are vitally connected through their relationship to the friction of space. Transportation is the means of reducing that friction, at the cost of time and money. Site rentals are charges which can be made for sites where accessibility may be had with comparatively low transportation costs.

People who are prepared to pay the highest price for improved transport provision (that is, to outbid rivals) will enjoy the most accessible locations.

This approach is clearly dependent upon some very stringent assumptions that need to be spelt out before we proceed further. We focus initially upon the residential location of households. The city under review is seen as a featureless plain with all production, recreational, and retailing activities concentrated at a single urban core (the central business district, or CBD). The population is homogeneous with respect to family size, income, housing demands, etc., but while building costs are largely unaffected by location, transport costs rise with distance from the CBD. With these assumptions, the sum of transport costs plus site rents is constant across the entire city. That is, if we take a ray out from the CBD to the perimeter of the city and concentrate exclusively on household decisions, we have the situation depicted in Figure 3.9. Total site rent in the city may be estimated as the volume of the inverted cone centered on the CBD.

An improvement in the transport system will result in a fall in land values at each location and an outward expansion of the city, the extent of this outward expansion being dependent upon the elasticity of demand for transport services.

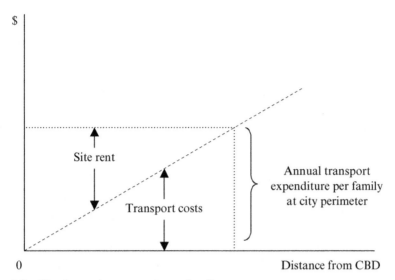

Figure 3.9   *The site rent/transport cost trade-off*

If the demand for transport is perfectly inelastic then the boundary of the city remains unchanged. If *AB* in Figure 3.10 is the initial rent gradient then, with a perfectly inelastic demand for transport services, the result of, say, uniformly lower public transport fares is to shift the gradient to *A'B*. The city's perimeter remains at *B*.

With a degree of elasticity, however, the reduced transport cost will encourage longer-distance travel to work and recreational activities and the eventual rent gradient is likely to settle at a position such as *A"B"* and the city's boundary to extend out to *B"*. It should be remembered that this simple model assumes that transport costs vary linearly with distance from the CBD and that individuals

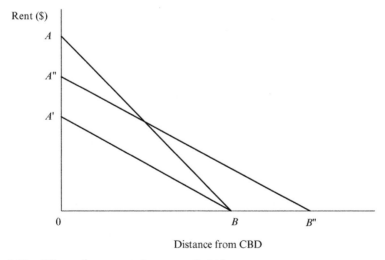

Figure 3.10   *Effects of transport changes on the bid-rent curve*

are identical. If this is not the case, then, as Herb Mohring (1961) has pointed out, the precise relation between transport cost and location patterns would be obtained simultaneously rather than sequentially as above. Further, the change in relative site rentals may also result in households wishing to own different sized plots of land; this complication is incorporated by allowing for some elasticity in the demand for quantities of land.

William Alonso greatly refined the model of urban location by extending beyond a simple consideration of residential land rent. The priorities of households differ and there is clearly competition in a free market land economy among the demands of industry, commerce, and various classes of households for different sites. In general, there are so-called 'agglomeration economies' to be enjoyed by industry and commerce from locating both close to each other and at the city core – they present an identifiable geographical entity (for example, medicine in Harley Street and bespoke tailoring in Savile Row in London, and Wall Street in New York), can be easily served by specialized suppliers, and can provide customers with a comprehensive range of services, etc. Consequently, given the potentially higher revenue associated with a core location, business tends to bid highly for central sites. Poorer people who cannot afford high transport fares and place a relatively low priority on large sites are willing to bid higher rents for inner area locations, while the wealthy will be more inclined to bid a higher rent for suburban locations.

Figure 3.11 shows the bid-rent curves for three groups of urban land user: business, poor households, and wealthy households. We see, in this very simple example, that business will outbid both classes of household for sites near the urban center, poorer households will locate adjacent to the CBD, while the wealthy will outbid the other groups for sites at the edge of the city. Clearly this is rather a stylized picture of urban land use and rents (Chapter 13 provides some further refinements), but it does offer some insight into the influence transport

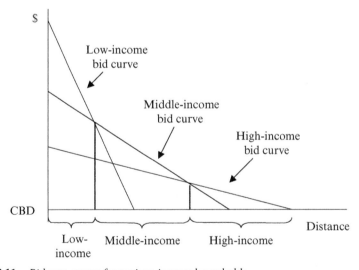

Figure 3.11   *Bid-rent curves for various income households*

can have on intra-urban location patterns. Quite simply, high transport cost activities, *ceteris paribus*, will be located at a short distance from the CBD and low transport cost activities will take locations further away.

General support for this pattern of land use in the United States is seen in Table 3.4, which shows that the spatial concentration of poverty increased steadily in the three decades to 1998, with over 25 percent of core metropolitan areas' populations being made up of the country's poorest 20 percent by the end of the period. But there has also been a continual overlapping suburbanization process, with 61 percent of the United States living in suburbs by 1990 compared to 36 percent in 1948. The advent of cheap motoring was a major cause of this.

Changes in transport costs may affect the amount of land taken up by various activities, and some of the basic implications can be illustrated using the bid-rent curve.

Transport Policies and Urban Bid-Rent Curves

Figure 3.12 replicates the curves seen in Figure 3.11 with $0 \Rightarrow P$ being the section around the CBD occupied by poorer people, $P \Rightarrow M$ that occupied by middle-income people, and $M \Rightarrow W$ that occupied by the wealthy. The introduction of improved public transport with low fares, for example, may well increase the willingness of poorer households to bid for locations further from the CBD and consequently the central ring of land use, as we see in the top section of Figure 3.12, may both widen and, more probably, move outwards to say P^*. As an example, the construction of the Washington Metro, with its relatively cheap, good-quality service, increased the willingness of people to pay for land parcels

Table 3.4 *Share of United States central-city population by income class and year*

Year	All metropolitan statistical areas/primary metropolitan statistical areas (%)	Central cities (%)	Suburbs (%)
Low income (national lowest 20%)			
1969	18.3	21.9	14.8
1979	18.5	23.7	14.5
1989	18.1	24.0	14.1
1998	19.0	25.5	14.9
Middle income (national middle 60%)			
1969	59.4	59.8	59.1
1979	59.4	59.0	59.8
1989	59.4	58.8	59.8
1998	58.8	57.9	59.3
High income (national top 20%)			
1969	22.3	18.3	26.2
1979	22.1	17.3	25.7
1989	22.5	7.2	26.1
1998	22.3	16.6	25.8

Source: US Department of Housing and Urban Development (2000).

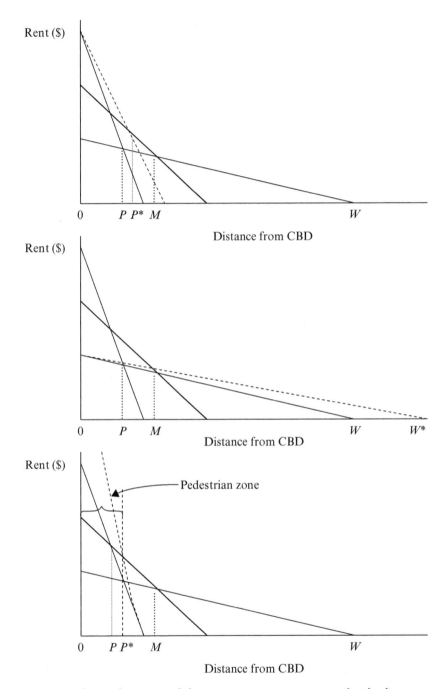

Figure 3.12   *The simple impacts of changing transport provision on urban land use*

near metro stations. Light rail can have a similar effect within urban areas as seen in Houston (Pan, 2019). Although not shown, the effect may well also produce a growth in economic activity at the CBD. In the urban center, retailers were even more willing to offer high rents for sites near metro services.

Alternatively, the construction of an extensive urban/suburban freeway network is likely to improve the access offered to car-owning, wealthy households, shifting their bid-rent curve upwards and to the right (the center section of Figure 3.12). The ring of land occupied by this group will thus be extended out beyond the original city boundaries (that is, from $M \Rightarrow W$ to $M \Rightarrow W^*$). Work in the United Kingdom on its motorway-building programs of the 1960s by Evans (1973), for instance, specifically attributes the 'flight to the suburbs' to 'the large-scale construction of urban motorways which increases commuting speeds and comfort for the commuter' and argues that the only way to get higher-income groups back into the central area is to '[m]ake the transport system slow, cheap and uncomfortable, and not fast, comfortable and expensive'.

Another possibility is that land-use planning may instigate a pedestrian-only zone around the CBD as seen in the bottom section of Figure 3.12. This will make it cheaper and more convenient for poorer households to move around and thus locations about the CBD more attractive places for them to live. Although the exact effect of such a policy depends upon its detailed design, in the bottom section of Figure 3.12 it is assumed that the result is that the belt of lower-income households expands out to P^*.

Of course, reality is a little more complicated than these examples suggest; for example, we have treated the city in isolation and as an abstraction, ignored variations in the geography of the area, assumed away any land-use planning agency, and treated location change as instantaneous. We have also ignored important feedback effects including the ability to change times of travel and routes, and to use modes of transport differently. The aim however, is to make it apparent that any attempt at formulating an urban transport policy, or any advance in transport engineering, will have important implications for urban form and on the people that live in the city even physically distant from the actual policy initiative.

Exhibit   *The impact of parking policy on house prices in the Netherlands*

Paid parking was initiated in 1935 in the United States in Oklahoma and is now widespread where there is limited off-street parking. Excess demand for parking leads to cruising as residents and visitors need to search for an available parking space. Appropriate parking prices reduce the number of parking places being demanded, and have the effect of reducing cruising for parking and associated traffic congestion costs.

The 1970s and 1980s saw car ownership increase in Amsterdam and Utrecht in the Netherlands with parking fees being used to ration spaces; see the table. The Mulder Act of 1989, allowing municipalities to extract revenues from traffic violations, including parking, witnessed stricter parking policy with higher parking tariffs and tighter enforcement. With parking discouraged in Amsterdam's center, drivers parked in surrounding areas leading to the introduction of paid parking in these areas. A similar development of paid parking occurred in Utrecht, which witnessed a large increase of its paid-parking area in the mid-1990s.

In Dutch cities, residents receive parking permits when paid parking is introduced to increase their political support. The implications of this policy on residents was assessed by examining the effect of its introduction on house prices for Amsterdam and Utrecht over a period of 30 years. A hedonic price index was used to allow for the effects of parking policies on house values making allowances for closeness to the city, size of property, whether the property was insulated, the attribute of a garden, etc.

As seen in the model results presented in abbreviated form, the introduction of paid parking (the first variable) had no significant effect on house prices in either Amsterdam or Utrecht. This finding is consistent with the idea that residents only vote in favor of a local policy when it has no negative impact on their house prices.

	Full sample	*Implementation areas*	*Amsterdam*	*Utrecht*
Paid parking	0.039***	−0.011	0.009	0.003
Paid parking × private parking	0.026**	−0.016	−0.026	−0.004
Outdoor parking	0.029***	0.064***	0.073***	0.086***
Garage parking	0.060***	0.093***	0.103***	0.087***
Log size	0.770***	0.774***	0.853***	0.839***
Log size distance to city center	−0.005	−0.004	−0.024	−0.185***
Log size × distance to city center^2	−0.003	0.002	0.001	−0.003

Notes: Variables statistically significant as * 10 percent, ** 5 percent, and *** 1 percent levels. Additional control variables affecting house values, such as garden, central heating, insulation, year of construction, distance from city center, zip code, were included.

See also: J. de Groote, J. van Ommeren, and H.R.A. Koster (2018) The impact of parking policy on house prices, *Journal of Transport Economics and Policy*, 52(3), 267–82.

3.7   Urban Wages

Transport costs not only influence urban land-use patterns, but they are also instrumental in determining spatial variations in urban wage rates. As Leon Moses (1961) pointed out, 'the wage differential, positive or negative, a worker is willing to accept is completely determined by the structure of money transport costs'. For simplicity, we assume that all employment is either concentrated at the city center or else spread evenly over the surrounding, mainly residential, area. All households are assumed initially to be in equilibrium, all enjoying the same level of welfare. Moreover, all workers are paid identical wages, work the same hours, and undertake the same number of commuting trips. Initially, then, net monies after work-trip outlays will vary among workers according to the nature of their intra-urban transport costs and the distance of their homes from the CBD. Variations in land values with distance from CBD, as we saw in the previous section, act as an adjustment mechanism to ensure uniformity of welfare. People living away from the urban core will pay more in transport costs, but their land rentals will be correspondingly lower.

In this simple world, however, a worker could improve their well-being by giving up their job at the CBD (and thus saving commuting costs) and working at one of the jobs which are spread evenly over the urban area and which are near their home. They would be willing to accept a lower income in this situation; indeed, they would be willing to sacrifice their wage rate down to the point where it is cut by as much as the commuting costs that are saved. Thus, there will be an equilibrium wage at locations nearer home than the CBD that will be lower than the core wage.

The result of this type of approach is the development of an urban wage gradient, the shape of which is determined by commuting cost factors. In Figure 3.13 the downward-sloping curve then represents the fall-off in wages from W at the CBD needed at each location to be paid to a worker as employment moves from the urban center. This decline represents the decreasing amounts of compensation required to be paid by an employer to attract workers who have easier commutes because they do not have to go to the CBD. The cost of enticing a local worker to a job at, say, location A is only W^* and well below that at the CBD. The worker living at A is indifferent between commuting to the CBD and earning $0W$ and working at home and earning $0W^*$. The commuter wage gradient curve traces out the wage rates at which a worker living at A would have to be paid to make them indifferent between working at home and at any intermediate site between A and the CBD. (It also shows the wage rates at which people living between A and the CBD will be indifferent between working at home and at the core.) The exact shape of these curves varies according to the types of jobs available and the quality and qulaifications of workers as well as the nature of the transport system (Autor, 2019).

If we introduce the notion of some secondary employment concentration, say at L, then reverse commuting may develop, especially if public policies support it (Cervero and Tsai, 2003). If employers at this subcenter require

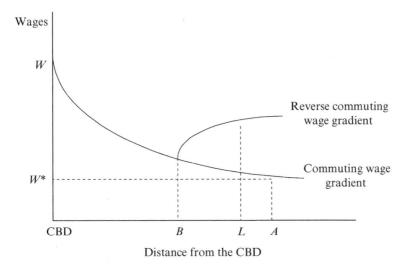

Figure 3.13   *Transport and wage costs*

amounts of labor that they cannot attract from households to the right of L they will need to compensate workers who travel out from areas between L and the CBD. Since the transport system tends to be less costly, in overall terms of money, time, and comfort factors (see Chapter 5 for more detail) for reverse commuting, the reverse commuting wage gradient is likely to be less steep than the commuting wage gradient. In this case, they can obtain the workers that they need by taking them from $B => L$ as well as to the right of L, with wages being determined by the reverse commuting wage curve. The main influence on reverse commuting costs *vis-à-vis* those for CBD commuters is the generally lower levels of traffic congestion away from the city center.

Just how does the wage gradient theory stand up to empirical investigation? There is remarkably little work on this question, but we can pull together some insights. Quite clearly the spread of national wage agreements, combined with imperfections in the land and transport markets (for example, public transport subsidies, the existence of company cars, and incomplete road networks), makes any exact testing of the theory difficult. American evidence from New York in the 1960s found wages to be higher in suburban counties than at the CBD and, even after allowing for variations in industrial structure, no wage gradient emerged (Segal, 1960). However, a little later, Rees and Shultz (1970) in their study of Chicago found a 'strong positive association of wages with distance traveled to work', but the wage gradient for blue-collar workers had its peak in the area of heavy industrial concentration (the south-west of the city) and sloped downwards towards the north-west. Similarly, analysis of the Panel Survey of Income Dynamics (basically looking at the activities of the same group of individuals over time) showed that '[u]rban wage gradients exist in America' (Madden, 1985).

More recently, Darren Timothy and William Wheaton (2001) have provided further confirmation of the trade-off between commuting times and wages in the United States, taking account of the larger shifts that are taking place in urban form, notably suburbanization. They used a very simple model:

$$W_i - W^0 = F_2(C_1), \qquad F'_2 > 0 \qquad (3.7\text{a})$$

$$C_i = F_1(E_i), \qquad F'_1 > 0 \qquad (3.7\text{b})$$

where:

C_i is the average commuting cost of workers in employment zone i;
E_i is the employment in zone i;
W_i is the wage rate in zone i; and
W^0 is the base metropolitan wage rate.

Using data for two large metropolitan areas, after adjusting for types of employment and such, they found that much of the 15 percent variation in urban wages could be related to commuting time differences between locations.

In the United Kingdom, Evans (1973) suggested that while a wage gradient could be discerned for Greater London there was little conclusive evidence of one elsewhere. Indeed, in provincial cities, clerical wages were often almost uniform across metropolitan areas. Clerical wages were, however, found to be higher in the City and the West End of London than in the suburbs.

Although these findings are not completely conclusive, the evidence supporting the wage gradient theory is at least balanced by that rejecting it. The problems are that the studies to date fail to allow for the multiplicity of factors other than transport that affect wage levels. We have already mentioned some of the problems – notably imperfections in certain markets – but to these we must add the tendency for employers to compensate workers for high transport costs by unrecorded payments (free meals, shorter working hours, more flexible time-keeping, etc.). Additionally, in some cities there are unrecorded advantages of working in the city center (better out-of-work and shopping facilities, increased career potential, etc.). The studies do not, therefore, refute the idea that transport costs influence urban wage patterns, but rather that the situation is more complex than the simple wage gradient theory suggests.

References

Allen, D.N. and Robertson, G.E. (1983) *Silicon, Sensors and Software: Listening to Advanced Technology Enterprises in Pennsylvania*, Institute of Public Administration, Pennsylvania State University.

Autor, D.H. (2019) Work of the past, work of the future, American economic, *Review, Papers and Proceedings*, 109, 1–32.

Button, K.J., Lall, S., Stough, R., and Trice, M. (1999) High-technology employment and hub airports, *Journal of Air Transport Management*, 5, 53–9.

Cairncross, F. (1997) *The Death of Distance: How the Communications Revolution will Change our Lives and our Work*, Orion Business.

Cameron, G.C. and Clark, B.D. (1966) Industrial movement and the regional problem, University of Glasgow Occasional Paper No 6.

Cervero, R. and Tsai, Y-.H. (2003) Job access and reverse commuting initiatives in California: review and assessment, *Transportation Research Record*, 1859, 78–86.

Chisholm, M. (1971) Freight transport costs, industrial location and regional development, in M. Chisholm and G. Manners (eds), *Spatial Policy Problems of the British Economy*, Cambridge University Press.

Cook, W.R. (1967) Transport decisions of certain firms in the Black Country, *Journal of Transport Economics and Policy*, 1, 344–56.

Diamond, D. and Spence, N. (1989) *Infrastructure and Industrial Costs in British Industry*, HMSO.

Edwards, S.L. (1975) Regional variations in freight costs, *Journal of Transport Economics and Policy*, 9, 115–26.

Evans, A.W. (1973) *The Economics of Residential Location*, Macmillan.

Eversley, D.E.S. (1965) Social and psychological factors in the determination of industrial location, in T. Wilson (ed.), *Papers on Regional Development*, Blackwell.

Fischer, L. (1971) *Die Berucksichtignung Raumordnungs Politiseler Zeilsetviengen in de Verkehrsplanung*, Strassenbahn und Strassenverkesstectnick.

Greenhutt, M.L. (1963) *Microeconomics and the Space Economy*, Scott-Foresman.

Gudgin, G. (1978) *Industrial Location Processes and Regional Employment Growth*, Saxon House.

Kain, J.F. (1964) A contribution to the urban transportation debate: an economic model of urban residential and travel behavior, *Review of Economics and Statistics*, 47, 55–64.

Madden, J.F. (1985) Urban wage gradients: empirical evidence, *Journal of Urban Economics*, 18, 291–301.

Mohring, H. (1961) Land values and the measurement of highway benefits, *Journal of Political Economy*, 69, 236–49.

Moses, L.M. (1961) Towards a theory of intra urban wage differentials and their influence on travel behavior, *Papers of the Regional Science Association*, 9, 53–63.

Owen, W. (1987) *Transport and World Development*, Hutchinson.

Pan, Q. (2019) The impacts of light rail on residential property values in a non-zoning city: a new test on the Houston METRORail transit line, *Journal of Transport and Land Use*, 12, 1310.

Pirog, S.R. III and Lancioni, R. (1997) US–Japan distribution channel cost structures: is there a significant difference? *International Journal of Physical Distribution and Logistics Management*, 27, 53–66.

Rees, A. and Shultz, G.P. (1970) *Workers and Wages in an Urban Labour Market*, University of Chicago Press.

Scholvin, S., Breul, M., and Revilla Diez, J. (2019) Revisiting gateway cities: connecting hubs in global networks to their hinterlands, *Urban Geography*, 40, 1291–309.

Segal, M. (1960) *Wages in the Metropolis*, Harvard University Press.

Stafford, H.A. (1985) Environmental protection industrial location, *Annals of the Association of American Geographers*, 75, 227–40.

Stevenson, R.L. (1879 [2004]) *Travels with a Donkey in the Cévennes*, Penguin.

Thomson, J.M. (1974) *Modern Transport Economics*, Penguin.

Timothy, T. and Wheaton, W.C. (2001) Intra-urban wage variations, employment location, and commuting times, *Journal of Urban Economics,* 50, 338–66.

US Department of Housing and Urban Development (2000) *State of the Cities*, HUD.

Van Es, J. and Ruijgrok, C.J. (1974) Modal choice in freight transport, in E.J. Visser (ed.), *Transport Decisions in an Age of Uncertainty*, Martinus Nijhoff.

Weber, A. (1929) *Theory of the Location of Industry*, University of Chicago Press.

Wegener, M. (2004) Overview of land use transport models, in D.A. Hensher, K.J. Button, K.E. Haynes, and P.R. Stopher (eds), *Handbook of Transport Geography and Spatial Systems*, Elsevier.

Whebell, C.E.L. (1969) Corridors: a theory of urban systems, *Annals of the Association of American Geographers*, 59, 1–26.

Zandiatashbar, A. and Hamidi, S. (2021) Transportation amenities and high-tech firm location: an empirical study of high-tech clusters, *Transportation Research Record*, 2675, 820–31.

4   The Demand for Transport

· ·

4.1   Demands for Transport

Chapter 3 considered the inter-relationship between land-use patterns and transport. This offered insights into some of the factors influencing the demand for
transport services. For example, one of the most pronounced characteristics of
the demand for transport is its regular fluctuation over time. In urban areas, the
demand for road space and public transport services is markedly higher in the
early morning and late afternoon than during the rest of the day. In the inter-
urban and international context, the demand for passenger transport fluctuates
regularly over a year with high seasonal peaks and peaks around public holidays.
With international freight transport, and especially shipping, there are long-term
cycles in demand.

   This tendency for peaks and troughs in demand is often a reflection of fluctuations in the demand for the final products made accessible by transport services.
In general, people wish to go on holiday to some destinations in the summer to
enjoy the warm weather, or the winter for skiing. Hence the seasonal peak in the
demand for highways, and rail and air services. Many businesses have traditionally found it efficient to operate standard hours (that is, from 'nine to five') with
the consequential concentration of commuter traffic. Whether the post-Covid
pandemic era will support this in future is another matter. Longer-term fluctuations in the demand for shipping services reflect the state of business cycles in the
trading nations – at the nadir of such cycles demand slumps; at the zenith it is
extremely buoyant.

   There are also pronounced variations in the demands for different modes of
transport according to the distance of a trip – a feature found for freight transport as well as passenger (de Bok et al., 2021). This is largely a function of the
technical features of the various modes that affect their overall attractiveness for
shorter or longer trips. Figure 4.1 offers a very generalized picture of the way that
conventional forms of transport dominate different lengths of personal trips. This
domination varies from walking and cycling being important for short journeys,
to air transport dominating inter-continental travel. Evidence supporting this is
seen from English data for short- and medium-length trips (Table 4.1), although
to be exact, the curves shown are not only related to demand, but also the availability of the various options.

   What is slightly different in the twenty-first century is that in many circumstances the traditional transport modes have been confronted with alternatives
to travel. This is particularly true when the purpose of trips is to meet friends
or to undertake tasks that involve transference of information – for example,

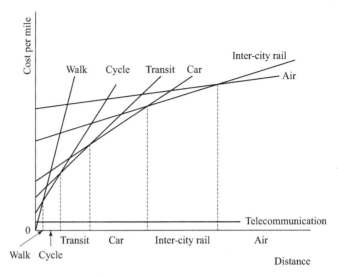

Figure 4.1 *Dominant modes of transport*

Table 4.1 *Average trip length by main mode (England)*

	2005	2010	2015	2019
Private:				
Walk	0.7	0.7	0.7	0.7
(Walks of over a mile)	1.4	1.5	1.4	1.4
Bicycle	2.4	2.8	3.0	3.3
Car/van driver	8.4	8.4	8.6	8.4
Car/van passenger	8.8	8.6	9.3	9.0
Motorcycle	9.8	9.9	11.1	8.0
Other private transport	18.4	17.1	15.0	15.3
Public:				
Bus in London	3.8	3.5	3.9	3.7
Other local bus	4.4	4.7	5.0	5.1
Taxi-/mini-cab	4.8	4.8	5.2	5.0
London Underground	8.5	8.5	8.8	8.6
Surface rail	32.7	30.6	32.7	32.3
Other public transport	22.9	25.4	19.5	16.2

Source: UK Department for Transport.

conferences and business meetings – or to engage in various forms of transaction involving, for example, shopping, finance, or marketing. In this case there has been a pronounced switching in demand away from transport in its conventional form to interactions involving some form of communication. In 2020, the long-term potential of telecommunications for transference of information became clear during the Covid-19 pandemic. This does not exclusively apply to person movements, but also to the uptake of electronic correspondence in place of paper communications by mail and courier.

The extent of competition between transport modes – the issue of cross-elasticity of demand that we return to later – only really relates to cases where there are genuine alternatives. If this is not so then one mode will dominate a market. Competition is thus normally at the margin. There are few real alternatives for tourists, for example, other than flying when it comes to long-distance travel across oceans.

In terms of aggregate demand, despite regular fluctuations, it has been suggested that over long periods of time there has been a remarkable stability in the demand for travel. Households, for example, on average make roughly the same number of trips during a day albeit for different purposes, over different routes, or by different modes. There may be more leisure travel, but there are fewer work trips and greater use is now made of air transport and the automobile at the expense of walking and cycling. It is also suggested that this situation reflects that there is a limit to the time people have available for travel, especially if they are to enjoy the fruits of the activities at the final destinations. They, therefore, seek to use some notion of a 'travel time budget' more effectively as travel technology and travel choices change.

As analysis of travel time budgets has advanced, it has become clear that the situation is more complicated than this, and that the constancy suggested above should be subjected to much closer inspection. In the United Kingdom, for example, there is evidence that average travel times have increased steadily throughout the twentieth century. Explanations are difficult to find, but one suggestion is that this is the result of rising incomes and that the constant time budget implied by Yacov Zahavi (1977) and others only holds for each income group. Zahavi, for example, found that people who made at least one motorized trip per day in an urban area, spent a constant 1.1 hours on their daily travels. Thus, people are moved from low-income groups with low travel time budgets to higher-income groups with associated higher travel time budgets. One example of a situation supporting this result is the Netherlands. In this case, 'travel time budgets' increased over the last three decades of the twentieth century, with time expenditure on travel per head increasing in relation to changes in travel costs and income levels. Such findings emphasize the importance of time as well as conventional variables in travel demand analysis and, as we see in the following chapter, considerable emphasis is placed upon the role that time costs play in transport decision-making.

Given this rather general, aggregate background we move to look in more detail at the influences and motivations that affect travel and transport-related demand. It seems appropriate to begin by considering the simple economic demand function as an *aide mémoire*.

4.2   Influences on Travel Demand

We begin by recapping some basic demand theory but adding some discussion of the peculiarities associated with transport. Demand is an abstract concept reflecting what individuals would like to consume under different scenarios. It is generally considered that the quantity demanded of a commodity, D_a, is influenced by its price, P_a, the prices of other goods $(P_1, P_2, \ldots, P_n)$, tastes, T, and the level of income, Y. The neoclassical demand curve entails focusing on the implications of price changes on demand holding the other factor constant, that is:

$$D_a = f(P_a, P_1, P_2, \ldots, P_n, T, Y) \qquad (4.1)$$

A fall in price has two implications for demand – the price of the activity under consideration falls relative to other prices (substitution effect) and more can be bought for a given income (income effect) – both of which stimulate the quantity of the good or service demanded. This means that normally there is a negative relationship between price and the quantity demanded, provided other elements in equation (4.1) remain constant (Figure 4.2). It gives the 'downward-sloping demand curve'. The elasticity of demand reflects the relative sensitivity of a change in the quantity demanded to a change in price.

The curve shifts, however, if there are changes in other elements of equation (4.1). An increase in income by allowing more to be bought at any price level moves it out, whereas a fall in the price of a substitute, but making the good relatively more expensive, pulls the demand at any price down. In some cases, as with fashion goods or where public attitudes alter, the demand curve may shift because of changes in 'taste', essentially a catch-all concept used to mop up effects not captured in income or price effects.

For calculation purposes, as with many areas of demand analysis, a log-linear specification of the form seen in equation (4.2) is often used to estimate the effects of the various factors on demand. This allows a simple interpretation of parameters such as elasticities, but does assume that, for example, the price elasticity of demand is the same at all price levels:

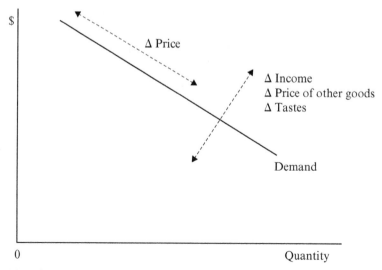

Figure 4.2   *The simple demand curve*

$$\ln Q_M = \alpha + \beta_1 \ln P_M + \beta_2 \ln Y + \beta_3 \ln P_N \qquad (4.2)$$

where:

Q_M is the quantity of mode M demanded;
P_M is the price of mode M;
Y is income; and
P_N is the price of an alternative, N.

All variables are expressed as logs (ln) and the parameters would normally be estimated using multiple regression analysis. The price elasticity (defined as $\{\Delta Q/Q\}/\{\Delta P/P\}$) is the parameter β_1 in a double logarithmic equation as in seen above; the income elasticity of demand, reflecting the sensitivity of the quantity demanded to income changes, is β_2, and β_3 is the cross-elasticity of demand reflecting the sensitivity of demand for mode M as the prices of alternatives vary.

While this simple framework holds for transport, as for all other goods and services, there are refinements and detail that need to be highlighted if one is to gain an understanding of the way the transport markets operate. The individual terms in the equation are, in fact, often not simple variables but, rather, represent complex compounds of several interacting factors (Litman, 2021). Price, for instance, is not simply the fare paid but must embrace all the other costs involved in obtaining the transport service (of which 'time costs', as we noted above, are generally held to be the most important), while it may not be total income that influences travel demand by individuals but rather income exceeding some threshold subsistence level. Further, there is the need to be very clear on what exactly it is that is being demanded: is it a trip *per se* or is it something more specific than this, for example, a bus trip or a journey over a route? Quandt and Baumol (1966) have gone so far as to suggest that it is not transport at all which is being demanded but, rather, a bundle of transport services. We look at this idea more fully in the context of forecasting in Chapter 12.

The emergence of behavioral economics has added to interest in these sorts of issues. Behavioral economists have, for example, produced numerous examples of when people do not make decisions, as assumed in standard economics, in isolation from the opinions of others. A Rolls-Royce may offer very similar transport services to a VW Beetle but it also offers prestige and status. On the other hand, some may see the fuel advantage of the Beetle as helping to enhance the ecological image of the user. In technical terms, there can be missing variables in any transport demand function simply because many attributes of transport are not only difficult to quantify, but are also not directly related to travel.

These types of problems and issues are clearly difficulties that cannot be entirely circumvented in general discussions of the influences affecting transport demand. They should be borne in mind as we move on to look in more detail at some of the items contained in the demand function as set out in equation (4.1).

4.3   Pricing a Transport Service

As has been suggested, the price of transport embraces considerably more than the simple money costs paid out in fuel, fares, or haulage fees. In transport modeling and quantitative work these other components of price (that is, time costs, waiting, insecurity, etc.) may be combined to form a generalized cost index of the type we discuss in Chapter 5 where we focus in more detail on cost, but here we concentrate on money prices and on the sensitivity of transport users to the price of transport services.

Generalizations are obviously difficult, especially across all modes of transport, but in many instances, it seems clear that price changes within certain limits have relatively little effect on the quantity of travel or transport services demanded. The demand for cargo shipping is, for example, very inelastic, in part because of the lack of close substitutes for shipping services, in part because of the short-term inelastic nature of the demand for the raw materials frequently carried, and in part because of the relatively low importance of freight rates in the final selling price of cargoes.

While, in broad terms, demand elasticities exhibit a degree of stability over time, they do not remain entirely constant. In part this is due to shifts in the demand function resulting from such things as rising incomes and changes in consumer tastes. Studies of urban public transport in the 1970s, for example, covering a variety of countries, indicate relatively low price elasticities with a direct fare elasticity of around –0.3 being considered normal. Smith and McIntosh (1974), looking at British urban bus undertakings, for instance, produce figures ranging from –0.21 to –0.61, but the majority fall at the lower end of the spectrum. Charles Lave's (1970) American work on direct fare elasticities, however, found an elasticity of –0.11 for transit trips in Chicago, implying the fare elasticity in the United States in this period was slightly lower than in the United Kingdom at that time.

Studies in the 1980s surveyed by Phil Goodwin (1992) tend to produce similar figures to Smith and McIntosh, although highlighting that the short-term elasticities found in 'before and after' studies of fare change are in the order of a third of the size of longer-term elasticities covering a reaction time in excess of five years.

The effect of price change on private car transport must be divided between the effect on vehicle ownership and that specifically on vehicle use. Most early United Kingdom studies of car ownership indicate an elasticity of about –0.3 with respect to vehicle price and –0.1 with respect to gasoline price (Mogridge, 1978). American empirical work suggests a rather higher sensitivity (the Chase Econometrics Associates model, for example, implies a –0.88 purchase price elasticity and a –0.82 fuel price elasticity), but responsiveness is still very low.

For car use, all the evidence suggests an extremely low fuel price elasticity in the short term, which may be attributed to changing patterns of household expenditure between vehicle ownership and use and people's perception of motoring costs. (We return to patterns of short- and long-run elasticities below.) Terence Bendtsen (1980) brought early findings together in an international comparison that found the petrol price elasticity of demand for car use to be –0.08

in Australia for the period from 1955 to 1976; –0.07 in the United Kingdom for 1973–74; –0.08 in Denmark for 1973–74 and –0.12 for 1979–80; and –0.05 in the United States for the period from 1968 to 1975. Oum et al. (1992) found a slightly greater degree of sensitivity when looking at seven studies covering the United Kingdom, the United States, and Australia: they yielded car usage elasticities in the range –0.09 to –0.52.

Exhibit   *Demand shocks on airline fares produced by high-speed rail transport*

China rapidly built the world's largest high-speed rail (HSR) network – about a third of the world's total. At the same time, it has seen considerable growth in its domestic airline industries which were freed from fare, if not capacity, regulation in the early 2000s. Over intermediate distances of 400 km to 1,000 km these modes compete for traffic. While much of the competition involves incremental changes in terms of fares and frequency, 'shocks' or jolts in the market have impacted on their respective demands. These shocks may be predictable, such as a large, discrete increase in capacity, or they may be unexpected, such as a major technical failure. While often unique in their nature, they can reveal the extent of cross-elasticity between these modes.

The launch of the Beijing–Shanghai high-speed railways (the Jing-hu HSRs) and the Wenzhou train accident can be looked at as two examples. The Jing-hu HSRs were opened on June 30, 2011, and carry the largest passenger volume in China. The line is 1,348 km with 22 stops, with a design speed of 350 kph. Air services also connect seven of the stops. On July 24, 2011, there was a major accident on the HSR resulting in 40 fatalities and nearly 200 injuries. The overall impact of the national HSR network was a significant reduction of ridership, and resulted in the government mandating a travel speed of 300 kph and a 5 percent reduction in fares.

A difference-in-differences analysis was used. This methodology uses longitudinal data from treatment and control groups to obtain an appropriate counterfactual for estimating a causal effect of some event, by comparing the changes in outcomes over time between the two groups. In this case the control group consists of airlines outside the influence of the new HSR route and the control group of those airlines that compete with the new HSR services. For the analysis, airline fare data from June 20 to July 24 – that is, 10 days before the opening to 24 days after – were used to assess the impact of the HSR entering the market. For the implications of the Wenzhou accident, the period 23 days before the incident to 12 days after was used.

Wei et al. (2017) find evidence of HSR substitution for airlines. The latter's average fares for services along the Jing-hu route declined by 30.6 percent upon the launch of the rail service, but the mean fares rose for these same routes following the Wenzhou rail accident, rebounding by 27.6 percent. In more detail, analysis shows a larger impact of the two HSR events on low-cost and regional airlines, on shorter (less than 1,000 km) and/or tourism routes, and on flights departing during the evening. This suggests that the HSRs serve as a low-end substitution in the Chinese airline market.

See also: F. Wei, J. Chen, and L. Zhang (2017) Demand shocks, airline pricing, and high-speed rail substitution: evidence from the Chinese market, Journal of Transport Economics and Policy, 51(4), 266–89.

Table 4.2 provides a survey of estimates of automobile and public transport elasticities from 1990. We immediately note the higher long-term elasticities in all cases, a topic we return to below, but also the relatively high-income elasticities reflecting the possibilities for modal switching or other changes in travel behavior as incomes change – an important consideration for policy-makers in developing countries.

If we move to the other extreme of the transport market and look at airline operations the evidence is that demand is slightly less elastic with long-term demand (estimated from cross-sectional data) emerging as elastic. What these coefficients, and indeed those cited above relating to other modes, often disguise are quite significant differences in the elasticities for different groups of travelers and between individual services. Mutti and Mural (1977), in an investigation of air travel across the North Atlantic air market, generally found inelasticity, but with variability between routes. Examinations of internal air traffic within the United States, however, produce much more varied results. Samuel Brown and Wayne Watkins (1968) and Gronau (1970) showed a remarkable degree of consistency by producing price elasticities of –0.85 and –0.75 respectively, but Jung and Fujii (1976) came to a somewhat different conclusion: air travel demand for distances under 500 miles in the south-east and south-central portions of the United States is price-elastic. To some extent variations in these findings are influenced by a common problem found in estimations of elasticities, they can be sensitive to the level of aggregation in the data deployed (Levin, et al., 2017).

Table 4.2   *Summary of demand elasticities provided by Graham and Glaister*

	Short/long run	*Elasticity*
Fuel demand with respect to fuel price	SR	−0.25
	LR	−0.77
Fuel demand with respect to income	SR	0.47
	LR	0.93
Traffic (car-km) with respect to fuel price	SR	−0.15
	LR	−0.31
Traffic (car-trips) with respect to fuel price	SR	−0.16
	LR	−0.19
Traffic (car-km) with respect to car time	SR	−0.20
	LR	−0.74
Traffic (car-trips) with respect to car time	SR	−0.60
	LR	−0.29
Traffic (car-km) with respect to income	SR	0.30
	LR	0.73
Freight traffic with respect to price	n.a.	−1.07
Car ownership with respect to cost	SR	−0.20
	LR	−0.90
Car ownership with respect to income	SR	0.28
	LR	0.74

Note: n.a. = not available.

Source: Graham and Glaister (2004).

The relevance of this earlier work, other than in its technical innovations, is clouded by the considerable institutional changes that took place from the late 1970s when air transport, as we discuss in Chapter 14, began to be deregulated. Table 4.3 provides a larger listing of some of the main studies that have examined air transport demand elasticities, including more recent ones. While no single figure emerges from these studies that can be isolated as the 'representative' fare elasticity, some general conclusions can be drawn.

There is a distinction between the fare elasticities for business and non-business air travel, with the latter being generally higher. This is a pattern also seen, as one might expect, in terms of the type of fare being paid. This conforms to the intuition that vacation travelers have more flexibility in their actions (destinations, times of flights, etc.) whereas business trips often fly at short notice.

Exhibit   *Fuel efficiency of United States cars following the 1973 and 1979 oil crises*

The oil embargo of 1973 resulting from the Yom Kippur War increased the world price of oil from $3 per barrel to nearly $12. The United States retail price for a gallon of regular gasoline rose from 38.5¢ in May 1973 to 55.1¢ in June 1974. In the wake of the Iranian Revolution, the global price increased to $39.50 per barrel in 1979. As can be seen from the table, the fuel efficiency of the United States' car fleet was poor in the early 1970s with the oligopoly of automobile manufacturers competing on design and size rather than miles per gallon. It has been estimated that the results of the two disruptions in the fuel market resulted in the annual cost of owning and operating a car by 1981 having risen by $2,400 compared with the pre-1973 period. About a third of this was due to new environmental regulations, including, in 1975, the establishment of corporate average fuel economy (CAFE) standards.

	Miles per US gallon			Real price of gasoline (1967 = 100)
	City	Highway	Harmonic mean	
1968	12.59	18.42	14.69	97.3
1969	12.60	18.62	14.74	95.4
1970	12.59	19.00	14.85	98.0
1971	12.27	18.18	14.37	87.6
1972	12.15	18.90	14.48	85.9
1973	12.01	18.07	14.15	88.7
1974	12.03	18.23	14.21	108.3
1975	13.68	19.45	15.79	106.0
1976	15.23	21.27	17.46	105.3
1977	15.99	22.26	18.31	103.7
1978	17.24	24.48	19.89	100.5
1979	17.70	24.60	20.25	122.2
1980	20.35	29.02	23.51	149.6
1981	21.75	31.12	25.16	150.8
1982	22.32	32.76	26.06	134.7
1983	22.21	32.90	26.01	126.1
1984	22.67	33.69	26.59	119.2

The market reaction to this has involved changes in the number of trips made, driving behavior, mode choices, and a market shift to smaller, more fuel-efficient automobiles. As the table shows, the two crises saw a downsizing of cars and a clear increase, with a lag, in fuel efficiency after 1974 and again after 1979. Overall, the fuel economy of the United States' fleet improved by over 50 percent between 1974 and 1984.

There was a significant increase in imports of smaller cars, most notably from Japan and Germany, which, besides fuel economy, were of a better quality. By 1980, domestic luxury cars with a gross weight averaging 4,500 pounds were no longer made and there began a phasing-out of rear-wheel-drive layouts in compact cars in favor of lighter front-wheel-drive designs. More cars offered fuel-efficient four-cylinder engines.

In terms of mileage traveled, however, while there were very short-term dips (from 1.306 billion in January 1974 to 1.284 billion in August 1967 and from 1.562 billion in May 1979 to 1.518 billion in September 1980) as the vehicle fleet adjusted, the steady growth in the American automobile soon returned to its upward trends. The impacts of the large and sudden fuel price increases were seen in the types and sizes of cars used rather than having any long-term effect on their use.

See also: R.W. Crandall, H.K. Gruenspecht, T.T. Keeler, and L.B. Lave (1986) Regulating the Automobile, Brookings Institution.

Table 4.3 *Examples of findings of air fare elasticities studies*

Study (publication year)	Focus of study	Values
Oum et al. (1992)[c]	Trip purpose (business/non-business)	−1.15 to −1.52
	Mixed or unknown	−0.76 to −4.51
Royal Commission	Business travel	−1.57 to −3.51
on National Passenger	Non-business travel	−4.38 to −4.50
Transportation (1992)[b]	Short trip (under 500 miles)	−1.16 to −2.70
	Long trip (over 500 miles)	−1.34 to −2.56
Straszheim (1978)[d]	First class	−0.65
	Economy, peak period	−1.92
	Economy, average	−1.48
	Economy, standard	−1.12
	Economy, promotional	−2.74
	Economy, high discount	−1.82
De Vany (1983)[a]	28-mile trip (one way)	−0.78
	400-mile trip (one way)	−1.02
	650-mile trip (one way)	−1.07
	1,500-mile trip (one way)	−1.14
	2,500-mile trip (one way)	−1.17
Gillen et al. (2002)[c,e]	Long-haul international business	−0.26
	Long-haul international leisure	−0.99
	Long-haul domestic business	−1.15
	Long-haul domestic leisure	−1.52
	Short/medium-haul business	−1.39
Bhadra (2003)[a]	Less than 250 miles	−0.67
	250–499 miles	−0.56
	500–749 miles	−0.74
	750–999 miles	−1.45
	1,000–1,249 miles	−1.82
	1,250–1,499 miles	−0.85
	1,500–1,749 miles	−1.08
	1,750–1,999 miles	−0.84
	2,000–2,249 miles	−1.06
	2,250–2,499 miles	−1.38
	2,500–3,000 miles	−0.86

Notes: a. United States data. b. Canadian data. c. Synthesis of previous studies. d. North Atlantic data. e. From a range of international studies.

The lower sensitivities associated with first-/business-class fares also reflect the service requirements of users who often seek room to work on planes and in lounges. The estimates of the elasticities are also sensitive to the length of service with shorter routes generally exhibiting higher fare elasticities, in part because other modes of transport become viable options.

The difficulty with many statistics on demand sensitivity is, therefore, that they are elasticities averaged over several groups. In fact, the price elasticity of transport, as with the price elasticity of other goods, should ideally be set in a specific context. In the case of transport, four broad types of classification are important and we consider each in turn. Table 4.4 sets aviation elasticities in the

Table 4.4 *Elasticities of demand for passenger transport (expressed in absolute values)*

Mode	Range surveyed		Number of studies
	Market demand elasticities	Mode choice elasticities	
Air[a]			
Vacation	0.40–4.60	0.38	8
Non-vacation	0.08–4.18	0.18	6
Mixed[b]	0.44–4.51	0.26–5.26	14
Rail: Inter-city			
Leisure	1.40	1.20	2
Business	0.70	0.57	2
Mixed[b]	0.11–1.54	0.86–1.14	8
Rail: Intra-city			
Peak	0.15	0.22–0.25	2
Off-peak	1.00	n.a.	1
All day[b]	0.12–1.80	0.08–0.75	4
Automobile:			
Peak	0.12–0.49	0.02–2.69	9
Off-peak	0.06–0.88	0.16–0.96	6
All day[b]	0.00–0.52	0.01–1.26	7
Bus:			
Peak	0.05–0.40	0.04–0.58	7
Off-peak	1.08–1.54	0.01–0.69	3
All day[b]	0.10–1.62	0.03–0.70	11
Transit system:			
Peak	0.00–0.32	0.1	5
Off-peak	0.32–1.00	n.a.	3
All day[b]	0.01–0.96	n.a.	15

Notes: a. The distinction between vacation and non-vacation routes is rather arbitrary and may partly account for the very wide range of elasticity estimates. b. This includes studies which do not distinguish between categories (peak, off-peak, or all day).
n.a. = not available.

Source: Adapted from Oum et al. (2008).

context of other transport demand elasticities. With the exception of HSR, the demand for airline services is more sensitive to price variations than modes, and there is also a wider dispersion of results across studies.

4.4 Trip Purpose

Trips are made for a variety of purposes and by a diversity of individuals or companies. Some are made at short notice and the price of the trip may be a relatively small consideration compared with scheduling, reliability, and speed. Decisions may also depend upon who is paying for the trip, whether it is the individual traveling or an employer. Another consideration is whether there is a group purpose in the trips, say a family holiday, or whether it is an individual traveling alone. Studies of travel demand, therefore, control for the purpose of the trip.

There is an abundance of evidence that the fare elasticity for certain types of trips is much higher than others. Business travel demand emerges from most empirical studies as relatively less sensitive to changes in transport price than other forms of trip. This is because business travel is often difficult to book in advance and in many cases there is a principal–agent situation. The principal (the owner of a business who pays for the trip) may be concerned about keeping costs down but the agent (the employee booking the trip) has less incentive to do so. Non-work trips are generally paid for by the traveler who is more interested in economy, and especially when leisure trips involving a family group are involved.

Over the years, Kraft and Domenich (1970) found that, in Boston, public transport work trips exhibited a fare elasticity of –0.17 compared with –0.32 for shopping trips, figures closely conforming to those found for public transport in the United Kingdom. Considering air traffic, Mutti and Mural (1977) attribute part of the variation they found in fare responsiveness on the North Atlantic routes to the fact that 'we expect personal travel to be more price elastic than business travel'. Straszheim (1978) subsequently provides confirmation of this view and isolates elasticities for different types of service. He concludes, 'First class fares can be raised and will increase revenue … . The demand for standard economy service is about unity, and highest for peak period travel … . The demand for discount and promotional fares is highly price elastic …'. Tae Oum et al. (1986) came to identical conclusions when looking at North American data. Quite clearly, therefore, it is dangerous to attempt to analyse transport demand without considering the specific type of trip being undertaken.

4.5 Levels and Methods of Charging

Users of different forms of transport (or, sometimes, different services of the same mode) are often confronted with entirely different methods of payment. Consequently, their perception of the price of a journey may differ from the actual monies expended. Early work by Sherman (1967), for example, has suggested that motorists perceive very little of the true overall price of these trips because they base decisions on a limited concept of short-term marginal cost. Harrison and Quarmby (1969) found that drivers perceived only between 50 and 60 percent of their own costs (fuel, tire wear, vehicle maintenance, etc.) and this did not include environmental costs and the costs of congestion imposed on others.

Users of public transport, on the other hand, are usually made much more aware of the costs of their trip-making by the requirement to purchase a ticket, usually prior to beginning their journeys. Nevertheless, given the range of season tickets (which permit bulk buying of journeys over a specific route) and travel card facilities (which permit bulk buying of journeys over a specified network), the distinction is not a firm one.

The empirical findings regarding season tickets and travel cards are very limited and are also not very helpful in providing general parameters. One reason for this is that season tickets are only purchased periodically, and allowing for other things that may occur between a fare change and a season ticket purchase decision is challenging. Season tickets may also come in a variety of forms – monthly, quarterly, and annual – with varying discounts. Peter White's (1981) review of the empirical information available on travel cards in the United Kingdom did, however, point to a much lower price elasticity for travel card systems than for conventional single ticket cash payment systems, findings subsequently supported by Mark Wardman (2014).

4.6 The Time Period

As with other purchasing decisions, people confronted with a change in transport price may act rather differently in the ultra-short run, the 'market period', the short run, and the long run. Immediate reactions, in the ultra-short term, to a public transport fare rise may, for example, be dramatic, with people, almost on principle, making far less use of services, even boycotting them, but knee-jerk reactions are extremely short-lived and are seldom considered by economists, although they are often of interest to politicians.

The ultra-short-term elasticity may, therefore, be extremely high but short-lived. This type of situation may be less common than is sometimes thought and, indeed, the reverse response may result in the slightly longer period. In the market, for example, people may appear relatively unresponsive to a price change either because they do not consider it a permanent change or because technical constraints limit their immediate actions. The demand for gasoline, a major input into modern transport, offers a good example of how its demand varies with significant price rises, a situation found during the 'oil shocks' of the 1970s, and more recently in 2007–2008.

In Figure 4.3 the price of oil rises from P_1 to P_2, and, ignoring any knee-jerk reactions in the ultra-short term, the gasoline purchased will change little. The transport users are locked into a pattern of behavior that makes reducing their fuel consumption difficult; this is the 'market period'. In the short run, however, individuals can change their travel patterns by switching modes, combining trips, and cutting out some travel, and businesses can reschedule the use of their vehicle fleets and modify their collection and delivery patterns. The demand, therefore, becomes more elastic in relation to the new price, and the amount bought falls to Q_2. In the long term, people can change the type of car they use, their employment, and their residential location, and industry can modify their entire supply chain. Hence the quantity of gasoline demand will fall to Q_3 in the figure, and the demand curve will flatten out further.

Table 4.5 offers more direct indications of how price and income elasticities can vary over time after a price shock in the gasoline market. Figure 4.4 makes

Figure 4.3   *Abstraction showing changes in demand elasticities for oil over time*

Table 4.5   *Price and income elasticities of gasoline demand by automobile users*

	Price elasticity	Income elasticity
Short run	−0.2 to −0.3	0.35 to 0.55
Long run	−0.6 to −0.8	1.1 to 1.3

Source: Basso and Oum (2007).

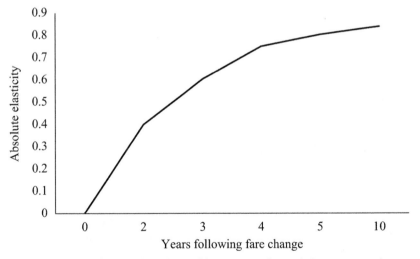

Figure 4.4   *Estimated United Kingdom public transport demand elasticity over the period after a fare change*

use of Goodwin (1992) to indicate the dynamic absolute fare elasticity of demand for United Kingdom transit fares.

In a more direct transport context, when considering the effect of general rises on commuter travel costs, the necessity of having to make journeys to work is likely to result in minimal changes in travel patterns in the short term but over a longer period, relocations of either residence or employment may produce a more dramatic effect. Teleworking has added to the options in recent years. This implies that one must take care when assessing elasticity coefficients, and it is useful to remember that cross-sectional studies tend to offer estimates of long-run elasticity while time-series studies reflect short-term responses.

4.7   The Absolute Level of the Price Change

Price elasticities are generally found to increase for both passenger and freight movements (de Bok et al., 2021) the longer the trip under consideration. This should not be seen simply as a function of distance but rather a reflection of the absolute magnitude of, say, a 10 percent rise on a $5 fare compared with that on a $500 fare. It is also true that longer person journeys are made less frequently, and thus people gather information about prices in a different way. Additionally, they often tend to involve leisure rather than business travel; this suggests that distance may be picking up variations in trip purpose. In the air transport market, for example, Arthur De Vany (1974) found in a classic study that price elasticity rose from –0.97 for a 440-mile trip in the United States to –1.13 for an 830-mile trip. For similar journeys, Richard Ippolito (1981) found the respective elasticities to be –0.525 and –1.0.

While it is important to treat elasticities with care because of these types of aggregation issues, there is a further reason for counseling caution when considering such parameters: there are several statistical methods employed to calculate elasticities and these can influence the values obtained. In some instances, these related to the time span of the elasticity being studied; some techniques are mainly used for short-term elasticity estimation while others are more relevant for cross-sections of data, and thus long-term elasticity calculations. The intention here is not to go into the technicalities of the various modeling frameworks, although some discussion of this is to be found in Chapter 12 when explicitly discussing demand modeling and forecasting, but rather to highlight what seem to be the two main trends:

- First, if aggregate data are used, for instance looking at demand for an entire railroad network, then, although it is far from universally true, elasticities tend to be higher than from 'discrete choice'-type models that use data at the individual service or customer level.
- Second, even within a modeling framework (be it involving the use of aggregate data or disaggregate data) the exact mathematical form of the equation used influences the elasticity calculated. Equation (4.2) highlighted the

Table 4.6   *Demand elasticities for North American rail freight transport (expressed in absolute values)*

Commodities	Log-linear	Aggregate logit	Translog	Discrete choice
Aggregate commodities	1.52	0.25–0.35, 0.83	0.09–0.29, 0.60	n.a.
Chemicals	n.a.	0.66	0.69	2.25
Fabricated metal products	n.a.	1.27	2.16	n.a.
Food products	0.02, 1.18	1.36	2.58, 1.04	n.a.
Iron & steel products	n.a.	n.a.	2.54, 1.20	0.02
Machinery	n.a.	0.16–1.73	2.27–3.50	0.61
Paper, plastic, & rubber products	0.67	0.87	1.85	0.07–0.09
Petroleum products	n.a.	n.a.	0.99	0.53
Stone, clay, & glass products	n.a.	2.03	n.a.	0.56
Transport equipment	n.a.	n.a.	0.92–1.08	2.68
Wood & wood products	0.05	0.76	1.97, 0.58	0.08

Note: n.a. = not available.

Source: Oum et al. (1992).

log-linear, or 'Cobb–Douglas', specification, the generic features of which we return to in Chapter 5. Table 4.6 provides some general guidance to these with respect to estimated elasticities of demand for rail freight transport elasticities for rail freight transport.

4.8   Income Levels

After housing and food, transport represents, at about 10 to 15 percent for a single-car-owning United Kingdom household, the largest element of expenditure out of income in industrialized countries. While there is ample evidence that transport is a normal good in the sense that more is demanded at higher levels of income, this generalization does not apply to all modes of transport or to all situations. As was seen in Chapter 2, at the national level, income exerts a positive influence over car ownership decisions, and we consider this relationship at a more disaggregate level below. But the situation is not so clear-cut with public transport use, and in some cases this mode clearly becomes an 'inferior good' with its use falling after some level of income has been attained. As incomes have risen and, with them, car ownership has become more widespread, public transport has in many situations proved to be an inferior good. Gwilliam and Mackie (1975) suggest that the long-run elasticity of demand with respect to income was of the order –0.4 to –1.0 for urban public transport trip-making in the United Kingdom during the 1970s. They argue that, although car ownership rises with income, and hence some trips are diverted from public transport, there is still a limited off-setting effect inasmuch as wealthier households make more trips in total. This effect would seem to be less relevant today with much higher levels of automobile ownership in developed countries.

The income elasticity of demand for many other modes of transport is seen to be relatively high, and especially so for modes such as air transport. John Taplin (1980), for example, suggests a figure of the order of 2.1 for vacation air trips overseas from Australia. By its nature air travel is a high-cost activity (the absolute costs involved are high even where mileage rates are low), so that income elasticities of this level are to be expected. There is also some evidence that wealth influences the demand for air travel, and a study of the Israeli market found a wealth elasticity of 2.06 (Alperovich and Machnes, 1994).

As with price, income changes exert somewhat different pressures on transport demand in the long run compared with the short. In general, it may be argued, a fall in income will produce a relatively dramatic fall in the level of demand, but as people readjust their expenditure patterns in the long term the elasticity is likely to be much lower. Looking at the responsiveness of car owner-ship levels to income changes, British and United States studies suggest a short-term income elasticity of between 2.0 and 4.5, while in the long run it appears to fall to around 1.5 (Button et al., 1982). However, as with price elasticities, the relationships between long- and short-term effects are not completely clear-cut. Reza and Spiro (1979), for example, produce an estimate of 0.6 for the short-run income elasticity of demand for petrol, rising to 1.44 in the long run, findings generally in line with what we saw in Table 4.5. If one assumes that gasoline consumption is a proxy for trip-making, then one could attempt to justify this in terms of a slow reaction to changing financial circumstances – a reluctance, for example, to accept immediately the consequences of a fall in income. In fact, the situation is likely to be more complex because the long run may embrace changes in technology, and possibly locations, that alter the fuel-consumption–trip-making relationship. Thus, these figures may still be consistent with the initial hypothesis regarding the relative size of short- and long-run income elasticities of demand for travel.

There is a literature on the possibility of a constant travel income budget akin to the travel time budget mentioned in Section 4.1 with households tending to spend a fixed proportion of their income on transport. Zahavi (1977), for example, in his examination of data from a large sample of urban transport users, noticed that the proportion of disposable income spent on cars by car-owning households at any income level appears to be approximately constant at a given moment in time. (United Kingdom data suggest a proportion of around 15.5 percent – slightly larger for low incomes – for 1971 to 1975.) The evidence for bus transport is less clear, but Mogridge suggests that while the proportion of dispos-able household income spent on bus travel seems to rise with income, a constant proportion still emerges if adjustments are made for the number of people in each household.

In the longer term there is evidence at the aggregate level that since the early 1980s there has been a steady increase in the overall proportion of income or disposable income allocated to travel in the United Kingdom. (This contrasts with a roughly constant proportion in Canada and the United States.) This may, however, be explained in terms of rising income levels but constant proportional travel budgets within each income group. But the conclusion concerning the idea of some overall budget mechanism governing individual travel decisions must be that the evidence available still leaves many questions unanswered and the theory still largely unproved. In an examination of 30 or so travel surveys from across the world, Andreas Schafer (2000) finds some consistency in travel money budgets for countries with about 0.85 cars per household, but the link is weak and only applies at a very aggregate level.

Exhibit   *Meta-analytical synthesis of demand elasticity results*

Meta-analysis is the statistical analysis of a collection of results from individual studies. It is a quantitative alternative to narrative discussions of research studies. The analysis uses probability-based statistics to summarize primary findings or to elicit moderator variables that influence variations in the results of these studies.

Most of these studies make use of meta-regression analysis and can be generalized as:

$$b_j = \beta + \Sigma_{k=1}^{k} a_k Z_{jk} + e_j; \quad j = 1.2, \dots, L$$

where:

   b_j is the reported estimate of β in the jth study in the L studies being examined;
   β is the 'true' value of the parameter of interest;
   Z_{jk} are independent variables that measure the relevant characteristics explaining
      variations between studies;
   α_j is a coefficient that reflects the biasing effect of study characteristics; and
   e_j is the error term.

Z_{jk} includes, specification variables (for example, the form of the empirical model, type of regression, and data sources), sample size, characteristics of the primary literature, and variables reflecting whether possibly relevant effects have been omitted from a primary study.

Wardman used meta-analysis to examine 1,633 price elasticities of demand found in 167 United Kingdom studies of car, rail, bus, and underground travel. Generally plausible relationships with journey purpose, mode, ticket type, area, and distance were found with anticipated differences between the short and the long run. The study makes use of the parameters obtained to imply general elasticities taking account of the variations in the primary studies' contexts, their technical specifications, and control variables they used. The results for United Kingdom passenger rail are seen in the table and compared to the fare elasticities laid down in the official *Passenger Demand Forecasting Handbook*. (Similar tables were calculated for other modes.)

As anticipated, the short-term impacts of rail fare changes are less than the longer-term implications. This applies to all fare categories. In general, the demand associated with changes in first-class and full fares is lower than that for discount fares. The former categories are more generally associated with business travel and commuter travel, whilst the discount fares are more often used for discretionary travel. By distance, work shows that, across the studies included, the long-run demand curve for rail travel is more sensitive to fare changes than is the short-run curve. Finally, the parameters suggested by the United Kingdom's *Passenger Demand Forecasting Handbook* would seem to be over-estimating the sensitivity of rail passengers' demand regarding fare changes.

Journey type		Short PTE	Short London	Short other	Inter-urban London	Inter-urban non-London
Season	SR	−0.18	−0.19	−0.31	−0.31	−0.28
	Static	−0.31	−0.33	−0.52	−0.52	−0.48
	LR	−0.36	−0.38	−0.61	−0.61	−0.57
	PDFH LR	−0.60	−0.50	−0.70	−0.75	−0.90
Non-season	SR	−0.37	−0.39	−0.62	−0.62	−0.57
(first &	LR	−0.73	−0.77	−1.23	−1.23	−1.14
standard)	Static	−0.63	−0.66	−1.05	−1.05	−0.98
	PDFH LR	−0.85	−0.80	−1.00	−1.05	−1.00
First	LR	−0.65	−0.69	−1.10	−1.10	−1.02
Full	LR	−0.70	−0.74	−1.19	−1.19	−1.10
Reduced	LR	−0.94	−0.99	−1.58	−1.58	−1.47

Notes: SR = short-run; LR = long run; static = intermediate between SR and LR; PTE = public transport executive; PDFH = *Passenger Demand Forecasting Handbook*.

See also: M. Wardman (2014) Price elasticities of surface travel demand: a meta-analysis of UK evidence, *Journal of Transport Economics and Policy*, 48, 367–84; and K.J. Button (2019) The value and challenges of using meta-analysis in transportation economics, *Transport Reviews*, 39, 292–308.

4.9   The Price of Other Transport Services

The demand for any transport service is likely to be influenced by the actions of competitive and complementary suppliers. (Strictly speaking, it is also influenced by prices in all other markets operating in the economy, but, with the possible exceptions of the land market, which was discussed in Chapter 3, and electronic communications, which we look at in Chapter 5, the importance of these is less great.) We have only touched upon the importance of motoring costs *vis-à-vis* the demand for public transport services and more is said on this topic later in the chapter. Moreover, there are the cross-price effects between modes of public transport. Table 4.7 presents the results from several different studies looking at elasticities of demand (both own fare and cross-fare) for transport in Greater London for 1970 to 1975.

The variation in results generally reflects the adoption of alternative estimation procedures, the inclusion of difference background, control variables, and time-lag allowances. One of the more interesting points is the almost total insensitivity of the demand for urban car use to the fare levels of both bus and rail

Table 4.7   *Greater London estimated Monday to Friday fare elasticities (1970 to 1975)*

Study	Elasticity of	With respect to	
		Bus	Local rail
Fairhurst & Morris (1975)	Bus	−0.60	0.25
	Rail	0.25	−0.40
Glaister (1976)	Bus	−0.56	0.30
	Rail	1.11	−1.00
Collings et al. (1977)	Bus	−0.41	n.a.
Lewis (1978)	Peak road traffic	0.03	0.06

Note: n.a. = not available.

Source: Glaister and Lewis (1978). This paper contains the full references to the studies cited.

public transport modes. This fact, which has been observed in virtually all studies of urban public transport, is the main reason that attempts by city transport authorities to reduce or contain car travel by subsiding public transport fares have proved unsuccessful.

The table suggests that there is likely to be more switching of demand between public transport modes as a result of one changing its fare structure than between that mode and private transport. Gilbert and Jalilian (1991) also provides cross-elasticities for London between public transport modes but throws up somewhat different results with the indication that bus travel in London is more sensitive to underground fares with a cross-fare elasticity of 0.90. Analysis of the cross-elasticity of demand between car and rail costs for inter-city rail travel in the United Kingdom, shows much less sensitivity: an average cross-elasticity of 0.09, falling to 0.027 and to 0.028 on some freeways (Acutt and Dodgson, 1995).

What emerges is that is that despite generally low levels of substitution between public transport modes passengers are particularly sensitive to in-vehicle access/egress and waiting time in choosing a mode and less so for fare variations. In general, rail demand is less sensitive to changes in bus demand than bus demand is to changes in rail demand. We also find that peak-hour demand more markedly switches between public transport modes than off-peak demand (Fearnley et al., 2018).

In other transport markets the cross-elasticity of demand may be higher, both between operators of the same mode of transport and between modes themselves. Rate reduction in non-conference shipping lines, for example, has periodically attracted considerable traffic away from the cartel, conference, and alliance carriers. Similarly, scheduled airlines have experienced a relative contraction of demand over time as low-cost carriers have entered the market.

Evidence on the cross-price elasticity of complementary transport services, such as feeder links to longer-distance trunk hauls, is scant. The expansion of the motorway network in the United Kingdom, the autobahns in Germany, and the freeways in the United States reduced motorway travel costs and increased the demand for certain feeder roads, while at the same time reducing it on competing routes. The exact implications of such network effects are much more difficult to trace out than changes in modal split but, in practical terms, are important features of the transport system.

The topic of cross-elasticities of demand between modes is returned to in Chapters 8 and 9 when discussing their importance when trying to divert traffic to less environmentally damaging and congestive forms of transport.

4.10   Tastes, Human Desires, and Motives

One of the items which influences equation (4.1) but not mentioned to date, that is often included in elementary discussion of demand, is the 'catch-all' variable, 'taste'. Traditional microeconomic theory assumes that consumers' taste stays constant when prices or income change. In practice this is a very strong assumption to make. For example, a regular commuter tries a new bus service, then this provides additional knowledge of the transport alternatives available. This may affect future commuting decisions.

While there may be circumstances in which such a term could and, indeed, should be included in the demand function, in general, tastes are more likely to influence the form of the demand equation – linear, log-linear, or whatever – and its location in price/quantity space. Consequently, a change in taste may be seen to affect the relationships between demand and the explanatory variables rather than result in some movement along a demand curve following the pattern of an established relationship. But situations do vary.

The economic meaning of 'taste' is seldom made clear, but in practice it seems to embrace all influences on demand not covered by the previous headings. Over time, tastes in transport certainly have changed. Globally, there has been an increased car orientation of society as people have moved towards private transport irrespective of cost or income considerations, while in freight transport the changing structure of the national economy (especially the switch from basic heavy industry to light industry producing high-value, low-weight products) has shifted the emphasis from price to other aspects of transport service. Both changes must to some extent be related to rising standards of living. With more wealth and greater free time there is likely to be an enhanced desire to benefit from the greater freedom and flexibility offered by private transport. A change in location patterns is also possible with larger residential plots away from urban centers now becoming attractive for many people.

Another aspect of 'taste' concerns inertia and asymmetry in decision-making (Goodwin, 1977). This has two implications:

- First, there may be discontinuities in the demand curve for transport, or at least parts of the demand curve reflect almost total insensitivity to price changes, as a result of habit and inertia on the part of individuals and firms. It may be explained in some cases quite simply by the fact that there are costs involved in seeking out information about alternatives, and continuing as before is thus the rational response until more major price changes occur.

- Second, there may be cases where responses are not symmetrical; a ratchet effect exists whereby the reaction to a price fall is not the same as the reaction to an identical price rise. Limited empirical work has been done on such 'path dependencies', although Blasé (1980) did find evidence of asymmetries in travel behavior in the context of fuel price variation and Dargay (1993) provided further support for this across a number of national studies.

Rather more effort has been put into the question of service quality. It is noticeable, for example, from empirical studies, that public transport demand is sensitive to changes in service quality, especially to any reduction in the speed or frequency of services. Again, this fact reflects the decreased importance attached to the purely monetary dimension. Market research in the West Midlands of the United Kingdom, for example, revealed that only 27.1 percent of people felt that keeping fares down would be the greatest improvement to local public transport; the remainder looked for service quality improvements, for example, 14.6 percent for greater reliability, 10.4 percent for higher frequency, 10.4 percent for more bus shelters, 10.0 percent for cleaner vehicles, etc. (Isaac, 1979).

An extensive survey by Armando Lago et al. (1981) examined a range of international studies concerned with urban public transport service elasticities. Their general conclusion, that services will generate less than proportional increases in passenger and revenue (that is, $\varepsilon_S < 1$), seems to contradict the above findings. But this may be misleading. To begin with, the survey looks at several service-quality attributes in isolation rather than at a package of service features. It also admits that many of the services sought by potential public transport users are qualitative rather than quantitative and hence are not amenable to the types of analysis reviewed. The survey also highlights the fact that service quality is far more important when the initial level of service is poor; the general elasticities found for peak-period ridership, for instance, are much lower than those for off-peak. The evidence presented suggests that service headway is one of the more important service variables; the studies examined indicates an elasticity of the order of –0.42 compared with, for example, –0.29 for in-vehicle bus travel time.

The evidence suggests that, as the modern world of inventory management and tracking has evolved, low price is also often no longer the dominant determinant of freight modal choice. In a survey conducted in the United Kingdom by the Price Commission as long ago as 1977, for instance, it was found that only in 52 percent of cases did consignors elect to use the cheapest road haulage operator available for local trips, 77 percent for intra-regional trips and 64 percent for trunk hauls. Subsequently, McGinnis' (1990) study of freight transport in the United States, for example, found that rates only became an important consideration after required service criteria were met.

The UK's Price Commission found that many companies were so unconcerned about finding the lowest price that competitive quotations were not sought. An emphasis placed upon vehicle suitability is seen to reflect customer concern about such factors as weather protection, systems for securing loads, and compatibility of vehicle with product. These are concerns unlikely to have been of paramount importance when heavy industry dominated the economy but are of much more a concern for more modern, high-technology firms and for large retailers. These firms were increasingly turning to 'just-in-time' production methods whereby inventories are kept to a minimum. To optimize such processes, reliability of supply is vital and companies were willing to pay the additional financial costs that this may entail. This is a subject considered in more detail in Chapter 10.

Exhibit   *The role of ancillary revenues in airline finances*

The fare an airline passenger paid prior to the trend towards economic liberalization from 1978 provided a package of services; for example, a seat with a given pitch in each class, meals, ability to change flights, and a relatively large checked baggage allowance. The 2000s saw this change as initially low-cost airlines offered a basic service at a low fare with other services being available for a supplement. Basically, a passenger bought a package of the services that they were willing to pay for; technically there was unbundling. Then additional services were added, including such things as insurance, hotel rooms, and car rental to the bundle for further fees.

The airlines did this to increase their load factors, bringing in travelers who did not want all the elements of the standard 'package', and to relate fares more closely to the costs of carrying individuals. The idea was that by not imposing the cost of services that a potential passenger did not value highly, they could price down the demand curve to fill seats by attracting those who would not fly. Additional items were added to allow pricing up for those willing to pay for them.

The table indicates, for United States and non-United States regions in 2012, a rough breakdown of the forms of ancillary revenues that were generated. The figure shows the results of an online survey conducted in 2011 by John O'Connell and David Warnock-Smith asking how likely people were to by buy accommodation, car rental, travel insurance, etc. in the future.

	À la carte services	Excess baggage fees	Onboard retail	Sales of miles	Hotels, car rental, insurance
Non-US carriers	15%	15%	10%	30%	30%
United States carriers	25%	20%	–	50%	5%

These results, combined with expert opinion and along with secondary data, indicate that airport car parking and checked baggage charges are the most accepted commission-based and unbundled products for airlines to sell.

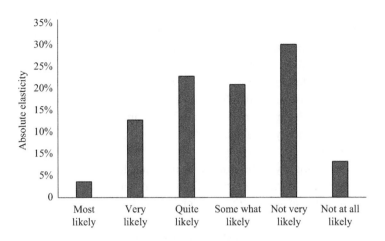

See also: J.F.O. Connell and D. Warnock-Smith (2013) An investigation into traveler preferences and acceptance levels of airline ancillary revenues, *Journal of Air Transport Management*, 33, 12–21.

4.11 The Notion of a 'Need' for Transport

The demand function indicates what people would buy given a budget constraint, but it is often argued that allocation of resources on this basis results in inequalities and unfairness because of differences in household income or other circumstances. There are, thus, some advocates of the idea that transport services, or at least some of them, should be allocated according to 'need' rather than effective demand. The concept of need is seldom defined, or at best rather imprecisely (Banister et al., 1984), but seems to be closely concerned with the notion of merit goods – that is, needs 'considered so meritorious that their satisfaction is provided for through the public budget over and above what is provided for through the market and paid for by private buyers'. The idea is that, just as everyone in a civilized society is entitled to expect a certain standard of education, medical cover, security, etc., so they are entitled to enjoy a certain minimum standard of transport provision. Looked at another way, the government, or other donor, provides such a good based on 'merit' because it can better provide for individual welfare than allowing consumer sovereignty.

One can point to several transport policy initiatives over time which are based upon this idea. The 1930 Road Traffic Act in the United Kingdom, for example, introduced, besides other things, road service licenses into the bus industry which embraced the notion of public need. The Traffic Commissioners interpreted this to mean the provision of a comprehensive network of services for an area, irrespective of the effective demand for specific routes. Licenses were granted on this basis and operators cross-subsidized the unremunerative services with revenue from the more profitable ones. More explicit were the social service grants given to the railways under the 1968 Transport Act whereby 222 services were subsidized for social reasons, once again despite deficit effective demand for their services. Additionally, the United Kingdom government has provided capital and operating cost subsidies to assist the shipping and air services to the remoter islands of Scotland.

In a different context, the 1978 Airline Deregulation Act in the United States has provided subsidies for services to small communities (the Essential Air Service Program) and the 1987 National Transportation Act in Canada provided explicitly for subsidies to 'essential' air services in the northern part of the country.

Allocation by some notion of need implies that the market is not used to determine the output or price of transport services. Figure 4.5 takes the simple case of a transit service that, under market conditions, would produce a fare of P_1 and offer Q_1 seats. If public policy requires that a higher level of services is warranted, say Q_2 seats, then this distorts the market. For a commercially driven market to offer Q_2 seats, a fare of P_2^* would be required, but only Q_2^* seats would be willing to pay this. For the Q_1 transit seats to be efficiently used, a fare P_2 is needed. The result is the necessity to subsidize the difference between this fare and the commercially necessary fare for Q_2 seats. We deal with some of the issues involved in transport subsidies, and alternative methods of finance, later in the book.

This notion of need rather than effective demand raises two important issues. First, exactly what is the nature of 'need'? And second, if one accepts that the concept has some operational meaning, how can it be incorporated into economic analysis? We look at these two questions in turn.

The need for adequate transport provision stems from the idea that people should have access to an acceptable range of facilities. It is, therefore, essentially a 'normative' concept. Transport is seen as exerting a major influence on the quality

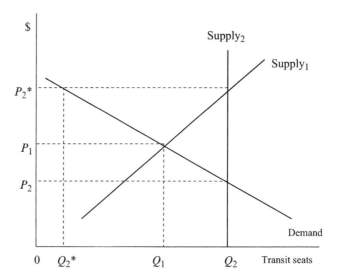

Figure 4.5 *Allocation by 'need'*

of the lives of people and a certain minimum quality should be ensured. The United Kingdom has traditionally emphasized this view of mobility; for example: 'The social needs for transport also rank high – the needs of people to have access to their work, shops, recreation and the range of activities on which civilized society depends' (UK Department of Transport, 1977). Defining the exact level of mobility in this context is difficult, but it is helpful to look at the groups who, for one reason or another, seem in need of transport services in addition to those who would be forthcoming in the market.

The most obvious group is the poor, who cannot afford transport. Transport expenditure forms a substantial part of a household budget and, consequently, those on the lowest income must make fewer trips, shorter trips, or trips on inferior modes of transport. A major problem is that, as we see later, as income levels rise, in general there is a tendency towards higher car ownership, leaving only depleted and expensive public transport facilities for those at the lower end of the income distribution. A household with a car in the United Kingdom tends, for instance, to make on average about 300 fewer bus journeys per year than comparable households without a car. But there are also wider issues, in that this change in the transport sector has implications for population distribution.

Higher car ownership in rural areas, and the resultant reduction in the demand for local public transport, has put pressure on rural bus and rail services. Between 1970 and 1974, for example, the National Bus Company in England, which was responsible for most rural services in England and Wales, reduced its bus kilometers by 7 percent. This, in turn, has been one of the causes of rural depopulation. Similar trends were seen in Chapter 2 with respect to the United States. There is a long tradition of rural public and special transit service operating and capital assistance from federal and state government. The US Federal Transit Administration has over 5,300 rural and inter-city transit programs, and there is special federal and state transport support for special mobility services transport. In addition, social services funding is available. The question then arises as to whether society in general needs a balance between urban and rural society.

While inadequate income poses one problem, there are other groups in society that are often felt to need assistance. The old, the infirm, and children are obvious examples where, irrespective of income, effective demand may be felt to be an inadequate basis upon which to allocate transport resources. The available evidence suggests that only about 10 percent of households in the aged or disabled category have private transport at hand. Even when a household does own a car (or has one made available through employment agreements), there are still members of it who may be deemed in need of additional transport.

Women enjoy less mobility than men, although the gap is closing, at least in wealthier countries. An early study of mobility by Hillman (1973), for instance, found that 70 percent of young married women in the outer metropolitan area of London had no car available for their everyday use – even 30 percent of those qualified to drive were in this position. Even in the mid-1990s, women in the United Kingdom aged between 26 and 59 years, the prime years of domestic caring responsibilities, only traveled about half the miles of men, making fewer trips and shorter trips. While there are national differences, the British pattern was far from atypical.

Although there have been changes since Hillman's study, the evidence is that women still enjoy both less mobility and accessibility than their male counterparts.

There are political-economy arguments, therefore, that these various groups are in need of adequate and inexpensive public transport services (or special transport provision in the case of the disabled) and that the normal market mechanism is inadequate in this respect.

If one accepts the notion that need is, in certain contexts, the relevant concept rather than effective demand, then, for practical purposes, this idea requires integration into more standard positive economic theory. (It should perhaps be noted that many people do not accept the idea of 'need' as an allocative device but advocate tackling problems of low income or disadvantage at their source through measures such as direct income transfers, but this is an issue outside our present discussion.) Perhaps the simplest method of reconciling the difficulty is to treat the monies paid out by government and other agencies in subsidies to social transport services, as the effective demand of society for the services. One can then perceive the situation as analogous to that of conventional consumer theory. Just as effective demand reflects the desire of an individual to purchase a service, so governmental response to need reflects society's desire to purchase transport services for certain of its members.

4.12 The Valuation of Travel Time Savings

The importance of travel time in transport economics should by now be apparent. While the action of travel involves some time costs, it is perhaps more useful to consider travel time in this chapter that focuses on demand and benefits rather than costs. This is because travel or transport time savings are normally considered to be a major component of any scheme designed to improve transport efficiency. As we see in Chapter 11, travel time savings form the major component of inter-urban road investment benefits – a situation also found in most fields of transport. For reasons of comparability with other forms of benefit, a vast amount of intellectual energy has gone into devising methods of placing money values on such benefits.

Two quite distinct methodologies have been developed for time evaluation, the distinction being made between time saved in the course of employment and time saved during non-work travel (including commuter trips when fixed working hours are involved). The distinction is drawn because work time involves lorry drivers, seamen, pilots, etc., not simply in giving up leisure but also in incurring some actual disutility from the work undertaken. Hence, if they could do the same amount of work in less time, these people would be able to enjoy more leisure and suffer less disutility (or the employer must pay them more to encourage a continuation of the same work hours with a higher output). Savings in non-work time do not, by definition, reduce the disutility associated with work and, consequently, although more leisure may be enjoyed, they are likely to be valued below work travel time savings.

The valuation of work travel time (which embraces all journeys made when travelers are earning their living) is made simpler if we accept the traditional economic idea that workers are paid according to the value of their marginal revenue product. On this basis, the amount employers pay workers must be enough to compensate them for the marginal time and disutility associated with doing the job. Thus, it becomes possible to equate the value of a marginal saving in work travel time with the marginal wage rate (plus related social payments and overheads). An alternative way of arriving at this cost-savings approach is by reflecting upon the opportunity costs involved – as Benjamin Franklin once said, 'remember that time is money'. Time savings at work permit a greater output to be produced within a given time period, which, again drawing on the marginal productivity theory of wage determination, will be reflected in the marginal wages paid. Official policy in many countries is to value work travel time savings as the national average wage for the class of the transport user concerned plus the associated costs of social insurance paid by the employer and a premium added to reflect overheads.

A major problem with the wage equivalence approach is that it assumes employees consider the disutility of travel during work to be the same as the disutility of other aspects of their work that they may be required to undertake if travel time is reduced. In many cases workers may consider the travel much less arduous than these alternative tasks. This implies that savings in work time travel should, in such cases, be valued at less than the wage rate plus additions. Also, some people may view travel time as highly productive – many rail and air travelers, for instance, certainly work on their journeys – suggesting that reduced travel time would not significantly alter output. Even time spent in car travel can be used to complete mental tasks – for example, Fowkes et al. (1986) found that about 3 percent of business travel time by car was spent working.

More recently, analysis of San Francisco Bay Area travelers found that, overall, commute time is not unequivocally a source of disutility to be minimized, but rather offers some benefits (such as a transition between home and work). Most people were found to have a non-zero optimum commute time, which can be violated in either direction – that is, it is possible (although comparatively rare, occurring for only 7 percent of the sample) to commute too little (Redmond and Mokhtarian, 2001). Examining the wage rate alone ceases to be a useful measure of work travel time savings in such cases.

While labor economics provides a useful foothold to obtain values of work travel time, rather more empiricism is required in the evaluation of non-work travel time. The behavioral approach involves using revealed preferences to consider trade-off situations that reflect the willingness of travelers to pay in order to save time. In other words, if a person chooses to pay $X to save Y minutes, then he/she is revealing an implicit value of time equal to at least (X/Y) per minute. More formally:

$$\Delta A = -\alpha \Delta T - \beta_1 \Delta C + \beta_2 \Delta E \tag{4.3}$$

where the relative attractiveness of the alternatives, ΔA, is the difference between the travel time cost, ΔC, and travel time, ΔT. The coefficients α and β_1 are both negative because a decrease in either the time or cost of a trip is seen to generate positive utility.

Empirical studies attempting to value non-work travel time in this way have looked at several different trade-off situations (a survey is offered by Waters, 1992), notably when travelers have a choice among:

* route;
* mode of travel;
* speed of travel (by a given mode over a given route);
* location of home and work; and
* destination of travel.

The standard approach in these trade-off studies is to employ a simple equation of the general form:

$$P_1 = \frac{e^y}{\left(1 + e^y\right)} \quad \text{where } y = \alpha_0 + \alpha_1 \left(t_1 t_2\right) + \left(c_1 t_2\right) \tag{4.4}$$

where:

P_1 is the probability of choosing mode (route, etc.) 1;
y is choice of mode (route, etc.); takes value of 1 for mode (route, etc.) 1 and 0 for mode (route, etc.) 2;
e is an exponential constant;
t_i is the door-to-door travel time by the j' mode (route, etc.); $i = 1,2$;
c_i is the door-to-door travel cost by the jth mode (route, etc.); $i = 1,2$; and
α_0, α_1, and α_2 are constants to be estimated.

A value of time can then be inferred by looking at changes in the dependent variable that result from a unit change in either the time or the cost difference. Strictly, it may be found as the ratio α_1/α_2 in equation (4.4).

Many of the early studies of non-work travel time concentrated on urban commuter trips because there was pressure at the time to provide information for cost–benefit analysis (CBA) of urban transport investment plans. In consequence, mode and route choice evaluation techniques were developed to a high level of mathematical sophistication. Early work by Michael Beesley (1965) specifically employed discriminant analysis to examine the journey to work-mode choices of employees at the UK Ministry of Transport during 1965–66. This technique essentially finds the trade-off value of time that minimizes the number of misallocations of commuters to alternative modes with different time and cost characteristics.

The upper part of Figure 4.6 considers the possible options available to a traveler when choosing between two modes. If the figure relates to Mode A, and only time savings and costs are important then Option 3 dominates. Conversely, Mode *B* will dominate Option 2 (where Mode *A* is slower and more expensive). But in some cases, travelers may not have such a clear-cut choice and will have to elect between Options 1 and 4 where there are trade-offs between time and money costs.

The lower portion of the figure gives some actual decisions by individuals regarding the choices that are made between the two modes (filled and unfilled circles). The line *AB* (where $\Delta C = \theta \Delta T$) provides the partitioning that leads to the minimum number of 'misclassifications' and reflects the trade-off between changes in travel time and travel costs being made. The slope of this line, θ, identifies the value of travel time savings.

The discriminate function used to determine the minimum number of mis-specifications takes the form:

$$Z_{ij} = \sum_{K=1}^{n} \alpha_k \left[f(X_{ki}, X_{kj}) \right] + \sum_{1}^{m} \beta_1 U_1 \qquad (4.5)$$

where:

X_{ki}, X_{kj} are the values of the *k*th attributes of the *i*th and the *j*th trip packages;
U_1 are user attributes;
α_k are parameters associated with the alternative systems;
β_1 are parameters associated with user characteristics; and

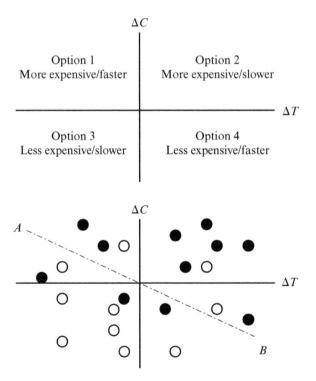

Figure 4.6   *The 'Beesley graph' of travel time–cost trade-off*

$f(X_{ki}, X_{kj})$ is a function that may take either of the forms $(X_{ki} - X_{kj})$ or (X_{ki}/X_{kj}).

Beesley estimated that commuter trip time savings were valued at between 30 and 50 percent of the gross personal income of the commuters. One of the main problems with this pioneering study, though, was that it failed to isolate in-vehicle travel time from the other components of journey time (for example, waiting and walking time). This defect was subsequently remedied in a larger study of mode choice in Leeds undertaken by David Quarmby (1967), which embraced seven variables including walking and waiting time as well as in-vehicle time. The findings indicated that savings in walking and waiting times are valued at between two and three times savings in in-vehicle time – parameters that have proved to be remarkably robust over the years.

Table 4.8 provides details of the non-work time values that have been revealed in these and subsequent studies. Many of these moved on from the discriminate approach to adopt logit and probit specifications (discussed in the context of car ownership modeling in Chapter 11) that offer more flexibility and more statistical measures of the quality of a model.

Model specifications can influence the travel time values obtained and care is needed in their selection. There is also a tendency to lump all non-work travel time together because it is not directly related to theories of labor productivity, but this may produce aggregation bias. Mark Wardman (2001), for example, in reviewing British value of travel time savings work found that the valuation of commuting time savings are about 35 percent higher than for leisure travel in London and south-east England, although only about 14 percent higher for work pertaining to other parts of the country.

Stated preference, or experimental, techniques, whereby hypothetical questions are posed to travelers to gain information about trade-offs they would be willing to make have become more common in recent years. A pioneering example was that of Lee and Dalvi (1969), who used questionnaires, rather than looking at actual choices, to discover the level of fare increase required before passengers switched from one mode of public transport to an alternative. Interestingly, in Manchester it was found that in-vehicle time, walking time, and waiting time were not separately important and travelers did not distinguish between them. Overall, it was estimated that non-work travel time was being valued at 15 to 45 percent of hourly income.

While most urban studies have tended to focus on mode choice decisions, the evaluation of non-work inter-urban travel time has tended to concentrate rather more on route and speed choice situations – although imperfections in travelers' knowledge of the latter make speed choice trade-offs suspect. Pioneering work on route choice by Paul Claffey (1961) looked at choices made between tolled and free roads in the United States and attempted to allow for differing accident rates and levels of driver discomfort when assessing the time/money-cost trade-offs. Mathematical weakness limits the value of this specific model but subsequent reworking suggests time differences are unimportant in route choices of this type.

Table 4.8   *Computation examples of estimated values of travel time savings*

Study	Country	Value of time as % of wage rate	Trip purpose	Mode
Beesley (1965)	United Kingdom	33–50	Commuting	Auto
Quarmby (1967)	United Kingdom	20–25	Commuting	Auto, transit
Thomas & Thompson (1970)	United States	86	Inter-urban	Auto
Lee & Dalvi (1971)	United Kingdom	30	Commuting	Bus
		40	Commuting	Auto
Talvitte (1972)	United States	12–14	Commuting	Auto, transit
Hensher & Hotchkiss (1974)	Australia	2.70	Commuting	Hydrofoil, ferry
Kraft & Kraft (1974)	United States	38	Inter-urban	Bus
McDonald (1975)	United States	45–78	Commuting	Auto, transit
Guttman (1975)	United States	63	Leisure	Auto
		145	Commuting	Auto
Hensher (1977)	Australia	39	Commuting	Auto
		35	Leisure	Auto
Nelson (1977)	United States	33	Commuting	Auto
Edmonds (1983)	Japan	42–49	Commuting	Auto, bus, rail
Deacon & Sonstelie (1985)	United States	52–254	Leisure	Auto
Hensher & Truong (1985)	Australia	105	Commuting	Auto, transit
Guttman & Menashe (1986)	Israel	59	Commuting	Auto, bus
Fowkes (1986)	United Kingdom	27–59	Commuting	Rail, bus
Chui & McFarland (1987)	United States	82	Inter-urban	Auto
Mohring et al. (1987)	Singapore	60–129	Commuting	Bus
Cole Sherman (1990)	Canada	93–170	Commuting	Auto
		116–165	Leisure	Auto

Source: Waters (1992). This paper contains the full references to the studies cited.

Dawson and Everall (1972), using a modification and looking at route choices of motorists traveling between Rome and Caserta and between Milan and Modena where the autostrada offered alternatives to ordinary trunk roads, found that observed trade-offs indicate that commuting and other non-work travel time was valued at about 75 percent of the average wage rate.

It is clear from the selection of studies cited above that non-work time savings are, indeed, valued below the wage rate, but it is equally clear that the values obtained from economic studies are extremely sensitive to the assumptions made and the estimation technique employed.

David Hensher (1979) goes further and points to the rather strong assumptions that are implicit in the not-uncommon practice of taking time values obtained from, say, a mode choice study and employing them in route or speed choice situations. He also questions whether enough consideration is given to the composition of time savings beyond the in-vehicle/waiting-time split and to preferences between constant journey speed (with a lower average) and faster, variable speeds (with a higher average). There is also the common practical problem that it is difficult to separate the influence of comfort and convenience factors from travel time savings.

In Britain the UK Department of Transport and its successors have since the 1960s recommended standard values of time for transport analysis purposes. The use of standard figures is to encourage uniformity in investment appraisal. While the work–travel time figures are open to only minor criticisms (and even quite major errors here would seem unlikely to distort decisions), the use of standard non-work travel time values has met with more serious criticism.

Empirically, non-work travel time values have generally been shown correlated with income levels (Ian Heggie's 1976 work being one of the few exceptions), but on occasions an average value across all income levels has been used for policy formulation purposes. The argument supporting this 'equity' value is that if time values were directly varied with income this would tend to bias project selection towards projects favoring the higher-income groups. In evaluation, the travel time savings of such groups would automatically be weighted more heavily than those of the less well-off. The Leitch Committee (UK Department of Transport, 1978) in the United Kingdom, however, rejected this line of argument because it is not consistent with the way other aspects of transport investment are evaluated. Since the overall distributional effects of transport investment may be treated more directly in the appraisal process (see Chapter 11), the notion of 'equity' values was rejected in favor of income-based time evaluations.

Even if generally acceptable values of travel time could be obtained, there are still difficulties associated with using them. One of the major problems is that some projects can result in a small number of large time savings while others produce a magnitude of extremely small savings. The problem becomes one of deciding whether 60 one-minute savings are as valuable as (or more valuable than) one saving of an hour's duration. It could be argued that travelers, especially over longer routes, tend not to perceive small time savings or cannot utilize such times. If this is so, it would tend to make urban transport schemes appear less attractive *vis-à-vis* inter-urban ones because the main benefits of urban improvements have been small time savings spread over thousands of commuters.

One suggestion is that a zero value should be adopted in these contexts: small travel time savings with a positive value only being employed once a hold level of saving has been reached (say ten minutes). This ignores the fact that small time savings may, in some circumstances, be combined with existing periods of free or idle time to permit substantial increases in output or in leisure enjoyment. Further, if there are non-linearities in the value of travel time this would imply that widely used trade-off methods of time evaluation based upon average time savings must be giving biased estimates of the value of travel time. The debate over the handling of small travel time savings is unlikely to be resolved easily.

Finally, there is the question of whether revealed or stated preference measures of the value of travel time savings are more 'accurate'. There is some indication from Table 4.9, which provides details of the travel time savings values used in the United Kingdom, that, in fact, they are relatively consistent – a finding consistent with Wardman's (2001) review. The table relates to the values used in COBA, the program used to assess road investments. The method of determining the values changed between 1988 and 1994 from a revealed to a stated preference approach. While there are some clear differences, the broad pattern is very similar considering the very different methods of estimation used.

Transport studies in less developed countries tend to adopt the convention that while work travel time savings should be given a monetary value based upon the cost-savings approach (although the wage rate is generally modified to allow for imperfections in the local labor market), savings in non-work travel time – especially in rural areas – are given a zero value. The justification for this is that the prime objective of improving transport infrastructure in the Third World is to assist in economic growth and thus the emphasis should be exclusively concentrated on economically productive schemes – leisure time is not seen as 'productive'. Thomas (1979) pointed to an anomaly, however, when this argument is carried into practice. While non-work travel time savings in rural areas are ignored, savings in vehicle operating costs for such travel is not. Not only is this inconsistent but it also has important distributional implications because the main beneficiaries of low operating costs are almost invariably high-income car owners.

4.13   The Demand for Car Ownership

While the demand for cars is not strictly a direct transport matter, it is in some ways more to do with industrial economics and the demand for consumer durables. The importance of the automobile in affective travel behavior, land-use patterns, and the environment makes it a matter of considerable interest to transport economists (Dargay and Giuliano, 2006).

Car ownership, as we saw in Chapter 2, has risen considerably since the First World War with only brief halts during periods of major military conflict and occasional decelerations in the trend during periods of macroeconomic depression. This upward trend is not unique to the United States or the United Kingdom but is also to be found in all other countries irrespective of their state of economic development, or the nature of their political institutions. The upward trend in car ownership is the result of both the considerable benefits that accompany car availability (notably improved access and greater flexibility of travel) and the long-term increases in income enjoyed by virtually all countries since the Second World War. The 'demonstration effect' has tended to accelerate the

Table 4.9   *Overall values of time used in United Kingdom road investment analysis*

	1994 study	COBA (1988)	COBA (1988) full income growth	COBA (1988) income elasticities	COBA (1988) income growth adj.10
Driver	–	–	–	–	–
Commuting	5.4	–	–	–	–
Other	4.4	–	–	–	–
Non-work total	4.9	5.6	6.2	5.9	–
Employee (Business)	6.7	–	–	–	–
Employer (Business)	14.7	–	–	–	–
Working total	21.4	19.1	20.9	20.6	–
Passenger	–	–	–	–	–
Commuting	6.0	–	–	–	–
Other	3.1	–	–	–	–
Non-work total	4.03	5.6	6.2	5.9	–
Employee (Business)	6.7	–	–	–	–
Employer (Business)	14.7	–	–	–	–
Working total	21.4	15.9	17.4	17.1	–
LGV	–	–	–	–	–
Hire & reward	45.0	–	–	–	–
Own account	35.0	–	–	–	–
Total	40.06	–	–	–	–
COBA 9	–	19.35	–	–	20.3
OGV/HGV	–	–	–	–	–
Hire & reward	45.0	–	–	–	–
Own account	35.0	–	–	–	–
Total	40.06	–	–	–	–
COBA 9	–	14.05	–	–	14.7
PSV	–	–	–	–	–
Scheduled coach	50.0–60.0	–	–	–	–
Motorway charter	23.0–33.0	–	–	–	–
Scheduled bus	17.0	–	–	–	–
Trunk road charter	0.0–25.0	–	–	–	–
Total PSV	–	84.17	–	–	88.4

Notes: All results are in 1994 £0.01/minute.

Source: Gunn (2008).

process in less developed countries as attempts are made to emulate the consumption patterns of more affluent nations.

Considerable effort has been focused on exploring both the rate of increase in vehicle ownership and reasons why this should differ between countries and between areas within a single country. Information on the underlying demand functions is sought for a variety of reasons. Car manufacturers need to know the nature of changing demands for new vehicles, both within the country and within their export markets, and to be able to forecast likely changes in the type of vehicles which are wanted. While work in this area often sheds some useful light on the workings of the car market, it is only of limited use to transport economists. By contrast, central government is generally more interested in the aggregate number of vehicles in the country, mainly for road planning purposes, but also, to a lesser extent, to assist the finance authority in its fiscal duties. Regional variations, which can be quite pronounced within countries (Table 4.10), are also of interest for strategic planning purposes, particularly for developing national and international road networks.

The theory underlying much of the early forecasting work looking at car ownership levels is closely akin to the management theory of a 'product life' cycle, where a product has a pre-determined sales pattern almost independent of traditional economic forces, although taste and costs are not altogether absent from the model. The logistic curve fitting model developed by the United Kingdom's Transport Research Laboratory (then the Road Research Laboratory and subsequently the Transport and Road Research Laboratory over the period), in its basic form, treats per capita vehicle ownership as a function of time (Figure 4.7), with the ownership level following a symmetric, sigmoid growth path through time until an eventual saturation level is approached (Tanner, 1978). Broadly, it is argued that long-term growth in ownership follows a predictable diffusion process. Initially, high production costs and unfamiliarity will keep sales low, but after a period, if the product is successful, economies of scale on the supply side coupled with bandwagon effects on the demand side would result in the take-off of a comparatively rapid diffusion process. Finally, there is a tailing-off as the market becomes saturated and everyone wishing to own a car does so.

Table 4.10   *Regional variations in Great Britain's car ownership patterns*

Region	Automobiles per 1,000 population	Average vehicle age
North-east	403	6.0
North-west	469	6.1
Yorkshire & the Humber	432	6.2
East Midlands	487	6.7
West Midlands	510	6.4
East of England	513	7.1
London	345	7.4
South-east	542	6.9
South-west	522	7.5
Total England	471	6.8
Wales	483	6.9
Scotland	433	5.8
Great Britain	480	6.7

Source: UK Department for Transport (2007).

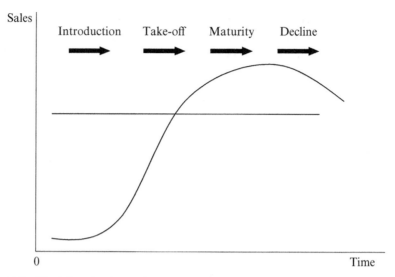

Figure 4.7   *The life cycle of a product*

The initial form of model was a logistic curve that simply traced out per capita car ownership over time using national car ownership data (Figure 4.8). The logistic equation took the form:

$$C = \frac{\alpha}{1 + \beta \exp(-\alpha c t)} \tag{4.6}$$

where:

    C is per capita car ownership;
    t is a time trend; and
    α, β, and c are parameters to be estimated.

For calculation purposes it was necessary to feed an exogenous value of 'saturation level' (the parameter α) into the equation. This was done either by judgment based upon such things as the proportion of the population who would be able to drive if there were no constraints on car ownership (for example, taking out the young and the infirm from the population) or by calculation 'mean reversion' parameters. The latter involved taking two periods of regional cross-sectional data on car ownership levels and regressing the levels of ownership in the base year against the changes in those levels. The constant term in the resultant equation (that is, when $\Delta C = 0$) is, *de facto*, the saturation level. Once the overall equation is fitted using up to point t in the figure then it is possible to extrapolate to produce forecasts.

    Historically, the Road Research Laboratory's (RRL) extrapolative approach provided relatively good forecasts in the United Kingdom in the 1960s (Table 4.11), but tended to be less reliable in later years and to suffer from over-prediction. Some of the difficulties were associated with problems

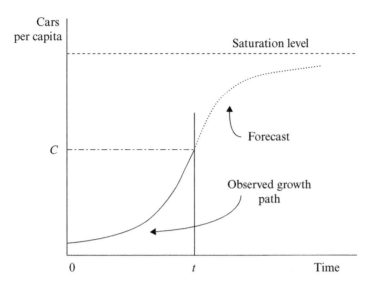

Figure 4.8   *The logistic growth curve approach to car ownership forecasting*

of estimating key parameters such as the ultimate saturation level, or with the correct configuration of the growth curve – in later work, a power function, which does not imply a symmetric sigmoid growth path, replaced the logistic (equation (4.7)). In addition, the time variable was supplemented by other variables to reflect changing costs of motoring and income. The resultant extrapolative model is still widely used to gain general insights into car ownership and to gauge the implications of policies regarding motoring costs, such as fuel taxation, on the future carpool:

$$C_t = \frac{S}{1 + \left(\dfrac{S - C_0}{C_0}\right)\left(\dfrac{Y_t}{Y_0}\right)^{-k_1 S}\left(\dfrac{P_t}{P_0}\right)^{-k_2 S_{-k_3 S_t}} e} \qquad (4.7)$$

where:

C_0 is car ownership per person at time t = zero;
S is the saturation level to which C is asymptotic as t increases;
Y_t is income per head;
P_t is 'cost of motoring'; and
k_1, k_2, and k_3 are constants.

Despite these limitations, this type of general framework can be useful when there are serious data constraints. Button et al. (1993) examined factors affecting car ownership levels across a range of very-low-income countries where there is little information on many of the economic variables that one would like to consider – in this case just data on income and time were used in a quasi-logistic equation.

Table 4.11   *Comparison of actual car ownership and RRL forecasts*

Year of publication	*Base year for calculation*	*(Forecast annual growth in cars per capita)/actual annual growth in pool 1975*	*Forecast car pool 1975*
1962	1960	1.14	1.13
1965	1964	1.57	1.57
1967	1966	1.67	1.68
1969	1968	1.84	1.84
1970	1969	1.66	1.66
1972	1971	1.62	1.58

Source: Button et al. (1980).

At least one school of thought rejects the underlying extrapolative philosophy as inadequate. It has been argued that car ownership forecasting should be based only upon explicit economic variables such as income and vehicle prices rather than 'proxy' variables such as time (the counterargument being that 'time' somehow encapsulates changing tastes). The final RRL forecasting framework attempted to meet this criticism by incorporating economic variables, but a time trend is still retained and the income and vehicle operating cost elasticities are not estimated internally within the model but derived from 'external' sources. The demand model developed by Bates et al. (1978), as part of a larger regional highway traffic model (RHTM) in the United Kingdom, in contrast is based entirely upon 'causal' variables, and all the relevant elasticities are estimated directly within the forecasting model. This type of framework is now widely used in economic forecasting, especially at the local level, but also for national studies.

The basis for the underlying model is in economic utility theory. It is assumed that the utility, U, that a household, n, gets from owning a thing, j, is represented by:

$$U_{j,n} = V_{j,n} + \varepsilon_{j,n} \tag{4.8}$$

where $V_{j,n}$ is a deterministic component and $\varepsilon_{j,n}$ is a random factor.

For estimation purposes, a multi-nomial logit model is generally used in the car ownership context, although in some cases alternatives are adopted, especially for local analysis where the interest may be in forecasting the number of cars per household rather than the national carpool. The logit model takes the general form:

$$V_n = \beta_n^1 + \sum_{k=1}^{p} \beta_{nk} X_{nk} \tag{4.9}$$

where:

p is the number explanatory variables;
β_n^1 is the 'alternative-specific' constant associate with n vehicles;

β_{nk} is the 'weight' for variable k in the utility of having n vehicles; and X_{nk} is the value of variable k for vehicle ownership level n.

To show what this means in practical terms, a simple form of the actual type of equation calculated is provided by Fairhurst (1975) in the context of car ownership, not in the United Kingdom as a whole, but in London:

$$\log \frac{P_0}{1-P_0} = c + b \log Y + d \log H + f \log(B+1) + g \log(R+1) \qquad (4.10)$$

where:

P_0 is the proportion of households without a car;
H is persons per household;
B is a bus public transport index; and
R is a rail public transport index.

The data used in these types of models are not the time-series registration statistics employed by the RRL, but rather a series of cross-sectional sets of statistics generally obtained from household surveys. For forecasting it is necessary to be able to predict reliably the level and distribution of future income and other variables. The approach also concentrates on the probability of households having a certain level of vehicle ownership rather than, as with the time-trend model, on forecasting the national average or regional ownership level; this conforms more closely to other recent trends in transport demand forecasting (see Chapter 12). In the case of the United Kingdom, for example, where the geographical size of the country makes national forecasting meaningful, this type of economic model makes use of data from the Family Expenditure Survey and the National Travel Survey. It relates household car ownership to household income, number of adults in a household, number of children in a household, number of employed household members, number of retired people, and the geographical nature of the location of the house.

This type of economic framework is now regularly used in aggregate analysis. Dargay (2002), for example, examines trends in the growth of car stocks over past decades and make projections of its development over the next 25 years for 82 countries at different levels of economic development, from the lowest (China, India, and Pakistan) to the highest (the United States, Japan, and European nations). The countries account for 85 percent of the world population and 93 percent of the vehicle stock. The projections are based on estimates of a dynamic time-series model and an S-shaped function to relate the vehicle stock to GDP. The estimates are used in conjunction with assumptions concerning income and population growth, to produce projections of the growth in the vehicle stock on a year-by-year basis.

Differences in the geographical demand for car ownership interest transport planners both because they need to be able to forecast future demand for links in the local road network and because, where ownership is low, social commitments may require that alternative public transport is provided. These models often need to be a little more detailed in terms of the variables included. For example, it seems likely that spatial variations at the local level may, once allowance has been made for differing income and demographic factors, be explained in terms of the quality of local transport services, as in the case of Fairhurst's work on London.

Good, uncongested roads combined with poor public transport increases the demand, *ceteris paribus*, for private car ownership. Regional econometric studies of car ownership have attempted to reflect this cost-of-transport effect by incorporating variables such as residential density in their models (it being argued that a densely populated area is normally well served by public transport while motoring is adversely affected by the higher levels of traffic congestion). More sophisticated local models have shown the frequency of public transport services to influence car ownership rates, at least slowing the rise in automobile ownership but not reversing it. If these studies are correct then there is some evidence that the long-term growth in car ownership may be contained by improving public transport services, although from a policy point of view the overall cost of such actions needs to be fully assessed.

4.14 What Does 'Behavioral Economics' Tell Us?

Most of our analysis so far of demand, excepting the discussion of habit and hysteresis, and to some extent need, is founded on the idea that individuals act as if they were *homo economicus*. It assumes that consumers have full information, make cognitive, non-emotional, optimal decisions, and that these decisions are marginal and independent of the actions of others. Psychologists however, are increasingly finding that people often exhibit inertia in their actions, they can be philanthropic, there is asymmetric information in their transactions, and they search within boundaries. While in many cases it is quite reasonable to use the conventional concept of *homo economicus* when discussing and quantifying many aspects of transport demand – people will buy less fuel if oil prices rise – in some circumstances this is not the case.

Because of this, there has been an increased interest shown by transport economists in behavioral economics (Garcia-Sierra et al., 2015). Broadly, this involves embedding study of the effects of psychological, cognitive, emotional, cultural, and social factors in the decisions of individuals and institutions, and how those decisions vary from those assumed in neoclassical economics. Put another way, these factors can mean that individuals appear to act irrationally when contrasted with the conventional neoclassical economics we are familiar with.

The transport decision considered may be of a long-term nature: choice of residential location or employment, whether to acquire a driving license, own a car or not, etc., or shorter-term choices of destinations, modes to use, routes to take, and the timing of trips. In practice, any of these decisions are complex and made in the face of imperfect information. This often means resorting to heuristics and the adoption of mental shortcomings. Human behavior as a result deviates from that postulated in standard neoclassical models. Behavioral economics, in recognition of this, has begun to play a role in policy-making, including in transport policy. In 2010 a Danish Network was created and a year later the United Kingdom Department for Transport published a *Behavioral Insights Toolkit* in 2011.

The mounting intellectual interest in behavioral economics is confirmed in the awarding of the Nobel Prize for Economics to such as Herbert Simon, George Akerlof, Daniel Kahneman, and Richard Thaler. Thaler's work on nudging, basically any aspect of choice architecture that alters people's behavior in a predictable way without forbidding any options or significantly changing their economic incentives, and his best-selling book, *Nudge: Improving Decisions on Health, Wealth, and Happiness* (Thaler and Sunstein, 2008), have brought behavioral economics to the public eye.

The approach is essentially inter-disciplinary; Kahneman, for example, was trained in psychology, and unlike many neoclassical economists does not have roots in engineering. While, as we see later, behavioral economics has impacted on some aspects of the supply theory of economics, including Leibenstein's work on X-efficiency, Robert Metcalfe and Paul Dolan (2012) and Filippini et al. (2021) highlight the ways in which it is increasingly influencing the analysis of travel demand and pushing through policy initiatives.

Examples of this, in terms of cartography and nudges, are when words like freeway, route, highway, parkway, etc., are used as designators to convey different impressions of the quality and nature of a road. In some cases, the categorization is used to nudge drivers to use specific routes. Differing colors for roads on an old-fashioned map, or the outlining of some, serve the same purpose. Google Maps with brighter colors highlighting more congested routes has updated this behavioral tool further. As Zhan Guo (2011) has demonstrated, the schematic transit maps of the kind used by the London Underground, which distort information about distances between stations to give a clearer perspective of possible linkages between lines, influence routes, and modes chosen. Results show that the elasticity of the map distance is twice that of the travel time, suggesting that passengers often trust the Tube map more than their own travel experience when deciding the best travel path. Intelligent transport systems, involving indicators of parking availability, act as 'boosts' to those whose apparently irrational behavior of cruising around to seek a parking place had, in fact, been the result of inadequate information.

Kahneman's 'prospect theory', when individuals assess their loss and gain perspectives in an asymmetric manner – for example, when losing \$1,000 could only be compensated by the pleasure of earning \$2,000 – has been applied to travel demand models and other markets (Li and Hensher, 2011). Figure 4.9 depicts a situation where a driver could take a 'short-cut' that could reduce a trip time by X minutes ($+X$) but, if there is congestion, may alternatively increase it by X minutes ($-X$). If the driver were risk-neutral then they would be indifferent

Exhibit   *When London Underground workers go on strike*

On February 5 and 6, 2014 a labor dispute caused a partial shutdown of London's underground. While some stations were closed, some stayed open. This allowed Shaun Larcom et al. (2017) to look the subsequent use of the 'Tube' by those travelers who were seriously affected by the strike and those who were not.

London's Underground has the eighth-largest number of stations in the world (270) and carries the 11th-largest number of passengers. In many cases it offers alternative routing options between an origin and a destination. The network is described by a schematic map showing only relative positions of Tube stations and of interacting surface rail stations. The distances between stations are thus distorted. A labor dispute led to a 48-hour partial closure of the systems strike from the evening of the February 5, 2014. Individual workers were left to decide their actions but enough went on strike to close 171 stations. The Circle, Bakerloo, and Waterloo & City lines were also closed. This was the first major disruption to the system in three years.

Larcom et al. gathered data from January 19 to February 15 for all modes of public transport excluding buses. Because Oyster cards – a rechargeable 'pay-as-you-go'-type plastic card – were used for about 80 percent of trips and also had individual numbers, these were used for route tracking of trips during the rush hour each day. Some idea of the scale of the data used can be seen since there were 19,301,730 data entries on January 24. Two panels of users were isolated: one (the unconditional) whereby no information of post-strike travel was used and the other (the balanced) where both pre- and post-travel details were included. This allowed comparisons between before and after behavior using difference-in-differences techniques.

It is found that the benefits enjoyed by travelers forced to experiment with alternative routing because of station closures, who remained with the new travel pattern (about 5 percent of the total), conservatively gained about 20 seconds per journey. Put another way, they would gain about four hours of commute time over 3.3 years. At an aggregate level, the time saved because of long-term modal adjustments was larger than the time lost due to the strike.

These findings suggest that many commuters had failed to find their optimal travel pattern before the strike and, by exploration, found a better, if not always optimal, pattern that continued to be used once the system again became fully operational. Explanations lie in the noisy information available, the stylized nature of the Tube maps, and the fact that different train lines travel at different speeds. The strike essentially provided a 'boost' to look at alternatives.

See also: S. Larcom, F. Rauch, and T. Willems (2017) The benefits of forced experimentation: striking evidence from the London underground network, *Quarterly Journal of Economics*, 132(4), 2019–55.

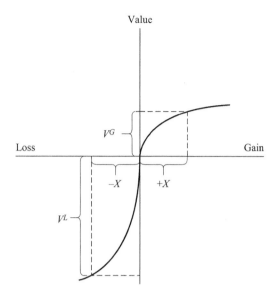

Figure 4.9   *The asymmetric nature of valuing a gain and loss*

between the options. But in most cases, because of the lower valuations drivers put on a minute gained as opposed to a minute lost, the value of the potential time savings from diverting (V^G) are less than the potential loss (V^L); the time-savings/value trade-off curve is stepped.

A common example of this, when it comes to trip-making, is that arriving early is not seen as being as important as arriving the same number of minutes late. A similar situation arises in terms of travel insurance, relative to the actual probabilities of a fatal accident: individuals over-insure themselves against an aviation accident and under-insure against an automobile accident.

The idea that individuals are only concerned about the effects of their actions on themselves is also coming under question in some contexts; the very notion of 'need' as an allocative mechanism is one indication of this. There is also plenty of evidence from drivers' behavior that many give way to other drivers when there is no self-benefit from doing so.

When it comes to speeding and traffic safety, Peer (2011) asked drivers to estimate how much time can be saved by increasing speed. The drivers generally under-estimate the time saved when increasing from a relatively low speed and over-estimate the time saved when increasing from a relatively high speed. This time-saving bias affects speed predictions in conventional demand models. Indeed, in predicting drivers' personal speed choices, the time-saving bias was second only to the frequency of committing ordinary violations and outperformed more conventional variables such as drivers' age, gender, education, the number of years a driving license has been held, monthly driving distances, and drivers' prior speeding violations and crashes.

Behavioral economic approaches are gradually finding that travel demand is particularly affected by novel, accessible, and simple measures. Simplicity is important because people respond more to things they understand. The increasing amount of information that providers now accumulate through big data suggests that fares and services can be more fine-tuned to customers' demands.

References

Acutt, M.Z. and Dodgson, J.S. (1995) Cross-elasticities of demand for travel, *Transport Policy*, 2, 271–7.

Alperovich, G. and Machnes, Y. (1994) The role of wealth in demand for international air travel, *Journal of Transport Economics and Policy*, 28, 163–73.

Banister, D., Bould, M., and Warren, G. (1984) Towards needs-based transport planning, *Traffic Engineering and Control*, 25, 372–5.

Basso, L.J. and Oum, T.H. (2007) Automobile fuel demand: a critical assessment of empirical methodologies, *Transport Reviews*, 27, 449–84.

Bates, J.J, Gunn, H.F., and Roberts, M. (1978) A disaggregate model of household car ownership, Department of the Environment and Transport Research Report 20, HMSO.

Beesley, M. (1965) The value of *time* spent in travelling: some new evidence, *Economica*, 32, 174–85.

Bendtsen, P.R. (1980) The influence of price of petrol and of cars on the amount of automobile traffic, *International Journal of Transport Economics*, 7, 207–13.

Blasé, J.R. (1980) Hysteresis in travel demand, *Transportation Planning and Technology*, 6, 109–16.

Brown, S. and Watkins, W. (1968) The demand for air travel: a regression study of time-series and cross-sectional data in the US domestic market, *Highway Research Record*, 213, 21–34.

Button, K.J., Fowkes, A.S., and Pearman, A.D. (1980) Disaggregate and aggregate car ownership forecasting methods in Great Britain, *Transportation Research Part A*, 14(4), 263–73.

Button, K.J., Pearman, A.D., and Fowkes, A.S. (1982) *Car Ownership Modelling and Forecasting*, Gower.

Button K.J., Ngoe, N., and Hine, J. (1993) Modelling vehicle ownership and use in low-income countries, *Journal of Transport Economics and Policy*, 27, 51–67.

Claffey, P.T. (1961) Characteristics of passenger car travel on toll roads and comparable free roads, *Highway Research Board Bulletin*, 306, Highway Research Board.

Dargay, J.D. (1993) Demand elasticities: a comment, *Journal of Transport Economics and Policy*, 27, 87–90.

Dargay, J.D. (2002) Road vehicles: future growth in developed and developing countries, *Proceedings of the Institution of Civil Engineers*, 151, 3–11.

Dargay, J.D. and Giuliano, G. (2006) Car ownership, travel and land use: a comparison of the US and Great Britain, *Transportation Research Part A*, 40, 106–24.

Dawson, R.F.F. and Everall, P.P. (1972) The value of motorists' time: a study in Italy, Transport and Road Research Laboratory Report, LR.

de Bok, M., de Jong, G., Wesseling, B., Meurs, H., van Bekkum, P., Mijjer, P., Bakker, D., and Veger, T. (2021) An ex-ante analysis of transport impacts of a distance-based heavy goods vehicle charge in the Netherlands, *Research in Transportation Economics*, 101091.

De Vany, A.S. (1974) The revealed value of time in air travel, *Review of Economics and Statistics*, 56, 77–82.

Fairhurst, H.M. (1975) The influence of public transport on car ownership in London, *Journal of Transport Economics and Policy*, 9, 193–208.

Fearnley, N., Currie, G., Flügel, S., Gregersen, F.A., Killi, M., Toner, J., and Wardmand, M. (2018) Competition and substitution between public transport modes, *Research in Transportation Economics*, 69, 51–58.

Filippini, M., Kumar, N., and Srinivasan, S. (2021) Nudging adoption of electric vehicles: evidence from an information-based intervention in Nepal, *Transportation Research Part D*, 97, 102951.

Fowkes, A., Marks, P., and Nash, C.A. (1986) The value of business travel time savings, Working Paper 214, Institute for Transport Studies, University of Leeds.

Garcia-Sierra, M., van den Bergh, J.C.J.M., and Miralles-Guasch, C. (2015) Behavioural economics, travel behaviour and environmental-transport policy, *Transportation Research Part D*, 41, 288–305.

Gilbert, C.L. and Jalilian, H. (1991) The demand for travel cards on London Regional Transport, *Journal of Transport Economics and Policy*, 25, 3–30.

Glaister, S. and Lewis, D. (1978) An integrated fares policy for transport in London, *Journal of Public Economics*, 9, 341–55.

Goodwin, P.B. (1977) Habit and hysteresis in mode choice, *Urban Studies*, 14, 95–8.

Goodwin, P.B. (1992) A review of new demand elasticities with special reference to short and long run effects of price changes, *Journal of Transport Economics and Policy*, 26, 155–70.

Graham, J.D. and Glaister, S. (2004) Road traffic demand elasticity estimates: a review, *Transport Reviews*, 24, 261–74.

Gronau, R. (1970) *The Value of Time in Passenger Transportation: The Demand for Air Travel*, Columbia University Press.

Gunn, H.J. (2008) An introduction to the valuation of travel time-savings and losses, in D.A. Hensher and K.J. Button (eds), *Handbook of Transport Modeling*, 2nd edn, Elsevier.

Guo, Z. (2011) Mind the map! The impact of transit maps on path choice in public transit, *Transportation Research Part A: Policy and Practice*, 45, 625–39.

Gwilliam, K.M. and Mackie, P.J. (1975) *Economics and Transport Policy*, Allen & Unwin.

Harrison, A.J. and Quarmby, D.A. (1969) The value of time in transport planning: a review, in *Report of the Sixth Round Table on Transport Economics*, European Conference of Ministers of Transport.

Heggie, I. (1976) A diagnostic survey of urban journey to work behaviour, in I. Heggie, (ed.), *Modal Choice and the Value of Travel Time*, Clarendon Press.

Hensher, D.H. (1979) Formulating an urban passenger transport policy: a re-appraisal of some elements, *Australian Economic Papers*, 18, 119–30.

Hillman, M. (1973) Personal mobility and transport policy, PEP Broadsheet 542.

Ippolito, R.A. (1981) Estimating airline demand with quality of service variables, *Journal of Transport Economics and Policy*, 15, 7–15.

Isaac, J.K. (1979) Price and quality in road passenger transport, *Journal of the Chartered Institute of Transport*, 38, 359–61.

Jung, J.M. and Fujii, E.T. (1976) The price elasticity of demand for air travel: some new evidence, *Journal of Transport Economics and Policy*, 10, 257–62.

Kraft, G. and Domenich, T.A. (1970) *Free Transit*, Heath.

Lago A.M., Mayworm, P.D., and McEnroe, J.M. (1981) Transit service elasticities: evidence from demonstration and demand models, *Journal of Transport Economics and Policy*, 15, 99–119.

Lave, C.A. (1970) The demand for urban mass transportation, *Review of Economics and Statistics*, 52, 320–23.

Lee, N. and Dalvi, M.Q. (1969) Variations in the value of travel time, *The Manchester School of Economic and Social Studies*, 37, 213–36.

Levin, L., Lewis. M.S., and Wolak, F.A. (2017) High Frequency evidence on the demand for gasoline, *American Economic Journal: Economic Policy*, 9, 314–47.

Li, Z. and Hensher, D.H. (2011) Prospect theoretical contributions in understanding traveler behavior: a review and some comments, *Transport Review*, 31, 97–115.

Litman, T. (2021) Transport demands and elasticities: how prices and other factors affect travel behavior, Report, Victoria Transport Policy Institute.

McGinnis, M.A. (1990) The relative importance of cost and service in freight transportation choice: before and after deregulation, *Transportation Journal*, 30, 12–19.

Metcalfe, R. and Dolan, P. (2012) Behavioural economics and its implications for transport, *Journal of Transport Geography*, 24, 503–11.

Mogridge, M.J.H. (1978) The effect of the oil crisis on the growth in the ownership and use of cars, *Transportation*, 7, 45–65.

Mutti, J. and Mural, Y. (1977) Airline travel on the North Atlantic, *Journal of Transport Economics and Policy*, 11, 45–53.

Oum, T., Gillen, D.W., and Noble, S.E. (1986) Demand for fare class and pricing in airline markets, *Logistics and Transportation Review*, 22, 195–222.

Oum, T.H., Waters, W.G., and Yong, J.-S. (1992) Concepts of price elasticities of transport demand and recent empirical evidence, *Journal of Transport Economics and Policy*, 26, 139–54.

Oum, T.H., Waters, W.G., and Fu, X. (2008) Transport demand elasticities, in D.A. Hensher and K.J. Button (eds), *Handbook of Transport Modelling*, 2nd ed, Elsevier.

Peer, E. (2011) The time-saving bias, speed choices and driving behavior, *Transportation Research Part F*, 14, 543–54.

Quandt, R.E. and Baumol, W.J. (1966) The demand for abstract transport modes, theory and measurement, *Journal of Regional Science*, 6, 13–26.

Quarmby, D.A. (1967) Choice of travel mode for the journey to work: some findings, *Journal of Transport Economics and Policy*, 1, 273–314.

Redmond, S. and Mokhtarian, P.L. (2001) The positive utility of the commute: modeling ideal commute time and relative desired commute amount, *Transportation*, 28, 179–205.

Reza, A.M. and Spiro, H.M. (1979) The demand for passenger car transport services and for gasoline, *Journal of Transport Economics and Policy*, 13, 304–19.

Schafer, A. (2000) Regularities in travel demand: an international perspective, *Journal of Transportation and Statistics*, 3, 1–31.

Sherman, R. (1967) A private ownership bias in transmit choice, *American Economic Review*, 77, 1211–17.

Smith, M.G. and McIntosh, P.T. (1974) Fares elasticity; interpretation and estimation, in *Symposium on Public Transport Fare Structure*, Transport and Road Research Laboratory Report, SR37UC.

Straszheim, M. (1978) Airline demand functions on the North Atlantic and their pricing implications, *Journal of Transport Economics and Policy*, 12, 179–95.

Tanner, J.C. (1978) Long-term forecasting of vehicle ownership and road traffic, *Journal of the Royal Statistical Society*, 141A, 14–63.

Taplin, J.H.E. (1980) A coherence approach to estimates of price elasticities in the vacation travel market, *Journal of Transport Economics and Policy*, 14, 19–35.

Thaler, R.H. and Sunstein, C.R. (2008) *Nudge: Improving Decisions on Health, Wealth, and Happiness*, Yale University Press.

Thomas, S. (1979) Non-working time-savings in developing countries, *Journal of Transport Economics and Policy*, 13, 335–7.

UK Department for Transport (2007) Transport statistics Great Britain 2007, DfT.

UK Department of Transport (1977) Transport policy, Cmnd 6836, HMSO.

UK Department of Transport (1978) Report of the advisory committee on trunk road assessment, HMSO.

Wardman, M. (2001) A review of British evidence on time and service quality valuations, *Transportation Research Part A*, 34, 171–205.

Wardman, M. (2014) Price elasticities of surface travel demand: a meta-analysis of UK evidence, *Journal of Transport Economics and Policy*, 48, 367–84.

Waters, W.G. (1992) Values of travel time savings used in road project evaluation: a cross-country/jurisdiction comparison, Australian Transport Research Forum.

Wei, F., Chen, J., and Zhang, L. (2017) Demand shocks, airline pricing, and high-speed rail substitution: evidence from the Chinese market, *Journal of Transport Economics and Policy*, 51, 266–89.

White, P.R. (1981) 'Travelcard' tickets in urban public transport, *Journal of Transport Economics and Policy*, 15, 17–34.

Zahavi, Y. (1977) Equilibrium between travel, demand, system supply and urban structure, in E.L. Visser (ed.), *Transport Decisions in an Age of Uncertainty*, Martinus Nijhoft.

5 Direct Costs of Transport

. . . .

5.1 Factors Influencing the Supply of Transport

The supply of any good or service is generally a positive function of its price. Suppliers, and stakeholders, are more willing to put the effort and resources into providing more output as prices rise. The detailed nature of the relationship is heavily influenced by the costs involved, although factors such as the motivation of suppliers are relevant. Private companies, for example, generally have different objectives from state-owned suppliers. This chapter, and the one that follows, look at the various costs associated with supplying transport services and at the relationships between the resources required to provide these services and the types and amounts of output finally 'consumed' by travelers and freight consignors. This chapter is specifically concerned with the production functions perceived by the direct providers of transport services, which relate the various factor inputs to the final services offered, and with the financial costs of these factor inputs.

There are two broad overlapping groups that have an interest in the supply of transport services. First, there are the stock-holders who shoulder the direct burden of financing the transport system and the services that are being supplied. These may be thought of as entrepreneurs in the case of small-scale businesses often found in sectors such as trucking and repair garage services or share-holders in the case of larger undertakings such as airline or shipping companies. But they may also be large corporations or government agencies in the case of large-scale operations. In the case of the public sector, the tax-payers are the stock-holders.

The second group, the stake-holders, include not only the stock-holders but also those who do not pay the direct costs of providing transport but nevertheless incur costs from its provision. These latter parties may include users in terms of fares and rates paid, but there are also those who have external costs imposed on them. This latter group may include those whose health is damaged by air pollution associated with transport and those suffering third-party injuries caused by accidents. The exact natures and orders of magnitude of these two broad groups vary considerably on a case-by-case basis.

The chapter differs from the following one in that it deals with direct costs as borne by the supplying agency: the stake-holders. These are normally, but not always, financial costs that are incurred as the result of purchasing factor services in the market (that is, the wages of labor, the interest on capital, the price of fuel, etc.). There is one very important complication. The actual cost of the travelers' or consignors' own inputs is the direct cost of making a trip. Transport is special (but not unique) in that the person being transported contributes their own time inputs and, when private motor transport is involved, their personal energies, skills, and expertise. Equally, with freight transport, the consignor of cargo bears the direct costs of having inventory tied up in transit.

The opportunity costs of this time and the utilization of acquired skills will, therefore, directly enter the production function for trip-making. We consider the external costs in the following chapter, although representing genuine resource costs does not directly influence the decisions of transport suppliers in their provision of transport services. In brief, therefore, this chapter is exclusively concerned with the perceived or reaction costs that influence the supply of transport services. It should be pointed out, however, that the separation of direct and external costs is something of an expositional device and that in practice this distinction is becoming increasingly blurred as official policies attempt to make transport agencies fully cognizant of the full resource implications of their actions.

All these factors influence the shape of the transport supply function which, in its simplest form, is seen in Figure 5.1. There is nothing special in the general sense about the supply curve of transport services. It is normally positively sloped, reflecting the incentive that higher prices have on suppliers to put more of their services on the market. The importance of the need for consumers, at least in terms of passenger movements, to put their own time into the delivery of transport services, however, often means that one should treat price in a broader sense to embrace time costs. This gives us a notion of 'generalized costs' that we discuss in some detail later.

The supply curve's position in price/quantity space is also influenced by where it is positioned *vis-à-vis* factors such as levels of income, the price of alternatives to transport (which may be teleworking or teleshopping in the short term, but can embrace relocating home or work in the longer term), and to the costs of the inputs required to provide the transport services (including the costs of the time of the travelers or of inventory holdings in the case of freight transport).

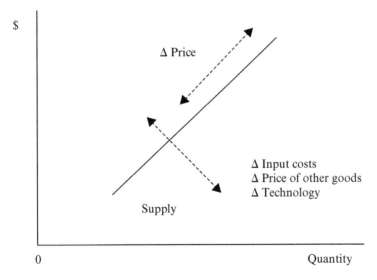

Figure 5.1   *The simple transport supply curve*

The financial costs of transport to immediate users have, as a broad generalization, been falling over time. The money costs of traveling from, say, Washington DC to San Francisco, for example, has fallen considerably over the past century relative to incomes in the United States with the improvements in air and road transportation, and it is certainly a lot quicker. This has been due to technical progress, but also more recently to changes in the regulatory regimes that have controlled the supply of transport – a subject we shall return to in detail in Chapter 14.

Not all transport users have enjoyed lower fares, especially in the short run. As technology and demand patterns have changed, so some modes or journeys have become more expensive, often because a superior service has replaced them. In other cases, the subsidies given to the various modes have changed, again affecting the costs to the final user. Table 5.1 provides, in very broad terms, details of how changes in passenger fares, measured in current prices, have varied since 1970 in the United States. What it does not allow for is the general rise in price levels over this period, which has been about 530 percent. Nor does it allow for the improved quality of transport services, the speed, or the length of journeys. There are wide variations by route or region and in part this chapter offers some reasons for these micro- and meso-differences. Other modes exhibit different patterns.

5.2 Fixed and Variable Costs

Direct costs can be divided in several ways but two are particularly relevant to transport, namely distinctions according to variability over time and distinctions among the parties responsible for incurring the various elements of cost. The first of these distinctions is discussed in this section.

In the long run, or so the introductory texts tell us, all costs are variable, but the long run is itself an imprecise concept (even a tautology) and the ability to vary costs over time differs among modes of transport. The long run in the context of a seaport is, for instance, very different from that in road haulage or in the bus industry. Port infrastructure is extremely long-lived, specific, indivisible, and expensive. It is impossible to consider the standard question associated with

Table 5.1 *Average public passenger transport fares in the United States (current prices)*

	1970	1980	1990	2000	2010	2018
Air carrier, domestic, scheduled	40.65	84.60	107.96	339.00	336.09	349.63
Class I bus, inter-city	3.81	10.57	20.22	29.46	n.a	n.a
Transit, all modes	0.22	0.30	0.67	0.93	1.21	1.60
Commuter rail	0.84	1.41	2.90	3.33	4.81	6.43
Inter-city rail/Amtrak	3.19	17.72	39.59	52.15	60.70	69.59

Note: n.a = not available.

Source: US Bureau of Transport Statistics.

long-run costs – namely, 'what is the cheapest way of providing a given capacity in the long run'? – when talking of time horizons 20, 30, or even 50 years hence. Trucking is different, capital costs are lower, physical durability less, and there is always the prospect of varying the use, within limits, of the vehicle fleet. Trucks are, unlike ports, mobile both among a range of potential employers and among a range of locations.

The nature of many costs, therefore, means that they may be considered fixed in the short term: there are temporal indivisibilities. The period under consideration will, as we have already seen, differ among transport sectors, but it will also differ within a single transport undertaking. Railway operators owning track and rolling stock offer a useful illustration of this.

A railway service involves using several factor services, many of these being highly specific and each with its own physical life-span. When it comes to considering line closures the essential questions revolve around deciding exactly which costs are fixed. Figure 5.2 offers a general illustration of the main cost items associated with a rail service together with an appropriate, although not exact, indication of the physical life of existing equipment. In the very-short term – the 'market period' since all other items have already been purchased (that is, they are fixed) – the only reaction a railway can make when confronted with a sudden change in demand is by adjusting extremely variable costs. These are costs notably associated with such factors as labor, fuel, and maintenance. However, if the railways are earning income to cover these costs then there is no justification for closing the line. Wagons last about ten years, and applying the same logic, these should be replaced after that time if returns exceed the costs of doing so.

After a period of about 18 years, however, locomotives become due for replacement. Consequently, locomotive costs become variable over a 15-year

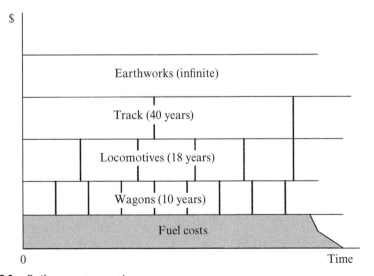

Figure 5.2   *Railway costs over time*

horizon and the managers must decide whether revenues justify replacement. Is 15 years, therefore, the long run? The answer is probably 'no' because other factors are still longer-lived, such as rolling stock for 25 years and track and signaling for 45 years. (Earthworks have an infinite life and once constructed do not enter further decision-making processes.) Further decisions regarding closure must, therefore, be made after 25 and 45 years even if the line earns enough revenue to cover its motive replacement needs. Consequently, the long run for railways, in this context, is anything up to 40 years with, in the interim, a series of successive short-run cost calculations having to be made.

The reverse calculations are made regarding the expansion of services. If the wagons are covering their costs to an extent that they would also cover the costs of additional locomotives then capacity expansion is commercially justified.

It should be quite apparent that the distinction between fixed and variable costs is a pragmatic device requiring a degree of judgment and common sense on the part of the decision-maker. In the short term – whatever that may be – some costs are clearly fixed, resulting in a falling short-run average cost of use until capacity is reached. Just to show the generality of the principles, we can switch to a different mode. Figure 5.3, for instance, may be seen as illustrating the average cost of the increased use of a ship ($SRAC_1$), which falls steeply until capacity is fully utilized. A second ship may then, if demand is strong enough, be brought into operation, exhibiting a short-run average cost curve of $SRAC_2$.

The fixed capacity constraint for each ship typifies that found in most modes of transport and tends to differ from the smooth, stereotypical, symmetrical 'U-shaped' $SRAC$ curves often assumed to be associated with manufacturing industry described in economics texts. While the upturn in the curve may not be quite as dramatic as shown, and not entirely vertical if, for example in our shipping case, a vessel steams more slowly or takes a shorter route, then there may be

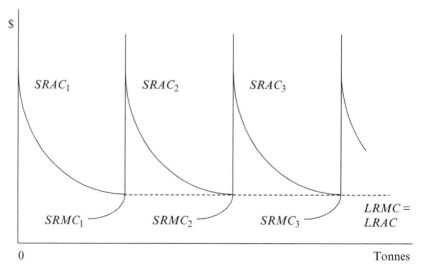

Figure 5.3   *The long- and short-run costs of shipping*

some curvature to the upward part of the curve. The long-run curve is, following elementary economics, formed from the envelope of the short-run average cost curves.

In many sectors of the economy the long-run average cost curve is not horizontal, as in our illustration, at least not to any high level of minimum cost, but is often found to be downward-sloping as a result of economies of scale. These economies may potentially take a variety of forms in transport and may be thought to vary according to the type of transport involved and the mode of operation being undertaken.

The standard method of examining for scale effects is to look at the cost elasticity of output. Evidence presented in a survey of studies of the rail, road haulage, and aviation sectors in the United States (Winston, 1985) suggests that scale effects exist in some modes with respect to output but not in others. All studies examined, irrespective of the modeling framework used, indicate scale effects in rail freight transport, but the empirical evidence is contradictory for road haulage – although the more recent of the studies, employing state-of-the-art econometric techniques, suggest constant costs. Studies of United States domestic aviation indicate there are no, or few, scale effects in the conventional sense, irrespective of how the cost function is specified (Johnston and Ozment, 2013). More specific studies tend to consider features of transport industries, fleet size, infrastructure, etc., and these are looked at in turn.

Economies Associated with Larger Vehicle Size

One approach is to look at costs with respect to size of vehicle or vessel. The classic example of this is in shipping, where capacity (in terms of volume) increases much faster than surface area, but this is also a feature of most other modes of freight transport. Thermal processes (such as engine size) also generally exhibit scale economies in all forms of transport, and crew numbers do not increase proportionately with the size of mobile plant. Figure 5.4 gives some rough indication of economies of scale in bulk carriers. The figure takes four size classes – Handy (up to 40,000 dwt), Handymax (between 50,000 and 60,000 dwt), Panamax (over 65,000 dwt), and Capesize (over 150,000 dwt) – and looks at the cost savings per tonne as size increases. The differentials are given for rough guidance. The exact economics of individual ships of any class varies according to such factors as age, design, speed, and so on. Similar general patterns emerge not only for other types of shipping – for example, Figure 5.5 gives data on container vessels – but size economies also exist, at least up to a point, for most modes of transport.

Diseconomies of vehicle size can be associated with such as the state of technology (there were limits to the size of ships until metal vessels emerged) and the quality of complementary services, such as transport infrastructure. Evidence produced in the early 1970s by Edwards and Bayliss (1971), however, suggests that there may be limits to the cost advantages of using extremely large road haulage vehicles, at least in the United Kingdom. Diseconomies of scale appear to begin

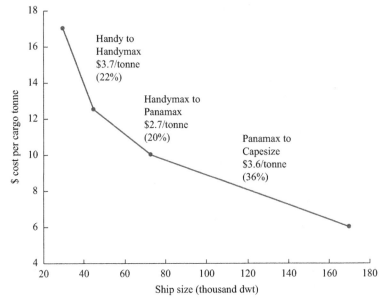

Source: Stopford (2009).

Figure 5.4 *Economies of scale related to ship size for bulk carriers*

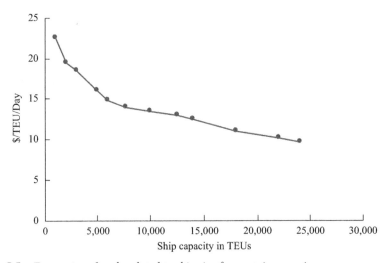

Figure 5.5 *Economies of scale related to ship size for container carriers*

setting in after about 11 tonnes carrying capacity has been reached. Evidence from Britain's Armitage Inquiry into heavy trucks, however, indicates that there are still economies of scale to be enjoyed by using commercial road vehicles in excess of the 32.5 tonnes gross maximum weight permitted in 1980 (see Table 5.2).

Scale may also be approached in a different way, namely in terms of the number of power units used to move a load. Ships, and many types of truck, have a physically fixed engine to capacity ratio, whereas railroads have separate

Table 5.2 *Estimated savings from increasing the maximum weight of trucks in the United Kingdom from 32.3 tonnes*

Maximum weight	Savings (%)
35 tonnes, 4 axles	5–7
38 tonnes, 5 axles	5–9
40 tonnes, 5 axles	7–14
42 tonnes, 5 axles	9–13
44 tonnes, 6 axles	11–13

Source: UK Department of Transport (1980).

locomotives pulling independent wagons. There are exceptions to this, including the Australian road trains whereby a single powerful ('prime mover') truck pulls a number of trailers, but they are limited (Zhang et al., 2020). Many of the economies of platooning (or 'flocking') come from a reduction in the overall weight of the locomotive unit needed to pull a large load and from the use of a single driver. Platooning of wagons (or even automobiles) also reduces the infrastructure required because of the strict physical regulation of wagons. This allows them to travel closer together than would occur with individual cab/ wagon units. Uniform speeds have fuel saving potential. A possibility of automated, driverless trucks offers the prospect of greater economies of consolidation as more wagons can be strung together and controlled remotely (Zhang et al., 2020).

While for engineering reasons for various economies of scale clearly do exist in utilizing larger units of mobile plant at least up to some point, it should be noted that it is often impossible to take advantage of them even when demand for transport services is high. In many instances there may be physical limitations associated with complementary inputs, such as loading bays, and the associated infrastructure cannot always handle the larger vehicles (ports and airports pose specific problems in this context), while in others the consignments of traffic are small and can be more efficiently handled in smaller vehicles. Returning to our maritime example, large ships on liner routes often incur heavy costs as frequent landings and embarkation of individual consignments require rearrangements of the entire cargo. This is one reason why improved hub-and-spoke operations are gaining in importance – see Section 5.3.

Economies of Scale in Infrastructure Provision

Transport demand is not spread evenly over space, but tends to be concentrated on links between specific trip-generating and trip-attracting points, for example journey-to-work trips are concentrated along links between residential and industrial estates; holiday air transport demand is highest between the main cities in the United Kingdom and popular recreational resorts in Spain, Greece, etc. Thus, there is a tendency in transport, as we saw in Chapter 4, for demand to be concentrated on certain portions of the network and, *ipso facto*, certain parts of the

Table 5.3 *Economies of large port operations*

	Vancouver	*Seattle*
Traffic	88,000	377,000
Number of berths	3	11
Wharfage	$23.63	$33.75
Handling & through-port charge	$81.27	$40.00
Vessel service & facility charge	0	$26.60
Tailgate loading	$22.28	0
Port charges per container	$127.18	$95.35

Source: Heaver (1975).

static infrastructure. Technically this concentration of traffic is possible because of substantial scale economies in infrastructure provision.

An examination of the costs associated with handling container traffic in an average port (Vancouver) and a large port (Seattle) in Table 5.3 (which assumes the charges paid by container traffic reflect port costs) reveals the economies enjoyed from scale. It seems in port operations that a fourfold increase in size reduces costs by approximately one-quarter. Similarly, with internal transport, John Tanner (1968) found some years ago that the cost of four-lane motorways was on average 78 percent of those with six lanes. However, it should be said that evidence of scale economies in road provision is not altogether conclusive. The findings of Keeler and Small (1977), looking at 57 freeway segments in the San Francisco area, favor constant returns, while Alan Walters (1968), again employing United States sources, finds evidence 'that there are increasing costs of (road) construction in urban areas'.

The difficulty here, as with other forms of infrastructure costing, is to isolate comparable construction costs from those costs associated with specific locations and geographies. In terms of railways, the move from a single- to a double-track system involves roughly a quadrupling of capacity by eliminating conflict between directions. Quadruple tracking should more than double capacity by permitting segregation by speed. Indications of such gains can be seen in the British estimates in Table 5.4 of the costs of these options (at 1967 prices) for similar geographies. As is often done, to spread costs of large investments over time, interest is taken as the cost of capital. We see that the average rail costs rise much less rapidly than increases in potential capacities. But there are wide variations in these costs dependent upon whether existing track is upgraded or entirely new track is laid, the nature of the traffic, the gradients and curves involved, the need for bridges and tunnels, etc.

Economies from Large Fleet Size

Larger fleets of vehicles may offer economies in maintenance, standardization (or, in some cases, the availability of a mixed vehicle fleet to meet variable demand), crew scheduling, etc., although administrative problems and remoteness of

Exhibit   *The container and world trade*

A major driver of the sevenfold increase in world trade from the early 1960s to the 1990s was the introduction of containerization. This was developed in the mid-1950s in the United States by Malcom McLean. Containers are robust, with steel-reinforced corners allowing stacking without causing damage. They are uniform in size, theft-proof, easy to load, and can be moved by ship, barge, truck, train, or plane (although air containers are smaller).

Prior to this, loading and unloading general cargo involved the handling of individual items of different dimensions and weights. There was some unitization using pallets, sacks, and so on, but this did little to reduce costs and ships spent two-thirds of their productive time in ports. The costs of bulk breaking meant that most maritime movements involved simple connectivity and limited hub-and-spoke movements. Containerization also saw pilfering pre-container reduced considerably, which brought down insurance costs.

Containerization is capital-intensive, requiring specialized infrastructure not only at ports and at inland origins and destinations, but also in trucks and railroad wagons, as well as investment in the boxes themselves. But productivity gains were huge – the first purpose-built crane in 1959 could load a 40,000 lbs. box every three minutes – more than 40 times the productivity of a longshore gang. These and other effects are seen in the table which assesses the effects of containerization in the United Kingdom and Continental Europe over the first five years of containerization.

	Pre-container: 1965	Container: 1970–71
Productivity of dock labor	1.7 tons per hour	30 tons per hour
Average ship size	8.4 gross registered tonnage	19.7 gross registered tonnage
Port concentration (number of European ports, southbound Australia)	11 ports	3 ports
Insurance costs (Australia–Europe trade for imports)	£0.24 per ton	£0.04 per ton
Capital locked up as inventory in transit (Hamburg–Sydney)	£2.00 per ton	£1.00 per ton

Bernhofen et al. (2016) looked at a large panel of product-level trade flows between 1962 and 1990 to examine the role of containerization on twentieth-century globalization. They assumed 1966 to 1983 as the period in which significant containerization occurred, with the four-year period before being 'pre-container' and the seven years after being 'post-adoption'. It was assumed other technologies were pretty stable over the 18 years.

Focusing on 22 industrial countries in which the uptake of containerization was seen as quicker and deeper, they compared the causal effects of containerization on international trade using non-containerized bi-lateral pairs as a counterfactual. Adjustments were made to allow for some countries trading more in products not amenable to containerization. Developments in institution trade arrangements were captured by variables reflecting membership of a free trade bloc and by both partners in trade being General Agreement on Tariffs and Trade (GATT) members.

Greater effects were found in trade between developed economies than either between developed and developing economies or between two developing economies. More traded goods were suitable for containerization. Regarding inter-developed economies' trade, the cumulative average effects of containerization over a 20-year time period were also much larger than the effects of free trade agreements or the GATT.

See also: D.M. Bernhofen, Z. El-Sahli, and R. Kneller (2016) Estimating the effects of the container revolution on world trade, *Journal of International Economics*, 98, 36–50.

Table 5.4 *Average cost per mile of rail track in the United Kingdom (1967, current prices)*

	Number of tracks		
	1	*2*	*3*
Interest	£3,020	£4,260	£7,900
Revenue of track & structure	£1,400–2,840	£1,986–3,442	£3,422–4,474
Signaling	£2,600	£4,030	£8,070
Total	*£7,020–8,460*	*£10,190–11,730*	*£19,380–20,430*

Source: Foster and Joy (1967).

decision-maker from customer may temper these advantages. Evidence on the presence of fleet economies of scale, however, is far from conclusive for all modes of transport and indeed there seems to be a gradual emergence of constant returns for many with limited scale economies in specialized forms of transport.

Historically, the analysis regarding bus operations has been rather confusing. The oft-cited United Kingdom statistical analysis by Lee and Steedman (1970), looking at the accounts of 44 United Kingdom municipal bus undertakings for 1966–67, suggests the notion of constant returns to scale, a situation agreeing with Williams' (1981) study of 11 American publicly owned operations. Wabe and Coles' (1975) examination of 66 United Kingdom operators, however, 'provides evidence that diseconomies of scale exist in the provision of bus services'. Koshal's (1970) work in India offers international support for the notion of constant returns in bus operations. The problem with most of these studies, however, is that they use econometric models which assume that the existence of scale effects does not extend over all levels of output.

The 1980s witnessed the development of more 'flexible' model forms in econometrics (a topic we address in more detail later in this chapter) which allow for variation in scale effects as output changes – for example, they allow for testing for a U-shaped cost curve. Button and O'Donnell (1985), applying such techniques to United States urban bus data, found that economies of scale do seem to exist up to a point, although diseconomies set in for the larger undertakings. This broadly conforms with studies both of Israeli bus fleets (Berechman, 1983) and for the United States inter-city bus industry.

Alan Walters' work on the trucking sector produced evidence of constant returns in the United Kingdom, although the large number of owner-drivers working in this sector makes exact costing difficult. Regarding United Kingdom aviation, the Edwards Committee found evidence of scale economies when there was fleet standardization but generally concluded that the optimal size of a fleet depends upon the task in hand. Looking at shipping, Tolifari et al. (1986) found evidence of scale effects in bulk fleets – see Figure 5.6. The difficulty with empirical work in this field, as well as in aviation, is the diversity of the market conditions that are encountered and the support that is often forthcoming from government to finance 'the nation's flag carrier'. As can be seen in the figure, the costs of a fleet with traditional registry (in one of the major industrial states) tend to be higher than when open registry (the adoption of a 'flag of convenience') is favored, because of the standards demanded by the former. As we see below, these scale effects also become rather clouded with the introduction of economies of density.

One indication of constant returns to fleet size is sometimes thought to be diversity in the scale of operators in a sector of transport: large companies competing directly against one or two vehicle firms suggesting that there is little advantage in large fleets. Road haulage is possibly the most extreme example of this phenomenon, as we see regarding the United Kingdom in Table 5.5, but throughout transport – except for areas directly regulated by government – one finds large and small firms competing.

Differential managerial skills may permit some firms to grow larger than others, but this does not imply technical economies of scale exist. They may also be supplying slightly different services, perhaps in qualitative terms, which are not

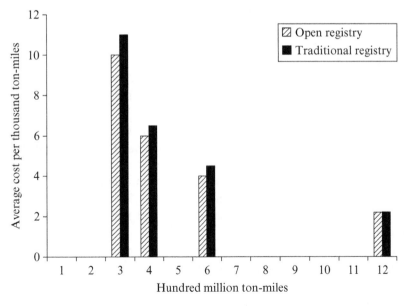

Source: Tolifari et al. (1986).

Figure 5.6   *Economies of scale in bulk shipping*

Table 5.5 *United Kingdom O-license holders and number of vehicles grouped by size of fleet (2015)*

Fleet size	Number of licenses	Number of vehicles
0	8,023	0
1	31,576	31,576
2 to 5	24,112	69,305
6 to 10	5,616	42,512
11 to 20	3,141	45,538
21 to 50	1,909	59,642
51 plus	858	99,487
Total	*75,235*	*348,060*

easy to quantify, and thus strict cost comparisons become difficult. Evidence of this type, therefore, may be capturing differential demands rather than any strict scale effect.

The variable costs of transport – those related to the rate of output – are generally considered to be dominated by labor and fuel items. They are usually seen as variable in the long term because the inputs involved are largely tied to the outputs delivered, and thus suppliers of transport can cut their costs if demand for their services declines. But often the costs of these inputs can also change dramatically in the short term, independently of actions by transport suppliers. Oil crises are one example of such instability but civil unrest and natural events like floods also pose challenges. In this case the transport supplier is suddenly confronted with a cost increase necessitating a rise in fares or freight rates being charged.

The importance of variable relative to fixed costs can vary considerably, even in the short term as seen by the increased importance of fuel costs for modes such as aviation in 2007 to early 2008, when oil prices rapidly rose to record levels. Since infrastructure costs are relatively fixed, it is, therefore, the cost of the mobile plant that is normally treated as marginal. Table 5.6 offers data on international airlines in a more stable period before the atypical fuel price fluctuations that began in the 1970s.

It should be noted that even in the long term the costs of mobile plant are, in aggregate, likely to exceed those of infrastructure, although individually vehicle costs in many cases are relatively small. The costs of aircraft operations come within a sector with very high costs per unit of mobile plant, while road haulage is a sector in which the total operational costs per vehicle are low. The importance of both direct and indirect labor costs and fuel costs, however, is apparent at both ends of the spectrum.

Remaining with airlines, while Table 5.6 offers average figures, the costs incurred vary considerably according to such things as type of aircraft, and their configurations, lengths of routes, traffic flow, flights per day, and so on.

Table 5.7 represents a broad average across many different types of airline operations. But variable costs differ not simply with the level of vehicle usage but also with the type of transport operation undertaken. Vehicles, for example,

Table 5.6   *Components of operating costs of scheduled international airlines (percent)*

	1980	1990	1999
Direct operating costs			
Flight operations	44	32	35
Flight crew	8	7	8
Fuel & oil	28	15	8
Airport & en route charges	5	4	7
Aircraft rental, insurance, etc.	3	6	9
Maintenance	11	11	11
Depreciation: aircraft & ground facilities	6	7	7
Total direct operating costs	*60*	*50*	*53*
Indirect operating costs			
Station/ground services	11	12	11
Passenger services	9	10	11
Ticketing, sales, & promotions	14	16	14
Administration & other costs	6	11	12
Total indirect operating costs	*40*	*50*	*47*

Source: International Civil Aviation Organization, *Digest of Statistics*, ICAO, from years indicated.

Table 5.7   *United States airlines' Boeing 757–200 flight operating costs (FOCs) in 2009*

Airline	Number of aircraft	Seats	FOCs per block hour	FOCs per seat hour	Utilization (hours/day)	Stage length (miles)
American	101	188	$2,568	$13.66	10.3	1,460
Continental	34	179	$2,568	$14.35	12.1	1,860
Delta	101	188	$2,357	$12.95	1.6	984
America West	12	190	$2,065	$10.87	13.1	1,167
Northwest	48	191	$2,260	$11.83	11.7	1,137
Trans World Air	20	179	$2,656	$14.84	11.8	1,405
United	98	186	$2,684	$14.43	11.2	1,281
USAir	34	182	$3,069	$16.87	11.1	1,254

Source: https://www.icao.int/mid/documents/2017/aviation%20data%20and%20analysis%20
seminar/ppt3%20-%20airlines%20operating%20costs%20and%20productivity.pdf.

have an optimal speed above or below which fuel costs tend to rise steeply; consequently, operations involving continually stopping and starting will, *ceteris paribus*, increase variable costs. Maintenance costs can also vary considerably with the type of terrain over which journeys are made. To some extent these variations may be off-set by employing specialized vehicles whose variable cost profiles conform most closely to the type of operation undertaken. In the airline context there exists a whole range of different aircraft designed to meet the needs of different operational patterns – airbuses for short-haul and large-volume traffic, wide-bodied jumbos for long-range operations, and so on.

Equally, Table 5.8, from one of the most detailed studies on the subject, gives some indication of the running and standing costs of different forms of operation

Table 5.8 *United Kingdom trucking, running and standing costs per mile (1977, current prices)*

	Fleet size	Bulk tankers	Tipping	Smalls & parcels	Long distance	Other general	Other sectors	All sectors
Running	100+	0.20	–	0.12	0.15	0.21	0.14	0.18
Standing	100+	0.27	–	0.30	0.18	0.31	0.42	0.28
Running	21–100	0.17	0.13	0.12	0.15	0.16	0.16	0.15
Standing	21–100	0.22	0.19	0.28	0.16	0.22	0.26	0.21
Running	1–20	0.19	0.15	0.12	0.13	0.12	0.16	0.14
Standing	1–20	0.31	0.12	0.19	0.19	0.14	0.25	0.18

Source: UK Price Commission (1978).

in the United Kingdom's trucking sector in the late 1970s. While these figures are not strictly variable and fixed costs, and they are very much case-specific in that trucking hauls are relatively short in Britain compared with, say, the United States, they do convey a general impression of how costs vary, even within sectors, with the type of transport operation performed.

The cost profiles also vary with the type of firm controlling the operations. Evidence from statistical studies of United States urban public transit systems, for instance, suggests that public ownership can lead to higher costs of provision. Karlaftis and McCarthy (1999), for example, found that Indianapolis experienced an annual 2.5 percent reduction in operating costs after privatizing the management of its public transit system. Ian Wallis (1980), in his study of urban bus operations in major Australian cities, gave a list of reasons why private operators enjoy lower costs in certain areas than their publicly owned counterparts:

*   greater flexibility and efficiency in use of labor;
*   relatively small proportions of maintenance and administrative costs;
*   lower basic rates of pay; and
*   lower wage/salary on-costs (taxes, pensions, etc.).

While in part cost variations may be explained in terms of either the size of the operator or the type of operation undertaken, cost differences may also reflect alternative operational objectives. There is ample evidence that large national airlines often employ high-cost modern equipment to enhance their image. But even at the level of local public transport, similar indications of X-inefficiency exist. Teal et al. (1980), for example, cite instances of local authorities preferring to operate their own para-transport system rather than make use of established private operators, despite demonstrably higher costs.

Labor costs, although flexible, are usually much less variable than fuel costs. This is not simply because of imperfections in the labor market (for example, fixed working hours, union agreements on redundancies, training costs, etc.), which often make it difficult to increase or reduce the size of the labor force – even in the sense of dividing up public transport crews to conform with daily peaks in travel demand – but also because of the nature of many types of transport operation. Once a form of transport operation has been decided upon, and capital invested, there are high labor costs associated with maintaining and servicing this equipment irrespective of the traffic carried. Further, once an undertaking is committed to a scheduled service, labor becomes a fixed cost in providing this service.

One of the major problems in this latter context is the technologically unprogressive nature of many forms of transport operations, which makes it difficult to substitute one factor input for another as their relative prices change. In the case of the mercantile marine, it has proved possible to substitute fixed for variable factors (notably capital for labor) as labor costs have risen, but this is much less easy in areas such as public transport provision. It is difficult to see how the basic operations of traditional taxi-cabs, for example, could be retained with a substantial reduction in labor input. Attempts to reduce labor costs in the urban public transport sphere in the United Kingdom, by introducing one-person-operated vehicles, did seem to have some limited effect on costs (for example, Brown and Nash 1972 estimated a 13.7 percent cost saving), but this should be a once-and-for-all step rather than the prospect of continual factor substitution.

5.3   Economies of Scale, Scope, Density, Experience, and Commonality

In recent years it has become increasingly appreciated that while economies of scale in their strictest form may be of considerable importance in many transport activities, there are instances where it is not simply the sheer size of the undertaking or activity that is the prime determinant of cost variation. Several other factors are of importance in the transport context.

Many transport undertakings provide a variety of outputs. Taking aviation as an example, at the most basic level these may be scheduled and charter services, but, in more detail, there is the matter of outward and return services, and, at a more detailed level still, each flight may be viewed as a specific product. The economic question then becomes one of deciding whether there are cost savings in one supplier producing this range of services rather than there being several suppliers each specializing. Where there are cost economies from multi-product production then economies of scope are said to exist. Just as with conventional scale effects, it is possible for economies of scope to exist at some levels of output but not at others. As a city expands, for example, there may exist economies of scope in bus service provision favoring a monopoly supplier, but as it gets larger and demand rises so these economies may disappear and several much smaller operators prove more cost-effective.

Technically, economies of scope are assessed when:

$$S = \{[C(Q^1) + C(Q^2)] - C(Q^1 + Q^2)\}/\{C(Q^1 + Q^2)\} \qquad (5.1)$$

where:

> $C(Q^1)$ is the cost of producing Q^1 units of output one alone;
> $C(Q^2)$ is the cost of producing Q^2 units of output two alone; and
> $C(Q^1 + Q^2)$ is the cost of producing Q^1 plus Q^2 units of together.

Economies of scope exist if $S > 0$. There are economies of scale if C/Q falls as Q expands.

There are also instances where there are cost economies from serving larger markets – it effectively allows the more intensive use of capital. Again, aviation provides an example of these so-called economies of density where larger markets enable higher load factors to be enjoyed and hence a lower unit cost per passenger.

Economies of scale, scope, and density can be obtained in various ways using a variety of network types. While we discuss each of these below, separately, in practice most transport undertakings combine them in a variety of ways.

Point-to-point Services

Point-to-point services simply offer services between two points – that is, connectivity as opposed to inter-connectivity. This is seen in Figure 5.7, where there are five cities that are all linked to each other by, for example, rail services offered by separate suppliers. This involves services over ten separate lines. There are no real economies of scope because each train carries passengers who are only concerned with getting to the destination of an individual service. What economies of scope do exist are on the demand side and come from some travelers wanting different qualities of service, for example, those who are willing to pay a premium for first-class service.

Linear Networks

Linear transportation services such as buses and railways that collect and drop passengers en route seek to capture economies of density and scale. For

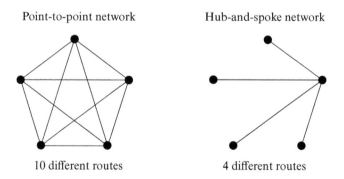

Point-to-point network   Hub-and-spoke network

10 different routes   4 different routes

Figure 5.7 *Point-to-point versus hub-and-spoke networks*

example, in the United States, Amtrak's north-east rail service from Washington DC to Boston makes stops on the way at other major cities such as Baltimore, Philadelphia, and New York, to drop and collect passengers. One reason for the fares scale Amtrak uses, and the schedules adopted, is to maximize revenues by maintaining a high-load factor by moving various groups of passengers between a variety of destinations. The challenge is that overtaking on railways is difficult without expensive provision of sidings. Buses, on the other hand, have more flexibility when operating linear route structures, as, for example, do airlines to some extent in Norway and Chile, where linear networks are common because of the geography of those countries.

Hub-and-spoke Networks

The coming together of these economies of scope and of density has also been characterized by the adoption of 'hub-and-spoke' operations. While United States domestic aviation is the most cited example of this phenomenon, with all the main airlines basing their services on flights to and from a limited number of hubs it is also found in shipping (with traffic into Europe coming by large ships to a small number of large ports to be distributed to other ports by smaller vessels) and in some spheres of bus operators (such as the importance of Victoria Coach Station in London as the hub for long-distance inter-city bus services in the United Kingdom).

Figure 5.7, as we have seen, offers an indication of the cost advantages of hub-and-spoke operations. With direct services between each city pair, as in the point-to-point operation shown in the left-hand side of the figure, there would need to be ten services provided, and many of those may be relatively thin with limited traffic. If, as in the right-hand side of the figure, traffic is hubbed through one of the cities, with passengers being consolidated at this hub to go onto their final destinations, then only four services are required. This allows larger aircraft to be used, and potentially higher-load factors enjoyed, thus reducing costs and fares. The penalty is that people traveling through, rather than stopping at, the hub airport will have longer flight times and spend some time waiting for their connecting flights.

For longer-distance travel, often international routes, there may be several changes. Figure 5.8 illustrates a typical 'dog-bone' or 'dumb-bell' route structure.

Figure 5.8   *The 'dog-bone' pattern of international hub-and-spoke operations*

Here a passenger wanting to travel from x to c would be routed as $x \Rightarrow A \Rightarrow B \Rightarrow c$, where A and B are major hub airports that consolidate traffic from cities x, y, z, ... , j traveling to a, b, c, ... , i. An example of these types of trips are found on North Atlantic air routes where, for example, an individual may fly with United Airlines from a small city in the United States to Washington DC, change plane and fly on to London, change planes and fly to a small European city.

Competition in this system is largely between inter-connected airline networks, often involving alliances. Figure 5.9 again takes the long-distance movement $x \Rightarrow c$, but now looks at the options that may be available when comparing different air cargo alliances rather than just the services of a single airline. The routing $x \Rightarrow A \Rightarrow B \Rightarrow c$ is retained as the base case, but the airline offering this may also have alliance ties with other carriers and push traffic through one or more of their hubs; this may make $x \Rightarrow C \Rightarrow A \Rightarrow B \Rightarrow c$ an option, or $x \Rightarrow C \Rightarrow D \Rightarrow c$. A competitive alliance may offer $x \Rightarrow F \Rightarrow G \Rightarrow c$. And so on.

Depending on schedules and routes served, there are thus numerous possibilities for moving cargo from x to c. From a costing perspective, the costs of these various combinations will differ for the combinations supplying airlines involved. In the context of a discussion of fuel price rises, each overall routing would require a different surcharge that would need to not only reflect the weight of the consignment but also such things as the different distances involved and the forms of equipment used by the various members of an alliance.

Radial Networks

In practice, we find that in many cases the large inter-connected network transport undertakings often compete not only with each other but with alternative forms of networks. In some cases this involves competition with networks that have little or no connectivity – they are, rather, a set of non-connecting services. Tramp shipping may offer this type of competition to the maritime liner networks. But more structured competition may be found in the airline sector whereby low-cost carriers operating 'radial' networks compete with the hub-and-spoke model of the traditional airlines. Looking again at Figure 5.7, radial networks would involve scheduled services between a 'base' and the four connected airports but no inter-lining of services at the base.

Figure 5.9   *Network competition in the air cargo sector*

When radial networks are adopted, they are generally accompanied by considerable commonality (or standardization). Remaining with the low-cost airline example, Ryanair and Southwest use a common fleet of derivatives of the Boeing 737 aircraft, while EasyJet and Frontier Airlines use planes from the Airbus 320 family. This concentration on a limited number of aircraft type produces a variety of advantages:

- The smaller the number of aircraft types, the lower the number of reserve crews needed (to cover for illness, etc.). Flexible swaps of crews are possible with one type, with less crew training being required.
- Fewer spare parts are need with common fleets, lower costs for storage, capital intensity of stock, and costs of obsolescence. Standardized maintenance processes lead to reduced labor costs, with mechanics only needing to be familiar with only one type of aircraft.
- Standardization means ground handling can be simplified and more cost-efficient. Carriers benefit from economies of scale in commonality of ground handling equipment and from less training of labor.
- Generally, ordering several planes of a single type will lower their unit price compared to ordering a mixture of planes from different manufacturers.

While a standardized fleet can produce significant cost advantages, there can be drawbacks. Carriers aiming at maximizing efficiency and their cost advantages by using a uniform fleet generally limit the types of services they provide. As noted earlier when discussing hub-and-spoke networks, airlines require types of aircraft that best suit their networks, and when offering a wide range of diverse services may be best served with a more diverse fleet. In the low-cost carrier case, there are limited variations in demand and routes and commonality may thus be advantageous. This contrasts with airlines such as Lufthansa, Air France, or Delta, which operate global hub-and-spoke systems involving high-demand trunk routes as well as lower-demand regional connections. These airlines require a more varied fleet. The more alike are routes and demand for the services, the more important will fleet commonality be in attaining maximum efficiency.

Economies of Experience

A further recent development is the appreciation that there is a 'learning-by-doing' element in many activities that can reduce costs, and in some cases also be a factor affecting demand. These 'economies of experience' tend to be under-researched in the transport sphere but technically exist when unit costs decline as more is produced or as a supplier stays in a market for an extended period. There may be several dimensions involved in this:

- *Goodwill.* When confronted with several carriers, potential users of aviation have varying levels of information, and especially about the quality of services. Risk aversion encourages a 'better the devil I know' mentality that favors incumbent suppliers. The need to combat this with advertising and promotions pushes up the costs of new entrants.

- *Knowledge.* Incumbent suppliers have more information about a market they serve and can tailor their services to specific customer groups. New entrants must sink resources into acquiring such information.
- *Organization.* New entrants must assimilate the requirements of new services within their networks and this entails learning costs throughout the remainder of their organizations.

As for evidence, one early study of United States domestic airline regulation found that after the opening of routes, incumbent carriers had a larger impact on markets than newly established carriers (Baker and Pratt, 1989). Similarly, analysis of Compass Airlines' entry into the Australian domestic market highlights the problems of establishing goodwill and brand loyalty (Nythi et al., 1993). Switching mode, in the United Kingdom it has been argued that these experience effects may have been advantageous to National Express, the largest bus operator, in the period following the deregulation of the inter-city bus network after 1980. National Express was the incumbent supplier and enjoyed, along with other things, considerable experience in the market that enabled it to dominate newcomers.

The natural way for a transport undertaking to enjoy the various cost advantages of scale, scope, and so on is for it to develop its own network and services on those networks efficiently. In many cases, however, suppliers try to accelerate this process by merging or taking over an existing network to add to their own. Mergers may take place for several reasons. In some cases – and we shall return to this in Chapter 7 – it may be to remove competition from a market to enjoy additional market power. Mergers involving overlapping transport networks are often seen as motivated in this way. In other cases, there may be synergies between non-overlapping (or at least involving limited overlap) that can add to economies of scope and density, and bring in economies of experience because they do not involve developing routes from scratch. Added to this, the enlarged network may generate economies of greater market presence on the demand side by offering a wider range of services to transport users.

The decision to merge networks occurs, therefore, when the incentives exist for the businesses involved, be they driven by rent-seeking or cost-saving motivations. For simplicity we assume that the benefits of, say, a shipping network are proportional to the number of customers (n) who use it, and that the constant of proportionality is unity. Then, following Metcalfe's Law, the value of the network is n^2. A simple calculation shows that combining two networks of size n_1 and n_2 yields:

$$\Delta v_2 = n_2\left(n_1 + n_2\right) - n_1^2 = n_1 n_2 \tag{5.2a}$$

$$\Delta v_2 = n_2\left(n_1 + n_2\right) - n_2^2 = n_1 n_2 \tag{5.2b}$$

Each network of sailings gets equal value (v_2) from the inter-connection. Those on a smaller network (2) each get considerable value from linking with the large number of nodes on the larger network (1), while many consignors of the latter may each get a smaller additional utility, but there are a lot of them. This offers scope for reciprocation, with the networks having free access to each other. The problem is that the large supplier may need to keep its market power to allow adequate price discrimination to recover costs and make an acceptable long-term return. In this case, the larger shipping company may merge with the smaller one and attain twice the value of offering inter-connecting services:

$$\Delta v_1 = n_1 \left(n_1 + n_2 \right)^2 - n_1^2 - n_2^2 = 2n_1 n_2 \qquad (5.3)$$

5.4   Specific, Joint, and Common Costs

When dividing out costs, according to the groups of services produced, it is often useful to allocate responsibility to specific users or consignors. While the fixed/variable cost dichotomy poses problems about the relevant time period to consider, cost responsibility raises issues of the traceability of costs. Some costs are very specific and can, therefore, be allocated quite easily – the stevedore costs of loading and unloading a cargo onto and off a ship is a case in point. In other cases, a degree of averaging may be necessary but, nevertheless, costs can generally be traced to specific groups or classes of user.

But there is also a whole range of other costs that may be either 'joint' or 'common' to a few users and are difficult to trace directly to any specific group. It is sometimes said that fixed costs may generally be treated as joint or common while variable costs may be treated as specific, but this is too simplistic. Many variable costs are, in practice, joint (for example, the fuel costs incurred in moving a train in one direction and bringing it back are joint to both movements) or common (for example, the basic maintenance costs of retaining a freight and passenger rail link), while certain fixed costs are clearly specific (for example, the capital costs of freight wagons have no connection with passenger demand).

In some cases, the technology is such that two products can be delivered at the same time: the textbook wool and mutton case. An example of this in transport is the combination of passengers being carried on the upper deck of commercial aircraft and freight on the lower deck. Allocating the fixed costs of the aircraft between these two uses, other than for specific features like seats, etc., is challenging. Nevertheless, airlines do carry both on many aircraft, as can be seen in the revenue composition in Figure 5.10.

Strictly, joint costs exist when the provision of a specific service necessarily entails the output of some other service. Jointness is a technical feature and exists at all points in time, that is, both before as well as after any investment decisions are made. Return trips (or 'back-hauls'), where the supply of transport services in one direction automatically implies the provision of a return service, are the classic examples in transport economics. The fact that true joint products are

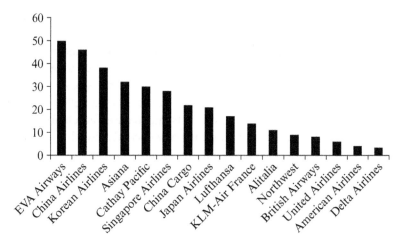

Figure 5.10   *Percentage of airlines' revenues from cargo*

produced in fixed proportions means there can be no variability in costs, making it logically impossible to specify the cost of, say, an outward journey when only the overall cost of the round trip is known. Joint costs are, consequently, non-traceable. This further implies that joint costs can only be escaped jointly, with services in both directions being withdrawn together.

In a market situation, joint costs pose few problems in practice (Mohring, 1976). If there is a competitive road haulage service offering a round trip between *A* and *B* and back again each week using *M* trucks then equilibrium rates would soon emerge for each service (that is, from *A* to *B* and from *B* to *A*). Although there are specific delivery, terminal, pick-up costs, etc., little difference exists between the costs of running the lorries fully loaded or empty and hence prices would be primarily influenced by the differences in the demand in each direction. In the short term, the combined revenues from the *A* to *B* and the *B* to *A* services may not be enough to cover joint costs, but in such a situation the number of trucks offered would soon fall below *M*, increasing the price of trips in both directions until joint costs are recovered. Excess revenue above joint costs would have the opposite effect. The key point is that differences exist in the demands for the out and return services and that different prices should be charged for each in equilibrium. Consequently, knowledge of the relevant demand elasticities together with that of joint cost permits the problems of traceability to be avoided. We return to consider this problem in more detail in our discussion of pricing in Chapter 6.

Common costs are like joint costs, in that they are incurred as the result of providing services to a range of users, but differ in that the use of resources to provide one service does not unavoidably result in the production of a different one. The classic example of common costs in transport is the provision of track facilities. A road may be used in common by lorries and cars, but the withdrawal of rights for hauliers still leaves costs to be borne by motorists. With several classes of user, it is often possible to trace certain components of cost to those responsible, but there is still usually a large proportion that is untraceable. We now turn to look at some attempts that have been made to allocate common track costs across different categories of traffic.

5.5   Problems of Common Cost Allocation: The Road and Rail Track Cases

The allocation of common track costs among users poses practical problems in transport and deserves specific attention. As Arthur Hadley put it in 1885, before becoming President of Yale University, 'God Almighty did not know the cost of carrying a hundred pounds of freight from Boston to New York'. The ways costs are allocated varies between countries in part because some facilities are publicly owned and some private. The inter-city road network in the United Kingdom, for example, is almost exclusively the responsibility of central government. Users, since the effective abolition of the Road Fund in 1937 and its legal death in 1955, make no direct, hypothecated payments to use the network – save for a small number of toll bridges and roads – but do pay considerable sums to government each year in the form of fuel tax, value added tax, car tax, and vehicle excise duty. The United States has had a national federal fuel tax since 1956, which in 2021 amounted to 18.4 cents per US gallon of gasoline and 24.4 cents per gallon of diesel fuel. The revenue goes into a Highway Trust Fund. Revenues go into the Highway Account which funds road construction and other surface transportation projects, and a Mass Transit Account to support mass transit. In addition, individual states have a variety of mechanisms for financing their road networks.

When deciding upon the desirability of making a road journey, potential users are to some extent influenced by these taxes. Therefore, attempts have been made, on the grounds of economic efficiency, to allocate accurately the public costs of road provision (both the construction and maintenance of the track) to users. The European Union, for example, wishes members to ensure that all road users pay at least their allocated short-run marginal costs of track provision and that the full long-term cost is recovered in total.

There are problems of deciding exactly what constitutes the total cost of road track provision in any period – for example, should the maintenance costs be estimated in the same way as depreciation in nationalized industries or a commercial business, or simply considered as they are incurred? And what exactly constitutes the capital cost of any one year?

National comparisons of annual expenditures against tax revenue suggest that most governments of industrial countries recover from road users more than is spent on road track provision. There is also certainly no reason why, as some have advocated, the ratio should approximate to unity. Part of the revenue raised from road users must be considered as a 'pure' tax in the same way as there are taxes on other expenditures. Also, there are social costs associated with road transport (see Chapter 6) and motoring taxes may, in part, be seen as a method, albeit a very imperfect one, of making road users aware of such costs.

Additionally, if prices in other sectors of the economy deviate from costs, there are sound economic reasons for this to be also the policy on roads.

Development of the United Kingdom's Road Track Costs Allocation Method

The experiences of the United Kingdom in developing mechanisms for the allocation of transport track costs in the 1980s offers an insight into the economic challenges involved and into the need for pragmatism when putting methodologies into practice.

While there is no sound reason why expenditure should match revenue in aggregate, it may still be desirable for each class of road vehicle to cover its allocated track costs. This is the view, for example, of the European Union (1998). It has also become increasingly important as public–private partnerships (PPPs) are playing a greater role in highway provision. The partners need to make contractual agreements covering the tolls levied on various types of uses (Button, 2016). Allocation of track costs to vehicle categories is, therefore, still important. The difficulty is that roads provide a common service to a variety of modes of transport (cyclists, motor cars, light vans, heavy lorries, buses, etc.) and the exact apportionment of marginal costs is, therefore, far from easy. The method of allocation developed by the UK Department of Transport is based upon a refined version of an approach pioneered in the 1968 'Road track costs' study which crudely attempts to allocate long-run marginal costs to different classes of road users. The methodology is similar to that developed in the 'Federal highway cost allocation study final report' which has been used in the United States since the late 1990s.

The calculations are done for the four standard categories of road: motorway, trunk, principal, and other. Of total capital expenditure (made up of the average expenditure over the previous year, the current year, and the forecast for the following year), 15 percent is allocated directly to heavy goods vehicles according to their maximum vehicle weight times the kilometers run, on the grounds that they necessitate higher engineering design standards. The remaining 85 percent is allocated out on passenger car unit (pcu) kilometers (pcu being an estimate of the amount of road required to accommodate a vehicle expressed in terms of car equivalents), on the argument that capital expenditure is determined by changes required in the physical capacity of the network.

Current maintenance expenditures are allocated according to a series of *ad hoc* calculations that attempt to relate the various component items (such as resurfacing, grass cutting, lighting, road markings, traffic signs, drainage, etc.) to different vehicle characteristics, namely their size, number of standard axles (high axle loadings doing considerable damage to road surfaces), and the use made of roads. The criteria used to decide how costs are affected by the vehicle characteristics are based upon 'expert advice from traffic engineers and research scientists'. Special items such as policing and car parks are treated separately.

Table 5.9 compares the cost allocations with revenues for different broad categories of road users in the United Kingdom, for 1989–90. When aggregated, road users cover their allocated cost, a situation which is also common in many

Table 5.9 *Allocated taxation/revenue ratios by vehicle type in the United Kingdom (1989–90)*

Vehicle class	Tax/cost ratio
Cars/light vans/taxis	3.4:1
Motorcycles	2.3:1
Buses & coaches	1.1:1
Trucks over 1.525 tonnes gvw	
Not over 3.5 tonnes gvw	1.3:1
Over 3.5 tonnes gvw	2.4:1
Other vehicles	2.4:1
All vehicles	2.6:1

Source: UK Department of Transport (1989).

other industrialized countries although not the United States. A similar picture is seen within vehicle classes, although again the United States is something of an exception, with many classes falling short in paying their fully allocated costs. In 2000, for example, while automobiles and buses broadly covered their costs, trucks did not. Additionally, even in countries where all sizes of heavy goods vehicle pay tax in excess of the public road costs attributable to them, there is considerable variation in the revenue/cost ratio and large vehicles with a small number of axles tend to have the lowest ratios. This may be particularly undesirable if these large vehicles are also responsible for generating a high level of external costs such as pollution and noise.

The UK Department of Transport's method of cost attribution has come under some criticism. At one level, the detailed allocation within the Department's framework in the 1970s was biased against heavy goods vehicles because of:

- the excessive emphasis on vehicle weight in the allocation of capital costs when much of the network's design is determined by vehicle speed;
- the assumption in the calculation that the network is of optimal size;
- the rather dubious nature of passenger car units as a measure of road capacity; and
- the 'standard axle' measure used in the calculations.

In particular, there may be an element of double counting when calculating heavy goods vehicle costs. Cars are accredited with a small allocation of maintenance costs, but this is only possible because of the high engineering standards of roads required to carry heavy goods traffic. Hence, goods vehicles are allocated both the additional costs of high design standards and the bulk of maintenance costs whereas with lower design specifications, suitable for cars only, cars would be allocated much higher maintenance costs.

This last point has been examined in some detail by Ken Small et al. (1989) in a study of the United States' road investment and pricing policy. The evidence seen in Table 5.10 strongly suggests that under the United States regime, where

Table 5.10   *Examples of actual and optimal road vehicle taxation in the United States (1988)*

Vehicle	Taxes (cents per mile)		
	Current	Marginal cost (existing roads)	Marginal cost (improved roads)
2-axle single unit			
28,000 lb	2.5	9.2	3.6
33,000 lb	3.0	23.8	9.3
5-axle tractor unit			
33,000 lb	4.0	1.2	0.5
80,000 lb	7.2	41.3	16.2

Source: Small et al. (1989).

certain federal road taxation revenues are partly hypothecated to road building and maintenance, the amount of investment has historically been suboptimal, resulting in pavements that are, from an economic prospect, too thin. The result is the need for high maintenance and reconstruction outlays relatively soon after a road is opened.

The economic evidence is that, if higher taxes had been introduced initially and higher-standard roads constructed, then subsequent taxation to finance maintenance would, on average, have been much lower than it inevitably will have to be if the network is not to deteriorate. The structure of the taxation should also have been adjusted to more closely correspond to the damage associated with various classes of user.

At a more fundamental level, Christopher Nash (1979) has suggested that the traditional road track cost approach is really asking the wrong question and that track costs should be allocated along altogether different lines. He suggests the more appropriate way is to adopt a sequential approach where greater emphasis is placed upon differing demand elasticities among road users. Specifically, he advises:

- Forecasting traffic growth rates by vehicle type using alternative assumptions about future taxation levels and structures.
- Estimating the full costs of catering for different traffic growth rates.
- Identifying the level and structure of taxes at which the revenue obtained from an incremental slice of traffic matches incremental costs both for traffic as a whole and for individual traffic types.
- To the extent that the resulting taxes fall short of government revenue requirements, raising taxes on vehicle classes along second-best lines (that is, according to demand elasticities).

Such calculations obviously place greater demands on informational sources, but they do offer a rather more realistic basis for track cost allocation as well as pricing consistent with principles adopted elsewhere in the transport sector.

Allocating Costs in a State-owned Railroad

Railway track cost allocation is carried out in a slightly different context because the railways, unlike the roads, have traditionally been responsible in most countries for providing both track and rolling stock. This has changed somewhat in some European countries, not only because in countries such as the United Kingdom rail operations have been separated from track provision, but because European Union regulations require open access to their networks and this necessitates track cost estimations for charging purposes. In countries such as the United Kingdom, the necessity for devising a method of allocation stems not simply from designs for internal efficiency but also to permit the allocation of common fixed costs between those services that are operated on commercial criteria (for example, inter-city services) and those that are operated on social criteria (for example, commuter services) and are given central government subsidies (Bowman, 2015).

Here we focus on the situation where, as is still common, state ownership of track and operations remains, and we look at some of the challenges faced in the past by British Rail – a largely multi-purpose passenger system. The intensity with which this subject has been studied provides insights of a more general nature.

In countries such as the United Kingdom, where track is often used by several types of service, the necessity for devising a method of cost allocation pre-privatization of rail track in 1993 stemmed not simply from a desire for internal efficiency but also from the need to allocate common fixed costs between those railway services that were operated on commercial criteria (for example, inter-city services) and those that were operated on social criteria (for example, commuter services) and were subsidized by the state. The situation in the United States is different. There, the tracks are largely owned by the freight railroads and Amtrak, the large national passenger carrier, and local services' short-haul providers. The various railroads largely allocate costs to meet their specific objectives. Class 1 freight railroads are, however, legally obliged to allow access to Amtrak services and only to charge a marginal cost for this.

One of the difficulties with railway operations is that common costs (which include signaling, termini, etc., in addition to track) form a substantial part of the total cost. Normal commercial practice would be to use a 'cost-plus' method of pricing so that each customer would pay a rate covering his/her specific costs plus a contribution to overheads. Provided this results in all costs being recovered in aggregate, the problem of common cost allocation is not a serious issue. Unfortunately, for the reasons mentioned above, plus the difficulty of devising a sufficiently sensitive price discrimination regime given the diversity of services offered (see Chapter 7), the railways have found it important to be able to allocate their track costs.

A major difficulty in this area is that the railways' 'jargon' often does not conform to conventional economic definitions. The railways talk of 'direct costs' and 'indirect costs', but the former (which embraces haulage costs, maintenance, marshaling, booking, insurance, and collection and delivery by road) is clearly different from the economic notion of short-run escapable costs (and may or may not exceed them). As the United Kingdom's Select Committee on Nationalized Industries stated in 1960, '[t]he direct costs ascertained by traffic costing methods are not the same thing as short run marginal costs. Nor do they correspond with the savings that would flow immediately from the discontinuance of a small part of railway activities'. Equally, indirect costs, as defined by the railways (that is, track, signaling, and general administration) are not sufficiently fixed costs that are common to all traffic. While certain costs (for example, earthworks) are invariant with traffic, it is often possible to allocate track and signaling costs to services according to causation. The type and density of traffic determine whether a single-track route is operated with no signaling or a multi-track, multiple-aspect signaling system is provided.

Stewart Joy (1973), the chief economist at British Railways, highlighted almost 50 years ago how these costs can vary with the quality of service – an express Category A service on double track with 12 trains a day cost £8,250 per mile per annum in track costs (at 1961 prices); a less frequent, Category B service cost £7,250; heavily used non-express Category C services cost £6,250; and slow, Category D services cost £3,500. It is possible with poorer quality services to have more basic signaling and lower track maintenance standards. Further, there are quite significant differences associated with the costs of track used exclusively for passenger services compared with track used only for freight. The Beeching Report, which brought about major reforms in the British rail system in the 1960s, found that a single track maintained to passenger standards costs at least £3,500 per mile per annum, but if it were only required to conform to freight standards it would cost £2,000 per mile per annum, and it has been argued this could have been reduced further.

The improvement in costing in the United Kingdom came about in part because of the 1968 Transport Act and the introduction of social service subsidies for specific routes – the system required identification and costing of those services and facilities whose cost should properly be borne or aided by the community. The common costs were allocated according to the so-called 'Cooper Brothers' formula (which was essentially an average, rather than marginal, cost type of framework) that endorsed the idea of allocating track costs in terms of gross tonne-miles and signaling costs on the basis of train miles. With homogeneous traffic flows evenly spread this is reasonable, but with mixed traffic and peaks in use the allocation technique is unlikely to match causation with costs.

British Rail moved in the late 1970s to a system of 'contribution accounting', which entailed breaking down revenue and costs into some 700 major subsectors (or 'profit centers'). These profit centers, which are composed of single traffic flows, groups of flows, or specific passenger services, are defined so that resources allocated to them can be specifically identified with a minimum of controversy. Even so, not all common costs could be so allocated and thus British Rail accounts revealed the surplus of revenue over directly attributed expenses that are a 'contribution' to the indirect costs. The sum of all avoidable costs recovered may not cover all business costs, however, and a 'basic facility cost' is likely to remain. British Rail argued though that this approach, given the high proportion of indirect costs, 'ensures a high level of certainty in profit assessment' (Dodgson, 1984).

The privatization of railways in the United Kingdom and the deregulation of private networks in countries such as the United States has meant that there has been more effort put into cost modeling of the type discussed elsewhere in this chapter. The American railroads, a largely freight mover, have traditionally varied in the ways that they have allocated their costs and generalization is not easy (Poole, 1962). The removal of most economic regulation under the 1980 Staggers Rail Act provided the Class 1 United States railroads with greater flexibility in their pricing and the ability to close or sell off unprofitable lines. With this came the need for more specific costing. The growth in importance of container traffic, with its own unique set of costing issues, has provided a further stimulus for more accurate costing, as has the common use of track with Amtrak.

Prior to 1980, the US Interstate Commerce Commission (ICC) regulated rates on a rate-of-return basis – essentially a cost-plus model. For this it assigned to each service those costs that could be directly and unambiguously attributed to it. In addition to these directly attributable costs, each service was assigned a portion of common costs in such a way that all such costs were allocated somewhere. This is what is often called a 'fully distributed cost approach'. In other words, the total allocated costs of C of a service were defined by an affine function of the form $C = F + my$, where F represents fixed costs insensitive to traffic volume, m is a constant marginal cost, and y is the level of output.

John Meyer (1958) and others criticized this approach over the years, pointing to the arbitrary allocation of common costs across services. In doing this they were resurrecting a point made in the late 1800s by Frank Taussig (1891), who argued that 'attempts have indeed been made at various times ... to apportion the expenses, and to assign to each item of traffic the sum which it cost ... . Yet surely the division is purely arbitrary'. Meyer also pointed to the inappropriateness of the ICC's assumption about output costs which assumed, for example, that it cost as much to haul 100 tonnes one mile as to haul one tonne 100 miles. While any attempt to allocate all costs to a particular output is unquestionably difficult, as we shall show later in this chapter, the degree of arbitrariness has been reduced somewhat with the introduction of econometric costing analysis.

From the two examples, road and railroad track costs, the problems of allocating costs common to several services are, therefore, seen to be difficult ones. Economic principles advocate the notion of seeking avoidable costs associated with specific users and then allocating these accordingly. The problem is in defining the base from which to begin the series of allocations; in the case of roads, are roads mainly designed for cars with lorries imposing additional costs, or are they there to provide a quality of service with the faster car traffic necessitating higher engineering standards? We have seen that it is possible to allocate many items on an avoidable cost basis although practical application may necessitate a high degree of averaging.

5.6   Transport User Costs and the Notion of Generalized Costs

Simple observation shows us that different types of transport are associated, in a very broad way, with the distances of trips. Walking and cycling, together with the riding of mopeds, are largely reserved for local travel, whereas air transport dominates long-distance movements. Similar generalizations can be given about freight transport, although in this case it is shipping that dominates long-distance movements, at least in terms of physical movements. Of course, there are cases where this very broad picture does not pertain. For example, where there are stretches of water to be covered, it is often by boat or aircraft if there is no road or rail infrastructure; and equally in mountainous regions where it is costly to build surface infrastructure, air transport can play an important role. The boundaries also tend to vary slightly with culture; the United States is a car-oriented society and many people, even for the shortest of journeys, would not consider walking or cycling.

Figure 4.1 in the previous chapter provided a very stylized picture of the boundaries of the various transport modes. The cross-over points represent 'distant boundaries' over which the modes compete. This competition takes a variety of forms. From the traveler's point of view, or that of a consignor of freight, a multiplicity of factors influences this type of decision.

Travelers in particular take notice of the time it takes to make a trip and the money costs involved, and, frequently, also the quality of the service offered. Consignors are concerned not simply with the financial costs of carriage but also the speed, reliability, and timetabling of the service. The demand for transport is not, therefore, simply dependent upon financial costs but rather on the overall opportunity costs involved. Transport is not unique in this, but it does differ from other services in that money costs may only form a relatively small part of overall costs. In terms of decision-making, the money cost of a trip may have minimal influence over whether it is undertaken or the transport mode preferred; a fact that may explain the considerable use of private motorcars even when 'cheaper' alternative modes are available.

User costs are also, according to Herb Mohring (1976), important in the urban public transport context for another reason. He argues that, in the context of very frequent public transport in cities, the main scale economy effects are associated with savings in passengers' time. These economies exist when the service is such that people do not arrive at a stop intending to catch a scheduled bus, but, rather, know that headways are so close that at any time the wait will be short. If say the average headway is ten minutes then the average wait, assuming random arrivals of passengers, will be five minutes. A reduction of headway to five minutes will reduce the average wait to two and a half minutes. Increased output of bus services, therefore, reduces average waiting time and thus the users' cost of traveling by bus.

In analysing transport demand or when forecasting future consumer response, it is often possible to assess responses to the individual components of overall cost, that is, money costs, time costs, inconvenience costs, and so on. In some situations, however, it has proved useful to have a composite measure. This may be true in situations where multi-dimensional cost functions are unwieldy or when a simple uni-dimensional measure, by focusing attention on general trends in cost, permits a clearer understanding of changes in the demand for transport services. A pragmatic device to reduce the wide range of costs involved in travel is to employ a single index expressing 'generalized cost'. This was a concept developed by Leon Warner (1962) as part of the Chicago Area Transportation Study.

The generalized cost of a trip is expressed as a single, usually monetary, measure combining, generally in linear form, most of the important but disparate costs that form the overall opportunity costs of the trip. On a rare few occasions, a generalized time-cost measure has been advocated to replace the financial index (Goodwin, 1974). The characteristic of generalized costs is, therefore, that it reduces all cost items to a single index and this index may then be used in the same way as money costs are in standard economic analysis. Simply, generalized costs can be defined as:

$$G = g(C_1, C_2, C_3, \ldots, C_n) \tag{5.4}$$

where G is the generalized cost and $C_1, C_2, C_3, \ldots, C_n$ are the various time, money, and other costs of travel. This permits the demand for trips to be expressed as a function of a single variable – that is, $Q_D = f(G)$. While, in simple indices, generalized cost is formed as a linear combination of time and money (or distance) costs, in most applied analysis the time and money components are divided into several elements (for example, walking time, waiting time, in-vehicle time, etc.). This results in an expression of the general form:

$$G = \sum_i M_i + \sum_j T_j \tag{5.5}$$

where M are the actual money costs of a journey (for example, fare or petrol costs) and T_j are the time costs (for instance, in-vehicle time and waiting time made up of the amount of time involved multiplied by the monetary value per unit of time). These were discussed in detail in Chapter 4.

For expositional ease, we take a fairly simple specific form of the generalized cost function that was used some time ago in the United Kingdom as part of the South-east Lancashire, North-east Cheshire (SELNEC) transport study conducted in the late 1960s (Wilson et al., 1969), which provides a useful illustration of actual application. It is dated, but it makes the key points rather neatly. The generalized cost index used in the combined trip-distribution–modal-split element of the analysis was of the form:

$$G_{ij}^K = a_1 t_{ij}^K + a_2 e_{ij}^K + a_3 d_{ij}^K + p_j^K + \zeta^k \tag{5.6}$$

where:

G_{ij}^K is the generalized cost of travel by mode K between points i and j;

t_{ij}^K is the travel time from i to j by mode K (in minutes);

e_{ij}^K is the excess time (for example, waiting time for public transport) for the journey from i to j (in minutes);

d_{ij}^K is the distance from i to j that acts as a surrogate for the variable money costs of trips (that are assumed proportional to distance);

p_j^K is the terminal cost (for example, parking charges) at j (in pence);

ζ^K is a modal penalty reflecting the discomfort and lesser convenience associated with public transport journeys; and

a_1, a_2, and a_3 are parameters which, since p_j^K and ζ^K have unit coefficients, value other cost items in monetary terms.

An important issue is how these costs should be treated in analysis of transport decisions. Economics is concerned with costs that influence behavior in the short term and with those that affect long-term decisions. In the short term, people may well only perceive a limited range of costs or not fully appreciate the full magnitude of some cost items. Nevertheless, it is this set of costs which influences their immediate actions. The problem of perception is generally associated with the external costs that travelers generate by ignoring their actions (see Chapter 6), but here we are concerned with the misperception of the costs they bear themselves.

People misperceive the costs of their journeys (or of moving goods) for several reasons:

- This is the first time the trip is being made and the trip-maker has incomplete information of the costs involved.
- The money or time cost may be so small that it is not worth taking into account.
- Certain variable costs may be regarded wrongly as fixed costs; included here would be the tendency for car users only to take account of petrol costs of journeys and ignore depreciation of the vehicle and its maintenance.
- Users may be unaware of the connection between a particular action and the costs to which it gives rise; for example, a fast driver may be unaware of the additional fuel costs he/she incurs.
- Habit can make regular trip-makers unaware of changing cost conditions over time even if they were fully cognizant of the full resource costs of their actions at some earlier point in time. This is more likely to be a problem encountered by car users than public transport travelers who face regular ticket purchases.

While the final three reasons for misperception result from poor or inadequate information, the first represents a departure from the conventional economic idea of maximizing behavior. While this poses interesting theoretical questions, there are reasons for arguing that the last three are likely to be of greater quantitative importance for transport economists. Lack of good information is likely to result in different travel behavior to that anticipated in full information situations. Whereas perceived generalized costs offer a basis for travel behavior analysis, it is actual resource costs that are appropriate for investment decision-taking. Where people accurately perceive the costs of their travel there is no difference between the perceived and resource generalized cost. Where there is misperception, however, resource costs, being the full opportunity cost of trip-making, will exceed the perceived costs and this may result in over-investment in transport facilities if adjustments are not made. (Of course, we are still ignoring external costs such as pollution, but these complicate rather than change the argument.)

The social welfare gains associated with an investment are assessed by comparing the resource costs with the benefits generated. The difficulty is that the actual traffic levels using the facility depend upon perceived costs. In Figure 5.11 we have a linear demand curve for use of a road with an initial perceived generalized cost of usage equal to P^1. A widening of the road speeds traffic, causing the perceived generalized cost to fall to P^2.

Exhibit   *Measuring perceived costs of driving*

While accountancy calculations may be used to estimate the resource costs of making a car trip, for the monetary costs perceived by the driver (which are needed for examining travel motivations) either revealed- or stated-preference methods have to be used. A stated-preference study conducted in 2001 involving questioning 416 Israeli drivers considered a variety of factors influencing drivers' perceptions of trip costs. These were:

- Fuel consumption is a variable cost affected by travel distance (F).
- Insurance is a fixed cost (I).
- Maintenance is a variable cost covering routine maintenance including tires and oil (M).
- Depreciation includes the reduced value of the car and interest rates. This is usually considered a fixed cost, but part of it is also a variable cost as the future value of the car is also a function of its mileage (D).
- Repairs refer to mechanical and accident repairs to the extent that they are not covered by insurance. They are distance-based (R).
- Licensing is a fixed cost (L).

It was found that the person vehicle size affected perceptions of the cost of using it, as did whether drivers were asked about daily costs or monthly costs. The first table below provides the various response rates and the values of vehicle costs as perceived by owners who answered both questions. The standard deviations are large, indicating rather poor perception among drivers.

In terms of which costs drivers consider when trip-making, the table below shows clearly the importance of fuel costs, although these are often combined with other factors. Very few respondents considered all four possible elements.

Average perceived cost per kilometer by vehicle size				
	Number of observations	Response rate (%)	Average (NIS)[a]	Standard deviation
All vehicle sizes (monthly estimate)	360	87	1.01	1.19
All vehicle sizes (daily estimate)	332	80	1.45	2.69
Small vehicles (monthly estimate)	110	88	1.01	0.97
Small vehicles (daily estimate)	103	82	1.03	0.76
Medium vehicles (monthly estimate)	204	86	1.03	1.23
Medium vehicles (daily estimate)	186	78	1.71	3.49
Large vehicles (monthly estimate)	46	90	0.77	0.55
Large vehicles (daily estimate)	41	80	1.30	1.07

Note: a. NIS = new Israel shekels.

	Comparison of cost elements			
Element mentioned	Number of cases	Response rate (%)	Average NIS[a]/km	Standard deviation
At least fuel (F)	400	96	1.03	1.21
Fuel (F) & maintenance (M)	73	18	0.94	0.57
Fuel (F) & insurance (I)	88	21	0.85	0.57
Fuel (F) & depreciation (D)	82	20	0.92	0.88
F & at least one other element	159	38	0.92	0.75
F & M, but not I or D	25	6	0.99	0.59
F & I, but not M or D	31	7	0.88	0.66
F & D, but not M or I	34	8	1.08	1.20
F & M and I	38	9	0.91	0.57
F & M and D	29	7	0.89	0.61
F & I & D	38	9	0.78	0.53
All four elements	19	5	0.87	0.63
None of them	14	3	0.70	0.65

Note: a. NIS = new Israel shekels.

Feeding the results into a regression model to examine factors affecting these variations in the perceived monetary costs of driving produced the following:

Perceived costs (NIS/km) = 1.00E + 00
+ 1.97E – 04 Engine size (cc)
+ 1.95E – 0.2 Vehicle age (years)
– 1.40E – 04 Vehicle use (km/month)
– 9.50E – 0.2 Gender
– 6.32E – 03 Person age (years)
+ 1.79E – 03 Commuting time (minutes)

The importance of the vehicle age and engine size is clear from the size of their coefficients, and supported by high t-statistics. The usage coefficient is negative, large, and highly significant, supporting the idea that the more a driver uses a vehicle the lower the perceived costs. It appears that longer-distance commuters have a higher perception of motoring costs. Overall, the results are suggestive of much lower perceived costs than the resources cost of car use in Israel.

See also: Y. Shiftan and S. Bekhor (2002) Investigating individual's perception of auto travel cost, *International Journal of Transport Economics*, 29, 151–66.

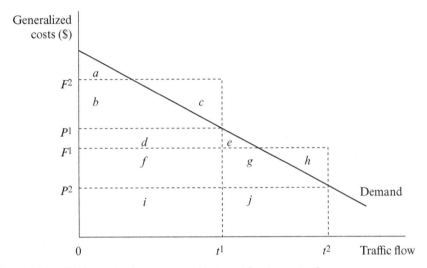

Figure 5.11   *Welfare gains from a cost reduction with misperceived transport costs*

If, however, the actual resource costs of trip-making along the road are F^1 and P^2 for the respective pre- and post-investment situations, then there will be 'deadweight' welfare 'losses' generated at both the t^1 and t^2 traffic levels. (At the preinvestment traffic flow, t^1, this loss is equal to area c and at the post-investment flow, t^2, it is h.) If no account is taken of this, however, the apparent consumer surplus gain from the road widening is equal to $(d + e + f + g)$. In fact, since the genuine resource costs are measured by F^1 and F^2, the investment will result in a net benefit of $(b + c + d + e - h)$. The area $(b + e + d)$ represents a straight resource cost saving under the demand curve by reducing the resource costs of travel, while $(c - h)$ reflects the change in deadweight welfare loss between the two traffic flow situations. Henry Neuberger (1971) generalized this calculation to take account of the effects of policies that alter costs and travel patterns over a network of roads.

The adoption of a single index idea of transport costs has permitted significant advances in transport forecasting and project appraisal to be made. This does not mean, however, that the concept is without its critics, nor that those choosing to ignore its existence have not made other advances. First, the inherent constraints implicit in the aggregating of the various cost components into a unique index restricts the separate elasticities of demand with respect to each individual cost component. One ends up with an elasticity with respect to generalized costs but cannot, for example, assess the particular effect of a reduction in travel time costs.

Second, there is concern about the long-term stability of money as the numerator. Because income rises over time, it is argued, the utility of money will fall relative to other items, especially time which is fixed in quantity. McIntosh and Quarmby (1972), therefore, argue that time should be used as the basis of measurement and the operational concept should be generalized time costs. Additionally, time is equally distributed (in the sense that everyone has 24 hours in a day) which circumvents some of the distributional difficulties of using money values of travel cost components. Third, even if the basic notion of generalized cost is accepted, there are critics who oppose the use of a 'universal' index for application throughout a country, for example of the form McIntosh and Quarmby (1972) put forward for the United Kingdom some years ago. A difficulty is that there is little evidence to support the universality of any weighting scheme employed. Although the use of official time valuations and formulae ensure consistency in approach, they may lead to inconsistencies in the results if the overall index is only accurate in certain sets of circumstances.

Generalized cost is, despite these criticisms, a useful tool in helping us to understand, in broad terms, how variations in travel cost can influence travel behavior. Above all, it is an extremely useful pedagogical device that can help policy-makers articulate their ideas and plans to a more general audience. It also serves as a pragmatic device for assisting in certain types of modeling and decision-making where, otherwise, no information would be forthcoming at all. In this context the index is likely to be an imperfect instrument, but, when used with sufficient circumspection, it can yield useful insights into the possible effects of alternative transport policies.

5.7   The Bunching of Public Transport Services

There often seems to be a bunching of buses on the roads, or a concentration of flights leaving at about the same time for a destination. In the bus case, this may be simply caused by traffic conditions that do not allow buses, with the frequency of their stops and their relative lack of dexterity, to keep up a schedule that on paper has more regular headways between them. In the airline case it can sometimes be explained by airport noise curfews or 'banks' of flights arriving and leaving to facilitate passengers making connections. But in many cases bunching, and similar service features, results from deliberate actions on the part of suppliers of services. This may be because demand peaks at certain times of the day and, therefore, that is the time that customers are willing to pay for having the 'bunch' of vehicles available.

This logic extends to the large number of taxi-cabs that are at certain times waiting at airports, railway stations, and other terminals. But the nature of supply and the product on offer can also lead to situations in which the bunching is less desirable. This can also occur in terms of where transport infrastructure, such as gas stations, is located. Setting aside planning controls, even where there is a relatively free choice, gas stations tend to be physically bunched.

The explanation for this phenomenon, and the account of the costs that it creates, can be traced back to the work of Harold Hotelling (1929) nearly a century ago. While his analysis was really designed to explain business location decisions and why manufacturers in markets with a limited number of large producers – known as oligopolies these days – tend to produce very similar goods, it also has relevance to the issue of transport service bunching. The analysis can be explained by recourse to Figure 5.12.

The distances between points $A \Rightarrow B$ and $B \Rightarrow C$ in the figure represent ten-minute intervals. If potential users are arriving continually, and at an even rate, then this flow can be taken as the horizontal line of uniform thickness joining A, B, and C. We introduce two bus companies, X and Y, that offer identical fares and an infinite capacity to carry passengers. Thus, passengers are indifferent as to which company's bus they make their trip in. Initially they both operate their services at 20-minute headways, each offering seats midway along a time period. The average wait for a passenger is thus five minutes: if someone just misses X's bus and must wait for Y's bus then they have a ten-minute wait, but someone arriving coincidentally in time for Y's bus has no wait. However, while this is an optimal situation, it is not an equilibrium because there is an incentive for the bus companies to reschedule. X, for example, may reschedule their service to run just prior to Y's bus, say at X^*. This will allow them to pick up virtually all the passengers who were waiting for Y's bus. Company Y, to remain in business, will then reschedule their service to, say, Y^*, and thus take away most of the passengers that would be waiting for the X^* service. This goes on until the companies time their 20-minute headways to coincide with each other – at $X^\dagger$ and $Y^\dagger$.

This is an equilibrium because there is no incentive for either supplier to change their services; alterations will mean smaller numbers of passengers. It is not, however, optimal from a passenger's perspective because now the average waiting time is ten minutes: missing the X bus means a wait of 20 minutes for

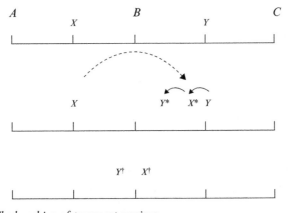

Figure 5.12   *The bunching of transport services*

either X's or Y's next service, with no wait for those that just turn up when a bus is due.

The nature of the competition and common costs for the two suppliers effectively cause an external cost for potential bus users, a topic we return to in Chapter 6. Of course, the example is excessively simple, but there are records from the early part of the twentieth century of bus companies engaging in a whole series of practices akin to this – for example, missing out passengers at some stops to move ahead of another company's buses to collect a large line of customers later on in a route (Foster and Golay, 1986). The degree of welfare loss due to a high level of waiting time is likely to be dissipated because consumers will not arrive at even intervals but will play their own 'games' with the bus companies to minimize their waits. Also, the equilibrium conditions tend to break down with more than two bus operators and when complex networks of services come into play.

5.8   Economic Performance

It is generally assumed that firms seek to minimize their costs, and this is a common assumption when considering transport markets. In practice, firms perform with varying degrees of efficiency. Further, performance can be measured in many dimensions; it may be in terms of whether costs of production are being minimized (X-inefficiency), whether output is at an optimal level (allocative efficiency), or whether resources are being wasted in protecting a particular, normally legal monopoly, market position (the so-called 'Tullock rent-seeking inefficiency').

We take the example of an airport and an airline and look at the potential implications for these various forms of efficiency when there are different market structures. The interest is in how actors seek to acquire rent (or profit) when there is no genuine capacity problem; in other words, when they can exercise market power. Figure 5.13 represents, for simplicity, the short-run costs (MC) and demand (D) for take-off slots associated with a single-runway airport. For ease of presentation the demand curve is drawn as linear, and the cost curve is horizontal. In most natural monopolies, because of various scale and scope economies, the cost curves would almost certainly be downward-sloping. Introducing this, however, while more realistic, adds complexity but not substance to the argument.

There is assumed to be adequate capacity to meet all effective demand currently in the market. If there were a binding physical capacity constraint at a level before QC, as strict classical theory would require, then the MC curve would become vertical at the point where capacity is reached. This does not affect the fundamental tenure of the rent-seeking argument as presented here, and is thus ignored. But in these circumstances, charges become a rationing device for the limited capacity and a reflection of the costs incurred in providing the existing capacity, as well as a means of extracting economic rent.

The issue is the simple one of the level and distribution of benefits from alternative allocating mechanisms assuming that only airlines and an airport

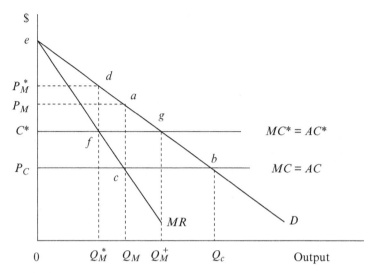

Figure 5.13   *Illustration of potential inefficiencies in a market for airport take-off/landing slots*

are involved. It is assumed, unless stated otherwise, that both the airlines and the airport are seeking to be economic rent maximizers. This may be a strong assumption for those in public ownership where there may be valid arguments for considering other possibilities such as 'satisficing' with a series of lower objectives being sought, but it does provide the ability to keep the analysis manageable.

The ultimate outcome will depend on the nature of the market and the power of buyers and sellers:

- *Competitive airlines/competitive airport.* This yields the standard Pareto first-best outcome of a price of P_C and an output of Q_C. The combined rent of buyers and sellers is maximized as the area ebP_C in Figure 5.13. The airlines enjoy the economic surplus from the use of the airport in this case because of the horizontal nature of the cost curve; with a positive slope the airport would also enjoy some rent, but with a negative slope it would be losing money. The same outcome in terms of overall slot use would emerge if the airport were a monopoly that is regulated, requiring it to marginal cost price its slots or allocate them using a Vickrey style of auction. The highest bidder wins but pays an amount equal to the second-highest bidder, although here the airport would extract the rents from the airlines.
- *Monopoly airline (or strong strategic alliance)/competitive airport.* Since the airport has no market power, the airline, or cartel of airlines, will be able to force it to price its slots down to the airport's marginal cost of providing the slots, P_C. The airlines will again gain the economic rents, again ebP_C.
- *Competitive airlines/single-pricing natural monopoly airport.* This is the traditional neoclassical case of a monopoly with slot prices reaching P_M and the number of slots limited by the airport to Q_M. The gains from the

airport's activities are shared between the airlines (eP_Ma) and the airport (P_MacP_C). But there is a welfare loss equal to the area abc – the Harberger (1959) 'deadweight loss triangle'. This is the sort of institutional structure that one could imagine under a regime where the airport sets its slot prices at P_M and then allows any airline to take up slots at this rate with subsequent slot-swapping allowed. If, once the slot fees have been paid, the airlines can buy and sell slots, then there would be transfers of benefits between them to the extent of aP_Cd with no effect on either the airport's rent or aggregate welfare.

- *Competitive airlines/single pricing institutionalized monopoly airport.* Here, the price and output combination is the same as the above, but the airport will potentially enjoy a smaller rent and overall social welfare will be less. There is likely to be rent dissipation in this type of situation. The airport, to retain its institutional monopoly, will be willing to expend up to P_MacP_C in potential economic rent to defend this position – for example, through lobbying, political support, advertising, or legal actions. Even a small amount of rent is preferred to none. Since such actions are essentially non-productive, at least in a non-Keynesian world, not only does it cost the airport money but it also represents a loss of social welfare.

- *Competitive airlines/perfect price discriminating natural monopoly airport.* In this case, through such actions as the auctioning of individual slots in a manner that allows first-degree price discrimination, the airport can extract slot prices down the demand curve. This action produces for the airport economic rent of ebP_C with the airlines having none. The outcome is Pareto efficient and maximizes welfare. *De facto* this means that the demand curve represents the airport's marginal revenue curve with price differentiation. The outcome is Pareto optimal.

- *Competitive airlines/single natural monopoly airport with X-inefficiency.* Harvey Leibenstein (1966) argued that monopolies have limited incentive to minimize their costs but rather they often operate in an 'inert area' where there is little pressure to seek maximum efficiency. (Figure 5.14 illustrates the notion of an inert area. Managers can make trade-offs between the profits they may make by affecting costs and the efforts they put into the business. The additional profits tend to taper away with additional effort because more problems are encountered. At some point, E^*, the additional effort ($E_{Op} - E^*$) is just not seen to justify the additional profit of ($\Pi_{Max} - \Pi$) required to maximize profits. Hence costs are not minimized.) This inertia may be brought on by a variety of factors such as the considerable managerial effort required to negotiate labor contracts when confronted by labor union demands. If this is the case then the cost curve will rise to MC^* in Figure 5.13 and the single profit-maximizing monopolist will limit the supply of slots to Q^*_M and extract rent amounting to $P^*_MdfC^*$ The airlines will be left with edP^*_M.

- *Competitive airlines/perfect price discriminating natural monopoly airport with X-inefficiency.* The situation here is that the airport will provide Q^+_M and

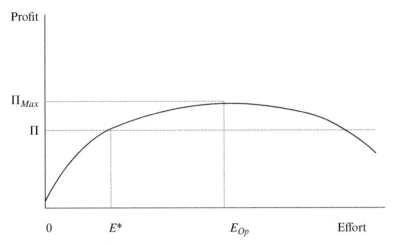

Figure 5.14   *The notion of inert areas*

enjoy economic rents of egC^*, with the airlines taking none. Compared with the single-pricing monopoly situation where there is no X-inefficiency, the aggregate social welfare is, however, reduced by P_Magc^*.

This categorization does not consider all possibilities – for example, there is no consideration of X-inefficiency among the airlines or of collusion between the parties, but it does indicate the importance of the institutional, as well as technical, characteristics affecting efficiency in determining the levels of profits generated and the recipients of this rent.

5.9   Costs and the Measurement of Economic Efficiency

One can consider whether a transport undertaking is efficient, or whether its efficiency changes over time, by looking at either the costs of producing its outputs, which is the way we have discussed the subject so far, or the output that is generated from the inputs used: productivity. These measures are mirror images of each other. Cost functions relate costs to output quantities and input prices; production functions relate output quantities to input quantities.

Productivity improvement can come about in several ways. It could reflect reductions in inefficiency using existing technology, a shift in technological knowledge and capabilities, and/or differences in environmental or operating circumstances that affect input/output use. An example of the latter is a transport firm operating in adverse terrain. It will require more inputs per tonne of cargo moved than firms operating in easy terrain; this is separate from questions of technological prowess. The concept of productivity of greatest importance is often that of technological change or 'shifts' in productive abilities. Improving efficiency using existing knowledge will encounter limits. Major long-term advances in industries and society's wealth are caused by changes in productive abilities.

Returning to the strict cost side of the equation, the traditional method of assessing whether an undertaking is efficient was to rely on accountancy procedures that involved compiling data in relation to the various cost categories of interest and connecting these to the firm's outputs in a largely intuitive manner, generally assuming a linear relationship between the various costs and outputs. While useful for short-term decision-making, the technique lacks any explicit causal link between inputs and outputs, which limits its usefulness for long-term decision-making.

Separating the impacts of fixed and variable costs is particularly problematic. In the transport context, a somewhat more advanced accountancy framework is described by Ken Small and takes the form:

$$C = c_1 RM + c_1 PV + c_1 VH + c_1 VM \tag{5.7}$$

where:

RM is route-miles;
PV is peak vehicles in service;
VH is vehicle-hours; and
VM is vehicle-miles.

The accounts imply constant returns to scale, with total costs (C) increasing by the same factor (c_1) as any common increase across all the right-hand-side variables. If, however, RM is kept fixed and the other factors increase by a common factor, then the increase in costs will be less than this, implying economies of density.

There are two broad approaches to quantitative performance ratings that are now more widely used than accountancy measures. The first are statistical or econometric estimations of production or cost functions and the second are non-parametric or programming approaches. Before looking at these in detail, there is also a more basic productivity indicator that entails 'benchmarking'. This is a generic concept referring to a process of identifying similar organizations or production activities, gathering quantitative and impressionistic data about the similarities and differences across the enterprises, and drawing conclusions about which are the most effective, and hence what other enterprises can learn from them. This may include quantitative performance comparisons but is not restricted to that. It often includes management organizational structures and practices. We do not discuss this in detail, but it is often used in practice (for example, by EUROCONTROL, the body overseeing European air traffic control, when comparing the efficiency of individual centers) and focuses on the more rigorous econometric and program approaches.

Statistical Cost and Production Functions

Statistical functions, with parameters normally estimated using regression analysis, are much more widely used in economic analysis. A statistical production function relates output to levels of inputs, but because it is difficult to estimate a production function when firms produce more than one output, cost function approaches have been developed based on duality theory. A cost function is the dual to production technology in that it translates in a one-to-one fashion. The cost function can also be applied to multiple-output situations. Duality theory also recognizes that input prices replace the need for explicit measurement of input quantities. A cost function specifies the minimum cost of producing a given output obtainable from an input vector given the production technology, that is:

$$C = C(w, y, t) \tag{5.8}$$

where:

C is the cost;
w is a vector of input prices;
y is a vector of outputs; and
t is the state of technology. (The production function approach relates outputs to inputs.)

Because the estimation involves the costing of producing, y, given the input vector, there is also the need to specify the motivations of the transport supplier and the technical relationship between the inputs and outputs involved. Traditional econometric methods for estimating cost or production functions implicitly assume that all firms are successful in reaching the efficient frontier, and deviate only randomly. If, however, firms are not always on the frontier, then the conventional estimation method would not reflect the efficient production or cost frontier against which to measure efficiency. For this reason, many studies now estimate frontier production or cost functions which recognize that some firms may not be on the efficient frontier. The reasons for this we explore in more detail in Chapter 6.

Logarithmically differentiating the cost function with respect to time decomposes the rate of growth of total cost into its sources: changes in input prices, growth of output, and rates of cost reduction due to technical progress:

$$\frac{\partial \ln C}{\partial t} = \left(\sum_{n=1}^{N} \frac{\partial \ln C}{\partial \ln w_n} \frac{\partial \ln w_n}{\partial t} \right) + \left(\frac{\partial \ln C}{\partial \ln y} \frac{\partial \ln y}{\partial t} \right) + \left(\frac{\partial \ln C}{\partial t} \right) \tag{5.9}$$

The rate of technical progress equals the negative of the rate of growth of total cost with respect to time, holding output and input prices constant. In a regression, this is the parameter measuring the shift in the cost function over time. When it comes to introducing technology into estimations, the accountancy approach, as seen in equation (5.7), assumes a linear relationship between inputs and outputs, often referred to as a Leontief technology. This means that there is no possibility of substituting one input for another in the production process.

The Cobb–Douglas cost function, while being limited by having constant returns to scale, has been widely used in transport studies; for example, historically in the analysis of economies of scale in the British bus industry by Lee and Steedman (1970), and American railroads by Keeler (1974). It has the advantage that it does allow some factor substitution in production, and it is relatively easy to estimate the coefficients in the model using regression techniques when expressed in natural logarithms. Its general form is:

$$\ln C = \beta_0 \sum_i \beta_i \ln y_i + \sum_j \gamma_j \ln w_j \qquad (5.10)$$

where i denotes the inputs and j the outputs.

There may be systematic differences between firms otherwise employing the same technology, for example, differences in terrain or market location. Network variables could allow for differences in terrain, weather, or exogenous characteristics of the market area served, such as more favorable directional flows of cargo and/or shorter average lengths of haul. Firm dummy variables (which by taking the value of unity or zero distinguish whether a firm is in a specific grouping or not) and firm-specific trend variables are sometimes incorporated to measure differences in productive efficiency across firms and over time. By controlling for these factors, the estimate with respect to time is a measure of the rate of technical change, that is, how the cost function is shifting over time. Bitzan and Keeler (2003) further separated out specific productivity changes (reduction in crew size and elimination of caboose) and show that there were sustained productivity gains in addition to the specific advances after railroad deregulation in the United States.

A major constraint in using stochastic frontiers such as the Cobb–Douglas specification (and others such as the constant elasticity of substitution model) is the need to specify the detailed form of relationship between inputs and outputs. Additionally, none provides functions akin to the 'U-shaped' functions that are the norm in economics as initially costs fall with production but ultimately rise as inputs become scarcer and thus more expensive. To circumvent this problem, variable 'flexible' forms of function have been developed. Perhaps the one most widely used in transport analysis is the translog model. This takes the general form in the case of total cost of:

$$\ln C = \beta_0 \sum_i \beta_i \ln y_i + \sum_j \gamma_j \ln w_j + \sum_i \sum_j \delta_{ij} \ln w_j \ln y_j \qquad (5.11)$$

$$+ 0.5 \sum_i \sum_k e_{ik} \ln y_i \ln y_k + 0.5 \sum_j \sum_l \Phi_{jl} \ln w_j \ln w_l$$

with the following cost share equations also being required:

$$S_j = \frac{\delta \ln C}{\delta \ln w_j} = \gamma_j + \sum_i \delta_{ij} \ln y_i + \sum_l \Phi_{il} \ln w_l$$

The flexible form approach does not need any prior specification of technology; it emerges from the estimation process. For example, in early work using the framework, Allen and Liu (1995) found that traditional ideas that American trucking was characterized by constant were incorrect and that results using a translog model showed they enjoyed increasing returns to scale; and Anne Friedlander (1993), by holding capital inputs constant, found increasing returns to density on the United States railroads, as did Caves et al. (1984) for airlines and Singh (2005) for Indian urban buses.

The usual emphasis in cost function estimation is on the overall results, that is, the parameter values such as the degree of scale economies and measure of technological change. These are based on the common relationship revealed by statistical estimation across the set of firms and years. For performance comparisons, one also looks at individual firms relative to the estimated cost function. In estimating a cost function from combined cross-sections of firms and time-series data, it is common to include firm- and time-specific variables to remove the mean effect of systematic departures from the industry norm of firms or years. This is done to correct for possible omitted variables in the regression. For example, a trucking firm might enjoy unusually low costs because of some overlooked network advantage – perhaps the cities it serves are closer together than those for other firms. The cost and output data for this firm could distort the coefficients being estimated across the industry.

This practice, though, can sometimes prove to be counterproductive. Expressed as a 'fixed effects model', dummy variables are used to remove the mean deviation of the firm's observations from the common regression estimate. The firm in question may, however, be the largest in the industry. It might be scale economies explaining the firm's superior performance, and one would want to have left the firm's data unadjusted precisely to help measure scale economies. In terms of productivity comparisons, the firm dummies are capturing some of what is being sought: how does the firm compare to others? If it has systematically lower costs and this cannot be explained by known variables, the residual may be taken as an indicator of managerial performance. The value of a firm-specific dummy variable could be a performance indicator, but again, it could be that there are other factors explaining the firm's apparently superior performance. It is, therefore, important to examine the deviations of firms and years to see if there are possible explanations that need to be taken into account.

The total cost function formulation assumes that firms adjust all inputs instantaneously as outputs change. However, they may not be able to adjust them all (especially capital stocks) as outputs change. To account for the short-run disequilibrium adjustment in capital stock, Gillen et al. (1990) in their work on airlines, and others, estimate variable cost functions, in which capital stock is treated as a fixed input, that is, the capital stock enters the cost function rather than the service price of capital. Separating out the influence of capital stocks and capital utilization is an important element in productivity studies, that is, distinguishing between productivity gains from capital investment or increased utilization of capital, as distinct from actual shifts in the function (technological change).

Productivity and cost measures, irrespective of the way they are derived, assume that the quality of service provided is constant. This is a long-recognized shortcoming of most productivity measures, and the criticism remains. In the absence of acceptable quality measures, productivity measurement is biased because it measures quantity changes but not quality. Improving quality absorbs inputs, but the higher-quality output is not recognized except partially by a shift in weights if prices for higher-quality services rise relative to others. The inability to incorporate service quality is a major weakness of productivity measures.

An issue related to quality is capital utilization. If the flow of capital services is measured as strictly proportional to capital stocks (that is, the capital depreciates with the passage of time rather than actual use), then productivity gains can be obtained via higher utilization of the fixed or indivisible capital stocks. But high utilization of capital may be accompanied by deteriorating service such as congestion delays. Insofar as the deterioration of service is manifested by increases in the use of other inputs, this will off-set the seeming productivity gain. But if congestion manifests itself in decreased service quality, standard productivity measures do not capture this. High utilization rates of capital may thus appear to imply high productivity, but this might, in part, be misleading if there is deterioration in unmeasured service quality.

Programming Measurements

Management programming methods directly compare quantities of outputs with quantities of inputs. The most widely used is data envelopment analysis (DEA), which is a mathematical programming technique that generates quantitative relative performance scores across 'decision-making units' such as bus companies or shipping lines, where multiple outputs and inputs are involved but there is no basis for assigning relative weights to the various inputs and outputs. Index numbers compare the growth in aggregate output to the corresponding changes in aggregate inputs. The aggregates are weighted sums of the growth rates of respective outputs and inputs, with economic weights (for example, revenues and costs) assigned to the outputs and inputs.

Programming measures of efficiency involve index number procedures that construct a ratio-type productivity/efficiency measure from measures of outputs and inputs. They are non-parametric; that is, they are a direct numerical calculation, in contrast to the statistical estimation used in the production econometric cost function approach. They may take several forms, including partial productivity ratios, such as DEA, and total factor productivity (TFP). Once a measure of productivity is developed, it can be 'decomposed' into sources of productivity gains to isolate pure technological change in contrast to other influences on productivity, such as X-inefficiency.

Partial productivity measures relate a firm's output to a single input factor such as revenue tonne-kilometers divided by the number of employees to measure labor productivity. This is tracked over time or compared with other companies or operations. However, the productivity of any one input depends on the level of other inputs being used; high productivity performance in one input may come at the expense of low productivity of other inputs. Despite this limitation, partial productivity measures remain in wide use, and can provide useful insights into causes of differential performance across firms operating in similar operating environments or over time within a firm when the operating environment and input prices remain relatively stable.

DEA becomes useful when firms employ several inputs and generally produce numerous outputs. It can be used for ranking the relative efficiency of decision-making units, say different urban bus fleets or airports, in this context. With multiple outputs and inputs, weights are usually needed to aggregate the various output and input categories to construct an index to rate different units. DEA uses linear programming to solve for a set of weights that will maximize each unit's or firm's performance rating relative to others in the dataset. In its most basic form, we can take a case where W and Z are the inputs in an airline-wide sample of n carriers and w and z are the corresponding observations of a typical airline. The airline's efficiency index, Θ, assuming free disposability and variable returns to scale, is the solution to the linear program:

Choose $\{\Theta, \lambda\}$ to: min Θ such that: $\Theta w \geq \lambda' W$

$$z \leq \lambda' Z$$

$$\lambda_i \geq 0, \Sigma \lambda_i = 1, i = 1, 2, ..., n \qquad (5.12)$$

An illustration is seen in Figure 5.15, which depicts production, rather than cost, frontiers. We consider the efficiency with which several bus companies with identical vehicle fleets use their labor input to provide peak (X) and off-peak (Y) services. The black dots represent the combinations of peak and off-peak passenger seat-miles each operator provides. Those enterprises on the 'old frontier' are deemed to be the most efficient users of their labor over the two periods, although no judgment can be made about whether company M, which offers a relatively large amount of peak services is preferable to N, which focuses on using its labor for off-peak services. To make that judgment one needs to know the demands for the different types of services. The filled stars indicate what may happen to the frontier over time as technology improves.

DEA can be a useful procedure for establishing relative performance scores where multiple outputs and inputs are present yet their relative importance (weights) are not evident. But it has its limitations. While other suppliers inside the frontier are relatively inefficient, being on the frontier does not imply maximum efficiency; all the companies may be inefficient but differ in their degrees of inefficiency. There are methods of measuring the extent to which suppliers fall behind those on the frontier, but these may be sensitive to the ways in which measurements are made; for example, is the measurement the vertical distance from the frontier, the horizontal distance, or some average of the two? The results are also sensitive to outliers. The shape of the frontier can differ considerably if there is, say, one supplier that is well away from the remainder. This can be seen in Figure 5.15 if instead of producer K in the second period being located

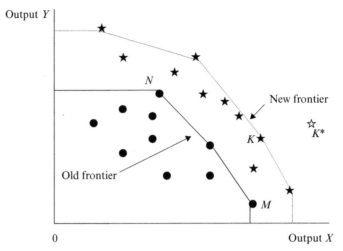

Notes: • denotes performance of firms in the first period; ★ denotes performance of firms in the second period.

Figure 5.15 *Production frontier for two outputs, observed at two different time periods*

as indicated, it is located at *K**. Finally, the technique does not in itself allow for any assessment of causality: it basically provides a ranking mechanism indicating levels of cost (or production efficiency), offering insights as to the underlying causes of the differences between suppliers.

Given the availability of easy-to-use software, there are numerous examples of applications of DEA in transport, for example Bookbinder and Qu (1993) who calculated DEA scores for seven large North American railroads and explored the effects of different numbers of outputs and inputs as well as reducing the number of firms. Another case study is by Oum and Yu (1994), who analysed OECD railways for the period from 1978 to 1989, employing two types of output measure and evaluating and interpreting the relative efficiency scores. Button and Costa (1999) examined the efficiency of local transport in several European cities, and Fare et al. (2007) looked at airlines, just to provide a few examples. Some studies have used both parametric and non-parametric techniques to confirm their findings, as, for example, did Good et al. (1965) when comparing the efficiency of European and United States airlines.

References

Allen, W.B and Liu, D. (1995) Service quality and motor carrier costs: an empirical analysis, *Review of Economics and Statistics*, 77, 499–510.

Baker, S.H. and Pratt, J.B. (1989) Experience as a barrier to contestability in airline markets, *Review of Economics and Statistics*, 81, 352–6.

Berechman, J. (1983) Costs, economies of scale and factor demand in road transport, *Journal of Transport Economics and Policy*, 17, 7–24.

Bitzan, J.D. and Keeler, T.E. (2003) Productivity growth and some of its determinants in the deregulated U.S. railroad industry, *Southern Economic Journal*, 70, 232–53.

Bookbinder, J.H. and Qu, W.W. (1993) Comparing the performance of major American railroads, *Transportation Research Form*, 33, 70–85.

Bowman, A. (2015) An illusion of success: the consequences of British rail privatization, *Accounting Forum*, 39, 51–63.

Brown R.H. and Nash, C.A. (1972) Cost savings from one-man operations of buses, *Journal of Transport Economics and Policy*, 6, 281–4.

Button, K.J. (2016) Public–private partnerships: a review of economic considerations with particular reference to transportation projects, *Transportation Planning and Technology*, 39, 136–61.

Button, K.J. and Costa, A. (1999) Economic efficiency gains from urban public transport regulatory reform: two case studies of changes in Europe, *Annals of Regional Science*, 33, 425–38.

Button, K.J. and O'Donnell, K. (1985) An examination of the cost structures associated with providing urban bus services in Britain, *Scottish Journal of Political Economy*, 32, 67–81.

Caves, D.W., Laurits, R., and Tretheway, M.W. (1984) Economies of density versus economies of scale: why trunk and local airline costs differ, *Rand Journal of Economics*, 15, 471–89.

Dodgson, J.S. (1984) Railway costs and closures, *Journal of Transport Economics and Policy*, 18, 219–36.

Edwards, S.L. and Bayliss, B.T. (1971) Operating costs in road freight transport, Report, UK Department of the Environment.

European Union (1998) Fair payment for infrastructure use: a phased approach in a common transport infrastructure charging framework in the EU, White Paper, Com(96)466.

Fare, R., Grosskopf, S., and Sickles, R.C. (2007) Productivity of US airlines after deregulation, *Journal of Transport Economics and Policy*, 41, 93–112.

Foster, C. and Golay, J. (1986) Some curious old practices and their relevance to equilibrium in bus competition, *Journal of Transport Economics and Policy*, 20, 191–216.

Foster, C.D. and Joy, S. (1967) Railway track costs in Britain, Report, *Development of Railway Traffic Engineering*, Institution of Civil Engineers.

Friedlander, A. (1993) Rail costs and capital adjustment in a quasi-regulated environment, *Journal of Transport Economics and Policy*, 24, 9–34.

Gillen, D.W., Oum, T.H., and Tretheway, M.W. (1990) Airline cost structure and policy implications, *Journal of Transport Economics and Policy*, 24, 9–34.

Good, H., Röller, R.D., and Sickles, R.C. (1965) Airline efficiency differences between Europe and the US: implications for the pace of EC integration and domestic regulation, *European Journal of Operations Research*, 80, 508–18.

Goodwin, P.B. (1974) Generalized time and the problem of equity in transport studies, *Transportation*, 3, 1–24.

Hadley, T. (1885) *Railroad Transportation: Its History and its Laws*, G.P. Putnams.

Harberger, G. (1959) Using the resources at hand more effectively, *American Economic Review*, 59, 134–47.

Heaver, T.D. (1975) The routing of Canadian container traffic through Vancouver and Seattle, Report, WESTMAC.

Hotelling, H. (1929) Stability in competition, *Economic Journal*, 39, 41–57.

Johnston, A. and Ozment, J. (2013) Economies of scale in the US airline industry, *Transportation Research Part E*, 51, 95–108.

Joy, S. (1973) *The Train that Ran Away*, Ian Allan.

Karlaftis, M. and McCarthy, P. (1999) The effect of privatization on public transit costs, *Journal of Regulatory Economics*, 16, 27–44.

Keeler, T.E. (1974) Railroad costs, returns to scale, and excess capacity, *Review of Economics and Statistics*, 56, 201–208.

Keeler, T.E. and Small, K.A. (1977) Optimal peak-load pricing investment and service levels on urban expressways, *Journal of Political Economy*, 85, 1–25.

Koshal, R.K. (1970) Economies of scale in bus transport II: some Indian experiences, *Journal of Transport Economics and Policy*, 4, 29–36.

Lee, N. and Steedman, I.W. (1970) Economies of scale in bus transport I: some British municipal results, *Journal of Transport Economics and Policy,* 4, 15–28.

Leibenstein, H. (1966) Allocative efficiency vs 'X-efficiency', *American Economic Review*, 56, 392–415.

McIntosh, P.T. and Quarmby, D.A. (1972) Generalized costs and the estimation of movement costs and benefits in transport planning, *Highway Research Record*, 383, 11–23.

Meyer, J.R. (1958) Some methodological aspects of statistical costing as illustrated by the determination of rail passenger rates, *American Economic Review*, 48, 209–22.

Mohring, H. (1976) *Transportation Economics*, Ballinger.

Nash, C.A. (1979) The track costs issue: a comment, *Journal of Transport Economics and Policy*, 14, 113–16.

Neuberger, N.L.I. (1971) Perceived costs, *Environment and Planning*, 3, 369–76.

Nythi, M., Hooper, P., and Heusher, D. (1993) Compass Airline; 1 December 1990 to 20 December 1991 – what went wrong? *Transport Reviews*, 13, 112–49 and 185–206.

Oum, T.H. and Yu, C. (1994) Economic efficiency of railways and implications for public policy: a comparative study of the OECD countries' railways, *Journal of Transport Economics and Policy*, 28, 121–38.

Poole, E.C. (1962) *Costs: A Toll for Railroad Management*, Simmons-Bordman.

Singh, K. (2005) Costs, economies of scale, in urban bus transport: an analysis of municipal undertakings in India, *International Journal of Transport Economics*, 32, 171–94.

Small, K.A., Winston, C., and Evans, C.A. (1989) *Road Work: A New Highway Pricing and Investment Policy*, Brookings Institution.

Stopford, M. (2009) *Maritime Economics*, Routledge.

Tanner, J.C. (1968) An economic comparison of motorways with 2 or 3 lanes in each direction, Road and Research Laboratory Report LR.203.

Taussig, F.W. (1891) A contribution to the theory of railway rates, *Quarterly Journal of Economics*, 5, 438–65.

Teal, R.F., Marks, J.V., and Goodhue, R. (1980) Subsidized shared-ride taxi service, *Transportation Research Record*, 778, 25–32.

Tolifari, S., Button, K.J., and Pitfield, D. (1986) Shipping costs and the controversy over open registry, *Journal of Industrial Economics*, 34, 409–27.

UK Department of Transport (1980) Report of the inquiry into lorries, people and the environment, HMSO.

UK Department of Transport (1989) The allocation of road track costs 1989/91, Department of Transport.

UK Price Commission (1978) The road haulage industry, House of Commons Paper HC 698, HMSO.

Wabe, J.S. and Coles, O.B. (1975) The peak and off-peak demand for bus transport: a cross-sectional analysis of British municipal operations, *Applied Economics*, 7, 25–30.

Wallis, I.P. (1980) Private bus operations in urban areas: their economics and role, *Traffic Engineering and Control,* 22, 605–10.

Walters, A.A. (1968) *The Economics of Road User Charges*, Johns Hopkins University Press.

Warner, S.L. (1962) *Stochastic Choice of Mode in Urban Travel: A Study in Binary Choice*, Northwestern University Press.

Williams, M. (1981) The economic justification for local bus transport subsidies, *International Journal of Transport Economics*, 8, 79–88.

Wilson, A.G., Hawkins, A.F., Hills, G.J., and Wagon, D.J. (1969) Calibration and testing of the SELNEC transport model, *Regional Studies*, 3(3), 337–50.

Winston, C. (1985) Conceptual developments in the economics of transportation: a *Journal of Transportation* interpretive survey, *Journal of Economic Literature*, 23, 57–94.

Zhang, L., Chen, F., Ma, X., and Pan, X. (2020) Fuel economy in truck platooning: a literature overview and directions for future research, *Journal of Advanced Transportation*, 2020, 2604012.

6 The External Economic Costs of Transport

· ·

6.1 Introduction

Chapter 5 was concerned with showing the types of financial costs directly confronting transport users and those providing transport services. It is clear from our everyday experience, however, that there are other costs associated with transport that are not directly borne by those generating them. Some affect those not traveling, such as when air travelers impose noise costs on those living below aircraft flight paths, and when road travelers inflict dirt and vibration on those living adjacent to major trunk routes while, at the same time, impeding the progress of pedestrians in towns. Maritime transport frequently pollutes bathing beaches with their oil discharges, and the construction of ports disrupts local breeding grounds for birds and sea life.

These are often seen as issues associated with mechanized transport, and especially automobiles and trucks. But this has, albeit on a different scale and in different forms, been an issue back into antiquity. In Roman times, road traffic was limited at night in cities because of noise nuisance, in the middle ages and later river flows were used to 'transport' dung and excrement, as well as offal and other waste products, away from cities. Draft animals were the cars and trucks of the time, and they left their mark on urban streets and on the 'fragrances' in the air.

These are external costs generated by transport users. They are inflicted on the non-traveling public, often those living nearby, but in the case of global warming emissions the victims may be thousands of miles away. They are now at the forefront not only of transportation debates but more generally as societies have become more concerned with quality of life and the larger issue of climate change.

But they are not the only form of negative externality. There is also traffic congestion. A car entering a congested stream of traffic slows other cars already in the traffic, an effect external to the driver but different from environmental effects in that the cost is contained within transport – strictly, it is a 'club bad'.

This chapter focuses initially on the former type of external effect – the imposition of uncompensated effects created by transport users on the general public or some part of it – and then moves on to look at the challenges imposed by various forms of traffic congestion. The latter being about managing the internal workings of the transport system more effectively by optimizing the external costs one set of users imposes upon another. But we begin with some definitions and some clarifications.

6.2 Externalities

Formally, in economics externalities exist when the activities of one group (either consumers or producers) affect the welfare of another group (consumers or producers) without any payment or compensation being made. They may be thought of as relationships other than those between a buyer and a seller, and do not normally fall within the 'measuring rod of money' or within a complete market.

There are also external benefits as well as costs, although these are generally thought less important in the transport sector. In the context of transport, wide streets often act as fire-breaks in addition to serving as transport arteries, and this may be thought of as an external benefit associated with urban motorways. Likewise, the drainage effects of canals are often an external benefit for agriculture. One reason why external benefits are less common than their negative counterparts is that there is an incentive for those producing them to bring them into the market and charge for them. A simple example of this may be when railway enthusiasts (often called 'foamers' in the United States and 'grisers' in the United Kingdom) enjoyed standing on railway platforms watching trains – a benefit generated by the railway company and enjoyed free by the enthusiasts. There are now often charges, however, for accessing platforms simply to view.

A vast theoretical literature has grown up since the Second World War, refining the rather complicated concept of external costs. There are, for example, often confusions between externalities and such things as public goods, which we return to later. While much of the detail of this work has a greater or lesser importance in a transport context, there are two major distinctions that need to be highlighted.

Pecuniary and Technological Externalities

The formal difference between these two categories of externality is that when the latter effects occur in production (or consumption) they must appear in the production (or utility) function, while this is not the case with pecuniary externalities. Pecuniary effects occur when, say, a firm's costs are affected by price changes induced by other firms' actions in buying and selling factors of production. An example can help to clarify this. A new motorway may block or destroy a pleasant view formerly enjoyed by the residents of an area. The fact that this directly enters the residents' utility function means that if no compensation is paid, this is a technological externality. If this new motorway also takes business away from a local garage and transfers it to a new motorway service station, then the reduced income suffered by the garage proprietor is a pecuniary externality since the effect is indirect, namely through changes in the prices charged by the two undertakings.

The distinction is a fine one – particularly since in practice both forms of externality usually occur simultaneously – but it is an important one. Technological externalities are real resource costs that strictly should be taken into account in decision-making if optimal efficiency is to be ensured. Pecuniary externalities do not involve resource costs in an aggregate sense, but they do normally have important distributional implications (in our motorway example, the service station gains while the local garage loses).

The fact that there may be pecuniary externalities associated with a project does not reduce the aggregate net benefit, but, rather, reveals that there are adjustments in the economy which influence who is to enjoy the gains and who is to suffer the costs. The distinction between technological and pecuniary externalities is, therefore, important in the appraisal of public sector transport investments where one is concerned with the incidence of the costs and benefits in addition to their overall level (see Chapter 11). The pecuniary external effects can, for example, raise matters of environmental justice (Haynes, 2004).

The Distinction Between Pollution and Congestion

Conventional welfare economics distinguishes between varieties of externality categories according to the different types of agents involved. Jerome Rothenberg (1970) offers a simple dichotomy that is possibly of more use in the transport context than some of the more complicated categorizations that have emerged subsequently. He distinguishes between two forms of what he calls 'generic congestion'. The underlying idea is that externalities result from attempts by different agents to share a common service that is not provided in discrete units earmarked for each (in a technical sense, it has 'public good' characteristics). The presence of other users already affects the quality of service that is rendered to each. Generic congestion may, in technical terms, be divided into:

*   *Pure pollution.* 'The essence of pollution … is that there are some other users who do abuse the medium – the polluters – while others are relatively passive victims of such abuse – the public. Jet planes make the noise, housewives are forced to submit to it'.
*   *Pure congestion.* 'If highway traffic is the classic example of congestion, then the central inter-personal distributive fact about it is that all users are using the medium (the public good) in much the same way, each is damaging service quality for both others and himself, and the ratio of self/other damage is approximately the same for all users … The whole user group loses homogeneously by their self-imposed interaction'.

Another way of looking at externalities, and one developed by Alain Bonnafus (1994), is according to the domain they affect. The alternative typology is illustrated in Figure 6.1. Here we see a succession of overlapping spheres that address the question of 'external to what'? The innermost sphere is essentially the firm (which may be any producer of transport services, say a bus company or a shipping line, but may also be treated as a driver of a car supplying transport services to him or herself). The agent is the perpetrator of the externalities.

The second sphere reflects what are often called 'Marshallian externalities' and captures what we have termed pure congestion: a truck entering a congested road and slowing down others further. The third sphere reflects what Alain

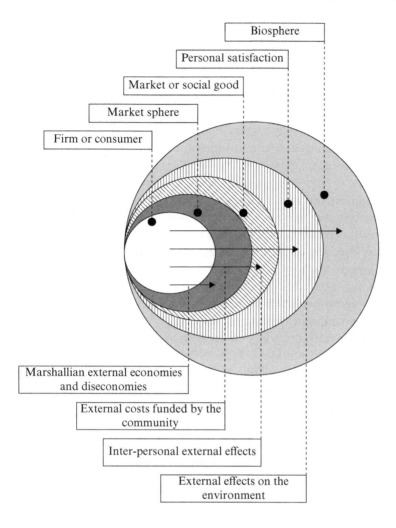

Figure 6.1   *The economic relationships between external effects*

Bonnafus sees as the external costs of a transport company paid for by the community. These are subsidies for operations and infrastructure maintenance not captured in user fees. The penultimate sphere reflects inter-personal external effects, such as lack of safety or noise. Finally, the outermost sphere embraces the quality of the larger, potentially global, environment that is affected by the emissions of the truck.

From an economic perspective, the advantage of this type of approach is that it provides an indication of where the market failings are in the broader scheme of things, and where the incidence of the external costs are being borne. The movement from conceptualization to practical valuation and analysis of alternative ways of dealing with the various forms of externality is, however, made no simpler. We do not, therefore, attempt to look at all the domains illustrated, but focus on those particularly relevant for transport, namely those involving pure pollution and pure congestion. We have already dealt with Marshallian externalities in Chapter 5.

6.3 Transport's Implications for the Environment

Transport pollutes the physical environment in several ways that can also be seen in a stylized manner in relation to their broad geographical and temporal incidence in Figure 6.2.

* It imposes many local environmental costs on those living, working, or taking recreation near major pieces of transport infrastructure. These include such factors as noise, visual intrusion, local air pollution (for example, particulates, lead, and carbon monoxide), and the disposal of obsolete vehicles. A major problem here is that, unlike many other forms of environmental intrusion, it is generally difficult to move transport facilities away from sensitive areas simply because users demand easy access and proximity to roads and to public transport terminals.
* There are trans-boundary effects such as emissions that contribute to acid rain (such as nitrogen oxides (NO_x)) and maritime spillages that have impacts some distance from the transport activities themselves. This poses challenges of inter-jurisdictional authority at the national level, and often within federal systems at the state level.
* There is the contribution of transport to the global environmental problems of global warming – such as emissions of carbon dioxide (CO_2) – and to upper-level ozone depletion – notably, chlorofluorocarbons (CFCs). As we see later in Chapter 8, these pose major challenges because of their long-term

Figure 6.2   *The time and spatial coverage of exhaust gases and other environmental intrusions*

effects and the need for coordinated, global approaches to handle them. Strictly, these CO_2 emissions are not pollution, CO_2 being a trace gas that appears in the atmosphere naturally with sources in groundwater, rivers and lakes, ice caps, glaciers, and seawater.

A very general indication of the contribution of transport to some of the atmospheric problems associated with light mechanized transport in the United States is offered in Table 6.1. Table 6.2 offers a similar breakdown for the United Kingdom, although covering all transport modes in this case. It is noticeable that many of the pollutants are becoming less of a problem per mile traveled, but of course, transport use is growing and partly off-sets this.

Many environmentalist groups argue for substantial reductions or total elimination of these adverse environmental effects, but this ignores the cost associated with removing such nuisances. While some people suffer from the environmental intrusion associated with transport, others clearly benefit from being able to travel more freely or move goods more cheaply. In almost all cases environmental improvements would reduce the net benefits enjoyed by transport

Table 6.1   *United States light gasoline and diesel vehicle exhaust emissions rates (grams per mile)*

	2000	2005	2010	2015	2018
Light-duty gasoline vehicles					
Total HC	1.617	1.020	0.786	0.499	0.350
Exhaust CO	16.028	9.759	7.121	4.898	3.941
Exhaust NO_X	1.681	1.079	0.901	0.518	0.289
Exhaust $PM_{2.5}$	0.037	0.023	0.017	0.011	0.008
Light-duty diesel vehicles					
Total HC	2.919	1.915	0.939	0.232	0.183
Exhaust CO	47.204	28.016	13.604	3.205	2.663
Exhaust NO_X	2.906	1.691	1.008	0.248	0.153
Exhaust $PM_{2.5}$	0.066	0.052	0.023	0.005	0.004

Source: US Bureau of Transportation Statistics.

Table 6.2   *Pollutants emissions from transport in the United Kingdom (thousand tonnes)*

	1995	2000	2005	Percent of national emissions in 2005
CO	4,180	2,500	1,124	46.5
NO_X	1,098	818	549	33.8
PM_{10}	53.6	38.6	33.7	22.5
Benzene	28.4	5.6	3.4	20.8
1,3 butadiene	7.4	3.8	1.6	60.8
Pb	1.049	2.2	2.1	1.7
SO_2	51.8	6.7	3.0	0.4

Source: UK Department for Transport.

users. Economists tend, therefore, to think in terms of optimizing the level of pollution rather than 'purifying' the environment entirely.

If we look at Figure 6.3, we see plotted on the vertical axis the money value of the costs and benefits of reducing the noxious fumes emitted by motorcars and, on the horizontal, the environmental improvements that accompany a reduction in such fumes. The marginal costs (MC) of reducing the emissions are likely to rise quite steeply. While more sophisticated filters may be fitted and fuel subjected to more extensive refining, both become increasingly costly to apply as the toxicity of the exhaust is reduced. Additionally, they reduce the efficiency of vehicles and may, in the case of improved refining, impose higher levels of pollution on those living around refineries.

The marginal benefits (MB) of 'cleaner' road vehicles, in contrast, are likely to fall with successive improvements. The public is likely to be relatively less conscious of lower levels of emission and be aware that many of the seriously toxic materials (for example, lead) are likely to be amongst the first to be removed in the clean-up program. Consequently, the marginal cost and revenue curves associated with improved emission quality are likely to be of the form seen in Figure 6.3.

There is quite clearly an optimal level of improvement (that is, $0E_1$), beyond which the marginal costs of further emission reductions exceed the marginal benefits. If the clean-up program reduced emissions to the point where further reductions would yield no additional benefit (that is, exhaust fumes would be considered 'pure', although this may not mean zero toxicity if individuals' perceptions are faulty), then the situation is not optimal. Improvements beyond $0E_1$ to $0E_2$, in fact, result in a net welfare loss equal to the shaded area ABE_2 in the diagram.

Consequently, when talking about the excessive environmental harm caused by various forms of transport it is important to remember that this is an excess above the optimal level of pollution, not above zero pollution or some perceived 'pure' environment. We return to this topic and methods of attaining the optimum in Chapter 8.

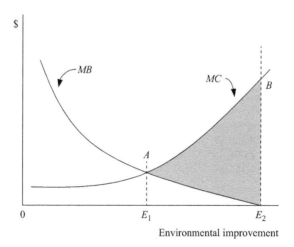

Figure 6.3   *The optimal environmental improvement*

6.4   The Valuation of Externalities

Physical measures of environmental damage are helpful, and a necessary input into analysing their economic implications, but the diversity of measurements used and impacts generated limit their usefulness. To compare the external costs and benefits of transport with other features of transport it is often found useful to convert such costs and benefits into monetary terms. This is no easy task but economists have developed several procedures that, at least in the case of some externalities, do provide reasonable guidance to the value of these external effects. In recent years the level of sophistication used in this process has risen considerably and only a very brief outline of some – the more common techniques – is set out below.

The various stages in valuation are seen in Figure 6.4. As can be seen, it is a sequential process embracing many disciplines beside economics; indeed, without good physical measurement and scientific understanding of the consequences of environmental intrusion, the economic analysis would not be possible. The immediate focus will be on the various techniques that go into 'monetization' of the various externalities, and in the following section we shall consider some of the empirical work that has been conducted.

Precedents

Consistency over time is the prime reason for suggesting that historical precedents could be used as a means of valuing certain aspects of the environment.

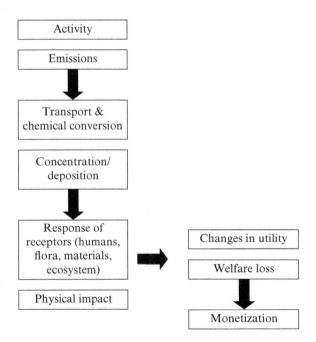

Figure 6.4   *The stages of putting a money value on an externality*

Precedents in this context largely comprise legal, judicial rulings on compensation for inflicting environmental damage. While having some superficial attractions, the procedure, however, has severe limitations.

The main applications of this approach in transport have been in terms of valuing injury and death in transport accidents although there are numerous instances of transport suppliers, and especially shipping companies, having to compensate for spillage of toxic pollutants and there are often rulings on compensation on such things as the additional noise nuisance associated with an airport expansion.

Precedents only exist where there are established rights and these extend to very few environmental attributes. Even without this practical limitation, the usefulness of the techniques is restricted by the nature of most legal systems. They normally apply to the need for victims (including relatives of people killed) of the incident to be cared for during the remainder of their lives. Consequently, where the environmental damage causes death, the 'cost' to the deceased is not considered. Equally, damage to flora and fauna is generally outside of the scope of legal rulings on compensation. Finally, where evidence has been produced looking at legal precedence, it tends to show little by way of a consistent pattern.

Averting Behavior

Many adverse environmental consequences of transport can be ameliorated by insulation. Noise nuisance can be reduced by double-glazing windows, the adverse effects of air pollution by installing air conditioning, and accident risk by the adoption of safer engineering design standards for transport infrastructure (for example, relating to road surfaces and air traffic control radar), the ways in which it may be used (for example, speed limits), and the design of the vehicles that use it (for example, air bags and seat belts in cars). A widely deployed technique for assessing the costs of environmental damage is to equate them with the cost of avoidance, often called the 'prevention expenditure' method.

The main problem is the difficulty of isolating specific expenditures made for environmental reasons from the implicit joint expenditure on other benefits accompanying, for example, double-glazing (such as reduced heating bills, etc.) or air conditioning (for example, a cooler room temperature). Noise insulation is also only partial in that it does not offer protection when in the garden or when windows are open. More fundamentally, there are questions about the optimality of the level of avoidance adopted. In terms of safety, for example, the aviation industry provides an extremely safe product but only at a tremendous cost. In terms of potential lives saved, each is implicitly valued more highly than, say, a life saved on the roads where the per capita safety expenditure is much lower.

This type of approach is the mirror image of looking at the environmental costs of lost production or the damage done in repairing the problems caused by environmental damage – for example, adding lime to water polluted by traffic-related NO_X emissions. The costs of pollution on health can be related to the days of work lost by, for example, more frequent asthma attacks due to fuel additives or from lack of sleep due to aircraft noise. Isolating these costs can be difficult; there is a need to make a full life assessment of their impacts on individuals or production.

Revealed Preference: Hedonic Prices

There are circumstances where consumers of environmental resources, through their actions, implicitly reveal the values that they place on them. They make trade-offs involving sacrificing some monetary benefits to limit the use of environmental resources, or to gain some environmental benefit. The classic case is the willingness of people to pay to live away from noisy airports or roads, or to pay a premium for a hotel room away from a busy street. But these choices, as we saw earlier with the discussion on generalized costs, also extend to travel time values that involve trade-offs between such things as external and internal attributes of modes and travel speeds.

The underlying theory can be discussed in terms of Figure 6.5, which plots the welfare enjoyed by an individual at various levels of wealth. The diminishing marginal utility of money gives, for example, the trade-off curve *I* for an individual living in a quiet, rural setting. The construction of an airport adjacent to the house imposes measurable noise costs on this person and, for every level of wealth, this pulls the trade-off curve down, that is, it becomes *II*. If the person was initially at a point *A* on *I* then the imposition of the noise will reduce welfare to level *B*. To get them back to their original welfare level, compensation of *BC* would be needed, this being sufficient to move the person around *II* until the original level of welfare was restored.

This approach assumes, however, that there is a finite level of compensation that satisfies the individual. If, however, one starts at an initial position *A**, then it is not altogether clear that this is so. This type of problem, for example, arose

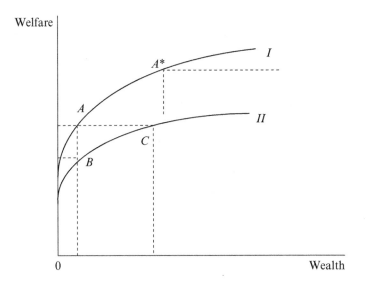

Figure 6.5   *The basic trade-off model*

as early as the late 1960s when the Roskill Commission in the United Kingdom was assessing sites for a Third London Airport and were trying to value the noise costs of aviation effects; eventually an arbitrary value was adopted for some individuals. Second, the onus of the technique as described above is on compensation. One would normally get a different value by taking the amount adversely affected individuals would be required to pay to bribe the authorities not to construct the airport (that is, the amount necessary to get back to the higher trade-off curve for the new level of welfare *B*).

In practical terms, revealed preference techniques normally require sophisticated econometric analysis. This is because most goods involve a variety of attributes of which environmental elements represent only a subset. In consequence, the normal approach is to use a hedonic price index that puts values on the diverse attributes of the good being examined (for example, the various features of houses in the noise case mentioned above). In general terms this means estimating:

$$C_h = F(c_1, c_2, c_3, \ldots, c_n) \tag{6.1}$$

where C_h is the consumption of housing services $c_1, c_2, c_3, \ldots, c_n$.

The specifications of individual models differ, indeed one of the problems with hedonic indices is that of model specification; but whatever form they take, they seek to isolate the 'price' of each characteristic in the equation.

Exhibit   *The economic costs of CO$_2$ emissions*

The social cost of carbon (SCC) is calculated using integrated assessment models (IAMs) of climate and the economy. Because of the longevity of many pollutants and the duration of their effects, the latter estimate the global damage resulting from greenhouse gas emissions over a century or more. They seek to capture the complex interplay between climate and the economy. Future climate damage is discounted to a current SCC value using a social discount rate.

Three widely used estimation model frameworks used to estimate the SCC of CO$_2$ are:

- The dynamic integrated climate change (DICE) model. This is essentially a neoclassical global economic growth model with CO$_2$ emissions treated as function of global GDP and the carbon intensity of economic activities, with the latter declining over time with technical progress. The damage function is calibrated on the sum of the damage to agriculture, coastal areas, energy use, health risk, recreation, cities, and the ecosystem. It assumes that climate damage increases more than linearly with temperature increases.

- The framework for uncertainty, negotiation, and distribution (FUND) model is a nine-region model of the world economy and its interactions with climate, running in time steps of one year from 1990 to 2200. It consists of scenarios for economy and population, which are perturbed by climate change and greenhouse gas emission reduction policy. Policy variables are energy and carbon efficiency improvement, and sequestering CO_2 in forests.

- The policy analysis of the greenhouse effect (PAGE) model uses simple equations to simulate the results from more complex specialized scientific and economic models. The damage caused by temperature increases includes economic and non-economic categories and are considered over eight regions. The model assesses lost output from global temperature changes.

Model	Study	SCC per ton CO_2 according to the study in the 2nd column	SCC per ton CO_2 according to the US Department of Energy ($ in 2010)
DICE	Nordhaus (2008)	$6[a]	$28
FUND	Anthoff et al. (2011)	$8[b]	$6
PAGE	Stern (2007)	$8[a]	$30
	Hope (2006)	$5[a]	–
	Hope (2013)	$106[b]	–

Notes: a. Value in 2000. b. Value in 2010.

Source: Van den Bergh and Botzen (2015). This paper contains the full references to the studies cited.

Studies using these methods have produced the results seen in the table. A higher SCC per ton indicates a greater gain from reducing carbon emissions at the margin. There is diversity between results even using the same method. The final column provides results from a US Department of Energy comparative study of the three models, using five emissions and socioeconomic scenarios, and assuming the same discount rate value of 3 percent. Each element in the column is average across the outcomes of the five scenarios.

Concerns have been expressed over the wide range of values of the SCC found not only across the three broad modeling frameworks, but also between studies using the same approach. Aside from differences in the technical modeling, there are also differences in the variables included and the discounts that are used. The functions used in the work do not handle 'tipping points' or extreme changes in climate well, nor do they allow for individual risk aversion to climate risk.

See also: J.C.J.M. van den Bergh and W.J.W. Botzen (2015) Monetary valuation of the social cost of CO_2 emissions: a critical survey, *Ecological Economics*, 114, 33–46.

This leads on to a further problem. It is necessary to have a substantial amount of information on the determinants of, in our example, housing selection processes just to gain an insight into the value of one environmental influence. Many hedonic studies employ a wide variety of variables. It is also important that the characteristics used are the ones perceived to be important to house occupiers and buyers: the perceived housing market attributes. It is not the actual set of characteristics that determine hedonic prices, but rather the characteristics as seen by those active in the housing market. This often leads to the implicit, but seldom accurate, assumption that all those in the market have complete information of all housing attributes. The assumption is also that all such attributes are sufficiently tangible and measurable to be incorporated into the econometric estimation.

Travel Cost Method

The travel cost method is a particular form of revealed preference analysis. New transport infrastructure can destroy recreation sites such as parks and fishing facilities that have been provided at a zero price. People, however, travel to such locations to make use of the natural amenities and thus incur a measurable travel cost both in terms of time and money. Use can be made of this information to gain some idea of the value of such facilities. This is a special case of the more general revealed preference approach (Smith, 1989).

Figure 6.6 offers guidance to the simplest travel cost approach. Surveys find that the number of visits to, say, a park from an origin A amounts to X_a, and from B amounts to X_b. Further, the actual average generalized travel costs (that is, including travel time costs) for these trips amount to P_a and P_b respectively from the two origins. A succession of further surveys looking at other origins enables the distance decay function to be derived. From this, the consumer surplus derived from visiting the park and enjoyed by an individual living at A is seen to be area $(A + B)$. Total surplus for those originating from A is then found by multiplying $(A + B)$ by the number of trip-makers originating from there. Similar calculations can be carried out for each origin to get the aggregate surplus.

Exhibit   *The economic costs of the* Amoco Cadiz *oil spill*

When the supertanker *Amoco Cadiz* ran aground 200 miles off the coast of Brittany in 1978 it resulted in the largest oil spill of its kind – 223 thousand tonnes – up until that date. Subsequent legal actions resulted in economists trying to place a value on the resultant environmental damage. This was a challenge, given the lack of data and the sensitivity of their results to the assumptions made, for example, did the authorities use the best knowledge available in their reactions?

Two types of case were heard, one initiated by the French government concerning the damage and clean-up costs of the incident, and the others by local authorities, individuals, and businesses adversely affected by the spillage. Five categories of cost are considered under two headings:

Costs of remedial actions

• Direct costs of clean-up

• Costs of restoration

Other physical effects

- Costs of lost tourism

- Costs of damage to amenities

- Damage to marine resources

Marginal effective analysis was used for evaluating the clean-up and restoration costs. Pumping of the oil, for example, was initially focused on the largest and most accessible deposits with efficiency per worker falling as the area became less polluted. Optimal pumping is when the marginal social benefit of doing so was equated with the marginal clean-up cost.

The question in defining the marginal cost of clean-up and of restoration by the French military was one of whether it should be valued as if a third party were brought in to do the work or as the additional cost of temporarily taking naval manpower from other duties. Essentially, this is a matter of whether the cost curve is long-run embracing the costs of having a reserve available to undertake these actions or a short-run cost curve of diverting existing manpower. Put another way, is the aim to calculate the option price that society is willing to pay to avoid an irreversible change in marine resources in the face of considerable uncertainty about the likelihood of a disaster, its implications, and the costs of dealing with it? The outcome was based on the former, and clean-up costs of between $103 and $114 million were awarded.

A different methodology was used for evaluating the second group of costs, the loss of tourism revenue for both the polluted and unpolluted areas affected by an adverse halo effect. Tourism effects were diverse and exact costs difficult to define. Indicators such as levels of flour deliveries were used to calculate the decline in the number of tourists. It was estimated that the spill effects lasted until 1979, equal to 2.9 million tourist days. Wage and profit rates were then applied to estimate the costs.

Amenities losses, being non-market effects, were valued using both contingent methods and travel cost approaches, although they were considered limited proxies in the court. In terms of implications for marine life, this was measured in lost fishing time and the damage done to boats and equipment (which was estimated by surveying fishermen). Lost income to the fishermen used estimates based on the market price of the types of fish caught and estimated lost catch. Similar methodologies were used to assess the costs to oyster farmers.

See also: F. Bonnieux and P. Rainelle (1993) Learning from the Amoco Cadiz oil spill: damage valuation and court's ruling, *Industrial and Environmental Crisis Quarterly*, 7, 169–88.

The main application of the technique is in evaluating specific types of environmental impact, but is of less use where there are several environmental factors involved and one wishes to evaluate them individually. Perhaps a bigger problem, however, is the need to specify the generalized cost function which itself should

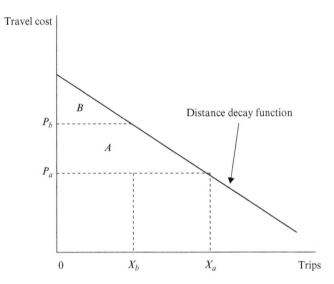

Figure 6.6   *The basic travel cost method*

include a monetary value of travel time. While, as we have seen, the work on the value of travel time is extensive, the subject is itself at least as controversial as that in the field of environmental evaluation.

Stated Preference

Stated preference techniques (often called 'contingency valuations' in the environmental literature), which have their basis in experimental economics (Smith, 1982), do not involve attempting to place values on environmental costs by observing actual trade-offs, but, rather, seek to elicit information on the trade-offs individuals would make when confronted with particular situations. It provides individuals with a mental experiment, a pseudo-market that involves decision-making within a controlled environment as far as the information they have and the options open to them.

The most widespread approach is asking, through questionnaires and surveys, or interactive computer games, a relevant group of individuals either what compensation they would need to keep them at their current level of welfare if some pre-defined transport-induced environmental degradation took place, or, alternatively, what amount would they be willing to pay to prevent this occurrence (Spash, 2008). The questions are set in an institutional context (for example, to make it clear what methods of finance are involved), and, to provide a market framework, the questioner initiates the process by suggesting an opening 'bid' to which the respondent reacts. The questions need to be couched carefully to ensure that the hypothetical trade-offs are clear and that the potential problems with the techniques are minimized.

Inevitably questions arise regarding the extent the information gained through a stated preference approaches is that which would emerge if an actual market existed. Strict comparisons are not possible since, by definition, no actual market exists in the stated preference context, but comparisons with other techniques can, at least, give some indication of consistency. In a number of case studies (which were not transport-specific), where stated preference techniques were deployed alongside other methods of evaluation, Pearce and Turner (1990) found that there was a 'reassuring' degree of overlap in the findings reported. Differences do, however, still exist and it is difficult to decide whether this reflects variations in the quality of individual studies or is a reflection of the usefulness of differing techniques.

One of the main problems in using the above set of procedures is that they do not all have the same theoretical underpinnings and this makes comparisons of results difficult. Is it valid, for example, to compare a value for noise pollution derived from an averting study with a value of air pollution derived from a stated preference study? It may also be argued that stated preference is more likely to yield meaningful results for local environmental effects such as traffic noise and road accidents because these affected people are more generally familiar with, and are thus capable of making, trade-offs in experimental situations.

6.5   The Magnitude of the Environmental Externality Problem

The discussion so far has provided a general account about the nature of the external environmental cost of transport and an account of some ways in which these may be usefully expressed for economic analysis. For example, Figure 6.3 presented hypothetical marginal cost and benefit curves associated with reducing motor vehicle exhaust emissions, but to make good practical use of these concepts, as we have emphasized, it is first necessary to measure physically the levels of pollution and then to put a monetary value on the units of pollution generated.

Here we look at the measurement problem and consider some of the ways in which pollution has been evaluated in practice and the results obtained. There is also an assessment of the economic importance of various forms of transport-associated environmental effects. These topics embrace many complex issues and have been subjected to major research efforts.

Noise

The noise caused by traffic is associated with many things and is increased by heavier traffic volumes, higher speeds, and greater numbers of trucks. Vehicle noise is a combination of the noises produced by the engine, exhaust, and tires. Defective mufflers or other faulty equipment on vehicles can also increase the loudness of traffic noise. From an economic perspective, it is often important to have engineering data on the courses of noise to assess optimal policies for remediation.

Noise associated with transport is a major problem. Early analysis includes a survey conducted by Market and Opinion Research in 1972 which found that 12 percent of respondents thought that excessive noise was one of the three or four most serious problems in Britain. In pre-unified Germany, Frenking (1988) found 65 percent of the population was adversely affected by road traffic noise, with 25 percent seriously affected; by way of comparison, this represented twice the problem of noise from neighbors and three times that from industrial noise. It is an especial nuisance in urban areas, in towns that suffer from a lot of through traffic (for example, located astride major trunk arteries, such as rail lines, motorways, etc.) and at locations around transport terminals, such as airports, bus stations, and car parks. It should also be remembered that noise is not only generated by traffic, but extremely high levels of noise are also often associated with the construction of transport infrastructure – up to levels of 110 dB when piles are being driven.

It has been estimated that over 110 million people in the industrial world are exposed to road traffic noise levels of more than 65 dB(A), a level considered unacceptable in OECD countries. While consistent data is somewhat sparse, there is also ample evidence that there are, in large part because of the nature of national land-use patterns, but also because of differing national legal structures, quite considerable differences between countries in terms of the populations affected by transport-related noise. Equally it is difficult, because of data limitations, to discern exact trends in population exposure to high noise levels. International comparisons provide tentative evidence of a decline in numbers suffering from serious noise problems – that is, over 65 dB(A) – in some countries but a rise in others, however there does seem to be a pattern of significantly increasing numbers of people falling into the gray area of intermediate noise nuisance of between 55 and 65 dB(65) (OECD, 1991).

Noise has several different effects on health and well-being. It affects activities such as communication (speaking, listening to radio and television) and sleep. These effects further induce psychological and physiological disorders such as stress, tiredness, and sleep disturbance. Noise can also contribute to cardiovascular disease, and, at high and prolonged exposure, hearing loss.

In practical terms there are, however, problems in measuring noise nuisance. First, noise nuisance depends upon both the intensity and the frequency of the noise. The 'A' weighted decibel scale (dB(A)) attempts to allow for this by offering a measure based on a weighted avenge of decibel readings where the weights reflect the level of unpleasantness caused by different frequencies and the decibels reflect the actual intensity of the noise. (While this measure is used in most transport-related work, a slightly different set of weights is employed in the perceived noise decibel (PNdB) used in the measurement of aircraft noise.) The dB(A) scale is logarithmic and Table 6.3 gives some examples of dB(A) measured peak noise of different forms of transport relative to other sources of noise.

The dB(A) scale is sometimes prefixed by a term such as L_{10} which means that it relates to a specific proportion of time (that is, L_{10} refers to the 10 percent peak noise level). On some occasions, decibel measures have been combined with other indicators of noise annoyance in a composite index. The Noise and Numbers Index (NNI) developed for the economic appraisal of the Third London Airport, for example, combined the average peak level of noise at an

Table 6.3   *Relative noise of different activities*

Perception example	Sound level dB(A)
Extreme jet take-off at 100 meters	120
Pop group	110
Loud car horn	100
Very loud heavy traffic	90
Noisy office	80
Loud busy street	70
Average office	60
Noisy normal conversation	50
Moderate quiet office	40
Quiet conversation	30
Quiet room	20
Very faint normal breathing	10
Threshold of hearing	0

airport (measured in PNdBs) with an indicator of the daily number of aircraft heard. The logarithmic nature of the NNI means that a one-unit increase in the index represents a greater increase in noise nuisance, the higher the existing level of the index.

A scale against which noise nuisances may be measured does not offer an economist trying to optimize noise emitted by transport much assistance in being able to place a monetary value on the noise so that the opportunity costs of different policies may be assessed. There are several ways in which noise has been evaluated, although revealed preference studies dominate in number.

In the 1960s, the Commission on the Third London Airport, in its pioneering study, considered changes in property values with higher noise levels and in so doing established an adoption of hedonic indices as an evaluation method (see also Chapter 11). Surveys were conducted at the existing Heathrow and Gatwick airports seeking the actual and predicted sale prices of properties at different distances from them. While the Third London Airport method is useful it does present some difficulties. House prices vary for many different reasons and not simply because of the noise levels inflicted upon them. House prices around Gatwick, for example, tended for a variety of reasons to be higher than Heathrow, which explains the greater fall in house values with respect to noise levels in the former. This does not invalidate the house valuation technique but it does suggest that values obtained by employing it should be used with circumspection and, more specifically, that a value for noise nuisance derived using it in one area may be inappropriate for transport studies elsewhere without adjustment.

A typical hedonic index of the type now used, albeit probably with fewer variables, is provided by Jon Nelson (1979):

$$\ln PV = 1.54 + 0.03(\ln X_1) + 0.20(\ln X_2) + 1.35(\ln X_3) + 0.02(\ln X_4)$$
$$+ 0.07(\ln X_5) - 0.33(\ln X_6) - 0.01(\ln X_7) \tag{6.2}$$

where:

> PV is a measure of property value differences;
> X_1 is a measure of the age of the house;
> X_2 reflects whether there is air conditioning;
> X_3 is the number of rooms;
> X_4 is the plot size;
> X_5 reflects whether the house has a riverside location;
> X_6 is time to reach employment; and
> X_7 is the 'noise exposure forecast' (NEF).

Examination of the NEF coefficient, the models calculated on data from around six major airports in the United States, thus suggests that a one-unit increase in NEF results in a 1 percent depreciation in a house's value. Table 6.4 provides some examples of the findings of such studies regarding airport noise.

Subsequently, Nelson (2004) applied meta-analysis to the negative relationship between airport noise exposure and residential property values. The analysis focuses on 20 hedonic studies covering 33 estimates of 23 airports in Canada and the United States that have looked at the percentage depreciation in property values per decibel increase in airport noise, or the noise discount. The weighted-mean noise discount across the studies is 0.58 percent per decibel, with country and model specifications having some effect on the measured noise discount; the cumulative noise discount in the United States is about 0.5 to 0.6 percent

Table 6.4   *Early estimates of noise nuisance on property values (percentage change per decibel increase)*

Study	Year	% in house price	Country
Abelson	1979	0.45	Australia
Collins & Evans	1994	0.45	United Kingdom
De Vany	1976	0.80	United States
Dygert	1973	0.60	United States
Emerson	1969	0.57	United States
Gautin	1975	0.35	United Kingdom
Levesqus	1994	1.30	Canada
Maser	1977	0.62	United States
McMillan	1978	0.50	Canada
McMillan	1980	0.87	Canada
Mieszkowski	1978	0.40	Canada
Nelson	1979	1.10	United States
O'Byrne et al.	1985	0.52	United States
O'Bryne et al.	1985	0.57	United States
Paik	1972	0.65	United States
Pennington et al.	1990	0.60	United Kingdom
Price	1974	0.83	United States
Uyeno et al.	1993	1.13	Canada

Source: Johnson and Button (1997). This paper contains the full references to the studies cited.

per decibel at noise exposure levels of 75 dB or less, while in Canada it is 0.8 to 0.9 percent per decibel. These are findings in line with the literature review conducted by David Gillen (2003), who found that aviation noise seems to reduce the prices of similar houses by about 0.45 to 0.9 percent for each decibel.

Atmospheric Pollution

Transport is a source of many harmful gases, and is one of the major contributors of several atmospheric pollutants. It is worth emphasizing, however, that while in some respects the environmental damage done by transport is increasing, in others, and regarding local pollution, there are reductions in many countries. Visual manifestations of this can be seen in the removal of the smog that used to hang over cities such as Los Angeles.

It is also worth remembering that exhaust fumes have a time and a spatial coverage. There is a time gap as the impacts move from one level to another. Figure 6.2 offered a broad picture of what happens. At the higher levels, the original impacts are connected to many other effects and systems, which are not exclusively related to transport. A potent cocktail of transport- and non-transport-related emissions, therefore, often exists. For ease of exposition, however, we deal with each of the main pollutants separately. The discussions below provide some indication of both these long- and short-term implications, as well as the nature of the spatial coverage, when this is particularly relevant.

Fuel additive emissions
To enhance engine performance, additives are added to fuels. While some are relatively benign in their environmental effects, others have caused increasing concern over time. The organic lead compounds added to gasoline as an anti-knock agent, especially when used by automobiles in confined urban spaces, have been singled out for particular attention. Lead is a metallic element that can be retained in the body in the forms of its compounds and can have an adverse effect on the mental development of children and affect the kidneys, liver, and reproductive system.

In industrialized nations, transport is the single largest source of lead emissions with some 50 percent of lead associated with transport, but the figure can approach 100 percent in confined urban spaces. However, the tightening of laws concerning maximum lead content in gasoline (for example, in the United Kingdom's case, from 0.84 grams per liter to 0.40 per liter in 1981 and a further reduction to 0.15 grams per liter in 1985) and the fostering of increasing use of lead-free gasoline through fiscal and other measures which we discuss further in Chapter 8, has caused major changes in most major industrialized countries.

Particulate matters
These embrace fine solids or liquid particles found in the air or in emissions such as dust, smoke, or smog. They are normally neither smelt nor tasted, nor seen by the naked eye, but can penetrate the body through the lungs and cause major health problems. Sources include the fine asbestos and other particles stemming

from wear and tear of tires and brakes as well as matter resulting from engine, and especially diesel engine, combustion.

Transport is the major source of particulate emissions in many industrialized countries including the United Kingdom and the United States. Particulate matter may be toxic, or carry toxic (including carcinogenic) trace substances absorbed into its surfaces. It also imposes costs on physical structures, for example, in terms of the need to clean and repaint buildings. There is, however, no scientific consensus on the size of particles that may be most harmful – for example, matter of less than 10 microns (PM–10) or 2.5 microns (PM–2.5) – making economic valuations difficult, and what estimates have been made generally relate to health aspects, and especially mortalities. In this context, however, McCubbin and Dellucci (1999) found that particulate matter, because of the severity of its health implications, was the most serious road-transport-generated pollutant in the United States. In terms of physical quantity emitted by transport in the States, PM–2.5 matter has fallen from 7.3 million short tons (2,000 lbs.) in 1991 to 2.61 in 2006, but PM–10 has risen to 18.42 million short tons from 18.4 over the same period.

Carbon dioxide emissions

The environmental concern here relates to CO_2 being generally seen by scientists as a major contributor to the greenhouse effect and consequential global warming: 'the balance of evidence suggests a discerning human influence on the global climate' (IPCC, 1995). CO_2 emissions result from the combustion of fossil fuels. It was estimated that, globally, transport contributed about 28.6 percent of CO_2 in 2018.

The contribution of CO_2 to the atmosphere varies considerably between countries but the industrialized countries as a whole are responsible for about 80 percent. Although detailed regional apportionment is difficult, Table 6.5

Table 6.5   *Share of transport CO_2 emissions*

	1971	1990	1998
OECD			
North America	25	29	30
Europe	14	20	23
Pacific	16	20	22
Non-OECD			
Africa	20	18	17
Middle East	14	20	18
Europe	10	9	13
Former USSR	9	9	8
Latin America	31	33	34
Asia (excl. China)	14	16	18
China	4	6	8
World	19	22	24

Source: IEA (2000).

provides some information on the division between the wealthier countries within the OECD and other countries at the end of the twentieth century. The general trend is clear. By 2017, the major emitting regions were Asia (29.6 percent) and North America (28.9 percent), with Africa responsible for 2.7 percent. (Population differences cannot account for this: Africa's population is about 1.22 billion, North America's 579 million, and Asia's 4.56 billion.)

Since CO_2 is a natural constituent of air (although only about 0.03 percent) it is not strictly a pollutant. Additionally, excess amounts of the gas have no detrimental effect on personal health. The problem is that there is mounting, although some would argue not yet conclusive, evidence that high levels of CO_2 in the atmosphere, by preventing heat from escaping from the planet, will lead to global climate changes.

The issue is not really one about the merits of the greenhouse effect *per se* (without it, estimates suggest the global average temperature would fall to about 19°C), but rather about the desirability of the effects which changes in its intensity will have. The exact geographical impacts of global warming, and its timing, are difficult to predict, and the long-term economic consequences are even harder to foretell. The types of problems which are feared, however, include: a rise in sea level as a result of thermal expansion of the sea and the melting of land ice; changes of climatic zones, for example, of desert regions and regions affected by tropical storms; detrimental effects on water resources in many areas; and problems of adapting agricultural production.

The wide-ranging potential impacts of global warming make it particularly problematic to place money values on them. The 'Stern review' (Stern, 2007) concluded that 1 percent of global GDP per annum needs to be invested to avoid the worst effects of climate change, and that failure to do so could risk global GDP being up to 20 percent lower than it otherwise might be.

Nitrogen oxide emissions
These pose difficulties when combined with other air pollutants or in areas where residents already suffer ill-health. In the latter case they can lead to respiratory difficulties and extended exposure can result in oedema or emphysema. At the trans-boundary or regional level, NO_X emissions converted to nitric acid and combined with sulfur dioxide (SO_2) form a significant component of 'acid rain' (or 'acid deposition') that has serious detrimental effects on ecosystems, for example damage to fresh-water fish stocks and deforestation. About 50 percent of NO_X emissions stem from the transport sector, and the rest from the energy and industrial sectors, although in many countries their output is falling. In the United States, it fell from 26.9 short tons in 1970, to 22.6 short tons by 2000, and to 18.2 short tons in 2006. The decline in transport-associated NO_X is largely due to the widespread adoption of auto catalysts; from 1990 all new cars in Norway, Sweden, Austria, and Switzerland had these fitted, and most other industrialized countries quickly followed.

Carbon monoxide emissions

Carbon monoxide (CO) can have detrimental effects on health by interfering with the absorption of oxygen by red blood cells. This may lead to increased morbidity, and adversely affects fertility. There is also evidence that it affects worker productivity. CO is especially a problem in urban areas where synergistic effects with other pollutants mean it contributes to photochemical smog and surface ozone (O_3). Concentrations of O_3 at lower levels have implications for the respiratory system. CO emissions result from incomplete combustion, which is most likely to occur at low air/fuel ratios in the engine. These conditions are common during vehicle-starting when the air supply is restricted.

In the 1980s some 90 percent of all CO emissions originated from the transport sector in most industrial countries, and about 80 percent were associated with automobile use. The figure reached 100 percent in the center of many built-up areas. CO emissions from transport more than halved in the United States in just over 35 years from 1970 to 100.6 million short tons in 2006. As with the United Kingdom (see again Table 6.2), in the United States transport accounts for about half of CO emissions.

Sulfur dioxide emissions

Emissions of this colorless but strong-smelling gas can result in bronchitis and other diseases of the respiratory system and they are, in conjunction with NO_X emissions, the major contributor to acid rain. Transport is directly responsible for about 5 percent of SO_2 emissions with diesel fuel containing more SO_2 per liter than gasoline. What is more important, coal-fired electricity generation is a major source of this gas and thus there are further transport implications both for electric rail transport and the manufacture of transport vehicles. Modern diesel engines are being adopted in wealthier countries, reducing the sulfur problem, and enhanced technology is combating the levels of SO_2 associated with coal-fired electricity generation.

There have been several studies at various levels of spatial aggregation to try to place an economic value on the costs acid rain imposes on forestry and the benefits of policies to reduce it. Estimates by Chestnut and Mills (2005), for example, of the quantified health and environmental benefits of the US Acid Rain Program totaled over $100 billion annually for 2010.

The trend in SO_2 emissions in general, including transport, has been downwards in many higher-income countries. Table 6.6 provides a decade of data for the United States showing the overall decline in SO_2 emissions since 2009 by type of activity. The direct use by transport (highway vehicles and off-highway) has clearly fallen dramatically both in absolute terms and in relative terms compared to the overall levels of sulfur emissions.

Volatile organic compounds

These comprise a wide variety of hydrocarbons (HC) and other substances (for example, methane, ethylene oxide, formaldehyde, phenol, phosgene, benzene, carbon tetrachloride, CFCs, and polychlorinated biphenyls). They generally

Table 6.6 *United States emissions of sulfur dioxide (million tons)*

	2009	2011	2013	2015	2017	2019
Highway vehicles	0.04	0.03	0.03	0.03	0.03	0.01
Off-highway vehicles	0.21	0.13	0.09	0.06	0.04	0.04
Fuel combustion	7.97	5.52	4.02	3.20	1.81	1.44
Industrial processes	0.70	0.58	0.53	0.48	0.44	0.44
Waste disposal & recycling	0.02	0.02	0.03	0.03	0.03	0.03
Miscellaneous	0.15	0.20	0.18	0.15	0.22	0.22
All sources	9.09	6.48	4.87	3.95	2.77	2.17

Source: US Bureau of Transportation Statistics.

result from incomplete combustion of fossil fuels, although evaporated gasoline from fuel tanks and carburetors is increasingly contributing to releases of aromatic HC such as benzene.

When combined with NO in sunlight, HC and some volatile organic compounds (VOCs) can generate low-level ozone, the main component of photochemical smog. Besides producing respiratory problems and causing eye irritations, some of the compounds are suspected of being carcinogenic and possibly mutagens or teratogens (which can result in congenital malformations). Excluding methane, emissions of which largely stem from agricultural sources, about half of VOC emissions in industrialized countries are generally associated with road traffic and the proportion in developing countries tends to be rising. About 30 percent of all VOC emissions are directly related to transport.

Accidents

Transport is a dangerous activity. Every year more than 1.17 million people die in road crashes around the world, and over 10 million are crippled or injured. These accidents can concern not just those involved in transport itself but also third parties. The dangers inherent in the transport of dangerous and toxic substances are, in fact, increasing this latter problem. From a purely statistical perspective, road transport resulted in 39,888 lives being lost in the United States in 2014, amounting to 124 deaths per million inhabitants, and only slightly less in the European Union. There are quite wide variations at a lower level of aggregation in the chances of being killed in a transport accident. For example, within the European Union in 2013/14 the number of road fatalities per million inhabitants ranged from 29 in the United Kingdom, 51 in Malta, 48 in the Netherlands, and 22 in Sweden through to 66 in Lithuania and 77 in Poland.

It should, however, be pointed out that in many high-income, developed countries the number of fatal road accidents is decreasing – for example, road fatalities for the United Kingdom reveal 4,753 deaths in 1991, falling to 3,743 in 1997, to 3,368 in 2004, and 1,752 in 2019 (the year before Covid effects began) with the general pattern repeated for injuries. For Germany, the decline has been even more pronounced, falling from 11,300 fatalities in 1991 to 5,842 in 2004, and to 3,036 in 2019 while for Italy the figures for 1994, 2004, and 2019 are 7,036, 6,122, and 3,173 respectively.

This is not, however, the situation in many low-income countries where, as private transport is expanding, the number of fatalities continues to rise. There is about a 70 percent greater chance of dying in a road accident in Africa than America, and a 185 percent greater chance than in Europe. Increased amounts of hazardous waste are being transported each year, and the related problem of spillage is also adding to the risks borne by third parties throughout the world, but particularly so in lower-income countries.

If one considers the accident rates by mode then road transport incidents dominate statistics, although, because of variations in modal split between countries, there are national variations in their relative importance. Some indication of different accident rates by mode and over time for the United States is, for example, seen in Table 6.7.

Interpretation of such data does, however, pose some problems: there is the point of comparison against which numbers of accidents should be set. Commercial aviation is, from a statistical perspective, generally cited as the safest mode of transport, but this may not be the case viewed in terms of time exposure.

Valuing the external accident costs of transport poses a particular problem (Jones-Lee and Loomes, 2003). Accident risks are partly internalized within transport in the sense that individuals insure themselves against being harmed by them. However, many travelers have no insurance, or, where it has been taken up, it is based on a misperception of the risks involved. Where there are also third-party risks involved in the possibility of accidents is during the transporting of dangerous goods or toxic waste. Attempts to devise methods for valuing accident risk have a long history, especially regarding fatal accidents.

Table 6.7   *Transport accidents in the United States by selected mode*

	Air	Highway (thousand)	Railroad	Waterborne
Fatalities				
1995	964	41.8	1,146	1,016
2000	764	41.9	937	888
2005	603	43.5	887	777
2015	406	35.5	749	700
2019	452	36.1	899	697
Injuries				
1995	452	3,593	14,440	6,165
2000	357	3,260	11,643	5,112
2005	302	2,728	9,402	4,095
2015	283	2,455	9,130	3,357
2019	259	2,727[a]	7,914	2,989

Note: a. 2018 data.

Source: US Bureau of Transportation Statistics.

The methods of valuation currently in use, however, still differ between countries, and agencies within countries. Some adopt cost avoidance calculations, others use lost-production/consumption-type techniques, but the use of revealed and stated preference methods is becoming more widespread. The lost-production (or export) method essentially asks what output the economy forgoes if, for example, someone is killed in a road accident – essentially a discounted calculation of the difference between what that person could have been expected to produce over the rest of their life and what they could have been expected to consume. The obvious problem is that a pensioner's death would be accorded a positive value with such a procedure. The lost consumption (or *ex ante*) method avoids this problem by assuming that the individual would gain utility by not dying and thus does not net out lost consumption, the ability to enjoy this consumption acting as proxy for the welfare of remaining alive.

Analysis based on microeconomic principles looks at choices that people make when trading off safer travel against riskier options and estimates the willingness to pay for the reduced risk. The revealed preference work focuses on actual choices, such as driving faster, which saves time but is more dangerous, or driving more slowly, which is more costly in time.

There is still no universally accepted value for accident prevention, and countries adopt a variety of valuations, and in some use different values according to mode or circumstance. The United Kingdom for example, uses a figure of about £1.93 million in 2020 for a statistical life saved in road project appraisal based on stated preference analysis, and £216,915 and £16,722 for serious and slight non-fatal accidents respectively. The United States used a value of up to $9.6 million in 2017 for a fatality, and Canada used $6.31 million in 2018. Academic studies also show some variability in their results. An early review of such studies in the United States, the United Kingdom, and Sweden using mainly stated preference methods concludes that the most reliable estimates from such studies give a distribution of values of life in 1989 with a median of $1.1 million and a mean of $3.4 million (Jones-Lee, 1990).

While reservations must be expressed over the method of valuing lost life (in terms of lost production) and some of the other forms of accident damage, these types of figures can also be aggregated to give very broad national overall costs of accidents – for example, the American Automobile Association estimated that the costs of property damage, lost earnings, medical costs, emergency services, legal costs, and travel delays due to road accidents amounted to $164.2 billion in 2007. It must be remembered, however, that such figures are gross of the internalization that takes place through insurance markets, and do not include the costs of lost lives and injuries.

Visual Intrusion

Transport infrastructure and mobile plant is frequently visually intrusive and often far from aesthetically pleasing. In addition, particulates and gases emitted by transport scatter and absorb light, adversely affecting visibility. The problem is measuring these effects. Some attempts have been made in the past to assess the intrusion of motorways on the landscape by looking at the percentage of the skyline obscured, but this approach only considers one dimension of a multi-faceted problem. Transport infrastructure must be viewed in the context of its surroundings – a new freeway located in formerly unspoiled countryside is likely to be viewed differently from one that blots out an unsightly waste tip. Design is also important. Also, it should be remembered that vehicles are as intrusive as infrastructure and large trucks or buses are, for example, often totally out of place in unspoiled areas or 'historic towns'. Whether it is the actual size of vehicles that is alarming or simply the level of traffic flow is difficult to disentangle.

A newer problem is that caused by the eyesores created by the difficulties of disposing of the old hardware of transport. The problem not only embraces disused infrastructure of road, rail, and maritime transport but also increasingly the vehicles themselves: cars, ships, and railway wagons. Variations in the number of scrapped vehicles over time are due to a variety of factors, including changes in fuel prices (Jacobsen and van Benthem, 2015), but as the overall vehicle population grows, disposal problems increase. Nevertheless, the weight of passenger cars, vans, and other light goods vehicles scrapped in the European Union in 2019 was 6.9 million tonnes; 95.1 percent of the parts and materials were reused and recovered, while 89.6 percent were reused and recycled.

Pollution of Water Systems

Water systems, both fresh and saline, suffer considerable pollution and other environmental damage from transport. Maritime transport itself results in both accidental and intentional releases of waste and oil into the seas, lakes and rivers, and ports, especially those requiring significant amounts of dredging, and are disruptive to wildlife. Other modes, however, can also cause damage including the run-off from roads and airports of liquids such as de-icing fluids, and the diversion of natural water-courses to allow for the construction of infrastructure.

Although most oil spillage (53 percent of incidents) is the result of transfers, major oil spillages due to maritime accidents attracts considerable attention: for example, the *Atlantic Express* spilled 287,000 tonnes of oil in 1979; the *ABT Summer*, 260,000 tonnes in 1991; the *Castillo de Bellver*, 252,000 tonnes in 1983; and the *Amoco Cadiz*, 233,000 tonnes in 1978. The quantity of oil spilt is not, however, a good indicator of the environmental damage done. The *Exxon Valdez* incident in 1989, for example, because it occurred in a scenic area, Prince William Sound on the Gulf of Alaska, is considered the most expensive in history despite the spillage being 37,000 tonnes. The costs of this in terms of clean-up ($2.2 billion), lost production in fishing and other industries ($300 million), and lost fishing output in south-central Alaska ($108 million), besides damages paid by the ship's owner, are large, although strictly difficult to calculate exactly because of problems of double-counting (Cohen, 1995). For example, while south-central Alaska may have lost business, other areas may have gained and some of the costs that have been included in calculations for damages paid by the ship's owners are already reflected in the direct damage and clean-up cost estimates. Ships are also generally insured and this means that at least part of the cost of spillage is internalized, as with many forms of accident risk.

There are also technical issues in physically assessing damage from spillage prior to any efforts at placing monetary values on them. A spill on marshland in winter does minimal damage to plant life, for example, because it has died back naturally and weather conditions can affect the rate of evaporation and toxicity of oil (Talley, 2001). There is also damage to water systems from indirect transport-related events, for example oil released when ships sink and on-shore maritime fuel storage tanks are damaged due to earthquakes and adverse weather.

Vibrations

Low-flying commercial aircraft, heavy goods vehicles, and railway wagons create vibrations that can affect buildings. Vibration within vehicles also adversely affects drivers and passengers. Vibration within a 'cabin' starts from the engine and the response of the vehicle to the road surface. Vibration varies in response to the load of the vehicle; there is more vibration as the load becomes lighter. The most widely reported injury for whole-of-body vibration is back injury.

Again, useful measures are elusive. While it is known, for example, that ground-borne vibration is related to axle loads, it has proved impossible to relate this effectively to any measure of structural damage. The evidence suggests, however, that the physical damage caused may be less than is sometimes claimed. Improved engineering techniques have reduced the damage caused by road transport and much of the damage formerly thought 'caused' by heavy lorries is more likely to have simply been 'triggered' by them. As Whiffen and Leonard (1971) pointed out half a century ago, '[a]ttention can be drawn to vibration by the rattling of doors, windows, lids of ornaments, mirrors, etc. The association of these audible and visible signs with the possibility of damage to the building results in exaggerated complaints about vibration, even though, in fact, there may be no risk of damage'. Vibrations may still be a cost in an economic sense, however, even if there is no structural damage to buildings. This is not a new problem: Martin (1978) found that 8 percent of the United Kingdom's population was considerably bothered by vibrations from road traffic. Since then, our knowledge of the implications of low-frequency noise has increased considerably, with evidence of discomfort, irritability, and sensitivity arising from sleep disruption (Araújo Alves et al., 2020).

Community Severance

Roads, railways, canals, and other transport arteries often present major physical (and sometimes psychological) barriers to human contact. An urban motorway can cut a local community in two, inhibiting the retention of long-established social ties, and, on occasions, making it difficult for people to benefit from recreational and employment opportunities on the other side of the barrier. A rail line can do the same. Although it may be possible to obtain estimates of the potential pedestrian and other delays, and reassignments resulting from the imped-ance, suppressed trips are much harder to identify. Severance also has important links with amenity; as Susan Handy (2003) puts it, 'the quality of a place, the way it looks, sounds, smells and feels ... affects the way people experience a place'.

Giving the largely qualitative implications of community severance full quantification, let alone any economic valuation, is not an immediate prospect. Progress has, however, been made since the late 1970s when the United Kingdom's Jefferson Report found that 'the overall conclusion is that no acceptable way is seen of extending the assessment of severance beyond an individual examination of some of the perceived effects except, perhaps, by means of subjective state-ments in appropriate cases'. Anciaes et al. (2016), for example, consider a number of ways in which community severance may be measured and its effects on health evaluated. They base their analysis on four questions: Are there barriers restrict-ing mobility and accessibility? Who is affected? How do people travel? And where do they go? Quantification of severance is then assessed by metrics that consider time losses, making use of examples from a variety of national approaches. What is still missing is any quantification of the mental costs of limiting mobility or access, or the feeling of isolation.

6.6 Energy Use

Energy use *per se* is not strictly an environmental concern in itself; it is more a matter of the types of energy used and in what context. The various energy sources have associated with them different environmental implications. Even wind power must be generated by man-made equipment usually involving the use of other energy sources, and wind farms can create local micro climates in their locations. There are broader issues about the non-renewable nature of oil, the main fuel used by transport.

To move anything requires energy. Transport, therefore, is a user of energy. The amount and types of energy that are used, however, have varied consider-ably over time as technology has changed. Much of it used to be in the form of the food given to animals, beasts of burden, or simply human consumption of calories in various forms. Renewable sources of energy, wind, and water power, have been widely exploited and still are, although often in somewhat different ways. Wind power, for example, is more often used indirectly as a means of generating electricity than for propelling ships or Chinese wheelbarrows. Much of modern transport since the advent of the steam engine has, however – and excepting some less developed countries where the beast of burden often still plays a major role – relied on non-renewable sources of energy such as coal, oil, and natural gas.

The levels of current and projected use of energy by the transport industries are particularly impressive. While there are national differences, a pretty clear

Table 6.8 *Energy consumption by sector in the United States*

	Quadrillion British thermal units						
	1995	*2000*	*2005*	*2010*	*2015*	*2019*	*2020*
Residential	34	34.5	32.5	31	32	32.5	31
Commercial	28	27	28	27	27.5	28	24
Industrial	18	21	22	22	20.5	21	21
Transport	15	17	17.5	18	18	17.5	16

Source: https://www.statista.com/statistics/239790/total-energy-consumption-in-the-united-states-by-sector/.

universal pattern of energy use emerges. Table 6.8 for example provides some information on relative final demand for energy by the main economic sectors in the United States. Transport accounted for some 17 to 17.5 percent over annual energy use over the 25 years to 2019, after which the Covid-19 pandemic of 2020 reduced absolute consumption somewhat as the United States along with the rest of the world's economy went into recession. In terms of oil demand, however, because of the need for a mobile source of power, transport has been the dominant sector throughout the pre-Covid period. For example, the United States consumed about 20 million barrels of oil products per day, of which 14 million barrels were used for transport, 9 million of these being gasoline. But a succession of global and national initiatives are now in place, designed to, amongst other things, reduce transport's dependence on carbon-based fuels such as oil. Relatively, though, transport is still expected to account for 30 percent of final oil demand in 2030, remaining the largest single consumer.

The exact effects of these global environmental initiatives are uncertain. Historically, a major factor that has contributed to the rise in energy demand for transport has been technology changes and stemming from these in particular has been the increasing use of road transport (see again Chapter 2). Future trends are likely to change the relationship. The global number of registered gasoline-powered cars and diesel commercial vehicles in 2003 was, respectively, about 589 and 224 million, but by 2020 the world's vehicle fleet was estimated to be 1.06 billion passenger cars and 363 million commercial vehicles. But many forecasters are suggesting international agreements, such as those reached at the COP26 UN Climate Change Conference, will reverse this trend as policies associated with containing global warming effect a disconnect between vehicle numbers and oil consumption. For example, hybrid and electric vehicles will become a larger part of the car park, reducing carbon emissions per mile. The challenge for the forecaster is to predict the number of miles driven.

But it is not just the number of vehicles that matter when it comes to emissions; technical factors also come into play. For example, there is fuel efficiency. The average new passenger car in Europe consumes about 6.5 liters of fuel per 100 kilometers, whereas the average passenger car in the United States uses over 40 percent more to cover the same distance. Part of this can be explained in terms of distances traveled: longer trips in America may be seen to justify more 'comfortable' vehicles but in addition there are important taxation differences. Retail gasoline prices in Europe include taxes in the range of 60 to 75 percent, compared with only 20 to 25 percent in the United States. There may also be cultural differences in the way various societies see large, less fuel-efficient vehicles, but these are more difficult to quantify.

Transport is not homogeneous and can be broken down in several ways to reflect its use of energy. The focus has largely been on the use of non-renewable energy resources, and especially oil, although electricity, an indirect energy source, is used by many rail systems and local trams. Electricity can be generated in a variety of ways, from oil, natural gas, coal, nuclear sources, hydro power, wind power, and so on, and thus its environmental implications are not always transparent. If, as many forecasts suggest, electric-powered personal vehicles, possibly with many being autonomous, have economic advantages in some markets, they will take an increasing market share from gasoline vehicles (Holland et al., 2016). Much of the energy mix will depend on local and national policies being pursued regarding gasoline, electric, and autonomous vehicles (Holland et al., 2021). This is a time of transition.

Given considerable variations in the efficiency of generating plants, one would really like an indicator of the amount of fossil fuel used to provide the energy to produce a given unit of transportation. Additionally, most of the data available on energy consumed in transport relate to the final movement and offer few insights into the full costs of transport provisions that embraces the energy needed to supply and maintain transport infrastructure and the manufacture and maintenance of vehicles. We also have limited knowledge on the way transport affects the use of resources in the broader economy – for example, on the effect that transport-intensive industries such as tourism have on energy consumption in final production such as hotels, restaurants, and the manufacturing of souvenirs, as well as in the movement of the tourists themselves.

In terms of its immediate effects, Table 6.9 looks at energy consumption by various transport modes in the United States. The dominant role of gasoline as an energy source is clear and reflects the widespread use of automobiles for personal travel. Other countries have somewhat different relative patterns that depend, in part, on the nature and size of their national economies and geography (for example, whether they produce and move large amounts of raw materials), but also on the transport policies that have been favored (for example, whether public transport has been strongly supported and levels of fuel taxation).

While much of the interest in energy consumption until the 1990s focused on its use in developed Western economies, the subsequent rapid economic expansions of large developing countries, especially Brazil, India, and China, has led to a shift in attention.

With its growth in GDP and aggressive expansion of transport infrastructure, China, for example, saw a fourfold increase in freight traffic and a sixfold increase in passenger traffic between 1980 and 2000. Cars for short trips and planes for

Table 6.9 *Fuel consumption in the United States by the main transport modes*

	1980	*1990*	*2000*	*2010*	*2016*
Air					
Certificated carriers					
Jet fuel (million liters)	32,249	46,228	52,631	40,990	42,273
General aviation					
Aviation gasoline (million liters)	1,968	1,336	1,260	818	780
Jet fuel (million liters)	2,900	2,510	3,679	5,513	5,440
Highway					
Gasoline, diesel, & other fuels (million liters)					
Light duty vehicle, short wheelbase, & motorcycle	265,683	264,067	277,375	334,474	346,319
Light duty vehicle, long wheelbase	90,078	134,802	200,395	133,756	143,160
Single-unit 2-axle 6-tire or more truck	26,206	31,635	36,200	53,811	58,062
Combination truck	49,350	61,070	97,155	106,677	111,876
Bus	3,854	3,388	4,210	7,329	8,426
Transit					
Electricity (million kWh)	2,446	4,837	5,382	6,534	6,604
Motor fuel (million liters)					
Diesel	1,632	2,464	2,236	2,365	2,233
Gasoline & other non-diesel fuels	42	129	89	383	439
Compressed natural gas	n.a.	n.a.	165	486	632
Rail, Class I (freight service)					
Distillate/diesel fuel (million liters)	14,778	11,792	14,006	13,949	12,814
Amtrak					
Electricity (million kWh)	254	330	470	555	516
Distillate/diesel fuel (million liters)	242	310	359	240	1,908
Water					
Residual fuel oil (million liters)	33,887	23,948	24,264	17,262	11,091
Distillate/diesel fuel oil (million liters)	5,595	7,816	8,560	8,076	8,498
Gasoline (million liters)	3,982	4,921	4,256	4,179	8,792
Pipeline					
Natural gas (million cubic feet)	17,971	18,684	18,185	19,476	19,749

Note: n.a. = not available.

Source: US Bureau of Transportation Statistics.

long trips increasingly dominated passenger traffic in the country, as growing incomes allowed more people to utilize these fast and comfortable means of travel. From 1980 through 2002, passenger traffic grew from 228 billion to 1,413 billion person-kilometers with highways' share increasing from 32 to 55 percent of total

Table 6.10   *Energy consumption by transport in China (1990–2000)*

Mode	Energy consumption (ktoe)[a]			Consumption share (%)		
	1990	*2000*	*Ratio*	*1990*	*2000*	*Change*
Railways	14,851	13,017	0.88	27.8	13.5	–14.2
Highways	25,495	65,516	2.57	47.6	68.1	+20.5
Waterways	11,407	11,988	1.05	21.3	12.5	–8.8
Civil aviation	1,222	5,090	4.16	2.3	5.3	+3.0
Pipelines	550	605	1.10	1.0	0.6	–0.4
Total	*53,524*	*96,214*	*1.80*	*100.0*	*100.0*	*0.0*

Note: ktoe = kilotonne of oil equivalent.

Source: China Energy Research Society (2002).

person movements. Passenger aviation traffic grew more than thirtyfold, its share of aggregate passenger movements growing 9 percent. Railway passenger traffic, while nearly quadrupling in volume, however, saw its share of the market declining from 61 to 35 percent. Since the early 2000s, China's expanded high-speed rail network has, however, absorbed some of the increase in overall long-distance passenger transport that would have likely otherwise used road or air modes.

As the result of the rapid traffic growth and the changing modal split, the transport share of national energy use grew from under 5 percent in 1996 to nearly 9 percent in 1999. The share of energy used by road transport in China officially grew from roughly 48 percent in 1990 to 68 percent in 2000, and most of this is in the form of oil consumption (Table 6.10). The share of civil aviation also grew rapidly, albeit from a very much lower base.

Most of the analysis of transport energy use focuses on its importance in moving vehicles of one form or another, but both the mobile plant used in transporting goods and people, and the associated infrastructure, rely on significant amounts of energy in their construction and maintenance. While difficult to quantify, for example, the production of over 50 million cars, nearly 14 million light commercial vehicles, and three million heavy commercial vehicles in 2006 obviously consumed an immense amount of energy.

As with many things, there is an intellectual curiosity about the links between transport and energy use, but there are also important public policy issues to be considered. Energy is used in virtually all forms of activity and there is a need to ensure that it is used to maximum effect and in ways that ensure any external affects are not excessive. In economic terms, the market for energy is, however, far from perfect for a variety of reasons. These stem partly from the intrinsic nature of the 'commodity' (largely associated with market failures linked to economies of scale in supply and externalities), but can also be due to the institutional environment in which energy is provided (especially government intervention failures that often are seen in terms of allocating property rights and regulatory capture). These imperfections, in turn, affect the ways in which transport users view energy and the ways in which they use it, and the forms and quantities in which it is supplied.

Much of the energy used in transport comes from finite sources: oil reserves, coal, wood, and natural gas. In economic terms, this is not a major issue if prices are appropriate and reflect the genuine, long-term opportunity cost of the use of these resources. In many cases, the drawing-down of the reserves of these resources may still be consistent with a genuinely 'sustainable' scenario in the Brundtland Report sense (World Commission on Environment and Development, 1987) of ensuring that future generations enjoy the same resource base as current generations, if at the same time alternative energy sources are being created – for example, the creation of hydroelectric or wind capacity. In terms of the notion of sustainable development, future generations will still have the same resource base as the current one, albeit it in a different form.

The challenge is to ensure that there are mechanisms and signals to guarantee that the energy base is not diluted excessively by transport use. In the past there have been significant shifts in the energy used in transport, with coal, and then oil, taking over from oars and sails in shipping for example. Market forces have largely driven these shifts; slaves became expensive as rowers, and sailing ships became too unreliable for expanding trade networks and hence steamships took over. One thing that has been learned, however, is that predicting the depletion rate of any resource is difficult. Stanley Jevons' famous concern in 1865 that coal supplies would soon be exhausted and, in consequence, the rail and steamship industry would, amongst others, become non-viable is a good example of how static analysis linking non-renewable resource depletion and transport can be misleading. But equally, the move from wood to coal and then to oil boilers on ships showed how the market can respond to potential shortages through stimulating the development of alternative technologies.

The economic problem is that for transport markets to function they must have appropriate price signals from the energy market. The semi-cartelization of many energy markets, with institutions such as the Organization of the Petroleum Exporting Countries (OPEC), and of many markets that supply the hardware of transport, such as the automobile and airframe manufacturers, coupled with political involvement, means that these signals are far from perfect. Consequently, the exploitation of any non-renewable resources is seldom optimal, irrespective of any externality considerations. The issue, however, is more of a generic one rather than being transport-specific, because market and institutional failures extend across all uses of energy.

6.7   Introduction to Traffic Congestion

The demand for transport is not constant over time. In large cities there are regular peaks in commuter travel while on holiday routes; both within a country and to overseas destinations, there are seasonal peaks in demand. Transport infrastructure, although flexible in the long run, has a finite capacity during any given

Table 6.11   *Traffic congestion in major United States cities (2005 and 2017)*

Large metropolitan areas	Annual delay per traveler (hours)	
	2005	*2017*
Los Angeles	72	119
San Francisco–Oakland	60	103
Washington DC	60	102
Atlanta	60	73
Dallas–Fort Worth	58	67
Houston	56	75
Detroit	54	61
Miami	50	68
Phoenix	48	62
Chicago	46	73
New York–Newark	46	92
Boston	46	80
Seattle	45	78
Philadelphia	38	62

Source: Texas Transportation Institute.

period. One cannot, for example, expand and contract the size of an airport terminal to meet seasonal fluctuations in demand. When users of a particular facility begin to interfere with other users because the capacity of the infrastructure is limited, then congestion externalities arise and time is wasted (Table 6.11). What we see, in terms of travel in some major cities at less than the authorized speed limit, is that large amounts of time are spent in traffic delays and that these delays are becoming longer over time. We also see considerable variation in the economic costs between cities, and that the 'ranking' of cities by their congestion levels has changed between cities between 2005 and 2017.

One could argue about whether the measure of congestion reflects the real economics of delays. Speed limits, for example, generally depend on the engineering standard of roads and on safety on considerations rather than on notions of optimal congestion level. Some degree of congestion is almost unavoidable if facilities are not to stand idle most of the time. The question is just how much congestion is desirable. Since people accept a low level of congestion but resent excessive congestion; because of the time and inconvenience costs imposed, there is some implied notion of an optimal level of congestion that is not captured in engineering criteria – a topic returned to later. There may, for example, be thresholds of congestion for different journey purposes (Sweet, 2014).

It is not just roads that experience congestion. It can be found in most modes of transport and can be either on links or at nodes. Table 6.12, for example, looks at air traffic control delays in Europe, but there are delays at airports as well. Remaining with Europe, for example, in 2006, 31.8 percent of flights were delayed by at least 15 minutes out of London's Heathrow Airport, 31.3 percent from Madrid, 30.7 percent from London Gatwick, and 28.6 percent from Paris Charles de Gaulle.

Table 6.12   *European air traffic flow management delays*

	Average daily traffic	*% of flights delayed[a]*	*En route delays (million minutes)*	*Airport delays (million minutes)*
1997	19,658	7	15.5	5.4
1998	20,681	9	21.7	5.7
1999	22,064	12	36.3	7.0
2000	23,071	9	24.4	7.4
2001	23,001	8	20.8	6.8
2002	22567	9	11.9	6.0
2003	23,197	6	8.0	6.8
2004	24,238	4	7.6	7.3
2005	25,244	4	8.9	8.7
2006	26,286	5	10.2	8.2

Note: a. A delay is defined as 15 minutes or more behind schedule.

Source: EUROCONTROL Performance Review Unit.

One should add, with reference to previous sections, that congestion does not only impose costs on the traveler in terms of wasted time and fuel (the pure congestion cost) but the stopping and starting it entails can also worsen atmospheric and other forms of pollution. The problem is particularly acute with local forms of pollution because road traffic congestion tends to be focused in areas where people work and live. Road traffic poses some of the greatest congestion problems and offers a useful basis of analysis.

The economic costs of road congestion can be calculated using the engineering concept of the speed–flow relationship. If we take a straight one-way street and consider traffic flows along it over a period at different speed levels then the relationship between speed and flow would appear as in Figure 6.7. Flow is dependent upon both the number of vehicles entering a road and the speed of traffic. Hence, at low volumes of traffic, when vehicle impedance is zero, high speeds are possible, constrained only by the capability of the vehicle and the legal speed limits, but as the number of vehicles trying to enter the road increases, so they interact with existing traffic and slow one another down. As more traffic enters the road, speed falls, but, up to a point, flow will continue to rise because the effect of additional vehicle numbers outweighs the reduction in average speed. This is the normal flow situation.

At the point where increased traffic volume ceases to off-set the reduced speed, the road's 'capacity' is reached at the maximum flow. (This is the road's engineering capacity and differs from the economic capacity that is defined as the flow at which the costs of extending the capacity are outweighed by the benefits of doing so.) Absence of perfect information means that motorists often continue to try to enter the road beyond this volume, causing further drops in speed and resulting in the speed–flow relationship turning back on itself. These levels of flow are known as forced flows. There is often a degree of 'learning from experience' that can improve the quality of decision-making and in practice, without any

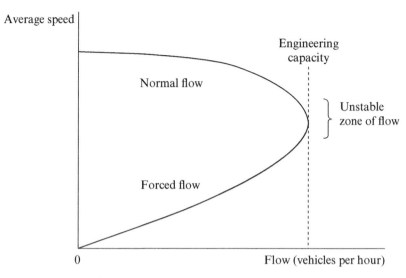

Figure 6.7   *The speed–flow relationship*

intervention, flows would settle around the zone of instability during rush-hour periods. A cross-sectional study of the main urban centers (Table 6.13) conducted half a century or so ago suggests that this zone of instability occurs at speeds of about 18 kph, but the situation is little changed today.

The actual form of the speed–flow relationship and the engineering capacity of any individual road will depend upon several factors. Clearly, the physical characteristics of the road, its width, number of lanes, etc., are of central importance and may be treated as long-term influences. Short-term factors include the form of traffic management and control schemes in operation (traffic lights,

Table 6.13   *Traffic speeds in selected cities*

City	Year	Population (million)	City center traffic speed (kph)	
			Peak hour	Off-peak
New York	1970	13.3	16.0	26.0
Detroit	1970	4.0	17.7	–
Salt Lake City	1970	0.9	27.0	–
London	1971	7.4	20.6	–
Birmingham	1965	1.1	22.1	–
Leeds	1965	0.5	18.0	–
Paris	1970	6.4	16.9	–
Athens	1971	2.7	15.5	24.0
Copenhagen	1967	1.7	14.5	–
Stockholm	1969	1.3	18.0	–
Calcutta	1971	7.5	11.0–16.0	19.0
Singapore	1972	2.2	21.0	–

Source: Thomson (1977).

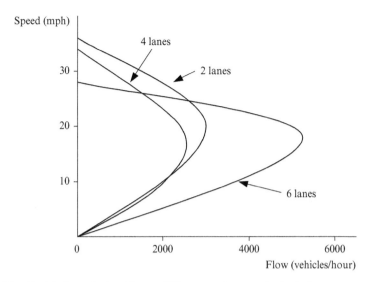

Figure 6.8 *Speed–flow relationships on different road categories in Sydney*

roundabouts, etc.). Finally, the type and age of vehicles combined with their distribution may influence capacity.

A typical set of speed–flow relationships which illustrate these points are, for example, offered by Neutze (1963) in his study of Sydney's arterial road system. Information obtained from over 400 locations on main roads in the city was used in the exercise, the results of which are seen in Figure 6.8. As one might expect, the capacity of six-lane roads exceeds that of either two- or four-lane roads, although at most traffic densities the speed is slightly higher on the two- rather than the four-lane roads. The explanation for this is that traffic management policies slow down flows of the four-lane roads because roadside parking is permitted and thus the capacity of curbside lanes is severely restricted, and they also tend to pass through more densely populated areas with more restrictive traffic management controls.

The speed–flow relationship provides a key supply-side input into the analysis but it is road space that is demanded. A theoretical framework linking the two elements is described by Alan Evans (1992). Relaxing the basic assumptions of the model can lead to modifications to the speed–flow relationship, for example Verhoef (2005) has shown that in some contexts it is not backward-bending at the saturation level but becomes vertical. The density function, the number of vehicles on a road at any one time, is also important in this type of analysis.

In Figure 6.9, element B shows the standard speed–flow relationship with the maximum flow depicted as F_{max}. This is traced round to the travel cost–flow diagram in element C. People essentially demand to join a road and this demand is seen as the demand curve, D, in element A of the figure. This diagram also depicts the relationship between travel cost and traffic density – the MC being the rising marginal cost of congestion each additional motorist imposes on others

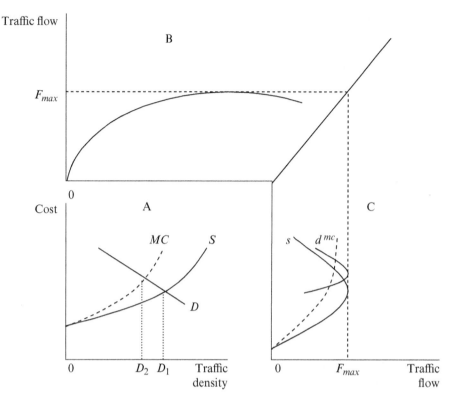

Figure 6.9   *The speed–flow relationship and the demand curve for road space*

using the road. The curve rises as the number of vehicles increases. The S curve represents the cost of joining the road as seen by the additional motorist, in effect his or her cost of trip-making ignoring the consequences of his/her actions for the others on the road.

The curves in element C of the figure, concerned with travel cost–flow relationships, are derived from elements A and B. The s curve is the average cost relating to congestion in a simple interaction model (see below) and the mc is the associated marginal curve. These relate directly back to the speed–flow relationship. Generalized costs (see Chapter 5) provide the vital link between physical traffic flows and cost. Broadly, faster travel in urban areas means cheaper travel in terms of generalized costs: vehicles are used more effectively and travel times are reduced. The S curve in Figure 6.9 represents the average generalized cost of trip-making at different levels of traffic flow. It is a reverse of the speed–flow curve seen in Figure 6.7, with the positively sloped portion concerning the negatively sloped section of the speed–flow curve; this stems from the inverse relationship between speed and generalized cost. The mc curve is the associated marginal curve that takes into account the congestion costs the additional user places on the existing traffic flow. The d curve is a derived demand curve reflecting the way in which the desired traffic flow changes as the cost of travel changes because the number of vehicles put on the road changes.

The actual traffic density that will emerge without any form of traffic restraints is where the demand for road space equals the average cost (S) of joining the road: D_1. This exceeds the optimal level, where road users take account of the impedance they impose on others, which is where MC is equated with demand. Moving across to the flow diagram, which is much more frequently found in the academic literature, the optimal traffic flow is where the mc curve intersects the derived demand curve.

6.8 The Economic Costs of Congestion

Most analysis of congestion focuses purely on segment A of Figure 6.9. It is usually presented in the form seen in Figure 6.10, with the AC curve representing the average cost of congestion at each level of traffic flow, and the MC curve the cost of additional traffic to existing flow. The optimal flow is, as we have seen above, where MC and demand are equated (F_2) while the actual flow, because road users ignore the congestion that they impose on others, tends to be F_1. A further interpretation can be placed on the AC and MC curves. The curves reflect the average and marginal generalized costs associated with different flows: they show all the time and money costs borne by road users when trip-making. In this sense they may be representing 'social costs' in the limited sense that they are the costs to the society of road users.

However, any individual user entering the road will only consider the costs they personally bear. They will, in most circumstances, either be unaware of or unwilling to consider the external congestion costs they impose on the other road users. Consequently, the individual motorist will only consider the average costs experienced by road users and take no account of the congestive impact of their

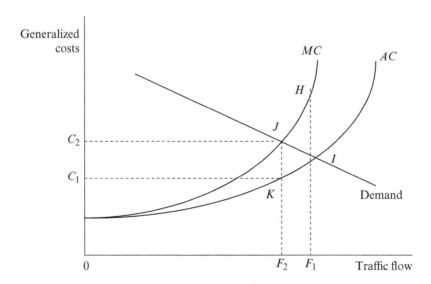

Figure 6.10   *The economic inefficiency of congestion*

trip on other vehicles. It is frequently argued that the MC curve, therefore, relates to the marginal social cost for the new trip-maker and existing road users of an addition to the traffic flow while the AC curve is equivalent to the marginal private cost curve – that is, the additional cost borne and perceived by the new trip-maker alone. The difference between the AC and MC curves at any traffic flow reflects the economic costs of congestion at that flow.

It is often important from a policy perspective to gain some idea of the actual costs associated with excessive congestion. From a social point of view the actual flow, F_1, is excessive because the F_1th motorist is only enjoying a benefit of F_1I but imposing costs of F_1H. The additional traffic beyond the optimal level F_2 can be seen to be generating costs of F_2JIF_1, but only enjoying a benefit of $(F_2JIF_1 - HJI)$, where HJI is a deadweight loss. A traffic flow lower than F_2 is also suboptimal because the potential consumer surplus gains from trip-making are not being fully exploited. Of course, this does mean that even at the optimal traffic flow there are still congestion costs, the area between the MC and AC curves up to traffic flow F_2, but these are more than off-set by the benefits enjoyed by those using the road.

While the work on congestion costs is extensive, estimating the overall costs associated with excessive congestion is not simple. Work looking at the money value of lost travel time has a long pedigree; information on such costs is of commercial value to public transport suppliers who may trade off faster services against higher fares. The exact cost depends upon the mix of traffic and the reason trips are being made. Periodically crude estimates, of the type produced by the United Kingdom's Confederation of British Industry (CBI) in 1988, are made of the costs of time wasted in congestion (about £15 billion per year for commercial traffic in the prices of the time) but these estimates, and subsequent ones based on questionnaire surveys tend to suffer from major theoretical and measurement problems. In the CBI case the calculations were based on scaling up the responses to a small survey of distribution companies that were asked to assess the costs traffic congestion was imposing on their operations. Besides the small size of the sample and the inherent dangers of aggregation, there was no effort to define a base-line level of optimal congestion as a basis for comparison nor was there any effort to net out the costs that the distributors were imposing on others but not paying for.

A more rigorous approach is to consider the opportunity cost of lost travel time (see Chapter 5). These vary by the nature of the road involved. Using the figures adopted by the UK Department of Transport when appraising road schemes, David Newbery (1988), as the result of careful calculations, produced marginal congestion costs by road type in the United Kingdom (Table 6.14). While these figures are in themselves dated, they represent solid analysis and show the differing levels of costs imposed by an additional vehicle joining the various traffic streams. Aggregation gives an estimated annual congestion cost in the United Kingdom of about £12,750 million for 1989–90.

Later studies of road congestion costs in the United States include Winston and Langer (2004), who reviewed congestion costing methods, and, using their

Table 6.14   *Estimated congestion costs by road type in the United Kingdom (1989)*

Road type	Marginal cost (pence per mile)
Motorway	0.26
Urban central peak	36.97
Urban central off-peak	29.23
Non-central peak	15.86
Non-central off-peak	8.74
Small town peak	6.89
Small town off-peak	4.20
Other urban	0.08
Rural dual carriageway	0.07
Other dual carriageway	0.19
Other rural	0.05

Source: Newbery (1990).

own model, came up with annual costs of $37.5 billion annually (2004 prices), a third of which consisted of freight vehicle delays. Weisbrod et al. (2001) evaluated the economic productivity costs of congestion, particularly to businesses for distribution, and reduced economies of scale and agglomeration, finding them to range from $20 million to $1 billion per year in typical metropolitan regions. The costs vary significantly by industry, with higher costs in industries that involve significant distribution costs or rely on specialized employees. The Texas Transportation Institute (2019) has developed a congestion index to calculate congestion costs in major American cities and converted these into cost measures. The Institute estimated that 2017 traffic congestion across the 494 urban areas examined cost $179 billion nationally, with each commuter averaging 54 hours in congestion.

6.9   Refinements on the Basic Congestion Model

The analysis of congestion, as set out, is based upon a very simple modeling framework: a linear road, no junctions, homogeneous traffic, and drivers who are all equally skillful. In practice, as we would expect from our discussion of the speed–flow relationship, the total cost function varies with the details of the transport system under consideration. Also, considerable traffic congestion stems from 'incidents' such as accidents, emergency road repair, and breakdowns that do not fit comfortably into the simple framework. Traffic incidents account for up to an estimated 60 percent of delay-hours. Although they are random events, they cause significant delays when traffic volumes approach road capacity. In uncongested conditions an incident causes little or no traffic delay, but a stalled car on the shoulder of a congested road can cause 100 to 200 vehicle-hours of delay on adjacent lanes.

William Vickrey (1969) distinguishes five types of congestion relevant in this rather more complex world. While these are couched in terms of road congestion, they are equally applicable to most other modes of transport – one can quite simply substitute air-lane or waterway for roads. The types of congestion are:

- *Simple interaction.* This occurs at comparatively low levels of traffic flow where the number of mobile units is small. Delays are minimal and usually result from slow and careful driving on the part of users who wish to avoid accidents. Total delay tends to vary as the square of the volume of traffic, so that each additional motorist causes a delay to *each other* road user roughly equal to that which the motorist suffers. This is essentially the type of congestion we have been concerned with above.
- *Multiple interaction.* This occurs at higher levels of traffic flow where, although the road capacity is not reached, an additional vehicle causes considerably more impedance to each other vehicle than with simple interaction. Empirical evidence suggests that for every minute the marginal user is delayed, other vehicles each suffer a delay of three to five minutes.
- *Bottleneck situations.* These occur when a particular stretch of a road (or other piece of transport infrastructure) is of more limited capacity than either the preceding or subsequent links in the network. If the flow is below that of the capacity of the bottleneck, then either simple or multiple interactions may occur, but once the capacity is reached, and if this is sustained for any length of time, then queues develop. An exceptionally high level of congestion is then likely to arise.
- *Triggerneck situations.* When a bottleneck situation results in queues of traffic, these may impede the general flow of traffic even for those not wishing to use the section of road with limited capacity. At the extreme, congestion may become so severe that the traffic comes to a complete standstill and can only flow again after some vehicles have backed up.
- *Network and control congestion.* The efforts of traffic engineers and managers (by the introduction of different traffic control devices) may reduce congestion costs at certain times of the day, or, for example, in the case of bus lanes, for specific types of traffic, but increase them at other times or for other modes. This results from the general bluntness of most traffic control schemes, which may help solve major problems but do, at times, create other, albeit usually less significant, difficulties. This type of congestion was not fully appreciated until the mid-1970s and had earlier led to excessively high estimates of urban congestion costs. Previously it was assumed that congestion tended to be of the simple or multiple interactive kind. But, as succinctly expressed in a United Kingdom 1975 policy document, 'Transport policy: a consultation document', '[o]nce account is taken of the limitations placed upon urban traffic speeds by factors such as the incidence of traffic lights and the multi-purpose nature of urban road networks, traffic speeds associated with even very low levels of congestion can be expected to be quite low – almost certainly below 20 mph in central areas'.

In addition to these five types of traffic congestion that can arise when the infrastructure is fixed, Vickrey also points to the more general problem of transport congestion in the economy. In the context of urban areas, roads in the United States take up 30 percent or more of the land area of city centers, while in Western Europe the figure is between 15 percent and 20 percent and in Third World countries about 10 percent. The question then becomes one of whether in the long term the general welfare of urban society is being excessively reduced by too much transport infrastructure congesting city centers. The acceptance of this view makes it rather difficult to define meaningfully optimal levels of transport provision in the traditional welfare sense.

A further problem is that many travelers, and especially road users, have a very poor perception of their own private costs. Indeed, in the case of car users the perceived cost of many trips may only embrace the time involved. In such cases the perceived AC, while reflecting some of the costs to a motorist thinking of joining a traffic stream, is an inadequate basis for calculating the MC curve which embraces the congestion costs to other road users. The appropriate policy curve in these circumstances is MC^*, which is based upon the resource costs of making trips rather than just the perception of the additional user. As we see in Figure 6.11, the implication of this is that congestion may well be somewhat higher than is sometimes estimated.

Congestion, or to be more exact excessive congestion, has been shown to imply a 'dead-weight' welfare loss and to reduce the economic efficiency of any transport system. In recent years there has been some debate, however, about whether this welfare loss is compensated by other beneficial effects of congestion that are not immediately apparent in the standard, static, marginal cost type of analysis. These arguments tend to follow three broad lines: those focusing on issues centering on the distributional effect of congestion on different groups in society, those concerned with more straightforward efficiency problems, and those that take other forms of cost into account.

The main costs imposed by traffic congestion are usually found to be time costs (although there may also be fuel and other components of generalized costs

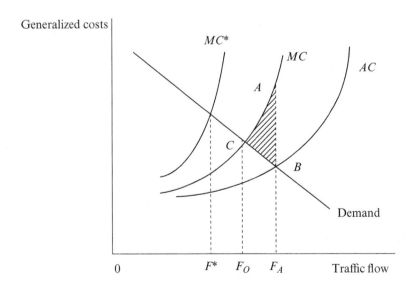

Figure 6.11   *The problems of misperceived private costs*

to be considered). Queuing up for the use of a transport facility and slowing down its consumption takes up the user's time. Measures to reduce the demand, increase the supply, or the introduction of market prices to optimize congestion (all of which are discussed later in the book) impose some form of either financial or welfare loss which, following simple efficiency criteria, must be lower than the congestion costs saved but still must be borne by someone.

Those who favor the retention of a high level of congestion as a method of allocating scarce transport facilities argue that, since in the short term time is evenly distributed to everyone – that is, there are 24 hours in every person's day – it is a more equitable method of allocation than many alternative techniques. If a traveler really wants to make a journey, he or she will be willing (and able) to wait, whereas if a high congestion-deterring charge is levied, his/her financial budget constraint may make it impossible to make the trip.

While there seem to be some grounds for this type of argument if one accepts that transport is unique in requiring a substantial time input for its consumption (a proposition that is far from self-evident), in the longer term the wider distributional issue is probably more effectively tackled by direct income redistribution measures. There seems no reason, in the general case, for singling out transport rather than several other economic activities for this special treatment. In addition, even when goods have in the past been provided free of charge, there is empirical evidence that, despite the equal distribution of time, it is the rich who tend to obtain them and, *ipso facto*, a disproportionate share of the benefit (Barzel, 1974).

Moving to the second mitigating argument in favor of allocation by congestion we turn to efficiency considerations. Congestion is seen by some as a complementary method of allocating certain types of facility, supplementing rather than competing with other, usually monetary price mechanisms. The dead-weight loss associated with congestion may in some situations, it is claimed, be outweighed by other forms of welfare benefit. In some instances, people – for example, those on aircraft stacking at congested airports – use time spent in queuing productively, while in other instances the dead-weight loss associated with suboptimally excessive congestion may be exceeded by administrative or other costs of achieving optimal utilization of the transport facility. As we see in Chapter 8 this has been one argument used against introduction of sophisticated metering devices for urban road pricing.

More generally, it is argued that, since transport users are far from homogenous, different groups of users will value time differently and hence a system with both time-allocated and financially allocated facilities could well be optimal. If analogies are made with other forms of economic activity, from retailing to car manufacturing, then both money and time are used for allocation. For example, one can get fast, personal service at a small local store, but prices are likely to be higher than at a large, possibly distant, supermarket where queuing is normal at checkouts.

This sort of approach is in general use for some forms of transport, with many countries, for instance, having fast, tolled motorways running parallel to slow, free trunk roads. Also, one can often choose between expensive, readily available air services or cheap standby facilities that often involve queuing or waiting for a flight. With a given distribution of income, this increased choice necessarily increases welfare that may, in turn, off-set any, or at least part of, the dead-weight loss incurred on congested parts of the system. Essentially there is product differentiation taking place in response to variations in the opportunity cost of time among consumers.

The difficulty with this argument is that in many cases physical factors make it impossible to provide different types of transport service. In other cases, economies of scale are sufficient to make the provision of alternatives excessively wasteful. One approach, favored by theoreticians, may be to decide upon the optimal flow, and only let that flow on to the road or facility at any one time, leaving a queue of potential users waiting. The optimal flow in this sense being such that the length of the queue of traffic wishing to use the road would make the opportunity time cost of waiting equal to the money price at which the traffic flow is optimal. It is difficult to see how this could be put into practice on urban roads, although it may be appropriate for making optimal use of facilities such as bridges or ferries where queuing is practicable. The information costs of estimating optimal queue lengths may also prove an insurmountable practical problem.

Finally, a high level of congestion may itself be optimal (even with the dead-weight losses it imposes and where neither of the former lines of argument are applicable) when other forms of cost are also considered. It may be, for example, that the transaction costs of moving from an over-congested to an optimally congested situation exceed the conventionally defined benefits of eliminating a dead-weight loss. The transition costs involved in removing an externality such as excessive congestion are of three broad types: the cost per unit of reducing the externality, initial lump-sum costs of organization, and information/enforcement costs of carrying the action through.

To remove excessive congestion would, in virtually all cases, involve costs in one or more of these categories and it could well be that in many cases such transaction costs could be very high. A related point is that the actual reduction of congestion to the optimal level for transport users may mean spreading other forms of external cost (generally noise and air pollution) to a much wider group of non-users in the community. Raising landing fees at over-used major airports, for example, is likely to divert traffic elsewhere and place environmental costs on people living near other, formerly under-utilized airports.

Congestion may in these circumstances, where the demand for transport concentrates the incidence of environmental costs on a relatively small group in the community, be felt to offer a more acceptable use of transport infrastructure than if congestion is reduced but this results in demand being spread geographi-cally. This is more likely if the initial congestion is concentrated in relatively insensitive areas, but its reduction would increase the environmental nuisance experienced in residential or other sensitive locations.

6.10   Some Broad Aggregate Calculations

The discussion so far has focused on individual external costs and provided, in places, some estimates of their possible magnitudes. Here we provide just a few examples of larger studies that have sought to place monetary values on a range of transport-related externalities. The problems with most of these studies are that they largely rely on secondary sources and there is, in some cases, a lack of consistency in the way various effects have been measured and evaluated. Second, placing monetary values on individual externalities at the micro, case-study level is difficult because such partial-equilibrium work assumes that 'other things remain constant', and most especially that income remains constant and that the prices of other goods remain constant. Clearly, at the macro level, any effort to estimate the willingness to pay for one externality reduction will reduce the income available to pay for the optimization of another. Equally, reducing, say, noise nuisance to an optimal level will affect the price of noise and thus make it difficult to evaluate the willingness to pay for, say, increased safety. Unless these factors are embraced in the macro-level calculations, there is an inherent upward bias in the valuation of external transport costs.

In addition, there are often important correlations in terms of the impact of various external factors. Reducing congestion costs, for instance, not only allows transport infrastructure to be utilized more efficiently by its users but often also reduces environmental costs because, for example, automobiles are not continually stopping and starting, or aircraft do not have to circle so much before landing. The correlations are not always positive. The fitting of a catalytic converter, while reducing NO_X emissions, increases fuel consumption and thus CO_2 emissions; and while smoother tires produce less road noise, they have less traction and can lead to more accidents.

Notwithstanding these problems, Emile Quinet (1994) first tried to use the best information available to give a general, minimum estimate of the monetary costs of the damage transport imposes on the environments of industrialized countries. His figures are, however, conservative because they cover only some of the damage done by transport, and because only lower estimates for each social cost considered are used in the calculations.

Table 6.15 provides another assessment of the external costs (including congestion) that have been specifically associated with the use of automobiles in the United States. Table 6.16 is a table at the meso level looking at estimates of some of the relative external costs of car use in a European city. It is not, however, a complete list of atmospheric gas releases.

The analyses show, as is typical, that the costs of congestion per mile exceed those of pollution and other environmental effects, although climate change effects are excluded. It should be remembered, however, that congestion is only external to those using transport, while the environmental costs are external to the transport system. The data suggest, however, that the largest social gains come from removing the imperfections within the transport system, rather than from removing the costs that are external to it.

Table 6.15   *Estimated externality costs of automobile use in the United States*

	Cents per gallon	Cents per mile
Central values for marginal external costs		
Fuel-related costs		
Greenhouse gases	6	0.3
Oil dependency	12	0.6
Total	*18*	*0.9*
Mileage-related costs		
Local pollution	42	2.0
Congestion	105	5.0
Accidents	63	3.0
Total	*210*	*10.0*

Source: Parry et al. (2007).

Table 6.16   *External costs of urban car use in Brussels (€ per vehicle mile)*

	Gasoline		Diesel	
	Peak	Off-peak	Peak	Off-peak
Congestion	1.856	0.003	1.856	0.003
Air pollution	0.004	0.004	0.042	0.026
Accidents	0.033	0.033	0.033	0.033
Noise	0.002	0.008	0.002	0.008
Total	*1.895*	*0.047*	*1.932*	*0.068*

Source: Proost and Van Dender (2001).

References

Anciaes, P.R., Jones, P., and Mindell, A.S. (2016) Community severance: where is it found and at what cost? *Transport Reviews*, 36, 293–317.

Araújo Alves, J., Neto Paiva, F., Silva, L.T., and Remoaldo, P. (2020) Low-frequency noise and its main effects on human health: a review of the literature between 2016 and 2019, *Applied Sciences*, 10, 5205, https://doi.org/10.3390/app10155205.

Barzel, Y. (1974) A theory of rationing by waiting, *Journal of Law and Economics*, 17, 73–9.

Bonnafus, A. (1994) Summary and conclusions, in Organization for Economic Cooperation and Development, Internalizing the Social Costs of Transport, Report, OECD.

Chestnut, L. and Mills, D.M. (2005) A fresh look at the benefits and costs of the US Acid Rain Program, *Journal of Environmental Management*, 77, 252–66.

China Energy Research Society (2002) Energy policy research 2002.1, Report.

Cohen, M.J. (1995) Technological disasters and natural resource damage assessment: an evaluation of the Exxon Valdez oil spill, *Land Economics*, 71, 65–82.

European Commission (2006) European energy and transport trends to 2030: update 2005, Report, Office for Official Publications of the European Communities.

Evans, A.W. (1992) Road congestion: the diagrammatic analysis, *Journal of Political Economy*, 100, 211–17.

Frenking, H. (1988) Exchange of information on noise abatement policies: case study on Germany, Report, OECD.

Gillen, D. (2003) The economics of noise, in K.J. Button and D. Hensher (eds), *Handbook of Transport and the Environment*, Pergamon.

Handy, S. (2003) Amenity and severance, in K.J. Button and D. Hensher (eds), *Handbook of Transport and the Environment*, Pergamon.

Haynes, K.E. (2004) Transportation location and environmental justice: a US perspective, in D.A. Hensher, K.J. Button, K.E. Haynes, and P.R. Stopher (eds), *Handbook of Transport Geography and Spatial Systems*, Elsevier.

Holland, S.P., Mansur, E.T., and Yates, A.J. (2016) Are there environmental benefits from driving electric vehicles? The importance of local factors, *American Economic Review*, 106, 3700–29.

Holland, S.P., Mansur, E.T., and Yates, A.J. (2021) The electric vehicle transition and the economics of banning gasoline vehicles, *American Economic Journal: Economic Policy*, 13, 316–44.

IEA (International Energy Agency) (2000) CO_2 emissions from fuel combustion 1971–1998, Report, IEA.

IPCC (Intergovernmental Panel on Climate Change) (1995) IPCC second assessment synthesis of scientific–technical information relevant to interpreting Article 2 of the UN Framework Convention on Climate Change, Report, IPCC.

Jacobsen, M.R. and van Benthem, A.A. (2015) Vehicle scrappage and gasoline policy, *American Economic Review*, 105, 1312–38.

Johnson, K. and Button, K.J. (1997) Benefit transfers: are they a satisfactory input to benefit cost analysis? *Transportation Research Part D*, 2, 223–31.

Jones-Lee, M.W. (1990) The value of traffic safety, *Oxford Review of Economic Policy*, 60, 39–60.

Jones-Lee, M.W. and Loomes, G. (2003) Valuation of safety, in K.J. Button and D. Hensher (eds), *Handbook of Transport and the Environment*, Pergamon.

Martin, D.J. (1978) Low frequency traffic noise and building vibration, Transport Research Laboratory Supplementary Report, SR.429.

McCubbin, D.R. and Dellucci, M.A. (1999) The health costs of motor-related air pollution, *Journal of Air Transport and Policy*, 33, 253–87.

Nelson, J.P. (1979) Airport noise, location rent, and the market for residential amenities, *Journal of Environmental Economics and Management*, 6, 320–31.

Nelson, J.P (2004) Meta-analysis of airport noise and hedonic property values: problems and prospects, *Journal of Transport Economics and Policy*, 38, 1–28.

Neutze, G.M. (1963) The external diseconomies of growth in traffic, *Economic Record*, 39, 332–45.

Newbery, D.M. (1988) Road damage externalities and road user charges, *Econometrica*, 56, 295–316.

Newbery, D.M (1990) Pricing and congestion: economic principles relevant to road pricing, *Oxford Review of Economic Policy*, 6, 22–38.

OECD (Organisation for Economic Cooperation and Development) (1991) *Fighting Noise*, OECD.

Parry, I.W.H., Walls, M., and Harrington, W. (2007) Automobile externalities and policies, *Journal of Economic Literature*, 45, 373–99.

Pearce, D.W. and Turner, R.K. (1990) *Economics of Natural Resources and the Environment*, Harvester Wheatsheaf.

Proost, S. and Van Dender, K. (2001) The welfare impacts of alternative policies to address atmospheric pollution in urban road transport, *Regional Science and Urban Economics*, 31, 383–411.

Quinet, E. (1994) The social costs of transport: evaluation and links with internalisation policies, in *Internalizing the Social Costs of Transport*, European Conference of Ministers of Transport.

Rothenberg, J. (1970) The economics of congestion and pollution: an integrated view, *American Economic Review, Papers and Proceedings*, 60, 114–21.

Smith, L.V. (1982) Microeconomic systems as an experimental science, *American Economic Review*, 72, 923–55.

Smith, V.K. (1989) Taking stock of progress with travel cost recreation demand methods: theory and implementation, *Marine Resource Economics*, 6, 279–330.

Spash, C.L. (2008) The contingent valuation method: retrospect and prospect, *Environment and Planning C*, 26, 34–53.

Stern, N. (2007) Stern review: the economics of climate change, Report, Cabinet Office – HM Treasury.

Sweet, M. (2014) Traffic congestion's economic impacts: evidence from US metropolitan regions, *Urban Studies*, 51, 2088–110.

Talley, W.K. (2001) Oil spillage and damage costs: US inland water tank barge accidents, *International Journal of Maritime Economics*, 2, 217–34.

Texas Transportation Institute (2019) Annual urban mobility report, TTI.

Thomson, J.M. (1977) *Great Cities and their Traffic*, Gollancz.

Verhoef, E.T. (2005) Speed–flow relations and cost functions for congested traffic: theory and empirical analysis, *Transportation Research Part A*, 39, 792–812.

Vickrey, W. (1969) Congestion theory and transport investment, *American Economic Review: Papers and Proceedings*, 59, 251–60.

Weisbrod, G., Vary, D., and Treyz, G. (2001) Economic implications of congestion, NCHRP Report 463, Transportation Research Board.

Whiffen, A.C. and Leonard, D.P. (1971) A survey of traffic induced vibrations, Road Research Laboratory Report, LR418.

Winston, C. and Langer, A. (2004) *The Effect of Government Highway Spending on Road Users' Congestion Costs*, Brookings Institution.

World Commission on Environment and Development (1987) *Our Common Future*, Oxford University Press.

7　The Pricing of Transport

7.1　The Principles of Pricing

Pricing is a method of resource allocation. There is no such thing as the 'right' price, but rather there are optimal pricing strategies that permit specified goals to be obtained. The optimal price, for example, to achieve profit maximization may differ from that needed to maximize welfare or ensure the highest sales revenue. In some cases, there are no attempts to devise a price to maximize or minimize anything, but rather prices are set that permit lower-level objectives (for example, acceptable levels of security or market share) to be attained.

Often linked to this is the matter of who is setting the price. Prices may be set to achieve certain objectives for transport suppliers in terms of their welfare (this is normally the case with private enterprise transport undertakings) while in other cases prices may be set to improve the welfare of consumers (as has been the case with some publicly owned transport undertakings). The distinction here can be a fine one and many undertakings consider that the employment of the pricing mechanisms to achieve their objectives is automatically to the benefit of customers.

One of the major problems in discussing pricing policies in practice is to decide what exactly the objective of pricing is. A good example is port pricing, where there has been a traditional blurring between the 'European' doctrine of setting prices to facilitate the economic growth of a port's hinterland and the 'Anglo-Saxon' approach that attempts to ensure that ports cover their costs and, where possible, make a profit with respect to the effects on the wider local economy (Bennathan and Walters, 1979). In providing local transit services, there are often conflicts between setting prices that allow use by lower-income groups and pricing so that the system does not get excessively congested at peak, rush-hour travel times.

When the private sector sets the price, much depends on the market power exercised by the supplies of the transport system and those using it, and this in turn is affected by the prevailing market structure. If the supplier operates within a highly competitive market, then there is no opportunity for the transport company to control the price; the market sets it. If, in contrast, and at the other extreme, there is a single monopoly supplier and numerous customers, then the transport undertaking can dictate prices to a large extent, but always must be cognizant of losing business and net revenue, by setting them too high. In intermediate cases, the various actors involved play 'games' with each other, jockeying to gain the most benefit, be it consumer surplus or profit.

The nature of market power and the ways in which it may be exercised depends to a considerable extent on the nature of the market itself. There are

Table 7.1   *Features of various market structures*

Feature	Perfect competition	Perfectly competitive	Monopoly
Profit maximization	Yes	Yes	Normally
Barriers to entry/exit	No	No	Yes
Perfect mobility of inputs	Yes	Yes	No
Ubiquitous information	Yes	Yes	No
Large number of firms	Yes	Maybe	No
Homogeneous service	Yes	Maybe	Yes
Firms confronted by the cost function	Yes	Yes	Yes
U-shaped AC functions	Yes	Maybe	Maybe
Profits	Normal	Normal	Monopoly rent

many different forms of market and it is beyond the scope of this volume to explain all of them. Table 7.1, however, provides a very brief outline of the main features of competitive, contestable, and monopoly markets; forms that are often said to exist in transport. They are not the only ones, but the aim is to give an indication of the various parameters that determine market behavior rather than to be comprehensive.

This chapter looks at the appropriate pricing policies to adopt for transport undertakings, considering a variety of objectives and when those involved are confronted by different market conditions. In simple terms, in the transport context it is about maximizing the benefits from transport given that there are resource and other constraints on what can be provided. While the later sections focus on criteria concerned with maximizing the social benefits of transport that embrace the interests of both suppliers and uses, this section briefly reviews the prices likely to exist in situations where transport enterprises are interested in purely commercial criteria (defined here as the pursuit of their own self-interest, which often, although not always, involves profits). The chapters that follow consider, along with other things, the role of pricing of the environment and of congestion.

7.2   Matching Supply with Demand

Traditional neoclassical economics assumes that profit maximization is the motivation behind the activities of private enterprise undertakings. The actual price level in this case depends upon the degree of competition in the market and the costs of production. Where competition is considerable then no single supplier has control over price and must charge that determined by the interaction of supply and demand in the market (Adam Smith's 'invisible hand'). In this perfectly competitive environment, it is impossible for any supplier to earn super-normal profits in the long term because of the incentives such profits have on new suppliers entering the market and increasing aggregate supply. Following the same logic, economics tells us that in the long run price will be equated with the marginal (and average) costs of each supplier.

In contrast, a true monopoly supplier has no fear of new entrants increasing the aggregate supply of transport services and has the freedom either to set the price or to stipulate the level of service they are prepared to offer. The effective constraint on the monopolist is the countervailing power of those demanding the service that prevents the joint determination of both output and price. However, given the absence of competition and the degree of freedom enjoyed by the monopolist, it is almost certain that a profit-maximizing price will result in charges above marginal and average cost (the only exception being the most unlikely situation of a perfectly elastic market-demand curve). This is one reason why governments have tended to regulate the railways, ports, and other transport undertakings with monopoly characteristics, or to supply the transport services themselves.

This simple description of textbook situations does, however, hide certain peculiarities that may arise in some transport markets. Since the actual unit of supply, the vehicle, is mobile it is possible for the overall transport market to appear to be essentially competitive, but the individual suppliers to price as if they were monopolists or, at least, exercise some monopoly power. The unregulated urban taxi-cab market is an example of this. In Figure 7.1, D_M is the market demand for taxi-cab 'rides' per hour in a market supplied solely by cruising taxicabs. The cost of taxi cruising activities is almost constant irrespective of whether a fare is carried or not, and to stay in business the cab operator must charge fares which permit such costs to be recovered.

In the figure, the iso-profit curve for a single operator indicates combinations of fare and ridership that allow a normal profit to be earned. It is constrained to a minimum fare (P_2) by the physical impossibility of carrying more than R_2 passengers an hour. Also, it is unlikely that a fare above P_2 would ever be feasible; potential users would simply not accept it. For the overall market, fares must exceed P_1 if taxi-cab services are to be offered, but is not the true long-term floor level of fares. Because potential customers are seldom positioned exactly

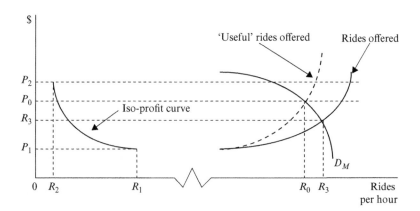

Figure 7.1   *Taxi-cab fare determination*

where empty cabs are cruising, there must be an excess of rides offered above total demand if enough rides are to be supplied; this is indicated by the 'useful' rides curve.

This lack of synchronization means, in effect, that the 'rides-offered curve' in Figure 7.1 is not a true supply curve since it is dependent upon demand conditions. At higher fares, the rides offered will increase but even at the intersection with the total demand curve (with R_3 rides offered) there will still be unsatisfied demand (Shreiber, 1975), that is, the number of taxi rides taken is less than the number demanded. This is because the taxis may not be at the same location as potential customers. Only if cabs were always exactly where they were wanted would demand always be satisfied. The demand will, in normal circumstances, only be fully satisfied at a price above the intersection – say P_0 – because at this and higher prices the ratio between rides demanded and the number offered will correspond to the rate of occupancy. This is so because the number demanded is then assumed equal to the number of rides taken, and there are no frustrated passengers who give up waiting because they are unable to obtain a ride.

The actual fare level may be set at any point above P_1 but below P_2, hence the apparently perfect taxi-cab market does not have a unique price. However, there are reasons to suspect that the final price will be nearer P_1 than P_2, thus permitting the earning of super-normal profit by the cab operators. It also means that those who still wish to pay the fare and use taxi-cab services will have a good service provided for them – the rides offered being well in excess of those demanded – although the short waiting time and abundance of capacity is likely to be wasteful in resource utilization.

The tendency towards high fares is caused by the monopoly power enjoyed by any individual taxi at the point of hire. Unlike normal perfect markets, individual suppliers are not normally confronted with perfectly elastic demand schedules for their services but when hailed by a potential customer are virtual monopolists able to charge a high fare for their services. People seldom turn away a cab, upon hearing the fare, to hail another one – the low probability of a lower cab fare does not justify it: once fares are at the higher level there is, therefore, no incentive for individual cabs to cut their fares, because to customers they all appear alike and no additional business is attracted (that is, revenue for any cab acting differently will inevitably fall).

Of course, the cab market is somewhat more complicated than the simple model suggests (there are, for instance, cab ranks, and it may be possible to differentiate cabs by color schemes, etc.), but the fear that cabs could exploit local monopoly power of the type described and keep fares suboptimally high is one reason why authorities in most major cities control fare levels. While this may be justified, it is hard to see why at the same time most cities outside of the United Kingdom regulate the number of taxi-cabs operating within their domain; if fares are deemed optimal at P_0 then rides offered will automatically adjust to R_0 and there is no need for official regulation of capacity which can seriously distort the market (Beesley, 1973).

While it is possible that the simple picture of perfectly competitive price determination is often complicated in the transport sector, it is equally true that the basic model of monopoly also on occasion needs modification. There are few if any natural monopolies in transport: there are normally competitive modes even if the one in question tends to be monopolistic in character. Users of transport services often have the alternative of either changing their method of production (in the case of freight transport) or pattern of consumption (with passenger modes) so that transport is itself competitive with different forms of human activity. In some cases where these countervailing forces are weak or the introduction of competition would mean wasteful duplication of services, government may institutionalize a monopoly but by controlling price and other commercial aspects of its operations prevent the exploitation of customers. Much of the regulation initiated in a wide range of countries in the 1930s and 1940s, which is discussed in Chapter 14, was ostensibly introduced for this sort of reason.

Exhibit   *The issue of predatory pricing*

The US Supreme Court in 1986 defined predatory pricing as 'pricing below an appropriate measure of cost for the purpose of eliminating competitors in the short term and reducing competition in the long run'. The Court's criteria for proving predation were based on market power, predatory conduct, and recoupment. (Recoupment being the ability of an incumbent supplier to recover revenues lost during the period prices are reduced, to force out a competitor.)

In practice, few cases of predation have been proved in transport markets. Large incumbents may set prices that offer a reasonable long-term profit but which are not large enough to stimulate new suppliers who will encounter entry costs: 'limit pricing'. If there are no market-entry and -exit costs as in contestable markets, then fear of hit-and-run competition will automatically exclude incumbents making abnormal profits. But there may also be other ways of deterring market entry.

The traditional approach to predatory behavior, with its foundation on microeconomic theory, was questioned by the US Department of Transportation (US DOT) in 1971. In its place the DOT favored a more structure-conduct-performance-based approach, looking at the actual behavior of suppliers over networks rather than simply the existence of monopoly power on any individual route: a wider concept of a 'domain of power'. It also recognized in the airline case that carriers can deter competitors through the use of long-term contracts with suppliers, control over infrastructure (for example, of slots and gates), and the benefit of greater financial resources.

To examine the different views, Ashutosh Dixit et al. (2006) studied airline concentrations at the 50 largest US domestic airports between 1991 and 1999, including 17 major hubs and two slot-controlled airports, and, in addition, looked at the specific behavior of a major airline.

One of the issues addressed was the response of incumbents to new market entry and also their re-entry. Fifteen routes of a major airline were selected when there were market entries by discount carriers, and 15 when there was none. Comparisons of these groups showed the major airline increasing average fares by 15 percent between 1994 and 1999 on routes where there was no discount airline competition. Of the routes where there was competitive entry (ten in 1993 and five between 1997 and 1998), fares were reduced.

Considering the markets where there has been a competitor (or competitors) entering the market but which have subsequently left it (see figure), the dominant carrier initially cut its fares but then increased them to the same or higher levels than before the competitive entry. There are also two cases of entry and re-entry by discount carriers and in both cases the incumbent responded with fare cuts, subsequent fare rises, and then cuts again when competitive re-entry occurred. This is all in line with the Supreme Court criteria.

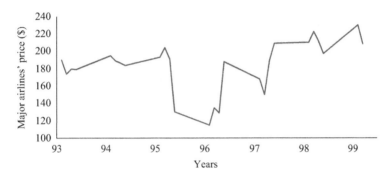

See also: A. Dixit, G.T. Gundlach, and F. Allvine (2006) Aggressive and predatory pricing: insights and empirical examination in the airline industry, *Journal of Public Policy and Marketing*, 25, 172–87.

The fear of potential competition, especially in the long term, tends to lead to the regulation of the activities of quasi-monopoly transport suppliers even when government intervention is minimal regarding other transport modes. Table 7.2, for example, offers information on some of the regulations imposed on taxi-cab services.

The pricing policies pursued by liner conferences, when shipping companies combine to monopolize scheduled maritime services between major ports, offer another illustration of this problem. Sturmey (1975) argues that conferences do not price to maximize immediate profits but rather to maximize the present value of the flow of revenue from the market. More discussion of detailed pricing of consignments by conferences is contained in Section 7.5, while here we focus on the relevant general principles.

The emphasis on revenue reflects the concern with market size, while that on the present value shows that long-term objectives dominate short-run considerations. If, in Figure 7.2, the intention was to maximize profit in each market, then price would be set, assuming the conference enjoyed a short-term monopoly position, at P_M with a monthly output of Q_M. If sales-revenue maximization (subject

Table 7.2 *Examples of taxi-cab regulation in the early 2000s*

Country – city	Fare regulation	Entry regulation	Period	Restrictions
Belgium	Yes	Yes	5–10 years	1 vehicle per 1,000 inhabitants/ personal & non-transferable
Czechia	Yes	No	–	Non-transferable
Denmark	Yes	Yes	10 years	Non-transferable
France – Paris	Yes	Yes	–	100 new licenses per year
Germany	Yes	No	5 years	License quota & fee
Hungary	Yes	–	–	–
Ireland	Yes	No (2000)	–	License quota & fee
Italy	Yes	Yes	–	4.5 per 10,000 inhabitants/1 license per person
Japan	Yes	No (2002)	–	–
Korea	Yes	Yes	–	–
Netherlands	Yes (2004)	No (2002)	–	–
Norway	City dependent	Yes	–	Neither tradeable nor transferable
Sweden	–	No (1990)	–	–
Switzerland	City dependent	Yes	3 years	Neither tradeable nor transferable
US – Seattle	No (1979)	No (1979)	–	–
Romania	Yes	Yes	–	4 vehicles per 1,000 inhabitants

Source: Salanovaa (2011).

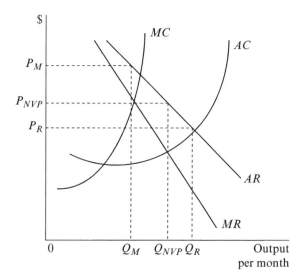

Figure 7.2 *Pricing of shipping conference services*

to cost recovery) is the objective then price P_R is charged (expanding output to where the MC curve hits the horizontal would violate the break-even constraint).

In practice, however, Sturmey argues that conference rates are found to be below P_M because the high short-term profits would encourage competition to enter the market; they are also unlikely to equal P_R because the conference looks beyond the immediate period although there is no *a priori* method of telling whether they will be above or below this level. The conference is likely to base its pricing policy on a relatively long time horizon, hypothesized by Sturmey to be the period over which the scale of productive enterprise is unchanged, but long enough to allow for additional capital equipment, which duplicates exist-ing equipment, to be installed – although not long enough for all factors to be considered truly variable. The net revenue over this period, discounted to yield its current worth, is then seen as the key variable to maximize. The conference rate is, therefore, likely to be, say, at P_{NPV} in Figure 7.2 at which the maximum present value (the value of the flow of net revenue as perceived today) is obtained without attracting new entrants.

7.3   Marginal Cost Pricing

As was pointed out in the previous section, the pricing policy adopted by any transport undertaking depends upon its basic objectives. The traditional, classi-cal economic assumption is that firms price so that profits are maximized. More recent variations on the theory of the firm suggests that many undertakings adopt prices that maximize sales revenues when in an expansive phase, or simply price to ensure that certain satisfactory levels of profit, security, market domination, etc., are achieved when a defensive stance is adopted – 'satisficing behavior', to adopt Herbert Simon's term.

The sales-revenue-maximizing ideas of William Baumol (1962) illustrate the sorts of deviation that this implies from conventional profit-maximizing ideas. In Figure 7.3 the total cost and revenue curves associated with different levels of output are depicted. The profit-maximizing business will produce an output of Q_Π, but the sales-revenue maximizer will continue producing to the point Q_R, where total revenue is highest subject to cost recovery. Costs in this case may be viewed as embracing a reasonable return for the owners of the transport undertaking.

Whatever the underlying operational objective, the theory of the firm assumes that the supplier is intent on maximizing his or her own welfare, be this defined in terms of profits or higher-level objectives.

Welfare economics takes a rather wider view of pricing, looking upon it as a method of resource allocation that maximizes social welfare rather than simply the welfare of the supplier. In some cases, since the good or service is provided by a public agency, this may be equated with maximizing the suppliers' welfare. In other instances, controls or incentives may be applied to private companies so that their pricing policy is modified to maximize social rather than private welfare. This may take the form of restrictions on pricing flexibility, or the taxing and subsidizing of firms so that their prices are socially optimal.

Social optimality has a wide variety of meanings but in broad terms it means maximizing the joint net social surplus – that is, the total revenue (*TR*) plus

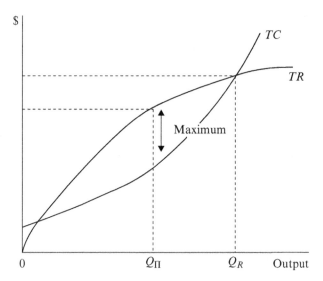

Figure 7.3 *Sales-revenue-maximizing output*

consumers' surplus (*CS*) generated by an undertaking minus the total cost (*TC*). We can, therefore, define the objective of public policy as the maximization of:

$$SW = TR + CS - TC \qquad (7.1)$$

Figure 7.4 takes the example of charging for rail freight capacity as an illustration of how the optimal price is arrived at. For expositional ease, assume that there are constant costs and that the railway undertaking is a monopoly. If it seeks to maximize its profits it will charge P_M, which in terms of equation (7.1) will produce total revenue of $P_M b Q_M 0$, consumer surplus of $ab P_M$, and total costs of $P_{MC} e Q_M 0$, resulting in a social welfare level of $abe P_{MC}$. While this may yield the maximum profit to the railway, it is not, however, the price that maximizes social surplus. That price is the price at which marginal cost is equated with demand. At this price, the total revenue is $P_{MC} d Q_{MC} 0$, consumer surplus is $ad P_{MC}$, and total cost is $P_{MC} d Q_{MC} 0$, which gives a total social welfare exceeding that associated with the profit-maximizing price by an amount *bed*.

In other words, social welfare is maximized when price is equated to marginal cost. What marginal cost pricing does, in effect, is to result in transport services being provided up to the point where the benefit for the marginal unit is equated with the costs of providing that unit. The policy is a well-established one in economic theory, and, indeed, formed the basis for United Kingdom public enterprise pricing from 1967.

Traditional theory also tells us that such a condition prevails in the long term when perfect competition exists, even though each firm is attempting to maximize its own profits. The ability to exercise any degree of monopoly power, however, permits a firm to price above marginal cost so that it can achieve additional profit at the expense of reduced output and at costs to the consumers. The price

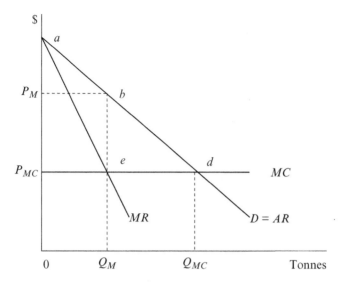

Figure 7.4 *Marginal cost pricing*

charged by a profit-maximizing monopolist will force some potential consumers to forgo consumption despite their willingness to pay for the costs of their
activities. Indeed, it was the fear of monopoly exploitation that led to controls
being imposed on railway pricing in the late nineteenth century and has led to
the United States controlling rate fixing by shipping conferences operating from
its ports.

  While it has been shown that adopting marginal cost pricing maximizes
social welfare, the exact definition of the appropriate marginal cost has been left
vague. More specifically, there is the question of whether long-run ($LRMC$) or
short-run marginal cost ($SRMC$) pricing is the more appropriate (short-run being
when there is a fixed capacity that can be modified only in the long run). $SRMC$
pricing has the advantage that it ensures existing capacity is used optimally but
does not take account of capital and other fixed cost items. Jack Wiseman (1957)
was concerned with this problem since, he argued, the shorter the time period
under consideration, the lower will the $SRMC$ appear and, *ipso facto*, the price
charged to users. This concern is misguided, however, because if there is fixed
capacity, as is almost always the case with transport in the short term, a premium
should be added to $SRMC$ as an effective rationing device to contain excessive
demand. Price is, after all, an allocative device.

  Figure 7.5 shows the demand for a passenger railway service with capacity
Q_1. The marginal cost of carrying each additional passenger is constant until
the capacity of the system is reached, whereupon the $SRMC$ becomes infinite.
If a price of P_1 is charged with $SRMC_1$, then demand will exceed capacity by
$Q^*_d - Q_1$. In these circumstances, where demand will exceed absolute capacity
using $SRMC$ pricing policy, a mark-up to price level P^*_1 is appropriate to ration
the available seats. The extra revenue thus generated in excess of $LRMC$ provides
an indication that it would be beneficial for the capacity of the railway service

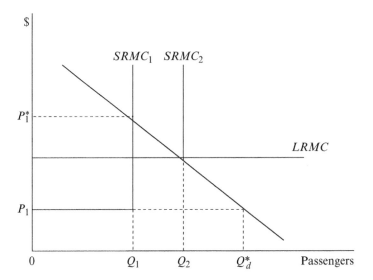

Figure 7.5   *Short-run and long-run marginal cost pricing*

to be expanded. The optimal scale of service will, in fact, be offering capacity Q_2, where the price charged to travelers is equated with $LRMC$ (and the upturn of the $SRMC_2$ curve). We see, therefore, that the long-run optimum is where $P = LRMC = SRMC$. In some cases (for example, airports or motorway systems), indivisibilities may make it impossible to provide exactly the optimal capacity Q_2, and a choice must then be made between a suboptimally small system or a suboptimally large one. In these circumstances, decisions must be based upon weighing the full costs and benefits of the alternatives against one another.

7.4   Difficulties of 'Second-best' Situations

The preceding analysis contained several implicit, as well as the stated explicit, assumptions. It assumed that all other prices in the economy are set equal to marginal cost. A variety of factors – some economic, others political or institutional – mean that all other prices in the economy are not equal to marginal cost. The problem, again couched in terms of the railway example, then becomes one of deciding whether marginal cost pricing is, in these circumstances, appropriate in the railway context.

For simplicity we assume that there is only bus and rail transport in the economy. Further, the bus sector is under monopoly control and fares are set above the marginal costs of providing services. The issue is one of whether the railways should marginal-cost price or adopt some alternative strategy that would maximize social welfare. In Figure 7.6, we have the production possibility curve for bus and rail services and, additionally, denote A as the traffic mix which would result in maximum social welfare; it is tangential to the highest attainable indifference curve.

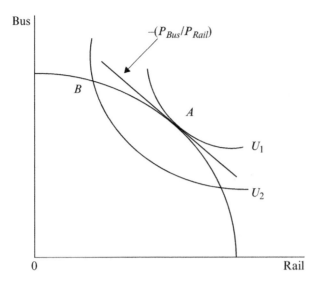

Figure 7.6   *Second-best problems*

Extending the analysis of Figure 7.4, because this combination maximizes social welfare, the two modes will be charging marginal costs at this point. Since, however, we have said that bus fares are above marginal cost $(P_{Bus} > MC_{Bus})$ the attainable position on the production possibility frontier with the actual price ration if rail adopts marginal cost pricing $(P_{Rail} = MC_{Rail})$ is *B*, which is on a lower utility curve, namely U_2. The question then arises as to whether the railways, by deviating from marginal cost pricing and adopting a 'second-best' pricing strategy, can enhance total social welfare.

The simplest approach to the second-best in these conditions, as established by Lipsey and Lancaster (1956/57) is that rail should adopt fares which deviate by the same proportion from marginal costs as do those of bus. In other words, it is possible to attain social welfare level U_1 by adopting prices that conform to:

$$\frac{P_{Rail} - MC_{Rail}}{MC_{Rail}} = \frac{P_{Bus} - MC_{Bus}}{MC_{Bus}} \tag{7.2}$$

What this effectively does is ensure that the two modes are comparable in terms of their relative attractiveness. In practice the calculations are more complex and Nilsson (1992) offers an illustration of how second-best prices could be determined for Sweden's freight rail services in conditions where road transport is not paying its full marginal costs. A general problem is that here we are only looking at transport, but while the second-best rule will ensure the social optimal mix of transport use there may be problems with other prices in the economy. If they all remain set at marginal cost but both rail and bus are priced along second-best lines above marginal cost, then transport will be relatively expensive when compared to other possible expenditures. Ideally, all prices should deviate by appropriate percentages from their marginal costs in these circumstances.

Under some conditions the problem may not be serious and, from a purely pragmatic stance, it may be more efficient to charge marginal cost prices than to bear the costs of working out any optimal adjustments. In other cases, deviations from marginal cost principles elsewhere in the economy may be so remote that they have minimal influence on the demand for transport. Under such conditions, and assuming the distortions cannot be removed, Davis and Whinston (1967) demonstrate that piecemeal optimization within separate sectors of the economy using marginal cost pricing is optimal. Ed Mishan (1962) suggests that since in many cases people spend a fixed amount of their income upon transport, there is, therefore, only a very low cross-elasticity of demand between transport as a whole and other goods consumed in the economy. This situation means that the issue can be reduced to optimizing the allocation of traffic between forms of transport, on a piecemeal basis, rather than having to consider the allocation of expenditure between a certain form of transport and all other goods. If, in our example, all competing forms of transport apply marginal cost pricing principles, then these should also be adopted by the railway service.

While Mishan's empirical approach has a certain practical common-sense appeal for some forms of transport – such as inter-urban passenger transport – it has less applicability in the freight sector or in the context of international travel. Freight costs have a considerable bearing upon both final prices charged for products and the location of the manufacturing industry; these are also the main reasons for the attempts at the macro-macro level to develop a Common Transport Policy within the European Union and why transportation at borders has been such an issue in the creation of the North American Free Trade Agreement (NAFTA).

If all other inputs to industry are priced above marginal cost because, say, of the monopoly power of suppliers, but transport is priced at marginal cost, then this could lead to an over-development, from the national efficiency point of view, of transport-intensive industry (although it is possible that relatively 'cheap' transport could break the monopoly power of the suppliers of other inputs forcing them, in the long run, to price at marginal cost). International air and sea transport has the complication that, except in certain well-defined areas, many nations consciously subsidize their 'flag bearers', enabling them to charge rates below $LRMC$ and, on occasions, even below $SRMC$. Any single operator charging fares based on marginal cost in this situation would find itself unable to attract the optimal volume of traffic, and thus some deviation from the marginal cost principle may be necessary.

The existence of monopoly and other distorting influences in the economy has been shown to necessitate some variations to marginal cost pricing in certain transport sectors. The key to the degree to which prices should deviate from marginal cost is clearly the sign and magnitude of the cross-elasticities of demand between transport and other goods and services in the economy. The practical difficulty in many cases is not the derivation of the appropriate theoretical model but rather our inadequate knowledge of the size of the cross-elasticities. The evidence that is coming forward tends to be piecemeal. Additionally, most of the evidence is only related to intra-transport cross-elasticities with extremely few estimates of transport/other goods cross-elasticities.

7.5 Price Differentiation, Price Discrimination, and Yield Management

There can be quite significant differences in the fares paid by those on a specific plane or train in most cases, but also for cargo rates on ships. Some of this is attributable to cost differences – things like superior service. But, in addition to this, these different prices may be used as a rationing device to allocate out scarce resources, limited capacity being available at the last minute requiring higher prices to ration it amongst those seeking a late seat or berth. This is effectively yield management in its traditional sense. There is also price discrimination, whereby transport service suppliers seek to gain as much revenue as each individual user is willing to pay above costs.

Second-best pricing and the like are forms of price discrimination: different users of a transport service pay different prices not entirely related to their attributed cost. So far we have discussed such discrimination largely in terms of imperfections in other markets and the need to make adjustments to marginal cost prices in the transport market of interest to reflect these external distortions. The adoption of marginal cost pricing can, in certain circumstances, however, also result in an undertaking making a financial loss even when other markets are working correctly. It is this type of situation that we now address.

The Basic Idea of Price Discrimination with Decreasing Costs

The classic example of this is the decreasing cost industry where, because of high initial capital costs, the setting of charges equal to $SRMC$ will result in a financial deficit. The railways are often cited as an example of an industry where marginal cost pricing may ensure optimal utilization but leave the undertaking with a financial deficit. In Figure 7.7 the railways are assumed to be a monopoly supplier of freight services and, indeed, although it is not shown, if a monopoly profit-maximizing price were adopted then abnormal profits could be earned. The adoption of marginal cost pricing (P_{MC}), however, with the downward-sloping AC and MC curves, at least over the relevant range, will result in a loss shown by the shaded area. A break-even situation could be attained by average cost pricing (that is, charging P_{AC}), but this would mean that $Q_{MC} - Q_{AC}$ potential rail travelers, willing to pay the additional costs they impose, are priced off the service.

In these circumstances the adoption of marginal cost pricing is essentially a welfare decision and if the undertaking does make a financial loss this is attributable to the pricing policy pursued rather than the incapacity of the service to be financially viable. The fixed costs of the service may be met in these cases by subsidy or by operating a 'club' system with potential users paying a fixed sum for the right to travel by rail and a mileage rate (or some other 'cost'-related variable fee) to reflect use. It could be argued that the fixed rates of road vehicle taxation combined with fuel duties reflect a type of club arrangement, but, if so, the system is extremely imperfect. In the United Kingdom, for example, at the very crudest level of analysis, there is very considerable variation in the ratio of license fee to fuel tax revenue that bears no relation to their relative expenditures on investment and maintenance (Table 7.3). This is a picture repeated in virtually all countries. Returning to Figure 7.7, if each user was charged a different price so that it reflects his or her willingness to pay, and output was limited to the point where MC equals demand (that is, Q_{MC}), this would yield a revenue of $0abQ_{MC}$, which may be compared with the total cost of providing the service, namely $0P_{MC}bQ_{MC}$. Using this first-best discriminatory pricing approach, the costs are fully recovered and a profit of $P_{MC}ba$ is being earned. Of course, price discrimination does not always guarantee full cost recovery, which depends on the revenue raised *vis-à-vis* the costs involved. Further, one should also note that perfect price discrimination, as described, results in the marginal cost level of output; in fact, it results in social welfare maximization but with all the benefits being derived by the provider of the transport service.

Figure 7.8 illustrates a situation, and one that does occur with certain forms of transport service, where even first-best price discrimination will not produce full cost recovery. Here, at no level of output does average revenue exceed average cost. It is impossible in this type of situation for costs to be recovered by charging a single price to all users even if monopoly-pricing policies are adopted. In this case even a club arrangement is incapable of preventing the service from being unprofitable. There may be justifications for keeping the service operating with the losses financed through subsidies if there are wider benefits to be enjoyed outside of those generally linked to transport; the service may, for instance, have

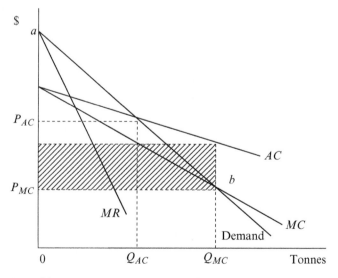

Figure 7.7   *Second-best average cost pricing with degreasing costs*

Table 7.3   *Road costs and user payments in the United Kingdom in pence per vehicle-kilometers (1998)*

Cost or revenue category	Fully allocated costs		Marginal costs	
	Low	High	Low	High
Costs				
Cost of capital for infrastructure	0.78	1.34	n.a.	n.a.
Infrastructure operating costs & depreciation	0.75	0.97	0.42	0.54
Vehicle operating costs (PSV)	0.87	0.87	0.87	0.87
Congestion	n.a.	n.a.	9.71	11.16
Mohring effect (PSV)	n.a.	n.a	−0.16	−0.16
External accident costs	0.06	0.78	0.82	1.40
Air pollution	0.34	1.70	0.34	1.70
Noise	0.24	0.78	0.02	0.78
Climate change	0.15	0.15	0.15	0.15
VAT not paid	0.15	0.15	0.15	0.15
Subtotal of costs	*3.34*	*7.20*	*12.32*	*17.05*
Revenues				
Fares (PSV)	0.84	0.08	0.84	0.84
Vehicle excise duty	1.10	1.10	0.14	0.14
Fuel duty	4.42	4.42	4.42	4.42
VAT on fuel duty	0.77	0.77	0.77	0.77
Subtotal of revenues	*7.14*	*7.14*	*6.17*	*6.17*
Costs–revenues	*−3.79*	*0.07*	*6.15*	*10.88*
Revenues/costs	*2.13*	*0.99*	*0.50*	*0.36*

Notes: Road sector costs exclude costs attributable to pedestrians, bicyclists, and motorcyclists; vehicle excise duty at the margin relates to heavy goods vehicles (HGV) and public service vehicles (PSV) such as buses.

n.a. = not available.

Source: Samson et al. (2001).

a strategic value or it may be deemed a 'merit good', a concept first suggested by Richard Musgrave (1957) in the context of low-cost housing, which society ought to provide to enable isolated communities to continue in existence.

In summary, in the more conventional case, if subsidies are to be avoided, two-part tariffs are impractical, and average cost pricing is deemed inappropriate, then price discrimination can still be used to finance the service. Essentially, price discrimination involves charging 'what the user will bear' provided they cover their marginal costs. In other words, it involves attempting to define the maximum amount each consumer, or, more realistically, each identifiable group of customers, is willing to pay for the service. The demand curve reflects 'willingness of users to pay' (the *AR* curve becomes the *de facto MR* curve) when a transport enterprise price-discriminates and a perfectly discriminating supplier will charge down this curve. First-best price discrimination is however rare, and more pragmatic approaches to price discrimination are pursued in practice.

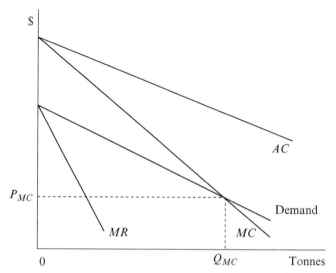

Figure 7.8   *Decreasing costs with demand always inside the average cost curve*

Differentiation by Type of Customer/Commodity

In many cases a transport undertaking itself provides several services (for example, first- and second-class rail services) and it also has a remit to make a prescribed level of profit, or to break even, rather than to maximize profits. Given these conditions, and assuming the cross-elasticity of demand for the different service is negligible, Baumol and Bradford (1970) stated that the price of any services should be set equal to its *SRMC* plus a mark-up inversely proportionate to the service's price elasticity of demand (ε). Hence, where the demand for a service is highly inelastic a substantial addition should be added to marginal cost. Where the demand is perfectly elastic, *SRMC* pricing is applied. In this way revenue *SRMC* can be obtained to meet the financial target without distorting the allocation of traffic between services.

If cross-elasticities are not zero, which is the common case, then the simple rule must be modified to ensure that the relative quantities of goods sold respond to the proportions that would occur if marginal cost pricing were applicable. The rule, for example, for substitutes is that optimal prices should be derived so that 'all output be reduced by the same proportion from the quantities which be demanded at prices equal to the corresponding marginal costs'. This is often called 'Ramsey Pricing' after earlier work in the United Kingdom by Frank Ramsey (1927).

Assuming the railways offer two products, express and commuter rail services, then they should, following this principle, price such that:

$$\frac{\left(P_{exp} - MC_{exp}\right)}{P_{exp}}\varepsilon_{exp} = \frac{\left(P_{com} - MC_{com}\right)}{P_{com}}\varepsilon_{com} \qquad (7.3)$$

It is not always possible, for practical reasons, to discriminate perfectly: the administrative costs of operating the system may be too high or exact knowledge of the pertinent demand curves unavailable. These, for example, are the reasons cited in the 1960s by British Rail for their reluctance to adopt more sophisticated costing and policies – the diversity of services provided made it impracticable. In other cases, it may be felt socially undesirable to charge 'what the user will bear' because of distributional consequences. Passengers with a lower elasticity of demand may be from the poorer sections of the community and unable to transfer to alternative modes of transport. It may still be justified, even in these circumstances, to provide services even if not all costs are recovered by the operator, providing that the potential revenue if discrimination were adopted exceeds the costs of the service. If this is the case, a subsidy is required to bring actual revenue up to potential revenue and, to some extent, the British government accepted this in the 1968 Transport Act when, for a period, it introduced specific social subsidies to maintain several railway services.

While price discrimination is relatively uncommon outside of the transport sector it is a familiar feature of pricing policy within it, and indeed has become more common as information systems have developed and sophisticated electronic means of levying fares and freights have emerged. Truelove (1992) provides an apt description of these pricing practices of British Rail in the 1990s before privatization, illustrating that even then they were widely practiced.

The distinction between first and second class can be further refined by the exclusion of discount fares from peak weekday and holiday trains, by the limited availability of old people's and students' discounts, and the reduction in supplement for travel in first-class carriages at weekends, when leisure travel is heavy and business travel almost negligible.

Another well-documented example of third-degree price discrimination has long been provided by shipping conferences, and now by shipping alliances. These act as quasi-monopoly suppliers of regular liner services between major ports, but they also often compete with non-conference liners and tramp shipping that may enter markets when rates rise. Consequently, one can hypothesize an inverted S-shaped demand curve for individual liner services over any route. Given the high capital costs associated with shipping, there is adequate evidence that, prior to the widespread use of containers, without price discrimination most conference lines would have become unprofitable, and even with containers, and the apparent homogeneity of the 'boxes' being moved, price discrimination is still a necessary commercial practice.

A detailed look at the Australia–Europe Conference by Zerby and Conlon (1978) produced a breakdown of rates that clearly shows the high degree of price discrimination exercised by these maritime cartels. Figure 7.9 reproduces their average revenues for each type of cargo carried in 1973–74 and when traced out this corresponds closely to the type of demand curve hypothesized. The low-value bulk cargoes (that is, ores and metals) are carried at (or sometimes below if ballast is required) the average incremental costs of loading and unloading. While the high-value products are carried at considerably higher rates, the tapering off in

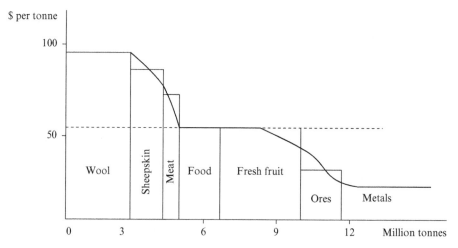

Figure 7.9   *Average revenues from cargoes carried by the Australia–Europe Conference (1973–74)*

rates caused by potential competition from air transport is seen to be effective at the top of the price range.

Price discrimination not only permits suppliers to recover their costs, but also helps travelers and consignors in that services can be retained even if, in some cases, it is necessary to differentiate the quality of service provided as well as the fare charged. International air travel offers some examples of this type of situation where differential prices are charged over a route according to the specifications of the types of service the travelers are willing to pay for. The gradual breakdown of the International Air Transport Association's (IATA) system of regulating airfares across the Atlantic in the 1970s was accompanied by the introduction of cut-price services such as 'Skytrain', operated by Laker Airways (Abe, 1979). No-frill flights were introduced at low fares with seat allocation dependent upon the willingness of potential passengers to queue for tickets which could be purchased until six hours prior to take-off. Subsequently this type of service has been modified and regular scheduled airlines now offer a variety of ticketing arrangements on their flights. A clear segmentation of the market had been recognized.

Figure 7.10 provides an illustration of the sort of situation that has emerged; for example, if there are three different groups of potential travelers with separate demand curves (D_1, D_2, and D_3), then three separate fares should be charged (P_1, P_2, and P_3) to maximize the consumers' surplus enjoyed. P_1 is charged for the highest-quality flight, equaling the marginal cost of service, with lower fares for poorer-quality flights. On the surface it appears that $0N_1$ passengers will travel first class, reaping a consumer surplus of ABP_1, and N_1N_2 passengers will pay P_2 for the slightly lower quality of service and enjoy a consumer surplus of *HIG*. This ignores the possibility that first-class travelers may switch to the poorer-quality but cheaper services (that is, there may be some 'revenue dilution'). In fact, travelers N'_1N_1 could switch and increase their

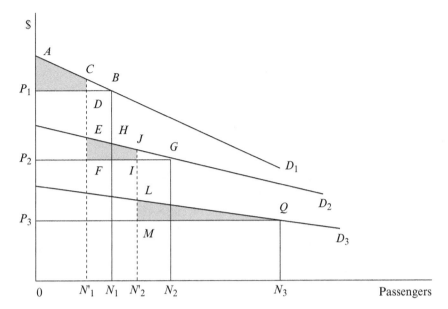

Figure 7.10   *Price discrimination according to service quality*

welfare. Similarly, N'_2N_2 passengers appear to be the probable number of customers for the poor-quality service, but again a further N_2N_3 may be induced to
join them by the lower fare. Whether people do take advantage of the possibility
of switching to cheaper but less convenient forms of service is uncertain, but the
availability of the range of services means the total potential consumer surplus
(the shaded areas) will exceed that generated if only a single price and service
package were available.

Dynamic Yield Management

There is also the practice of what has become known as yield management in the
air transport market, but is also used by other transport modes. Essentially, it is the
ability of management to gain additional revenue above costs from a pre-defined
activity (for example, a scheduled flight or sailing) when there is a need to ration
out capacity. For instance, there may be several people who want to book late for
a flight but the number of remaining seats is small. The airline will then push up
fares to ration out these seats to those willing to pay the most. This is not strictly
the same as price discrimination because the supplier is not trying to get all the customers' consumer surpluses but rather recover costs and allow those who gain most
from a service to have access to it. It is often called 'dynamic yield management'.

It has become a key element in, for example, the scheduled airline industry
where the chief executive of one major operator, R.L. Crandall, former President
of American Airlines, stated, 'I believe that yield management is the single most
important technical development in transportation management since we entered
the era of airline deregulation in 1979'. But it is also used elsewhere, including the
maritime sector.

The use of computer reservation systems (CRSs) by airlines enables an airline to adjust the fares offered on a given flight, the seats available at each fare, and the preconditions for booking at any fare. The preconditions (combined with some relatively minor quality differentials inherent in first-class, business-class, and coach-class areas of an aircraft) introduce product differentiation into the management equation while the various fares charged for what are, in many ways, very similar services represent the price differentiation element. The combinations offered and the adjustments made by an airline as the time of any flight departure approaches are designed to ensure the yield from the pre-determined decision to offer that service covers costs and allocates seats efficiently.

The technique is somewhat different from that of the classic economic model of price discrimination where management increases revenue by charging different groups of customers (differentiated by their price elasticities) different prices for the same product. The cost of serving each customer is, in the classic model, identical. There is, however, normally some qualitative or other form of product differentiation involved in yield management which implies cost differentials in the provision of services to customers. First-class air travel does cost an airline more than discount travel. Equally, however, the existence of economies of scope may mean that the supplier of a range of different services can keep unit costs lower than several suppliers each specializing in the services being offered. In overall resource terms, therefore, yield management may provide for the development a more efficient market structure.

The set of decisions confronting industries practicing successful yield management is often complex. The interactions and options available are numerous fare levels, fare structures, constraints, and capacity distribution to be decided simultaneously. This leads to a further common feature of yield management, namely sequential decision-making. The form this takes varies between both sectors and firms within sectors, but a broad indication of the decision sequence adopted by many airlines when considering a scheduled service is set out in Figure 7.11. In this case, the nature of the technology does permit a degree of interaction between some of the stages (for example, discount levels and allocation of seats to different fare classes) as the time of the flight approaches.

Empirically, separating out yield management, which is a resource allocation technique, from price discrimination, which is a revenue-maximizing technique, is difficult in practice and inevitably murky. But some insights into the degrees to which prices may vary for a service can be gleaned.

An example of what this means in practice can be seen in Figure 7.12 which looks at fares offered by regularly 'data scraping' the web pages of the airlines involved to see how fares are adjusted over time as departure approaches. The 'fares-offered' curves for a monopoly service indicate the degree to which available prices fluctuate, a reflection of the number of remaining seats, the fares being offered by the competitor, and the expected demand levels of potential customers at different times before take-off (last-minute business travelers, for example, tend to be willing to pay more for a seat and *de facto* compete for them). The fares offered rise towards take-off – but part of this may be attributable to rationing out

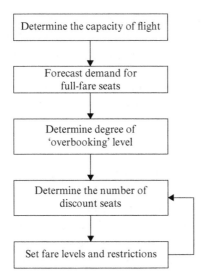

Figure 7.11   *Stages in arriving at yield-maximizing revenue in scheduled aviation*

the increasingly scarce number of unsold seats, and part to the effort of the airline to distinguish between leisure travelers who know their itinerary well in advance and are seeking cheap travel and business travelers who often must fly at the last minute and are willing to pay more.

Another form of differentiation by time of purchase that combines second- (entailing discounts for bulk buying) and third-degree price discrimination is found in the air cargo sector (Bowen and Leinbach, 2004). The link between forwarders, who act on behalf of freight shippers, and airlines is normally initially through

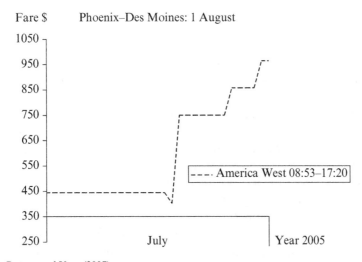

Source: Button and Vega (2007).

Figure 7.12   *Temporal-fares-offered curves for return services from Phoenix to Des Moines (leaving August 1 and returning August 5, 2005)*

their acquisition of allocated or bloc one-way capacity on airlines. This entails airlines six to 12 months before a flight's departure offering capacity to freight forwarders through essentially auctioning arrangements. The freight forwarders offer 'bids' (generally in terms of price per kilogram at the point of origin) based on the anticipated demands of their customers, the shippers. The remaining capacity, the cargo capacity, is then offered for sale one month before the flight departure.

Differentiation by Length of Journey/Haul

Price differentiation is not only by type of traffic or quality of service but may also be by length of journey. David Friedman (1979) offers a classic example of such a policy in the context of long-haul/short-haul differentials on American railways. The practice of charging short-haul traffic a higher mileage rate on railways than long-haul, despite attempts to legislate to the contrary, was common in nineteenth-century America. Friedman's justification for this practice demonstrates that without it there may arise quite serious distortions in transport infrastructure provision.

As an example, suppose there is a railway link between three towns, A, B, and C, where B is located between the other two towns. There is also river transport (priced at marginal cost) available between A and C offering an identical service to the railway but offering no communication for town B. The fixed, sunk cost of the rail link is such that:

$$C_{AC} = C_{AB} + C_{BC} \qquad\qquad (7.4)$$

that is, the sunk cost of the line from A to C is the sum of the two component sublinks. Also, on the same basis, the variable cost is:

$$V_{AC} = V_{AB} + V_{BC} \qquad\qquad (7.5)$$

Figure 7.13 shows the respective demand schedules for transport between the different pairs of towns. The railways may maximize their profits by charging down the demand curves D_{AB} and D_{BC}, where there is no competition from riverborne transport, to the point where marginal (that is, variable) cost is reached. Where competition does exist over the long route between A and C, the railways, to attract customers, will want to charge at most the rate offered by the river transport (call this R_{AC}). The railways will, however, accept traffic at rates below R_{AC} but above the variable cost. The areas WAV_{AB}, XDV_{BC}, and $R_{AC}EFV_{AC}$ show the revenues enjoyed by the railways on different links. If R_{AC} is lower than either the highest position of D_{AB} or D_{BC}, then there exists long-haul/short-haul discrimination in addition to discrimination within each type of traffic. In other words, identical goods with identical demand for transport schedules would be charged more per mile for a short haul than for a long haul.

The sum of the revenues in the diagram offers a measure of the social value of building and operating the ABC railway line. The aggregate producer surplus

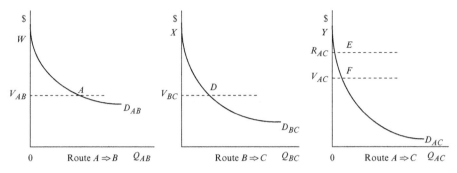

Figure 7.13   *Revenues from discriminating pricing according to length of haul*

generated should be set against the fixed costs of provision, which, together with calculations for *AB* and *AC* separately, indicate the long-term desirability of keeping the entire line open or only segments of it. Without long-haul/short-haul discrimination the railway would either have to give up some of its long-haul business or fail to capture some of the consumer surplus generated on short haul. Whatever the case, the railway's incentive to invest would be distorted and some economically desirable lines would not be operated.

Countervailing Power

The extent to which a supplier can engage in price differentiation depends on the degree to which the customer 'allows' it to price down the curve and the competition that is encountered in the market. For example, while the airline sector, where markets have been allowed to operate, has practiced extensive price discrimination, the operating margins have been well below other industries (Figure 7.14) which were of the order of 5.6 percent in the 1990s and early 2000s. This is mainly due to competition, but in other sectors, such as shipping, the power of customers is important. This ability to essentially resist the monopoly power of a large transport supplier is reflected, to a large extent, in the 'countervailing power' enjoyed by the potential transport user.

The development of the idea of countervailing power is usually credited to Kenneth Galbraith and his book, *American Capitalism*. This very 'unGalbraithian' volume essentially argues that large-scale enterprises in oligopolistic or monopoly markets often have much less flexibility than conventional theory postulates to exploit their power because of the existence of monopoly power at other points in what we would now call, as we saw in Chapter 1, the 'value chain'. The interest was initially stimulated by the observation that large buyers often enjoyed significant discounts when purchasing from suppliers. While there may be cost reasons for this, such as economies of density in shipping and handling, the outcome may also be the result of the strong bargaining power of the purchaser.

Essentially, what is seen is a situation where, rather than having original competition in a market, the competition is between the various buyers and sellers up and down the value chain – there are, according to this approach,

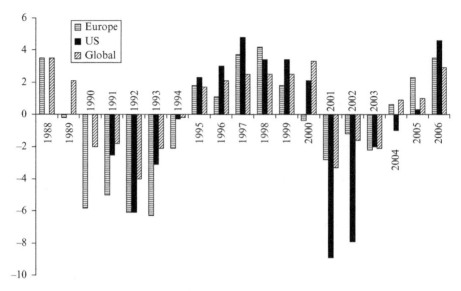

Notes: (i) A lack of a bar indicates a missing observation and not a zero operating margin.
(ii) Memberships of the various reporting bodies vary over time and thus the reported margins
reflect the associated carriers at the time of reporting.

Sources: Boeing Commercial Airplane; Association of European Airlines; Air Transport
Association of America; International Air Transport Association.

Figure 7.14   *Airline operating margins: global, European, and United States*

bi-lateral monopolies or oligopolies at various points in the chain (a bi-lateral
monopoly being a situation where there is a single buyer and seller of a given
product in a market). The level of concentration in the sale of the product results
in a mutual interdependence between the seller and buyer in price determination.
The notions of price-taking inherent in more standard neoclassical economics
are not upheld.

Countervailing power, Galbraith argues, prevents a large business from fully
exploiting customers: 'In a typical modern market of a few sellers, the active
restraint is provided by competition but from the other side of the market by
strong buyers … . At the end of virtually every channel by which consumers
goods reach the public there is, in practice, a layer of powerful buyers'. Basically,
market power on one side of a market 'create(s) an incentive to the organization
of another position of power that neutralizes it'.

It is perhaps useful to put Galbraith's ideas, together with other forms of
market forces, into a wider context. Figure 7.15 offers a simple illustration of
the various types of direct and countervailing powers that may affect the pricing
decisions of an undertaking providing transportation services. The Figure is relatively comprehensive, embracing ideas such as countervailing power, regulations,
the fear of public disquiet and complaint over excessive prices (the idea of 'voice'
put forward by Albert Hirschman in his 1970 book, *Exit, Voice, and Loyalty:
Responses to Decline in Firms, Organizations, and States*), contestability, and so

Figure 7.15   *Forces affecting a firm's pricing decisions*

on, as well as original competition (the traditional name for competition within the market).

Not all have agreed with this outcome, and the idea of countervailing power from the time of Galbraith initiating his ideas has been the subject of some skepticism. Academics such as George Stigler (1954), for example, questioned in a variety of ways whether the ability of large purchases of factors of production from monopolists in the value chain really had the incentive to pass on any savings to final customers; why not keep the rent themselves? Stigler was strong in his criticism of the concept:

> [I]t simply is romantic to believe that a competitive solution will emerge, not merely in a few cases, but in the general run of industries where two small groups of firms deal with one another suddenly all the long-run advantages of monopolistic behavior have been lost sight of in a welter of irrational competitive moves.

The theory is messy in the sense that it does not, except in very stylized situations, produce a neat-equilibrium, optimal outcome, but rather results in prices and outputs determined by games played by the various parties involved and influenced by their power in the market. These may be short-term equilibriums but are not optimal. There is no canonical model. The degree to which the outcome approaches either monopoly or competitive outcomes depends on the strength and strategic aptitudes of the various parties involved. A variety of things can influence these factors.

One indicator of the extent of countervailing power is the ability of, say, an airport to price-discriminate between airlines that may want to operate from it.

The ability to first-degree-discriminate, involving charging different prices for each take-off or landing depending on willingness to pay, is rare and unlikely

Figure 7.16   *Third-degree price discrimination between low-cost and legacy carriers*

to be a practical proposition for an airport even if it does enjoy considerable monopoly power and there are numerous airlines seeking slots. The information and administrative requirements are too large. A more viable proposition to consider is third-degree price discrimination whereby the market for airport services can be segmented and where the segments have different elasticities of demand. At the most basic level we can think in terms of segmentation between low-cost and traditional, full-service carriers.

We can take the simple case of a profit-maximizing airport that is serving both a low-cost carrier and a legacy carrier. In Figure 7.16 the airport decides its output by equating its overall marginal costs (MC_M) with its overall marginal revenue (MR_M). The price levied on the airlines will then be at the point on the average revenue curve directly above the flights attracted (AC_M) not illustrated in the figure. However, landing fees are normally a larger part of a low-cost airline's costs than for a traditional, legacy carrier. This makes the former more sensitive to the level of such fees. To increase its revenues, therefore, the airport can try to charge separate fees to its two potential customer groups; for example, it may use slot auctions (Button, 2008). It would effectively do this by drawing a horizontal line through the $MC_M = MR_M$ point and carry this over to the separate markets for low-cost and legacy carriers. This intersection gives the combined profit-maximizing output for the airport. Taking the resultant marginal cost across to the separate marginal revenue curves of the different categories of carrier optimally shares out slots between them. Prices for the low-cost carriers (P_{LCC}) and the legacy carriers (P_{LC}) are then determined by the average revenue curves corresponding to these slot numbers.

The types of issues associated with these conditions were explored by Francis Edgeworth in the nineteenth century, and have subsequently attracted considerable attention within the industrial organization fraternity with an interest in game theory. Figure 7.17 provides a simple, and extreme, example with a monopsony buyer (say a large airline) negotiating landing slot charges with a monopoly airport.

Initially at one extreme, we treat the airport as a monopolist with numerous potential airlines wanting to use its slots. In this case we get the standard textbook situation where the airport will set its output where marginal cost equals marginal revenue (Y_1) and set price to clear the market (that is, price will be P_1).

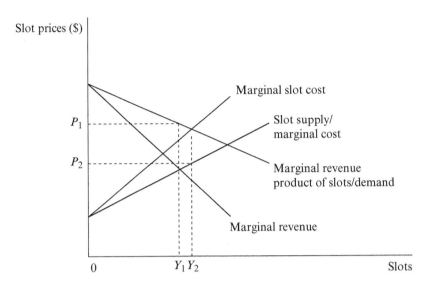

Figure 7.17   *Price and output under a pure bi-lateral monopoly*

In contrast, if an airline (or a strong alliance of airlines) has monopsony power, and the airport is confronted with competition from alternative facilities, then the price of a slot will be P_2. This is because the market-supply curve for slots will be positively sloped with a market-slot curve above it. The marginal revenue product curve of slots – the additional revenue the airline obtains by buying an additional slot – is downward-sloping, reflecting diminishing marginal productivity. To maximize its revenue, the airline will buy slots up to the point where the marginal cost of a slot is equated to the marginal revenue it will generate (that is, Y_2 slots), for which the market clearing price is P_2.

The situation where there is bi-lateral monopoly generally leaves the outcome indeterminate with a market price somewhere between P_1 and P_2. The resultant price and output combination will depend on the bargaining skills of the two parties and that, of course, will be a function of their game-playing skills. While one can relate to this in the case of a large hub-and-spoke airline negoti-ating slot rates at its main hub airport, there are other points in the value chain where these types of bi-lateral monopoly or oligopoly may emerge. Of relevance, here, is the monopoly power of labor unions in their dealing with airports and the airframe manufacturers with the airlines.

What is clear, irrespective of the power of airports and airlines in the example, is that the final consumer – passenger or shipper – does not benefit greatly from a bi-lateral monopoly situation further up the value chain. The sharing-out of economic rents seen in Figure 7.15, between the two providers of intermediate services, is an effective extraction of consumer surplus from the final users of air transportation services. The situation may also pertain in other cases where there are imperfections up the value chain that result in non-competitive prices being pushed down the chain and being imposed on passengers and freight consignors.

Testing for the existence of countervailing power in any market is challenging. It is difficult to discern, for example, whether the fact that a large-scale buyer of a product from a large producer gets a discount because of the scale economies of such transactions or because the buyer can drive a hard bargain by virtue of its purchasing power. Much of the general empirical work trying to ascertain whether countervailing power has any significant impacts on markets uses a structure–conduct–performance framework, looking at links between supplier profits, or mark-ups, and on supplier concentrations with the additional consideration of buyer concentrations. Limited work of this type, however, has been performed on the aviation sector. There has been some work trying to benchmark different airports' efficiency, generally using data envelopment methods, but normalizing for the characteristics of airports is difficult, especially when using programming techniques.

One of the problems in exploring countervailing effects is that the market power on either side of the market varies considerably by context. The situation depicted in Figure 7.15 of a monopoly confronting a monopsony is very seldom seen, and more common are oligopolistic bi-lateral structures where the market powers on both sides are defused by continual games being played between the buyers and suppliers themselves. Turning specifically to aviation, in some cases groups of clustered airports are under common ownership, as with the main London airports, giving them considerable regional monopoly power, whereas in other cases there may be alternative terminals within proximity; in the United States a two-hour drive between airports is generally seen as providing competition. Additionally, many airports have their rates regulated – for example, in the United Kingdom the British Airports Holdings (BAH) is price-capped by the Civil Aviation Authority (CAA) – making econometric analysis of market power difficult. Air services are also not homogeneous, and nor are the airlines providing them, making generalizations difficult.

The degree to which airports can segment in this way, however, depends on the extent to which the airlines can dilute the revenue being collected by the airport – essentially their ability to prevent differential fees. Many airports are used by a small number of airlines, and in some cases even large airports rely on a single carrier for 80 percent or more of their business. The extent to which airports practice third-degree discrimination has not been rigorously examined, although a study by Jacobs Consultancy (2007) did find differential passenger charges for low-cost terminals at Budapest, Kuala Lumpur, Marseille, and Singapore airports.

While airports may exercise some forms of price differentiation by carrier type, it becomes more difficult to separate out the effects of cost variations from charging policies based upon willingness to pay. Even in the cases cited, low-cost carriers are often based in separate terminals that offer passengers more limited, less grandiose, and generally less well located facilities. For example, Richard de Neufville (2006) cites Geneva, Berlin, Kuala Lumpur, Paris Charles de Gaulle, Singapore, and Warsaw airports as situations where specific facilities for low-cost carriers have been provided. In effect, different fees may largely be reflecting different costs and not strict price discrimination by demand.

The fact that only a few cases[4] of clear third-degree price discrimination seem to exist could be suggestive of airlines being able to exercise a considerable degree of countervailing power. This would seem to be illusory because of capacity problems at major airports in many parts of the world, and particularly Europe, and regulatory regimes that force airports to set charges based upon narrow accountancy costing principles. The form exists when, given the capacity of an airport, the nature of the demand curves for potential low cost and legacy carrier users are such that profit maximization leads to a high price that only the traditional, legacy airlines are willing to pay.

7.6   Pricing with Stochastic Demand

Our discussion of price discrimination as a method of recovering costs has to date made the rather heroic assumption that the supplier of transport – be it ship owner, railway manager, airline operator, or whatever – has perfect knowledge of the demand situation being confronted. Most transport managers have, from past data and employing 'managerial intuition', some notion of the average level of demand for their services and some idea of how this demand fluctuates. With yield management, regularly posting and changing the fares offered can often give a pretty good idea of short-term demand conditions. In practice, though, the assumption of complete or near-complete information is often unrealistic. This is particularly so over longer periods. The specific problem of systematic and regular known short-term peaks in demand is considered in the following section; here we concentrate on irregular fluctuations in demand of a stochastic nature. A transport undertaking may, for instance, know that fluctuations are about 20 percent of the average daily demand, but have no way of telling whether tomorrow's demand will be, say, 7 percent above the average or 14 percent below it.

The introduction of this notion of 'stochastic' demand requires a slight modification to the marginal cost pricing approach. The conventional arguments for discriminate pricing revolve around the idea that simple marginal cost pricing will, because of declining average cost, result in the supplier incurring a financial loss. Ralph Turvey's (1975) widely accepted position formulated nearly five decades ago is that the problem should be expressed in terms of the difficulties associated with matching the services supplied (usually vehicle journeys) with those that are demanded (usually passenger journeys) when a fixed timetable is operative.

Approached in this way, the problem is one of defining a price structure which will cover all relevant costs but which will, at the same time, ensure reasonable utilization of the transport capacity available. Two broad approaches emerge. The first of these depends upon having fairly reliable information about demand and its range of fluctuation, while the second relies upon good information on all relevant costs. Here, we concentrate on the first approach and, especially, the load factor for a service.

If fares are fixed so high that the number of people wishing to use the service never exceeds the available capacity, then, as a result of the fluctuating demand condition, there will frequently be substantial numbers of empty seats and resources will be wasted. Alternatively, if the fares are set so low that capacity is always fully utilized, then many people, who often have spent time queuing for the service, will, again because of demand fluctuations, find themselves unable to obtain a seat. Clearly, common sense suggests a compromise between these extremes will meet the requirements of both supplier and potential traveler. Turvey's pragmatic solution is that operators should structure their fares so that on average a certain percentage of seats will remain empty.

To some extent this is the situation that has developed with yield management on the scheduled airlines where passengers have even greater flexibility by being able, via booking early, to ensure themselves a seat if they wish rather than risk disappointment, but at the cost of forfeiting the fare if they do not make the flight. The situation was also evident on the streets of central London in the past where parking meter fees were fixed so that on average 15 percent of spaces were vacant although, of course, from experience we know that at times it is impossible to find a vacant parking space while at others they are in abundance. One might also point to the 'standby capacity' kept by British Rail until the 1968 Transport Act, which it was claimed acted to cope with long-term fluctuations in demand for railway services.

To cover costs in this type of situation without recourse to either direct or cross-subsidization it is likely that price discrimination is necessary. Any of four standard types of discrimination (that is, by type of passenger, degree of comfort, regularity of use, and/or seat availability) could be used for this.

Where knowledge of demand fluctuations is less precise, then Turvey's second and rather more pragmatic approach may be applicable. Here fares can be determined by simply dividing available costs of the service by the passengers carried and the service only runs if such fares broadly correspond to those on the remainder of the transport system. Additional revenue may then be gained on an *ad hoc* basis by raising fares for those groups where willingness to pay exceeds the cost-based fare. The actual avoidable costs can be estimated, where there is uncertainty about initial traffic levels, using the following formula that, for simplicity, is couched in terms of a passenger railway service:

$$\begin{aligned}&[(\text{Probability that marginal passenger will necessitate as extra} \\ &\qquad\qquad \text{carriage}) \times (\text{Cost of extra carriage})] \\ &+ [(\text{Probability that marginal pasenger will necessitate an extra} \\ &\qquad\qquad \text{train}) \times (\text{Cost of extra train})]\end{aligned} \tag{7.6}$$

Because this probability $LRMC$ curve represents costs as an increasing function of the number of passengers and since this is itself a decreasing function of the fare charged, there is likely to be a fare structure in which such marginal costs are recovered.

Whether the fare is optimal, however, depends upon timetable flexibility; so far we have implicitly assumed a given timetable. The overall fare is set at the level of the marginal social cost of an extra passenger, in other words equal to the frustration and inconvenience he/she causes to other potential but disappointed travelers by occupying a scarce seat. The combination of timetable and fare that equates the marginal cost, so defined, with the marginal financial cost is thus an overall optimum. In practice, of course, imperfect knowledge of demand situations, plus the need to make timetabling and pricing decisions simultaneously, makes it unlikely that such an overall optimum will be attained except by chance.

7.7 The Problem of the Peak

Most forms of transport, both freight and passenger, experience regular peaks in demand for their services. Urban public transport (upon which our attention will be focused later) experiences peaks in demand during 'rush hours' each weekday morning and evening. While there is considerable variation between cities, typically rush hour lasts from about 6 to 10 am and from 4 to 7 pm local time, with some people traveling places during their lunchtime causing a mini rush hour from noon until 2 pm. Urban freight transport also has peaks in demand to match the seasonal needs and operating practices of customers. In London, for example, most deliveries are made between 7 am and 1 pm. Over a year, air, bus, and rail services meet peaks in demand from holiday traffic during the summer months and over public holidays, while within a week there are marked differences between weekend and weekday demand levels. Over an even longer period, shipping is subjected to cyclical movements in demand as the world economy moves between booms and slumps.

The difficulty in all these situations is to determine a pattern of prices that ensures that transport infrastructure is used optimally, provides a guide to future investment policy, and ensures that all relevant costs are recovered. Unlike the previous section, we are concerned here with problems arising from systematic variations in demand, frequently over a relatively short time period during which adjustments cannot be made in capital equipment to ensure that price is always equated with $LRMC$. The problem is essentially one of indivisibility in the time dimension of supply relative to demand and is, therefore, a form of the joint production problem. Problems of this kind do occur in other sectors of the economy, but transport, like electricity and some other forms of energy, cannot be easily stored to reconcile systematic changes in demand with smooth, even production. Reconciliation can only be effectively achieved through price adjustments or shortages and excesses in the market.

Before proceeding to look at the peak-load pricing problem it is worth noting that there exists a parallel spatial/directional problem of joint costs in transport which can be treated in an identical way to that of the peak. This involves the question of deriving appropriate rates for front-hauls and back-hauls – a situation often found in the provision of unscheduled road haulage, or freight and shipping services. Basically, there is a high demand for a service in one direction (the front-haul) but a lower one for a return service (the back-haul); that is, demand is uni-directional in nature whereas supply consists of round-trip journeys. This situation is directly analogous to the peak-load situation, with the front-haul being the spatially directional equivalent of the peak, and simple substitution of word 'yields' the appropriate analysis.

Perhaps the most widely discussed peaking problem involves urban public transport and bus services. The size of most urban bus fleets is determined by the demand for public transport services during the morning and evening commuter rush hours. Typically, over half the passengers carried during a day travel during the main peak periods. In Manchester, for example, 1,090 buses were required to meet rush-hour demands in 1966 while only 400 were used during the midday period. Comparable figures for Birmingham Corporation Transport Department in 1969 were 1,500 and 327 vehicles respectively. Bus road crews may also be considered as a joint cost since numbers are determined by peak demand. It is seldom possible to cover both daily peaks with one shift, hence either two shifts are required, or else split-shifts must be introduced usually involving inconvenience payments (often equal to the standard wage) being paid for time between peaks. The total wage bill for road staff, which amounts to about 50 percent of the total cost of most British bus operators, is, therefore, almost invariant with demand and may be treated as a joint cost of providing peak and non-peak services.

To determine optimal prices let us assume that during a 12-hour period a bus operator is confronted by two different demand situations, each of six hours' duration. In Figure 7.18, D_1 is the low, off-peak demand situation and D_2 the peak-level demand curve. The $SRMC$s of operation (fuel- and mileage-dependent depreciation) are assumed constant at level $0a$ until the capacity of the bus fleet, which initially is assumed as fixed, is filled, whereupon they become infinite. In the short term, with capacity fixed, the objective is to maximize social welfare by

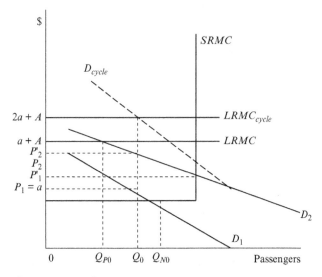

Figure 7.18   *The optimum peak price*

making optimal use of the fleet. In this case the off-peak and the peak demands should be priced at their respective *SRMC*s. The fares should, therefore, be P_1 and P_2 at the off-peak and peak respectively, with corresponding passenger numbers Q_{P0} and Q_{N0}.

Changes in capacity brought about by varying the fleet size do not influence *SRMC*s except to the extent that the capacity constraint is pushed further to the right if vehicles are added and to the left if they are withdrawn. *LRMC*s are treated as constant at a level A. Since the capacity is joint to both subperiods, changes in capacity should be determined by the combined demand of peak and off-peak periods, that is, the full cycle of activities (Hirschleifer, 1958). Consequently, it is D_{cycle} that is the relevant demand curve (because this represents the vertical summation of D_1 and D_2). Further, it is $LRMC_{cycle}$ that is the relevant long-term cost curve, because this represents the combination of the short-run costs in the two periods plus fixed costs; that is, $2a + A$. The situation is analogous to that of a collective good.

The optimum long-run capacity in the case illustrated, and assuming there are problems of indivisibilities, involves a contraction of capacity to $0Q_0$. The non-peak travelers will then pay P'_1 and peak travelers P'_2. Given the way the D_{cycle} and $LRMC_{cycle}$ curves are derived, the combined revenues from off-peak and peak fares will exactly equal the costs involved. Also, the off-peak fare now exceeds *SRMC* and capacity is fully utilized around the clock, the pricing differences reflecting differing strengths of demand. In summary, changes in capacity, because they are joint to both periods, now depend upon the sum of the differences between price and the capacity's operating costs per period relative to the cost of providing new capacity for the entire cycle. That is, investment is justified if:

$$[(P_1 - a) + (P_2 - a)] > B \qquad (7.7)$$

It is relatively simple to extend the analysis to any number of subperiods, which may be of unequal duration, by weighting the different periods according to their fractional importance in the entire cycle.

In practice, the situation is often somewhat more complicated than that depicted, because passengers are not rigidly confined to either period but may switch trips between them if differential fares are levied. Unfortunately, little empirical work has been conducted on this, but it is quite possible that our implicit assumption that D_1 and D_2 are independent is often unrealistic and allowance needs to be made both for their own and for cross-elasticities. Also, of course, it may be necessary to take cognizance of interdependencies between the demand for urban bus travel as a whole and the possibilities of switching to private transport.

While there is a firm economic basis for peak-load pricing, its implementation has been piecemeal. An early example was the pricing policy pursued in the Manchester–Salford area in the United Kingdom between the summers of 1970 and 1975 (Tyson, 1975) and there are differential metro fares in American cities, such as Washington DC. Some American airports have attempted to introduce

Table 7.4   *Pricing structure at New York, LaGuardia Airport (2002)*

Type of charge	Minimum charge
Operation during peak (8 am to 9 pm), non-scheduled carriers	$100
Operation off-peak, non-scheduled carriers	$25
Operation during peak (8 am to 9 pm), scheduled carriers	$50
Operation off-peak, scheduled carriers	$20

Source: Port Authority of New York and New Jersey, Aviation Department, Schedule of charges for air terminals, 2003; Port Authority of New York and New Jersey, Guidelines for constructing an economically defensible peak-hour flight fee.

peak pricing but, as with facilities such as Boston Logan, it has met with legal problems, and at other places, such as LaGuardia (Table 7.4), it hardly reflects the magnitude of demand variations (Schank, 2005). It is also employed at the major airports in the United Kingdom, although the primary objective has historically been to raise revenue for investment rather than as a strict short-term capacity-rationing device. First attempts to introduce peak-load pricing date back to 1972 when the BAA established a runway movement charge at the busiest time of day at Heathrow. Passenger peak charges were implemented in 1976. Both the differential between peak and off-peak charges and the definition of peak periods have changed considerably over the years. The ratio of peak to off-peak fees increased over the years until the mid-1980s. Several differentiations for peak landing fees have been tried but these were eventually succeeded by a uniform peak-hour fee. The charter airlines in Europe in the 1990s – the mainstay of the tourist industry before the emergence of low-cost carriers – also practiced peak-load pricing when setting their fares. In their case, this reflected seasonal variations in tourism demand patterns.

7.8   Transport Subsidies, Operational Objectives, and Pricing

Many sectors of transport enjoy quite substantial levels of either central or local government subsidy. (Table 7.5 shows the percentage of transit costs recovered in some of the world's major cities, and Figure 7.19 provides some detail about the situation regarding recent time tends in London's transport subsidies.) Because they represent payments for transport services by non-users, subsidies complicate the pricing problem.

To some extent the type of problem created depends upon the form of subsidy given. If a central or local government provides the subsidy for a specific service, then it may be seen as representing that government's demand for that service and treated alongside the demand of other customers; the service subsidies given by local authorities to specified bus services in the United Kingdom under the 1985 Transport Act may be categorized in this way, as may many of the subsidies to franchised services in other European countries and in some American cities (Morlock, 1987). From a pricing/operational point of view such subsidies are relatively easily assimilated into standard economic models. This is

Table 7.5   *Levels of operational transit subsidies in various cities*

City	Percent subsidy	City	Percent subsidy
Perth	72	Brussels	27
Adelaide	60	Munich	54
Brisbane	46	Stockholm	33
Melbourne	76	Vienna	41
Sydney	45	Hamburg	38
Phoenix	72	Copenhagen	34
Denver	81	London	7
Boston	76	Paris	39
Houston	72	Singapore	−15
Washington	50	Tokyo	−5
San Francisco	65	Hong Kong	−36
Detroit	77	Kuala Lumpur	−35
Chicago	54	Surabaya	−27
Los Angeles	57	Jakarta	−1
New York	53	Bangkok	7
Toronto	39	Seoul	3
Frankfurt	55	Beijing	80
Amsterdam	60	Manila	−12
Zurich	40		

Source: Newman and Kenworthy (1999).

so in the United Kingdom case where the routes to be subsidized are put up for competitive tender, a process that is designed to ensure the minimum subsidy is paid for the designated service. Further, the evidence from London, and from similar systems in the United States, is that there are cost efficiency gains (after allowing for administrative and monitoring expenses) of about 20 percent over more general subsidy arrangements.

When lump-sum subsidies are given to transport undertakings for general revenue purposes, however, problems arise in deciding upon the best methods of using the subsidy and the appropriate charge to levy on customers. It is difficult to devise pricing and operational objectives which ensure that management uses the fixed subsidies efficiently to attain the welfare objectives for which they are intended. A few possible objectives have been cited as offering a way around this problem.

It has been argued that commercial criteria (with profit-maximizing pricing) in this situation would lead to monopoly exploitation and be counterproductive in terms of the social objectives justifying the subsidy, while a social-welfare-max-imizing criterion (with marginal cost pricing) would break the link between costs, prices, and output, and lead to probable X-inefficiency: the provision of services at excessive costs. To circumvent these problems, and to provide clear pragmatic guidelines for lower-level management, London Transport attempted in the late 1970s to maximize passenger mileage subject to a budget constraint (that is, that costs are recovered after the fixed-sum subsidy has been taken into account). Operationally, when the criterion is applied at the margin, this means:

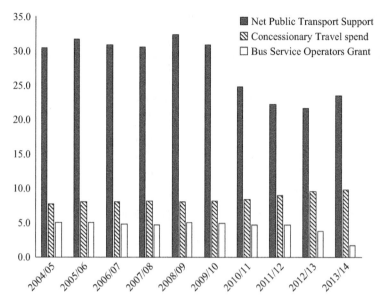

Note: Public transport support is monies spent by authorities to provide unprofitable 'socially necessary' services generally by tendering them out to private operators. Concessionary fare reimbursements are monies paid to compensate bus operators for carrying certain types of passengers, such as the aged or physically impaired, at low or zero fares.

Figure 7.19 *Net government support per passenger journey for London bus travel (current £)*

Reduce price as long as the increase in passenger mileage resulting exceeds the loss of revenue multiplied by the shadow price of public funds; increase bus mileage as long as the increase in passenger mileage resulting is greater than the net addition to the financial loss multiplied by the shadow price of public funds. (Nash, 1978)

The criterion, therefore, permits adjustments to the system operated so that costs are met (after allowing for the subsidy) and relatively junior management can assess the desirability of alternative courses of action. The criterion is, however, demonstrably inferior in theoretical terms to a pure marginal cost pricing strategy: price discrimination and cross-subsidization may result which push fares on inelastic services above marginal operating costs so that revenue is available to finance services which exhibit a relatively high elasticity (and thus easily provide an increase in passenger miles). It is quite possible, therefore, for a service to be operated for which the level of demand is never high enough to permit price to cover marginal costs.

It is possible, at the expense of complicating the criterion, to devise weighting schemes which can be attached to passenger miles on various routes to reflect their importance to the decision-maker, and schemes do exist which yield the same results as marginal cost pricing. Whether it is justified to adopt such weights must be an empirical question, depending on the loss of welfare that may accompany the simple unweighted passenger-miles-maximization approach relative to the administrative costs of implementation. Dieter Bos (1978) has also pointed to the distributional implications of the criterion and suggests that positive distributional effects may justify a certain level of welfare loss although, again, the exact distribution effect cannot be determined by *a priori* argument. (Empirical evidence in London suggests, however, that the London Transport scheme did have desirable distributional implications.)

7.9   Market Instability, Suboptimal Supply, and the Empty Core

To recap, economic theory tells us that, when there are no fixed costs, bargaining between suppliers and customers will ensure that prices are kept to a minimal level that allows suppliers to recover all costs over the long term, and the marginal cost of meeting customer demand represents the entire cost of production. The problems come when there *are* fixed costs, or indivisibilities in the cost function.

The traditional view of fixed costs was developed when the bricks, steel, and mortar of industrial plants had to be paid for. It was largely seen in relation to manufacturing, or in the context of a services industry, in terms of the immobile hardware involved: rail track and bridges. This seemed logical at the time because fixed costs are defined as invariant with the amount of production and the physical plant and infrastructure of the time fitted this description. Fixity is, however, a relative concept, and while, as we have seen in Chapter 5, a rail track may be seen as fixed over a long period, a railway locomotive may be seen as fixed over a shorter time until it needs replacement. In other words, some costs of production are fixed over the given decision period, while the train still operates, but become variable when replacement is needed. While the locomotive keeps functioning, the use made of it will be influenced by the marginal costs of maintenance, crew, fuel, and so on.

But with service industries, and especially those involving scheduled services, the fixed costs are somewhat different in detail, if not in their strict definition. While airlines and conference shipping lines, for example, do use expensive hardware, this is not their underlying fixed cost problem. Indeed, the largest costs of airlines have traditionally been their labor. These in the traditional sense are generally, but not entirely, seen as variable costs. Even aircraft are now seldom owned by the carriers but are leased, sometimes on a wet-lease that includes crew. The result is that airlines are increasingly becoming 'virtual carriers' that act to bring together packages of services owned by others and thus are encumbered with few fixed costs themselves in the traditional economic sense.

Fixed costs in a modern service industry, including airlines, however, can take a different form. An airline is committed to a scheduled service some six months or so before the flight: it is committed to have a plane, crew, fuel, gates, landing and take-off slots, etc., available at a given time. This does have an advantage that fares are often collected before the airline has to provide the service, but in a highly competitive market this is generally more than off-set by the limited amount of revenue that is ultimately collected. The commitment to a scheduled

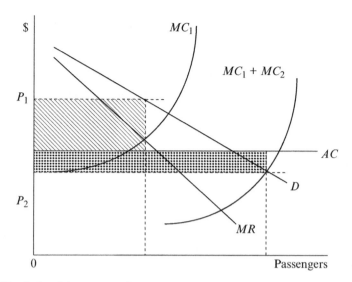

Figure 7.20   *Indivisibilities in supply*

take-off time poses the traditional cost recovery problem associated with any decreasing cost situation: costs cannot be recovered by charging a single marginal price.

The problem can be seen in Figure 7.20. Here we have a situation where there is a single air (or ship or bus) scheduled service that has a marginal cost curve of MC_1, an average cost curve of AC, and is confronted with a market demand of D. Being a monopoly provider, it will set its price at P_1 and enjoy monopoly profits of the shaded area above AC curve. A second carrier, attracted by these profits, can enter the market with identical equipment and will push out the marginal cost curve to $MC_1 + MC_2$. The result in this competitive situation, where price is set equal to marginal cost, is that fares will decline to P_2, resulting in a combined loss for the two suppliers equal to the shaded area below the AC curve. There must, therefore, be some mark-up above marginal prices to sustain the two carriers. As we have seen, airlines and other suppliers in modern deregulated markets largely engage in second- and third-degree price discrimination and charge passengers and shippers different prices to try to extract as much revenue as possible. In general, this is temporal price differentiation.

While this approach can allow revenues above marginal cost to be generated when a service has some degree of monopoly power (for example, no competing flight to the destination within a reasonable time frame), the problem is that with a fixed schedule in a competitive market, the various airlines set take-off times for each destination at about the same time. This leads to intense competition to fill seats and forces fares down to levels that do not allow all the costs of individual services to be met. It is worth filling a seat once offered with anyone willing to pay for its marginal cost.

Empirical analysis supporting the logical basis of the temporal-fares-offered curve has been well established in studies of European and American

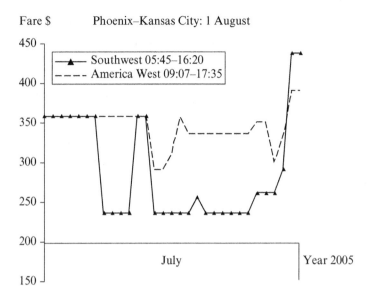

Fare $ Phoenix–Kansas City: 1 August

Source: Button and Vega (2007).

Figure 7.21   *Temporal-fares-offered curves for return services from Phoenix to Kansas City (out August 1 and returning August 5, 2005)*

air transport markets. Figure 7.12 above, just as an example, looks at a United States monopoly market and illustrates the consistent rise in fares as the time of departure approaches. This pattern is also found on the numerous other routes where this technique has been applied, and holds irrespective of whether the monopoly airline is a low-cost carrier or pursues the traditional, full-service business model.

Figure 7.21 shows the sort of temporal-fares-offered curve that emerges when two carriers offer nearly identical services, differentiated largely by a small difference in departure times. Again, the pattern is consistent and can be examined in detail in other works. This is also from the United States and shows the volatility that arises, and the lack of a significant and consistent rise in fares towards take-off is clear. Other studies looking at services where there are more than two competitors show a further flattening-out of the temporal-fares-offered curve, with near commonality of fares offered by all up to take-off, as one would expect in the large numbers case.

It also leads to suboptimal levels of investment despite excess capacity during peaks in the cycle. The fact that full costs are not recovered, and that ultimately an airline will withdraw a service or go out of business, is known as the 'empty core problem'. It is neither a new concept – it was developed in the 1880s by a largely forgotten Oxford economist, Francis Edgeworth – nor is it one that has limited application. In the long term, as potential investors become aware of this problem, they will reduce or cease to put new capital into the industry.

Overall, there are several conditions in which there may be no core and, hence, a market may not be sustainable. These occur when there are relatively large fixed costs, avoidable (set-up) costs, indivisibility, network effects, or severe fluctuations in demand. An unsustainable market may also exist when some suppliers enjoy a degree of institutional or financial protection, and when there are significant variations in the costs of suppliers. In practice, many public utilities, transport industries, and some manufacturing industries meet these criteria.

The lack of a core can broadly result in two outcomes depending on the reactions of the players in the market. If the transport suppliers think they can beat out competitors in the market, then there will be instability as suppliers keep entering and leaving the market. Alternatively, if potential suppliers are more rational and realize that their market entry will result in excess capacity and an inability to recover full costs, then they will not enter. The result is that there will be a suboptimally low capacity provided. Looked at in another way, there are indivisibilities in the aircraft or ships scheduled and the overall capacity will be lower than would occur if they were perfectly divisible.

The fact that this economic conundrum applies to the scheduled airlines (Button, 2003) and the scheduled shipping industry (Pirrong, 1992) has been appreciated for some time, but largely ignored in policy formulation. The complexity of the underlying economic model has hindered the communication of the issue to decision-makers. This situation also runs counter to some traditional, often ideological, views of competition policy which hold that there can 'never be too much competition'.

7.10 Indirect Pricing

In some cases, there are excessive transactions costs involved in directly pricing a user of a transport service, or if it is not possible for technical reasons. The outcome in many cases is an adjustment to the price of a complementary good; in the case of a publicly owned transport facility, this means *de facto* a tax. An example of this in the United States and many other countries has been the pricing of road use from the 1930s when the road system began to be improved and largely paved. Tolls paid on turnpikes had been a traditional way of pricing many major roads, but with the advent of the widespread adoption of the motor vehicle, the excessive congestion created around manual toll booths saw a fuel tax come in as a replacement.

There are important trade-offs to consider when using indirect pricing. It may reduce the transaction costs of collection, which may involve savings for the supplier of transport services, other users, or third parties, but it is not an efficient price. It does not directly reflect the use of the transport system and thus does not optimize that use. A fuel tax, for example, is poorly correlated to the costs of individuals' road use; payments vary by engine size and where the vehicle is used, which may not be where the costs are incurred. There may be jurisdictional issues when, for example, fuel is purchased in one location but the driving is largely done in another. There is also the danger that because of the lack of direct accountability, the authorities may manipulate the indirect charge to raise revenues not directly related to the costs of the facility. (This is distinct from a pure sales or purchase tax that is a clear form or government revenue collection and is levied on many items.) Finally, the charge may end up serving several purposes.

There have been efforts made to see to what extent these surrogate prices do reflect actual costs of use. But this is not easy. In addition to the micro issues of how to allocate costs to categories of road user, trucks, cars, and so on, there is the issue of what items to include (for example, is air pollution a road cost in the conventional sense?), and how to value them. Even when it comes to items such as capital costs there are problems. Road investments are lumpy and outlays vary considerably year by year. The 'pay-as-you-go' method simply takes the annual expenditure, which may be considered a rather simplistic approach given the volatile nature of investment. The 'public enterprise' approach looks at a road as an investment and considers how much interest would have to be paid to borrow the money required to make that investment. While there are some sound economic grounds for this methodology, it does involve somewhat strong assumptions in calculating the capital tied up in the system and the interest that would be required to finance this capital.

There are also issues about how costs should be allocated between users of common infrastructure. Trucks, for example, cause more pavement damage than do cars but because they go more slowly, design standards for bends, for example, could be more flexible. If the pavement depth were designed optimally for trucks then there would be less maintenance required and the allocation of operating costs of the track would be less for larger vehicles. Simply looking at taxes and other non-user-based charges and treating them as prices is not helpful. In one sense, the methods of pricing much transport infrastructure is a little like charging a premium on butter to cover the costs of bread, but allowing consumers to take as much bread as they wanted. The charges do little to make consumption of bread efficient. Likewise, most surrogate charges for transport infrastructure do little to ensure it is used optimally or to offer guidance as to when capacity needs to be adjusted.

Despite these problems, there may be practical considerations that make using indirect pricing a tractable and reasonable second-best approach. This may be so in some countries where there are complex regulatory systems and there is a need for a significant flow of funds for investment. The distinction between the transport service and the complementary good may also be somewhat blurred.

An example of this is often found at airports that provide direct services to airlines but also provide a variety of services on the ground to passengers. This is often referred to as the 'two-till' approach to financing an airport's activities. Figure 7.22 provides an illustration of the sort of circumstances in which this may arise. In more mature countries, where there is a significant traffic flow but growth in traffic is relatively slow, there is more incentive to extract extra revenue for passengers. This situation is compounded when the income of that country is

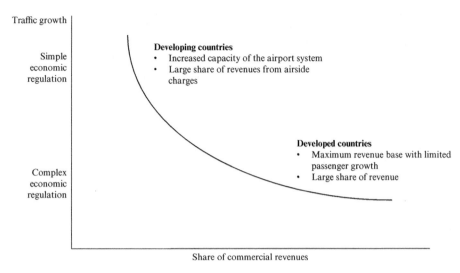

Source: Juan (1995).

Figure 7.22   *Financing airports from two 'tills'*

high and travelers are willing to pay for additional airport services. When incomes lower and airports are subjected to less regulation, the tendency is to rely much more on direct income from airlines; it is also easier to collect than through a multiplicity of retail concessions and the like. Whether the use of commercial revenues leads to more efficient use of resources than charging higher rates to airlines is, however, debatable. While it may be relatively easy to isolate the costs of the air services charges from commercial services offered on the ground, a differential amount of monopoly power may lead to distortions in investments and in pricing. How to handle this issue has, for example, been a major policy issue at London's airports (Starkie, 2001).

References

Abe, M.A. (1979) 'Skytrain': competitive pricing, quality of service and the deregulation of the airline industry, *International Journal of Transport Economics*, 6, 41–7.

Baumol, W.J. (1962) On the theory of the expansion of the firm, *American Economic Review*, 52, 1078–87.

Baumol, W.J. and Bradford, D.F. (1970) Optimal departures from marginal cost pricing, *American Economic Review*, 60, 265–83.

Beesley, M.E. (1973) Regulation of taxis, *Economic Journal*, 83, 150–72.

Bennathan, E. and Walters, A. (1979) *Port Pricing and Investment Policy for Developing Countries*, Oxford University Press.

Bos, D. (1978) Distribution effects of maximisation of passenger rules, *Journal of Transport Economics and Policy*, 12, 322–9.

Bowen, J. and Leinbach, T. (2004) Market concentration in the air freight forwarding industry, *Tijdschrift voor economische en sociale geografie*, 95, 174–88.

Button, K.J. (2003) Does the theory of the 'core' explain why airlines fail to cover their long-run costs of capital? *Journal of Air Transport Management*, 9, 5–14.

Button, K.J. (2008) Auctions: what can we learn from auction theory for slot allocation? in A. Czerny, P. Forsyth, and H.-M. Niemeier (eds), *Airport Slots International Experiences and Options for Reform*, Ashgate.

Button, K.J. and Vega, H. (2007) The temporal-fares-offered curves in air transportation, *Journal of the Transportation Research Forum*, 46, 83–100.

Davis, O.A. and Whinston, A.B. (1967) Piecemeal policy in the theory of second-best, *Review of Economic Studies*, 34, 323–31.

De Neufville, R. (2006) Accommodating low-cost airlines at main airports, *International Airport Review*, 1, 62–5.

Friedman, D.D. (1979) In defense of the long-haul/short-haul discrimination, *Bell Journal of Economics*, 10, 706–708.

Hirschleifer, J. (1958) Peak loads and efficient pricing: comment, *Quarterly Journal of Economics*, 72, 451–62.

Jacobs Consultancy (2007) *Review of Dedicated Low-cost Airport Passenger Facilities*, Commission for Aviation Regulation.

Juan, E.R. (1995) *Airport Infrastructure: The Emergence Role of the Private Sector, Cofinancing and Financial Advisory Services*, World Bank.

Lipsey, R.G. and Lancaster, K. (1956/57) The general theory of second best, *Review of Economic Studies*, 24, 11–32.

Mishan, E.J. (1962) Second-thoughts on second best, *Oxford Economic Papers*, 14, 205–17.

Morlock, B.K. (1987) Privatizing bus transit: cost savings from competitive contracting, *Journal of the Transportation Research Forum*, 28, 72–81.

Musgrave, R.A. (1957) A multiple theory of budget determination, *Finanzarchiv*, 17, 333–43.

Nash, C.A. (1978) Management objectives, fares and service levels in bus transport, *Journal of Transport Economics and Policy*, 12, 70–85.

Newman, P. and Kenworthy, J. (1999) *Sustainability and Cities: Overcoming Automobile Dependence*, Island.

Nilsson, J.E. (1992) Second-best problems in railway infrastructure pricing and investment, *Journal of Transport Economics and Policy*, 26, 245–59.

Pirrong, S.C. (1992) An application of core theory to the analysis of ocean shipping markets, *Journal of Law and Economics*, 35, 89–131.

Ramsey, F. (1927) A contribution to the theory of taxation, *Economic Journal*, 37, 47–61.

Salanovaa, J.M., Estrada, M., Aifadopoulou, G., and Mitsakis., E. (2011) A review of the modeling of taxi services, *Procedia Social and Behavioral Sciences*, 20, 150–61.

Samson, T., Nash, C.A, Mackie, P.J., Shires, J., and Watkiss, P. (2001) Surface transport costs and charges: Great Britain 1998, Report, UK Department of the Environment, Transport and the Regions.

Schank, L.L. (2005) Solving airside airport congestion: why peak runway pricing is not working, *Journal of Air Transport Management*, 11, 417–25.

Shreiber, C. (1975) The economic reasons for price and entry regulation of taxicabs, *Journal of Transport Economics and Policy*, 9, 268–79.

Starkie, D. (2001) Reforming UK airport regulation, *Journal of Transport Economics and Policy*, 35, 119–35.

Stigler, G.J. (1954) The economist plays with blocs, *American Economic Review*, 44, 7–14.

Sturmey, S.G. (1975) *Shipping Economics*, Macmillan.

Truelove, P. (1992) *Decision Making in Transport Planning*, Longman.

Turvey, R. (1975) A simple analysis of optimal fares on scheduled transport sources, *Economic Journal*, 85, 1–9.

Tyson, W.J. (1975) A study of the effect of different bus fares in Greater Manchester, *Chartered Institute of Transport Journal*, 37, 334–8.

Wiseman, J. (1957) The theory of public utility price: an empty box, *Oxford Economic Papers (New Series)*, 9, 56–74.

Zerby, I.A. and Conlon, R.M. (1978) An analysis of capacity utilisation in liner shipping, *Journal of Transport Economics and Policy*, 12, 27–46.

8 Containing the Environmental Costs of Transport

. . . .

8.1 Introduction

Chapter 6 offered evidence on the magnitude and the diversity of the external economic costs associated with transport. We now move to consider the various methods of confronting the problems posed by negative externalities. This chapter focuses on those issues involving the environmental while Chapter 9 is concerned with excessive traffic congestion.

It should be emphasized that the public policy focus on the external costs of transport, while glaring in the developed world, is much less intense in many less-wealthy countries. The affluence in Western nations has transferred part of the desire from improving material living standards to that of improving (or retaining) environmental quality. The marginal utility of additional financial income, it is often argued, is for most people in the West of less value than a cleaner, quieter, and safer environment in which to live. This is a comparatively recent phenomenon when it comes to transport economics, with books on the subject written in or before about 1960 giving scant attention to environmental externalities.

Although increasingly concerned with matters such as deforestation, water pollution, and soil erosion, most Third World countries still retain some of this comparative indifference to the environmental impacts of transport: their generally poor living standards and inadequate transport systems necessitate that effort be directed almost exclusively at improving material output. This is despite mounting environmental problems, including those stemming from the release of global climate change gases. What has changed over time is that more larger countries have moved up the economic ladder – such as China, India, and Brazil – and are becoming more engaged in environmental dialogues.

We have seen in Figure 6.1 that, ideally, externalities should be contained to the point where the costs of further reductions exceed the marginal social benefits (as stated in the early 1970s by the United Kingdom's Royal Commission on Environmental Pollution, 'pollution should be reduced to the point where the costs of doing so are covered by the benefits from the reduction in pollution'). It should be re-emphasized that this is unlikely to mean zero pollution or zero congestion but rather optimal levels of external cost; a congestion-free road system would mean periods of wasteful idleness. To achieve this optimum, several possibilities recommend themselves and the objective of this chapter is to evaluate the effectiveness of the main ones.

These options are largely assessed in terms of their economic implications, but in practice there are important political (most notably the lobbying power of various groups) and wider social concerns (involving such things as 'environmental justice') that come into play when policies are being considered. There is considerable analysis of these broader aspects in the economic literature, but these are not dealt with in any detail here.

8.2   The Main Economic Approaches

When it comes to the environment, the adverse economic effects of transport result from a chain reaction (Figure 8.1), starting with market failures such as inappropriate pricing and investment policies. Most notably these negative third-party externalities affect the costs perceived by those in the transport sector who react to input prices that do not appropriately reflect the external costs. Basically, there is too much transport and often the wrong sorts of transport being supplied. This in turn causes excessively damaging environmental effects such as noise, emission of global warming gases, and water pollution. The ultimate welfare effects are felt further down the chain in the form of higher environmental damage to health, sustainable local biosystems, and reduced long-term productivity.

From a policy perspective, the diagram is useful because it shows that economic policies designed to reduce, or optimize, the environmental costs associated with transport may be introduced at various points in the chain. If, for political reasons or because of transactions costs, it is not possible to tackle the market failures *per se*, there may be relatively cost-effective second-best approaches that can be applied further down the chain. For example, by building sound-walls along the sides of streets to reduce excessive noise, restricting motor access areas to noise-sensitive areas, or planting forests to act as carbon sinks. These second-best approaches, however, may distort other markets and this needs to be borne in mind when assessing their merits.

At the more specific instrument level, a broad indication of the range of policies which can be applied to limiting the external costs of the motor vehicle are set out in Table 8.1. As can be seen, policies can broadly be divided between

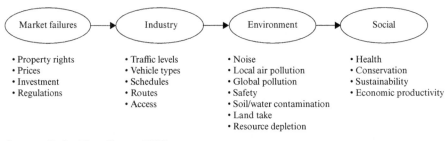

Source: Derived from Button (2001).

Figure 8.1   *The stages in the environmental cost chain*

Table 8.1 *Taxonomy of policy instruments to control the environmental impacts of motor vehicles*

	Market-based incentives		Command-and-control instruments	
	Direct	*Indirect*	*Direct*	*Indirect*
Vehicle	Emissions fee Tradeable permits	Differential taxation Tax allowances for new vehicles	Emissions standards	Compulsory inspection & maintenance of emissions control systems Mandatory use of low-polluting vehicles Compulsory scrappage of old vehicles
Fuel		Differential fuel taxation High fuel taxes	Fuel composition Phasing out of high-polluting fuels	Fuel economy standards Speed limits
Traffic		Congestion pricing Parking charges Subsidies for less polluting modes	Physical constraints of traffic Designated areas	Restraints on vehicle use Bus lanes & other priorities Information systems

those based on market-oriented approaches and those involving command-and-control measures. In practice, however, 'baskets' of instruments that reinforce one another are usually employed. The table also reflects the ability of policy-makers to direct their attention at various aspects of the transport problems with policies possibly being aimed at the vehicle, the fuel used, or at affecting the level and composition of traffic.

While it is useful at times, both for illustration and to retain a link between theory and policy, to refer to actual measures employed by transport authorities, the emphasis is on the direct economic implications of the alternative approaches rather than their political or social virtues. Broadly we proceed by initially looking at the strict market approach to the subject (the 'Coasian solution'), and then move on to consider fiscal instruments and the internalizing of external costs by charging those who generate them (the 'Pigouvian solution'). Variants of both are also looked at before considering command-and-control measures.

8.3 Marketable and Tradeable Permits

Much of the work of Nobel Prize-winning economist Ronald Coase (1960) focused on the effects that complete or imperfect markets for property rights have on creating excessive social costs. The solution to this problem he saw as ensuring that individuals have more complete ownership over property rights and that they can trade these rights to maximize the efficient use of resources. This generally involves marketable or tradeable permits. The owner, say, of some rights to pollute a river to some legal extent may sell those rights to another individual or company. The term 'tradeable permits' is sometimes also used to describe this concept, but on other occasions relates to the situation when the owner of legal rights to pollute may trade these with another individual or firm for rights to carry out similar pollution at a different place or time. A transport example of the latter is the trading of landing and take-off slots at major airports.

A more concrete example of the use of marketable permits was the Kyoto round of negations that led to an international protocol on the release of global warming gases from 2005 regarding global carbon emissions and *ipso facto* the release of global warming gases. The system devised gave participating countries an allocation of carbon and allowed them to trade these amongst themselves. The countries, or individuals and firms within them, that can make the most effective use of carbon will then buy additional amounts in a carbon market from those that have allocations but cannot use them effectively. In this way the allocations end up in uses that yield the greatest economic gains. Transport largely fell outside of this particular system but there have been specific markets devised for modes such as aviation.

The general way marketable permits work is illustrated in Figure 8.2. In this diagram, which largely replicates Figure 6.1, the *MNPB* curve, drawn linearly purely for the sake of simplicity, shows the net benefits that the perpetrator of the externality (emissions in our example) gain from that activity. There are diminishing returns as more emissions are generated. The *MEC* curve reflects the marginal costs of emissions that are assumed to rise as they increase – for example, small

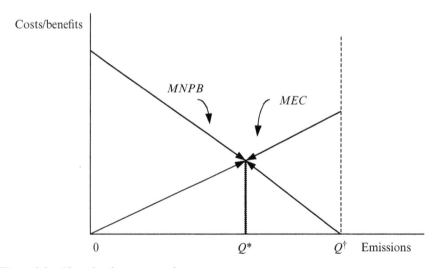

Figure 8.2   *The role of property rights*

emissions of NO_2 cause little damage, but as they mount up, increments become more serious.

If there are no property rights, in other words the perpetrators can use up as much of the environmental resources as they wish at no cost, then emissions will rise to point $Q^\dagger$ in the diagram irrespective of the costs involved. There are also no incentives to emit beyond this level: it is an equilibrium. If, on the other hand, those affected by the pollution have the rights to clean air then there will be no pollution: again, an equilibrium point, despite the net benefits that would be generated if a degree of pollution were allowed.

Ideally, when the optimum level of emissions is at Q^*, the net benefits are maximized. To reach this point, and for it to be an equilibrium, Coase argues that rights to the atmosphere should be created and trade in them permitted. Assuming that those adversely affected were given these rights, then some of the individuals would be willing to sell these rights to the emitters who would have a willingness to pay. Trade would continue as long as there were enough potential emitters willing to buy rights from the polluted that were not so severely affected; in other words, until an equilibrium is reached with emission levels at Q^*. Alternatively, the initial allocation of rights could be given to the emitters. The marginal emitters would be willing to be bought out by the most severely affected polluted and this trade would again continue until emissions are at Q^*.

It does not matter in this context from a long-run perspective who is initially granted the property rights to the atmosphere. The ultimate trading leads to an optimal outcome. The initial allocation could be by an auction (in which case the government would get a windfall once-and-for-all gain), it could be by lottery, it could be according to current use, and so on. This is more of a political economy than an economic matter because it has obvious distributional effects – those with the initial allocation (or the government in the case of auctions) make a short-term financial gain – but not long-term resource efficiency effects.

While theoretically the Coasian approach has intellectual merit, it has limitations. To allocate property rights to, in the example, the atmosphere there is a need to be able to define the units being traded. While this can be proxied in the case of something like greenhouse gas emissions by using tons of carbon, this is not so easy with things like noise or visual intrusion. There is also the issue of policing to ensure contracts agreed upon are upheld, and there are the transaction costs involved in the buying and selling of the rights themselves. Efficient trade also assumes that markets work perfectly, and there is no monopoly power present.

Despite these challenges, tradeable permits, or at least policies containing their main elements such as cap-and-trade which is considered below, have been used to deal with specific transport-related externalities, in addition to more generic problems such as global warming gas emissions. They were used, for example, in the United States to remove lead from gasoline in the 1980s and as part of the efforts of the European Union's Emission Trading Scheme to reduce CO_2 emissions from aircraft.

A less strict market approach is that inherent in the corporate average fuel economy (CAFE) standards affecting the fuel efficiency of new vehicle fleets in the United States and discussed below. Here there is no monetary trading but car manufacturers can adjust the types of vehicles being made (intra-company trading) conditional on average fuel burn standards being met which allows for flexibility in their production to reflect costs and market demand.

Exhibit   *Marketable permits for lead in gasoline*

Lead was introduced into gasoline in the 1920s to boost the octane level of the fuel and to reduce engine 'knock'. The 1970s saw measures to reduce the lead content of the fuel as catalytic converters, which were damaged by lead, were phased in to reduce hydrocarbon (HC), nitrous oxides (NOx), and carbon monoxide (CO) pollution levels, and as it became accepted that lead in fuel had adverse effects on human health and, in particular, on the brain development of small children. The 1970 Clean Air Act Amendments gave the US Environmental Protection Agency (EPA) the power to require new cars to use unleaded fuel and be fitted with catalytic convertors.

In the light of further medical evidence, from 1979 the EPA accelerated the decrease in pollution from pre-1975 vehicles by requiring refineries to reduce the average lead content of gasoline, the agency thus deploying a tradeable permit mechanism. Different standards were applied to the permissible lead content according to refinery size. Large refineries with a productive capacity of over 50,000 barrels a day, or refineries that as a corporate group had a capacity of over 137,000 barrels per day, had to produce gasoline containing on average less than 0.8 grams of lead per gallon per quarter for the first year and 0.5 grams for the following two years. Smaller refinery limits were based upon five standards dependent on scale of production. How the refineries were to meet their standards was up to them. This gave flexibility in terms of technology and also product mix because the standards were an average across fuel types. The EPA subsequently tightened and modified the system in 1982 (when a new standard of 1.1 grams was set) and in 1983.

Refineries could buy and sell lead rights amongst themselves to come under the maximum lead content stipulation. Those that could not individually meet the standards could 'buy' into a group of over-achievers and, by dint of averaging, all could comply with the 1.1-gram requirement. The EPA used the term 'constructive allocation' to describe it. In 1985 refineries that had more than met the standard also had the option of 'banking' (basically carrying over) any lead rights into the next quarter. This was designed to provide refineries with more temporal flexibility. The lead content of gasoline was then reduced successively in 1985 and 1986, with all inter-refinery averaging and banking ceasing in 1988, and all lead additives banned in 1996.

The figure shows the annual reduction of lead in United States gasoline for the 25 years after 1970. From 1979 to 1988, the regulations on refineries accounted for about 36 percent of the lead reduction that occurred.

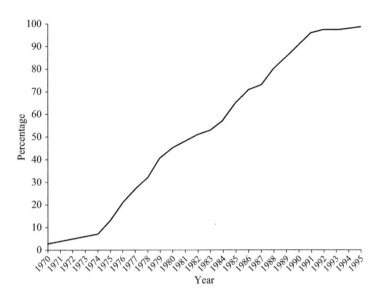

Actual data on the effects of the trading scheme is empty space. The EPA did not collect any. What evidence there is regarding banking suggests that the pre-banking permit price for 0.1 grams of lead was $0.01 and after its introduction was $0.02 to $0.05, suggesting the marketable permit program produced several hundreds of millions in abatement costs. In a dynamic context there were likely additional savings to refineries associated with their ability to smooth out transaction costs. These savings probably exceeded the $226 million the EPA had projected, given the scale of banking that transpired.

See also: R.W. Hahn (1989) Economic prescriptions for environmental problems: how the patient followed the doctor's orders, *Journal of Economic Perspectives*, 3, 95–114; *and* R.G. Newell and K. Rogers (2003) *The US Experience with the Phasedown of Lead in Gasoline*, Resources for the Future.

8.4 The OECD's 'Polluter-pays Principle'

There is an inevitable problem with optimizing externalities, as pointed out by Coase himself, and this involves the perspective with which one looks at an externality. Coase argued that externalities could theoretically be removed by allocating environmental property rights, either to polluters or those adversely affected, and allowing trade to take place in these rights. There are clear practical problems with doing this, not the least of which is that of policing the system, but the idea does pinpoint the symmetrical nature of externalities. Should those who suffer be protected or should those who benefit be compensated for desisting from their current transport activities? While from an efficiency perspective there is no clear answer, international agencies such as the OECD (1975) have taken the line that morally those who pollute should pay for the excessive damage they cause the environment – the so-called 'polluter-pays principle'.

Emissions Charges

The concept of emissions charges is not a new one and can be traced back to the publication of Arthur Pigou's work on *The Economics of Welfare* in 1920. The idea is that the authorities take responsibility for the environment – in effect they become the property right holders, and charge users of the environment an appropriate price (or tax) for that use. Figure 8.3 provides a standard type of visual illustration of how such a charge would apply to road transport. We see the marginal cost of road users (*MPC*) rise. Because road users only take account of the cost of trips they incur themselves, they will keep making trips until the flow is F_1. The traffic, however, creates (for example) noise that when added to the costs of fuel and time in making trips pushes up the full marginal cost at each level of flow to *MSC*. If this were taken into account, then motorists would reduce their traffic and the flow would fall to F_2. The optimal environmental charge designed to reflect the noise costs on residents is the difference between the *MSC* and *MPC* at this flow as illustrated. The road users, by having the marginal costs of their trips pushed up from P_1 to P_2, are discouraged from making trips that do cover this full cost and thus the flow falls to F_2.

Strictly, this diagram could be a little deceiving. It assumes that imposing a pollution charge will affect traffic flow, which it may, but in fact there may be other ways in which a road user could deal with an environmental charge. In terms, of say, a charge on noise, a road user could suppress the noise without making fewer trips, or at least not significantly fewer; or, with a carbon tax, could buy smaller-engine vehicles to conserve fuel but not seriously affect travel patterns. In other words, part of the impact of an emissions charge would be to pull the *MSC* cost down in Figure 8.3.

The more technically correct diagram would be to have emissions on the horizontal axis to directly link the charge with the *de facto* effect on the environmental cost. One can easily trace out that the environmental result would be the

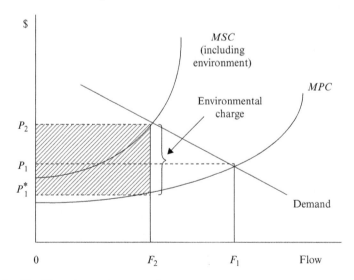

Figure 8.3   *The Pigouvian environmental tax*

same as when emissions are perfectly correlated with traffic flow. It is deliberately drawn this way, however, to allow the discussion to move to the need to target policies and to measure their impacts in relation to the externality involved. For example, high fuel taxes may be a good way of reducing certain emissions, such as CO_2, but the ability to change vehicle types means that traffic flows may be unaffected. For handling congestion problems, as we see in the next chapter, there is a need for direct measures affecting trip-making.

Pigouvian-style charges, while not common, are increasingly being used in transport, the best-known example being the differential tax on leaded petrol that virtually all industrialized countries outside the United States adopted in the 1980s, but some airports also vary landing/take-off fees according to the noise nuisance aircraft create.

While the basic concept is not difficult to appreciate, it has been refined and argued over since the 1920s. Perhaps the most important of these debates reflects the fact that it is the authorities who impose the Pigouvian tax who are the main beneficiaries of them. Unlike tradeable permits where markets allow for compensation through the pricing mechanism, there is no such automatic structure with charges because the revenues collected go to government. It is then a political matter regarding who subsequently enjoys them. Historically, it has often been debates over the use of revenues that have been the main obstacles to the use of environmental charging.

There are also problems in the calculation of the optimal pollution charge or price, since it is necessary to have reliable information about the *MPC* and *MSC* curves. As we have seen in Chapter 6, knowledge in this area is scant and although the use of, for example, hedonic house price indices may shed some light on the monetary importance of noise nuisance, they are far from perfect and normally offer little insight into the shape of the curves involved or the responsiveness of people to financial incentives.

At a rather more theoretical level, it is possible to question whether the polluter-pays principle is being correctly applied in Figure 8.3. We have implicitly assumed that the road users should buy the right to pollute in the area, but this could be turned on its head, and the proposition presented that road users should buy the right to relatively clean air, that is, the road users should be paid a subsidy of an amount equal to the emissions charge $(P_2P^*_1)$ depicted in the diagram to curtail their activities. Again, as with the Coase case, the question is essentially a moral–legal one involving property rights; although there may also be practical considerations involving the administrative costs of introducing either prices or subsidies, these should also be considered.

As William Baumol and Wallace Oates (1988) have stressed, one of the problems of charging polluters is that information about the *MSC* curve is imperfect, and that, even if some initially arbitrary price is charged, there is no indication of whether this is too high or too low. The usual 'trial and error' method of pricing used in industry is, therefore, not appropriate.

Since information about the *MSC* curve is necessary for virtually all optimal containment of noise and emissions, irrespective of the method used,

Baumol and Oates argue in favor of pricing on the grounds that it will cause fewer distortions than other policies. Their arguments found favor with the OECD, which maintained that '[t]he costs of these measures (to ensure that the environment is in an acceptable state) should be reflected in the cost of goods and services that cause pollution in production and/or consumption'. Figure 8.4 considers two modes of transport, trucking (A) and railways (B), and relate the marginal net private benefits associated with using each mode to the noise nuisance emitted.

These curves are unknown to the authorities but it may be decided that it would be beneficial to do something about noise pollution rather than leave it at a high level. In these circumstances one may wish to reduce noise emissions by say 15 percent, and to use polluter charges to achieve this. Baumol and Oates demonstrate that a uniform charge on both road haulage and railway noise is the appropriate 'second-best' policy to pursue. In the figure the marginal abatement costs (MAC) of noise emissions by one unit for each of the two modes are plotted. These curves are not known with any degree of exactitude to policy-makers. A mandatory reduction of 15 percent for each mode would result in emissions being reduced to A and B for trucking and railroads respectively.

While the desired objective has been satisfied, what one sees is that the MAC costs involved differ as between the modes – they are higher for road than for rail. It would be more cost-effective to reduce noise by a greater amount on the railways than on roads quite simply because it is cheaper per unit to cut emissions in the former. A noise emissions charge of P per unit per decibel would automatically achieve the aimed-for improvement because it would be more of an incentive to cut pollution where it is cheaper to do so (a level $B^{\dagger}$ for rail) and have smaller reductions where the costs of abatement are higher (to $A^{\dagger}$ in the case of road haulage).

The Baumol and Oates argument highlights that if a standard is to be aimed for, then the most efficient way of attaining it is by using fiscal instruments. One can see the importance of this in many transport contexts. Because of its very nature much transport activity is a mobile source of environmental intrusion, but the domains in which it operates often differ in their sensitivity to its presence.

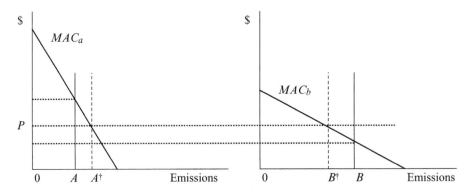

Figure 8.4   *The advantage of fiscal instruments when there is uncertainty*

Different airports, for example, because of their locations and prevailing wind conditions, impose different noise envelopes on their surrounding populations. The actual physical noise associated with any aircraft type may, therefore, impose different costs at different airports.

To set a standard that all aircraft should reduce noise levels by a specified amount would thus be inefficient. A charge, on the other hand, which would bring about the same overall noise reduction would give the flexibility to airlines to use their quieter aircraft at locations where noise is a major nuisance and their older, noisier ones where the problem is less severe.

The polluter-pays principle tends to be favored by many academics but it is not without its critics. Clifford Sharp (1979), for example, questions the distributional implications and argues that in some instances an environmental improvement may be obtained as efficiently by means of progressive taxation without the possible regressive effects of pollution charges. Essentially, the argument revolves around the fact that the benefits from any environmental improvement are closely related to income. A poor person would probably have a preference for no pollution charges (and *ipso facto* lower final money prices) than a wealthier person whose marginal utility of income is lower. Hence, from a distributional point of view, a subsidy of $P_2P^*_1$ in Figure 8.3 to the airport to suppress aircraft noise, financed from a progressive taxation system, will have the same environmental effect but none of the regressive features of the pollution charge.

While hardly common, pollution charges have been used in transport with some success. One clear illustration of where fiscal incentives (in this example, coupled with regulation) have proved particularly effective has been in reducing the levels of lead (Pb) pollution. Many countries have introduced significant tax differentials between leaded and unleaded gasoline but, equally, many have also initiated regulations regarding the fuels that can be sold. In particular, the banning of normal gasoline (providing the tank capacity for garages to stock unleaded fuel and leaving only the more expensive super) has effectively further reduced the real choice open to most automobile users in the Netherlands, Switzerland, the United Kingdom, and Germany. The combined impact of these measures in the United Kingdom was a rise in vehicles using unleaded gasoline from 0.1 percent of the car park in March 1988 to 25.9 percent in October 1989. Similarly, in the pre-unified Federal Republic of Germany the percentage of automobiles using unleaded rose from 11 percent in 1986 to 28 percent in 1987.

To date, however, fiscal policies have tended to be piecemeal, usually focusing on modes of transport rather than directly on transport externalities and, generally, with the explicit objective of reducing the effect of different modes rather than optimizing them. This suggests that the social objective of government policy has been one of satisficing rather than optimizing although it has been argued that the actual effect of some regulations has been excessive.

Schwing et al. (1980), for instance, suggested that the United States Clean Air Act of 1970 imposed car exhaust emission levels that were far too stringent, with a consequential welfare loss. Table 8.2 presents the results of their cost–benefit study. While the high benefit estimate suggests some welfare advantage from the Act, the underlying assumptions required to reach this conclusion are deemed very unrealistic. Optimal levels for toxic exhaust emissions were estimated to be 0.73 percent, 0.31 percent, and 0.82 percent control for NOx, CO, and HC respectively.

The acceptability of this type of work would be questioned by environmentalists in terms of both the items included in the cost–benefit calculations and the valuations placed upon them. The problem, common to most studies of environmental aspects of transport, is the inadequacy of knowledge both about the actual physical impact of the various external effects generated by transport and about the values society places upon them. Until some clear understanding of these matters is obtained it is difficult to see how the external effects of transport are likely to approach the optimal level.

Cap-and-trade

Cap-and-trade emission control policies are a hybrid between a strict market approach along Coasian lines and the setting of strict standards. A maximum amount of emission is set based upon political and scientific considerations and then this is allocated by the buying and selling of permits within this constraint. One of the aims of this is to introduce more information into the market, the ceiling, and to thus add more stability.

An example in the context of transport is the European Union Emissions Trading System (EU ETS). This started in 2005 and includes over 11,000 energy and manufacturing plants in Europe with a net heat in excess of 20 MW accounting for 41 percent of the Union's greenhouse gas emissions. From 2012, parts of the aviation sector were included in it. These covers flights where both take-off and landing are within the EU. Initially, the Union planned to include all flights even if the take-off or landing was outside of its geography; this is referred to as 'full scope'. But after protests from mainly the United States and China, the system was modified to a reduced scope, which 'temporarily stopped the clock'. The allowances under the EU ETS specific to airlines are European Union Aviation Allowances (EUAA). If airlines need additional allowances, they can also purchase regular European Union Allowances. EUAA issued for 2013–20 corresponded to 95 percent of the emissions of 2008–12. From 2021 onwards, there is

Table 8.2   *Impacts of the United States Clean Air Act of 1970*

Benefit estimate	% Control level			Benefit (10^9)	Cost (10^9)	Net benefit (10^9)
	HC	CO	NO			
Low	0.98	0.97	0.94	9	65	−56
Prime	0.98	0.97	0.94	34	65	31
High	0.98	0.97	0.94	102	65	37

Source: Schwing et al. (1980).

to be a linear annual reduction until 2064, when no additional EUAA allowances will be issued. The last European Union Allowances would be issued in 2057.

Carbon Off-setting

A carbon off-set is a reduction in emissions of carbon dioxide or other greenhouse gases made in order to compensate for emissions made elsewhere. For example, a shipping company could off-set the carbon generated in its activities by tree planting, supporting wind farms and biomass energy, constructing biogas digesters, or building hydroelectric dams. The off-set, providing it reduces carbon emissions by the same amount as that generated by transport, meets the polluter-pays principle irrespective of the form it takes. That, however, inevitably raises questions over the imposition of other forms of externalities – for example, wind farms are not seen as aesthetically pleasing to all. The Kyoto Protocol has sanctioned off-sets as a way for governments and private companies to earn carbon credits that can be traded on a market-place.

The idea, however, that buying an off-set will instantly erase transport's carbon footprint is overly simplistic (Becken and Mackey, 2017). Newly planted trees take years before becoming significant carbon absorbers, and that is only when forests stay protected for long enough to reach that point. Such cases where the carbon off-set is sold before it has been achieved are known as 'forward crediting'. Furthermore, many projects entail monoculture forestry with just one species being planted. This supports very little biodiversity and is more susceptible to fires and disease.

The accounting process, translating emissions reductions from projects to carbon off-sets that can be sold, is complex. For example, estimations of emissions from air travel are usually generalized across types of aircraft, fuel use, routes, and other factors, because it is not feasible to measure the emissions of specific flight. In forestry projects, the amount of carbon absorbed varies widely depending on the species of tree, and climate and soil conditions. Implementing a project can also release emissions, which needs to be accounted for to ensure that only net reductions are claimed.

Any off-set project should have 'additionality'. The project would not have happened without the off-sets. Some emission-reducing activities naturally occur in compliance with existing regulations, or because they are profitable investments. Ensuring the off-set plays an indispensable role in whether or not a project is implemented is problematic; it deals in hypotheticals.

The project's carbon reductions should be permanent, without causing any eventual emissions that reverse the original effects. For instance, while plantations store carbon, they run the risk of releasing it if the trees end up being cut or burned down. Some projects keep a buffer reserve of off-set credits, which are used to compensate for any credits that are inadvertently voided. They can also mitigate risks from the outset to reduce chances of a reversal occurring.

Voluntary carbon-set programs have been adopted by a number of major airlines, and have been put forward by the International Civil Aviation Organization

(ICAO) as its main instrument for reducing carbon emissions. For example, in Europe, British Airways has a scheme allowing passengers to buy credits for protecting threatened forests, and EasyJet is engaged in off-setting projects in Peru and Ethiopia. In the United States, Delta uses avoided deforestation projects as an off-set. But there are issues with these schemes.

The ICAO's Carbon Offsetting and Reduction Scheme for International Aviation (CORSIA), set in train in 2016, has the goal of carbon neutral growth from 2020. Being phased in from 2021, aircraft operators should purchase carbon credits from the carbon market. The scheme is voluntary for all countries until 2027. As emissions below 2020 levels are grandfathered, CORSIA regulates 25 percent of aviation's international emissions applying to international flights as representing 60 percent of aviation emissions.

Economic comparisons between aviation off-set programs and cap-and-trade policies (such as the EU ETS discussed earlier) have provided some *ex ante* assessment as to their potential effects. Taking Sweden as a case study, Larsson et al. (2019) examined the possible effects of these policies on air travel emissions from 2017 to 2030. Their analysis shows that when emissions reductions in other sectors are attributed to the aviation sector as a result of the EU ETS and CORSIA, carbon emissions are expected to reduce by –0.8 percent per annum. However, if non-CO_2 emissions are included in the analysis, then emissions will increase. This is less than what is needed to achieve the 2°C reduction target. When looking at both domestic and international flights, and at total emissions, not just the increase, it has been estimated that 12 percent of aviation emissions will be off-set due to CORSIA in 2030 (Scheelhaase et al., 2018).

8.5 More on Environmental Standards

Figure 8.3 indicated that charging a pollution price might optimize external costs. It is equally possible, however, that rather than operate through the pricing mechanisms the desired, environmentally optimal level of traffic could be obtained by using command-and-control instruments; that is, the establishment of legal or in some cases voluntary standards covering pollution, noise, and safety.

The setting of environmental standards is long established, as the oft-cited night-time banning of chariots in classical Rome illustrates. Their use is now extensive and covers such wide-ranging things as the establishment of 'noise abatement zones' in the United Kingdom, and the controls embodied in a series of Road Traffic Acts that have, since 1973, laid down regulations regarding car silencers and exhausts. The CAFE standards define the fuel efficiency of new vehicles in the United States (see Section 8.8) and most industrial countries now insist gasoline-powered cars are fitted with catalytic convertors and use unleaded fuels. There are controls over where oil-tankers may clean their tanks and when aircraft may take off. Individuals are required to wear seat belts in many countries and the use of cell phones while driving is often illegal. The list of standards and regulations is long and continues to grow.

They also change over time, as we see later regarding vehicle fuel efficiency. As another example, noise standards were introduced in the United Kingdom at the manufacturing stage for new lorries in 1970 with limits of 91 dB(A) for vehicles with engines over 200 hp and 89 dB(A) for less powerful lorries, while from March 1983 new vehicles coming into production had to meet more stringent requirements of 88 dB(A) and 86 dB(A) respectively. Supranational legislation has gained in importance recently with the European Union setting vehicle noise limits from the early 1990s. The Civil Aviation Act of 1971 laid down regulations about night movements over built-up areas in the country, and specifies overfly patterns for aircraft. The speed limits operative on roads in virtually all countries are primarily designed to reduce accident risk – with some supplementary positive effects, on occasions, on fuel economy.

The compulsory wearing of seat belts in many countries is also to reduce accident costs. Similarly, the periodic testing of vehicles and the licensing of lorries, aircraft, etc. are to ensure that minimum safety and environmental standards are achieved. In many overseas countries the regulations are more stringent (for example, the removal of lead from petrol in the United States, and stricter annual checks on pollution emissions from internal combustion engines in states such as New Jersey and Oregon) or take different forms (such as airbags in cars in the United States), but their intended effect is the same: to reduce the marginal environmental, including external accident, costs of transport.

While all the above represent physical regulations to contain pollution, they should strictly be divided between those controls that act directly to contain the externality (for example, noise emission legislation), the third component of Figure 8.1, and those that control transport in such a way as to reduce the external costs (for example, lorry routes and aircraft flight path regulations). The effects of these alternative broad sets of physical controls are not the same.

Actual emission standards act directly to limit the external effects permitting other characteristics of operations to be adjusted freely. Operational regulations impose much more stringent controls, severely limiting the alternative courses of action open to the operator. With noise emissions standards for aircraft flying over an area, for instance, an airline can either conform and pay the costs of suppressing noise or avoid the area in question; with operational controls, the latter option is available. This point should be borne in mind during the more general discussion of physical controls, which follows. We shall return to the question of operational restrictions, traffic calming, and vehicle routing in more detail later.

One justification for adopting command-and-control methods is that they can have lower administrative costs. For example, the imposition of a zero lead content requirement for gasoline is relatively easy to understand and to enforce. It may not be optimal, and the effects across different users may not be fully efficient, but the transaction costs are relatively small. Allowing different individuals to have different amounts of lead in their fuel according to, say, their willingness to pay is quite clearly going to be difficult to price and to administer. In more strict economic terms, the transactions costs of pricing *à la* Pigou, or marketable permits along Coasian lines, are just not cost-effective. But there may be other reasons for adopting standards.

While in the simple case illustrated in Figure 8.3 the effect of an optimal standard produces an identical level of road transport activity (and, *ipso facto*, environmental intrusion) to an optimal pollution charge, it can be argued that, with more realistic assumptions, the pricing approach offers a superior solution to the externality problem even where administrative costs are similar.

When information about the exact shape of the *MEC* curve is poor, the use of standards is demonstrably less efficient than the Baumol–Oates charging approach seen in Figure 8.4. If, to achieve the 15 percent reduction in transport noise used in our example, both road and rail were compelled to cut their noise emissions (that is, to $0A^t$ and $0B^t$ respectively), then it is clear from the diagram that the marginal net private benefits generated by the two modes are no longer equal (at the new emission levels, $MAC_a > MAC_b$). Consequently, social welfare could be improved by lowering the standard for road haulage and increasing it for rail. Unfortunately. in the real world, lack of perfect knowledge of the *MAC* curves means that the optimal differentiation of standards is likely to be impossible to define. Thus, in this imperfect situation, the polluter-pays principle is almost certainly going to prove superior to the use of emission standards.

It is also probable that pollution pricing will prove more flexible than standards. While transport infrastructure may impose external costs of visual intrusion it is normally the mobile unit that generates the greatest external costs. Given the differing income levels and preference patterns in various parts of a country, one could re-interpret the *MAC* curves in Figure 8.4 in terms of the marginal abatement associated with a single mode, but operating in different parts of the country. In this case the uniform emissions charge would be both theoretically superior and, in addition, reduce the costs to transport undertakings of reducing their noise emissions. The imposition of different standards for each area means that operators must either ensure that vehicles moving between areas conform to the most stringent standards, or have specific, variously suppressed vehicles designed to conform to local regulations. Both options are likely to be wasteful. With a charging regime, the operator can select a vehicle mix that minimizes their overall costs of operation: vehicles numbers may be suppressed or pay the emissions price, or they may be subjected to a combination of the two.

Moving to a more dynamic situation, where technology is variable, Maler (1974) suggested that pollution prices have important advantages over regulations for the encouragement of a rapid adoption of cleaner technologies. His argument rests upon the implicit assumption that transport suppliers, when confronted with either a pollution price or emissions standard, assume this price or standard to be fixed in the medium term irrespective of their individual actions. Consequently, they will always assess the benefits to themselves of adopting new operating methods or technologies against existing prices or standards. In Figure 8.5 we show the marginal private costs of reducing exhaust fumes for a truck operator confronted with the existing technology (MC_1) and with the new technology (MC_2). The MC_2 curve is inside MC_1 because it is cheaper to suppress vehicles with the new technology at all noise levels. On the assumption that the authorities have full information on MEC and can, therefore, define the optimal level of traffic noise we see that either a pollution charge of $0P$ or a standard of $0C$ will ideally be in force.

If the pricing policy is pursued, the trucker will find it financially worthwhile to quieten their vehicle by CD_1 (costing CD_1B) and pay $0CBP$ in charges. With a standard, they pay no pollution charges, but it costs them CBD_1 to conform to the noise regulation. However, if the new technology is available, an individual trucker will perceive, *ceteris paribus*, the benefits of adopting it as ABD_1D_2 if there is a charging policy operative, that is, the trucker will reduce their emissions with the new technology to $0H$ (costing AHD_2) and pay charges of $0PAH$. The incentive to adopt the alternative technology with the emissions standard is only D_1EBD_1, that is, the cost of conforming to the standard with the new technology rather than the old. Thus, the pollution charging policy offers an incentive of the shaded area, ABE, in excess of an emissions standard to move to the cleaner technology.

One possible option is a combined environmental tax/standards approach whereby all vehicles are obliged to meet a set standard and there is a scale of emissions-related 'fines' for vehicles that exceed this. If the standard were rigorous and well below the existing level of emissions (that is, consistent with the optimal level of pollution with the cleaner technology in our example above), then this would be as effective as the pricing approach and at the same time offer a firm target for vehicle operators to aim at. Such a tax/standards approach may, however, be particularly appealing at the vehicle manufacturing stage where new technology can most easily be injected into the transport sector in a gradual manner.

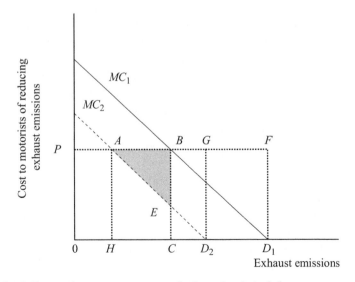

Figure 8.5 *Pollution charges, emissions standards, and technical change*

8.6 Transport Subsidies and the Environment

To try to stimulate the greater use of less 'polluting' transport, in the broadest sense, there has traditionally been a widespread use of subsidies. These are politically attractive, largely because they involve a diffuse contributor base but a focused receptor base. We exclude here the plethora of subsidies that are designed primarily to meet social objectives, such as ensuring acceptable levels of mobility, meeting the needs of the physically disadvantaged, and providing access to remote regions, but are concerned explicitly with subsidies aimed at changing travel patterns with the objective of encouraging more environmentally benign forms of transport.

In practice, however, it is important to note that these are not normally 'Pigouvian subsidies' that are explicitly paid to individuals to desist in generating external costs, but, rather, indirect subsidies to encourage the adoption of other activities that are associated with lower levels of external or other adverse economic impacts. In terms of surface, personal travel the conventional wisdom is that an efficient public transport system with adequate load factors is more energy-efficient than the automobile.

There are general issues regarding subsidies of any kind, such as whether it is reasonable to use taxes collected from the general public to essentially subsidize public transport and car users, and whether it is possible to have an efficient subsidy regime that is not highly X-inefficient and captured by the transport-providing agencies and their employees. But from a pure efficiency perspective, for the types of subsidies given to stimulate less environmentally intrusive modes of transport, there needs to be a reasonably high cross-elasticity of demand between modes for public transport subsidies to be effective. We shall return to this later.

Thus, an alternative to operating directly upon the transport undertaking generating externalities (either pollution or congestion) is seen to be the offering of a carrot to transport users to switch to more socially desirable modes. This line of reasoning has been widely used as a partial justification for the large subsidies given to support the railways and urban transport services. In the United Kingdom, the Railways Act of 1974, for example, permitted government grants of up to 50 percent of the costs to be paid to British Rail customers for the installation of sidings and the provision of rolling stock following an assessment of the environmental harm of the lorry movements which would be avoided if the investment concerned went ahead. The 1968 Transport Act initiated a system of centrally and locally financed public transport operating and capital subsidies (the latter of which have since been abandoned), with the objective of containing the growth in private motor traffic in large urban areas.

In the United States, net federal subsidies from 1990 to 2002 meant that for every thousand passenger-miles, transit got $118 in subsidy, although not all of this was justified on environmental grounds. In addition, there were extensive state and local support initiatives for public transport, although their motivations have not always been clear.

In a perfectly competitive world, there would be no justification for this type of policy, but in a situation where marginal cost pricing is not universal and where political expedience leans against the introduction of measures such as road pricing, subsidies may offer a pragmatic second-best approach to the externality problem.

Where the cross-elasticity of demand between transport and other goods is negligible and the overall demand for transport is totally inelastic – a situation not unrealistic in the context of commuter travel in many large urban areas – the optimal subsidy to a zero externality-generating transport mode will have the same effect on the use of an externality-generating mode as pollution charges.

In Figure 8.6, the overall demand for transport, which is supplied by a combination of private cars and a light rapid transit system, is fixed. Cars have associated with their use external costs that can be expressed as the difference between the MPC_C and the MSC_C. The light rapid transit system has no such externalities associated with its use (that is, $MSC_{LRT} = MPC_{LRT}$) and for simplicity we assume it is a constant cost form of transport. The free market outcome, where no cognizance is taken of externalities, will be a division of traffic at point $0Q^\dagger$ in the diagram. The optimal solution is a split of Q^*, which may be brought about either by charging a Pigouvian pollution charge of the level indicated in the figure or, alternatively, by subsidizing the public transport mode by an identical amount. The modal split effects are the same.

If aggregate demand is not perfectly inelastic then the optimal subsidy is more difficult to define, although it may still offer a second-best solution to the externality problem. Figure 8.7 shows the cost conditions for the externality-generating mode (the car) with a demand curve for its services of D_C. It also shows the cost (C_{PT}) and demand (D_{PT}) for the public transport mode. A subsidy for the public transit mode will cause D_C to shift to the left (say to D'_C),

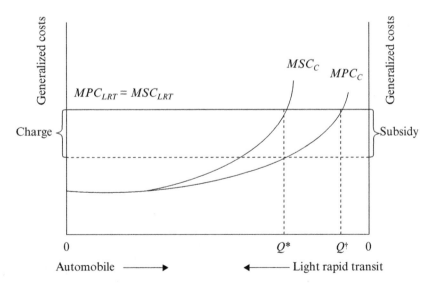

Figure 8.6   *Optimal subsidy to a non-polluting substitute mode with fixed aggregate demand for travel*

reducing the dead-weight welfare loss associated with the initially suboptimally high level of car usage. Unless, however, the demand for car use is pushed so far left that it intersects the cost curves in some areas where $MPC_C = MSC_C$, a dead-weight loss will remain.

As with Figure 8.6 the subsidy itself will also result in some loss of welfare. The fall in the cost of car use as people switch to public transport will have the effect of pulling back the demand for the latter to D'_{PT} and thus reduce the amount of funds needed to fund the optimal subsidy. The ultimate cost of the subsidy is the amount per transit user times Q_{PT}, which exceeds the area of net consumer surplus enjoyed at the subsidized fare level by wxy. If the dead-weight loss saving associated with the reduced level of demand for car use is $abcd$ (that is, the area between MSC_C and MPC_C as D_C shifts to the left), then the optimal subsidy can be defined as that which maximizes the difference between the gain from reducing the dead-weight loss of excessive congestion minus the efficiency cost of the subsidy. In the diagram, this is the subsidy that will maximize $(abcd - wxy)$.

The practical difficulty with this approach is that the optimal subsidy may be extremely large and, theoretically, if the cross-elasticity of demand between modes is low, may even result in negative fares. The use of public transport subsidies in urban areas has been questioned for this very reason. This is a topic that we covered in Chapter 4, where it was found that price cross-elasticities between bus and car are generally low, with service cross-elasticities somewhat higher.

Specifically, early survey work by Michael Kemp (1973) on modal transfers found that in general the direct fare elasticity for urban public transport was low (–0.1 to –0.7), suggesting that substantial subsidies are necessary to attract passengers to public transport irrespective of whether they constitute new travelers or those diverted from private cars. Baum's (1973) work looking at the possible

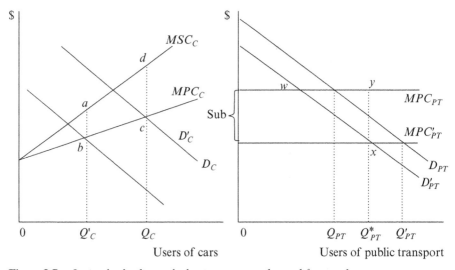

Figure 8.7   *Optimal subsidies with elastic aggregate demand for travel*

effects of offering free urban bus transport was even less optimistic, his analysis yielding elasticities in the range from –0.1 to –0.4 for Britain, the United States, and West Germany. Later, after surveying some 50 empirical studies of both long- and short-term cross-elasticities, however, Goodwin (1992) concluded that, in the short term, bus demand remains inelastic enough to make revenue-raising by fare increases an effective policy, but demand increases by fare reductions limited. But in the longer run the effectiveness of the first policy is reduced, and that of the second is increased.

Finally, De Witte et al. (2006) compared the introduction of 'free' public transport for students at Brussels' Flemish-speaking colleges and universities in the 2003–2004 academic year with French-speaking universities and colleges in the city. They found an increase in public transport use among students benefit- ting from the measure, but also that the group of non-benefitting students not only outnumbered the benefitting students when it came to using public trans- port, the STIB, but also used it more frequently. By contrast, the train, which is not free, is used more frequently by Flemish-speaking students. This is somewhat counterintuitive to the introduction of 'free' public transport for the latter. It appears that there are many other factors affecting the uptake of free goods than just the zero price.

Exhibit   *The 'Ubernomics' of app-based ride-hailing*

Options available for personal urban mobility increased with the arrival of on-demand, app-based ride-hailing (often called ride-sourcing) in the 2010s. The computer platforms of Uber, Lyft, DiDi, etc. allow taxi-like services by connecting consumers to nearby drivers. Initially, this matched car owners with spare seats to customers who needed to travel to places poorly served by public transportation or conventional taxis. Subsequently, individuals have acquired vehicles specifically to be drivers and to meet the demands of app-based vehicle-hailing markets.

Ride-sourcing drivers are largely attracted to the occupation because of the flexibility it offers, the level of compensation, and because they can adjust their work hours to smooth flows of income. They are also more similar in terms of their age and education to the general workforce than to taxi drivers and often had full- or part-time employment before joining. Drivers and riders also often operate in two 'homes' by using several ride-sourcing platforms. This can minimize the 'request to pick-up time', thus offering gains to both parties.

A customer is paired with the nearest driver and can actively track a vehicle once hired. Payment is automatically made through the app. The transportation network companies (TNCs), such as Uber, do not own vehicles, provide training, pay driver expenses, provide insurance, or accept liability. They market themselves as digital platforms that link independent contractors with customers.

Ride-sourcing services are often seen as competitors to taxi-cabs that have a history of being highly regulated with respect to driver qualifications, fares, etc. These regulations meant that much of the time cabs were idle as fares were sought. There was a divergence between the rides being offered and useful rides being made available at locations where potential riders were seeking service. App-based ride-hailing services, being a part of the 'gig economy' often involving part-time work, added greater flexibility to the supply of rides, reducing mismatches between the positioning of drivers and ride seekers.

Increased revenue comes from product differentiation (for example, premium, shared, and food delivery services). This allows a wider range of vehicles to enter the market and more users with diverse requirements to be served. With some drivers having vehicles that can provide a range of services, this generates economies of market presence by speeding up the matching of rides to riders. TNCs also make use of 'surge pricing' to attract more drivers at peak periods and to ration demand.

Considerable economic/legal debate has surrounded the role of drivers in Uber types of markets regarding whether they are self-employed or work for Uber. In one sense the drivers act independently, as is the case in much of the taxi-cab industry, but there are often different legal responsibilities. TNCs have sought to disclaim employee status, depriving drivers of social insurance among other benefits, and to deny liability to third-party victims for damages due to auto accidents or sexual assaults arising out of their business.

There were initial thoughts that ride-sourcing would reduce the demand for driving. The evidence, however, is that, whatever efficient gains there are in terms of vehicle utilization, the increased overall demand for shared rides generally results in more congestion and this is focused in times and space. Traffic peaks are now often in the evening in areas of social activity rather than daytime jobs or shopping. The traffic system has not traditionally been designed to cope with this.

There are safety and security issues associated with ride-sourcing. It was anticipated that the probable uptake of ride-sourcing by individuals who would previously drink and drive would decrease accidents. Comparing accident trends in areas of California with and without a TNC presence, one study found ride-hailing availability significantly reduced traffic-related fatalities for basic services. A wider American study, however, found the staggered arrival of ride-sourcing across cities to be associated with a 2 to 4 percent increase in fatalities, although this study made no allowance for a parallel fall in fuel prices on traffic demand. A study of Austin, Texas revealed a fall of 17 to 40 percent in accidents after Uber had been operating for four years.

See also: K.J. Button (2020) The 'Ubernomics' of ridesourcing: the myths and the reality, *Transport Reviews*, 40, 76–94; *and* J.D. Angrist, S. Caldwell, and J.V. Hall (2021) Uber versus taxi: a driver's eye view, *American Economic Journal: Applied Economics*, 13, 272–308.

8.7   Protecting the Sufferers

The strategies examined so far have relied upon either forcing the generator of externalities to change their production process or encouraging the adoption of a different method of operation. We have only touched upon the idea of insulating the public from environmental intrusion (that is, in the context of aircraft landing path controls and lorry routes). Insulation in the short term may be achieved either by directing traffic away from sensitive areas or by physically protecting people and property (for example, with double-glazing for sound insulation), while in the longer term new investment permits a more efficient separation of transport from those sensitive to its wider impact (the main reason for the official rejection of the Roskill Commission's recommendations on the siting of a Third London Airport in the 1970s was that an inland site would be excessively damaging to the country's environment – see Chapter 11).

Fairly typical of the approaches favoring command-and-control approaches was the Armitage Report produced 40 years ago in the United Kingdom, which went as far as to recommend the establishment of 'Lorry Action Areas' to protect residents living in a limited number of areas but who suffer from the worst environmental effects of road freight transport. Specifically, such areas would involve:

- the installation of double-glazing in houses, which would reduce considerably the major problem of noise in homes;
- grants for repairs to houses physically damaged by lorries;
- maintaining road surfaces to high standards, which would reduce vibrations;
- minor road improvements to reduce accidents and to reduce noise by, for example, the use of noise-absorbing road surfaces;
- the building up of pavements or the erection of bollards to reduce the problems of vehicles cutting corners and of damage to buildings through physical contact; and
- in the worst cases of intense local nuisance by a specific generator of lorry traffic, compensation for discontinuance action taken by a planning authority in respect of a site with planning permission or existing use rights.

The difficulty with protective options, both long- and short-term, is that their effects often extend beyond simply protecting sensitive groups in the community and their overall cost may be considerable. Limiting the flight paths of aircraft can both increase the risk of accident (by forcing the adoption of less safe climbing and turning patterns) and increase the cost of operations (especially energy costs). Similarly, lorry routing both necessitates higher infrastructure costs and often leads to longer trip distances.

In the long term it should, theoretically, be easier to design the spatial economy so that transport's effect on the environment is significantly lower. Options include:

- sterilization of land between nuisance and dwellings;
- use of non-sensitive buildings (for example, light industry) as barriers between nuisance and sensitive areas;
- design dwellings so that little-used rooms face the nuisance rather than living rooms or bedrooms; and
- make use of self-protecting developments – for example patio-style housing – to reduce intrusion.

Such designs obviously generate additional costs and only provide a partial solution to the environmental problem. Like most of the shorter-term protective measures they only ameliorate those aspects of environmental costs inflated while people are at home. Land-use planning may offer some limited protection at other times especially in the reduction of accident risk – but it is unlikely to separate transport completely from the non-traveler.

One should also perhaps include under protective measures the notion of traffic calming. This entails the use of such things as road humps, speed tables, raised junctions, reduced carriageway widths, and 'changed road surfaces' both to slow traffic flows and to encourage the use of particular 'suitable' links in the network or alternative modes. Essentially the idea is to make streets more attractive and liveable. In Europe, traffic calming has tended to come about as part of wider packages and has often been tied to legal speed limits of 30 kph or, in the Netherlands, to a walking pace limit. The latter is part of the country's *Woonerven* – where all road users have equal rights to road space. In the United Kingdom, traffic calming schemes have come about more as part of a policy to reduce urban traffic speed for safety reasons – about 70 percent of schemes have this as a primary objective. Evidence from Germany suggests that serious casualties fell by up to 50 percent in areas where it has been introduced, for example by 44 percent in Heidelberg after traffic calming was initiated.

There are also some positive environmental externalities associated with some types of urban design. Obesity and many forms of illness are associated with a lack of physical activity. The way that cities are built and the way individuals move about in them influence the amount of physical activity that citizens 'enjoy', and lack of facilities within walking or cycling distance necessitates the use of mechanized transport with minimal physical activity. The design of urban areas can thus be perceived as a way of helping to counteract some of the adverse effects on personal well-being by fostering a healthier life-style.

8.8   Energy Use

We now spend some time looking in detail at some economic aspects of transport energy policy. In many cases the instruments used are from the generic toolkit outlined above, but the roles they play are of importance because of the very high correlation between energy use and form and different components of atmospheric pollution. Ensuring that there is no excessive use of a scarce, finite resource such as oil is also of importance.

There is theoretically a wide range of policy tools that can be deployed to affect the energy use of transport. Each has its characteristics and usefulness depending on the background assumptions that are adopted. Here we are selective and focus on some of the more important efforts that have been made to influence fuel consumption in transport. Longer-term policies involving land use and such policies as 'compact-city' design are explicitly omitted. These are large and multi-dimensional topics in their own right and take us beyond the boundaries of a chapter such as this.

Although theoretically there are numerous ways to influence energy use, a wide range of practical and political factors determine the policies that have been initiated to influence the energy consumption in transport. In some circumstances the costs of introducing, monitoring, and policing some policies, as with some specific environmental policies, simply make them impractical, at least in the purest forms. In other situations, there may also be trade-offs between improving energy efficiency and meeting other objectives, such as removing pollutants from the atmosphere or ensuring an acceptable level of traffic safety. An example of the former has been the removal of lead from gasoline in many countries, which reduces the fuel efficiency of internal combustion engines.

The policy tools that are in place, or have been used, to influence the type of fuel used in transport, as well as the aggregate consumption, are nevertheless quite extensive. The following is not intended to be comprehensive in its coverage but rather should be viewed as illustrative of the types of measures that have been put in place.

Leaving Things to the Market

One policy option that is often forgotten is to leave things to the market. After all, while there are market failures, there are also government intervention failures that may either worsen an original market failure or cause serious and unexpected distortions elsewhere in the system (OECD, 1992).

In practice, the market has been a significant influence on the types and amount of energy used by transport. Historically, for example, changes in prices have demonstrable medium- and long-term impacts on overall energy consumption in transport, most of which we have only appreciated in retrospect. Not all of these, however, have been directly related to the price of fuel. A simple transmission mechanism illustrates the difficulty of policy-makers trying to foresee energy changes and plan for the development of new technologies.

At the beginning of the twentieth century, automobiles were expensive and canals were limited in the their geographical coverage leaving coal-powered (either directly or after transformation into electricity) railway systems to dominate surface transport. The energy effect was brought about by the introduction of mass production of cars, initially by Fiat in Italy, but on a larger scale in 1913 by Henry Ford in the United States, aimed at gaining a market share in the very highly competitive automobile industry of the time. This brought down the costs of car production and subsequently the price of cars (from $910 for a touring Model-T in 1910 to $367 in 1925). In turn, this led to more use of cars and trucks (sales of the touring models were 16,890 units in 1910 rising to 691,212 in 1925), with a resultant switch in transport away from coal as the primary energy source to oil.

In the East German economy of the 1960s, market forces were largely ignored when policy moves towards greater car ownership at administered prices were initiated. The resultant centrally planned outcomes were the Wartburg and Trabant cars, and, by the time the Berlin Wall came down, there was a waiting time of nearly ten years to receive a not very comfortable, reliable, or efficient vehicle. The complexity of planning the design and production of cars proved too much for even the highly skilled planners of East Germany.

Fuel prices themselves are also powerful influences on consumption. Where there have been shortages of some forms of energy, either because of physical factors or institutional ones, markets can bring about changes. In the past there have been shortages of oil for political reasons. While there are short-term adjustment issues, the long-term effect of a fuel shortage and price rise is that fuel is used more efficiently.

An example is the impact on the fuel efficiency of the United States 'car park' after the oil crises of 1973 and 1979 (Crandall et al., 1986). The average energy efficiency of vehicles (and possibly the way they are driven) rose following both crises, albeit with a lag as the adjustment took place. A subsequent survey bringing together work on long-term gasoline fuel price elasticities indicates that about 20 to 60 percent appears to be due to changes in the vehicle miles driven, with 40 to 80 percent being due to changes in fleet composition (Parry et al., 2007). A more general rule of thumb, suggested by Goodwin et al. (2004) after reviewing numerous empirical studies, is that fuel consumption elasticities are greater than traffic elasticities, mostly by factors of 1.5 to 2.00.

Energy, because of the relative inelasticity of aggregate demand for its use, has traditionally been the subject of taxation. In many cases this has been for purely sumptuary purposes, but in other cases, as with the federally earmarked gasoline tax in the United States, it has been used as a proxy charge for some related consumption item; in the United States' case, to pay for the use of the road. In other cases, there have been environmental motivations, for example the differential taxes applied to gasoline and diesel fuels in many countries.

Fuel Taxation

Examples of taxes on the energy used by transport abound, although as mentioned earlier the exact motivations underlying them are not always clear. The US Energy Tax Act of 1979, for instance, was a law passed as part of the National Energy Act. One element of the act created the 'gas-guzzler' tax applying to sales of vehicles with official estimated gas-mileage below certain levels. In 1980, the tax was $200 for a fuel efficiency of 14 to 15 miles per gallon (mpg), and was increased to $1,800 in 1985. In 1980, the tax was $550 for fuel efficiencies of 13 mpg and below, and was changed in 1986 to $3,850 for ratings below 12.5 mpg. The gas-guzzler tax only applied to cars under 6,000 lbs., which made sports utility vehicles (SUVs) and other large passenger cars exempt.

In terms of using taxation as an instrument for encouraging energy conservation, or changes in the energy source used for environmental reasons, carbon taxes have been adopted in several countries. These are not transport-specific but are more holistic in their intent of making optimal use of resources more generally, although their impacts on transport are often large. In 1991, Sweden, for example, placed a tax of $100 per ton on the use of oil, coal, natural gas, liquefied petroleum gas, petrol, and aviation fuel used in domestic travel. Industrial users paid half the rate (between 1993 and 1997, 25 percent of the rate), and certain high-energy industries such as commercial horticulture, mining, manufacturing, and the pulp and paper industry were fully exempted from these new taxes. In 1997 the rate was raised to $150 per ton of CO_2 released. Finland, the Netherlands, and Norway also introduced carbon taxes in the 1990s.

In other cases, however, efforts at introducing such policies have failed. In 2005 New Zealand proposed a carbon tax to take effect from April 2007 and applied across most economic sectors, but the policy was abandoned in December 2005. Similarly, in 1993, President Bill Clinton proposed a British thermal unit (BTU) tax that was never adopted.

Vehicle Standards

Rather than directly regulate on the composition of fuels, or use the pricing mechanism, there have been efforts to influence energy consumption and pollution by legislating on the design of vehicles. The details adopted vary and here we highlight just some of the issues by looking at the European and North American cases.

There have been somewhat different approaches adopted in different countries. Returning to Figure 8.1, the approach of the Europeans has been largely on the environmental emissions themselves, by stipulating in agreements with their own industry and with manufacturers in Japan and Korea the maximum levels of pollution that new vehicles may emit. Table 8.3 shows the main standards set for gasoline cars. Other categories of vehicles have their own standards that must be met.

In contrast to this, the CAFE standards, first introduced by the United States Congress in 1975, are federal regulations that sought to improve fuel economy in the wake of the 1973 Arab oil embargo (Table 8.4). In other words, in terms of Figure 8.1 they impact on the industry. The regulations initially applied to the sales-weighted average fuel economy, expressed in mpg, of a manufacturer's fleet of current model year passenger cars or light trucks with a gross vehicle weight rating of 8,500 lbs. or less, which were manufactured for sale in the United States. Light trucks not exceeding 8,500 lbs. gross vehicle weight rating do not have to comply with CAFE standards. They constituted

Table 8.3   *European new gasoline automobile emissions standards (grams per mile)*

Date (first registration)	CO	THC	VOC	NO_X	$HC+NO_X$	P	PN[#/km]
January 1997	2.2	–	–	–	0.5	–	–
January 2001	2.3	0.2	–	0.15	–	–	–
January 2006	1	0.1	–	0.08	–	–	–
January 2011	1	0.1	0.068	0.06	–	0.005	–
January 2013	1	0.1	0.068	0.06	–	0.0045	–
September 2015	1	0.1	0.068	0.06	–	0.0045	6×10^{11}
September 2018	1	0.1	0.068	0.06	–	0.0045	6×10^{11}
September 2019	1	0.1	0.068	0.06	–	0.0045	6×10^{11}
January 2021	1	0.1	0.068	0.06	–	0.0045	6×10^{11}

Table 8.4   *Canadian company average fuel consumption (CAFC) goals and the United States' corporate average fuel economy (CAFE) standard (liters/100 km)*

Model year	Passenger car		Light-duty trucks	
	CAFC	CAFE	CAFC	CAFE
1978	13.1	13.1	–	–
1980	11.8	11.8	–	–
1982	9.8	9.8	–	13.4
1984	8.7	8.7	–	11.8
1986	8.6	9.1	–	11.8
1988	8.6	9.1	–	11.7
1990	8.6	8.6	11.8	11.8
1992	8.6	8.6	11.6	11.8
1994	8.6	8.6	11.5	11.7
1996	8.6	8.6	11.4	11.7
1998	8.6	8.6	11.4	11.7
2000	8.6	8.6	11.4	11.7
2002	8.6	8.6	11.4	11.7
2004	8.6	8.6	11.4	11.7
2006	8.6	8.6	11.4	10.9

Source: Adapted from Perl and Dunn (2007).

some half a million vehicles in 1999 and by 2021 their number had reached 320 million. From early 2004, the average new car had to exceed 27.5 mpg and light trucks exceed 20.7 mpg. Trucks under 8,500 lbs. had to average 22.5 mpg in 2008, 23.1 mpg in 2009, and 23.5 mpg in 2010. After this, new rules set varying targets based on truck size 'footprint'.

Whereas the United States' regime is statutory, the Canadians have a voluntary scheme to foster fuel economy: the company average fuel consumption (CAFC) agreement, which was established between government and auto manufacturers in 1978. Details of the joint goals set are seen in Table 8.5.

The US National Highway Traffic Safety Administration (NHTSA) regulates CAFE standards and the US EPA measures vehicle fuel efficiency. Congress

Table 8.5 *The economic costs of road injuries and morbidity (2015–30, $ 2010)*

	Economic loss ($ billions)	Percentage of GDP	Per capita loss
By World Bank region			
East Asia & Pacific	560	0.123	240
Europe & Central Asia	345	0.082	374
Latin America & Caribbean	115	0.116	184
Middle East & North Africa	103	0.166	227
North America	515	0.149	1,370
South Asia	121	0.155	64
Sub-Saharan Africa	38	0.120	33
By World Bank country income group			
Low income	11	0.120	14
Lower-middle income	202	0.138	64
Upper-middle income	621	0.144	237
High income	963	0.106	779
Global (166 countries)	1,797	0.120	231

Source: Chen et al. (2019).

specifies that CAFE standards must be set at the 'maximum feasible level' given consideration for: technological feasibility; economic practicality; effect of other standards on fuel economy; and the need of the nation to conserve energy. If the average fuel economy of a manufacturer's annual fleet of car and/or truck production falls below the defined standard, the manufacturer pays a financial penalty; thus, there is a very crude pricing mechanism involved. Fuel efficiency is highly correlated to vehicle weight, but weight has been considered by many safety experts to be correlated with safety, intertwining the issues of fuel economy, road traffic safety, air pollution, global warming, and greenhouse gases. Hence, historically, the EPA has encouraged consumers to buy more fuel-efficient vehicles while the NHTSA has expressed concerns that this leads to smaller, less safe vehicles. More recent studies tend to discount the importance of vehicle weight on traffic safety, concentrating instead on the quality of the engineering design of vehicles.

While there have been changes in the standards over time, Tables 8.4 and 8.5 both show that these have tended to be infrequent and that by, for example, European standards, the American fleet is relatively fuel-inefficient. Part of the problem seems to be difficulties in building political alliances strong enough to carry though measures that tighten the prevailing standards.

A further problem with the CAFE standard approach is that it can lead to an increase in highway externalities. While the CAFE standards, disregarding any undesirable stimulating effects they have on the sales of light trucks and SUVs (which are much less rigorously controlled), will increase the fuel efficiency of vehicles, they also make them cheaper to drive per mile. This can add to congestion and local environmental damage, including noise nuisance (Kleit, 2004).

Speed Limits

Engines of all types perform differently at different speeds and each has an optimal fuel performance speed. Given the operational cycle of any transport activity, as a generalization more energy is expended at the beginning of a movement, and in some cases at the end, than during cruise, although there is normally an optimal cruising speed. It is possible, therefore, to influence the energy efficiency of a transport system by regulating the speeds at which individual units operate over it.

Privately supplied transport operations, such as shipping and airlines, have financial incentives to conserve energy and, other things being equal, route ships and planes accordingly and set fuel-efficient schedules. The public authorities, cognizant of the wider impacts of transport, often off-set these energy goals to attain other objectives. The most obvious cases are the take-off and landing patterns at airports, which seldom are energy-efficient but take cognizance of noise nuisance envelopes.

While speed limits are usually imposed for reasons of improving traffic flows and for safety, there are examples of explicit, speed-based energy policies in transport. As an emergency response to the 1973 oil crisis, the United States Congress effectively imposed a national 55 mph maximum speed limit in 1974 under the Emergency Highway Energy Conservation Act by requiring the limit as a condition of each state receiving highway funds. The limit was unpopular, especially in western states that have long distances between cities or points of interest. Subsequent analysis by (Forester et al. 1984) was somewhat unclear on the implications of the measure on energy consumption. Congress lifted all federal speed limit controls in the November 28, 1995 National Highway Designation Act, fully delegating speed limit authority to the states.

Fostering Alternative Technologies

Taxation, vehicle design standards, and other measures, in addition to market forces, can, and have in many cases, affected the technology of transport and, *ipso facto*, energy use and efficiency. The higher fuel prices after the Israeli wars of the 1970s led to lighter vehicles using alternative materials for bodywork, and more fuel-efficient engines. In addition, however, there have also been some other explicit policies aimed at technology shifts with the aim of reducing the use of oil-based fuels.

There has been a long history, for example, of policies aimed at developing viable electric cars that can effectively be powered from a variety of energy sources, including hydro-generated electricity. Historically, in the early days, electric-driven cars were as numerous as gasoline, steam, or diesel cars, the first electric car being developed somewhere between 1832 and 1839, but seem to have gone out of favor because of maintenance issues and the costs of mass production. These are sometimes called, as in California, 'zero emission vehicles' (ZEVs), although from the wider geographical perspective, given the primary source of

Exhibit   *'Boris bikes'*

In August 2007, London mayor Ken Livingstone announced a cycle hire scheme. This became operational as Barclays Cycle Hire in July 2010 with 5,000 bicycles and 315 docking stations distributed across the City area and parts of eight boroughs. Boris Johnson had become mayor by then, hence the colloquialism 'Boris bikes'. Initially, the system required payment of registration and membership fees in exchange for an electronic access key, but this was changed to allow casual cycle hires by non-members who had a credit card.

The project was expected to cost £140 million for planning and implementation over six years, and was seen as the only Transport for London system to fully fund its annual cost of operation, a goal estimated to take two to three years. The 'on the road' cost involved was £28,000 per bicycle, with the docking stations costing around £200,000 each to install. An expansion in March 2012 involved 2,300 more bikes and 4,800 docking stations. In December 2013 an extra 2,000 bikes and 150 docking stations in west London were added.

In 2015, sponsorship of the scheme transferred from Barclays to Santander Cycles and by February 2018 covered 40 square miles of London with over 11,000 bikes and 800 stations. Ridership however, as seen in the figure, tended to have plateaued by about 2016 at around 10 million rides a year despite the bicycles benefitting from laws banning e-scooters on the sidewalk or the road, although this began to change in 2020 with trials beginning for the introduction of e-scooters.

Regular users register on a website for 24 hours or one year. They are given a key to release a bike from a docking station. From December 2010 casual users could join for hourly use. The first 30 minutes of each trip is free. Additional usage charges are £2 per 30 minutes or part thereof. Bicycles may be used any number of times within the access period, each use charged according to its duration.

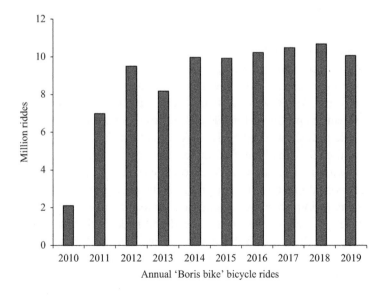

Annual 'Boris bike' bicycle rides

In the first three months, 95 percent of journeys did not exceed 30 minutes, earning access but not usage fees. The scheme generated £323,545 in usage revenue in under 100 days, with 72,700 of the initial 1.4 million journeys earning no revenue. In May 2012, Transport for London estimated the scheme would cost tax-payers £225 million by 2015–16, almost five times the maximum due from Barclays. Access fees were doubled in January 2013, hoping to generate £4–6 million annually. From 2016–17 Transport for London put £3.6 million into the scheme, effectively hiring 10 million bike rides. This amounted to 16.9 percent of the scheme's operating costs.

The scheme was criticized for allowing riders to have unlimited use by docking the bike every 30 minutes resulting in a dependence on late fees and penalties to make up revenues. The system also required the user to find docking stations close to the points of departure and destination, lacking one of the key advantages of bicycles, dock-less bicycles, and e-scooters. Coverage was also poor in south-east London, an area with a limited Tube network, and in outer London, where the scheme is almost non-existent despite most Londoners living there. Additionally, redistribution of bikes was hindered by the refusal of Westminster and of Kensington and Chelsea councils to allow bikes to be repositioned in their boroughs between 11.00 pm and 8.00 am, creating challenges in meeting morning peaks.

See also: M. Ricci (2015) Bike sharing: a review of evidence on impacts and processes of implementation and operation, Research in Transportation Business and Management, 15, 28–38.

energy, this is very seldom the case, and even if solar panels are used on vehicles, there is still the pollution associated with the production of these panels. National governments have regularly tried to foster the development of economically feasible electric car technologies by investing in R&D programs.

At a more local level, the California zero emission vehicle (ZEV) program, initiated in 1990 and followed in some other states as partial zero emission vehicle (PZEV) programs, was designed to catalyze the commercialization of advanced-technology vehicles that would not have any tailpipe or evaporative emissions (California Air Resources Board, 2005). It initially required that 2 percent of new vehicles produced for sale in 1998 and 10 percent of new vehicles produced for sale in 2003 would be ZEVs. After auto-makers argued that they could not meet the 1998 deadline, full implementation of the program was delayed until 2003 with interim measures to encourage the use of more PZEVs. In 2002, auto-makers sued the state over the program and were granted a preliminary injunction barring its implementation pending a final court ruling. During the ensuing legal debate, the state decided to go ahead and make revisions to the rule to sidestep the legal challenge, with the aim of restoring the ZEV program by 2005. Overall, these types of policies have not been conspicuously successful in bringing about sea changes in transport technology. For example, of the 4,000 to 5,000 electric cars built for California's ZEV mandate in the late 1990s, only about 1,000 remain on the road.

The European Union, through Joint Technology Initiatives in the 7th Research Framework Programme running from 2007 to 2013, provided increasing levels of funding for research into fuel cells and hydrogen with the intention of reducing the time needed to market such technologies by between two and five years.

While fully electric or hydrogen-propelled vehicles have proved elusive to develop on a commercial scale, the hybrid vehicle such as the Honda Insight and the Toyota Prius that combines electric propulsion with, generally, a gasoline engine has proved more successful. It offers, at prevailing prices, fuel efficiency, although at a higher capital cost, and in many cases is economically justified in the market-place. Policy has been instrumental by financing part of the R&D costs of the underlying technology, but in many cases local policies have provided an added inducement for its uptake. In the United States many local jurisdictions, for example, allow hybrids to use high-occupancy vehicle (HOV) lanes on highways even if they do not meet passenger requirements.

There are also initiatives to foster the use of telecommunications as an alternative to trips that are primarily for information exchange. This can apply to such things as teleworking (rather than commuting to work in an office), teleshopping, telebanking, and distance learning (Salomon and Mokhtarian, 2007). The Covid-19 outbreak in 2020 and the quarantine measures introduced in many countries led in the short term to far more activities becoming home-based. In terms of such activities as teleworking, there had already been a sizeable uptake of remote working (Figure 8.8).

While the debate over whether the advances in telecommunications in the long term have added to travel because of the complementary nature of the home-based activities, or reduced it because of its substitutability features, is

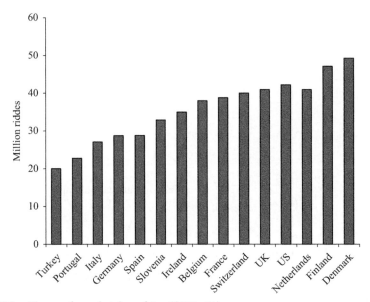

Figure 8.8 *Shares of people teleworking (2015–16)*

still the subject of much debate, policy-makers have put forward initiatives to increase its use as a transport energy policy initiative. Some of this has been in the form of information (for example, the US Office of Personnel Management and the General Services Administration have established this joint website on Telework to provide access to guidance issued by both agencies) and facilitation (for example, under United States law, federal executive agencies must establish policies under which eligible employees may participate in telecommuting to the maximum extent possible). Again, in the United States in 1996, the Clean Air Act, amongst other things, required companies with over 100 employees to encourage telecommuting. The European Union also reached a framework agreement to encourage more teleworking and to put in place laws that would help facilitate it across the member countries.

The difficulty is assessing whether telecommuting and similar activities, while unquestionably enhancing social welfare by giving firms and individuals more choices, result in less travel. There are inevitable 'buy-back effects' as time formerly used, for example, in physically commuting can be used for other forms of trip-making. Additionally, telecommunications may simply add to the conventional travel behavior of people and the way firms use their employees' time. This type of situation is illustrated in Figure 8.9.

There are assumed to be physical limits to the amount of travel an individual can do and the number of physical interactions possible. Improved transport and communications have undoubtedly improved the situation, but logic would suggest that there is some asymptote. While one may pull down this asymptote, or modify the growth path in physical inter-personal communications by fostering telecommunications after time T, there is also the possibility that the new technology will lead to a higher number of inter-personal communications, pushing up the overall communications asymptote without reducing the growth

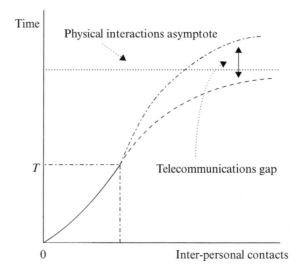

Figure 8.9 *The 'telecommuncations gap'*

in personal movements, the telecommunications gap reflecting this. If so, then the impact on the environmental damage associated with transport is left unaffected. Indeed, if there is a degree of substitution within the physical travel aggregate, then this may be more damaging to the environment if it involves trips through more sensitive areas of cities or at times of day when citizens are more sensitive to noise.

8.9   Safety and Accidents

Safety is a major concern in modern transport. Any form of movements of individuals and goods involves a degree of danger, but that has not stopped the development of modern transport. Indeed, while the opening of the Liverpool and Manchester Railway in the United Kingdom, the world's first inter-city railway, in September 1830, saw William Huskisson, the popular Member of Parliament for Liverpool, run over by the engine, the Rocket, and killed, this heralded the beginning of a period of 'railway mania'.

Today, traffic injuries are among the ten leading causes of death in the world, and they are the leading cause of death among young adults aged 15–29 years. Traffic accidents also produce 20–50 million non-fatal injuries with many of those involved incurring a disability. Table 8.5 extends this to the global situations. Table 8.5 offers estimates of the global economic costs of road accidents and sets them in the context of the world's GDP. The latter is important because the costs of accidents involve evaluation of the economic value of victims. Higher-income countries, therefore, have higher absolute costs, although differentials are not so great when set in the context of a country's overall economic condition.

There are numerous causes of accidents, but many are the result of irresponsible behavior by vehicle operators. On the roads, young and elderly drivers are more prone to accidents, but there is a strong correlation between drinking and driving. There are also some people who are quite literally, for no apparent reason, 'accident prone'. Although there are many factors contributing to the frequency and severity of road crashes, drunk driving is among the principal reasons for crashes in many countries; for example, 40 percent of fatal crashes in the United States in 2003 were alcohol-related, a percentage that has remained relatively stable over the past few years. Consistent with this, the National Highway Traffic Safety Administration, McCarthy and Tay's (2005) study of 2000 United States crash data, estimated that alcohol-related crashes imposed a $114.3 billion cost on society.

Safety is partly an externality and partly it is not. One policy approach is to internalize more of the costs of safety. This is done by such measures as legal responsibility for the costs of accidents in the form of compensation, a measure that is often accompanied by compulsory insurance. Such actions can, however, in some contexts because of moral hazard, prove counterproductive. Moral hazard is the prospect that a party insulated from risk (by, in this case, insurance) may behave differently from the way it would behave if it were fully exposed to the risk. It can arise because an individual does not bear the full consequences of their actions, and therefore has a tendency to act less carefully than would otherwise be the case, leaving another party to bear some responsibility for the consequences of those actions. With insurance, it is the other premium payers who bear the burden. For example, an individual with insurance against automobile theft may be less vigilant about locking a car, because the negative consequences of automobile theft are partially borne by insurance company.

One way of reducing the moral hazard problem is to change the insurance market, and one modification, the pay-as-you-drive (PAYD) insurance, that embraces actual miles driven for premiums rather than a flat-period sum, has been suggested. The aim would be to limit trips, rather than encourage them as the more traditional approaches do. Aaron Edlin (2003) has estimated that this would reduce the externalities associated with driving, including accidents.

If such internalization is not possible, or thought to be ineffective or impractical, other policies are commonly used to handle safety concerns. Focusing on road transport to keep the material manageable, although the experiences extend in general across all modes, policy initiatives often revolve around keeping some groups off the road entirely – for example, a minimum driving age – and deterrent measures such as driving bans if caught with alcohol in the system above a 'safe' level, fines for speeding or dangerous maneuvers, and imprisonment for extreme offenses. Training and testing of drivers are also common practice, and educational initiatives to discourage dangerous driving are common, although it is not clear that they always meet their objectives (Tay, 2004).

The reunification of East and West Germany in 1990 provided a natural economic experiment when one important change for East German motorists was a relaxation of the legal blood alcohol concentration (BAC) limit (Vollrath et al., 2005). There was no change in the legal limit for West German motorists. This offered the opportunity to analyse the immediate, short-term, and longer-term effects of raising the BAC limit in East Germany between 1992 and 1994. A major finding was that the relaxed concentration limits led to an increase in blood alcohol levels among East German drivers but generally did not increase the frequency of drinking and driving. The exception was younger drivers who not only increased their alcohol consumption after the relaxation in the legal limit but also increased their frequency of drinking and driving.

Also focusing upon drinking and driving policy, Mathijssen (2005) conducted a retrospective analysis of anti-drunk driving campaigns that the Netherlands implemented between 1970 and 2000. The study found significant deterrent effects following the introduction of a statutory alcohol limit, random breath testing and evidential breath testing, and changes in the enforcement level; but mixed effects for publicity and educational campaigns; and little effect for changes in penalties and driver improvement programs.

Speed is generally highly correlated with accidents, and speed limits are common for that reason. In April 1987, the United States federal government enacted the Federal Highway Bill that, among its other provisions, permitted states to increase speed limits on rural sections of their Interstate highways. This provided the basis for several natural experiments. Forty states responded to the enabling legislation by raising their speed limits, fueling an ongoing debate regarding the highway safety effects of higher speed limits. The results of annual cross-section–time series covering 1981 to 1989 for California, which raised speed limits in May 1987, found the higher speed limits to have no system-wide effects on fatal, injury-related, or property damage accidents (McCarthy, 1994). Redistribution effects, however, were identified in that counties with 65 mph highways experienced a significant increase in each accident category. Theodore Keeler (1994) also found, when looking at data for 1970 and 1980, that lower rural speed limits did little to reduce fatal automobile accidents.

Vehicle design and 'fittings' may also affect safety. These types of measures include such things as seat belts, air bags, and crash helmets on motorcycles, as much as the quality of brakes and suspension, the types of wind-shield glass and headlamp lighting, and so on. There is an economic problem forcing regulatory measures to ensure that the safest engineering technology, or at least a minimum stand, is adopted. People react to the new technical requirements. Lave and Weber (1970), for instance, suggested that mandated safety devices (seat belts, better bumpers, collapsible steering wheels) might lead to faster driving that could off-set the safety gains. More generally, Samuel Peltzman (1975) found that while technological studies in the mid-1970s implied that annual highway deaths would be 20 percent greater without legally mandated installation of various safety devices on automobiles, the effects of non-regulatory demand for safety and drivers' behavioral responses to the devices virtually off-set these. Sobel and Nesbit's (2007) study of changes in NASCAR safety rules offers support for this.

Saas and Zimmerman (2000), for example, studied the impact of United States state laws mandating helmet use by motorcyclists over a 22-year period and found helmet laws to be associated with an average 29 to 33 percent decrease in per capita motorcyclist fatalities. However, since voluntary helmet wearing rates are higher in harsher climates, the efficacy of helmet laws varied directly with the warmth of a state's climate. Repeal of helmet laws in the 1970s and subsequent re-adoption in the late 1980s and early 1990s had had roughly symmetrical effects on fatalities. It was also found that alcohol consumption and the number of police available to enforce traffic laws significantly affected motorcyclist fatalities.

In other words, safety regulations do not necessarily in themselves decrease accidents and deaths because of the off-setting effects on driver behavior and enforcement policies.

The effects of piecemeal approaches and of policy conflicts involving packages of measures were studied by Crandall et al. (1986). They were concerned about the conflicts which arose in the United States between the setting of safety standards (by Highway Traffic Safety Administration), emissions standards (by Congress and administered by the EPA), and fuel economy measures (set by Congress and administered by the EPA). While static conflicts emerged as technically unavoidable (for example, the safety regulations initiated in the United States between 1968 and 1982 pushed average car weights up by 136 lbs. and increased fuel consumption by 3.5 percent, which conflicted with measures aimed at fuel efficiency and emissions controls), the dynamic effects of uncoordinated policies, for instance, slowing down replacement of older, less socially desirable cars was a serious administrative failure.

An important point is that the level of safety expected from transport systems does tend to vary between countries. In part this is due to income differentials. As seen earlier in the book, the value society puts on reducing the chance of a fatal accident depends to some extent on the income of the people involved. There is ample evidence that when it comes to transport safety, poorer countries, in part because of their limited resource base, but also because of the high shadow prices involved, spend less on meeting what in other countries are taken as minimum safety standards (Jadaan et al., 2018).

References

Baum, H.J. (1973) Free public transport, *Journal of Transport Economics and Policy*, 7, 3–19.

Baumol, W.J. and Oates, W.E. (1988) *The Theory of Environmental Policy*, Cambridge University Press.

Becken, S. and Mackey, B. (2017) What role for offsetting aviation greenhouse gas emissions in a deep-cut carbon world? *Journal of Air Transport Management*, 63, 71–83.

Button, K.J. (2001) Are current air transport policies consistent with a sustainable environment? in E. Verhoef and E. Feitelson (eds), *Transport and Environment: In Search of Sustainable Solutions*, Edward Elgar Publishing.

California Air Resources Board (2005) California's air quality history key events, Report, CARB.

Chen, S., Kuhn, N., Prettner, K., and Bloom, D.E. (2019) The global macroeconomic burden of road injuries: estimates and projections for 166 countries, *Lancet Planetary-health*, September 3, e390–e398.

Coase, R.H. (1960) The problem of social cost, *Journal of Law and Economics*, 3, 1–44.

Crandall, R.W., Gruenspecht, A.K., Keeler, T.E., and Lave, L.B. (1986) *Regulating the Automobile*, Brookings Institution.

De Witte, A., Macharis, C., Lannoy, P., Polain, C., Steenberghen, T., and De Walle, S.V. (2006) The impact of 'free' public transport: the case of Brussels, *Transportation Research Part A*, 40, 671–89.

Edlin, A.S. (2003) Per-mile premiums for auto insurance, in R. Arnott, B. Greenwald, R. Kanbur, and B. Nalebuff (eds), *Economics for an Imperfect World: Essays in Honor of Joseph E. Stiglitz*, MIT Press.

Forester, T.H., McNown, R.F., and Singell, L.D. (1984) A cost–benefit analysis of the 55 MPH speed limit, *Southern Economic Journal*, 50, 631–41.

Goodwin, P.B. (1992) A review of new demand elasticities with special reference to short and long run effects of price changes, *Journal of Transport Economics and Policy*, 26, 155–70.

Goodwin, P.B., Dargay, J., and Hanly, M. (2004) Elasticities of road traffic and fuel consumption with respect to price and income: a review, *Transport Reviews*, 24, 275–92.

Jadaan, K., Al-Braizat, E., Al-Rafayah, S., Gammoh, H., and Abukahlil, Y. (2018) Traffic safety in developed and developing countries: a comparative analysis, *Journal of Traffic and Logistics Engineering*, 6, 1–5.

Keeler, T. (1994) Highway safety, economic behavior, and driving environment, *American Economic Review*, 84, 684–93.

Kemp, M.A. (1973) Some evidence on transit elasticities, *Transportation*, 2, 25–52.

Kleit, A.N. (2004) Impacts of long-range increases in the fuel economy (CAFE) standard, *Economic Inquiry*, 42, 279–94.

Larsson, J., Elofsson, A., Sterner, T., and Åkerman, J. (2019) International and national climate policies for aviation: a review, *Climate Policy*, 19(6), 787–99.

Lave, L.B. and Weber, W.E. (1970) A benefit–cost analysis of auto safety features, *Applied Economics*, 2, 265–76.

Maler, K.G. (1974) Environmental policies and the role of the economist in influencing public policy, in J.G. Rothenberg and I.G. Heggie (eds), *Transport and the Urban Environment*, Macmillan.

Mathijssen, M.P.M. (2005) Drink driving policy and road safety in the Netherlands: a retrospective analysis, *Transportation Research Part E*, 41, 395–408.

McCarthy, P. (1994) An empirical analysis of the direct and indirect effects of relaxed interstate speed limits on highway safety, *Journal of Urban Economics*, 36, 353–64.

McCarthy, P. and Tay, R. (2005) Road safety, alcohol and public policy, *Transportation Research Part E*, 41, 373–76.

OECD (Organisation for Economic Co-operation and Development) (1975) *The Polluter Pays Principle*, OECD.

OECD (Organisation for Economic Co-operation and Development) (1992) *Market and Government Failures in Environmental Policy: The Case of Transport*, OECD.

Parry, I.W.H., Walls, M., and Harrington, W. (2007) Automobile externalities and policies, *Journal of Economic Literature*, 45, 373–99.

Peltzman, S. (1975) The effects of automobile safety regulation, *Journal of Political Economy*, 83, 677–725.

Perl, A. and Dunn, J.A. (2007) Reframing automobile fuel economy policy in North America: the politics of punctuating a policy equilibrium, *Transport Reviews*, 27, 1–35.

Pigou, A. (1920) *The Economics of Welfare*, Macmillan.

Salomon, I. and Mokhtarian, P.L. (2007) Can telecommunications help solve transportation problems? A decade later: are prospects better, in D.A. Hensher and K.J. Button (eds), *Handbook of Transport Modelling*, 2nd edn, Pergamon.

Sass, T.R. and Zimmerman, P.R. (2000) Motorcycle helmet laws and motorcyclist fatalities, *Journal of Regulatory Economics*, 18, 195–215.

Scheelhaase, J., Maertens, S., Grimme, W., and Jung, M. (2018) EU ETS versus CORSIA: a critical assessment of two approaches to limit air transport's CO_2 emissions by market-based measures, *Journal of Air Transport Management*, 67, 55–62.

Schwing, R.C., Southworth, B.W., Von Buseck, C.R., and Jackson, C. (1980) Benefit–cost analysis of automobile emission reductions, *Journal of Environmental Economics and Management*, 7, 44–64.

Sharp, C.H. (1979) The environmental cost of transport and the public interest, *Journal of Transport Economics and Policy*, 13, 88–191.

Sobel, R. and Nesbit, T.M. (2007) Automobile safety regulation and the incentive to drive recklessly: evidence from NASCAR, *Southern Economic Journal*, 74, 71–84.

Tay, R. (2004) The relationship between public education and enforcement campaigns and their effectiveness in reducing speed related serious crashes, *International Journal of Transport Economics*, 31, 251–5.

Vollrath, M., Krüger, H.-P., and Löbmann, R. (2005) Driving under the influence of alcohol in Germany and the effect of relaxing the BAC law, *Transportation Research Part E*, 41, 377–93.

9 Optimizing Traffic Congestion

9.1 Economics and Optimal Traffic

As we saw in Chapter 6, excessive congestion leads to the inefficient use of transport infrastructure. Throughout the world, there has been a *pot pourri* of initiatives over the years to optimize congestion, not only on city streets but also on inter-urban roads and at seaports and airports. These initiatives have not proved conspicuously successful as we can observe in most cities and at many ports. Many of the policies that have been pursued, however, have been devoid of serious economic content. The aim of this chapter is to examine the types of approaches that economists have advocated for reducing excessive levels of traffic congestion – it is not about eliminating it – and what the outcomes have been when they have been adopted.

It is not only in the context of pollution that economists have advocated externality pricing. One idea for optimizing the level of congestion is to use the price mechanism to make travelers more fully aware of the impedance they impose upon one another. The suggestion is that motorists should pay for the additional congestion they create when entering a congested road or that aircraft should pay a premium to land at busy times of the day. In the case of road traffic, ideally, as with pollution charges, those causing congestion should pay the other road users adversely affected, but practically this is quite clearly impossible. Hence, the idea is that the relevant road authority or agency should be responsible for collecting the charges.

We spend some time looking at the theoretical and practical issues involved in doing this, and assess some of the congestion charging schemes that have been introduced into cities like London, Gothenburg, and Stockholm, and on inter-city highways.

Other measures, of a less direct and second-best kind, such as parking charges, public transit subsidies, the deployment of intelligent transport systems (ITSs), and investment in additional infrastructure, are also considered. In technical terms, while congestion charging or road pricing seek to equate the demand for transport use with the full costs of use, including the costs on other transport users (environmental costs are a separate matter), alternatives such as capacity expansion and the wider use of ITSs seek to push the costs of transport use down, whereas measures such as transit subsidies seek to decrease the demand for the congestion-causing mode through substitution effects.

While much of our attention is on the congestion seen on roads, congestion is a problem found in many other transport activities, as discussed in Chapter 6.

While the general economic approach to developing and assessing remedial policies is common across the various forms of transport, there are various nuances,
and we shall consider some of these later in the chapter.

The aim of this chapter is not to provide an encyclopedic coverage of all the
literature that has been generated on road pricing and other forms of congestion
charging, nor to catalogue all the efforts that have been made – largely failures
with a few successes – to adopt road pricing. It is not the intention to go into the
finer points of obtuse microeconomic theory. Rather, it is to consider some of the
challenges that confront the adoption of efficient fiscal policy instruments within
the transportation system using road pricing as an illustration. In doing this,
examples and case studies will be used so that readers unfamiliar with the idea of
adopting user charges as a means of improving traffic management will not find
it difficult to understand the basic concepts involved.

9.2 'Road Pricing'

Charging for road use has traditionally taken one of two forms. There have long
been tolled roads of the type initiated in Britain in the seventeenth century and in
the United States from 1795, when the Philadelphia and Lancaster Turnpike was
completed, where users pay a fee for use. These tolls – and the same is true where
they are used today – are intended to recover the cost of constructing and physically maintaining the road. Such tolls are not designed to allocate the road space
or to optimize congestion. When tolls vary it is normally related to the physical
damage done by a vehicle to the pavement and not to the impedance that such a
vehicle may impose on other road users.

More widely, road users are charged even less directly for their use of infrastructure through a variety of taxes that may (as in the case of the United States
federal gas tax) be hypothecated to be spent on the road network (often through a
road fund mechanism) or flow into the general coffers of the Treasury to be spent
as the government wishes. In general, these taxation systems have little to do with
making good use of road assets.

The role of an economic price, however, is threefold: to allocate what is
available, to indicate where that capacity needs to be changed, and to provide the
resources for financing that change. The acronym AIR sums this up. Traditional
tolls may serve the last of these purposes by recovering investment costs, but
they seldom meet the other two. Table 9.1 provides some very general guidance
as to the tasks that various forms of road charging are set to perform. From the
perspective of optimizing congestion, weight–distance truck tolls and general distance tolls for example provide limited support, although they are relatively easy
to enforce and meet many budgetary demands.

The adverse effects of inappropriate charges for the use of one asset, in this
case a road, are felt in complementary and competitive sectors. They occur when
authorities seek to contain the primary problem with a second-best approach
involving either restricting the use of complementary services (for example,

Table 9.1 *Technical tasks for various forms of road charging*

Road charging scheme	Entering/ exiting facilities	Presence in area	Position on road network	Distance traveled	Time/ congestion level	Vehicle class/ weight	Charges owed	Data communi- cation	Data storage	Payment billing	Enforce- ment
Facility congestion tolls	●				●	○	●	●	●	●	●
Cordon congestion tolls		●			●	○	●	●	●	●	●
Weight–distance truck tolls	○	○	○	●	○		●	●	●	●	●
General distance tolls		●	○	●	○	○	●	●	●	●	●

Notes: ● Required for the task; ○ Optimal but not required for the task.

Source: Adapted from Sorensen and Taylor (2006).

controls over parking) or stimulating the use of alternatives (such as public transit) – see Button (2006b). This seldom works.

On the expenditure side, road investments are made for a variety of reasons, often with quasi-economic justifications added as a veneer. Cost–benefit analysis, which is discussed in detail in the next chapter, is widely used in one of its variants to provide a social assessment, but the technique is far from perfect and subject to political manipulation.

More powerful in the age of the car has been the engineering approach of providing capacity to meet demand. While there may be some justification for this in some situations, the fact that there is no direct economic price per trip paid by road users for their activities means that 'demand' in this context is nothing like the notion of effective demand used by economists. The outcome is likely to be excess capacity and a geographical maldistribution of roads. The reluctance of citizens to accept the environmental effects of more large-scale investments in roads, coupled with the increasing costs of construction as successive projects move down the marginal-returns-on-investment curves, have to some extent stymied this build-to-meet-demand philosophy.

The distortions that result from inappropriate charges for the use of one asset, in this case a road, have also been felt in complementary and competitive sectors as the authorities have sought to initiate second-best policies to contain congestion. Attempts to discourage car trips terminating in a congested area by means of parking restrictions and fees leads to higher levels of through-traffic as well as additional congestion as terminating drivers seek the limited parking capacity that is available (Shoup, 2005). A significant amount of car movements in many cities involves drivers looking for somewhere to park. Subsidies to public transport reduce the incentive for it to be provided efficiently and at the lowest cost – the X-inefficiency problem.

To reduce urban road traffic congestion, national and local authorities have gradually been turning to policies with a degree of economic rationale underpinning them, rather than simply trying to build their way out of problems or providing ever-increasing amounts of subsidies to public transportation. There have been moves to use road pricing as a tool for rationing scarce road space to those who gain most from its use. This focus on roads, and notably on the pricing of automobiles, is not simply a reflection of the large number of people who commute by car, it is also linked to the size and geography of cities. Table 9.2 provides some United States data on the share of automobiles in commuting. While New York has a relatively small share of auto-commuters, it has some of the worst because of its compact geography and sheer size. But all the cities listed suffer from acute road traffic congestion issues.

The importance of appropriate pricing to make the best use of transportation infrastructure is certainly not new: the principles can be found in the work of French engineering economists of the 1840s. Unfortunately, for a variety of reasons, both practical and due to a lack of understanding by many of basic economic principles, road space is seldom priced in a way that optimizes congestion and, as a result, social welfare is not maximized. The modern principles of road

Table 9.2   *Mode split (percentage) for travel to work in United States cities with more than 30,000 commuters (2018)*

	Single driver	Carpool	Transit	Bike	Walk	Other	Home
New York	22	4	56	1	10	2	5
Los Angeles	70	9	9	1	3	2	6
Chicago	49	8	28	2	6	2	5
Houston	78	10	4	0	1	3	4
Phoenix	74	13	3	1	1	2	6
San Diego	74	9	4	1	4	1	7
San Antonio	78	12	2	0	2	3	3
Philadelphia	50	7	26	2	9	2	4
Dallas	77	11	4	0.20	2	1	5
Austin	75	8	3	1	3	2	8
San Jose	76	12	4	1	2	1	4
San Francisco	30	9	34	4	13	4	6
Columbus	78	10	3	1	3	1	4
Charlotte	75	10	3	0	2	2	8
Seattle	44	7	23	4	12	2	8

pricing go back over 80 years to the work of Arthur Pigou, and were expanded upon by the Nobel Prize-winning economists James Buchanan and William Vickrey, and by the former British Prime Minister Margaret Thatcher's main economic advisor Alan Walters (Button, 2020).

The idea is simple: since roads are not privately owned and access to them is not determined by the market, there is a need, if roads are to be used efficiently, for the authorities to set a user charge that, for any given capacity, ensures that socially optimal flows are attained – the road price. There is often confusion about what this means. Road pricing is solely concerned with making the best use of roads from the narrow perspective of users and is not concerned with third-party effects such as pollution that should be treated separately. Congestion may or may not be related to environmental damage; 20,000 solar-powered cars per hour on a road may congest it but cause minimal environmental damage, whereas 500 old, badly maintained diesel vehicles may cause no congestion but a lot of pollution.

Second, as another Nobel Prize-winning economist, Ronald Coase (1960), demonstrated, policies such as road pricing are not market solutions but the most effective way of achieving an externally determined target traffic flow. This flow is independently determined and is not the result of any market-based process. In the congestion case, where economic pricing has been adopted, this pragmatic objective is often there to constrain traffic to the legal speed limit.

The standard economic diagram illustrating the basic principles of road pricing is that originally found in the works of Walters and Vickrey, and although this is now seen as a gross simplification, it serves well to illustrate the essential aims of congestion charging. In Figure 9.1 we take the basic case of a straight, single-lane road with a single entry and single egress point, and with homogeneous traffic entering the road at regular intervals, although the intensity of entry can change. The average cost curve shows the generalized costs (a composite of money and time costs) of using the road for existing traffic, and is the cost observed by a potential additional user. The demand curve represents the utility that potential road users enjoy by joining the traffic flow at different levels of generalized cost. Individuals will join the traffic flow, provided they feel that the benefits to be enjoyed exceed the costs. In the diagram, this leads to a traffic flow of F_1.

The problem, however, is that by undertaking the very act of joining the traffic stream a vehicle slows all succeeding vehicles by some small amount unless there is excess capacity on the road. This may only be a few seconds for each vehicle, but when the flow is large this mounts up. This combination of the cost borne by the vehicle driver and the cost imposed on other vehicles is depicted as the marginal cost curve in the diagram. If motorists take these combined costs into account then the flow would fall to F_2. The idea of the road price is to make them cognizant of the congestion cost element by imposing a charge of $C_2 - C_1$ on each road user, this being the additional congestion costs associated with the marginal user at the optimal traffic flow. The result of this is a welfare gain amounting to HJI – traffic flow F_1F_2 only generated benefits to road users equal to the areas F_1F_2JI, but at a cost of F_1F_2JH.

The optimal road price is relatively simple to calculate, and may seem to require little information. Taking the average cost of making a trip to the vehicle user as:

$$AC = a + (b/v) \qquad\qquad (9.1)$$

where a is the cost per vehicle in \$ per mile, b is the value of travel time in \$ per hour, and v is traffic volume, then the total (TC) cost of a traffic flow of

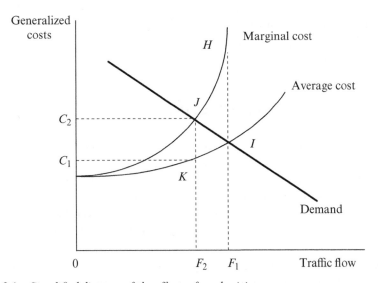

Figure 9.1 *Simplified diagram of the effects of road pricing*

q vehicles is equal to ACq. An additional vehicle joining the flow increases the overall cost to road users by:

$$MSC = \frac{dTC}{dq} = AC + \frac{dAC}{dq} \tag{9.2}$$

The congestion externality is given by $q(dAC/dq)$.

It takes little imagination to realize that over a complex network with numerous junctions, various road types, different vehicles mixes, and so on, the case in the diagram and equations is simple in the extreme and that calculating the optimal charge would be challenging. Indeed, this is sometimes used as a reason for not charging. The pricing of a computer, a car, or any other sophisticated product or service is far from easy but it is done, albeit far from ideally, and companies like Microsoft and Apple seem to be held in much higher esteem than many local politicians and traffic engineers. Private sector companies in Western-style economies make an educated guess at the appropriate direct price for their products and then adjust them in the light of experience; if there is a large demand for their product, then they raise prices and use the revenue to invest in additional capacity that will ultimately reduce costs and pries. They do not charge a low price and then let queues allocate the output.

Figure 9.1, despite its simplicity, also provides a way of looking at alternatives to road pricing as congestion containment policies. Expanding the capacity of a road by adding physical capacity or initiating better traffic management through intelligent transportation initiatives will shift the cost curves down and out and thus reduce the divergence between them at the point where demand equates with the average cost. Such actions are clearly not costless and still leave a divergence between the new actual traffic flow and the optimal flow given the added capacity. Effectively traffic increases to fill the additional road capacity available. Subsidizing public transportation will pull the demand curve for road use to the right, but again will still leave, albeit smaller, a traffic flow in excess of the optimum. Limiting or charging for parking will have similar impacts. We look at these effects in more detail in Section 9.9.

9.3   Applications of Urban Road Pricing

What is so surprising is that the principles of using pricing to allocate scarce resources, indicate where more are needed, and provide revenues to fund expansions – very simple economic ideas that are central in other parts of market economies – have taken so long to be applied to roads. Basically, if there is a shortage of something, prices rise to allocate it to those who benefit most from its use. The higher prices indicate that more capacity is needed, and generate the revenue to finance it.

Although it seems unlikely that many of the policy-makers who have moved towards road pricing as a means of reducing congestion are aware of the finer

Table 9.3   *Characteristics of eight major road pricing schemes*

City	Electronic system starting date	Entry charge for a small vehicle	Toll ring area (km²)	Average daily crossings	Annual revenue (millions)
Trondheim	1991	$2.40	50.0	74,900	$25.00
Oslo	1991	$2.40	64.0	248,900	$196.00
Bergen	2004	$2.40	18.0	84,900	$36.00
Stockholm	2006	$1.33 to $2.66	29.5	550,000	n.a.
Singapore	1998	$0.33 to $2.00	7.0	235,000	$80.00
Rome	2001	$3.75	4.6	75,000	$12.30
London	2003	$15.0	22.0	110,000	$320.00
Santiago	2004	$6.42	n.a.	250,000	n.a.

Note: n.a. = not available.

points of economic theory, a combination of desperation at the failure of traffic engineers to provide solutions to what is an economic issue, combined with a tightening of public funding, concerns about the environmental implications of continued massive infrastructure expansion, and the emergence of new technologies for fee collection, have created settings conducive to congestion pricing. We review some of these here, and Table 9.3 offers a few more details; Lehe (2019) goes into more depth.

In 1975 Singapore implemented a cordon-based variable pricing scheme with the aim of reducing congestion in the city's central business district (CBD). In 1999, the scheme was extended and now charges are applied to users on certain expressways and outer ring roads as well. Charges take effect on weekdays, from 7.30 am to 7 pm in the business districts, and from 7.30 am to 9.30 am on outer roads. Automated electronic road pricing was implemented in 1998.

Cordon tolling has been a very widely used strategy, with some initiatives that were first intended to finance additional engineering works evolving toward congestion charges. The deployment of cordon tolling, for example, was popularized by its use in a number of Norwegian cities primarily for revenue-generating purposes. In 1986, Bergen established the first urban toll ring as a supplementary funding mechanism for new roads, public transport, parking space, pedestrianization, and an environmentally improved city center. The cordon-based scheme only requires payment on entering the city center. There are six toll points around the city, with fees collected between 6 am and 10 pm on weekdays. Approximately 13 percent of the revenue is used to cover operating costs. Enforcement is dependent on digital video control. Because of the level and structure of the charges, there has been little impact on traffic levels and the system is not really a demand management tool in its current form. The toll ring was expected to cease operating in 2011 but was retained and a second ring added.

A toll ring scheme was initiated in Oslo in 1990 with the objective of financing additional roads capacity. Charges are in effect seven days a week at all times of the day. Electronic collection started in 1991. The current toll ring is expected to cease operations in 2007 but there is interest in having the Oslo system evolve into a genuine congestion pricing scheme. Trondheim introduced an area-wide variable pricing scheme in 1991, again to finance road infrastructure and public transportation. Since its inception, Trondheim has opted for differential rates being charged for the morning and evening rush hours and a lower rate between 10 am and 6 pm. An innovation to this system, which was originally cordon-based only, was the introduction of inter-zone charging in 1998.

In 1998 Rome implemented a cordon-based pricing scheme with the aim of preserving its historical areas. Payment is required to enter the city center and only residents and employees working in the area with secured parking spaces are permitted to enter the city center. Authorized non-residents, numbering about 35,000, are charged a flat rate. Charges are in effect six days a week, from 6.30 am to 6 pm on weekdays, and from 2 pm to 6 pm on Saturdays. Electronic pricing started in 2001 with 22 toll points around the city.

Santiago de Chile's scheme consists of a network of toll roads that cross the city from north to south and also surround it. In 2004, the first of four major toll road concessions involved the implementation of a pricing mechanism, and in 2006 two additional projects were completed. The main purpose has been reducing air pollution in the city, with the alleviation of excess congestion a secondary concern. There are three levels of charge depending on traffic speeds, the lowest being effective when the speeds are above 70 kph and the highest when speeds fall below 50 kph. Payment is required at all times when using any of the road concessions.

Central London has been the subject of an area pricing regime since 2003 (Leape, 2006). The charges apply to vehicles using roads in the city's core area between 7 am and 10 pm on weekdays, with a 90 percent discount for those living in the area, buses, and some other groups, and free entry for ultra-low-emission vehicles. Payment, £15 per day in 2020, is made through a variety of channels and there is the opportunity for retrospective payment.

During the first seven months of 2006, a full-scale cordon-based road pricing trial was implemented in Stockholm with the objective of reducing congestion and improving environmental quality. This was followed by a referendum in September 2006 to test views on making the scheme permanent, a proposal that received over 50 percent of the vote. Road users were obliged to install a free-of-charge transponder on their wind-shields and a smartcard could be bought at different locations, recharged, or linked to a bank account to make payments. Charges were in effect on weekdays from 6.30 am to 6 pm, and on Saturdays from 2 pm to 6 pm. A limit of $8.30 was set as the maximum a user could be charged per day. As with other schemes, users were able to make a payment after they used the roads. Violations were considered tax evasion as the scheme was classified as a governmental tax (Börjesson et al., 2012). A similar scheme was adopted in Gothenburg in 2013 (Börjesson et al., 2016).

Table 9.3 focuses on urban pricing schemes but some semi-urban schemes have involved a somewhat different approach that sets a level of service on a road and then adjusts the price to attain this. This has been deployed in the Interstate

15 scheme in California. In this case, the toll varies with traffic to maintain a target traffic speed with the road users being given the option of a 'free' road alongside the priced one. Information on average tolls for various times of the day is made available to help in route choice decision-making. Tolls can change every 15 minutes from 5.45 am to 7 pm as well as by day of the week. The minimum toll was 50 cents and under normal conditions it could go up to $4.00, although when road sensors detected extremely heavy traffic it could be as high as $8.00. The project was a three-year demonstration starting in 1996 that allowed single-occupant vehicles to use the existing I-15 high-occupancy-vehicle express lanes for a fee, with the aim of maximizing the use of the existing I-15 express lanes, to fund new transit and road improvements in the I-15 corridor, and to use a market-based approach to set tolls. The pricing project met its primary objectives, and by 2020 variable toll lanes, in a variety of forms, were to be found across the state.

9.4   Some Difficulties with Road Pricing

Theoretical economics, with its love of abstraction and mathematical exactitude, has long been drifting away from more traditional ideas of political economy. It is easy to show, as we have seen above, that with a few equations or diagrams, there are benefits to be gained by manipulating road user charges to contain excessive congestion. Implementation of such strategies, however, has been confronted by a plethora of practical and political challenges (Gu et al., 2018). In addition, these have not always been independent of each other, with opponents to road pricing using technical imperfections of any scheme as a justification for attacking the concept in its entirety.

Thus, despite the adoption of more economically based road charging systems in recent years, and indeed more economically based congestion pricing systems in other contexts, as we see later, road pricing is not the norm. There are many reasons why this is the case, some of which have been explored in detail by academics, but others remain speculative. From a review of public service atti-tudes, Peter Jones (1998), for example, listed the following reasons for opposition to road pricing:

- Drivers find it difficult to accept the idea of being charged for something they wish to avoid (congestion), and feel that congestion is not their fault but rather something that is being imposed upon them by others.
- Road pricing is not needed, either because congestion is not bad enough or because other measures are superior.
- Pricing will not get people out of their cars.
- The technology will not work.
- Privacy concerns.
- Diversion of traffic outside the charged area.
- Road pricing is just another form of taxation.
- Perceived unfairness.

We have touched lightly upon some of the issues, such as those associated with distributional impacts and the expenditure of revenues, when discussing the rationale for the systems that are now being used. The topic is a large one, however, and some more scratching of the surface is attempted here regarding several of the other factors that have proved impediments to improving the way roads are used. Additionally, it should be remembered, there is no single, ideal way of implementing road pricing, and the rejection of some schemes that have been put forward in the past may also have related more to their details than to the acceptability of the concept itself. While the basic theory of road pricing is, thus, comparatively straightforward, its detailed implementation has been subject to debate.

Political Ideology

Reluctance to adopt economic pricing principles may in part be due to a feeling that individuals have some form of 'inalienable right' to mobility and that pricing would restrict this. Matters of inalienable rights are complex, and this is not the place to discuss them in any detail. What is perhaps germane, however, is that rights are not free goods; there is an opportunity cost involved in acquiring and retaining them. The costs of providing ubiquitous mobility are high, and, while some may see ubiquitous mobility as desirable, the opportunity costs of achieving it are opaque in a world where there are inappropriate signals of the wider economic and social costs involved. Nevertheless, notions such as the 'freedom of the King's Highway' persist, and many are reluctant to pay for the use of roads irrespective of the economic consequences of current and future generations of excessive congestion.

In some ways, related to this notion of a right to mobility is the position taken in some countries that once a road has been built using public money, normally financed by taxation, then the public have the right to freely use the facility. This, for example, is a common argument voiced in the United States, and one of the reasons why road pricing in California has been limited to new facilities offering a better quality of service to the existing public roads; hence the charging regime is called 'value pricing'. The argument that, once paid for, a facility should be open to all runs against the basic ideas of economic resource allocation but has emotive appeal. Unless there is optimal capacity whereby user charges should just reflect upkeep costs, then there is a need to somehow ration the scarce road space so that its benefits are not diluted, and pricing is the way this is normally done in market economies and seems to work well.

Calculating the Road Price and its Impact

The simple analysis of the sort seen in Figure 9.1 assumes a lot, and especially that the demand for road space may be represented by a continuous function. In practice there may be kinks or discontinuities and indeed, theoretically, there may be no optimal road price because the demand situation is such that pricing would result in either too much traffic or too little, depending upon the levy charged.

This is a theoretical possibility. After all, the smooth curves used in basic analysis are only expositional aids and the actual form of the demand function is an empirical question that can only be resolved in the light of practical experience.

It is clearly difficult, perhaps impossible, however, to calculate the optimal road price, especially because it is often context-specific. Indeed, Table 9.4 provides a very wide range of calculations from some of the main studies. To begin with, the road price is simply the efficient way of attaining a traffic-related objective, and especially those pertaining to flow, speed, or traffic density. This objective is set by the authorities, often based on the views of traffic engineers who take into account such things as safety and road wear in their estimates. It is largely a subjective indicator of the type of performance that is wanted from the road. The road price is then set to limit traffic to attain the objective.

What this charge will need to be will depend on the costs perceived by motorists using the road; and this is largely a combination of direct costs and the implicit money costs of travel time. In practice neither is easy to calculate. The problem is that people's demand elasticities depend on their perceptions and not on objective measures. Hence, while the money costs of a trip will embrace such things as fuel costs and wear and tear on the vehicle, because these involve infrequent outlays, the road user tends to ignore most of them when deciding on a journey. Travel time poses a different sort of problem because, although it is recognized that 'time is money', to adopt the old saying, exactly how much money a minute of travel time saved is worth is open to some debate. As we have seen,

Table 9.4   *Early estimates of optimal road prices*

Study	Place	Road price at peak times (current prices)
Walters (1961)	Generic US urban expressway	$0.10–0.15/auto-mile
UK Ministry of Transport (1963)	Urban areas in Great Britain	£0.375/auto-mile
Greater London Council (1974)	Central London	£0.60/auto-day
Elliott (1975)	Los Angeles	$0.03–0.15/auto-mile
Kraus et al. (1976)	Twin-cities expressways 1970	$0.03–0.15/auto-mile
Keller & Small (1977)	Bay Area expressways 1972	$0.027–0.343/auto-mile
Dewees (1978)	Toronto 1973	$0.04–0.38/auto-mile
Cheslow (1978)	Berkeley 1977	$2.00/auto-trip
Spielberg (1978)	Madison 1977	$1.00/auto-trip
Mohring (1979)	Twin-cities	$0.66/auto-trip
Gómez-Ibáñez & Fauth (1980)	Boston	$0.5–1.0/auto-trip
Viton (1980)	Bay Area bridges 1972	$0.154/auto-mile
Starrs & Starkie (1986)	Adelaide arterial roads 1982	A$0.025–0.22/auto-km
Cameron (1991)	Los Angeles expressways	$0.15/auto-mile

Sources: Button (1984); Morrison (1986). These papers contain the full references to the studies cited.

there are a variety of techniques available for putting a valuation on time savings, but issues arise about such things as the appropriateness of the methods used (generically between stated and revealed preference techniques) and whether one can sum the value of many small savings to get the value of a large saving.

Difficulty in Devising a Practical Method of Collection

Congestion varies across road networks but it is quite clearly impossible to make a separate charge for each segment of a road network. The pioneering Singapore area licensing scheme was, for example, simple and just involved vehicles having to display a card to show that the driver had paid to enter the core area during designated times. From an economic perspective, this procedure had low transaction costs – the production and sale of permits was cheap and enforcement at entry points to the city became part of normal policing – and provided drivers with prior knowledge of potential costs upon which to base decisions regarding entering the city. It did not, however, provide any direct link to the congestion caused by a vehicle once it was in the city, and its application elsewhere in urban areas with far more entry and exit points would make enforcement more difficult and costly.

A general attempt at reflecting congestion more accurately is found in the Stockholm and Gothenburg schemes, where there are differential charges, but difficulties arise if this is taken too far because motorists are only retrospectively made aware of the congestion costs of their trips. Such systems are also likely to be more expensive to install and administrate, although recent advances in 'smartcard' technology have reduced this problem (Button and Vega, 2007).

Crude area licensing, even if enforced electronically as in London, is cheaper and, since permits must be purchased before entering specified urban zones, the full cost of a journey is made known to motorists before they enter congested streets – if they are still prepared to do so. The disadvantage of this simpler system is its insensitivity to changes in traffic conditions throughout the day. It is a trade-off between the price accurately reflecting the full economic costs of a trip and the ability to relay this to the potential road user.

Manual charging systems also inevitably lead to 'step tolls' in the sense that you either pay or you do not pay, and even when there is payment the price goes up in discrete jumps. The academic evidence is that there are considerable efficiency losses when such crude charges are imposed (Arnott et al., 1993).

The United Kingdom's Smeed Report on road pricing recognized as early as 1964 the limitation of this type of simple fee collection nearly 60 years ago and discussed various electronic options. The technology of the day was, however, limited and expensive. Things have changed and now a variety of alternatives are available and many have been adopted.

There are two broad ways of implementing more sophisticated forms of electronic road pricing. The first uses automatic vehicle identification (AVI), which records centrally the congestion costs of individual trips for each vehicle. The second does not identify individual vehicles but deducts the cost of using congested roads from a stored value medium where the proprietor of the system is not able to establish who is using the facility. This latter approach, which might usefully be called non-smartcard technology, can be extended to the use of smart-cards, similar to credit cards, which automatically debit the costs of trips directly from bank accounts or charge them to a credit card account (such as Visa or Mastercard).

There was early experimentation with equipment and operational practices in Hong Kong. On the operational side, the two-year experiment during the mid-1980s involved fitting over 2,500 vehicles with AVI together with the setting of electronic loops in the road surface at the edge of charge zones. When a vehicle crossed a boundary, a power loop energized its AVI that sent a message, via induc-tive receiver loops, to a roadside recorder. The technical and economic feasibility of the system used was found to have achieved 99 percent effectiveness and reli-ability against the criteria set for it.

There are, however, practical difficulties with the system. An early concern that emerged involved confidentiality of the information gathered. The issue is still a sensitive and possibly inevitable one in some countries. The Hong Kong experiment, while successful in showing that the technology used was reliable and that real-time adjustments to charges were possible, also raised concerns that the information collected could infringe on personal liberties. The electronic conges-tion charging schemes in Stockholm, London, Gothenburg, and elsewhere that have been initiated since that time have taken care to minimize the possibility of them being used for 'tracking', with powerful legal protections being built into the institutional structures in which they operate. The widespread use of electronic payment across a huge number of sectors also means a social acceptance of the mechanism has developed more generally.

The London system makes use of off-the-shelf camera-based automated number plate recognition technology to enforce speed limits. Video recognition closed circuit television cameras target optical characters on the number plates of vehicles at a rate of one per second even if the vehicle is traveling up to 100 mph. Charging is automated through computerized systems that deduct funds from the smartcards or through billing.

The systems now deployed in Stockholm, Norway, and Santiago use AVI involving the installation of a transponder or a smartcard that are detected by beacons installed at toll booths and other check points. The exchanges of infor-mation between the tag and radar are possible using simple radio frequency iden-tification technology. Regular users have their vehicles fitted with an electronic tag while visitors can make cash payments using specific lanes. Violators are identi-fied through camera-based recognition of the vehicles' license plates and charged a retrospective fee.

Singapore's second-generation scheme does not require a centralized com-puter system to keep track of vehicle movements since all charges are deducted from an inserted smartcard at the point of use, with records of transactions kept in the memory chip of the card belonging to the individual. As a further step to assure the public of privacy, all records of transactions required to secure payments from the banks are erased from the central computer system once this is done – typically within 24 hours.

In a sense, these types of devices are often just more efficient ways of cordon charging. While it is possible to develop these types of technologies to provide real-time charging that reflects the actual levels of congestion when a vehicle is using a part of the road network, they still suffer the major economic drawback that consumers should know the price of something before coming to the purchase decision. The problem is that the drivers' own actions affect the price that should be paid and this makes real-time charging extremely difficult in practice.

Efforts at circumventing this problem have been made. One approach is to provide advanced information on local traffic conditions so that a driver has more insight as to the likely road price to pay. Modern technology facilitates the provision of real-time traffic information on relevant parts of the network.

Distributional Effects

Technically, in economic terms, road pricing leads to a Hicks–Kaldor societal welfare improvement (a subject we shall return to when looking at investment criteria in Chapter 11). What this means is that, overall, while some people will be worse off as a result of the price (if they were not it would be a Pareto improvement), those who benefit will be able to compensate them and still retain some gains from the scheme. In the case of road pricing, it is the authority that imposes the charge that benefits from the revenues collected (represented as C_2JKC_1 in Figure 9.1), with the average road user being worse off. This leads to two related issues: first, defining exactly which road-using groups lose and by how much; and, second, whether and by how much the authorities should provide compensation. The first of these issues is dealt with here, and the second in the subsection that follows.

Under a road pricing regime, road use depends on the capabilities of potential users to pay the congestion charge. Whether this would result in undesirable regressive effects on social welfare is an empirical question. It is likely that surface public transport, as we see below when discussing London, would move more freely and would provide a better service for the lower-income groups that tend to patronize it. Also, the wealthy are likely to benefit from being able to 'buy' uncongested road space, a situation they value because of the importance they attach to time savings. In contrast, middle-income groups could be forced to switch from private to public transport, a mode they consider inferior.

Inter-personal welfare comparisons of this type are difficult to make, but it is possible, for example, that if some of the revenue from road pricing were directed towards further improvements in public transport (which may or may not mean heavily subsidized fares), then the adverse effects on the middle-income group could be substantially reduced. Whether this is socially acceptable or desirable is a political question.

All forms of pricing inevitably lead to differential consumption patterns that are to some extent influenced by income levels. Western-style economies accept this, partly because it prioritizes what people want to consume but also because income is itself seen as reflecting the endeavors of individuals. If there are concerns about the income distribution, this is treated as a normative issue that should be handled through redistribution as part of a political process. Road pricing is no exception to normal pricing principles. Much of the debate about the distributional effects of congestion charging centers on the ability of poorer individuals to be able to buy road space, but the poor are unable to buy many things. Thus, the problem is really one of income distribution *per se*, rather than of the price mechanism.

There is a second area of distributional interest, namely how the impacts of road pricing are spread over geographical space. In some instances, there is a clear link between this and the income distribution issue because of the correlation between land-use patterns and household incomes. In another context, however, there are concerns that road pricing will penalize businesses in areas where road users pay for their congestion effects as opposed to those that do not. The evidence on this is limited, but a study of the London road charging scheme by Quddus et al. (2007) found that although individual stores were adversely impacted by the road price, it did not affect overall retail sales in central London. Isolating the implications of the congestion charge is, however, not easy because of a failure of the Underground's Central Line during the initial period of its introduction, the heightened fear of terrorism at the time, and the on-set of a general macroeconomic downturn.

Expenditure of Revenue

Linked to the distributional issue, Clifford Sharp (1966) pointed out that the revenues from road pricing need to be re-allocated with a degree of circumspection. A distinctive outcome of the road price is that the revenue does not normally go to a private company that then makes commercially oriented decisions on how to spend it, but rather to a public agency that has less clear-cut criteria regarding the use of the revenue flow. This poses short-term practical as well as intellectual challenges. Sharp assessed some alternatives for using the revenues, including reducing other road user charges. This has an appeal if the funds are not being used to fulfil other explicit policy objectives, such as reducing CO_2 emissions from carbon fuels or acting as a sumptuary tax to finance other, socially approved expenditures.

In strict efficiency terms, the revenues should be used for purposes that yield the highest social return. Since in most cases large revenues from optimal congestion charges themselves indicate inadequate capacity, a strong case can be made that some should go into providing additional road capacity (Button, 2006a). A related but slightly different argument is that the $F_1 - F_2$ motorists priced off the roads in Figure 9.1 should receive some compensation. Direct transfers back to former motorists, however, pose the problem that they are likely to use at least part of the money to 'buy back' road space. An alternative method of compensating motorists adversely affected may be to use the road pricing revenues to construct more roads, but there are issues here. Daniel Graham and

Stephen Glaister (2006), for example, take a wide geographic perspective of road pricing across the entire United Kingdom's road network and find that while its introduction in urban areas would increase the revenues enjoyed by the relevant road authorities, revenues would fall on other parts of the network that are far less used.

Given that investment decisions should be based upon a much wider range of criteria than simply the revenues raised from road charges (see Chapter 11), an alternative approach would be to treat the revenues as a pure tax income and to use them as part of general public expenditure, and in this way wider problems of efficiency and distribution may be tackled. In this vein, from a pragmatic, political-economy perspective of forming coalitions of interests that would endorse road pricing, Phil Goodwin (1989) and Kenneth Small (1992) argued for spreading the expenditure of revenues across different interest groups, including road users (in the form of investment in additional capacity and intelligent transportation technology to better manage existing capacity), public transport authorities (in the form of capital and operating subsidies), and the general public (in the form of reduced taxation or increases in public-endorsed non-transportation expenditures). The trick, of course, would be to find the appropriate balance of this redistribution between the various groups that would carry local political opinion. This has proved, however, difficult in many cases.

Several efforts have been made to ask those affected how they would like to see the revenues from road pricing spent. Erik Verhoef et al. (1997) did an extensive survey in the Netherlands, and found that, in decreasing order, the preferences were for investment in more road capacity, reduction in vehicle taxation, reduction in fuel taxation, investment in public transportation, subsidies for public transportation, investment in carpooling facilities, general taxation cuts, and expansion of other forms of public expenditure.

In practice, most road pricing schemes do involve a high degree of earmarking of revenues, either because the local authority has needed to do this to get policies through or because central government has mandated it as part of its wider policy agenda. In the case of the toll roads in Norway, although not strictly a road pricing scheme, the revenues were specifically earmarked for local transport expenditures on roads and buses. In the United Kingdom, the revenues from London's congestion charging must, by national law, be spent on transport in London, but much of it goes to subsidize bus services.

Road Pricing is a First-best Solution in a Second-best World

Marginal cost pricing of road space is only strictly optimal if all other goods in the economy are also marginal cost priced; it forms a benchmark. To deal with situations where marginal cost pricing is not universal, there is a need to adjust the road price to reflect these distortions elsewhere in the system. For example, if the costs of public transport are set above their costs inclusive of congestion, then the charges imposed on roads should also be set above the simple calculation of the road price.

While the concept is relatively simply to follow, operationalization can be difficult, as shown by Verhoef (2002). The nature of pricing imperfections can be complex and extensive; they may also be positive, in the sense of reinforcing the road price, or they may conflict with it. They may also be within the road system; for example, introducing congestion pricing on some roads but not others affects the relative attractiveness of various routes and the economic activities located about them. At the micro level, charging for only some routes may deflect some traffic onto unpriced 'rat-runs', which that not only has adverse effects for congestion, but may also have adverse environmental implications. There is a danger that one region or city may not introduce road pricing, hoping to attract business from adjacent areas that do. Similar problems arise when it comes to airport and seaport pricing that are discussed later.

These types of problems can easily be seen in Figure 9.2, which shows a situation where there are two roads linking A and B, one free and the other with an optimal road price in place. (One could easily interpret the unpriced route as an alternative mode and the arguments would remain valid.) The roads are pure substitutes for each other in the sense of the generalized costs, using the sum of the monetized travel cost, c, plus the toll r where it is levied. The costs will be equal for both roads (following the so-called 'Wardropian' equilibrium principle), with people trading off lower monetized costs of a non-priced trip against the higher-priced but faster facility. Drivers are nearly identical in their preferences (for example, their values of time savings are the same), except when demand is not perfectly elastic.

Given the different prices, the challenge is to set a second-best charge for the priced road that maximizes the efficiency with which both roads are used. In general, this will be below the optimal road price when only one link is considered. This is because the charge on the priced road will improve the situation over conditions when there is no access fee. But this charge will divert some traffic to the other, unpriced road, adding to the level of congestion there. Thus, there is a trade-off in terms of improving travel conditions on the facility that is road priced, but worsening them on the route that remains free. Ideally both routes should have a congestion charge, but we are assuming that is not possible. It is the establishment of the optimal trade-off in this constrained case that necessitates the second-best pricing.

Priced road

A B

Free road

Figure 9.2   *The classic two-route second-best case*

9.5   Impacts of Road Pricing

There are numerous academic and official studies that have examined the potential effects of using road user charges of one form or another to reduce urban traffic congestion. Rather than rehash these, or try to produce some meta-analysis of their statistical conclusions, here we look briefly at what has transpired when road pricing has been adopted. One thing is clear, the evidence from the various road pricing schemes that have been initiated and heavily studied to date shows that drivers do respond to prices and that traffic congestion can be controlled through direct user charges. Besides the direct traffic effects on congestion, the initiatives have exerted secondary influences, many of which were generally anticipated but not on the scale that they have occurred.

There are inevitably problems in assessing the pure impacts of road pricing. All the schemes that have been introduced to date have been part of larger packages, and isolating the effects of any element is difficult. The Singapore area licensing, for example, was accompanied by additional bus capacity and investments in park-and-ride facilities as well as exemption for high-occupancy cars. Also, the charges themselves have inevitably embraced political compromise that, for example in the London case, resulted in significantly lower charges for residents and some types of road users such as taxis, trucks, and two-wheeled vehicles. Added to this can be unforeseen circumstances that affect the system, such as the closure for a period of the main Underground railway line in London at the time congestion charging was initiated.

The world is also not static, and traffic growth takes place over time. Consequently, there is a need for the level of congestion charges to change with circumstances. However, this makes it hard to estimate anything but very short-term *ex post* elasticities because of the problem associated with allowing for these background growth trends. The outcomes of any scheme at any point in time will thus be contextual on exactly how recently road pricing has been imposed and the extent to which it has been modified in the light of experience.

Table 9.5 provides details of the outcomes of some of the major urban road pricing schemes in terms of the direct effects on automobile traffic, on the traffic situation more generally, and on public transport. The pattern that emerges is clear and does not need much in the way of elaboration; road pricing where it has been employed has reduced the use of cars, improved traffic flows, and led to a modal shift toward public transport during peak periods.

There have also been secondary benefits, such as reduced traffic-generated environmental pollution, although this is difficult in practice to quantify and evaluate because people allocate their time saved from not being held up in traffic in ways that in themselves can result in adverse environmental consequences. Just as an example, it has been estimated that the Stockholm scheme reduced CO_2 by 10 to 14 percent in the inner-city area and by 2 to 3 percent in the surrounding area, although there was little impact on noise levels, while the London charging scheme produced an annual $6 million benefit in terms of reduced CO_2 emissions, and $30 million in lower accident costs.

Table 9.5   *The effects of major road pricing schemes*

City	Traffic effects	Congestion effects	Public transport effects
Singapore, 1975–98[a]	−44%; −31% by 1988	Average speed increased from 19 to 36 kph	Modal shift, from 33% to 46% trips to work by city bus, 69% in 1983
Trondheim, 1991	−10 %	n.a.	+7% city bus patronage
Singapore, 1998[b]	−10 to −15%	Optimized road usage, 20 to 30 kph roads, 45 to 65 kph expressways	Slight shift to city bus
Rome, 2001	−20 %	n.a.	+6%
London, 2003	−18% 2003 vs 2002; 0% 2004 vs 2003	−30%; 1.6 min/km typical delay 2003, 2004 vs 2002 (2.3 min/km)	+18% during peak hours bus patronage 2003, +12% in 2004
London, 2005[c]	Small net reductions −4% 2005–2006	−22%; 1.8 min/km typical delay	Bus patronage steady
Stockholm, 2006	−30% 2006 vs 2004	−30 to −50% journey time	+6%

Notes:
a.   Although called Area Licensing Scheme, the system was a cordon toll rather than an area license.
b.   Electronic fee collection introduced.
c.   New rate introduced.
n.a. = not available.

Not all the systems described are strictly road pricing; the Norwegian ones, for example, were introduced primarily for revenue-raising. In addition, while the Singapore scheme showed that road pricing can reduce congestion successfully, it also showed that the effect of any scheme seems rather more difficult to forecast than some advocates suggested. The actual details of this scheme are obviously tailored to the geography and political climate of Singapore and have not been exactly replicated elsewhere. It was also questionable whether the actual prices charged are truly optimal or whether they are excessively high, acting as a method of revenue collection for the government as much as an instrument of microeconomic resource allocation. Quite clearly transport may be a legitimate field for pure indirect taxation but in assessing the effectiveness of a road pricing scheme it is important to isolate the price efficiency aspect from that of taxation *per se*.

Of course, not all outcomes have been exactly as predicted. In very many cases, the authorities have under-estimated the power of pricing and the reduction in traffic has exceeded forecasts, and the revenue collected has been less than expected. Equally, public transport has generally been found to be a more popular substitute than expected once travelers are aware of the congestion costs of using cars, the park-and-ride facilities introduced in Singapore being a notable exception to this. This poses some operational challenges in terms of budgeting, scheduling, and the provision of public transport more generally, but has not seriously brought any scheme into difficulties.

Exhibit   *The initial London congestion charge scheme*

By 1998 traffic speeds across London were down to 10 mph. In the larger London Area drivers were spending about 30 percent of their time stationary during peak periods. Traffic management measures and public transportation subsidies had failed to halt the rising level of congestion. In 2003, however, a £5.00 daily charge (later raised) was imposed for driving or parking in central London between 7 am and 6.30 pm on weekdays.

The idea was based on the notion of road pricing initiated by Pigou in 1920 and 'discovered' in an obscure paper by Milton Friedman and a student by the mayor of London, Ken Livingstone. The congestion charge was imposed within six months of Livingstone's election. The system entails a toll ring with no effort to charge for the marginal costs of individual trips within the zone.

The £5.00 daily fee was based upon estimates from prior traffic studies, but in subsequent economic analysis was found to approximate to the marginal cost of driving two miles in inner London. Transactions costs for road users were minimized by offering a variety of ways (retail outlets, kiosks, call centers, and the internet) for pre-recording license information and for paying the charge. *Ex post* payment was also possible at a small premium within a defined time period, and a surcharge was added to payments made just prior to travel.

Enforcement was, given the photographic technology used, akin to that for speeding or other traffic violations. License plate numbers were recorded and non-payers were then sent penalty notices. There were immediate problems with identification because of the basic nature of the camera technology involved, and improved camera technology was introduced.

The short-term implications of the scheme are seen in the first table. A clear reduction in car traffic is seen, together with an increase in taxi and bus traffic. It should be said that this was before the development of hail-by-app cabs (for example, Uber), which have had a major subsequent impact on mode spilt. In terms of speed, all-day average network speeds rose from about 8.9 mph to 10.4 mph in the month after the charges were introduced.

Vehicle type	Year		Change
	2002	*2003*	
Cars	771 (47)	507 (35)	−34
Vans	287 (18)	273 (19)	−5
Trucks	73 (8)	68 (5)	−7
Taxis	256 (16)	312 (21)	22
Buses	54 (3)	65 (5)	21
Motorcycles	129 (8)	137 (9)	6
Bicycles	69 (3)	89 (6)	28
All vehicles	1,640 (100)	1,451 (100)	−12

Note: Traffic in thousands of vehicle-kilometers (and percent).

While these sorts of data provide indicators of traffic effects and the implications for modal split, they are inadequate indicators of economic benefits that reflect, amongst other things, the effects of charges on person travel and operating costs of the system. The second table provides a fuller social cost–benefit assessment of the charges completed by London Transport in 2006.

Annual costs (£ millions in 2005 prices)	
Administrative	5
Scheme operating	85
Set-up (opportunity costs/depreciation)	23
Traffic management (e.g., increased bus services)	20
Charge payer compliance	30
Total	163
Annual benefits (£ millions in 2005 prices)	
Time savings & reliability	
Car users	110
Vans and trucks	35
Taxis	40
Buses	42
Deterred drivers	−25
Reduced accidents	15
Reduced CO_2 emissions	3
Other resource savings	10
Total	230

The calculations suggest an annual social welfare gain of $67 million (in 2005 prices), but there are questions concerning some of the assumptions they make. For example, the demand and cost curves used do not take full account of the differentiated nature of road usage and the heterogeneous values of travel time. Further, the calculations are based upon first-best assumptions, namely that all markets are based on marginal cost pricing, but there are arguments that local labor markets would be affected according to how the revenues from the charging are spent. Linked to this is the question of efficiency. There may be net benefits associated with the London congestion charging regime, but this does not mean that resources are not being wasted. There may be inefficiencies in the infrastructure used and the ways in which the system is managed.

See also: J. Leape (2006) The London congestion charge, *Journal of Economic Perspectives*, 20, 157–76.

Enforcement has posed challenges to the authorities responsible for some schemes, although there seems to have been a learning process. Transport for London, for example, reported in 2006 that the number of penalty charge notices fell throughout 2005, with 21 percent fewer charges overall. In Rome, violations in the control zone resulting in fines fell from an initial 22 percent of the overall access flow to about 7 percent of those registered in 2005–2006. Reductions in traffic flows were mainly achieved through this reduction of illegal traffic entering the limited traffic zone. Better monitoring was made possible by the installation of electronic gates in 2001; illegal traffic decreased from an estimated 36 percent before their activation to under 10 percent after a year and a half.

9.6   Parking Policies

In some cases, often for political reasons but also possibly because it is more cost-effective to operate, a parking charging policy may appear preferable to road pricing as a means of containing congestion externalities. This is true if much of the traffic is terminating in the area concerned and there is a lot of circulating traffic seeking parking spots because of inadequate signage. Again, while the most extensive coverage of parking is in the context of urban car traffic, the principles can be equally valid for stands at airports or berths at seaports; for example, high stand charges for aircraft at air terminals can stimulate changes in flight patterns and traffic concentrations.

Parking is seldom provided and operated in an economic manner, and optimal fees are rare (Young, 2001). Parking can either be considered in a first-best world, where there is appropriate pricing elsewhere, including road pricing, or in a second-best context as a means of limiting traffic congestion when there are not appropriate prices charged for other goods and services (Button, 2006b).

The first-best approach is simply to set the parking charge equal to the marginal cost of parking, including the congestion costs of seeking a parking space. In practice, their detailed effects can be influenced by the institutional structure of an area; for example, any attempt to influence the parking market in one part of a city will influence the scale and nature of the induced externalities in adjacent boroughs by, depending on the nature of the policy, attracting or discouraging terminating traffic and affecting such things as the land value of office premises with parking facilities. Institutionally this can lead also to game playing by employers who argue for favorable parking concessions as a pre-requisite for them locating in any local administrative unit. As behavioral economics shows, these longer-term costs are generally more difficult to handle because of hysteresis. Once people change their activity patterns it is often difficult to encourage them to adjust to optimal behavior; there are stranded cost considerations and uncertainties to contend with.

A simple way to look at the role of parking fees in a second-best context is set out in Figure 9.3 (Verhoef et al., 1995). Quadrant A has the marginal cost and average cost curves (where we assume simple interaction congestion to be the only externality) but added to this is the cost of parking (reflecting the opportunity costs of a parking space and assuming for simplicity that individuals' parking durations are identical). This gives the combined costs curve of *TMC*. The optimal road price plus parking fee based on traffic density then become *RP* in the diagram. We now take the extreme case that for some reason the road price element of *RP* cannot be collected.

On the assumption that all vehicles paying appropriate prices which enter during the study period will find parking, then we can draw the 45° line in quadrant B of the diagram, which relates traffic density to parking occupancy. The parking fee for the period, *F*, required to achieve this is then mapped out in quadrant C. This demand curve again assumes that willingness to pay the set fee will guarantee a parking place; if this assumption is not valid because of

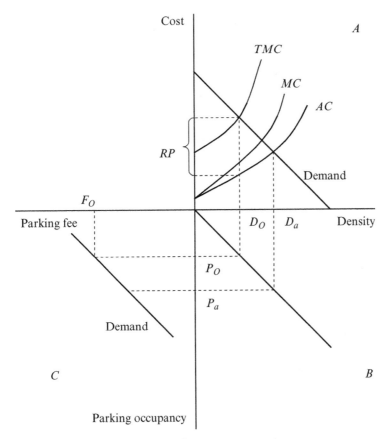

Figure 9.3   *A simple analysis of parking charges*

suboptimal capacity, the analysis requires modification. The demand curve for parking places is derived from the difference between Demand and the *AC* in quadrant A. The optimal parking fee here (F_O) is acting as a rationing device and its size could be adjusted accordingly if a suboptimal road price were initiated at some later date.

Parking policy has its own limitations. First, it only affects certain traffics. It obviously has little impact on through-traffic and, indeed, by deterring stopping traffic, it may encourage movements through the city centers. It also has distributional consequences. It bears more heavily on those making short journeys since the parking fee will form a relatively large part of the overall costs of their trips compared to those driving a greater distance. The policy is also likely to be relatively insensitive to actual levels of congestion since it is acting on a complement to road use rather than road use itself. From a practical perspective, many parking places are privately owned and hence direct control of prices is difficult for policymakers, although indirect measures, such as taxing land used for parking, provide a mechanism for tackling the problem.

There is also the question of just how sensitive parking decisions are to charging: the elasticity of demand. Table 9.6 provides some calculations for

Table 9.6   *Parking elasticities in Sydney*

	Preferred CBD	Less preferred CBD	CBD fringe
Car trip, preferred CBD	−0.541	0.205	0.035
Car trip, less preferred CBD	0.837	−0.015	0.043
Car trip, CBD fringe	0.965	0.286	−0.476
Park-and-ride	0.363	0.136	0.029
Ride public transit	0.291	0.104	0.023
Forgo CBD trip	0.469	0.150	0.029

Source: Hensher and King (2001).

Sydney, Australia, dividing parking locations up into more and less preferred sites. It provides both direct elasticities and cross-elasticities between locations. It shows, for example, that while a 1 percent rise in parking charges at preferred urban locations will reduce parking there by 0.54 percent it will increase parking at less preferred sites by 0.84 percent and fringe parking by 0.97 percent. In other words, simply raising parking charges at the most congested parts of the city can spread the demand for parking to other locations. Stated-preference analysis in Israel (Albert and Mahalel, 2006) finds that the demand elasticity regarding parking fees is considerably lower than for road pricing, again indicating a lack of traffic sensitivity to their introduction.

9.7   Congestion Pricing at Airports

Congestion in air transport arises at airports and during flights. As with road transport, the lack of a genuine benchmark for measuring congestion means that estimating congestion costs at different traffic levels or excess congestion levels in either context is difficult. The United States Federal Aviation Administration (FAA) and many other civil aviation organizations use a 15-minute delay on the published schedule as an indication of congestion, and on this basis 25 percent of flights suffered from excess congestion at the United States' major airports in 2006.

The economic cost of these delays is difficult to estimate because, unlike road traffic congestion where car drivers are trying to minimize their travel time and vehicle costs, commercial airlines are the direct customers for most airports' slots and in a deregulated world, airlines are largely motivated by profits. In other words, the nature of the opportunity cost associated with congestion is perceived differently when the user of a facility is a commercial entity than when it is an individual – the effects of congestion on an airline affect its bottom line, whereas the effects of road congestion on an individual are on that person's utility, which is usually modeled in terms of financial costs and the monetary value of lost time.

Airports vary in their physical form, ownership, and motivations. While there has been a gradual trend towards privatization in Europe, and especially in the United Kingdom, and modifications to the regulations regarding how they operate, United States airports are largely owned by local authorities of one kind or another. There are few, if any, fully privately owned airports in the world driven purely by unrestrained profit motives and this may, in part, explain why their efficient operations are often an issue of public interest.

Many airports are already congested (Table 9.7 gives data for major European facilities) and it is unlikely that runway capacity will in the foreseeable future expand in line with the projected increase in traffic, and certainly there will be many facilities where capacity will remain stagnant or grow much more slowly. There are often airports where demand is high but additional capacity will not be constructed because of local opposition to adverse local environmental effects. There are few quick-fix technologies on the horizon. Enhanced air navigation equipment and air traffic control practices, such as those being adopted in the United States under the NexGen initiative and by EUROCONTROL under the Single European Sky program, are likely to offer only temporary relief in terms of controlling flows into and out of airports. The challenge in these circumstances is to make the best use of the capacity that is available, and to adopt more efficient management practices.

The existing mechanisms for allocating take-off and landing slots generally rely upon administrative procedures. Many countries, or groups of countries such as the European Union, have regulations governing the ways slots are allocated, embracing a combination of formal and informal arrangements often overseen by a scheduling committee that includes incumbent users. It is normal to have some grandfathering element that favors existing users, and often there are limitations on the ability of incumbents to trade their slots with other carriers. To assist in coordination across airports, every flight requires a take-off and landing slot. There are also various inter-airport and airline meetings and, for international

Table 9.7 *Delays suffered by major European airlines at large airports in 2006*

Airport	Departures		Arrivals	
	Flights (%)	*Minutes (average)*	*Flights (%)*	*Minutes (average)*
London Heathrow	31.8	34.9	30.3	38.9
Madrid	31.3	45.7	33.1	44.3
London Gatwick	30.7	32.5	31.5	37.8
Paris CDG	28.6	38.1	23.4	37.4
Barcelona	27.2	43.4	28.0	41.2
Rome	26.3	41.8	22.8	42.0
Athens	25.2	40.2	27.7	41.0
Frankfurt	25.0	36.9	24.6	40.0
Dublin	24.4	44.6	29.5	39.7
Larnaca	24.3	50.9	30.1	49.8
Milan Malpensa	24.2	44.3	22.1	41.6
Lisbon	24.1	42.6	30.2	37.5

Source: Association of European Airlines.

routes, since 1947 the International Air Transport Association (IATA) has held twice-yearly schedule conferences now involving some 300 airlines and 200 airport representatives.

The situation is different in the United States where anti-trust laws mean that airlines simply schedule flights taking into account expected air traffic control and airport delays. An exception initiated in 1969 under the High-density Rule temporarily designated five 'slot-controlled airports' (JFK and LaGuardia in New York, O'Hare in Chicago, Newark in New Jersey, and Washington DC's Reagan National), where the federal government limited the number of aircraft movements during certain hours although the airlines from 1986 could buy and sell, or lease, the slots designated for domestic use amongst themselves. This regime has been modified several times since.

Although there are variations by country and airports, the fees charged for a slot are based largely on the size of aircraft, with some variations that reflect, for example, noise emissions, and determined on cost recovery criteria. This is a sort of unequally weighted Ramsey Pricing concept. Where there are fee differentials, they seldom embrace a full consideration of congestion costs. There is thus no reason to assume that this type of arrangement results in anything like the optimal use of slots at one airport, let alone across a network.

There are few incentives for re-allocation between carriers as the demand for their services fluctuates even when this is permitted. While there are wide variations, it is often difficult for new carriers to enter specific markets, and especially those dominated by a major airline. Equally, there are less than maximum incentives for incumbents to make efficient use of slots they retain in terms of the congestion that is imposed on other operators. Indeed, congestion may be used as an entry deterrent measure to limit competitive market entry.

While there is a temptation to simply transfer the road pricing concept to air transport infrastructure, there are differences. Roads are, for example, used by an atomistic set of independent 'customers' who cannot control the trips of others, whereas air transport facilities are used by a relatively small group of airlines that often have significant control over their actions. In some cases, a carrier is a near-monopsonist buyer of services at an airport. This is so at many of the most connected international hub airports in Europe and the United States (see Table 9.8). What one has in these circumstances are bi-lateral monopolies or oligopolies, with airlines providing countervailing power to the airports. Further, while it may be reasonable to apply continuous functions to the estimation of road traffic congestion, although cars are clearly discrete units, this is less sensible regarding aircraft movements that are far less numerous.

As alluded to earlier, there are also other differences that affect the measurement of congestion costs. While the analysis of production externalities is similar to the user-on-user externalities that form the basis of the economic analysis of road congestion, the motivation of the actors involved is not consumer surplus maximization (usually dominated by travel time costs) but rather producer surplus maximization. Commercial airlines in most markets are concerned only with profits when making operational decisions, and may well impose significant

Table 9.8 *Share of international flights by airline at Europe's and America's ten largest airports (2019)*

Airport	Connectivity[a]	Carriers	Share of flights (%)
Europe			
London Heathrow	317	British Airways	51
Frankfurt	309	Lufthansa	63
Amsterdam	279	KLM	52
Munich	259	Lufthansa	59
Paris Charles de Gaulle	250	Air France	50
Istanbul Airport	187	Turkish Airlines	79
Madrid	154	Iberia	46
Moscow Alexander S. Pushkin	150	Aeroflot Russian Airlines	80
Rome Fiumicino	139	Alitalia	43
Zurich	114	SWISS	54
North America			
Chicago O'Hare	290	United Airlines	46
Toronto Pearson Airport	251	Air Canada	59
Hartsfield–Jackson Atlanta	247	Delta Air Lines	79
Los Angeles	219	American Airlines	22
New York John F. Kennedy	186	Delta Air Lines	37
Dallas–Fort Worth	185	American Airlines	85
Miami	184	American Airlines	75
Houston George Bush	179	United Airlines	81
Newark Liberty	169	United Airlines	70
Vancouver	155	Air Canada	47

Note: a. Direct international destinations served.

Source: Official Airline Guide.

time costs on large numbers of their own passengers if this ensures high profits from the remainder, including those using connected services.

Figure 9.4 provides a simplified version of the use of a congestion charge regime for take-offs on a single runway on the premise that there are numerous airlines seeking rights: the atomistic case. The airport just charges an accountancy fee to cover costs. Functions are linear for ease of drafting and this does not affect the argument. With each additional flight, the marginal aircraft impacts other flights that the initiating airline does not take into account in its decision-making – seen as the divergence of the MC and the MC^* curves. The result is a flow through the runway of F_1 involving a marginal cost of MC_1. The flight, however, will impose congestion on other carriers' activities affecting their profitability as their costs rise and as customers' lower willingness to pay for a poorer service adversely affects revenues. The outcome is an aggregate producer surplus for the airlines at the airport of $\{a + c\} - \{g + h + i\}$ when there are F_1 flights. This will be zero if there is an atomistic market.

If there were a monopsony airline at the airport bearing congestion effects internally, it would take MC^* as its reaction function and manage a flow of F_2.

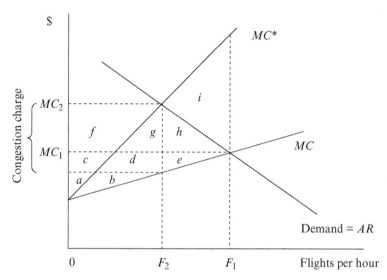

Figure 9.4   *Congestion costs at airports*

Such an airline can prioritize flights for take-offs at the airport and, to a lesser extent, en route by allowing overtaking. The resultant producer surplus to the airline is then $\{a + c + f\}$ which will be above zero. Similarly, with an airport employing marginal cost pricing akin to a road congestion charge, and thus levying a take-off fee that embraces congestion, the flights would be F_2.

While this simple analysis, essentially just a transfer of the Pigouvian framework to a situation where the infrastructure users are interested in economic rent maximization, can be insightful, it does miss some essential elements of runway economics. In the analysis, the degree to which any individual flight by an airline affects other flights depends, therefore, on the nature of the carrier operating the services and on the number of slots an airline uses. In many cases, where there is a dominant carrier, the impact of any flight is on the other operations of that carrier. What this intuitively means for charges is that, when there is a single dominant carrier operating from a not-for-profit airport not actively seeking to exploit monopoly power, there is no need to initiate congestion charges. There are potential problems, however, if the airport is itself rent-seeking. As with most bi-lateral monopoly situations, the slot prices will be bounded, but indeterminate, in this case. This is because a market dominated by a profit-maximizing monopoly tends to have high prices from users whereas a market dominated by a profit-maximizing monopsony tends to seek lower prices for those services.

When combined into a bi-lateral monopoly, the buyer and seller cannot both maximize profit simultaneously and are forced to negotiate. The resulting price could be anywhere between the higher monopoly and the lower monopsony prices depending on the relative negotiating power of each side. What theory suggests, however, is that, in formulating its case, the monopoly airline will think in terms of being able to internalize its congestion costs.

Where there is a degree of competition amongst airlines, however, congestion costs are not fully internalized and congestion pricing become relevant. Most airports are used by several airlines of different sizes with diverse scheduling desires leading to some degree of imperfect competition. In these cases, there will be some internalization of congestion costs but, from a social welfare maximization perspective, a need for congestion charges remains to internalize the remainder. The situation is made more difficult to analyse because the airports themselves usually confront some degree of competition from other airports or, especially in Europe, high-speed rail services.

In addition to this issue of pure market power, the air transport network is generally more complex than a road system in a very specific way. While most road movements are point-to-point (car drivers seldom change vehicles en route), most large airlines operate hub-and-spoke systems where people make trips via a hub, and changes of hardware for them are the norm. This means that carriers are concerned not only about the immediate implications of flight delays but also about the effects of this on connecting traffic and its own further network operations.

Further, whereas a car can wait almost indefinitely in traffic, an aircraft cannot be airborne indefinitely, reducing the flexibility of infrastructure to handle connecting traffic flows. Passengers would also be less than happy if an airborne flight was diverted to an alternative airport because its congestion fees were lower at that time.

Added to this is an issue examined initially by Eric Pels and Erik Verhoef (2004), namely the possibility in an oligopolistic business environment for strategic interaction between competitors that leads to non-competitive pricing. Basically, without congestion this will lead to prices in excess of the Pareto optimum for the airlines that collude, with the policy implication that, in the absence of any direct remedial action on the part of the authorities, there is a second-best case for subsidies.

But perhaps the biggest difference is that the literature on road pricing generally makes simplifying assumptions of homogeneous traffic and identical types of driver, which allows the MC curve also to be the cost curve related to the MC^* curve. This gives a determinant solution for the congestion charge. Put another way, with MC also representing the congestion-embracing-average-cost curve, MC_1 is both the average revenue in equilibrium F_1 and the average cost. The types of assumption made regarding roads, however, seem less applicable to runways, and the MC curve unlikely to be identical to the average-cost curve. We just list a few of the complications.

First, as noted previously, it may not seem reasonable to assume the curves are continuous; with 5,000 cars an hour on a road, continuous functions may seem an acceptable assumption, but with 40 landings on a runway they are much less justifiable. Second, many runways involve mixed flows of take-offs and landings with different time and fuel requirements. Third, typically air traffic is highly heterogeneous involving different sizes and types of aircraft. Fourth, because of laws regarding flying hours, the crew costs may vary between flights if connecting movements are missed. What these and other inconveniently realistic features would typically mean is that there would be no stable AC and MC curves (that is, adding a marginal flight may change the average cost for infra-marginal flights, so the curve is not stable). In this case there is no way of estimating an optimal congestion charge.

While in some ways more complex than roads, air transport infrastructure is also simpler in dimensions that make some forms of congestion charging, and especially auctioning, easier. It involves relatively small networks compared with the complexity of most urban road systems and, despite some differences in technical requirements, have a much more homogeneous set of users. A look at the vast number of theoretical papers on urban networks seeking optimal traffic flows, and *ipso facto* charges, all of which are based on a plethora of simplifying assumptions, illustrates the complexities involved. Further, while this work no doubt maximized the adrenalin flow of the authors that accompanies dancing an intellectual jig, it would seem to have little impact on policy. The road prices introduced in places such as Singapore and London involve nice round numbers, and the speed targets on the Interstate 15 in California's variable charging projects have been equally robust rather than being founded in economic science.

Considerable intellectual effort has been expended on defining appropriate pricing principles for airport slots, focusing mainly on the ways administrative fees could be modified to make better use of them. The resultant output has included looking at making greater use of pricing for cost recovery when there is no congestion, but has largely been focused on situations where there are at least some periods where demand under the current charging regime exceeds the capacity of the system.

Moving to the empirical analysis of airport congestion, much of this has involved looking at whether dominant airlines do internalize their costs. Daniel's pioneering work (Table 9.9) suggests that there is very little internalization by the larger carriers, but his analysis suffers from being based on a single airport and from focusing on just Northwest Airlines within a narrow cost-minimization context. The focus on one airport may be a reasonable approach if it is the only one subjected to serious congestion, but if there are other facilities in a similar situation then a network analysis becomes germane. Additionally, the simulation models deployed do not have a closed-form solution and thus it is not possible to discern what drives the non-internalization.

Subsequent work, notably by Jan Brueckner (2002) and Mayer and Sinai (2003), has looked across a range of airports to gain empirical breadth, and modified the models they used to meet the technical limitations of earlier formulations. New data sources also allow for econometric analysis of causes for different behavior patterns of airlines rather than just simulations. Using the number of flights that are delayed for 15 minutes or more as the indicator of excess congestion, Brueckner finds that delays do decrease where there is airline domination at an airport but the degree of internalization is small.

Adopting the excess of flight time over the minimum feasible flight time as their indicator of delay, Mayer and Sinai come to the same conclusion. Where there is competition between airlines at an airport, then each should take a share of the congestion costs imposed on others in proportion to their market share – for example, American and United Airlines each has roughly half the traffic at

Table 9.9   *Econometric studies of internalization of congestion at airports*

Study	Case	Model	Findings
Carlin & Park (1970)	LaGuardia Airport, New York, 1967–68	Numerical calculation and regression	While full marginal cost pricing is not possible, proportional marginal cost pricing does offer some efficiency gains
Morrison (1987)	US technical data on airline costs for 1980	Numerical calculations	Equal weighted Ramsey Pricing would redistribute welfare from commuter and local service carriers to cargo, international, and trunk carriers
Morrison & Winston (1989)	US delay data for May 1988	Looked at a road-pricing-regime-type model of atomistic pricing	Atomistic pricing would generate significant welfare benefits
Daniel (1995)	Minneapolis–St Paul Airport in 1990	Bottleneck congestion model and a time-homogeneous stochastic queuing model	Demand peaking means that congestion pricing can generate large savings by smoothing out demand
Martin-Cejas (1997)	Uncongested Spanish airports	Simulations looking at Ramsey Pricing	Allows for cost recovery
Daniel (2001)	Minneapolis–St Paul Airport in 1990	Stochastic bottleneck model	Congestion pricing would transfer welfare back from private aircraft operators and their high-income passengers to common travelers on commercial aircraft
Daniel & Pahwa (2000)	Minneapolis–St Paul Airport in 1990	i. Standard peak-load pricing model ii. Deterministic bottleneck model iii. Stochastic bottleneck model	Similar traffic patterns are produced by the models using weight-based fees, but a variety of patterns emerge when congestion pricing is used
Brueckner (2002b)	25 most congested airports in the US in 1999	Econometric analysis of delays using six different specifications	When an airport is dominated by a monopoly airline then the costs of congestion are fully internalized
Mayer & Sinai (2003)	Flights between airports with at least 1% of US flights, 1988–2000	Econometric analysis of delays using regression with and without fixed effects	Hubbing is the primary cause of traffic delays and this largely reflects optimal use of runway capacity
Harback & Daniel (2007)	27 major US airports, 2003	Deterministic bottleneck model of congestion	The idea that dominant carriers internalize self-imposed congestion costs is rejected and full congestion pricing is found to be optimal
Morrison & Winston (2008)	74 US airports for 2005	Morison & Winston (1989) congestion measure	Optimal and atomistic congestion pricing generate welfare gains with the latter being slightly greater

Source: Button (2008). This paper contains the full references to the studies cited.

Chicago O'Hare International Airport, and should thus each pay half of the costs that it imposes.

This is not, however, the finding of Harback and Daniel (2007), who looked at 27 large United States airports using structural models of landing and take-off queues, rather than econometric techniques, for empirical verification. It also differs from Brueckner's and Mayer and Sinai's findings in that an input measure of delays (the delays generated by each aircraft) is used rather than an output measure (delays experienced by each aircraft). The result, tested on data for 2003, is that in most cases there is no internalization of congestion costs by dominant airlines. The rationale seems to stem from Stackleberg oligopoly game theory, although other gaming models may be relevant. Essentially, the dominant carrier uses its ability to manipulate congestion to deter market entry by competitors, a limit pricing, which leads the dominant firm to act as if it had the costs of its rivals or potential rivals. If it were to internalize its congestion it would release capacity that could be taken by a competitor, allowing the latter the potential of reaping economies of scope and density, and of market presence.

What much of the work on airport congestion pricing does not completely embrace is the issue of full cost recovery. In conditions of a competitive supply of runway capacity and constant cost, the link is a simple one: appropriate charges indicate where capacity is needed and provides the revenues to complete new works. This quickly breaks down where supply is not competitive and there are obvious technical non-linearities in the long-term cost function; runways are not divisible. The empirical work on this is limited, but Morrison and Winston (2008) indicate that only charging for congestion caused to other carriers *à la* Brueckner would lead to $4.6 billion less revenue at United States airports than a regime of atomistic congestion charges akin to road pricing. Cost recovery then poses a range of additional issues in terms of the supplementary methods of finance, be these subsidies of one kind or another, or Ramsey Pricing.

There are difficulties in the general approach of these studies, besides specific limitations inherent in each. Here we focus on the data and definitional problems in trying to determine congestion costs. Consideration of transaction costs and information availability is, as Coase (1960) pointed out, important in determining the best mechanisms for asset allocation. Much of the slot analysis work focuses on the operating impacts of congestion on airlines' costs and time costs for passengers, but airlines are the final purchasers of the infrastructure.

Airlines are rent-seekers and use a variety of practices to extract rent from their customers – most notably second-degree price discrimination with frequent flyer programs that offer effective discounts for multiple flights and a combination of second- and third-degree price discrimination through yield management practices that involves posting a menu of fares, but where this menu changes by user groups according to their preferences about the timing of bookings. Because airlines take advance bookings, the immediate effects of congestion charges on revenue would be minimal, but the longer-term implications may be larger. In this context, even if an airline is profit-maximizing, it may prioritize its actions by net revenue flow rather than cost savings in terms of the ways it adjusts its flight sequencing. The empirical problem is that suitable information on revenues per flight is not available, although this is needed to estimate the congestion cost.

Added to this, as Brueckner (2005) points out in a theoretical contribution, on the cost side there are indivisibilities in the provision of airline services that make assessments of flight prioritization difficult, and especially so when there are hub-and-spoke operations. There are problems of scheduling different sizes of aircraft over various stage lengths and ensuring equipment compatibility as well as fulfilling technical requirements regarding such things as periodic refueling and maintenance inspections. In addition, crew changes need to conform to statutory flying hour regulations and there are operation constraints such as gate availability. Much more than in the road traffic congestion case, the internalization process within this context is inevitably one of a constrained optimization process and assessment of the degree to which this is done requires more complex assumptions about relevant functions. Whilst these considerations may be built into theoretical models, they are difficult to incorporate into empirical analysis and, in turn, into estimation of actual charges.

As mentioned earlier, one difference between road congestion and airport congestion is that the airline market is not atomistic and this difference offers an alternative practical approach to handling congestion. An underlying problem with congestion charging and its analysis is that it involves making external judgments about the optimal congestion charge. While the approaches examined in Table 9.9 are essentially about situations where there is excess demand under current charging regimes, and the role a Pigouvian-style price may play in optimizing this, they do not focus on how optimal slot charges may be implemented. They do not look at arrangements that would automatically reveal these fees and impose them on users. The alternative approach to setting congestion charges is to create appropriate institutional structures that coincidentally reveal optimal prices while allocating efficiently a given capacity.

One suggestion for significantly improving the slot allocation situation is the adoption of some form of auctioning system (Button, 2007). This is a mirror image of congestion charging where some expert sets a congestion charge and users willing to pay this price purchase capacity. Instead, the expert sets a level of capacity and then allows bidding for that capacity, generally in the form of an auction. Auctions have become a subject of increasing interest as markets have been deregulated and authorities have become interested in attracting more private finance. Indeed, the idea of using auctions for allocating airport slots is not new and the Nobel laureate Vernon Smith and his associates (Rassenti et al., 1982) used the problem in their early work on experimental economics. Their use for allocating air transport facilities is now attracting the interest of the European Union and some national governments.

Strictly, the standard Coasian line of reasoning implies that the initial allocation of slots, be it by lottery, auction, a handover to incumbents, or whatever, should, if, subsequent secondary markets are permitted, make no difference to the long-run efficiency with which they are used. Auctions are but one way of allocating property rights. There is no need for an expert economist or engineer to externally set congestion prices once the allocation has been made. There will be a short-term transfer of rents between airports and carriers, and subsequently between various carriers after secondary trading, but the outcome is that carriers that can make the most efficient use of slots will be able to obtain the numbers they require either through their bidding at an auction or through secondary trading, and will buy and sell slots as markets change.

In practice, there are matters of political economy to consider as well as the technical nature of subsequent secondary markets. The way that slots are allocated is a concern; windfall gains accrue if incumbents are given property rights that would not be enjoyed by those wishing to join the market. It is thus no accident that many legacy carriers find voice in supporting this give-away approach. Lotteries spread the windfall rents randomly but there do arise issues about who can participate and whether there are any payments to be made by winners. There is also the matter of whether the lotteries should be for pairs of slots, combinations of slots, or groups of slots. An extensive secondary market would be needed because the initial allocation is likely to be far from optimal.

But even if auctions are adopted, there are issues akin to those inherent in road pricing, including that of ensuring that costs of maintaining existing capacity are recovered, and how to finance and prioritize capacity expansion. With charges, this involves notions of maintenance cost allocations between users and cost recovery that have to be embraced within the charging regime. While auctions of runway slots are certainly not free from problems, they do partially circumvent the need for excessive calculations.

The primary aim of a well-structured periodic auction of slots is to make sure that the winner is the carrier that will generate the most profit from the use of a slot or bundle of slots. Ideally, it is a neutral process whereby exogenous information has no influence. In addition, an appropriately structured auction, through the revenues it raises, both provides signals as to whether additional capacity is needed and provides initial resources for capacity expansion. Indeed, the collection of a bid from the auction transfers the value of a slot to the airport and avoids the concerns with arbitrary initial allocations whereby airlines enjoy the wide-fall gains. Incorporating secondary markets into the structure allows for fine-tuning as markets evolve and to make technical adjustments for imperfections in the auction procedure.

Thus, as with congestion charging, auctioning of runway slots has its problems and it is perhaps helpful to discuss these in a comparative context. The number and duration of slots that is seen as making efficient use of a runway have to be determined and this, like a congestion charge, is an external judgment. But it is very much akin to the real economic decisions made by industry every day: coffee is normally sold in cafés in cups and there is the issue of defining exactly what constitutes a 'cup'. While modeling, by definition, abstracts from reality, there are institutional constraints that implicitly shape both, including the definition of slots as well as 'coffee cups'. Roads are designed to engineering standards that affect, for example, the speeds at which one can drive and remain on the surface, and this is in addition to institutional issues such as speed limits and driving restrictions for safety and environmental reasons. These are largely taken as axiomatic in the road pricing analysis.

Runways are similarly restricted with stall speeds limiting the number of take-offs and landings per hour, as well as institutional requirements dictating headways and hours of operation. While in the road case these factors can be incorporated in the assumptions needed for a continuous traffic flow (for example, in the maximum engineering flow) without much disruption, they are important for runways that only involve 60 or so movements an hour. The technical and institutional constraints that are part of airport operations essentially determine the capacity in terms of very discrete units. This makes the modeling of congestion pricing difficult.

If auctions are adopted, there are further issues to consider. One approach is a once-and-for-all auction with rights transferred to the airlines and the other is a concession arrangement with periodic auctions of slots but with airports retaining property rights. The former has considerable theoretical attraction, in that there is no requirement to externally determine the optimal frequency of auctions for concessions, but it may well be preferable to avoid the 'New York Cab Medallion Problem'. The latter involves existing holders resisting any expansion in capacity to protect their monopoly powers and highlights difficulties in increasing and allocating new capacity.

In practice, slot delineations, again as with estimation of a road price, cannot be treated as independent of wider considerations. In the case of road pricing there is the problem of the allocation of capacity to non-vehicle users, most notably pedestrians. Their pricing seems to be singularly ignored in the academic literature but they, and cyclists in some countries, probably constitute the largest number of movements on urban roads, and the greatest congestion. The parallel at airports is non-aircraft movements on aprons. Added to this, there are matters of interactions between traffic at junctions and how this should be handled. In the case of urban traffic systems, light sequencing is partly designed to facilitate high flow but also to take into account access needs of those on secondary roads and the overall safety of road users. The use of complicated runway configurations and the need to use runways for both take-off and landings are the aviation parallels.

Another difficulty often raised is the matter of how auction revenues should be used; they effectively transfer economic rent from carriers to the airport authority (be that a private or public agency). This is not a difficulty absent from congestion charging in atomistic markets, and deciding what to do with road pricing revenues has generated a small library of publications. If the airport is a rent maximizer then the auction becomes a form of price discrimination with each slot being sold at a price that reduces its value to the purchasing airline to that yielding a normal profit. The airline holding a slot would use it efficiently, including taking account of any internal congestion considerations. The airport would use the revenue to make investments that offer the highest return irrespective of the sector involved. Strictly, if an airport is congested then there are grounds for using the revenue for capacity expansion and the return would justify this.

Finally, while the general literature, which is not considered here, on auctions is extensive, no fully efficient and practical auction structure for allocating slots emerges, just as there is no ideal form of congestion charging. Although it poses some problems of its own, secondary trading in slots can provide a viable adjustment mechanism to correct for the worst misallocations of a primary auction and allow airlines to adjust their slot portfolios to meet take-off and landing requirements. But these also need structuring. As institutional economists frequently point out, markets do not arise and function in a vacuum but rather operate with a structure of formal laws and governances.

In practical terms, normally there is a place for trade to take place – in the twenty-first century this can be an electronic exchange – and there is the need for oversight of transactions, and methods of recording to ensure property rights are transparent. These are not problematic and, indeed, exist in embryonic forms in several airport slot markets already and seem to impose minimal transaction costs. A more important concern is the possibility that the market will prove to be imperfect, with monopoly power distorting its efficient functioning. There may be serious concerns that participants will 'bank' certain slots and that other airlines need to make efficient use of those slots they already have. The extent to which this can occur often depends not only on the underlying nature of the airline market and the details of the secondary slot market, but also on the generic nature of competition laws in the country.

9.8   Seaports Congestion

Roads are not the only area where congestion pricing has been advocated. Walters (1976), for example, argued 46 years ago that appropriate marginal cost pricing (including congestion charges) is 'no panacea for ailing or congested ports, but it does supply a useful set of principles to deploy in the discussion of port pricing policy'. Although the general economic principles for optimal port pricing are identical to road pricing, in some circumstances the nature of the shipping industry may result in complications. In the road context there is a monopoly supplier adopting social pricing policies coupled with competition for road space amongst many, uncoordinated potential users. While most ports conform to this type of market situation, in some instances the port authorities are confronted by a monopoly (or, more likely, a cartel) of shipping companies while in others there may be competition between hub ports for business (Haralambides, 2002).

Figure 9.5 shows the demand curve for shipping (the demand for port services may be seen as proportional to this) in terms of total import and export traffic. The port is assumed to have constant marginal handling costs, $0H$, which are passed to the ship owners as port charges. The shipping companies, if competitive, would then charge these customers an additional amount, RH, to reflect their own average costs, to give a total shipping rate of $0R$. The AC of shipping will itself rise after a certain point as port congestion forces queuing to load

Figure 9.5 *Port congestion pricing*

and discharge. Since the AC curve does not reflect the true costs of increasing traffic the port authority should, on welfare economic grounds, levy a congestion charge of AB. Assuming there is no potential for modifying the types of ships in service or the methods of cargo handling this will reduce the tonnage passing through the port from $0T_1$ to the optimal level $0T_2$. This is identical to the road pricing case.

Suppose that instead of a competitive shipping market, the port was used exclusively by a closed liner conference. There are now two important differences. First, the conference, being the sole operator, will bear the costs of congestion itself – the congestion costs are internalized. Second, the conference is likely to act as a monopolist (although, as we have seen in the previous chapter, countervailing powers act as a limited constraint in practice) and be more concerned with the marginal revenue curve than with demand. Thus, the ship owner will charge customers a rate of $0S$ for their services which comprise: port fees, $0H$; their own costs, including that of congestion, HU; and economic, monopoly, rent, US. The tonnage passing through the port is now suboptimally small at $0T_3$.

Although it may be argued that in this situation the optimal use of the port could in some situations be achieved by not charging a congestion toll and by reducing port fees below $0H$, this rather evades the real problem, namely the monopoly power of the shipping conference. Such a policy also places excessive power in the hands of the conference when negotiating with port authorities the fees (and, *ipso facto*, the subsidy) to be charged. The solution here is to tackle distortions at source, namely in the shipping market, rather than maladjusted port prices.

There are occasions when ports do add a surcharge for exceptional congestion. This, for example, occurred in many British, Chinese, and American container ports after the outbreak of the Covid-19 pandemic, although these surcharges have also been a reflection of higher operating costs due to labor shortages. These and other costs are passed through to shipping rates and affect the overall costs in the supply chain. Shippers have thus prioritized their consignments in the short term.

9.9 Non-pricing Options for Reducing Congestion

The traditional approach to handling traffic congestion, be it on the roads or elsewhere, in the absence of appropriate economic pricing, has been to increase capacity (which may entail civil engineering works or softer options such as the use of informatics) or to try to attract passengers or freight to less congested facilities such as public transport or the railways. These approaches have largely been advocated because they do not alienate road users, who, in terms of coalition theory, form a powerful lobbying group, and partly because of the capture of the system by engineers and others who have a vested interest in infrastructure investments. We look at the implications of some of these alternatives.

Invest in More Capacity

The oft-called 'engineering approach' to traffic congestion that tended to dominate thinking in the post-Second World War period was to build more capacity to meet demand; basically to 'predict and provide'. But, as was seen in Chapter 8 and earlier in this chapter, because there is congestion does not necessarily mean that there is a shortage of capacity; it is often the result of inappropriate use and incorrect pricing. Adding capacity in these circumstances can be wasteful and seldom reduces the congestion problem in the long run.

Figure 9.6 replicates the standard congestion diagram (essentially Figure 9.1) with a suboptimal traffic flow of F_1. An optimal road price would bring traffic levels back to the flow where MC_1 is equated to Demand (that is, at point B). In efficiency terms this means that without an appropriate charge, the traffic flow F_1 results in a social, or 'dead-weight' loss equal to the area ABC.

Increasing capacity affects the cost curves in the diagram; it pushes them down and to the right because at any flow the generalized cost is lower. The extra capacity need not come from physical investment but may be the result of introducing improved traffic control or information systems. If the additional investment pushes the marginal and average costs down to AC_2 and MC_2 then the traffic flow will increase to F_2. At this flow, however, there is still excessive congestion resulting in a dead-weight loss of abc, quite simply because the optimal use of the road after its expansion or the introduction of some enhanced informatics would be where MC_2 is equated with demand (that is, at point b in the figure).

If the demand curve is highly elastic, it is clear from the diagram that congestion costs would be little reduced by pulling the cost curves down. This situation is often couched in terms of a sort of Parkinson's Law of traffic at work: the so-called the Pigou–Knight–Downs paradox, or simply Downs' Law. Basically, this

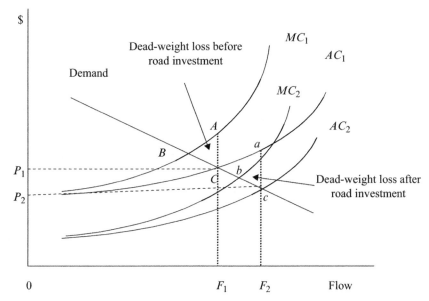

Figure 9.6   *The effects of expanding capacity on road congestion*

says that road traffic expands to fill the road space available. And there is empirical support for this.

One way of looking at the effects of infrastructure expansion on traffic congestion is to examine the effects of national construction programs. In an econometric study of highway spending and the cost of traffic congestion (as measured by the Texas Transportation Institute) in 74 urban areas in the United States covering 1982 to 1996, Winston and Langer (2006) found that, 'on average, one dollar of highway spending in a given year reduced the congestion costs to road users only eleven cents in that year'. Part of this may, of course, be because the investments were not optimal, but nevertheless the congestion-reducing effects do not appear large. In another study examining United States urban data from 1983 to 2003, Duranton and Turner (2011) found support for the fundamental law in highway building, the extension of the Interstate highway system being met with a proportional increase in traffic.

While aggregate expansion of capacity may not have much impact on congestion levels, investment in specific categories of highway may. Mixing traffic (buses, cars, trucks, bicycles, etc.) can worsen traffic flows because of their differing engineering features, such as speed and acceleration, and compound the problems of vehicle interaction. One policy approach is to separate traffic types and to construct mode-specific infrastructure. Truck-only lanes, for example, are under study as tools to combat road congestion, enhance safety, and reduce other external costs of road traffic.

The benefits of separating cars and trucks depend on several factors: the relative volumes of cars and trucks, the congestion delay and safety hazards that each vehicle type imposes, the values of travel time for each type, and the lane capacity indivisibilities. The optimal assignment of heavy vehicles to truck lanes, however, would still need the support of an allocative mechanism to optimize traffic flows on those lanes. In this context André de Palma et al. (2008) finds that priced lane for one vehicle type is generally more effective than hard restrictions on the number of entrants. The benefits of all forms of intervention, though, are sensitive to whether the proportions of cars and trucks are commensurate with lane capacities.

But even when it was appreciated that unrestrained use of infrastructure means its inefficient use, decision-makers were still reluctant to adopt economic pricing, their focus often continuing on maximizing throughput rather than optimizing its use.

One of the reasons that capacity expansion has been a way of optimizing congestion is that an implicit assumption of many traffic forecasting models is that the demand curve for road use is perfectly elastic, whereas the evidence from the road pricing schemes that have been initiated suggest that this is far from being the case. We shall return to this issue when discussing the economic aspects of transport forecasting modeling.

Improved traffic management, including the adoption of electronic ITSs, has the same effect as building more capacity. It allows more vehicles to use a road, but, without any system of limiting entry, simply leads to additional traffic bringing the flow back to the initial level. As an example, the perennially congested south-western stretch of the M25 ring road around London has been fitted with an experimental automated traffic control system called Motorway Incident Detection and Automatic Signalling (MIDAS). This consists of a distributed network of traffic and weather sensors, speed cameras, and variable-speed signs that control traffic speeds with little human supervision, but has done little to alleviate traffic problems.

Subsidize Fewer Congestion-causing Modes

Some modes of transport can technically make more efficient use of infrastructure than others, and thus there are arguments advanced for stimulating their use rather than congestion-inducing modes such as the motorcar. In the road context, the most common approach is to subsidize public transport modes. Buses, trams, and metro systems can in most circumstances when fully loaded move more people than the motorcar for a given land-take. In terms of the standard congestion diagram, subsidizing, say, a bus service shifts the demand for car use down and to the left, as seen in Figure 9.7. The welfare implications are that, whereas without any congestion initiatives there is a loss of ABC, by attracting some travelers from the car to a bus the loss declines to abc. Congestion costs remain, because the lower generalized costs of road use will cause some people who did not travel before to make trips, but they are normally reduced.

This type of policy has attractions, especially in circumstances when the subsidies also benefit low-income public transport services. There are, however, often difficulties. For the subsidies to stimulate a significant traffic effect, there must be a relatively high-fare cross-elasticity of demand. As we have seen in Chapter 4,

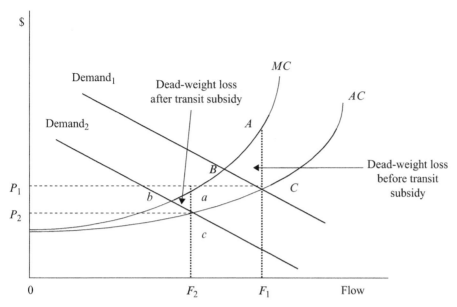

Figure 9.7   *The effects on road traffic of subsidizing rapid transit*

the cross-elasticities between modes often tend to be relatively low. The general evidence suggests that lowering fares often has little impact when it comes to attracting traffic to buses; at the extreme one can witness the reluctance of school-children to use free and convenient 'yellow buses' once they can drive a car. There is some limited support for the position that improved service (speed, frequency, and reliability), and especially in terms of rapid transit systems, can affect modal transfers to some extent, but this is an expensive option.

The second issue is that there are generally dead-weight losses associated with subsidies that we touched upon in Chapter 7, and just highlight again in a slightly different way.

First, a subsidy will result in a simple loss in terms of waste in the public transport sector. In Figure 9.8 it is assumed that the public transit undertaking, which for simplicity we assume has its own track, is run effectively and is eco-nomically priced. Further, and just for ease of exposition, it is assumed that the marginal cost of each public transport passenger is constant, thus giving an initial fare of F_1. A subsidy is then introduced to reduce fares to F_2 to attract travelers from their automobiles. The cost of that subsidy is the shaded area F_1F_2bc: the subsidy times the number of passengers that ultimately use the public transport. Part of the subsidy goes to the P_{as_1} passengers who are already riders, and the rest to those who give up their cars. Those already on public transport enjoy a transfer of money from tax-payers; this has no resource effects if prices elsewhere in the economy are optimal, although there are differential effects on bus-riders and tax-payers.

The amount that is needed to stimulate the $P_{as_1} - P_{as_2}$ transfer to public transport entails a degree of waste. In this case it is equal to an amount abc in the figure. This is a loss because while the P_{as_1}th transfer needs the full subsidy

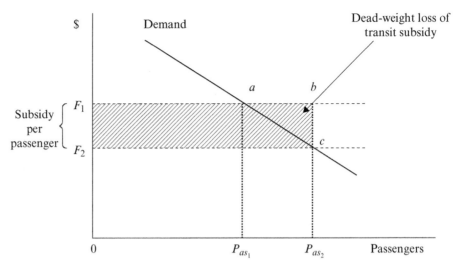

Figure 9.8 *The dead-weight losses of subsidies*

to cause the transfer, the P_{as_2}th person needs very little. But, in addition to this, there is also the potential for significant X-inefficiency in terms of the ways that subsidies are used. Much depends, as we saw in the previous chapter, on the way in which subsidies are awarded to public transport suppliers.

9.10 'Micromobility'

The notion of 'micromobility' is far from new. Walking and horse-riding are, of course, the traditional forms, but more recently the term refers to small, light-weight vehicles operating at speeds typically below 15 mph and driven by users. It includes the likes of bicycles, push-scooters, e-bicycles, e-scooters, e-skateboards, Segways, and electric pedal-assisted bicycles. While favored because of many positive environmental attributes, such as being low noise generators and fuel efficient, they are also seen as a way of reducing local traffic congestion. They not only take up little space while in motion but also when they are parked. Added to this, many of them are amenable to ride-sharing, and especially so with the development of GPS systems for locating them, smartphones for booking them, and electronic payment allowing the use of dockless technologies.

As a public transport mode, some forms of micromobility, such as Segways, were limited in their uptake probably because they require some practice to ride and involve high investment costs. But the short-term rental of bicycles, initially in Copenhagen in 1995 but then in Washington DC and other United States cities, became popular. By 2016 there were 42,000 shared bicycles across the United States. A key development occurred in 2013 when dockless bicycle-sharing emerged. Low initial and operating expenses, combined with local authority financial support in some cities, made the mode convenient and economical for customers. The arrival of the e-scooter soon followed, superseding the dockless bicycle in many places. Bird, a company based in Santa Monica, California, first deployed e-scooters in 2017. Within a year, the company expanded to over 100 United States cities and 11 international cities, and supplied over 10 million rides. Spin, based in San Francisco, started as a bicycle-sharing business and began to switch to e-scooters when the Ford Motor Company purchased it for nearly $100 million in 2018. Lime, which also started as a bicycle-sharing business, expanded into e-scooters in 2018 and by early 2020 was operating in over 100 cities in the United States, along with 27 international cities, accumulating over 11.5 million rides. The arrival of Covid-19 in 2020 stymied the rapid growth of the mode for at least a period.

E-scooters often meet a demand that current services do not, or only do so in a second-best way (Button et al., 2020). They may, therefore, not be a good substitute for congestion-causing automobiles or conventional forms of public transit. Their use may be as an alternative to walking or using another micromobility mode. Scooter rides are, for example, typically under two miles, which is often a distance too short for hailing a taxi or a transportation network company ride with, say, Uber. Robert Noland (2019), studying journey purposes of about 80,000 Bird and Lime e-scooter trips in Louisville, Kentucky, where 82 percent of commuters drive alone and 9 percent carpool, found that the average trip duration by scooter between August 9, 2018 and February 28, 2019 was 15.59 minutes and distance was 1.33 miles. Similar average distances were recorded in Indianapolis.

E-scooters, and most other micromobility modes, also generate a variety of safety and other issues. Their use on side-walks poses problems for pedestrians by creating congestion and endangering them. Nikan Namiri et al. (2020), for example, found that between 2014 and 2018 more than 39,000 e-scooter injuries occurred in the United States, with the annual number involving millennials increasing from 582 to 5,309 over the period. One-quarter of the injuries involved a broken bone, and one-third were to the head, double the rate of bicyclists' injuries. There is also a question mark over the financial viability of e-scooter companies. They operate in a very competitive market with free entry and exit, and few made a profit prior to the Covid-19 disruptions. These are common features of a lack of an economic core of the type discussed in Chapter 7. The resultant market instability reduces the likelihood that commuters and others will adopt e-scooter-riding on a large scale.

References

Albert, G. and Mahalel, D. (2006) Congestion tolls and parking fees: a comparison of the potential effect on travel behavior, *Transport Policy*, 13, 496–502.

Arnott, R., de Palma, A., and Lindsey, R. (1993) A structural model of peak-period congestion: a traffic bottleneck with elastic demand, *American Economic Review*, 83, 161–79.

Börjesson, M., Eliasson, J., and Hamilton, C.J. (2016) Why experience changes attitudes to congestion pricing: the case of Gothenburg, *Transportation Research Part A*, 85, 1–16.

Börjesson, M., Eliasson, J., Hugosson, M.B., and Brundell-Freij, K. (2012) The Stockholm congestion charges – 5 years on: effects, acceptability and lessons learnt, *Transport Policy*, 20, 1–12.

Brueckner, J.K. (2002) Airport congestion when carriers have market power, *American Economic Review*, 92, 1357–75.

Brueckner, J.K. (2005) Internalization of airport congestion: a network analysis, *International Journal of Industrial Organization*, 23, 599–614.

Button, K.J. (1984) Road pricing: an outsider's view of American experiences, *Transport Reviews*, 4, 73–98.

Button, K.J. (2006a) How should the revenues from congestion pricing be spent? in G. Roth (ed.), *Street Smart: Competition, Entrepreneurship, and the Future of Roads*, The Independent Institute.

Button, K.J. (2006b) The political economy of parking charges in 'first' and 'second-best' worlds, *Transport Policy*, 13, 470–78.

Button, K.J. (2007) Auctions: what can we learn from auction theory for slot allocation? in A. Czerny, P. Forsyth, D. Gillen, and H.M. Niemeier (eds), *How to Make Slot Markets Work*, Ashgate.

Button, K.J. (2008) Issues in airport runway capacity charging and allocation, *Journal of Transport Economics and Policy*, 42, 563–85.

Button, K.J. (2020) The transition from Pigou's ideas on road pricing to their application, *Journal of the History of Economic Thought*, 42, 417–38.

Button, K.J. and Vega, H. (2007) The costs of setting up and operating electronic road pricing in cities, *Traffic Engineering and Control*, 48, 6–10.

Button, K.J., Frye, H.F., and Reaves, D. (2020) Economic regulation and e-scooter networks in the USA, *Research in Transportation Economics*, 84, No 100973.

Coase, R.H. (1960) The problem of social cost, *Journal of Law and Economics*, 3, 1–44.

De Palma, A., Kilani, M., and Lindsey, R. (2008) The merits of separating cars and trucks, *Journal of Urban Economics*, 64, 340–61.

Duranton, G. and Turner, M.A. (2011) The fundamental law of road congestion: evidence from US cities, *American Economic Review*, 101, 2616–52.

Goodwin, P.B. (1989) The rule of three: a possible solution to the political problem of competing objectives for road pricing, *Traffic Engineering and Control*, 29, 495–7.

Graham, D.J. and Glaister, S. (2006) Spatial implications of transport pricing, *Journal of Transport Economics and Policy*, 40, 173–201.

Gu, Z., Liu, Z., Qixiu, C., and Saberi, M. (2018) Congestion pricing practices and public acceptance: a review of evidence, *Case Studies on Transport Policy*, 6, 94–101.

Haralambides, H.E. (2002) Competition, excess capacity, and the pricing of port infrastructure, *International Journal of Maritime Economics*, 4, 323–47.

Harback, K.T. and Daniel, J.J. (2007) (When) Do hub airlines internalize their self-imposed congestion delays? *Journal of Urban Economics*, 63, 613–30.

Hensher, D.A. and King, J. (2001) Parking demand and responsiveness to supply, price and location in Sydney central business district, *Transportation Research Part A*, 35, 177–96.

Jones, P. (1998) Urban road pricing: public acceptability and barriers to implementation, in K.J. Button and E.T. Verhoef (eds), *Road Pricing, Traffic Congestion and the Environment: Issues of Efficiency and Social Feasibility*, Edward Elgar Publishing.

Leape, J. (2006) The London congestion charge, *Journal of Economic Perspectives*, 20, 157–76.

Lehe, L. (2019) Downtown congestion pricing in practice, *Transportation Research Part C*, 100, 200–23.

Mayer, C. and Sinai, T. (2003) Network effects, congestion externalities, and air traffic delays: or why not all delays are evil, *American Economic Review*, 93, 1194–215.

Morrison, S.A. (1986) A survey of road pricing, *Transportation Research*, 20A, 87–97.

Morrison, S.A. and Winston, C. (2008) Another look at airport congestion pricing, *American Economic Review*, 97, 1970–77.

Namiri, N.K., Lui, H., and Tangney, T. (2020) Electric scooter injuries and hospital admissions in the United States, 2014–2018, *Journal of the American Medical Association Surgery*, January 8, doi:10.1001/jamasurg.2019.5423.

Noland, R.B. (2019) Trip patterns and revenue of shared e-scooters in Louisville, Kentucky, *Transport Findings*, April, https://doi.org/10.32866/7747.

Pels, E. and Verhoef, E.T. (2004) The economics of airport congestion pricing, *Journal of Urban Economics*, 55, 257–77.

Quddus, M.A., Carmel, A., and Bell, M.G.H. (2007) The impact of the congestion charge on retail: the London experience, *Journal of Transport Economics and Policy*, 41, 113–34.

Rassenti, S.J., Smith, V., and Bulfin, R. (1982) A combinational auction mechanism for airport time slot allocation, *Bell Journal of Economics*, 13, 369–84.

Sharp, C.H. (1966) Congestion and welfare, an examination of the case for a congestion tax, *Economic Journal*, 76, 806–17.

Shoup, D. (2005) *The High Costs of Parking*, American Planning Association.

Small, K.A. (1992) Using revenue from congestion pricing, *Transportation*, 19, 359–81.

Sorensen, P.A. and Taylor, B.D. (2006) Innovations in road finance: examining the growth in electronic tolling, *Public Works Management and Policy*, 11, 110–25.

Verhoef, E.T. (2002) Second-best congestion pricing in general static transportation networks with elastic demands, *Regional Science and Urban Economics*, 32, 281–310.

Verhoef, E.T., Nijkamp, P., and Rietveld, P. (1995) The economics of regulatory parking policies, *Transportation Research Part A*, 29, 141–56.

Verhoef, E.T., Nijkamp, P., and Rietveld, P. (1997) The social feasibility of road pricing: the case study of the Randstad Area, *Journal of Transport Economics and Policy*, 31, 255–67.

Walters, A.A. (1976) Marginal cost pricing in ports, *Logistics and Transportation Review*, 12, 99–105.

Winston, C. and Langer, A. (2006) The effect of government highway spending on road users' congestion costs, *Journal of Urban Economics*, 60, 463–83.

Young, W. (2001) Parking and traffic control, in K.J. Button and D.A. Hensher (eds), *Handbook of Transport Systems and Traffic Control*, Pergamon.

10 Economics and Transport Logistics

10.1 Introduction

The novel coronavirus (Covid-19) pandemic of the early 2020s highlighted the importance of good transport logistics. Globally, the need to move medicines, equipment, and sometimes patients put strains on the conventional supply chains in the medical field. Official lockdowns and quarantines, in addition to the sickness itself, affected workers and closed down many industrial production nodes, as well as removing numerous links in national transport networks (Guan et al., 2020). Tackling this required a rapid reorientation of complex supply lines. This, however, occurred after a period of considerable advances in the way that transport logistics was viewed and applied, and this aided the flexibility of its response.

Rapid changes in computer technology and communications over the past half-century and the arrival of 'big data', together with more flexible and rapid transport, has inevitably produced a more complicated market for transport services. Overlapping this have been developments in production technology and the emergence of a sophisticated financial system. And spatially coinciding with this has been the creation of global markets. To take advantage of these developments there has been considerable integration of various supply chains, with, at the same time, greater diversity in the nature of these chains. Economic factors have been instrumental in the forms by which transport has fitted into these chains while economists have been heavily engaged in analysing them.

Economists have long recognized that transport services are not provided in isolation. The very fact that they appreciate that transport providers are confronted by a derived demand curve makes this explicit. It has also been made clear in our earlier discussion of the value chain concept. For a variety of reasons, not least of which were the technical ability to do it and a rapidly growing demand for international trade facilitation, the larger notion of transport logistics began to be developed in the 1990s. This is effectively a more holistic way of looking at transportation, in effect redefining its boundaries to move outside of the simple movement of goods or people from A to B.

Optimizing supply chains is very much a matter of maximizing the efficiency of resource allocations and considering the best way of using scarce resources. It is about opportunity costs and thus it is about economics. Many of the findings of the work that has been done in the supply-chain field, however, have tended to appear in the management literature, or specialized logistics publications, rather than in mainstream economics journals. This is not the place to consider why this is so, although there has certainly been an element of the practical leading the theoretical in many of the developments that have taken place in supply-chain management, and much of the recent economic literature, supply modeling, and analysis has tended to be rather abstract in its orientation (Friesz and Kwon, 2007). Here we focus on the main areas where there are differences or refinements in the way that economics is applied, compared to that which is often covered in the more conventional transport economics texts.

The chapter is largely about the private provision of logistics services, but this provision is always within institutional and policy frameworks. The latter are largely taken as given, and only discussed when of immediate relevance to the economics of an issue. But they are relevant and one reason why modern transport logistics has grown in importance in business is that there have been significant changes in the legal constructs under which transport services, and trade more generally, can be delivered.

In addition, the focus is largely on the private sector businesses, although there are also issues involving the provision and management of public sector transport infrastructure. For example, the scale and quality of publicly owned transport road and rail networks, airports, and seaports affect such things as warehouse distribution, trans-shipments, and the extent to which just-in-time management of the supply chain is possible. This also raises economic issues of a different kind, namely how to appraise public infrastructure investments. The conventional cost–benefit procedures that we consider in Chapter 11 would appear inadequate to the extent that they do not fully encapsulate the benefits throughout the supply chain. This is not a topic dealt with in any depth here, but really reflects the limited partial equilibrium nature of the economic cost–benefit approach.

10.2   Transport Logistics

Transport logistics has a long history. In many ways, it is the adoption of transport economic principles within a larger supply-chain concept. Definitions of what exactly transport logistics entails are not always precise, but the general idea is that it involves relationships between transport and integrated approaches to logistics and supply-chain management. In other words, it involves the movement of goods through the supply chain, but is more than just the freight transport aspect and embraces the full commercial and operational frameworks within which the movement of goods is planned, managed, and finally carried out.

The modern, large-scale academic study of civilian transport logistics started around the early 1990s, when many of the current approaches were originally developed, but there was both an implicit interest in it which went back centuries, and a more systematic study of military logistics from classical times.

Logistics has always been important for the military, and transporting men and equipment to the battle-front in a timely and coordinated fashion has since the time of Alexander the Great given armies a decided advantage. The advent of mechanized transport and of massive, often conscripted armies has made the task more complex but possibly also more important. One reason for the failure of the German army to capture Paris in 1914, for example, was the inadequacy of transport logistics support; in effect it was impossible to move the number of men and their supplies through northern France to conform with the needs of the Schlieffen Plan. More recently, the overwhelming military success of Operation Desert Storm in 1990 was in part due to the transport logistics expertise of US General William (Gus) Pagonis.

The crucial role of logistics in the civilian sector has been recognized by the appointment of logistics experts to the boards of many major corporations, positions formerly largely reserved for financial, marketing, and production executives. There are also many companies that specialize in transport logistics, in addition to the in-house divisions of companies, and in many instances this involves international activities as the 'global economy' grows and the supply chains grow longer and more complex. The educational establishment has also not been slow to recognize the modern role of logistics and many of the prestige business schools around the world offer options in logistics as elements of their MBA programs.

This change has come about for a variety of reasons; some are economic in their nature while others stem from the emergence of new technologies. Before looking at some of these in a little more detail, two over-riding trends have been important in shaping the form of modern logistics. First, the length of freight hauls has increased due to wider outsourcing and new approaches to centralization, inventory holding, and terminal capacity. This means that production is now more transport-intensive. Second, there has been a 'time compression' in production and distribution that has put pressures on the system for more rapid delivery of intermediate and final goods. This, in turn, has reduced inventory holdings, making the production chain more vulnerable to disruptions in the transport system.

At the more meso level, in terms of technology, the advent of the container in the 1960s, and the fact that Malcom McLean did not seek any patent on his invention, revolutionized the way that movement of semi-bulk cargoes could be conducted, reducing the costs of movement almost immediately. In 1983 United States foreign ocean-borne commerce was 694.4 million metric tons; ten years later, this had increased to 884.4 million metric tons. Ten years after that, it had magnified to 1,167.9 million metric tons, nearly doubling in just 20 years. Growth of this magnitude is only physically possible with the use of containers.

The container not only cuts the costs of individual movements by a single mode of transport, but speeds up and cuts the cost of trans-shipments and con-solidations between modes, making inter-modal transport a viable form of freight movement. Inter-modal freight transport is movement of cargo in a container using multiple modes of transport (rail, ship, and truck) without any handling of the freight itself when changing modes. It also allows for easier handling of mixed types of cargo on a single mode: a container can have its own refrigeration unit or can be a 'tank' within a container-sized frame. The standardization of the unit being carried allows for economies of scale in the cost of manufacturing ships, wagons, etc. A container is also relatively easy to track, and can be sealed to enhance security.

The types of goods being carried have also changed, in part because of the availability of container transport and in-vehicle storage facilities (for example, refrigeration). There are more high-value, less-bulking commodities being moved, and their origins and destinations are more dispersed than with most primary products. Their value means that holding large inventories can be costly and that there are often economies in minimizing warehousing and storage. Inventory management requires reliable delivery to ensure that goods and components are available at the right time and undamaged. 'Just-in-time production' requires complex logistics, including information systems, to ensure the generalized cost of the supply chain is minimized.

Supply chains vary in their form and scale depending on factors such as whether they are domestic or international, involve perishable goods, are mainly bulk commodities, the costs of inventory holding, and whether special services are required, such as refrigeration (Meixell and Gargeya, 2005). They can also vary by direction, for example involving the movement of bulk commodities in one direction and exotics, such as agricultural products, in the other. They are also frequently multi-modal, often involving collection and delivery by one mode but trunk haul by another. In some circumstances there may be considerable inter-action between the freight supply chain and passenger transport; for example, trucks and cars share road space, and many 'passenger' aircraft carry freight in their belly holds.

In terms of economics, the logistics supply chain may be thought of as a set of interdependent markets, or in some cases a single market, for transportation services. Figure 10.1 provides a very simple illustration of the air cargo supply chain.

In depicting this, we assume that air is the chosen mode of transport, which will itself be an economic decision; in some circumstances road or rail may be an option, and in a few cases, maritime transport. The shippers may either send goods directly through their own regional distribution centers, may engage an integrated carrier, such as UPS or FedEx, that offers door-to-door multi-modal services, or may go to a freight forwarder that basically offers wholesale services. The decision on which option to take is economic and involves considering the generalized costs of the alternatives *vis-à-vis* their respective services. This is a market decision. But there are also submarkets in the chain. While the shipper may select a specific airfreight forwarder, that forwarder will obtain capacity from air cargo carriers by bidding for space.

Looked at from the supply side, the various air cargo chains that co-exist reflect the different business models that exist which in turn can be explained in economic terms. Ronald Coase (1937) provides the classic economic reason for different types of industrial structure, and why firms exist. The main reason stems from the existence of transaction costs. He argues that a firm's interactions

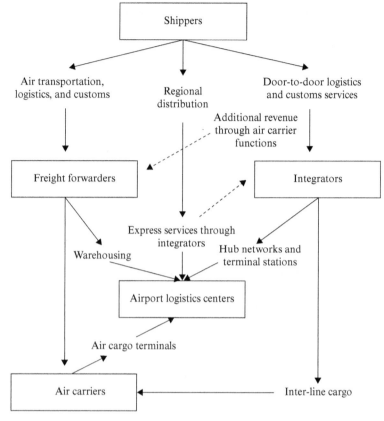

Source: Derived from Kasarda et al. (2004).

Figure 10.1   *The supply chain for air cargo*

within a market may not be under its control, but the firm's internal allocation
of resources are. Consequently, the integrated suppliers that manage the chain
internally cater mainly for small, high-value goods that require rapid and reliable
service, whereas the use of forwarders reflects the need for less structured but
cheaper services that accompany more general cargoes.

10.3   The Costs of Warehousing and Inventory Holdings

Savings in freight travel time are an important, although not always the most
crucial, indicator of improvements in the efficiency of freight transport. The
methods of valuing such savings for use in the economic analysis of firms, or for
forecasting aggregate traffic flows in transport infrastructure planning, are akin
to those that are used in valuing passengers' travel time savings (see Chapter 4).
The savings, however, can be related to several units –for example, to truck trips,
ship sailings, or rail wagons – in addition to the actual item being transported.
Table 10.1 offers a survey of the sorts of results that have emerged across a range

Table 10.1   *Value of time in goods transport by rail, inland waterways, trucking, and air transport*

Publication	Country	Data	Method	Value of travel time savings
Rail transport				*€ per transport hour*
Inregia (2001)	Sweden	SP	Logit	0 (shipment)
De Jong et al. (2004)	Netherlands	SP	Logit	918 (train)
Air transport				
Inregia (2001)	Sweden	SP	Logit	13 (shipment)
De Jong et al. (2004)	Netherlands	SP	Logit	7935 (full carrier)
Trucking				
Small et al. (1999)	United States	SP	Logit	174–267
Bergkvist (2001)	Sweden	SP	Logit+WML	3–47
De Jong et al. (2001)	France	SP+RP	Logit	5–11
Fowkes et al. (2001)	United Kingdom	SP	Logit	40
Inregia (2001)	Sweden	SP	Logit	0–32
Kurri (2000)	Finland	SP	Logit	1.53
De Jong et al. (2004)	Netherlands	SP	Logit	4.74
Rail transport				
Vieira (1992)	United States	SP/RP	Ordered Logit	0.65
Kurri et al. (2000)	Finland	SP	Logit	0.09
De Jong et al. (2000)	Netherlands	SP	Logit	0.96
Inland waterways				
Blauwens & Van de Voorde (1998)	Belgium	RP	Logit	0.09
De Jong et al. (2004)	Netherlands	SP	Logit	0.05
Trucking				
Kurri et al. (2000)	Finland	SP	Logit	1.53
De Jong et al. (2004)	Netherlands	SP	Logit	4.74
Fowkes et al. (2004)	United Kingdom	SP	Logit	0.08–1.18

Notes: SP = stated preference models; RP = revealed preference models.

Source: Adapted from De Jong (2008). This chapter contains the full references to the studies cited.

of studies covering inland waterways, air transport, railroads, and trucking, taking account of the country to which the study relates, the type of data used, and the methodology adopted.

There are wide variations in the results, and drawing general conclusions is not simple. Much depends on what is being carried: saving a few hours for a ton of coal may not be worth a great deal, but delays in supplying a crucial component for a damaged piece of equipment may be very costly. Modes of transport can also be important because of their particular security and safety features as well as their position in the supply chain. We also note that most of the studies that have been undertaken have used stated-preference techniques and these would in general seem to generate relatively high values for time savings than the small number of revealed-preference studies cited.

Freight is not always on the move in the logistics supply chain, but is periodically held in storage. The economics of warehousing is essentially about efficient inventory holding. The role of a warehouse is that of storage. Referring again to Figure 1.2 in Chapter 1, warehouses can also be seen as providing for consolidation and points between elements in the value chain, but we leave discussion of that role until the next section. Warehousing, within the narrow, traditional context, serves several functions (Ackerman and Brewer, 2001):

- Accumulations of raw materials for distribution further down the supply chain.
- Storage of in-process inventory at various points in the logistics pipeline.
- Storage of finished goods near the point of production.
- Storage of wholesale or retail inventory pending distribution to final customers.

From an economics perspective, warehousing is a clear cost. There are the fixed and variable costs of the warehousing activity, but there are also the costs of holding inventory in the system. There are the direct costs of having assets sitting in a warehouse, but added to these are the costs of physical decay of the products, their potential redundancy in the supply chain (a major concern for fashion items), and the danger of theft or damage being done. The benefits of warehousing come from reducing risk in the system, for example by having spare stock to meet contingencies, and from allowing economies of scale in production and in transport. In the context of the latter, it allows larger units to be transported less frequently.

One aspect of inventory optimization that has gained in importance in recent years relates less to the area served by a producing unit and rather more to the area served by warehouses. Changes in transport technology and information systems combined with the increased importance of high-value, low-weight manufactures in the economy has brought forth new physical distribution systems. The traditional model (Figure 10.2) assumed a trade-off between warehousing and transport with the costs of operating warehouses rising with their number but transport costs falling, assuming a constant throughput of goods. The optimal number of warehouses would be determined by minimizing the combined costs of warehousing and transport (that is, Q_w).

Modifications have incorporated the costs of holding inventories, essentially warehousing and handling, into the calculations that, in the simplest of terms, argue that variations in the costs of holding inventories follows the 'square root law'. This law effectively says that safety and cycle inventory requirements are related to the square root of the number of warehouses in the system. Hence, moving from a system of ten depots to an entirely centralized system would reduce inventory requirements by 68 percent. This has provided justification for companies reducing the number of warehouses and with this the market area served by each. The break-even point for degrees of warehousing, however, is sensitive to prevailing costs of holding inventories – in effect to the interest rate.

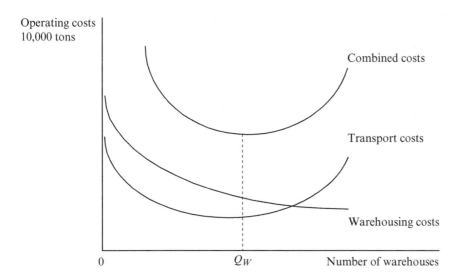

Figure 10.2   *Trade-off in transport and warehouse operating costs*

Reducing warehousing essentially means that more inventory is being held in the narrower transport system, in containers on trucks or rail cars, or in the holds of ships or aircraft (transit inventory). This has been made more attractive as the cost of tracking and tracing have fallen as telecommunications and related technologies have advanced in sophistication and fallen in cost. This has not only made the transport system more internally efficient, but, by providing more information to consignors, has given the ability to reduce inventory holdings. This is the basis for just-in-time production, or lean logistics. Some of the claimed gains that can result from just-in-time, as opposed to conventional, production are listed in Table 10.2.

The challenge is to find the optimal mix between using more transport to facilitate greater frequencies of deliveries, and greater reliability in those deliveries, and the reduction in inventory holdings. What a manager is trying to do is to optimize his or her stock, which consists of three elements:

Target stock = Forecast demand next period + Forecast demand in lead time + Safety stock

The problem is that the forecast elements have inherent uncertainty in them, and so the safety stock acts as a buffer. Improved transport systems, packaging, and information systems have effectively reduced the scale of inventory holdings required for safety purposes. Much of the rise in just-in-time practices came with the advent of 'dependent demand inventory' systems from the late 1960s, which, rather than traditional approaches that relied on forecasts premised on total demand being made up of a number of independent separate demands, focused attention on the interdependent needs for delivering a target near-term output.

Table 10.2   *The benefits of just-in-time production*

Area of improvement	Description
Productivity	Manufacturing productivity can improve by 20 to 40%
Lead times	Lead times can be reduced by more than 90%, reducing the need to carry finished goods inventories
Flexibility	Improves production flexibility, by allowing changes to the manufacturing schedule to meet changes in market demand
Market power	Market position is strengthened by the ability to supply on short notice, with greater flexibility and greater reliability
Quality	Consistency of quality improves
Inventories	Substantially reduces inventories, often by 60 to 80%
Floor space	Manufacturing floor space requirements are reduced by 30 to 40% because there is no 'waiting' inventory stacking on the floor
Investment	Capital required to operate a business is significantly reduced, estimated reductions being 25 to 50%

Source: Warne and Rowney (1986).

The possibility of more frequent deliveries means that the period over which demands are made is shorter and thus uncertainty is reduced. It is not just reduced lead times (the period between an order being placed and the delivery of that order) that are important, but also the reliability of delivery. Rail transport, for example, in the United States is often used in just-in-time manufacturing systems because of its reliability rather than its speed. Of course, higher costs of meeting short lead times need to be taken into account in the arithmetic. Figure 10.3 offers a simple illustration of the situation.

Conventional management requires that there is always a large safety stock of inventory to cope with unexpected contingencies. Alternatively, it has large and infrequent deliveries of stock that it holds in its warehouses. Just-in-time inventories are small in magnitude but the number of deliveries is larger. To maximize

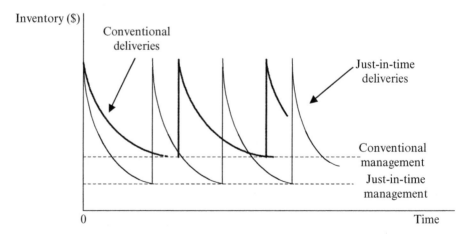

Figure 10.3   *The economics of just-in-time production*

efficiency, the manager has to set the cost of alternative delivery patterns against the level of stock that is being warehoused.

10.4   Consolidation and Trans-shipment

Warehousing is simply a storage function and adds little value to the supply chain other than providing insurance through the holding of safety stocks. In other words, a more dynamic form of warehousing involves consolidation and trans-shipment, a direct element of value added to the logistics supply chain. In this sense, when warehousing is used in this way, it becomes part of a hub-and-spoke structure that enables the suppliers in the system to benefit from economies of scope and density in the logistics chain, just as airports do in the provision of air passenger services (see Chapter 5).

To look at the optimum level of consolidation, it is useful to break down the costs involved along the lines of Figure 10.4. The diagram considers the problem in terms of the optimal payload for a delivery vehicle. The line-haul costs of moving goods to and from the consolidation point fall with the size of consignment carried due to scale effects, until the maximum physical or legal average payload on a vehicle is reached. If only haulage costs were to be considered in the warehousing decisions, then this would represent the optimal payload. However, there are also the resource costs involved with warehousing and consolidation itself: the provision of depots, handling staff, administrative costs, etc. These terminal costs are likely to rise with the level of warehousing and trans-shipment. Consequently, the logistics supply-chain manager, when considering options and

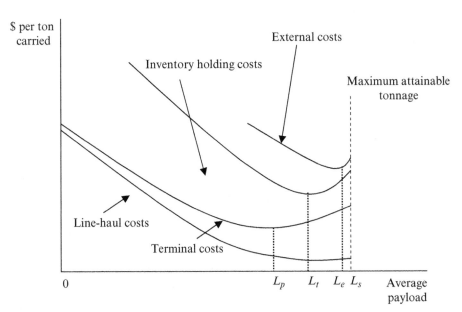

Figure 10.4   *Freight consolidation costs (represented cumulatively)*

taking both broad elements of cost into account, will feel the optimal level of consolidation would imply an average payload of L_t in the diagram.

So far, we have only looked at the terminal and movement costs confronting the transporter; however, the final customer awaiting delivery will also have costs that vary with trans-shipment levels. The greater the amount of warehousing and the larger the final average payload per vehicle, the fewer the number of deliveries that will be needed. Longer frequencies between deliveries push up the costs of stock-holding for customers and the overall level of inventories held. Thus, the time costs of increased consolidation rise with the average payload, suggesting that, overall, final recipients of goods would prefer a level of consolidation consistent with an average payload of L_t in Figure 10.4.

The diagram shows a clear distinction between the direct costs influencing the transporter's optimum and those factors affecting the final customer of the service, and it is the bringing together of these elements that supply-chain logistics embraces.

As we have seen in Chapter 6, there are also wider external costs influencing those not directly concerned with transport operations; these include those affected by vehicle noise or fumes or who have their own travel disrupted by freight vehicles. Generally, increased consolidation and higher payloads will reduce these costs, because fewer trips are needed, even if just-in-time production is part of the process, to transport the same volume of goods, and consolidation generally means less environmentally intrusive vehicles can be used in sensitive areas (Button and Pearman, 1981). Hence, from society's point of view, the optimal level of consolidation in the diagram is when all costs are minimized, that is, at point L_e.

10.5   Mode Choice

Logistics is not a transport-mode-specific activity and entails the use of a diversity of modes, either within a single logistics provider's own fleet or using forwarders and consolidators who make use of third-party transport suppliers. The way mode choices are made within a supply chain are, in economic terms, not that conceptually different from the way individuals make decisions about whether to, say, make a trip by car or bus. It is all about opportunity costs. We consider the more technical aspects of modeling and forecasting in greater detail in Chapter 12 and here just provide a flavor of the type of models that are used. We also focus on the more micro models, rather than models that are used, for example, in national network planning (Button, 2005).

One way of looking at the decision-making process of logistics service providers is to treat the alternative modes as a bundle of attributes – availability, speed, cost, capacity, security, safety, and so on – and then select the mode that comes closest to meeting the providers' requirements given their financial and other constraints. This was the approach developed some years ago by Baumol and Vinod (1970) when considering a situation where speed and economy of service are important; adding more factors complicates the mathematics but not the logic.

Speed is important to minimize the amount of 'inventory on wheels', essentially the lead time, and regular services to termini are usually preferred by consignors for their own production purposes, the possibility of delays necessitating keeping a larger safety stock. Initially the problem of safety stocks is assumed away and an iso-cost equation of this general form is used:

$$e = vp/(Kvp - 1) \qquad (10.1)$$

where:

e is the reciprocal of the shipping cost per unit of commodity;
v is the reciprocal of the average time required to complete a shipment;
p is the reciprocal; and
K is set equal to the expected annual variable cost of handling.

Allowances need to be made for uncertainty in delivery and safety stocks, and doing this provides an operational model of the form:

$$C = T/e + T/(pv) + a/s + wsT/2 + wh\{[s + (1/v)]\}\,T^{0.5} \qquad (10.2)$$

where:

C is the expected annual variable cost of handling;
T is the amount transported per year;
a is the cost of ordering and processing per shipment;
w is the warehousing cost per unit per year;
s is the average time between shipments; and
h is a parameter derived from the Poisson distribution used to simulate the stochastic elements of the problem.

The final items in equation (10.2) reflect the fact that when the timing of deliveries is uncertain, slow deliveries require larger safety stocks which increase the costs of warehousing. A shipper will select the mode of transport that will complete the delivery at the lowest annual variable cost of handling.

This approach provides guidance as to the mode that would be selected for a consignment, but not the total demand for the services of any given mode. The latter may, however, be of interest for the providers, either in the public or private sectors that provide infrastructure and operational capital (truck fleets, rail cars, ships, etc.). Aggregate demand can be assessed if it is assumed that profit maximization is the goal of the providers (which is largely realistic, say for United States railroads but not for state-owned roads); that the demand curve is linear, of the form $Dc = j - kT$; and that the safety stock is proportional to the total volume of shipments (rather than the square root specification used in equation (10.2)). This then gives:

$$T = (1/b)\{Dc - 1/e - 1/(pv) - ws/2 - wh[s + (1/v)]^{0.5}\} \qquad (10.3)$$

where Dc is the price difference between origin and destination and b is a constant equal to $-dDc/dT$.

This illustrates the fact that the annual tonnage shipped will be larger, the greater the price difference between the destination and the origin, the smaller the time taken between shipments, the smaller the time taken by a shipment, and the flatter the slope (b) of the demand curve for the commodity. However, these intuitively satisfying conclusions come at a price. The linear specification of the model is convenient for estimation purposes but may deviate significantly from reality.

The analysis of Baumol and Vinod (1970) is about warehousing and inventory management; it does not fully take account of consolidation and trans-shipment that is an integral part of many supply chains. This is often a multi-modal (inter-modal) activity – for example, using shipping for the long haul, and trucks and rail for access and egress to and from ports. The question then often becomes one of whether to use the same transport mode for the entire trip – say the truck as in Figure 10.5 – or to use a combination of modes and trans-ship or consolidate at some point in the system.

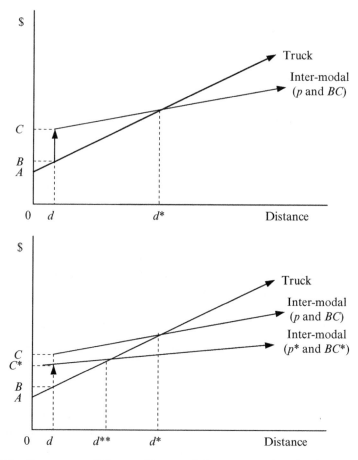

Figure 10.5   *Cost per ton of direct and inter-modal transport with and without support for trans-shipping and rail rates*

Figure 10.5 offers a simple example of what this means and the implications of technical change, or policy shifts, in terms of mode split (Beuther and Kreutzerberger, 2001). This considers an option of moving freight from A to B using either a truck or a rail/truck combination. The upper diagram shows a comparison between trucking which is a loading/unloading cost of $0A$ plus a trucking rate of r per mile. The cost by inter-modal road and rail is $0A$ plus AB (the cost of using a truck over distance $0d$) plus the trans-shipment cost of BC plus a rail rate of p per mile. The cut-off point in the figure, when inter-modal transport becomes less costly than rail, is at $0d^*$. The relative mile rates of the r and p, combined with the trans-shipment costs, determines this point. If there are technical changes, which one may think of in terms of the advent of container technology, whereby these parameters are reduced so that $BC^* < BC$ and $p^* < p$, then this will shift the comparative advantages of the alternatives; the threshold distance would decrease to $d^* < d$ for inter-modal transport.

A further aspect of mode choice is the extent to which third-party logistics, the employment of an outside transport operator and logistics suppliers, should be engaged and the degree to which a company should operate its own private transport fleet ('own account operations' in the United Kingdom). Many of the largest fleets of trucks are used to haul a company's own products, as can be seen in Table 10.3. There were more than 200,000 companies, excluding farmers, operating private fleets in the United States in 2018 and these accounted for 68 percent of the outbound freight.

Surveys conducted over the years, such as that in the United Kingdom and reported in Table 10.4, suggest that simple costs of carriage do not dominate decisions regarding whether third-party carriage use, but broader notions of costs and quality of service, such as reliability, security, and flexibility, also play a role. While the exact weights placed on the individual items inevitably vary with industrial sector and the size of companies, as well as changing over time, the items listed remain much the same. Globalization, lead-time reductions, customer orientation, and outsourcing have, for example, been important considerations

Table 10.3   *Largest private truck fleet operators in the United States (2018)*

Company	Industry	City	Vehicles[a]
AT&T	Utilities & like services	San Antonio	66,879
PepsiCo	Food products	Plano	62,400
Comcast Corp.	Business or home services	Philadelphia	37,000
Waste Management	Sanitation	Houston	32,056
Verizon Communications	Utilities & like services	Elmont	20,011
Time Warner Cable	Business or home services	Charlotte	19,903
Quanta Services Inc. & subs	Construction	Houston & subs	18,920
Republic Services Inc.	Sanitation	Phoenix	18,652
Waste Connections & Operating Co.	Sanitation	The Woodlands	15,574
CenturyLink	Utilities & like services	Denver	15,319

Note: a. The composition of vehicle fleets can vary considerably between operators. AT&T, for example, had 49 tractors and 66,830 trucks whereas PepsiCo had 14,300 tractors and 48,100 trucks.

Table 10.4   *Reasons for electing to use a company's own truck fleet*

Factor	Score
Reliability	14.9
Control	13.0
Customer relations	9.4
Speed of delivery	9.2
Flexibility	7.8
Cost versus price	7.4
Ability of 'own account' to meet timing constraints	6.6
Price is subordinate to service considerations	6.5
Specialized capacity	5.5
Speed of response	5.1
Adaptability	3.6
Consistency	3.5
Avoidance of damage of consignment	3.4
Security	2.6
Other (non-financial)	1.1
Other (financial)	0.5

Source: UK Department of Transport (1979).

since the 1990s. Further, new firms from different fields have entered the market, competing with traditional transport and warehousing firms to offer different packages of service attributes (Hertz and Alfredsson, 2003).

10.6   Urban Logistics

Many of the challenges in logistics involve collection and delivery in urban areas; often called the 'last-mile problem'. This may be misleading because urban freight transport can involve four types of movement: in, out, within, and through, and clearly the latter may not be the last mile of a trip. At the same time, because collection and delivery is often done by road transport that uses a common infrastructure with passenger modes, and can involve numerous stops, urban distribution can add more than proportionately to larger traffic congestion problems.

What constitutes urban freight transport in this context is not, however, clearly defined. There has, for an example, been a considerable reduction compared with 50 years ago, in the number of household deliveries of goods; people collect them from stores, and particularly large hyper- and supermarkets. Should this be treated as part of this 'last-mile problem' or is it part of consumption behavior? The issue may be seen in terms of whether the purpose of a trip is explicitly to transport freight, but even here it is not always easy to separate out the urban logistics part of a multi-purpose trip from, say, that part involving getting to or from work (D'Este, 2007). We have a joint product situation in these circumstances.

Table 10.5 provides a categorization of the various commercial transport segments serving the urban market. It shows quite distinct market segments meeting

Table 10.5   *The market sectors of urban freight*

Market sector	Truck type	Commodity	Load type	Route	Trip type
Courier	Small	Mixed	LTL	Variable	Very complex linked trips
General carrier	Intermediate size	Mixed	LTL or FTL	Variable	Variable – simple or linked trips
Specialist commodities (e.g. bulk liquid)	Large	Specific	FTL	Regular	Mostly simple trips
Over-sized/hazardous	Large	Specific	FTL	Fixed	Simple trips
External	Large	Mixed or specific	FTL	Regular	Simple trips – external to/from a single point

Note: LTL = less than truck-load; FTL = full truck-load.

the demands for carriage of various types of commodity. From a transport economic perspective, no single market structure emerges. Couriers, for example, that often include integrated suppliers such as FedEx, DHL, and UPS, offer extensive networks of service with multiple local pick-up and delivery points – often a *de facto* personal service – and there are clear economies of scope and density involved. Other, more specialized types of service have simpler networks and are thus more amenable to competitive supply.

Improving urban logistics can have significant economic benefits for their users. Table 10.6 offers a few examples of both the importance of local freight transport, but also some of the gains that have come about by enhancing the system. Of course, there have also been failures when inappropriate changes have been made. As with any activity, the costs of change must be set against the benefits, and in the urban logistics case there are such issues as the relative costs of changing the entire distribution network as opposed to making marginal changes to elements of it. The more complex the network, the more difficult it is generally to change the entire system.

Table 10.6   *The estimated benefits of improved urban distribution systems*

Supply-chain study	Scope of study	Estimated savings
Kurt Salmon Associates	US dry grocery sector	10.8% of sales turnover (2.5% financial, 8.5% cost); total supply chain $30 billion, warehouse supplier dry sector $10 billion; supply chain cut by 41% from 104 to 61 days
Coca-Cola supply chain	127 European companies focused on cost reduction from the end of manufacturing line	2.3–3.4% of sales turnover (60% to retailers, 40% to manufacturers)
ECR Europe	15 value-chain analyses (10 European manufacturers, 5 retailers), 15 product categories, 7 distribution	5.7% of sales turnover (4.8% operating costs, 0.9% inventory cost); total supply chain saving of $21 billion; UK savings $2 billion

Source: Adapted from Fiddis (1997). This paper contains the full references to the studies cited.

The nature of urban logistics systems and retail systems differs between countries, and this can partly be explained in terms of the market power within the specific supply chain and the motivations of the various actors. For example, Alan Mitchell (1997) pointed to the fact that most German and French retailers traditionally tended to be privately owned or franchised operations and largely motivated by volumes of sales and price when planning their strategic positioning.

In contrast, United Kingdom firms tend to be publicly quoted companies motivated by margins, and thus have a more constructive approach to their suppliers, including transport services. The United States system also differs because there is greater market segmentation, wholesalers have more power in the supply chain, and there is more focus on customer promotions and greater government intervention in the market, especially regarding anti-trust issues. These factors determine the bargaining ability of the transport suppliers in the market and the types of services that are demanded from them. In the United Kingdom, for example, the shift has largely been to one controlled by retailers, with their needs being pushed through to the transport market. This, combined with the long-established deregulated trucking market (following the 1968 Transport Act) that offers significantly lower cost services, has meant the widespread use of third-party logistics in the United Kingdom, but a slower uptake in the United States.

10.7   Green Logistics

Chapters 6 and 8 focused on some of the major environmental challenges imposed by transport, and on the economic implications of some of the ways of reducing, if not always removing, them. Here we focus specifically on the economic aspects of reducing the environmental costs of the larger freight supply chain. This has been a subject of increasing interest as trade, both within and between countries, has grown and the supply chain has become more extended. Interest has extended beyond traditional environmental groups and government to embrace trade bodies and many logistics service suppliers.

The supply chain makes use of a diverse range of transport inputs that in turn impact upon the environment. These differ sometimes from the environmental externalities associated with passenger modes because they can involve what is carried as well as the pure transport-generated environmental externalities, but from an economic perspective can largely be treated in the same way. While there are market incentives for the private sector to adopt greener logistics supply chains, official policies have also been deployed, mainly to reduce energy consumption. A range of policy options are available, but while there are a variety of approaches, the pros and cons of the alternatives, with some minor nuances, are largely the same as with passenger transport (Martin et al., 1995). They often entailed the types of measures outlined in Chapter 8 for transport more generally, but in addition there are often specific measures covering elements of the logistics supply chain. Table 10.7 provides details of the potential impact of some strategies that have been considered to foster fuel consumption and thus also

Table 10.7   *Macro studies on fuel consumption of impacts of alternative logistics structures*

Country	Time period	Main measures	Changes in energy consumption	
			Business as usual	With rationalization
Netherlands	1990–2015	Increased fuel efficiency; consolidation of loads; reduced empty running; large modal shift to rail	+47	−46
Germany	1988–2010	Improved fuel efficiency; large modal shift to rail; higher vehicle utilization; shorter distances traveled	+55	+28
United Kingdom	1995–2020	Halving the rate of ton-miles growth to 10% per decade; large modal shift to rail & water	+56	−4.4

Source: Adapted from McKinnon (2003).

CO_2 emissions. What they do not show, however, are the detailed mechanisms for bringing this about, nor the costs that these changes would impose on the supply chains involved.

Logistics also plays a reverse role in the larger production process in terms of product returns, source reduction, recycling, material substitution, reuse of materials, waste disposal, and refurbishing, repair, and remanufacturing. This is known as 'reverse logistics'. The combination of making the transport element of the overall supply chain more environmentally benign and the role of reverse logistics in optimizing the use of resources in the entire production process through the facilitation of recycling, refurbishment, and so on of products is known as 'green logistics'. It is a wider approach to the interactions of transport and the environment than simply making transport *per se* less environmentally intrusive (Rodrigue et al., 2001). From a narrow economic perspective, the commercial advantage to the transport industry of such things as recycling and refurbishment is that it can provide return loads and thus reduce the back-haul problem.

Recycling and refurbishment is growing in importance, not just for environmental reasons but also as a simple commercial proposition. Some examples of the gains from recycling compared to entirely new extraction and processing include 95 percent energy and air pollution savings for aluminum, between 40 and 73 percent for paper, 5 and 30 percent for glass, and 20 and 60 percent for steel. The amount of recycling that takes place varies by commodity and between countries; for example, the United Kingdom recycled 42 percent of steel packaging in 2002, with Belgium recycling 93 percent, Germany 79 percent, and the Netherlands 78 percent. The European average

Table 10.8   *Amounts of hazardous goods moved in the United States (2017)*

Mode	Million tons	Billion ton-miles	Average miles per shipment
For-hire truck	932.7	92.1	153
Private truck	882.2	34.7	28
Rail	90.4	61.7	640
Water	304.2	60.9	72
Air (incl. truck & air)	0.3	0.2	1,333
Pipeline	679.8	n.a.	n.a.
Parcel, postal, & courier	0.3	0.2	949
Other	78.1	75.3	4

Note: n.a. = not available.

Source: US Bureau of Transportation Statistics.

was 60 percent. Outside of Europe, the figure for Australia was 43 percent, Korea 47 percent, the United States 59 percent, South Africa 63 percent, and Japan 86 percent.

Some materials moved are also hazardous – especially certain chemicals – and command-and-control instruments involving routing, timing, and packaging are often adopted to minimize any external costs of spillage (Hancock, 2001). This applies to cargoes carried by water, pipeline, and air, as well as road and rail. The amounts involved are quite large, about 10 percent of the total ton-miles of freight movement being done in the United States. Table 10.8 offers some indication of the ways in which this is moved and the distances involved. The importance of railroads and multi-modal transport for long-distance movements is clear.

Command-and-control instruments are preferred over pricing largely because of the transaction costs involved. It is relatively easy to highlight hazardous loads by signs on vehicles and this makes enforcement of such things as routings and use of specified infrastructure, such as designated lanes on freeways, relatively easy. There is clearly, however, a quasi-pricing mechanism involved through the insurance market and in many cases compulsory insurance coverage is used to complement command-and-control instruments.

10.8   International Logistics

The major growth in international trade has both been facilitated by innovations in international logistics and has been a driving force for new approaches to logistics. The introduction of the container from the late 1960s significantly cut both the financial and the time costs of freight movements. Institutional changes, both at the global level (including tariff reforms under the auspices of such agencies as the World Trade Organization) and domestically in many countries (which have enhanced the efficiency with which goods can be moved to and from gateways, international ports), have been complementary to this.

There has also been a move towards internationalization of freight transport service suppliers. This has involved the formation of strategic alliances in shipping and cargo airlines, and in the United States and abutting countries between the freight railroads. The economic rationale for this is parallel to economies of scope, density, and market presence found in the passenger airline sector discussed earlier in the book. In addition, there have been direct international mergers and take-overs that have brought about even greater integration. Some of these have involved very large companies, such as the mega-shipping lines P&O Nedlloyd and AP Moller Maersk, which merged in 2005.

Figure 10.6 offers a very stylized picture of what generally has happened regarding freight movements before and after either technology changes (such as the adoption of the container), mergers, or, more often, the relaxation of institutional barriers to international trade. Not only was there a shift to more cross-border trade, but also the amount and complexity of goods movements within the nations involved increases.

This type of pattern has been observed in the European Union since the removal of internal restrictions of trade from the early 1990s and as additional countries have joined periodically since 2000. While the creation of the European Economic Community under the Treaty of Rome in the late 1950s had intended to introduce free trade between member states, progress was slow. After 30 years, as we see in more detail in Chapter 14, there remained serious obstacles to the movement of goods. Some indication of the administrative costs of international border crossings within Europe prior to the Single European Market initiative are seen in Table 10.9. Estimates made by the European Union in 1996, after

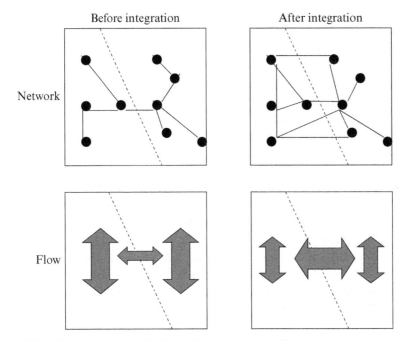

Figure 10.6   *Freight movements before and after international integration*

Table 10.9   *Estimated annual cost of administrative formalities and border controls in Europe before the Single Market initiative*

	$ billions (1988)
Administration	9
Delays	1
Public spending on customer operations	1
Lost business opportunities	5 to 19
Total	*16 to 30*

the removal of border controls under the Single European Market initiative that came into effect in 1992, suggest that logistics costs fell by as much as 27 percent between 1987 and 1992. About half of this saving was realized in the transport sector as idle time at borders was reduced and service reliability improved.

10.9   Big Data, Supply Chains, and Economics

The economic efficiency of any supply chain is heavily dependent on the quality and relevance of the data on both sides of the various micro markets involved. Exact definitions in any dynamic field of study or application is seldom easy. Broadly, big data can be seen as a field that analyses systematically extracted information relating to datasets that have traditionally been too large or complex to be dealt with by traditional data-processing application software. Entwined with this is the increased use of business analytics. This offers the ability to gain insight from data, applying mathematics, econometrics, simulations, and applied statistics to improve the quality of decisions (Selod and Soumahoro, 2020).

Transport logistics examples include global positioning systems and other location-aware technologies that are producing data which are specific down to particular latitude and longitude coordinates and seconds of the day. Another is the data continually gathered from large commercial aircraft in flight, monitoring their technical performance and allowing more efficient planning of highlighting needs and aircraft rotation. From the public sector perspective, collecting detailed information of traffic flows and delays at junctions across a network can enhance the efficiency of traffic signal sequencing.

Just considering the two aviation examples given, the ability to more rapidly and accurately predict weather patterns allows for adjustments in flight paths, while engine monitoring facilitates pre-emptive actions to prevent technical failures. Both help reduce costs and enhance the value of aviation in supply chains, effectively pushing up the production function of transport service suppliers.

The take-up of big data by those engaged in logistics and supply-chain management has been gradual (Wang et al., 2016). While definitions remain a little fuzzy, in 2014 survey data collected by the consultants Accenture from over 1,000 executives engaged by global companies found 97 percent of respondents were interested in implementing big data analytics. But it was also found that only 17 percent had implemented it internally or were outsourcing its implementation. The rationale for implementation was that not only can big data and business analytics reduce costs, but by improving visibility it can increase the logistics services demanded and, with that, revenues. Better information regarding consumers' habits and preferences allows both services to be tailored more closely to those being sought as well as pricing that extracts maximum revenue. Those still waiting were concerned, however, about investment costs, security, and privacy. Deciding how to incorporate big data analytics into companies' business models was a consideration as well.

Big data is also an almost necessary requirement for competitive modern logistics markets. The neoclassical ideal of perfect information is something of a straw man, but big data and associated analytics can enhance competition and increase economic welfare. Just as it can increase information enjoyed by transport service suppliers in the chain, it can make more visible to customers the relative qualities, prices, and other attributes of these transport firms. Big data can provide benchmarks. Often, those seeking logistics service have multiple criteria for making their selections. Big data is increasingly being used in conjunction with techniques such as analytical hierarchic processes which break down complex problems into separate small-size subproblems, to help with this (Ekici, 2013).

In the context of modeling transport markets, while much of the data used are quantitative, big data does offer sources of qualitative data in some circumstances. This generally involves the use of subjective assessments on the part of consumers or users when past series of hard data are not available or there are gaps in them. There are challenges in using big data even when data series are complete:

- Its volume accumulates data noise and incidental homogeneity.
- Volume creates high computational costs and algorithm instability.
- High variety requires different techniques and methodologies.

These factors generally produce heterogeneity, experimental variation, and statistical bias that are not well handled by standard econometric techniques designed to analyse smaller datasets. More robust and adaptive methodologies are, therefore, often adopted.

10.10 Security

One of the traditional concerns of supply chains is that of security. At one time or another, all elements of transport networks have historically found themselves prone to attack both in conventional wars and by terrorists (broadly defined). While the focus of these attacks has in the past often involved links and terminals in inter-urban networks – airlines/airports, railway lines/railway stations, etc. – the local, urban, and suburban elements of logistics chains have not been left unscathed. In the twenty-first century, attacks have also extended beyond the hardware of logistics networks to include their management. Examples include ransomware attacks on such things as pipelines. The 2021 ransomware attack on the Colonial Pipeline Company IT system resulted in the shutting down of the pipeline supplying oil to most of the eastern United States.

Security is a large subject and the focus here is on the vulnerability of shopping malls – important urban and suburban interfaces between inbound flows of goods to retail outlets and outbound flows from retail outlets to final consumption (Button, 2008). They are an integral part of the supply chain and also an element that is both high-profile and difficult to secure. We also add a few words on shipping matters.

Shopping malls provide important retail outlets that offer shoppers economies of scale and scope in their purchasing and economies of market presence for retailers in their selling. They have grown significantly in number in the United States and in many other countries over recent years, with increases in their size and range of facilities provided. They also often act as major recreation centers containing cinemas and food outlets in addition to stores selling commodities to take away. Strolling and 'hanging out' in malls can also provide a distraction for teenagers. Overall, from a security perspective, they represent large gatherings of citizens that offer possible targets for terrorists. Indeed, the US Department of Homeland Security categorizes shopping centers, along with other easily accessible public places, as 'soft targets'.

Traditional concerns with security, involving theft and attacks on individuals, have focused on the location of malls. Older malls located in middle-income groups and accessible only by automobiles were previously considered relatively 'safe' but with increasing suburbanization and changing demographics this is now less the case: 65 percent of United States and Canadian malls of over 400,000 square feet are located in areas with above-average crime risk, with 25 percent being in areas with three times or more the national crime risk. Mall design and that of its surrounding area also plays a role in crime rates. Crime tends to be higher in malls with spots that are attractive to juveniles and 'non-shoppers', and where there are crowded stores offering easy access.

Much of the discussion of mall security and terrorism has relied on anecdotal evidence, perhaps not unexpectedly given the nature of the 'games' that are played with potential terrorists. Their features would seem to make them very vulnerable to terrorist attacks of various kinds: they have multiple entrances and exits, are open to the public, have numerous potential places for concealment, often have adjacent car parking, have frequent deliveries, attract numerous shoppers, and employ large numbers of workers. Additionally, since their initial introduction in 1956, many of the larger malls in the United States (some 1,200 or so) and elsewhere are enclosed with extensive air conditioning and ventilation systems making them potential targets for toxic chemical or biological attacks. Other developments in the supply chain have seen the greater containerization of consignments reducing considerably the transparency of what is being delivered.

Security has thus always been an issue at malls and it is the emphasis that has changed. Traditional security has been focused on preventing petty crimes

Exhibit   *Costs and benefits of transport security*

The September 11, 2001 attacks in the United States on the World Trade Center and the Pentagon brought forth a 21-layered response from the Transportation Security Administration. This involved 15 pre-boarding and deterrence and 6 in-flight security measures; see the table.

Pre-flight	In-flight
Intelligence	Passenger resistance
International partnerships	Trained flight crew
Customs & border protection	Hardened cockpit doors
Joint terrorism task force	Federal Air Marshal Service
No-fly list & passenger pre-screening	Law enforcement officers
Crew vetting	Federal Flight Deck Officer Program
Visible inter-modal protection response teams	
Canines	
Behavioral detection officers	
Travel document checker	
Checkpoint/transportation security officers	
Checked baggage	
Transportation security inspectors	
Random employee checks	
Bomb appraisal officers	

Subsequently, Mark Stewart and John Mueller sought to estimate the costs and benefits of three of the main security measures designed to reduce the likelihood of a direct replication of the 2001 attack. They broke down the net benefits of each into the following components:

$$Net\ Benefit = p_{attack} \times C_{loss} \times DR - C_{security}$$

where:

p_{attack} is the probability of a successful attack is the likelihood that a successful terrorist attack will take place if the security measures were not in place;

C_{loss} is the losses sustained in the successful attack include the fatalities and other damage – both direct and indirect – that will accrue as a result of a successful terrorist attack;

DR is the reduction in risk is the degree to which the security measure foils, deters, disrupts, or protects against a terrorist attack; and

$C_{security}$ is the costs are those of providing the risk-reducing security measure required to attain the benefit.

The three security measures examined were: the installation of physical secondary barriers (IPSB) to restrict access to the hardened cockpit door during door transitions, the use of the Federal Air Marshal Service (FAMS), and the Federal Flight Deck Officer (FFDO) Program. Measures such as scanning checked bags or canines were not explored because they were not relevant to the 2001 attacks. Only measures aimed at stopping undetected boarding of aircraft, hijacking of aircraft, and success in entering the cockpit were examined.

Specifically, in doing this they examined doubling the budget of the FFDO program to $44 million per year, installing IPSBs in all aircraft at a cost of $13.5 million per year, and reducing funding for FAMS by 75 percent to $300 million per year. The break-even cost–benefit analysis then finds the minimum probability of an otherwise successful attack required for the benefit of each security measure to equal its cost.

It was found that the IPSB is cost-effective if the annual attack probability of an otherwise successful attack exceeds 0.5 percent or one attack every 200 years. The FFDO program is cost-effective if the annual attack probability exceeds 2 percent. However, more than two otherwise successful attacks per year are required for FAMS to be cost-effective. A policy that includes IPSBs, an increased budget for FFDOs, and a reduced budget for FAMS may be a viable policy alternative, potentially saving hundreds of millions of dollars per year with consequences for security that are, at most, negligible.

See also: M.G. Stewart and J. Mueller (2013) Terrorism risks and cost–benefit analysis of aviation security, *Risk Analysis*, 33, 893–908.

of theft, minor material damage to the fabric of buildings, and assaults on individuals – collectively called 'crimes' hereafter for brevity. These problems continue. For example, in a 1995 survey for the National Retail Federation, the University of Florida found that the average discount store in 1994 had 0.09 crimes against customers, ranging from simple assault to rape and murder. That translates into a rate of about 20 crimes against customers per year for chains the size of Walmart and Kmart. This problem of criminality is now overlapped by concerns about the possibility of terrorist attacks.

Globally, malls have not been immune from attacks in the past: there have been over 60 terrorist or terrorist-inspired attacks of various sizes at shopping malls since 1998 in 21 countries including the United Kingdom, Turkey, Israel, Russia, and Spain (LaTourrette et al., 2006). Most of these attacks have involved explosives of various types, but there have also been incidents involving firearms and chemicals. The events of September 2001 have heightened concerns in the United States and elsewhere that shopping malls may more frequently become explicit targets for major attack. There is also increased concern about other forms of major assault at malls. For example, a bombing took place in October 2002 in Vantaa, Finland, in a local Myyrmanni shopping mall killing seven people, including the bomber, and injuring 166. The shopping center was particularly crowded, with almost 2,000 people in it, including many children who had come to see a clown performance.

There have already been some actual and thwarted terrorist attacks at American malls, although on a relatively minor scale. Five people were killed and four injured in a shooting at a Salt Lake City mall in 2007 by a Bosnian, for example. There have also been abortive attempts at terrorism. In November 2007 Nuradin Abdi, a Somali living in Ohio, pleaded guilty to planning, with other al-Qaeda operatives, to blow up a Columbus-area shopping mall.

Nevertheless, and for a variety of economic, political, and social reasons, the attention paid to shopping mall security has been much less than to many other parts of the transportation supply chain such as airports, airlines, and chemical and oil movements.

One of the problems is that the retail industry has treaded warily for commercial reasons. Customers expect shopping centers to be free and open, and mall owners and operators have been reluctant to introduce stringent security measures, as airports have done, that might limit shoppers' access, or scare them off altogether. Though security officers are usually uniformed, for example, they are not intended to appear threatening and frequently serve a variety of roles as well as security.

Although the Nobel Prize-winning economist, Gary Becker (1968) and others have enhanced our understanding of crime prevention in general, the analysis of terrorism and its prevention is a relatively new area of study for economists, much of the social science interest in the field coming from sociologists and political scientists. Much of the traditional economic analysis of crime has focused on deterring criminals, but this is of limited relevance in situations when the perpetrator is intent on committing suicide. Inevitably there has been some theoretical economic analysis of the appropriate role of public sector and private sector insurance, essentially revolving around the degree to which the threat of terrorism constitutes risk or uncertainty, on the moral hazard issues of various compensation policies, and on the optimal ways to allocate the costs of counterterrorism measures. There has also been applied analysis seeking to cost the macro costs of terrorism on economic performance. Here we are more concerned with embracing some of these things within an assessment of how optimal security levels may be defined.

One of the problems in trying to apply economics to a subject such as mall security is that many of the actions are driven by subjective factors, often influenced by only partial information, which are difficult to quantify given the lack of large amounts of prior data. This makes it difficult to work out probabilities of attacks and their costs.

The situation is compounded because, unlike the consideration of safety where there is no feedback mechanism, the perpetrators of terrorist acts modify and adjust their methods and targets as security measures reduce the vulnerability of previous types of target. They essentially play games with the security agencies; for example, in some cases they switch targets because they have achieved their objectives by having diverted considerable security efforts to the old category of target. This means that much of the difficulty lies in the uncertain nature of terrorism in Frank Knight's (1921) sense of there being no easily calculable probability distributions associated with attacks. Initially, however, we look at a Gaussian approach and assume that such probabilities can be calculated.

Figure 10.7 provides a diagrammatic representation of the situation with security measured in some undefined way. This allows an assessment of the

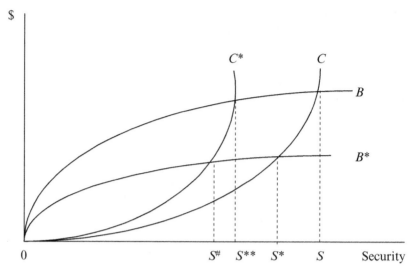

Figure 10.7 *The determinants of optimal security provision*

optimal level of security that should be provided in simple cost–benefit terms. *C* is an upward-sloping marginal-cost-of-security curve based on the reasonable assumption that each increment of security costs more as the most basic measures are exhausted. The *B* curve indicates the marginal benefits of additional security with the flattening of the slope reflecting the decline in additional benefits associated with the more detailed security measures. The optimal level of security in this case is at *S*.

These curves, however, can for analytical purposes usefully be decomposed. Increased security provides benefits in terms of both a reduced threat of material (including physical injuries to people) damage in the mall (separated out as *B**) and greater psychological 'comfort' to those shopping, or having family or friends shopping in the mall (the distance between the *B* and *B** curves). The extent to which this psychological 'comfort' exceeds the actual dangers that exist depends to a large extent on the information that is available to potential shoppers. While there may be no good estimate of the reduced chance of being involved in an attack on a mall, there are benefits from simply seeing security measures in place even if there is no objective method of assessing their effectiveness, although conversely people are sensitive to such things as media coverage of threats that push out the mental benefits of greater security actions. There may also be benefits that are external to those using and working in a mall, for example to those living in the neighborhood.

The cost curve also has its complexities. Attacks on malls can inflict both material damage on the fabric of the buildings and the vitality of the shops in it, and injury and death on individuals. The *C** curve is drawn to separate out the minimum marginal costs of incremental units of security, including the additional inconvenience costs to all parties as well as financial outlays, but the actual full economic costs may deviate from this. (While the *B* and *C* curves are drawn as smooth functions, in practice there may well be kinks if, for example, shoppers have threshold tolerance levels to the degrees of intrusion that security will impose on them.) The incentive to provide security at the lowest cost may not be there and, in consequence, X-inefficiency may be present in providing security measures pushing the cost curve up. Potential inefficiency arises in these types of situations because objectives tend to be opaque and many of the costs are only indirectly borne by those responsible for the security provided.

The problems of providing security on the lowest cost curve are compounded if there is asymmetrical information concerning the effectiveness of security measures – for example, security experts and consultants have an incentive to exaggerate the challenges being faced (consultants after all being rent-seeking economic agents operating in a commercial market). In effect, there is the potential for a degree of 'regulatory capture' of the security system by those involved in providing it.

On the other hand, the costs of security measures may reduce insurance premiums and other forms of crime in the mall. The costs may also be off-set to some extent by the supply chain adjusting at other points, either up or down, as other actors adjust their behavior. In these circumstances the cost curve will be lower than that depicted in the figure. The trade-offs involved are empirical questions and inevitably will differ between malls.

Given these complexities, some suboptimal outcomes may emerge. For simplicity, we assume that gains at other points in the supply chain off-set some of the costs of enhanced security and any X-inefficiency associated with it. In other words, $\{C^* - C\}$ is the difference between the actual and the narrowly defined minimum cost curve of on-site security.

If the attention was purely on the commercial damage that can be caused by acts of terrorism, as for example may be the case with private insurance companies, then security will be under-supplied by $\{S - S^*\}$. But even if the psychological benefits of more assured security are not ignored, then there may be inefficiencies in the provision of security measures leading to inadequacies of $\{S - S^{**}\}$ in their provision if the agencies responsible do not minimize their costs. If both full benefits are under-estimated and costs and the provision of security measures are not carried out efficiently then the resultant level of security, $S^{\#}$, could be well below the social optimum.

The conventional public policy approach to this sort of optimization problem is to apply cost–benefit or cost-effectiveness analysis, but this is difficult in this case because terrorism involves both uncertainty owing to the limited number of previous events, and game-playing owing to the reactive function of the terrorists. To get a genuine handle on the shapes of these curves perhaps the best tools available are experiments. These may involve some form of conventional simulations that can help assess static uncertainty, or more interactive approaches deploying experimental economics that can capture the adaptive behavior of terrorists to security measures.

While it is generally impossible to identify and quantify many of the costs and benefits of securing transport facilities, there are important questions about who should pay the costs if the terrorist threat is to be handled efficiently.

Shopping malls, as an example, are generally owned by the private sector and traditionally they have provided significant amounts of security within their facilities. Indeed, much of the protection is provided by private security (Davis et al., 2006). Mall owners and operators have had a vested interest in doing this, and in cooperating with police forces and other private parties (for example, the security personnel employed by individual retailers with a mall and the transportation companies involved in deliveries). Public confidence in the security of people and property is an important marketing tool for a mall operator.

Given the nature of traditional crime, mall operators have the option of passing on some of the risk of any breakdown in this type of security – for example, compensation claims – through insurance markets. They can also, as most have done, internalize some of the risk by enhancing their private policing. On the premise that they act rationally, shoppers in the mall also have a personal interest in protecting themselves (after all, compensation for being killed by a mugger is hardly ideal!) and their property, and often have the option of taking out insurance. Individual shops within malls have differing levels of attraction to criminals and may thus add additional security.

In another context, namely international freight movements, the United States government (though authorities in other countries have adopted similar policies) have played upon this private sector interest and developed initiatives such as the Customs–Trade Partnership Against Terrorism (C-TPAT) that fosters public–private cooperation throughout the global supply chain (Brooks and Button, 2006). Firms that participate conduct a comprehensive self-assessment of their security practices using guidelines developed after consultation with the national government. This avoids excessive checking by the government and affords the logistics supply flexibility in its operations on the premise that any failure in the security arrangements will hit the supplier commercially.

The general problem with security is that the threat posed by terrorists is different in that it largely involves uncertainty, with little knowledge about any underlying probability functions, if indeed any exist, rather than risk. The actuarial approach to the challenge is thus far from perfect, and certainly incomplete. The potential costs of a major terrorist incident are also extremely high. Returning to our primary example, these factors make it virtually impossible for a mall operator to either completely insure internally, or through the financial market, against terrorist attacks. This is one reason why Figure 10.6 is very broad in its nature; the precise quantification of any of the curves shown is virtually impossible. We can point to additional costs associated with security measures in several transport contexts. Table 10.10, for example, provides a comparison of the costs explicitly borne by airline travelers for security measures in 2002 immediately after the September 11 attacks in the United States, and these are only partial. They do not include costs embedded in higher fares.

There is the added problem that a major attack on a mall could have serious and much wider economic and geographical repercussions than those simply relating to the shopping facility. This can be seen and treated as a standard externality problem if these effects have relatively small impacts on overall price levels

Table 10.10 *Average security charges per traveler at airports (2002)*

Country	Average charge per passenger
Canada	$14.50
Germany	$10.57
Israel	$8.03
France	$6.88
Australia	$5.19
United States	$5.00
Netherlands	$4.13
Russia	$2.04
Italy	$1.90
United Kingdom	$0.00

Source: Waters and Yu (2003).

and incomes in the larger economy, but, if this is not so (which may well be the case), then the conventional tools of microeconomics break down. The standard *ceteris paribus* assumptions of neoclassical analysis do not hold. The issue becomes one of so-called 'political risk', although strictly, given the subjective nature of the issue, it is more about 'political uncertainty'.

These market failures necessitate a degree of public involvement in terms of specifying and possibly providing security and (if this fails) resources to cope with many of the aftermath effects. These are obviously not problems unique to transport security, but they certainly do exist when it comes to looking at appropriate economic strategies concerning transport infrastructure and operations.

Where the line is drawn between private and public sector responsibility is partly a technical one, which largely depends on where uncertainty becomes the dominant concern but also embodies normative judgment involving public perception of what the exact role of government should be. While normally the actual implementation of policies is seen in terms of narrower economic efficiency considerations – essentially the undertaking of a cost–benefit calculation of the effectiveness of public and private actors – when security arises there is often a high degree of subjectivity involving public perceptions. This was seen in the debates in the United States over whether private operators should implement new airport security measures after the 2001 terrorist attacks or whether it should be by a federal agency. Also indicative of this is that, while there is evidence that private security does not reduce security in malls, many shopping mall operators in the United States actively seek a local police presence in their facilities, often a police station, to give added public confidence.

References

Ackerman, K.B. and Brewer, A.M. (2001) Warehousing: a key link in the supply chain, in A.M. Brewer, K.J. Button, and D.A. Hensher (eds), *Handbook of Logistics and Supply-chain Management*, Pergamon.

Baumol, W.J. and Vinod, H.D. (1970) An inventory theoretical model of freight transport demand, *Management Science*, 16, 413–21.

Becker, G. (1968) Crime and punishment: an economic approach, *Journal of Political Economy*, 76, 169–217.

Beuther, M. and Kreutzerberger, F. (2001) Consolidation and trans-shipment, in A.M. Brewer, K.J. Button, and D.A. Hensher (eds), *Handbook of Logistics and Supply-chain Management*, Pergamon.

Brooks, M.R. and Button, K.J. (2006) Market structure and shipping security, *Maritime Economics and Logistics*, 8, 100–20.

Button, K.J. (2005) Can freight transport models be transferred across the Atlantic? in A. Regiani and L. Schintler (eds), *Methods and Models in Transport and Telecommunications: Across Atlantic Perspectives*, Springer-Verlag.

Button, K.J. (2008) The economics of shopping mall security, *Journal of Transportation Security*, 1, 127–39.

Button, K.J. and Pearman, A.D. (1981) *The Economics of Urban Freight Transport*, Macmillan.

Coase, R.H. (1937) The Nature of the Firm, *Economica*, 4, 386–405.

Davis, R.C., Ortiz, C., Rowe, R., Broz, J., Rigakos, G., and Collins, P. (2006) An assessment of the preparedness of large retail malls to prevent and respond to terrorist attack, Report, US Department of Justice.

De Jong, G. (2008) Value of freight travel time savings, in D.A. Hensher and K.J. Button (eds), *Handbook of Transport Modeling*, 2nd edn, Elsevier.

D'Este, G. (2007) Urban freight movement modeling, in D.A. Hensher and K.J. Button (eds), *Handbook of Transport Modeling*, Elsevier.

Ekici, A. (2013) An improved model for supplier selection under capacity constraints and multiple criteria, *International Journal of Production Economics*, 141, 574–81.

Fiddis, C. (1997) *Manufacturer-retailing Relationships in the Food and Drink Industry: Strategies and Tactics in the Battle for Power*, Parson Publishing.

Friesz, T.L. and Kwon, C. (2007) Strategic freight network planning models and dynamic oligopolistic urban freight networks, in D.A. Hensher and K.J. Button (eds), *Handbook of Transport Modelling*, 2nd edn, Pergamon.

Guan, D., Wang, D., Hallegatte, S., Davis, S.J., Huo, J., Li, S., Bai, Y., Lei, T., Xue, Q., Coffman, D., Cheng, D., Chen, P., Liang, X., Xu, B., Lu, X., Wang, S., Hubacek, K., and Gong, P. (2020) Global supply-chain effects of COVID-19 control measures, *Nature Human Behavior*, 4, 577–87.

Hancock, K.L. (2001) Hazardous goods, in A.M. Brewer, K.J. Button, and D.A. Hensher (eds), *Handbook of Logistics and Supply-chain Management*, Pergamon.

Hertz, S. and Alfredsson, M. (2003) Strategic development of third-party logistics providers, *Industrial Marketing Management*, 32, 139–49.

Kasarda, J.D., Green, J., and Sullivan, D. (2004) Air cargo: engine of economic development, Center for Air Commerce, Report, University of North Carolina at Chapel Hill.

Knight, F.H. (1921) *Risk, Uncertainty and Profit*, Houghton Mifflin.

LaTourrette, T., Howell, D.R., Mosher, D.E., and MacDonald, J. (2006) Reducing terrorism risk at shopping centers: an analysis of potential security options, Report, RAND Corporation.

Martin, D., Cannell, W., and Gwilliam, K. (1995) Reducing the impact of freight transport on global warming: the potential of technical solutions, *World Transport Policy, and Practice*, 1, 11–17.

McKinnon, A.C. (2003) Logistics and the environment, in D.A. Hensher and K.J. Button (eds), *Handbook of Transport and the Environment*, Elsevier.

Meixell, M.J. and Gargeya, V.B. (2005) Global supply chain design: a literature review and critique, *Transportation Research Part E*, 41, 531–50.

Mitchell, A. (1997) *Efficient Consumer Response: A New Paradigm for the European FMGG Sector*, Pearson Publishing.

Rodrigue, J-.P., Slack, B., and Comtois, C. (2001) Green logistic, in A.M. Brewer, K.J. Button, and D.A. Hensher (eds), *Handbook of Logistics and Supply-chain Management*, Pergamon.

Selod, H. and Soumahoro, S. (2020) *Big Data in Transportation: An Economics Perspective*, World Bank.

UK Department of Transport (1979) Road haulage operators' licensing report of the independent committee of enquiry into road haulage operators' licensing, Report, HMSO.

Wang, G., Gunasekaran, A., Ngai, E.W.T., and Papadopoulos., T. (2016) Big data analytics in logistics and supply chain management: certain investigations for research and applications, *International Journal of Production Economics*, 176, 98–110.

Warne, J. and Rowney, M.J. (1986) The Toyota just in time production system and early experience with ZIPS (Zero Inventory Production System), Report, TTC.

Waters, W.G. and Yu, C. (2003) Air security fees and highway safety, Proceedings of the 38th Canadian Transportation Research Forum Annual Conference.

11 Investment Criteria: Private and Public Sector Analysis

11.1 Transport and Infrastructure

Adam Smith in his classic book, *The Wealth of Nations*, certainly thought that transport in 1776 had a major and positive role to play in fostering economic well-being, and spent considerable time explaining this, and that government has an important responsibility in ensuring adequate transport infrastructure is provided:

> The third and last duty of the sovereign or commonwealth is that of erecting and maintaining those public institutions and those public works, which, though they may be in the highest degree advantageous to a great society, are, however, of such a nature that the profit could never repay the expense to any individual or small number of individuals, and which it therefore cannot be expected that any individual or small number of individuals should erect or maintain.

The preceding chapters have been primarily concerned with making the best use of an existing transport network or fleet of vehicles. They have, therefore, principally focused on short-term problems involving the management, regulation, and pricing of an established transport system. They were concerned with emphasizing the central role of marginal cost pricing (including social costs) in encouraging the optimal utilization of transport facilities. The discussions have thus largely taken the stock of transport infrastructure as given and been concerned with making the most efficient economic use of it.

There is, however, a longer-term aspect to be considered, namely possible changes in the size or nature of the basic transport system by either investment or disinvestment. (The latter may take the form of allowing quality deterioration by reduced maintenance of a transport network rather than physical removal of a link.) In the case of road haulage, and airline and shipping operations, the commercial nature of decision-making bodies means that changes are normally analysed in terms of their financial repercussions. With road track, railways, and port authorities, which in most countries are owned by public agencies, the provision of basic infrastructure is usually determined by looking at much wider economic considerations.

Before moving on to look at some of the key techniques employed in investment analysis, it is helpful to consider the scale of transport infrastructure that exists, and to provide some information on variations in modal provision and technology. We have already seen in Chapter 2 the considerable amount of transport infrastructure – roads, railway track, etc. – that has been developed over the years; basically, the stock of network capital. It is also clear from what we saw in Tables 2.6 and 2.7 that road infrastructure provision far exceeds that of rail in most of the larger, wealthier industrial nations. This stock is also growing. The United States railroad network, for example, expanded from 178,000 kilometers in 1993 to 202,500 in 2020, that in Japan from 20,300 to 27,300, and China's from 59,000 to 146,000. Perhaps more pronounced has been the investment in road networks.

The global situation is, however, variable. The picture is, for example, slightly different in the former communist states in Europe (and even more so in many less developed countries) that have relatively extensive rail networks *vis-à-vis* their road systems, although things are changing with developments in logistics and higher levels of car ownership.

In addition, it is not simply a matter of the quantity of the capital stock; its quality is also of considerable importance. The market-based economies of the Organisation for Economic Co-operation and Development (OECD) states, for example, recorded 63 percent of the Netherlands' rail network as being double-tracked, compared with 69 percent of the United Kingdom's and 45 percent of France's, while Bulgaria and Hungary only had 23 percent double-tracking, and Poland just 15 percent. Taking another parameter, while there are considerable variations in the electrification of rail networks in industrialized countries because of the type of traffic they carry, and the freight/passenger mix, they generally still have more extensive systems than in the post-communist states. For example, out of 31,000 kilometers of line, nearly 12,000 were electrified in the western states of pre-1990 Germany, but out of 14,024 kilometers in the former East Germany only 3,475 kilometers were electrified, and in Poland, of 26,545 kilometers only 6,296 were electrified. With political and economic reforms, Poland now has about 11,900 kilometers electrified, and Hungary has increased its electrified system from 2,300 to 2,800 kilometers.

There have always been significant variations between countries in terms of the proportion of national resources that are invested in transport infrastructure. This can be explained in terms of different geographies and industrial needs.

While the capital stock of transport infrastructure is large and huge sums are spent on its expansion and maintenance, the evidence is that investment in transport, and especially rail transport, tended to slow down in the latter part of the twentieth century compared to the 1960s and 1970s, and, in some cases, disinvestment may well have taken place. In the case of rail, this manifested itself as a 4.1 percent reduction in the rail network of OECD countries between 1970 and 1985, although effective capacity may well have increased as electrification and double-tracking programs were carried through. One reason for this was that many networks, such as the United States Interstate highway system, neared completion, and most industrialized countries had extensive transport networks in place by the 1990s. This trend has been reversed somewhat (Table 11.1) during the first decades of the twenty-first century, although the pattern still varies across countries.

Table 11.1   *Investment in transport infrastructure in selected countries (€ millions)*

Country	Infrastructure investment as % of GDP			
	Rail		Road	
	2016	2019	2016	2019
Canada	796.5	1,366.3	7,042.7	7,543.2
France	8,614.3	11,630.0	9,216.0	9,816.0
Germany	5,192.0	6,948.0	12,870.0	16,650.0
Italy	3,847.0	2,855.0[a]	3,755.0	6,555.0[a]
Japan	9,174.7	n.a.	32,575.9	30,027.2[b]
United Kingdom	13,511.1	13,298.4	8,561.4	9,642.6
United States	12,473.3	11,587.1	85,589.4	93,962.2

Notes: a. 2018. b. 2017.
n.a. = not available.

Source: Organisation for Economic Co-operation and Development.

The growth in globalization and the removal of trade barriers at the macro level, and the spread of urbanization at the more local levels, added impetus to the notion that additional capacity was needed in the early part of the twenty-first century. The changes in Europe, and the Trans-European Networks (TENs) initiative of the European Union which we discuss in Chapter 13, can also be likened to the development of transport networks of the kind fostered in Canada and the United States in the nineteenth century as a tool for political integration.

Economists look at transport investment from two broad perspectives. At the macro and meso levels there is interest in the ways and extent to which it contributes to the economic advancement of a region or a country, a topic we deal with later in the book. In the 1930s, for example, the construction of the autobahns in Germany were used as a way to stimulate employment, and the construction of the Federal Highway System in the United States was a major macroeconomic stimulus. More recently, the American Recovery and Reinvestment Act of 2009 had a significant transport investment component to it, as has the macroeconomic policy following the Covid-19 pandemic. At the microeconomic level, which is our main concern here, the interest is in the efficiency of individual transport investments, and the returns that they generate in either narrow financial terms or in wider, social terms. Project appraisal is necessary because investment resources are not infinite and there are many potential options in terms of the ways in which they may be used. Looking at the efficient use of these resources is our focus here.

11.2   Basic Theories of Investment Policies

Simple economic theory provides straightforward guidelines for investment decision-making; essentially, it involves pricing and output decisions where the constraints of a fixed production capacity (for example, a given fleet or rail network) cease to be binding. This is something that was introduced in Chapter 5 when considering long-run costs.

In Figure 11.1, which is a more complete picture of the cost curves shown in Figure 5.3, we consider an example of a profit-maximizing airline with a fleet exhibiting short-run average and marginal cost characteristics of $SRAC_1$ and $SRMC_1$ respectively, and confronted by the demand curve D (with marginal revenue MR). Ideally, a price P_1 will be set and seat-kilometers Q_1 offered. The long-run marginal cost ($LRMC$) is, however, below marginal revenue at this output, and, with this size of fleet, gives an inducement to expand output in the long term by acquiring more capacity.

Greater seat availability will, however, force prices down, but – and this is important in the example – it may also make it more economical to increase the aircraft fleet size. In the diagram, and assuming throughout that profit-maximizing prices are charged, the fleet could be expanded to correspond to $SRAC_2$ and $SRMC_2$. Here the long-run optimum situation is achieved with marginal revenue equated to long-run and short-run costs and with profit maximization resulting. If the firm were concerned with social rather than commercial profit-maximization criteria and adopted instead marginal cost pricing, then the $SRMC_3$ and $SRAC_3$ curves become relevant because with this objective function it is the setting of $D = LRMC = SRMC$ which is important. Greater capacity is still needed for this (hence the $SRMC_3$ and $SRAC_3$ curves) and optimal long-run output will be higher at Q_3 seat-miles with fares lowered to P_3. At this price and output, social surplus is maximized, although, since $P_3 < LRAC$, in the long run a financial loss will be made.

The basic principles are simple, and come straight from the elementary economic literature; the difficulty comes in the transport context in putting them into

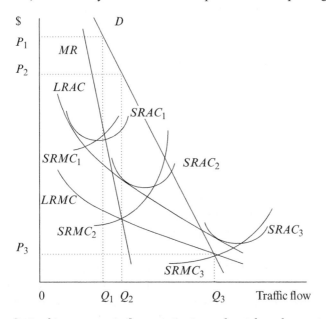

Figure 11.1   *Optimal investment: profit maximization and social surplus maximization*

practice. In many cases investments are not divisible and, hence, the $LRAC$ and $LRMC$ curves are disjointed segments, or even points, which do not intersect with demand. This is an extremely common situation in transport and it does pose serious problems in many operational cases.

It is not difficult, for example, to envisage routes where the available vehicles (be they planes, buses, or whatever) are either too small or too large to be optimal, and it is even more common in the case of infrastructure where, for instance, a two-lane motorway may be inadequate to cope with normal demand but a three-lane one is too capacious; you also must build a complete runway at an airport because planning to construct 20 percent of one does not make a great deal of sense. Further, there is the problem of what exactly is meant by 'cost'; is it simply the costs borne by the investor, or, because of market imperfections such as externalities, are there other costs that should be taken into account? There is also the matter of how inclusive the number of alternative investments to be considered is; in many cases there is a wide variety of alternative ways in which resources can be invested and selection processes can become important (Mackie and Simon, 1998).

While we have treated the commercial and social criteria of profit maximization and marginal cost pricing as amenable to presentation on one diagram, in practice most socially orientated undertakings look at a much wider range of costs (notably many of the externalities discussed in Chapter 6) when deciding upon investment than do those motivated by purely financial considerations. Coupled with this is the fact that the diagrammatic analysis assumes that, irrespective of the operational criteria, prices are optimal in the short term and thus can act as an aid and guideline to investment decision-making. Also, despite the sophistication of forecasting techniques (see Chapter 12) it is unlikely that the transport provider is completely aware of the exact form of the long-run demand curve confronting it; and may have a very poor idea of the full costs of constructing new facilities. Indeed, the fluctuating nature of demand for transport (especially long-term cycles in demand associated with national and international economic conditions) means that it is rather more of a stochastic concept than a deterministic phenomenon as depicted.

There is the added institutional problem that transport investments are seldom made in isolation from other changes to the transport system. For example, larger suppliers of transport services in the private sector that have the potential to exercise monopoly power are generally subjected to economic regulations to prevent such exploitation. Regulatory policies regarding external costs may also change during the construction of a large project. The result is that in practice a sort of 'muddling through', to use Charles Lindblom's (1959) jargon, turns out to be the reality with continual modifications being made to the project even after its construction has begun.

Given all these difficulties, together with the general inadequacy of information enjoyed by most transport suppliers of their current levels of cost, let alone future costs, it is not surprising that investment analysis in transport has received considerable interest. The high costs and long-term implications of infrastructure investments in road and rail track, and sea- and airports, has led to attention being directed at these areas. At the academic level they also pose difficult questions because, in many cases, facilities are provided at prices unrelated to cost, or made freely available to users. Additionally, there are frequently widespread ramifications for transport users elsewhere or for the non-users living in surrounding areas.

11.3 Commercial and Social Approaches to Investment

Transport infrastructure is provided in a variety of institutional settings, ranging from purely commercial structures to ones that are totally socially oriented, and is financed in many ways, ranging from user fees to taxes. Just considering air traffic control systems, the United States Federal Aviation Administration (FAA) is financed largely from taxes and has no strict financial remit, whereas NAV Canada is a non-profit, private corporation that levies user fees, the Australian air traffic control body is a government corporation financed from user fees, and the United Kingdom's National Air Traffic Services (NATS) is a price-regulated, for-profit, public–private partnership (PPP) that imposes user fees (Button and McDougall, 2006). But there is also diversity within countries, and sectors within them.

The administrative structure of transport in many countries means that most types of infrastructure are supplied with the intention of maximizing overall economic efficiency – that is, they are appraised in terms of their social value, assuming they are optimally utilized at marginal cost prices. There are clearly exceptions to this where profit maximization is seen as the primary objective, as with the United States railroads. Even when conducting assessment of a single project, or a series of closely related ones, the complexity of funding mechanisms can mean that a combination of techniques are adopted to meet the requirements of different stock-holders and this can even involve different approaches by various levels of government that have a financial stake in the project A simple review of the ways in which highways are financed in the United States (Table 11.2) highlights the complexity of the problem.

Financial Appraisal

Historically a lot of transport infrastructure has been provided by the private sector, and even some that has been publicly provided has been done using commercial criteria. Indeed, there are arguments that there are cycles in which the private sector, and, *ipso facto*, financial considerations, have played a greater or lesser role in transport investments. While this may apply when there are new modes emerging, for example the railroads taking over from canals for the movement of freight in the mid-nineteenth century, there have also been shifts of emphasis within modes. An example is the private engagement in turnpike investments in the eighteenth and early nineteenth centuries, reverting to government

Table 11.2 *Sponsors and features of highway financing in the United States*

Sponsor	Major features of financing	Examples
Private equity investors	Finance and develop the project using private resources	Dulles Greenway (VA) 91 express lanes (CA)
Private, non-profit entity	Issues tax-exempt debt backed by tolls (and without recourse to taxes) and oversees the project under the terms of the agreement between the state and a private developer	TH 212 (MN) Southern Connector (SC) Interstate 895 (VA) Tacoma Narrows Bridge (WA) Arizona toll project (AV)
Special-purpose public	Issues tax-exempt debt backed by tolls (and without recourse to taxes) and oversees the project under the terms of the agreement with private developer	E-470 (CO) Orange County transportation corridor agency (CA)
State agency	Issues tax-exempt dept backed by tolls (and without recourse to taxes)	Some turnpikes
State agency	Issues tax-exempt dept backed by taxes	Most highway projects that are financed by debt
State agency	Finances highways on a pay-as-you-go basis using states taxes and fees plus federal aid	Most highways

Source: US Congressional Budget Office (1998).

investments in highways in the early twentieth century, to the concessions for private investors that became common in the 1990s.

Differences in the perspectives of the investors depend largely on whether the focus is on the stock-holding (concerning only the people who make the investment) or the stake-holding (embracing those who not only put the finance into the system but also are affected by its larger outcomes). The former focuses primarily on commercial criteria and the financial returns that an investment can generate, and the latter on wider social criteria.

In technical terms the simple differences between the basic commercial and social welfare-maximizing approaches are seen in Figure 11.2. The profit maximizer is only interested in 'producer surplus', the difference between money paid out to make the investment and the subsequent revenue earned, whereas the broader approach takes account of both the 'producer surplus' and the 'consumer surplus', the amount society would have been willing to pay for the investment beyond the costs incurred, the combination forming the social surplus.

The distinction between the two approaches may be seen in more detail by contrasting the discounting approach used by large profit-orientated firms (and public corporations instructed to operate commercially) with the discounting approach of undertakings concerned with economic efficiency. (The discounting process is a simple weighting of different items of cost and income according to the time period at which they occur, more distant items being given less emphasis in the calculations.)

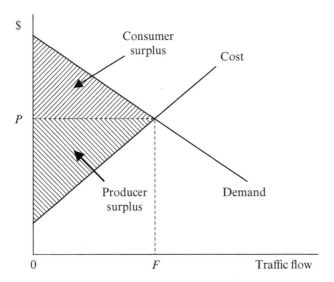

Figure 11.2   *The simple difference between the financial and social cost–benefit approaches*

More formally, a commercially motivated firm will, in the absence of a budget constraint, accept investments when the financial net present value is positive; that is:

$$NPV_P = \sum_{t=1}^{t=k} \left(\frac{P(R_t) - P(C_t)}{(1+r)^t} \right)$$ (11.1)

where:

NPV_P is the financial net present value;
$P(R_t)$ is the probable revenue that would be earned in year t from the investment;
$P(C_t)$ is the probable financial cost of the investment in year t;
r is the rate of interest reflecting the cost of capital to the undertaking; and
k is the anticipated life of the investment.

A positive NPV_P, therefore, tells the businessperson that it is worthwhile undertaking an initial investment, that is, it tells them that a movement from zero output in Figure 11.1 to output Q_1 with the associated short-run costs of $SRAC_1$ and $SRMC_1$ is commercially desirable and that a profit above both long- and short-run costs will be earned. A more normal case, where an expansion of operations is being considered involving some new capital outlay, requires the additional discounted profits from the investment to be compared with the additional discounted costs. If the resultant incremental NPV_p is positive, then the investment is justified on profitability grounds. In terms of the diagram, a movement down the $LRMC$ curve to output level Q_2 with the short-run marginal costs of $SRMC_2$ would yield a positive incremental NPV_p *but* subsequent investment to take one down the $LRMC$ curve to output Q_3 would not.

The Cost–Benefit Approach

In contrast to the stock-holder approach, investments involving the public sector generally involve economic efficiency being assessed using some form of cost–benefit (or 'benefit–cost') analysis (CBA) that, again in the absence of a budget constraint, suggests that schemes with a positive social net present value should be undertaken where:

$$NPV_{SW} = \sum_{G=1}^{G=x} \sum_{t=1}^{T=K} \left(\frac{aP(B_{GT}) - bP(L_{GT})}{(1+i)^T} \right) \qquad (11.2)$$

where:

NPV_{SW} is the social net present value;
$a_m P(B_{GT})$ is the probable social benefit to be enjoyed by individual m in year T as a result of the investment's completion, and B_{GT} is given a weighting a, to reflect society's welfare preference;
$b_m P(L_{GT})$ is the probable social cost imposed on individual m in year T as a result of the investment's completion, and L_{GT} is given a weighting b, to reflect society's welfare preference;
i is the relative social weight attached to a cost or benefit occurring each year;
K is the anticipated life of the investment; and
G is the number of individuals affected.

Again, in terms of Figure 11.1, a positive *NPV* implies that the social surplus associated with an investment exceeds the discounted costs – that is, the demand curve at the final output is equal to or above the *LRMC* curve. An additional investment will be economically justified if the discounted value of incremental social benefit exceeds incremental costs. Contrasting this with the commercial criteria, the NPV_p associated with moving down the *LRMC* curve from output Q_2 to Q_3 is negative but the incremental *NPV* would be calculated to be positive.

Not only is the cost–benefit type of analysis more comprehensive in terms of the items considered, but it also redefines many of the items retained from commercial criteria. For example, the costs of imported raw materials used in a potential road construction project in a Third World country would be valued at market prices if a commercial undertaking were responsible for road investment decisions.

If a public body undertakes road investment using wider social criteria, then it would look beyond the immediate financial indicators and at the 'shadow' prices of imports so that the scarcity of foreign exchange and the limitations of adequate finance for imports is reflected in the decision-making. In some investments use is made of formerly unemployed factor services – for example, unemployed labor where the opportunity cost of employment in a transport scheme is really zero or the opportunity cost of the leisure they now forgo. A commercial concern would cost such inputs at the wages that have to be paid, but in a cost–benefit study they may not be considered a cost at all, or, more probably, would be costed so that genuine resource costs are incorporated in the calculations.

A further very important distinction is that the social efficiency approach takes cognizance of the distributional effect of the investment (the a_m and b_m terms in equation (11.2)). This is often difficult to do although various schemes for weighting costs and benefits have been advanced by theoreticians. In practice there is a tendency to employ rather crude methods. Often, as in the case of the planning balance sheet approach discussed below, such methods have been used in urban infrastructure investment appraisals, which involve the simple setting out in tabular form of the impacts of a scheme on the different user and non-user groups affected, or, as with the COBA inter-urban road appraisal methods previously used in the United Kingdom, which carried out a partial CBA with no allowance for distributional effects and subjected the results of this to further debate at public inquiry.

In other cases, the social analysis may not be complete – it may focus only on the internal social efficiency of the transport system and ignore its wider implications on the environment, etc. In an evaluation, a new mode of high-speed ground transport, the magnetic levitation rail system (Maglev), Elhorst and Oosterhaven (2008) compare the results of an integral CBA that embraces environmental and wider economic effects with those of a conventional partial CBA that only looks at transport effects, and conclude that the additional economic benefits due to market imperfections vary from –1 percent to 38 percent of the direct transport benefits, depending on the type of regions connected and the general condition of the economy. Initially, however, it is useful to explain in a little more detail the broad differences between a financial appraisal and a social analysis of an investment.

11.4 Public–Private Partnerships

Public–private partnerships (PPPs) are a well-established part of transport policy. PPPs involve a government, or its agent, signing an agreement with a private company or consortium to supply it with services, with the private sector actor being involved in various elements of designing, building, temporarily 'owning', and running the physical assets. PPPs are long-term development and service contracts between government and a private partner. The European Union, for example, supports PPP initiatives by channeling funds through the Loan Guarantee Instrument for Trans-European Transport Network Projects. This consists of a European Investment Bank guarantee for subordinate debt in the form of a stand-by liquidity facility to be provided by commercial banks.

PPPs have a relatively long history. Their modern origins are often traced to the construction of Amsterdam town hall in 1662, and PPPs existed in France in 1666 with their use in the building of the Canal du Midi in Toulouse. In the United States, they date back to the Philadelphia and Lancaster Turnpike in Pennsylvania, which was chartered in 1792. The global upsurge in interest in them came in the 1970s when there was a focus on accelerating infrastructure investment, with transport forming a large part of the initiative.

PPPs were seen as part of an alternative service delivery mechanism designed to provide new ways of providing public services. Initially, they largely involved contractual arrangements between the private and public sectors to provide and operate relatively small-scale physical infrastructure (roads, sea-ports, etc.), but this situation broadened out somewhat in the late 1990s to embrace information technology and social facilities. The widening was partly due to concerns about the problems that straightforward privatization of large scale had encountered in places like Latin America. The public sector saw PPPs as a way of accelerating investment beyond traditional tax and borrowing chan-nels, while the private sector saw it as a way of spreading risk. A listing of some of the main heavy transport PPPs that were initiated is seen in Table 11.3 (see also Button, 2016).

These differences in the perspectives reflect varying interests between stock-holders (concerning only the people who make the investment – the private sector element of a PPP) and stake-holdings (embracing those not only putting finance into the system but also affected by its larger outcomes: the public more gener-ally). The former focus on commercial criteria, and the financial returns that an investment can generate, and the latter on wider social criteria – a subject covered more rigorously below. In welfare economic terms, a profit-maximizing private investor is only interested in producer surplus, the difference between money paid out to make the investment, and the subsequent revenue earned, whereas the broader approach takes account of both producers' and consumers' surpluses, the latter being the amount society would have been willing to pay for the investment beyond the costs incurred.

A major motivation for the private sector engaging with the public is to reduce their risk. The private sector pays more in interest, a risk premium, to raise capital because of the possibility of it defaulting. The public sector, because of its power to tax, does not have the same problem. This leads, with other factors, to a series of problems of drawing up contracts between the two parties (Hart, 2003):

- *The nature of partnerships.* Virtually all PPPs involve a degree of bi-lateral oligopoly and often, where highly specialized infrastructure is concerned, bi-lateral monopoly. In terms of large-scale investments, and the limited number of private sector investors capable of financing such projects, the negotiations underlying a PPP involve the exercise of market power. Conventional, neoclassical economic ideas of competitive equilibrium, the outcome of a bi-lateral monopoly or oligopoly situation, as discussed in Chapter 7, are normally indeterminate, depending on the bargaining skills of the parties involved.

  In many cases, the private sector developer (or a strong alliance of devel-opers), by dint of size and specialism, have considerable monopsony power, while the government agency is confronted with competition for its scarce resources from alternative uses. In cases where the public sector can foster competition between private developers for the market, the bargaining posi-tion is reversed. The resultant price and output combination will, in either case, depend on the bargaining skills of the two parties, and that, of course, will be a function of their respective game-playing abilities.

In general, however, whatever the outcome, the final cost of supplying the investment to the economy will be higher than that which would emerge with perfect competition on both sides of the market. Thus, irrespective of the power of the private firms and the government agency involved, the final consumer does not generally benefit greatly from a bi-lateral monopoly situation in terms of immediate costs. The gains are generally seen in acceleration in investments.

- *Initial contract.* The main challenge with the initial contract concerns its clarity and coverage (Hart, 2003). To be successful, a PPP must indicate the roles, responsibilities, financial liabilities, etc., of both the public and private partners.

- *Boundary of contract.* The degree to which unbundling (the passing over to the private sector of traditional public sector responsibilities) occurs can be looked at in a number of ways, and indeed the ways it can be carried out are also numerous. They may involve design, build, finance, operate, and maintain (DBFOM) concessions, or design, build, finance, and maintain (DBFM) concessions, or build, own, operate, and transfer (BOOT) concessions, and there are other variants. Additionally, details within each PPP, of any type, can vary considerably. There are also various categories of leasing that may be seen as PPPs, and the financial commitments of the two sectors can take a variety of forms.

  From a practical perspective, there are few independent elements of infrastructure, and there are also often interdependencies involving the investment in and operation of facilities. This raises questions about the appropriate boundaries of any PPP: which elements should be public and which private? For example, should the investment be public and the maintenance of a road be private? Forms of concessions can also differ in terms of the structure of the market imposed. In the context of South American airports, for example, there have been diverse approaches to concessions with some countries combining a number of airports within a concession package, while others have separate PPPs for each airport (Button, 2008). Much depends upon the extent to which the public sector believes there are economies of scope and density in having an integrated airport system as opposed to airports competing with each other.

  Many concessions involve commitments to build and finance, as well as manage, existing infrastructure. The decisions regarding the optimal approach in such cases have as much to do with the inherent nature of transaction costs within firms as they have to do with their method of provision. It is essentially a practical matter. If there are managerial synergies or high costs of unplanned coordination, then there are arguments for grouping activities in a PPP arrangement. The transaction costs of many standalone entities are higher than those when they are bundled. In terms of unbundling infrastructure investment from its subsequent operations, a situation

Table 11.3 *Examples of heavy rail infrastructure public–private partnership projects*

Project	Design/ construction period	Concession period (years)	Route length (kms)	Investment costs	Public funds	Contract type
Channel Tunnel rail link	1966–2003/2007	90	109	£5.8 billion	£2,010 million	DBFM
Öresund road–rail link	1991–2000	25–30	38	€2 billion	100% state guarantee	DBFM
HSL-Zuid Amsterdam to Belgium	2000–2007	25	100	€6 billion	€110 million per year	DBFM
Alice Springs–Darwin rail	2000–2004	–	–	A$1.2 billion	A$559 million	–
Taipei–Kaohsiung high-speed rail	2000–2007	35	335	US$18 billion	–	DBFOM
Perpignan–Figueres high-speed rail	2005–2009	50	45	€1.1 billion	€540 million + €62 million per year	DBFM
Diabolo rail link Brussels	2007–2012	35	3	€540 million	€250 million + track & signaling	DBF
Liefkenshoek rail link Antwerp	2008–2013	38	16	€840 million	€50 million per year	DBFM
Tours–Bordeaux high-speed rail	2010–2016	44	340	€7.2 billion	< 50%	DBFOM
GSM-R network France	2009–2015	15	14,000	€1 billion	€160 million	DBFOM
Lisbon–Madrid high-speed rail	2009–2013	40	165	€7.8 billion	–	DBFM
Nimes–Montpellier high-speed rail	2011–2016	–	80	–	€1.62 billion	DBFM
Brittany–Pays de Loire high-speed rail	2011–2017	–	182	€2.85 billion	–	DBFM
Rio de Janeiro–São Paulo–Campinas high-speed rail	2011–2017	40	–	US$18.7 billion	–	DBOF
Ylivieska rail link	2011–2014	20–30	76	€660 million	–	DBFM

Notes: DBFM = design, build, finance, and maintain. DBOF = design, build, operate, and finance. DBFOM = design, build, finance, operate, and maintain. DBF = design, build, and finance.

Source: Hanson (2011).

more akin to conventional provision, again transactions costs are involved, but in this case there is the matter of whether better-designed infrastructure reduces operating costs; essentially interactions are viewed sequentially rather than at the same time.

- *Honesty*. Corruption may take several forms regarding PPPs. In terms of the private sector, corruption can stem from the large incentive required to pull in the necessary private resources. In terms of the public, corruption is more in terms of economic capture. Officials and public servants subjugate the public's interest to those of their private interests, although overt breaking of laws is also present in some cases. Often, this type of corruption entails governments making inefficient decisions to improve the chances of re-election, and in particular continuing or bailing out projects that should be terminated. One reason that the issue of pet projects can occur, making simple comparisons between public and private ownership, is that the public sector is generally intrinsically more complex than the private, although the situation can vary on a case-by-case basis. Because of this, it is hard to make rules regarding ownership. To contain these sorts of problems, and in particular those of cost over-runs as officials seek to complete their 'pet' projects, fixed-price contracts for the private party and a budget cap for the public financing can temper political misbehavior by allowing scrutiny of public liabilities.

- *Renegotiation*. Regarding transportation, Guasch et al. (2008) found that 53 percent of concessions awarded in Latin American countries during 1989–2000 required renegotiation, and on average this was done just 3.1 years after an award. Vining et al. (2005) provide some North American transportation examples of the detailed issues that can lead to renegotiations and the various costs involved.

There are often quite legitimate reasons why a PPP breaks down once physical construction has begun; for example, unexpected rises in costs, or the encountering of unforeseen technical problems; basically the contract is incomplete. In these cases, there are often justifications continuing with the project; these may be centered in terms of bygones-being-bygones and the marginal gains to both parties of the additional costs are justified, or because of high transaction costs in seeking new partners to continue the work after relationship-specific investments have been made. In other cases, however, a private contract may 'low-ball' a contract by making an exceptionally low offer to contract for the work with the expectation that it can subsequently renegotiate at a higher price. The challenge is then to find the appropriate level of flexibility: too much, and undesirable opportunistic renegotiations are likely to be necessary; too little, and opportunities for welfare-enhancing renegotiations will be lost.

Long-term contracts can be one way of circumventing some of these problems, especially if the private actor can reduce its risks by having long-term contracts with its suppliers: a form of hedging. But, given the nature of risk, defining comprehensive contracts that allow for all contingencies is almost impossible. One way around rigid contractual structures, which can minimize transaction costs but which sacrifice opportunities to make PPPs more economically efficient, is by allocating and addressing future downside risks appropriately, to make them more flexible. But even this can fail, thus PPP contracts are seldom set in stone and renegotiation may be anticipated, given the longevity of many concessions and the temporal variability of demand.

11.5 The Theory of Cost–Benefit Analysis

While there are many complexities in undertaking commercial investment appraisal (for example, allowing for risk of unexpected changes in demand, deciding upon appropriate methods of raising capital, etc.), it is public sector transport investment that has attracted the greatest attention. The wide-ranging and long-term effects of most major changes in transport infrastructure necessitate the employment of sophisticated methods of project appraisal and of comprehensive techniques for decision-making. The underlying notion of CBA that forms the explicit (and, on occasions, implicit) foundation for much of this work has already been alluded to in previous sections. While the algebra set down there suggests a comparatively simple set of standard calculations, the theoretical model is itself based upon a set of much more complex assumptions which makes the application a far more tortuous exercise than it might at first appear. Indeed, there is evidence that the optimism once felt for CBA as the panacea for all transport investment appraisal problems has gradually evaporated and the confidence felt in the strength of CBA calculations no longer exists.

This and the following sections attempt, in broad terms, to explain the CBA methodology and to point to recent innovations in theory and practice. The subject matter of CBA has now become so vast that the treatment here must, by necessity, be rather limited. We begin by looking at the basic welfare economics underlying the technique, and the direction this is moving (Atkinson, 2011). This highlights some of the key assumptions upon which it is based.

The simple outline of CBA in the previous section emphasized the notion of selecting investments that maximize social surplus rather than just pecuniary returns. One of the major problems in this is that of inter-personal comparisons of welfare. Is it possible to say social welfare has risen if one group becomes better off at the expense of another? This represents a common situation in transport where users tend to benefit at the expense of non-users, or amongst users, travelers using one mode gain at the expense of another. CBA attempts to circumvent this conceptual problem by making use of 'hypothetical compensation tests'. Strictly, since we only have a notion of the ordinal ranking of individuals' priorities, inter-personal welfare comparisons can only be made in very limited circumstances. The Pareto criterion, which underlies most modern welfare economics, states that an action can only definitely be said to be socially desirable if at least one agent benefits and no one suffers any diminution of welfare.

Diagrammatically, in the upper portion of Figure 11.3 we have two individuals, A and B, who enjoy various levels of welfare recorded on the horizontal and vertical axes as U_A and U_B. If we have a finite collection of goods and services available (including transport services), together with a fixed level of costs, then the well-being of A and B will depend upon how these goods, services, and costs are distributed between them.

The utility possibility frontier represents the maximum possible welfare they could enjoy given different distributions of the goods, services, and costs. Initially, the goods etc. are distributed so that point X on the pre-investment frontier is achieved (that is, A enjoys a utility of $0U_A^*$ and B of $0U_B^*$). The goods, services, and costs could be redistributed so that any other point on pre-investment could be obtained but no point outside of it. Suppose now that a transport investment results in the bundle of goods, services, and costs changing and that position Y beyond the pre-investment frontier is reached. This would be deemed a Pareto improvement because both A and B are better off. Indeed, any *ex post* position within the 90° zone marked (such as Y) would be Pareto-superior to X since, even on one of the limits, at least one person is better off while the other, at worst, retains their original utility level.

The strict Pareto criterion is of little use in practice as most transport schemes have either direct or indirect net adverse effects on some members of the community. The suggested method of allowing for this, developed in the late 1930s, is to adopt a hypothetical Pareto criterion and decide whether, after the investment, it would be possible to redistribute the impacts in such a way that no one is worse off but there is still some residual gain to others. Whether such redistribution occurs is felt to be a normative issue and should be treated as being within the domain of politics rather than economics.

There are two broad approaches to the hypothetical compensation criteria. The first, initially advanced by Nicholas Kaldor (1939), forms the basis for most CBA studies and suggests that a scheme is socially desirable if the beneficiaries could compensate the losers and remain better off. In the upper part of Figure 11.3, Y is Kaldor-superior to X (although not strictly Pareto-superior) because Y is on the post-investment utility possibility frontier that passes outside of X. Hence, the bundle of goods, services, and costs which generate the post-investment frontier could be redistributed from Y to Y^*, which is Pareto-superior to X.

Whether the government instigates a tax/subsidy scheme to cause such a movement along the post-investment frontier is considered a political issue; Kaldor (in a discussion of the repeal of the nineteenth-century Corn Laws!) simply argues that it could be done. John Hicks (1940) favors a similar approach but adopts pre-investment weights for his criteria. Specifically, he argues for a project's acceptance if those who lose as a result of its implementation cannot bribe the gainers not to do it without becoming worse off themselves. In the figure, Y is Hicks-superior to X because, with the pre-investment package of goods, services, and costs that permitted the post-investment frontier to be attained, it is impossible for A (the loser) to bribe B (the beneficiary) not to support the investment.

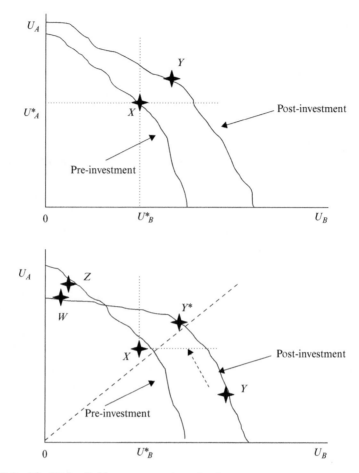

Figure 11.3 *The Hicks–Kaldor compensation criteria*

The problem with the Kaldor and Hicks approaches is that they may, in some circumstances, contradict one another. For example, in Figure 11.3, although combination W is Kaldor-superior to X, we can see that X is Hicks-superior to W. Further, even if one only used the Kaldor test and the investment was completed and position W attained, it then becomes possible to show that it is, again following the Kaldor criteria, socially beneficial to disinvest and return to X. (Similar types of problems exist with the Hicks test.) Paul Samuelson (1961) argues that the problem will always exist if the pre- and post-investment utility possibility frontiers cross and that comparisons in such circumstances are invalid.

This is an extremely restrictive view. Provided the two positions being compared are on the same side of any intersection of the frontiers, then the two criteria give consistent assessments and there are no problems of 'reversibility' (Skitovsky, 1941). Figure 11.3, for instance, shows a situation where Y meets both the Hicks and the Kaldor hypothetical compensation tests and may, therefore, be considered socially superior to X. There is also no question of advocating reversibility once the investment leading to Y has been undertaken. Whether, in practice, transport analysts need to test for these problems is an empirical question that has, to date, been inadequately explored. At least one experienced economist in the CBA field suggests that the Skitovsky criteria may be violated on more occasions than is sometimes supposed.

A different problem may arise when appraising a series of piecemeal investments. It is possible, because of the relative nature of consumer surplus that underlies all these tests, for a series of small investments each to pass the Skitovsky test but for the eventual outcome to be socially inferior to the initial position. In Figure 11.4, if we have an initial position of E on the pre-investment frontier, then an investment that permits F to be reached satisfies Skitovsky's criterion (and, indeed, Samuelson's); further, a move from F to G, following additional investment, may be approved and, likewise, a subsequent move from G to H, which again meets the Skitovsky test. However, despite the fact that we have seen that $E < F < G < H$ in terms of hypothetical compensation tests, it is clear in Figure 11.4 that E is preferable, on Skitovsky grounds, to H. Each of the series of small changes appears desirable, but the final, overall outcome leaves society worse off.

If this problem was only a theoretical curio there would be no need for concern, but unfortunately this does not seem to be the case. Numerous examples of piecemeal decision-making leading to a subsequent diminution of social welfare can be cited in urban planning, but in the context of transport perhaps the most worrying problem concerns the growth in car use since the Second World War at the expense of urban public transport (Mishan, 1967). For simplicity, we take a concentric-shaped city with employment concentrated in the

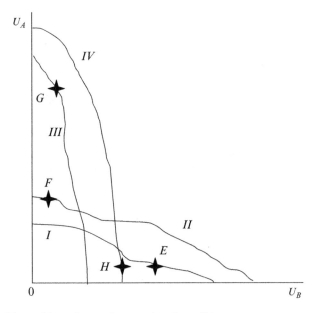

Figure 11.4   *The problem of assessing a series of small investments*

center. The urban core is surrounded by a ring of residential estates. The analysis is short-term and assumes that this land-use pattern is fixed. It is now possible to define three phases:

- *Phase I.* All commuters have only one mode of transport available to them and travel to work by means of public transport – taking ten minutes is the norm.
- *Phase II.* One commuter buys a car and drives to work, taking five minutes, leaving the other travelers unaffected by his/her action and still taking ten minutes to reach work by public transport
- *Phase III.* Many commuters, observing the advantage enjoyed by the car driver, begin to buy and use cars that, with the congestion they generate, increase driving time to work to 15 minutes and, due to the impedance caused by the cars, slows public transport so that commuters using this mode now suffer a 25-minute journey. In the longer term, because of the technologically unprogressive nature of public transport, the service may be withdrawn (following the syndrome of few passengers ⇒ higher fares and poorer service ⇒ even fewer passengers, etc.), leaving a choice of car purchase or walking to work. The result is a 'prisoner's dilemma' type of situation, where individually each commuter would prefer the original situation, rather than the new undesirable equilibrium, but cannot attain it by uni-lateral action.

The example illustrates the difficulties which may arise as the result of decisions based upon relative welfare measures: each commuter thought that he or she would benefit by investing in a car because they did not take cognizance of the whole set of decisions being made. Ideally, a CBA study should appraise all the systems or sequences of potential investments other than assess individual components of a program of events. The urban planning process, discussed in Chapter 12, is an area where this is relevant.

While most CBA studies of transport projects have concentrated on efficiency considerations, relying upon the hypothetical compensation criteria, it may be seen as important that some allowance for distributional impact should be incorporated. Specifically, it is argued that a project should only be accepted using the hypothetical type of criteria if the outcome improves the income distribution. For example, in the lower part of Figure 11.1, we assume that an improved income distribution means greater equality of welfare and thus corresponds to a movement closer to the 45° line depicted. Thus, Y, on the post-investment policy frontier, is both Skitovsky-superior to X and offers more equality because it is closer to the 45°, equal utility, line. It is important to note that it is the outcome that is being considered and not potential redistributed packages of the post-investment collection of goods, services, and costs. As we see in Section 11.5, there are several ways in which this distributional element may be incorporated within CBA studies.

11.6   Coping with Network Effects

The discussion above applies to all CBA applications, but a difficulty of applying the technique to transport investment decisions is the need to incorporate
adequately the wide-ranging effects that a change in one part of the transport
system has on the rest of the network. Most transport infrastructure forms a
link in a much larger, interacting network and, consequently, changes in any one
link tend to affect demand on competitive and complementary links. Although
this sort of complexity exists for virtually all forms of transport, the problem
of assessing the overall effect on road transport of improving a single link has,
because of the dominance of this form of transport in modern society, attracted
most attention.

If there are two roads, one from X to Y and the other from X to Z, where Y
and Z are to some degree substitute destinations, then an improvement in route
XY will affect three groups. We will assume for simplicity that all demand curves
are linear and that the pre-investment traffic flows on XY and XZ are T_{XY} and
$(T_{XZ} + R)$ respectively. The three groups of users to consider are then:

1   Existing users who remain on their original routes (that is, T_{XY} and T_{XZ}).
These will enjoy a gain in consumers' surplus because those on route XY
will now be using a higher-quality facility while those on XZ will benefit
from reductions in demand for this route as some former users switch to
the improved XY. If this latter traffic, which has diverted from XZ to XY, is
denoted as R, then the total benefit to those remaining loyal to their initial
routes may be represented as:

$$T_{XY}(C_1 - C_2) + T_{XZ}(C_1^* - C_2^*) \qquad (11.3)$$

where C_1, C_2, C_1^*, and C_2^* are the pre- and post-investment costs by roads XY
and XZ respectively.

2   Generated traffic consisting of people who did not previously travel (that
is, G_{XY} and G_{XZ}). On average (given the linear demand curves), each of
these groups of new road users will benefit by half as much as existing, non-
switching traffic. (Some will obviously be marginal trip-makers and only just
gain by making a trip, while others are intra-marginal and enjoy nearly as
much additional consumer surplus as the non-switchers.) The total benefit
of the investment to this group will thus be:

$$0.5G_{XY}(C_1 - C_2) + 0.5G_{XZ}(C_1^* - C_2^*) \qquad (11.4)$$

3   Diverted traffic that switches from route XZ to route XY because of the
investment (that is, R). The switch, given the free choice situation open to
travelers, must leave this group better off – they would not have switched otherwise – and the additional welfare they enjoy can be seen to equal half of the
difference in benefit between the cost reductions on the two routes, that is,

$$R\{(C_1^* - C_2^*) + 0.5[(C_1 - C_2) - (C_1^* - C_2^*)]\}$$

which may be reduced to:

$$0.5R[(C_1 - C_2) + (C_1^* - C_2^*)] \tag{11.5}$$

The total benefit of the investment is the summation of these three elements, namely:

$$TB = T_{XY}(C_1 - C_2) + T_{XZ}(C_1^* - C_2^*) + 0.5G_{XY}(C_1 - C_2)$$
$$+ 0.5G_{XZ}(C_1^* - C_2^*) + 0.5R[(C_1 - C_2) + (C_1^* - C_2^*)] \tag{11.6}$$

Figure 11.5 shows this diagrammatically. The left-hand part of the figure represents the supply and demand situations on route XY and the right-hand part represents those on route XZ. On route XY we see that demand has increased the supply of road space but that demand for its use has declined because the relative generalized cost of using XZ changes as traffic diverts from it to the improved facility.

Using the notation in the diagram, we know that $Q_{XY} = T_{XY}$ and that $Q'_{XY} = (T_{XY} + G_{XY} + R)$, therefore:

$$0.5(Q_{XY} + Q'_{XY}) = (T_{XY} + 0.5G_{XY} + 0.5R)$$

Similarly, since $Q_{XZ} = (T_{XZ} + R)$ and $Q'_{XZ} = (T_{XZ} + G_{XZ})$ we know that:

$$0.5(Q_{XZ} + Q'_{XZ}) = (T_{XY} + 0.5G_{XY} + 0.5R)$$

Substituting this into equation (11.6) we discover:

$$TB = [0.5(Q_{XZ} + Q'_{XZ})(C_1 - C_2) + 0.5(Q_{XZ} + Q'_{XZ})(C_1^* - C_2^*)]$$

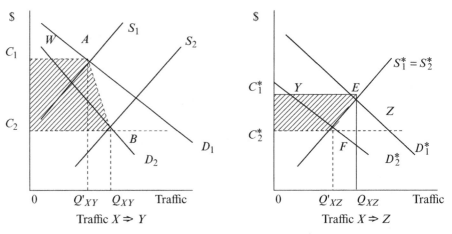

Figure 11.5   *Social benefits over a transport network*

or more generally, this is the oft-cited 'rule of half':

$$TB = 0.5 \sum_{N} (Q_n + Q_n^*)(C_n + C_n^*)$$ (11.7)

This net benefit is equivalent to the shaded areas seen in Figure 11.5. The rule of half can be applied to all transport schemes that interact with other components of the transport system where demand curves are linear. (It must, however, be used with a degree of circumspection when routes are complementary, where demand for the non-improved links may shift to the right, but the broad principle applies.)

The method of handling interdependencies outlined above was initially developed in the late 1960s as part of the London Transportation Study, but it does rely upon a rather strong implicit assumption that the income elasticities of demand for routes XY and XZ are equal. The problem is that there are many possible sequences in which the price changes on routes XY and XZ could follow; each would yield a different level of aggregate social welfare. For instance, if the chain of price changes is $(C_1, C_1^*) \Rightarrow (C_2, C_1^*) \Rightarrow (C_2, C_2^*)$ then the consumer surplus gain in the diagram would be $\{(C_1AXC_2) + (C_1^*YFC_2^*)\}$. But if the sequence is $(C_1, C_1^*) \Rightarrow (C_1, C_2^*) \Rightarrow (C_2, C_2^*)$ then the aggregate benefit would be $\{(C_1WBC_2) + (C^*_1EXC_2^*)\}$.

The general measure set out in equation (11.7) assumes that the demand fluctuations are linear in their own prices and with respect to cross-price effects; if this is so, then the measure would give identical results to both the sequences outlined above (which would themselves yield identical benefit estimates). Whether such assumptions are valid is debatable, but Foster and Neuberger (1974) argue that any deviation is unlikely to be of any practical significance in practical evaluation exercises. Certainly, given the other major difficulties of evaluation and measurement, the 'rule of half' provides a robust and useful guide to the user benefits of transport schemes.

11.7 Cost–Benefit Analysis in Practice and Variations on the Theme

Our attention, to this point, has focused on the theoretical ideas and concepts underlying CBA. We now turn to look more directly at its application in transport fields. The equation set out above (equation (11.2)) gives a formal mathematical definition of CBA, while Prest and Turvey (1965) give the verbal counterpart:

> CBA is a practical way of assessing the desirability of projects, where it is important to take a long view (in the sense of looking at repercussions in the distant as well as the immediate future) and a wide view (in the sense of allowing for side effects of many kinds on many persons, industries, regions, etc.) that is, it implies the enumeration and evaluation of all the relevant costs and benefits.

CBA has, over the years, formed the basis of investment appraisal of many major transport schemes in the United Kingdom (for example, the M1 motorway, the Victoria Line underground railway, the Channel Tunnel, London's system of ringway or beltway urban motorways, and the siting of a third London airport) and elsewhere. It has also become a tool in more routine decision-making, for example, to assess railway social service subsidies in the late 1960s and as a component of inter-urban road investment appraisal in the form of COBA and its subsequent modification, New Approach to Appraisal (NATA).

The United Kingdom situation, however, is a specific case. Elsewhere, there can be important variations in the forms of appraisal used to assess transport projects, some more comprehensive and others less so. Table 11.4 offers a broad overview of the differing nature of decision-making processes in several major European countries adopted from the 1990s. Over-riding these when European Union financing is involved are standard Union appraisal frameworks that have to be applied. The United States, being a federal system, has both a manual for conducting CBA for national highway investments as well as each state having its own approach for allocating its own resources (US Federal Highway Administration, 2020).

Major transport infrastructure appraisals, such as that conducted by the Roskill Commission in the late 1960s when looking at possible sites for a new London airport, have generally sought to provide a comprehensive economic assessment. But many CBA studies are less ambitious. The COBA computer program that was for many years employed as part of the inter-urban road appraisal process in the United Kingdom, for example, emphasised consistency of methodology over the comprehensive coverage of all costs and benefits. COBA made use of traffic forecasts derived from a standardized procedure and used them to compare discounted monetary valuations of travel time changes, variations in vehicle operating costs, and impacts on accident rates with the capital and maintenance costs of a project. While this provided an indication of the costs and benefits to traffic and the Exchequer, information on third-party effects, such as environmental impacts, were, until the early 1990s, treated separately. They were

Table 11.4   *The nature of transport infrastructure decision-making in European countries*

Country	Systems approach	Master plan	Inter-modal cooperation	Time horizon	Private financing
France	S	M	S	Long	M
Germany	M	W	M	Long	S
Italy	S	M	S	Short	S
Belgium	S	S	S	Short	S
Sweden	M	M	S	Medium	S
Denmark	M	M	M	Short	S
Norway	M	M	S	Medium	S
Finland	S	S	S	Medium	S
Switzerland	W	W	M	Long	S

Notes: S = scarcely developed. M = partially developed. W = well developed.

Exhibit   *The Third London Airport Study*

The Third London Airport Study, The Roskill Commission, which reported in 1971, established the modern textbook CBA approach to large-scale investment appraisal. In this case, however, it was not a full CBA study because it was assumed that a new airport was necessary for London anyway and that the economic benefits were deemed virtually equal for all possible sites.

The growth in United Kingdom air traffic grew rapidly throughout the 1950s, and by the early 1960s the question of a possible third London airport began to emerge. By 1961, it was forecast that the two London airports, Heathrow and Gatwick, when considered together, would exceed capacity from about 1973 and there was a need for a new, two-runway airport by 1980. After several attempts to look at alternatives in essentially a piecemeal way, a Commission was established in 1968. This, under Mr Justice Roskill, was '[t]o enquire into the timing of the need for a four-runway airport to cater for the growth of traffic at existing airports serving the London Area, to consider the various alternative sites, and to recommend which site should be selected'.

	Cublington	Foulness	Nuthampstead	Thurleigh
Capital costs				
Construction of airport	184.0	179.0	178.0	166.0
Airport services	14.3	9.8	14.5	11.6
Extension/closure of Luton Airport	−1.3	10.0	−1.3	−1.3
Road & rail development	11.8	23.4	15.5	6.5
Relocation of defense & public scientific establishments	67.4	21.0	57.9	84.2
Loss of agricultural land	3.1	4.2	7.2	4.6
Impact on residential conditions	3.5	4.0	2.1	1.6
Impact on schools, hospitals, etc.	2.5	0.8	4.1	4.9
Other	3.5	0.5	6.7	10.2
Total	288.8	252.7	284.7	288.3
Current costs				
Aircraft movements	960.0	973.0	987.0	972.0
Passenger users	931.0	1,041.0	987.0	931.0
Freight users	13.4	23.1	17.0	13.9
Airport services & operations	60.3	53.1	56.2	55.6
Travel costs to/from airport	26.2	26.5	24.4	25.4
Other	12.4	7.5	8.5	7.2
Total	2,003.3	2,124.2	1,988.1	2,005.1
Benefits (relative to Foulness)				
To common/diverted traffic (net of costs)	–	n.a.	–	–
To generated traffic	44.0	n.a.	27.0	42.0
Total (cost minus differential benefits)	2,248.1	2,376.9	2,245.8	2,251.4

Note: The table is only a partial reflection of the results obtained and does not, for example, include the sensitivity analysis conducted.
n.a. = not available.

The implication of the question posed involved considering where and when an airport should be built – not whether one should be built. This meant that in some ways it became a social cost-effectiveness study: finding the site with the lowest social costs attached to it. The initial list of 78 sites was reduced to an intermediate list of 29, before detailed consideration of Cublington, Foulness, Nuthampstead, and Thurleigh.

While the study team favored Cublington as marginally superior to the other sites, subsequent parliamentary debate over-ruled this in favor of Foulness. Although even this revised proposal was later abandoned, the study proved useful in showing up some of the practical difficulties in conducting a CBA study of a scheme which has extremely wide-ranging and diverse impacts – many of them posing serious problems of evaluation.

The present values of the various cost and benefit items for each alternative discounted from 2006 back to 1975 values and in millions at 1970 prices are given in the table. In all, the final analysis comprised 20 factors for consideration. All the estimations made were essentially based upon informed judgements.

Many of the items had shadow values placed upon them to allow them to be represented in a common unit. Noise nuisance, for example, was valued using hedonic indices. These considered the market value of housing at various distances from the noise envelopes created by aircraft taking off and landing at airports. These values were broken down by such things as the sizes of plots, the sizes of the housing units, the number of features of each house – bathrooms, bedrooms, etc., – whether there was a garage, distance from shopping facilities, etc., as well as the noise impact they were subjected to. Normalizing for all features but noise nuisance and setting this off against house values provided an economic cost of the noise.

Regarding travel time costs to/from the various locations, values were placed on the loss of work due to travel to and from an airport and on leisure time adjusting for the average incomes of business and leisure travelers. These were further broken down by mode of transport used (cars, light vans, and public transport), making allowances for occupancy levels. The values used were based upon theoretical considerations that work time costs were ultimately borne by the employer and thus the extra wages and supplementary payments to workers was used. For leisure, a fraction of this derived from empirical studies was adopted. Similarly, the costs at the airport of boarding, taxing, etc., were included, together with the costs to airlines of the different routings they would have to fly.

The site at Cublington was recommended by the Commission but the government rejected this and accepted a dissenting report by Colin Buchanan, a member of the Commission, which recommended that a new airport should be developed at Foulness (later known as Maplin Sands) in Essex. Subsequently, plans for a new airport were replaced by a smaller-scale redevelopment of Stansted Airport, a site not short-listed by the Roskill Commission.

See also: E.J. Mishan (1970) What is wrong with Roskill, Journal of Transport Economics and Policy, 4, 221–34; and Roskill (Commission on the Third London Airport) (1971) Report, HMSO.

considered, and largely in qualitative terms, in public inquiries into which COBA quantitative outputs were also fed.

Despite the widespread adoption of CBA by the transport sector, there has been a gradual disillusionment with the all-embracing, stereotypical appraisal implied by Prest and Turvey. This has manifested itself most strongly since the rejection of the Roskill Committee's recommendation regarding the siting of a third London airport and became noticeable at public inquiries into new road proposals in the late 1970s and early 1980s. While the criticisms of CBA as a method of socially evaluating transport investments have been extensive, they are perhaps most adequately summed up by Aaron Wildavsky (1966): 'Although cost–benefit analysis presumably results in efficiency by adding the most to national income, it is shot through with political and social value choices and surrounded by uncertainties and difficulties of computation'. A former Chairman of British Rail, Peter Parker, summarized the attitude evolving in the United Kingdom when he argued that there is a need for an approach that

> can be understood by ordinary intelligent people [and] incorporates the methods of analysis developed by welfare economists over the last decade or so [and] gets away from the naive position adopted by the early cost–benefit men which seemed to imply that every consideration could be perfectly weighted and that, therefore, there was a single best solution.

The responses of analysts to these dissatisfactions with mechanical CBA procedures took two broad lines. The first was an attempt to modify the original CBA framework (as exemplified by equation 11.2) with some allowances made to meet the major criticisms. Effort was put into evaluating externality items included in a CBA account and to placing more reliable values on time-saving attributes of schemes. Advances on this front were more rapid in some countries than in others. Sweden, for example, used a variety of techniques to enable a diverse range of effects, often expressed in monetary terms, to be brought into the appraisal process. The position in the United Kingdom was to seek a consistent process following experimentation in embracing a limited number of environmental factors within COBA (UK Department of Transport, 1992).

Additionally, techniques have evolved that introduce allowances for the distributional effects of schemes – an area neglected in earlier work which concentrated on overall impact – and for the risk and uncertainty that the predicted cost and benefit streams will diverge from that forecast. Theoretically, distributional effects can be allowed for by weighting the costs and benefits according to the different groups affected. Unfortunately, it has been demonstrated at the theoretical level that in many investment situations the applications of such weights (which may be based upon measures reflecting income tax liability) to cost and benefit items can still lead to the acceptance of projects which benefit the rich to the detriment of the poor. Consequently, there is a case for treating distributional considerations independently of efficiency.

Risk and uncertainty about probable outcomes pose even more difficult problems. With risks there is some knowledge about the likelihood of errors in forecasts and this can be incorporated in the analysis by indicating the range of probable long-term effects of investment, together with an indication of the probabilities of different levels of costs and benefits occurring. Unfortunately, there is no such knowledge of possible error with uncertainty, and consequently adjustments tend to be made according to intuition or 'skilled judgment'. With many transport projects, the costs of under-engineering are likely to be higher than those of comparable over-engineering (the 'premature' physical disintegration of the United Kingdom motorway system being a good example) and thus there is a tendency to over-react to the possibility of uncertain outcomes.

While these advances in traditional CBA techniques went some way towards meeting criticism of early studies in the field, they tend to complicate the estimation and decision-making frameworks and, hence, to move even further from the openness sought by the Minister for Transport and the Leitch Committee on Trunk Road Investment appraisal in the 1970s. One offshoot of CBA which retains the notion of social welfare maximization but also makes the CBA account accessible to the proverbial 'educated layman' is the planning balance sheet (PBS), which was initially devised and developed over a series of case studies to help urban planners. We discuss the PBSs in more detail below.

The second response to the critics is to move entirely away from the notion of a social welfare maximization CBA approach and to adopt a lower-level, but possibly more operational and manageable, approach to investment appraisal. This, for example, is the approach that has increasingly been followed in France since the late 1960s.

Broadly it is argued that, like most large private companies, public transport undertakings have insufficient information about the stream of costs and benefits (including social items) associated with the different policy options open to them and should, therefore, attempt to meet broad minimum levels of achievement rather than to maximize net benefits. This notion of 'satisficing' fits in with the attitude of most mature industrial concerns towards managerial decision-making (Simon, 1959). Although this second type of response to the critics of CBA is, to date, still comparatively under-researched in the transport field, several multi-criteria investment appraisal techniques have been developed, often only at an abstract level, in related areas of study such as regional and national resource planning (Dimitriou et al., 2016).

The PBS approach mentioned above, although firmly founded in the CBA tradition, offers a methodology that is sufficiently flexible to adaptation for both maximizing and satisficing frameworks. It has two main merits: first, it shifts the emphasis of analysis away from the total measure of net benefit to the distribution of the costs and benefits among affected groups; and, second, it circumvents many of the problems associated with expressing all costs and benefits in money terms.

The technique involves setting down, in tabular form, all the pros and cons associated with alternative investment options. These socioeconomic accounts are expressed in monetary values wherever possible but should this prove impracticable then physical values are used and, if quantification is not possible, ordinal indices or scales. The accounts are subdivided to show the effect of different

schemes on the groups affected, and this offers guidance to distributional implications. The accounts are compared with pre-determined planning goals (and these
instrumental objectives may imply either maximization or satisficing objectives)
which are selected as reflective of community preferences. Alternative investment
plans are ranked under each objective heading using ordinal ranking procedures
and the ranks are then added together to produce a ranking of the investments
with respect to the objectives taken as a whole.

A technique of this general kind met with approval from the Leitch
Committee in the United Kingdom as a tool in inter-urban road investment
appraisal. The Committee felt 'the right approach is through a comprehensive
framework which embraces all the factors and groups of people involved in
scheme assessment' (UK Department of Transport, 1978b). The project impact
matrix, as the Leitch Committee called their variation, sets out a 'general framework' of about 80 relevant measures of the effects of transport schemes. As
with most PBS studies the final account produced was extensive but Table 11.5
provides a summary. The intention is to use such an account to make pair-wise
comparisons between the magnitude of the effects associated with different
investment alternatives, or, where the problem is deciding upon a specific project
in isolation, to compare them with some instrumental objectives.

The PBS-type approach has, despite its attractions, some inherent limitations. It depends upon crude ranking criteria and scaling methods. The selection of instrumental objectives is itself highly subjective and, although it does
force the decision-maker to make his/her underlying value judgments explicit, it
can result in some conflict between interested parties. There is also the danger
that the subjectivity of these objectives and trade-offs is forgotten in the mass
of data incorporated in the accounts. The PBS has the advantage over some
of the more mechanical approaches where numbers are simply fed into some
computer program (such as COBA, developed in the United Kingdom for trunk
road investment appraisal) in that the construction of the initial socioeconomic
account can often be educational and can shed considerable light on salient questions the decision-maker should be asking.

While PBS can be considered as an extension of CBA, it may also be viewed
as a primitive form of a 'multi-criteria decision-making technique'. Multi-criteria
decision-making techniques fall into the second category of advances outlined
previously, in that they are concerned more with the meeting of certain low-level
aims than with maximizing social welfare. They involve weighting the different
effects of an investment to reflect social priorities, but the weights reflect success
at attaining certain objectives rather than maximizing an output.

Several multi-criteria approaches have been devised, each attempting to
achieve a multi-dimensional compromise between the wide diversity of goals and
objectives that are embodied in any form of public choice. Approaches differ in
their methods of presentation, the level of mathematical sophistication involved,
and the amount of data input required. Several of the techniques rely upon
geometrical representation to produce multi-dimensional scalings, while others
involve a considerable degree of intuition. Of greatest practical value in transport

Table 11.5   *The project impact matrix suggested by the Leitch Committee in the United Kingdom*

Incidence group	Nature of effect	Number of measures	
		Financial	*Other*
Road users directly affected	Accident savings	1	3
	Comfort and convenience	–	–
	Time savings	6	–
	Vehicle operating cost savings	5	–
	Amenity	–	2
Non-road users directly affected	Demolition or disamenity to owners of residential, commercial, & industrial properties	–	22
	Demolition or disamenity to users of schools, churches, public open spaces	–	15
	Land-take, severance, & disamenity to farmers	–	7
Those concerned with the intrinsic value of an area	Landscape, scientific, & historical value	3	–
		(+ verbal description)	
Those indirectly affected	Sterilization of natural resources, land-use planning effects on other transport operators	–	6
		(+ verbal description)	
Financial authority	Cost & financial benefits	19	7

Source: Adapted from UK Department of Transport (1978a).

are some of the weighting techniques, of which there are numerous variations. Maurice Hill's (1968) goal achievement matrix, for example, offers an explicit treatment of various goals and applies a set of pre-determined weights to them so that each option can be assessed in terms of goals achieved. To facilitate this, the goals are related to physical measures (for example, minimum traffic speeds, acceptable accident rates, reduced levels of specified toxic exhaust emissions, etc.) to reflect the extent to which they have been achieved. The final goal achievement account employs the weighted index of goal achievement to determine the preferred course of action.

The problem with all useful multi-criteria procedures is the derivation of weighting schemes that reflect the relative importance of physical 'goals' or 'objective instruments'; seldom will a public sector transport scheme do all that is hoped for. The traditional CBA approach, albeit in a maximizing context, avoids this problem by using monetary values as weights. While there is evidence that those responsible for decision-making in the publicly controlled sectors of transport favor movement towards multi-criteria appraisal techniques, the practical problems are unlikely to permit the widespread use of such approaches – beyond the project impact matrix type of analysis – soon.

These types of modifications to the cost–benefit approach are likely to lead to a more consistent treatment of environmental effects, but there is a more fundamental point about infrastructure provision. It has been argued that the conventional CBA approach to appraisal, because of its inherent assumptions regarding pricing, can lead to over-investment in transport infrastructure and excessive transport use. In Figure 11.6 we show various combinations of prices charged for road use, and, on the vertical, various levels (in money terms) of investment. There will be some optimal price–investment mix, such as P^*/S^*, which is optimal. This would be the socially efficient outcome if road users were charged optimal prices (embracing all external considerations) for their journeys.

Suppose, however, that the price in effect does not fully reflect costs; then, since there would be a heavy demand for road use, the conventional CBA approach would imply that more investment than S^* is required. Curve *I* traces out the relevant optimal price–investment combinations that would emerge. In fact, the low price is generating demand beyond the optimal level and thus the overall amount of traffic on curve *I* at points to the left will be suboptimally large. William Wheaton (1978) argues, therefore, that investment should be limited along a *P/S* curve such as *II*. The additional congestion occurring at any price below P^*, because of the limited additional investment in capacity, will in effect constrain traffic flows to the optimal level. The reasoning behind this conclusion is summarized by Wheaton in the following way:

> Such a reduction will increase congestion, and this helps to discourage the demand that has been 'artificially' induced by underpricing. It is important to remember that second-best investment does not call for building fewer roads as the price of driving is lowered. That would result in 'excessive' congestion. Rather it requires accommodating less of the induced demand than would be met if a simple cost–benefit analysis were applied.

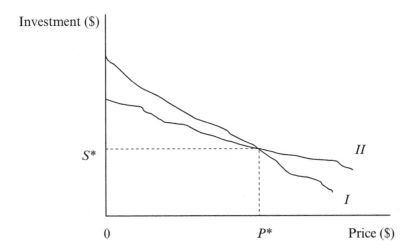

Figure 11.6   *Second-best investment with suboptimal congestion pricing*

Applying this to the question of environmental policy, the relevance is mainly in terms of just how much investment in new infrastructure is economically justified when transport prices do not reflect true costs. The standard methodology tends to ignore the imperfections which exist in terms of transport users not paying for the full costs of their activities and thus to favor high levels of investment. Wheaton's analysis essentially implies that in these conditions, where money prices are ineffective, second-best criteria determined by travelers' time costs (that is, congestion) can be used to limit travel to a level closer to the optimum.

The conditions for achieving this second-best situation may, however, prove to be complex. In terms of equity there may be a further argument in favor of such an approach, in that time is allocated even across individuals. Practically, there are difficulties in working out the optimal second-best strategy and, in overall environmental terms, given the proportionately higher pollution, noise, and other costs associated with congested roads, it is not altogether clear what the ultimate overall social outcome would be.

11.8   Comparability Between Appraisal Techniques

If scarce investment funds are to be allocated to best effect within the overall transport sector and between it and the rest of the economy, it is clearly important that in some way comparisons are made between the potential effect of using funds in projects evaluated on commercial criteria and using them where social evaluation techniques such as CBA are employed.

Accepting that for institutional or administrative reasons there is no hope of a common method of assessment being employed in practice, then one possible method of comparing projects between sectors is to develop comparability criteria that reduce social and financial costs and benefits to a common denominator. Essentially a mathematical relationship between net social and net financial returns must be found. In certain highly restrictive situations this may prove to be feasible. It is theoretically possible, under simplistic assumptions, to reduce everything to either a common financial or common social basis; we will assume, however, that we are assessing a potential investment aimed at improving an inter-city rail service (where profit-maximizing levies are charged) and wish to convert the net reserves obtained into social welfare terms. Social welfare is assumed here to refer to social surplus (that is, combined consumer and producer surpluses), as is standard practice in welfare economics.

Figure 11.7 shows the demand curve for the existing rail service to be linear (D_1 with marginal revenue curve MR_1) and that the improvement will result in a parallel shift of this curve to D_2. The average and marginal costs of using the service are assumed to be constant, irrespective of custom with MC_1 ($= AC_1$) being the relevant curve prior to improvement, and MC_2 ($= AC_2$) being operative afterwards.

With these assumptions, the demand curves are easily represented: D_1 as $P = a - kQ$ and D_2 as $P = b - kQ$, where P is price, Q is the level of traffic flow,

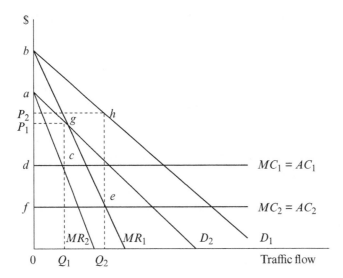

Figure 11.7 *Comparability between commercial and social investment criteria*

and k is the slope of the parallel demand curves. With profit maximization (that is, output at the point where $MC = MR$), it is seen from Figure 11.7 that $Q_1 = (a-d)/(2k)$ and $Q_2 = (b-f)/(2k)$. Integrating under the relevant marginal revenue curves shows that the improved rail service would increase profits by {Area (*bef*) – Area (*acd*)}, which is:

$$0.5(b-f)Q_2 - 0.5(a-d)Q_1 = \frac{1}{4k}\left[(b-f)^2 - (a-d)^2\right] \qquad (11.8)$$

The increase in consumers' surplus associated with the improved rail service is obtained from integrating under the relevant demand curves but above price. In this case the integration yields Area (*bhP₂*) – Area (*agP₁*), which equals:

$$0.5(b-P_2)Q_2 - 0.5(a-P_1)Q_1 = \frac{1}{8k}\left[(b-f)^2 - (a-d)^2\right] \qquad (11.9)$$

Since social surplus is composed of producers' surplus (that is, profit) plus consumers' surplus, it is apparent from adding equation (11.8) to equation (11.9) (and then comparing back to equation (11.8)) that the gain in social welfare, resulting from rail investment in this profit-maximizing situation, is 1.5 times the profit which would be earned. It seems possible, therefore, in the circumstances, to be able to convert profits earned into a comparable social surplus by multiplying by 1.5.

How useful is this conversion factor likely to be in practice? This only applies to user costs and does not permit the inclusion of external factors, either in terms of pollution or congestion, which limits its usefulness in urban transport appraisal or for certain types of infrastructure, such as airports, which are environmentally intrusive. Further, even within the strict confines of user-benefit analysis the conversion factor crucially depends upon a series of limiting assumptions. The factors which have been found to influence the ratio include:

- the shape of the *MC* curve before and after the investment;
- the shapes of the demand curves before and after the investment;
- the extent of price discrimination;
- the pricing policy pursued and the nature (if any) of its deviation from profit maximization;
- the consistency of the pricing policy employed as investment alters the cost and demand conditions;
- the incidence of externalities including network effects; and
- the extent to which revenue and benefit streams differ in their availability for reinvestment.

Given the sensitivity of the '1.5 rule' to these various factors, it is hardly a practicable method of introducing comparability into transport investment decision-making.

The comparability ratio approach assumes an investment is undertaken and then prices set to achieve some economic objective, usually profit maximization. Financial returns are then compared to social returns. Starkie (1979) argues that a more practicable approach is to determine a common basis for pricing first and then adjust capacity accordingly. The basic idea stems from work on the railways by Stewart Joy (1964), who looked exclusively at freight investment, but Starkie generalizes the approach to all forms of transport investment. It is assumed that the correct economic price for each mode is determined along the second-best pricing lines formalized by William Baumol and David Bradford (1970), and that investment, or disinvestment, should be adjusted until *LRMC*s are equated with the revenues obtained. This means that prices are set to cover *SRMC* with a mark-up in proportion to the inverse of the price elasticity of demand for each mode. The mark-up then reflects 'what the user will bear' towards the cost of capacity provision (that is, consumer surplus above *SRMC*). If this mark-up, combined with the revenue covering *SRMC*, does not meet the full *LRMC* then capacity should be reduced until an equality is established. If such a pricing regime produces a surplus in excess of *LRMC* then, *ceteris paribus*, there is a case for expanding capacity.

The fundamental idea is that if sufficient price discrimination is applied then all potential consumers' surplus is transferred to the supplier and, *ipso facto*, net revenue can be equated with social surplus. Its main advance is the importance which it places on pricing and the recognition that in the long run it is possible to fine-tune investment at the margin. Such an approach obviously removes the need to conduct comparability studies but it has its limitations. The main difficulty is that, while it may be possible in some areas to apply the discriminate pricing Starkie advocates, and mainly those undertakings directly controlled by government, in other cases private provision of transport facilities makes it rather difficult to ensure that the Baumol/Bradford rules are being applied.

Consequently, it is difficult to see how it could be decided what is the correct level of overall investment in the publicly owned sector of transport *vis-à-vis* the aggregate for the private sector. Because much public investment is assessed on social criteria and virtually all private sector investment is assessed on commercial criteria, many of the problems of comparability remain. (This problem is avoided in Starkie's empirical work, which focuses on road and railway track investment.) Further, the approach once again emphasizes user benefits but does not allow for external factors, especially the environmental effects of transport on non-users.

11.9 Assessing the Effect on National Income

It has been suggested that, rather than expand financial surplus by a comparability ratio, or force some form of common pricing on all sectors of transport, an entirely different measure of the net value of investment, applicable to all forms of transport project irrespective of ownership, may be preferable. The effect of transport on national income, for example, could be used as a substitute for the combined consumers' and producers' surplus generated. However, besides the practical difficulties involved in estimating the change in national income associated with alternative transport investments, the measure throws up an additional problem that involves the more fundamental question of whether the national income approach really does offer a reasonable and acceptable guide to the relative desirability of alternative investments. (We should perhaps note at this stage that national income, in this context, refers to the accountancy concept used in macroeconomics rather than the wider notion of national income referred to by Wildavsky earlier in the chapter.)

We can consider Figure 11.8 and assume that demand will not shift following a change in capacity. Further, if we assume the transport undertaking acts as a monopolist in its pricing policy, then we can see that an investment that reduces marginal costs from MC_1 to MC_2 will increase social surplus by (*hgcd*) in the diagram and profits by (*hdef*) – (*gcba*). The reduction in costs will also produce a higher national income. If the Laspeyres index is used (that is, the change in output valued at the pre-investment price), the rise will be measured as Q_1cjQ_2. If the Paasche approach is favored (that is, the change in output is valued at the post-investment price), however, the addition to national income is found to be only Q_1idQ_2.

There is no reason for the social surplus measure to correspond to the national income measure (or for different estimates of the latter to correspond) except in rather unrealistic circumstances. Nor, indeed, need it correspond to the profit generated. Of more practical importance, there is no reason why alternative investment possibilities will be ranked consistently by the different methods.

The reason why social surplus and national income measures (and, indeed, financial measures) need not correspond, nor rank consistently, stems from the fact that they measure entirely different things. Social surplus both includes

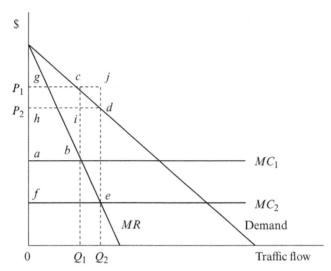

Figure 11.8 *The national income change approach to transport investment appraisal*

leisure benefits emanating from a project and explicitly incorporates allowances for the diminishing marginal utility associated with the increased consumption of travel. The national income measure does neither: it concentrates exclusively on goods and services traded in conventional markets, and assumes either a fixed pre- or post-investment price level.

Herbert Mohring (1976) demonstrated that the only time the two types of measure yield identical numerical results is *'If* a change takes place which increases the output obtained from a given set of primary resources, and *if* the primary resources allocated to market activities do not themselves change, and if the same pricing rules are used in consumers' surplus as in national income change benefit calculations' (emphasis original). Clearly, this means that in practice, the national income measure is likely to differ from either the financial or social surplus measure of benefit and hence is simply an alternative method of ranking and appraisal. It is different but not necessarily superior. Given the practical difficulties of estimation in most advanced economies its usefulness seems limited. In less developed countries, though, it may be a more viable appraisal technique if distributional and welfare considerations are felt to be of secondary importance to boosting the national product. Transport projects that help stimulate national income growth in these circumstances may be given priority over others.

The practical problems of incomparability between investments in different transport sectors has not gone unnoticed by United Kingdom and other transport authorities. The problem is particularly acute in publicly owned inland inter-urban transport where government policy in countries like the United Kingdom have distinguished between different types of service, some of which must show a financial return and others a social return. While the moves towards privatization and deregulation from the 1970s (see Chapter 14) have rather blurred the distinction, the problem of allocating resources between commercial and social transport services remains.

Certain measures have been introduced in the United Kingdom that attempted to standardize some elements of appraisal procedures across the two groups. Since the late 1960s, for example, discounting techniques were employed in all sectors using a nationally stipulated rate of discount. Some minor changes in the basis of calculation took place subsequently but such techniques remained the main tool of appraisal for a long period. The differences between sectors are just the items discounted; in one case it is simply the fare revenues, while in the other it is user benefits (usually calculated in terms of the financial value of the money, accident rate, and travel time changes associated with the investment).

The official position, until relatively recently, was that, although there may be a need to take distributional or environmental factors into account when doing either type of calculation, the pricing policies pursued mean that revenue may be equated with social surplus in the financially based calculation. Comparability then becomes unnecessary. The rationale behind this view was summarized by the Department of the Environment, the argument being that although 'the mechanics of assessment differ ... in ordinary circumstances British Railways pursue a policy of market pricing which ensures that *most benefits to users are fully reflected in the revenue collected*' (emphasis added). A Select Committee was not convinced, however, that inconsistencies did not remain and advocated the establishment of an Interurban Directorate to tackle the problem.

The Leitch Committee in the United Kingdom, when looking at trunk road investment, examined comparability in more detail and recommended that consistency could only be achieved if those undertakings employing financial techniques extended their analysis to embrace the wider social-surplus-based procedures of appraisal. As we have seen, the type of CBA envisaged, however, is somewhat more comprehensive and transparent than that currently used for road investment appraisal in the United Kingdom, which concentrates solely on user benefits. Further, to gain an even greater degree of consistency, there is a need to bring port and airport investment into the general CBA framework and widen the scope of appraisal away from the purely financial aspects which tend currently (with some significant exceptions) to dominate decision-making in these spheres.

While the notion of common CBA techniques being applied throughout the publicly controlled inter-urban transport system may have certain apparent advantages – in Germany and some other European countries it is used for all inter-urban road, rail, and waterway analysis – the Leitch study recognized that the private ownership of coastal shipping and pipeline limits the degree of comparability. Essentially, the widespread use of CBA within the publicly owned sector (which, in fact, goes beyond the road/rail situation considered by Leitch) may produce consistent investment decisions within this sector but does not determine the optimal size of public *vis-à-vis* private sector investment. In effect, very limited progress has been made towards a common method of economic assessment for road and rail investments in the United Kingdom, and some other countries.

11.10   Some Institutional Considerations

From a policy perspective, while there are reasons to ensure that adequate transport is available to facilitate economic development, and thus infrastructure
investments are made efficiently, there are market imperfections that can prevent
this from happening. One set of constraints encountered in most countries
is associated with planning requirements (Plotch, 2015). These can delay the
construction of a facility and affect its design and operations. We will not deal
directly with these issues here, because they vary considerably between countries,
but will rather focus on issues of finance and efficient operations. Financing
can pose particular problems in poorer countries, or even regions within more
prosperous nations, if they do not have an adequate tax base or access to more
sophisticated money markets. The scale of much transport investment also means
that they often get entangled in macroeconomic policy and the cycles of public
expenditure that accompany this.

Just taking the example of airports (although roads or seaports would serve
equally well): airports are relatively expensive to build, and, because of their
monopoly status in many locations, are often not operated efficiently. To reduce
the X-inefficiency, there have been moves in many countries to make airport
operators more commercially oriented. The national approaches aimed at inject-
ing more commercial pressures into the provision of airport services have varied.
Much of the interest that is now emerging is either in the privatization of some
aspects of airport activity or in engaging the private sector in some partnership arrangement with the state. In part this is because an airport is effectively
a composite entity consisting of units offering a variety of services: land access,
parking, concessions, terminals, runways, ground handling, fire and response
units, security, etc. Commercialization does not have to be applied to all these
activities, and may be pursued in a piecemeal way if politics or economics dictate.

Approaches differ according to the state of the local air transport market,
which is, in turn, often linked to the stage in economic development of the region
concerned. For example, airports can vary in terms of their potential revenue
flow from different sources – for example, slot fees and concessions – and this can
affect the degree of privatization or deregulation that is possible and the form it
is most likely to take.

Much depends on the state of the regional air transport market. The
forecasts of relatively slow longer-term growth in air traffic in and between the
developed countries (for example, estimated at about 2.6 percent a year to 2039
within North America, 3.3 percent within Europe, and 2.5 percent between North
America and Europe) means that their major airports will increasingly become
dependent on commercial or non-aeronautical revenues to enhance their revenue
stream. This in turn can pose problems in terms of regulation, as has already been
seen in the debates over the imposition of the price-capping regime used in the
United Kingdom.

While still relatively small, the protected growth of many air markets involving regions of developing countries offers the potential for increased airside

revenue in situations where there are potentially fewer social constraints involving such things as noise and land-take on building additional capacity or where there is already adequate capacity. The scope for raising significant commercial income is much less, however, because of lower initial traffic bases. It also suggests, though, that the regulatory regime overseeing a privatized airport system needs to be less sophisticated because it must only deal with airside issues, making the potential for various forms of regulatory capture smaller.

The problem for regions of the poorest developing countries, however, is that even though their air traffic flows may in aggregate be growing, this is from a low base and they still seldom generate sufficient revenue to cover the full costs of operations. Airports are essentially decreasing cost entities for which cost recovery can be difficult, especially in a situation where there is competition from other airports. This makes pure privatization options less tenable and the need for outside assistance from aid agencies or from government more relevant. PPPs offer another alternative (Button, 2008).

The wide variety of circumstances around the world has led to a diversity of approaches to commercialization of airports. Some have involved complete divestiture of former state assets to the private sector, albeit with some oversight of how the airport is operated, but in other instances the withdrawal of the state has been less complete.

The management contract approach retains government control, but involves contracting out specified elements of airport services – parking, hotels, retail concessions, etc. – for periods of time. This normally involves some form of auction. The system is in line with the notion of 'competition for the market'. Long-term contracting involves giving over the operational side of an airport, sometimes including investment commitments in additional capacity, for an extended period with the authorities retaining a degree of strategic control. The financing required normally entails bringing specialized international companies with the expertise to manage an airport, or system of airports, together with finance houses that can provide the necessary support for large-scale service activities. These types of concessions are widespread in South America, where local expertise and finance is limited, but there is reluctance for the state to divest itself of aviation assets.

Many developed countries have also pursued similar philosophies when expanding the involvement of private enterprise, but falling short of complete divestiture (Button, 2007). Many United States airports have adopted various concessionary schemes – for example, Boston, Pittsburgh, and Reagan National Airport in Washington DC have entered into concessionaire agreements, for the entire operations at Pittsburgh and for specific terminal buildings at the other airports. At Chicago O'Hare airport, parking has been contracted out, and the Port Authority of New York and New Jersey, which owns several airports, has a variety of agreements covering such things as the operation of terminal buildings and the supply of heating and cooling at some of its facilities. There is also a tradition in the United States of significant airline involvement in providing check-in facilities and baggage systems.

Complete privatization of major airports is uncommon, although increasing. In most cases there is concern that a privately owned airport will exercise its monopoly power to extract rent from customers. The challenges are to devise and operationalize appropriate regulatory regimes to monitor and direct these large companies in the public interest; often price-capping is deployed. The ongoing debates about full privatization concern such things as whether single airports, or as with Argentina, systems of airports, should be privatized, and when they are privatized, what should be regulated? Should it be all airport activities or just those directly aviation-related?

In their overview of various governance options, Michael Carney and Keith Mew (2003) focus correctly on the government being involved in both seeking to improve the efficiency of their airports and at the same time trying to direct the gains to specific groups rather than leaving management with full autonomy in their actions. This involves complexities that, while common to businesses in developed countries, are unfamiliar in many parts of the world. As a result, this has added to the growth in international firms specializing in airport management, including ownership, to allow the development of common, best-practice methods of operation while at the same time being innovative in creating bespoke models for different circumstances.

References

Atkinson, A.B. (2011) The restoration of welfare economics, *American Economic Review*, 101, 157–61.

Baumol, W.J. and Bradford, D.F. (1970) Optimal departures from marginal cost pricing, *American Economic Review*, 60, 215–43.

Button, K.J. (2007) The implications of the commercialization of air transport infrastructure, in D. Lee (ed.), *The Economics of Airline Institutions, Operations and Marketing 2*, Elsevier.

Button, K.J. (2008) Air transport infrastructure in developing countries: privatization and deregulation, in C. Winston and G. de Rus (eds), *Aviation Infrastructure Performance: A Study in Comparative Political Economy*, Brookings Institution.

Button, K.J. (2016) Public–private partnerships: a review of economic considerations with particular reference to transportation projects, *Transportation Planning and Technology*, 39, 136–61.

Button, K.J. and McDougall, G. (2006) Institutional and structural changes in air navigation service-providing organizations, *Journal of Air Transport Management*, 12, 236–52.

Carney, M. and Mew, K. (2003) Airport governance reform: a strategic management perspective, *Journal of Air Transport Management*, 9, 221–32.

Dimitriou, H.T., Ward, F.J., and Dean, M. (2016) Presenting the case for the application of multi-criteria analysis to megaproject infrastructure appraisal, *Research in Transportation Economics*, 58, 7–20.

Elhorst, J.P. and Oosterhaven, J. (2008) Integral cost–benefit analysis of Maglev rail projects under market imperfections, *Journal of Transport and Land Use*, 1, 65–87.

Foster, C.D. and Neuberger, H.L.I. (1974) The ambiguity of the consumer's surplus measure of welfare change, *Oxford Economic Papers*, 26, 66–77.

Guasch, J., Laffont, J.-J., and Straub, S. (2008) Renegotiation of concession contracts in Latin America: evidence from the water and transports sector, *International Journal of Industrial Organization*, 26, 421–42.

Hanson, I.G. (2011) Review of public–private partnerships in heavy railway infrastructure projects, COST Symposium Public Private Partnerships in Transport: Trends and Theory, Lisbon.

Hart, O. (2003) Incomplete contracts and public ownership: remarks, and an application to public–private partnerships, *Economic Journal*, 113, C69–C76.

Hicks, J.R. (1940) The valuation of social income, *Economics*, 7, 105–24.

Hill, M. (1968) A goal achievement matrix for evaluating alternative plans, *Journal of the American Institute of Planners*, 34, 19–29.

Joy, S. (1964) British Railways' back costs, *Journal of Industrial Economics*, 13, 74–89.

Kaldor, N. (1939) Welfare proposition and interpersonal comparisons of utility, *Economic Journal*, 49, 549–52.

Lindblom, C.E. (1959) The science of muddling through, *Public Administration*, 19, 79–88.

Mackie, P.J. and Simon, D. (1998) Twenty-one sources of error and bias in transport project appraisal, *Transport Policy*, 5, 1–7.

Mishan, E.J. (1967) Interpretation of the benefits of private transport, *Journal of Transport Economics and Policy*, 1, 184–9.

Mohring, H. (1976) *Transportation Economics*, Ballinger.

Plotch, P.M. (2015) What's taking so long? Identifying the underlying causes of delays in planning transportation megaprojects in the United States, *Journal of Planning Literature*, 30, 282–95.

Prest, A.R. and Turvey, R. (1965) Cost–benefit analysis: a survey, *Economic Journal*, 75, 683–735.

Samuelson, P.A. (1961) Evaluation of social income, capital formation and wealth, in P.A. Lutz and D.C. Hague (eds), *The Theory of Capital*, St Martins.

Simon, H.A. (1959) Theories of decision-making in economics and behavioral science, *American Economic Review*, 49, 253–83.

Skitovsky, T. (1941) A note on welfare propositions in economics, *Review of Economic Studies*, 9, 77–88.

Starkie, D.N.M. (1979) Allocation of investment in inter-urban road and rail, *Regional Studies*, 13, 323–36.

UK Department of Transport (1978a) Report of the Advisory Committee on Trunk Road Assessment, HMSO.

UK Department of Transport (1978b) *COBA 9 Manual*, Department of Transport.

UK Department of Transport (1992) Assessing the environmental impact of road schemes: standing advisory committee on trunk road appraisal, Report, HMSO.

US Congressional Budget Office (1998) Innovative financing of highways: an analysis of proposals, Report, US Congress.

US Federal Highway Administration (2020) *Operations Benefit-Cost Analysis*, TOPS-BC User's Manual FHWA.

Vining, A.R., Boardman, A.E., and Poschmann, F. (2005) Public–private partnerships in the US and Canada: 'There are no free lunches', *Journal of Comparative Policy Analysis: Research and Practice*, 7, 199–220.

Wheaton, W.C. (1978) Price-induced distortions in urban highway investment, *Bell Journal of Economics*, 9, 622–32.

Wildavsky, A. (1966) The political economy of efficiency: cost–benefit analysis, systems analysis and program budgeting, *Public Administration*, 26, 292–310.

12 Transport Planning and Forecasting

12.1 The Development of Transport Planning

The preceding chapters have concentrated primarily upon pricing and investment decisions for individual modes of transport in isolation: the pricing of public transport, urban car users, etc. Little has been said about the coordination of pricing and investment decisions across whole sectors of transport. Coordination, as Adam Smith pointed out, will come about automatically in a perfectly competitive market framework where marginal cost pricing principles are universally applied. Indeed, there has been considerable emphasis on coordination through the market in the development of inter-urban transport policy in countries such as the United Kingdom and the United States, but extending more broadly, from the late 1970s as we shall see in Chapter 14. Concern over safety and the environment is now often considered to be the main interest of the authorities and, within a quality licensing and quality regulatory framework, competition both within and between inter-urban modes is often encouraged.

There is, however, generally some planning of infrastructure provision in most countries, either by central or local government. At the international level there are coordinated plans for strategic highway, air traffic control, and high-speed rail developments. Some involve integrated planning of all transport systems, as in the Trans-European Networks program of the European Union, while others, including the Pan-American Highway linking almost all of the Pacific coastal countries of the Americas, are mode-specific. The extent and nature of this planning varies considerably between countries, as well as between modes and regions within them. The main objective in these cases is often the avoidance of duplication, especially in relation to major development projects with a long period of gestation, and the adoption of a high degree of technical consistency.

In other areas of transport activity, and especially in the urban context, this feeling has declined somewhat in recent years, necessary to introduce a high degree of planning, with central and local government intervention to improve the overall efficiency of local transport provision. The role that transport may play in other spheres of economic activity is one reason for this (improved transport, for example, may form part of a social welfare policy and is currently seen as central to the revitalization of local economies in depressed inner-city areas), but a more general explanation may be found in the magnitude of the imperfections of the urban transport markets. The justification for urban transport planning in this context was usefully summarized some years ago in a United Kingdom Department of Transport (1977) policy document, *Transport Policy*:

The many activities concentrated in urban areas must be accessible to people and the economic and social life of cities depends on enormously diverse and complex patterns of travel and destination. Yet there is not enough road space in large towns and cities for people to travel as much as they like and how and when they like. This can be one source of grievance. Another is that intrusion of dense traffic brings objectionable and sometimes intolerable noise, fumes and vibration.

We have already seen, in Chapter 6, the extent of the external effects of transport and have subsequently considered ways in which they may be tackled individually. A comprehensive marginal pollution pricing regime combined with comparable social investment criteria could, for example, ensure optimality. Political resistance to such an approach, combined with disquiet over the possible distributional repercussions and the practical problems of implementation, have so far tended to rule out the full-scale use of market mechanisms to regulate the urban transport sector. This does not mean that the pricing mechanism is not used, but rather that it forms part of a much larger package of policy instruments which are combined with the intention of improving the overall efficiency of urban transport in meeting the objectives of society.

Planning history and philosophies differ between countries, but there are some general themes that are common (Lay, 2005). Technology changes have often been a driving force; for example, the advent of the steam locomotive brought with it the need for strategic planning as fixed networks of rail had to be laid, which led to early traffic surveys and forecasts of traffic flows to enable priorities to be developed and costs to be calculated. The emergence of street cars and underground transport systems from the late 1850s meant that urban transport planning began to emerge, with government acting as facilitator for the private sector.

Exhibit   *Blue-print planning: L'Enfant's transport plan for Washington DC*

Pierre Charles L'Enfant developed the plan for Washington DC, the new United States capital, in 1791. The underlying legislation specified that the capital should be situated on the Potomac River between the Eastern Branch (the Anacostia River) and the Conococheague Creek near Hagerstown, Maryland. Thomas Jefferson, the secretary of state, had modest ideas for the capital. L'Enfant saw the task as far more grandiose, believing that he was also devising the city plan and designing the buildings. There was limited economic thought in L'Enfant's subsequent blue-print. It was design-driven.

L'Enfant developed a Baroque plan featuring ceremonial spaces and grand radial avenues, while respecting natural contours of the land. There was a system of intersecting diagonal avenues superimposed over a grid system. The avenues radiated from the two most significant building sites that were to be occupied by houses for Congress and the Presidency. L'Enfant stated that the avenues were to be wide, grand, lined with trees, and situated in a manner that would visually connect ideal topographical sites throughout the city, where important structures, monuments, and fountains were to be erected.

Open spaces were as integral to the capital as the buildings to be erected around them. Washington's current road network largely follows L'Enfant's plan.

Little economic thinking went into the blue-print plan. Ideas of even rudimentary cost–benefit analysis were absent. There were no serious comparisons with alternative road layouts. The grid street pattern offers efficiency in moving traffic, and modern road use makes use of uni-directional traffic flows over much of the system, with movements being in opposite directions along parallel streets. The intersecting diagonals, however, produce bottle-necks.

Little thought was given, either, to the management of traffic flows. Lights and traffic circles (roundabouts) now offer some increased capacity at major junctions, and there are parking controls. Nevertheless, Washington suffers from acute traffic congestion problems as highlighted by former city mayor, Adrian Fenty, in his comment that 'roughly 250,000 commuters drive solo into Washington daily, making them both polluters of our air and freeloaders of our infrastructure'.

See also: C.M. Harris (1999) Washington's gamble, L'Enfant's dream: politics, design, and the founding of the national capital, *The William and Mary Quarterly*, 56, 527–64.

By the end of the nineteenth century, transport planning had reached a stage that would be recognized today. It had become a sequential process (Weiner, 2008):

* *Political.* This is planning at the conceptual level and considers broad social and economic goals.

- *Development.* This is planning at the strategic and systems level, embracing factors such as land-use and service levels.
- *Transport.* This is conducted at the corridor level, considering transport demand management and infrastructure provision.
- *Facility.* This entails the implementation of the plan, with the provision of track capacity and its design.

In more detail, the history of urban transport planning in the United Kingdom, as a case study, is comparatively short, originating in the recognition that urban life-styles and cities themselves would change once ownership of private cars became widespread. The physical planners of the immediate pre- and post-Second World War periods were concerned with redesigning cities and transport infrastructure to meet the requirements of an automobile age. Abercrombie, in the County of London Plan of 1943, for example, typified much of the philosophy of the period in his proposals for the university quarter of Bloomsbury and the area around Westminster, by advocating the application of the precinctual principle. Traffic was to be diverted around these areas on good-quality arterial roads, with the precincts served by a limited number of local access routes. While this idea, which was American in origin, was never applied to the two sites studied by Abercrombie, the broad principle was employed in the post-war reconstruction of Coventry.

The 1947 Town and Country Planning Act institutionalized planning by making anyone wishing to develop land seek permission from the local authority. The basis for decision-making regarding land-use changes were a series of proposal maps which traced out proposed land uses for a horizon of ten years or more. The 'Town Map' was a legal document that both took time to prepare and required cumbersome procedures to be gone through prior to changes being accepted.

The system had the advantage that it allowed land to be set aside for schools, residential development, and so on, but only limited land was allocated to road construction. Further, since funds were not always available for rapid construction programs, in many places where land was allocated for transport corridors it led to blight and lack of maintenance of buildings that might at some unspecified future date be taken for road building. These were problems since a central theme of the physical planning approach to the urban transport problem was that improving the local transport network could alleviate excessive traffic congestion.

As traffic grew, alternative solutions were sought. While the initial approach to urban planning had been a narrow one, two important developments occurred in the 1950s and 1960s which strengthened the concept. First, although some planners, such as Abercrombie, took a broad geographical view of urban problems, the focus of most early planners tended to be local, seeking piecemeal solutions to specific traffic problems. In the 1950s there was a widening-out. Local highway authorities were encouraged by central government to produce joint plans for local road networks and the joint plans produced by the authorities in the

Manchester area (the SELNEC Highway Plan of 1962) and by the Merseyside area authorities (in 1965) bear witness to the success of this policy. Second, and not entirely independent of coordinated highway planning, came the recognition of the strong links between land use and transport planning.

The Buchanan Report (UK Ministry of Transport, 1963) provided firm evidence of the need to coordinate the two areas of planning. Buchanan was concerned about the environmental cost of traffic, and argued that urban road networks should not be expanded to the extent needed to reduce congestion to some pre-defined levels, as was then the accepted practice, but rather changes in transport and urban land-use systems should be assessed in terms of the costs of reducing congestion while maintaining some pre-defined environmental standard. If the costs of expanding the transport network without violating the environmental standard proved excessive to the community then traffic should be restrained until the environmental limit was attained.

Once it became recognized that not only was there a need to consider objectives other than simply congestion in transport planning, especially since transport is an integral part of a much wider urban economic system, it became apparent that physical planning needed to be replaced by a more comprehensive planning framework. The coordinated approach which resulted embodied 'structure planning', which sets out policies for the development of land, transport, and the local environment.

The United Kingdom's Town and Country Planning Act of 1968 embodied the idea of structure planning while the creation of the Department of the Environment in 1970 integrated overall responsibility for urban and transport planning into one organization. The 1968 Transport Act created several passenger transport authorities (PTAs) in major conurbations that were given responsibility for public transport operations within their areas. The PTAs were themselves committed to drawing up policies (within a year) and plans (within two years) to provide 'a properly integrated and efficient system of public transport to meet the needs of [the] area'. While the commitment to draw up structure plans necessitated liaison and coordination between local planning and highway departments and the PTAs, in practice land-use, road building, and public transport responsibilities remained separate – indeed in some cases the agencies had different boundaries.

The Local Government Act, 1972, integrated the existing PTAs, plus three newly created ones, into a reformed local government structure. The Act placed further emphasis on the need for coordinated transport planning in urban areas and each urban authority was compelled to produce a Transport Policy and Programme (TPP) setting down the strategy and objectives that were being followed. The TPPs have been used since 1975 as a means of assessing the level of central government financial aid to local urban transport undertakings (via the Transport Supplementary Grant) and emphasis has been placed on integrating transport planning with the wider issues of land-use planning and social policy in the area. The aim of this structure, therefore, has been to distribute grants to reflect local transport needs, and to reduce central government control.

The move to structure planning, which still forms the basis for local transport policy today, resulted in two major changes in the types of approach adopted by local transport agencies. First, there has been a trend towards more structured and phased planning; the Tyneside Study of 1968, for instance, produced an immediate action program, a transportation plan for a 15-year horizon and a general urban strategy plan to the end of the twentieth century. The TPP framework encourages a continual monitoring and updating of plans within a rolling framework. Second, planning is no longer viewed simply in terms of investment but now embraces the short-term management of existing resources. In part this may be a reflection of the changing objectives of urban transport planning but it is also the consequence of a greater economic awareness in planning that there is an opportunity cost associated with all actions involving the employment of scarce resources.

12.2   The Ethos of Transport Planning

The movement away from physical transport planning to structure planning in the 1960s increased the economic input into the transport planning process, although the development of modern planning methods must be attributed mainly to civil engineers, statisticians, and mathematicians rather than economists. One of the main problems of urban land-use/transport planning is the enormous range of possible options available, although this is much less of a difficulty in a country such as Britain, where urban land-use patterns are long-established and not susceptible to rapid change; in such cases, one is seeking the optimal transport system for the existing urban structure. A sequential approach to urban transport planning may, therefore, be appropriate with the four different levels of planning outlined in Section 12.1 taking place viewed as system designs:

1   design of broad land-use plan;
2   design of strategic transport plan;
3   design of detailed land-use plan; and
4   design of detailed transport plan.

(There may be some feedback between numbers 3 and 4 in the sequence.)

The transport planning process itself is complex and entails far more complex institutional and technical issues than can be fully considered here. In general, as we have seen, it can be broken down into several stages, each involving a certain amount of economic input to it. There is no firm or accepted best-practice method of drawing up a transport plan, since different agencies favor different detailed approaches. Broadly, however, the process may be typified by the various stages set out in Figure 12.1, but this must be seen very much as a stylization, intended rather more to show where economics can contribute to the transport planning process, than as a representation of any actual planning procedure. A few comments are justified on each of the stages.

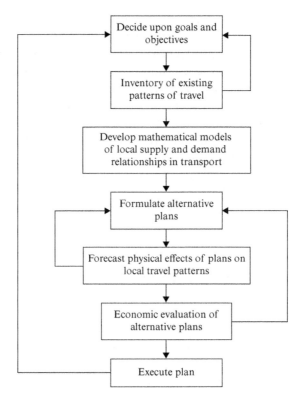

Figure 12.1   *The urban transport planning process*

Goals and Objectives

As we have seen above, the objectives of urban transport planning tend to change over time, periods where there is an emphasis being placed upon social and environmental considerations often being followed by a focus on improving the efficiency of the system. The general objectives of policy need to be made specific to permit trade-offs between alternative goals at a later stage of the planning process. The economist's contribution at this stage is that of a balancing agent, often counteracting engineering pressures for the emphasis of the plan to be on improving traffic flow or adopting capital-intensive solutions to environmental problems. The notion of 'opportunity cost' is essential if resources are to be used efficiently. The economist may also act as a sieve, pointing out the incompatibility or contrary nature of certain goals. Since goals and objectives are often formulated at the beginning of the planning exercise, before full information on existing transport problems have been obtained, they may be redefined after later stages in the sequence.

Inventory of Existing Transport System

Information is gathered about the nature of the local transport system and travel patterns both by sampling and counting people in the act of transport and by obtaining information from firms and households about their travel behavior and requirements (Stopher, 2008). Additional information is often extracted from official sources such as the Census, the National Travel Survey, and the Family Expenditure Survey. The types of surveys conducted and the questions asked have changed over the years as a result of important developments in transport forecasting. As we see in later sections, much more emphasis is now placed on understanding why people travel rather than on modeling flows of traffic.

Consequently, more detailed information of household characteristics is now sought, although the greater efficiency of modern measuring techniques means that the actual sample size has tended to fall (from over 10,000 households in the large studies of the late 1960s – the last substantial household survey in the United Kingdom, that of the West Yorkshire Transportation Studies, sampled 12,322 addresses – to considerably fewer than 1,000 today).

The broad-brush approach has given way to seeking greater insights into representative travel behavior. For example, while the US Federal Highways Administration (1973) set out guidelines for surveying household trip-making patterns in the 1970s, more recently there have been advances for collecting broader information on household activity patterns to help link these with travel behavior (Stopher, 1992).

One reason for this is that the types of planning issues under review have changed with time, with large road building programs tending to be replaced by traffic management and public transit policies. But modeling has also evolved. There has been a shift away from the more mechanical types of approach to travel patterns, and more of a focus on understanding factors that influence them. The development of stated preference techniques in recent years, for example, has furthered our understanding of the underlying nature of travel decisions. Quite clearly, since the basic aim is to seek information on existing conditions of supply and demand for urban transport services, economists can contribute to formulating the types of questions to ask as well as the forms of model in which information will be fed.

Mathematical Simulations of the Local Transport Market

The following sections look at modeling and forecasting techniques, and their economic underpinnings, but it is important to emphasize at this stage the basic requirements of the simulation models. Transport markets are complex and to produce models which replicate all their details is both difficult and, more importantly, likely to be too cumbersome for later forecasting work. Ian Heggie (1978) suggests that the pre-requisites of a good transport model are that it:

• assists in understanding and explaining behavior;
• aids policy formulation; and
• provides robust predictions.

The models of travel and transport demand are used for forecasting; therefore, it is important that the explanatory factors can themselves be predicted with some degree of certainty. The models are also used to assess the effects of different planning options; thus, it is important that they are simple to use and permit the effect of several alternative strategies to be explored. One of the major limitations of early models was that they were cumbersome to manipulate, limiting the possible policy options that could be assessed.

Formulating Alternative Plans

The complex and wide-ranging effects of any change in an urban transport system makes it very difficult in practice for more than a limited number of detailed plans to be fully formulated. A comprehensive plan consists of a package of projects and schemes, and for a large city the possible combinations forming such a package are immense. In some cases, only one planning alternative is drawn up in detail after a preliminary sifting of other possibilities at an earlier stage in the planning process.

Usually, the planning alternatives considered are a little more numerous and, besides the 'do nothing' situation, which may act as a benchmark, generally involve at least one public-transport-orientated package, one private-transport-based proposal and probably one rather more central alternative, offering a mix of private and public transport. Since the plans themselves are later evaluated, this approach should not be as restrictive as it appears. Following the forecasting and/or the evaluation stage new light may be shed on the detailed effect of alternative plans, and new compromise packages of projects emerge. Without feedback of this kind, it would be quite possible, given the vast range of alternative plans that are feasible for most large cities, to miss the potentially most beneficial alternative.

Forecasting the Physical Effects of Alternative Plans

Transport forecasting is looked at in detail in Sections 12.3 to 12.6, the modeling and forecasting stages being both central to the planning process and having a very substantial economics component. The key aspect of forecasting is that it provides the planner/decision-maker with useful information about the long-term implications of plans, emphasizing those areas where there are significant differences in the consequences of the alternative plans. Given the fact that transport is going to exist in the urban setting, irrespective of the plan adopted, and providing a 'do nothing' option is assessed, then it is the relative performances of plans that are important. Additionally, it is important that the final decision-makers are aware of the underlying assumptions of the forecasts, so that they can assess the reliability and strengths of the traffic forecasts. To this end, most forecasts are now presented as a range of likely outcomes under alternative assumptions.

Economic Evaluation

The economic evaluation of plans normally involves employing some variant, albeit in a less formalized format, of the cost–benefit analysis (CBA) approach outlined earlier. The comprehensive nature and emphasis on distributional effects which characterizes the planning balance sheet makes it an attractive technique in the urban planning context. It is also sufficiently 'open' as to permit the various consequences of plans to be related directly to the objectives of the planners.

With traditional CBA, not only are there problems of placing monetary values on many items, but also members of the urban community often view the final output of a single net present value of benefits with suspicion. General practice involves the inclusion of public participation at the evaluation stage, often in the form of public inquiries. In some cases – such as the Layfield Inquiry into the Greater London Development Plan in the United Kingdom – such inquiries can result in quite substantial revisions of the plan to be adopted. Evaluation of something as complex as a transport plan is, by necessity, a political process, but economists can assist the decision-maker by ruling out plans which are *clearly* inferior to others while at the same time giving a systematic presentation of the pros and cons of the final short-list of alternatives.

The inherent value judgments built into all forms of CBA make it a powerful aid in evaluation, but it is unlikely ever to provide an automatic, purely technical decision-making calculus, indeed it is debatable whether such a mechanical approach is to be desired.

Implementation

While it is often possible to implement some parts (usually traffic management components) of a transport plan almost immediately upon acceptance, other components (usually those involving infrastructure changes) are much longer-term in nature. It is important, therefore, that actions are phased so that costs are kept at a minimum. Additionally, over time objectives change and 'errors' in forecasts become apparent, and this may necessitate revisions of the plan. Consequently, there are feedbacks from the implementation stage back to the early stages of the planning process; in other words, modern planning is seen as an ongoing, rolling process of adaptation and change. It is often important, in this context, to ensure the maximum flexibility in the implementation program.

The preceding paragraphs have painted a thumbnail sketch of the transport planning process, highlighting the role economics can play. It is thin on detail and hides many of the subtleties of the planning exercise: readers interested in this specific aspect of transport economics are strongly advised to refer to one of the excellent texts now available on the subject. The following sections consider the economic problems of transport modeling and forecasting. These areas, together with plan evaluation, have become increasingly the preserve of economists and involve the application of modern microeconomic theory.

12.3 Traffic Modeling and Forecasting

At the outset it should be said that the objective here is not to provide anything like a comprehensive account of how traffic is modeled for planning purposes; this is a subject that extends well beyond our scope. What we do is provide an indication of the types of models that have been adopted, their limitations from an economic perspective, and some information on some of the more economically oriented approaches that are gradually coming to the fore. In the past, much of the work in this area has been dominated by engineers who have been rather neglectful of the ways in which travelers make decisions, relying instead on notions of flows derived from the physical sciences.

To conduct successful planning exercises, or indeed many other forms of policy development, it is, however, essential to have reliable forecasts of the probable effect of different policy options. General qualitative assessments can often provide useful insights into the effects of different policies, but good planning decisions require that we have more exact information of the detailed quantified relationship between travel and transport and the factors that influence them. Engineers, for example, need projections of future traffic flows when designing roads and other infrastructure. Recent years have witnessed a substantial growth in work attempting to specify and calibrate econometric travel demand models. Not everyone feels that economists are making great progress. As a general comment on economic forecasts, John Kenneth Galbraith observed: 'The only function of economic forecasting is to make astrology look respectable'.

In the United States, the increased role of the federal authorities in funding both inter-state transport facilities and local, urban transit systems had a similar effect. The need to allocate large sums to durable transport infrastructure schemes in the Third World motivated the World Bank to pursue a similar course. More recently still, the general move towards more careful project appraisal at the micro level has led to the development of stated preference techniques employing market-research-style procedures to transport forecasting.

Accuracy of Transport Forecast

Having noted the growth of work in the field, it is only fair to deviate and point to the quantitative limitations of what has been done before moving on to the technical details of methodology. In his classic paper on the methodology of positive economics, Milton Friedman (1953) emphasized the need for a good model to predict relatively well. In practice, however, very little retrospective work is done assessing the predictive abilities of models in transport economics.

An early assessment of traffic forecasting in the United Kingdom by Mackinder and Evans (1981) did not paint a very complementary picture of the engineering-based methods used at the time: '[A]n assumption of zero change from the base year would not have produced larger forecast errors ... . [F]or trips the errors would have been considerably less [than those obtained from a transport model]'.

A study in the late 1980s of 41 road schemes in the United Kingdom concluded from a comparison of actual and projected flows that only in 22 cases were the actual flows within 20 percent of the original forecast. Of the remainder, flows ranged from 50 percent below to 105 percent above the original estimate (UK House of Commons Committee of Public Accounts, 1988). The forecasts for the M25 London orbital road, for instance, were that on 21 of the 26 three-lane sections the traffic flow would be between 50,000 and 79,000 vehicles per day in the 15th year, whereas the flow within a very short time was between 81,400 and 129,000.

A noted exception is found in Dan McFadden's (2001) forecasts. These deploy a random utility mode split model to examine the construction of the Bay Area Rapid Transit (BART) system in the San Francisco area. The quality of his results may help explain why he was awarded the Nobel Prize in Economic Science, although it has not stopped the continued use of engineering consultants' four-stage modeling sequence for transportation forecasting. Capture is as endemic in transportation work as elsewhere. (While the conventional aggregate gravity model forecasts a 15 percent mode share for BART, his disaggregate forecast was 6.3 percent and the actuality was 6.2 percent. Despite this, BART has never adopted disaggregate modeling as a policy tool.)

Pickrell's (1989) study of grant programs funded by the United States federal Urban Mass Transportation Administration found that all ten urban public transport projects examined produced major under-estimates of costs per passenger (for example, the costs for the Miami heavy rail transit were 872 percent of those forecast, for Detroit's downtown people mover they were 795 percent of those forecast, and for Buffalo's light rail transit project they were 392 percent of those forecast). While inaccurate costing was one element of the problem, the forecast patronage in all cases was over-optimistic. Indeed, only the Washington heavy rail transit project experiences actual patronage that is more than half of that which was forecast. Some of the differences can be explained by difficulties in predicting future values of explanatory variables such as demographic changes, automobile costs, and the service level which the public transport service would offer, but Pickrell argues that important questions must also be raised over the structure of the models employed, the ways in which they were used, and the interpretation of output during the planning process.

Updating of this work by looking at cost and ridership forecasts for 47 United States transit systems indicates only limited improvements over time. Figure 12.2 provides details of the forecast versus out-turn investment costs. A positive value indicates over-estimation, while a negative value indicates under-estimation. Visual inspection shows that most transit systems do not perform as well as forecasted in terms of ridership, nor are they constructed consistent with their estimated costs; there are significant over-runs. For example, in the case of the Los Angeles Orange Line, ridership was under-estimated by more than 200 percent.

But there have been changes. During the period prior to Pickrell's study, visual inspection clearly suggests that ridership was over-estimated while capital costs

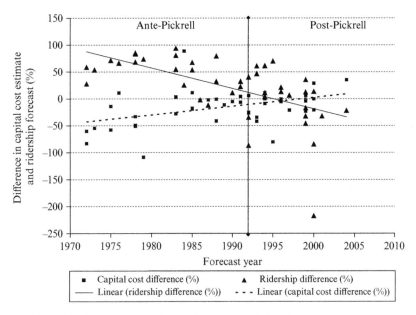

Figure 12.2   *Ridership forecast and capital cost estimate trends*

were under-estimated. However, during the post-Pickrell period, there has been a slight reversal of this. Further, post-Pickrell values are smaller than ante-Pickrell values (generally within 50 percent difference), implying an overall improvement in the forecasting and estimation process. The linear trend lines showing the differences in ridership forecasts and capital cost estimates reinforces this notion of improved forecasts; the differences moved closer to 0 percent line. Of course, external factors change with time (including land-use characteristics, transit system types, and transit technology), and corrections are needed to reflect this.

More recently, Bent Flyvbjerg et al. (2002), looking solely at cost estimations for 258 transport infrastructure projects (including rail, fixed-link, and roads) found they are generally under-estimated and are systematically misleading. Rail projects had the largest error where actual costs were 45 percent higher than estimated. Flyvbjerg (2007) later argues for techniques including benchmarking or reference class methods, to be developed to improve economic and financial risk assessment and management in transport policy and planning.

The Challenges of Forecasting

It is quite clear from these findings that forecasting traffic is far from easy. While these problems are diverse and some rather technical, several general comments on the application of econometric analysis to transport forecasting highlight the difficulties that have been encountered in constructing travel demand models.

First, transport is by its nature a derived demand but equally, as we have seen in previous chapters, it interacts with land-use and location patterns. There is, therefore, logic in developing a forecasting model that allows for these very close

Exhibit *Accuracy in traffic demand forecasting*

Considerable efforts go into the long-term demands for transportation and the costs of constructing and maintaining the required infrastructure. As an extensive number of *ex post* studies, and those of Flyvbjerg, have shown, however, the forecasts produced are generally not very accurate. The evidence is that demand for infrastructure is often over-estimated, and costs are under-estimated – for example, nine out of ten projects are subject to significant cost over-runs.

Railway projects

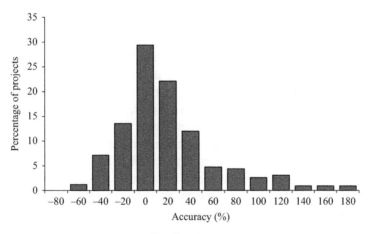

Road projects

Differences in the extent of these biases depend on the nature of the investments concerned. As we see in the figures, plotting the accuracy of passenger traffic forecast for 27 rail and 183 road projects from 14 countries across three continents, the most severe errors are related to rail projects; on average, rail traffic is over-estimated by over 100 percent compared to an average under-estimation of about 9 percent for roads. Rail errors also have a more bell-shaped error distribution. (Accuracy is the percentage by which the out-turn traffic fails to meet that predicted; a lower value on the horizontal indicates greater over-prediction.) The problem of misleading forecasts for road planners emerges as less serious than for the railways, and less one-sided.

Looking at the data over time, there are no indications that forecasts have become more accurate, indeed between 1969 and 1998 they may have become less accurate. Regarding rail, there also seems to be no difference in accuracy between forecasts made when a project commenced and when it was concluded. In the case of roads, the degree of under-estimation is, with some variation, largest when forecasts are made nearer the completion of the project. This latter situation seems to be due to 'assumption lag'. The forecasters in some countries seem to be slower to adjust their assumptions as planning and construction moves forward.

Inaccuracies also seem to grow with the costs involved in rail projects, but this is not the case with roads, although they do increase with larger projects when measured in terms of vehicles involved. The latter result has also been seen regarding aviation forecasting.

Those involved in traffic forecasting often provide specific reasons for deviations from the outcome values. These 'soft' data indicate that, for rail, uncertainty over the distribution of traffic and a deliberate 'slanting of forecasts' appear as dominant causes. The effect is to bias subsequent cost–benefit analysis in favor of rail investment. With respect to rail, uncertainty about overall traffic growth and over land-use development are major issues. There appears to be much less political interference in road traffic forecasting, and in the ultimate forecasts that are accepted, than is the case with railways.

See also: B. Flyvbjerg, M.K. Skamris Holm, and S.L. Buhl (2005) How (in)accurate are demand forecasts in public works projects? The case of transportation, *Journal of the American Planning Association*, 71, 131–46.

linkages. This is obviously not an easy thing to do but it is unlikely that reliable long-term forecasts will be forthcoming if transport and land-use models are treated in tandem rather than developed within an interactive framework. Indeed, using the type of interlinked land-use and transport model set out in Figure 12.3, it was shown that interactive effects over time account for a significant portion of the economic benefits of a transport scheme (Berechman and Gordon, 1986).

Moving on to the actual transport modeling framework, traditional micro-economic analysis specifies a demand relationship relating quantity demand to price and assumes that this relationship only changes (that is, shifts) when factors other than price vary. In transport demand analysis it is easy to incorporate the 'shift' variables into a modeling framework because their values are essentially determined outside the transport system (for example, income changes or changes in taste). The 'control price' variable is much more difficult. As we have seen, price is a broad concept in transport, embracing time, comfort, and other factors, in addition to simply the monetary cost of a trip. While generalized cost offers one method of reflecting the multi-dimensional nature of the price variable there is a tendency in forecasting work to employ changes in the ease of access as a proxy for price. Accessibility is nothing more complicated than an index that reflects the ease with which people can achieve the various activities they wish.

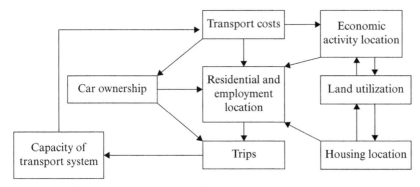

Source: Webster et al. (1988).

Figure 12.3   *Urban land-use and transport interaction model*

Transport systems are extremely complicated, comprising many modes of travel, varieties of routes, and combinations of different potential travel patterns. The sheer number of links and possibilities in any non-trivial transport network has inevitably resulted in simplifications having to be adopted by forecasters to permit calculations to be reduced to manageable proportions. Further, the 'product' being offered by the transport system is also unique in that a passenger-mile at a particular point on the network at a specific time may be performing a completely different function to another passenger-kilometer at another time and at a different point in the system.

While not always designed to handle the land-use/transport interaction effects, these latter types of problems have resulted in the emergence of three broad types of forecasting framework, each with its own characteristics and each with its advantages and defects. Each of these has many variants, but they can generally be thought of as sequential, disaggregate, and interactive frameworks. They are looked at in turn. While the discussion is couched primarily in terms of forecasting the demand for person movements, much of the traffic carried by the transport system is freight. The demand to move commodities differs quite substantially from person movements in the sense that it is, normally, uni-directional, while person trips are usually circular (that is, from home to work to home). The types of forecasting frameworks used to look at goods traffic are, however, essentially the same as for person movements, modified usually only in terms of the actual variables used. The three main approaches are now reviewed in turn.

12.4   Sequential Travel Demand Forecasting

Sequential models attempt to reduce the complexity of travel demand forecasting and making the handling of large databases easier by breaking the complicated patterns of demand for travel into, usually, four submodels (McNally, 2008). This approach has a long history, starting with the Detroit and Chicago Transportation

Studies of the 1950s, and is still, despite serious limitations, the dominant form of modeling used today; for example, it is used within the US Government's Urban Public Transport Planning System (UPTPS). The stages are:

- First, the trip generation/attraction model (the trip-end model) is used to forecast the number of trips originating and ending within pre-defined geographical zones of the study area (these might be countries in international travel studies or smaller areas within a city in urban land-use studies).
- Second, the total zonal trips are 'distributed' between origin–destination pairs of zones.
- Third, for each flow between different zones, a modal choice model is calculated to explain the split of traffic between the alternative forms of transport available.
- Finally, the traffic flows between each pair of zones and by each mode of transport are assigned to specific routes on the transport network.

In the context of freight modeling, which we discussed in Chapter 10, the parallel submodels represent transactions, flows, mode changes, and network assignments, with an industrial location model added to make the links between industrial activities and freight vehicle movements explicit. A vehicle-loading submodel is also sometimes added to shift the emphasis from the vehicle to the consignment.

Figure 12.4 provides an example of the sequential approach as developed by the regional highway traffic model (RHTM) team in the United Kingdom, and

Figure 12.4   *The United Kingdom's regional highway traffic model (RHTM)*

used to assist specifically in national road planning. It is typical of the series of sequences used in most other countries, including the United States. Mode choice submodels are excluded because of the dominant position filled by motorcar traffic. The approach set out is useful in distinguishing between the data analysis, computer simulation, and calibration aspects of the overall modeling and forecasting process.

The sequential framework may, therefore, be seen as moving from an aggregate overall traffic model to quasi-disaggregate forecasting with each successive submodel in the sequence acting as a check on the one following. In econometric terms the sequence is recursive. Attempts have been made (for example, in work forming part of the appraisal of the Greater London Development Plan) to introduce feedbacks from later to earlier submodels in the sequence on the grounds that one cannot really forecast, say, mode choice without knowing probable levels of congestion on each route, and this latter knowledge only becomes available after the assignment stage. A land-use forecasting model that attempts to describe the effect of changing land-use patterns on transport usually precedes the transport model sequence. Ideally, because land use is itself partly affected by transport conditions, there should also be feedbacks from the assignment submodel to land-use patterns, but to date this has proved to be practicably impossible.

Trip-end submodels are usually estimated on a household basis using either multi-variate regression techniques or category analysis. The former statistically relate the number of trips made by households to the socioeconomic characteristics of the households (for example, income, number of residents, car ownership, social status, etc.) and the type of environment in which they are located. The concentration on the household is now widely accepted as standard practice to reduce statistical problems that appear when data are grouped excessively (for example, by geographical zone). Category analysis is simpler, involving the construction of a multi-dimensional matrix with each dimension representing a socioeconomic variable stratified into several discrete classes or categories. For example, households may be divided into four income classes, three car ownership classes, and two location classes, giving in total 24 categories of household, each with its own average trip-generation level. Forecasts are obtained by predicting the number of households falling into each category at the target date, and multiplying by the relevant average trip generation rate. The total zonal trips in the example above would be predicted as:

$$T = \sum_{t=1}^{24} n_k r_k \qquad (12.1)$$

where n is the future number of households in category k, and r is the corresponding trip rate.

Revealed preference approaches to trip distribution models are of two broad types. Growth factor models involve extrapolating existing patterns of trips between alternative origins and destinations with projected trip-end estimates acting as constraints on the total number of trips leaving or entering any individual zone. They are little more than mechanical procedures based upon past behavior patterns and suffer from inabilities to allow for new zones being created. They have also gone out of favor because they require a substantial amount of data input.

The second group, simulation models, are more overtly economic in their nature. The gravity model is the most commonly used member of this group and has the attraction of having a precise economic interpretation. The underlying concept is also widely used in other areas of transport analysis such as when looking at the importance of transport costs in labor mobility, which will be discussed in Chapter 13.

Gravity models differ in form, but all exhibit terms reflecting the relative attractiveness of destinations and terms that measure the effect of impedance caused by the nature of the transport system. In early work, attractions were specified simply in terms of the population sizes of the zones of attraction, but in more recent studies a multiplicity of factors have been included, frequently varying with the journey purpose under consideration. Similarly, the crude notion that distance is a full reflection of impedance has given way to the incorporation of various forms of generalized cost measures.

The interactive version of the gravity model takes the general form:

$$T_{ij} = T_i T_j A_i A_j B_{ij}(C_{ij}) \qquad (12.2)$$

$$\text{subject to: } A_i = \left[\sum_j T_j B_j f(C_{ij}) \right]^{-1} \text{ and } B_j \left[\sum_i T_i A_i f(C_{ij}) \right]^{-1} \text{ where:}$$

T_{ij} is trips between zones i and j;
T_i is the total number of trips originating in zone i;
T_j is the total number of trips destined for zone j;
C_{ij} is the generalized cost of travel between zones i and j;
A and B are 'fuzz factors' – sometimes justified as indices of inverse accessibility – to ensure that total trips distributed across the whole study area originating from i do not exceed T_i and those destined for j do not exceed T_j.

This doubly constrained model assumes that trip-makers are competing for a limited number of opportunities in any specific zone, and has clear applications to modeling the demand for work or school trips where job and educational opportunities can be assumed to be independent of the transport system. In many cases only one constraint (either T_i or T_j) is imposed; for example, with inter-urban freight demand, one is often only interested either in the way movements fan out from a city or depot or in the way they converge on it. Urban non-work demand models are also often based upon origin-constrained models with less concern about destinations. On other occasions it may prove necessary to relax the constraints to facilitate easier fitting of the models, constrained versions of the gravity model usually requiring specific computer software for calibration.

An alternative simulation model considers the opportunities available in different zones to meet the needs of travelers.

The intervening opportunities model assumes that people try to keep their trips as short as possible and only lengthen them if nearer destinations do not prove acceptable to their needs. Individual residents in each zone are assumed to consider opportunities for the location of their conduct of specific activities (residence, work, shopping, etc.) at various places, starting from the base zone and fanning out to other zones in increasing order of difficulty in reaching them. Each time an opportunity is considered, there is a given, constant chance that it will be selected. The model takes the general form:

$$T_{ij} = T_i[\exp(-LV_j) - \exp(-LV_{j+1})] \qquad (12.3)$$

where V is the possible destination just considered, and L is a constant representing the probability of the possible destination being accepted (if considered).

While this type of approach has an intuitive appeal, it does suffer from the problem that, empirically, L seems to vary with V rather than remaining constant. Adjustment techniques to correct for the 'wandering' of L values are available, but their use seems to violate the notion of constancy. Empirical studies indicate that the results obtained using the intervening opportunities model are no better than those from gravity models. Attempts to develop the opportunities framework by considering competing rather than intervening opportunities (by basing the underlying probability function on the ratio between the trip opportunities in a zone and its competing opportunities) offer no improvements in a forecasting context but complicate the estimation process considerably.

In some instances, as for example with inter-urban road traffic forecasting in the United Kingdom, there had been a tradition to employ a 'fixed trip matrix' which assumes that the total number of trips (that is, the trips generated and attracted) is unaffected by the new transport scheme. The total traffic, which may well grow due to changing socioeconomic conditions, is simply redistributed as a result of the change in transport policy or infrastructure investment. If new traffic is generated, however, this result may prove distortive.

In Figure 12.5, Demand represents the true aggregate relationship between the cost of travel and the traffic flow. As a result of, say, a road investment, the cost of trip-making falls from P to P^*, with traffic increasing to F^*. Assuming there has been no shift in demand due to changing income or other socioeconomic factors, the traditional model would assume that demand had remained fixed at the all-traffic flow – in other words, that the implied demand curve is Demand*. This means that the benefit enjoyed by the generated traffic ($F^* - F$), and represented by the shaded area in the diagram, would be excluded from the subsequent appraisal stage. This is another reason why there are often feedback links which, in this case, result in the trip-end models being re-run incorporating some allowance for this generation effect.

Modal split models allocate traffic flows to types of vehicles. In some cases, for example, with urban freight transport or long-distance international

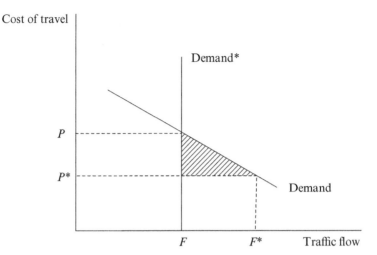

Figure 12.5 *The fixed trip matrix*

passenger transport, one mode so dominates a sphere of transport activity that no mode choice submodel is required, although this is exceptional. The traditional method of splitting origin–destination traffic flows by mode involves the use of diversion curves. These show the proportion of traffic likely to favor a particular mode given its relative cost (or other) advantage over alternative modes. If we are concerned with two forms of transport, a and b, then a typical model might be:

$$\frac{T_{ij}^a}{T_{ij}^a + T_{ij}^b} = \frac{1}{1 + e^{-\lambda(C_{ij}^b - C_{ij}^a)}} \tag{12.4}$$

This yields a diversion curve of the general form seen in Figure 12.6. Normally a series of curves are estimated by subdividing the traveling population (for example, by income) and modes (for example, by service ratios).

In some studies mode choice is modeled prior to distribution using trip-end or interchange models. The former are often used in highway-orientated origin-and-destination studies where the emphasis is on car travel with public transport being treated as little more than a residual to be subtracted from the trip-end predictions prior to assignments being made. The emphasis on variables such as car ownership and income, and the general neglect of public transport characteristics, limits the usefulness of this approach in urban transport planning. Interchange models are more commonly used in public transport feasibility studies and, consequently, concentrate on comparative time, cost, and service differentials between competing modes. Models of this type take the form:

$$T_{ijm} = a_0 X_{ij}^{\alpha 1} (F_{ij}^M)^{\alpha 2} (F_{ij}^b)^{\alpha 3} (H_{ij}^M)^{\alpha 4} (H_{ij}^b)^{\alpha 5} \tag{12.5}$$

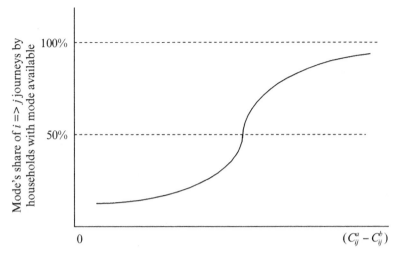

Figure 12.6   *Diversion curve of traffic between modes 'a' and 'b'*

where:

X_{ij} is a matrix of exogenous economic and social variables;
F_{ij}^{M} is the financial cost by mode M;
H_{ij}^{M} is the time cost by mode M; and
the superscript b indicates the money/time cost by the best mode.

Models of this type have a foundation in economic theory but estimation of parameters $a_1 - a_5$ poses serious statistical problems.

The final submodel, route assignment, compares the travelers' preferences for routes with the characteristics of the routes available. Early approaches relied upon diversion curves like those used in modal choice work but the development of minimum-path algorithms combined with improved computing facilities has permitted the introduction of more sophisticated techniques. A major problem in assignment is the possible need to constrain traffic flows on each link in the transport network to the capacity of the link. If the capacity constraint is omitted then an 'all or nothing' assignment results and no allowance is made for the congestion that accompanies high traffic volumes. Further, travelers use all routes, both the initially cheap and the not so cheap, especially when overall cost differentials are small. The introduction of capacity constraints permits this to be reflected in the model by adjusting link speeds (and hence costs) as the assignment proceeds and congestion levels rise.

In summary, the sequential method of forecasting broadly involves developing a series of mathematical models taking the general form:

$$T_i = f(X_i); \ T_i = f(X_j) \tag{12.6a}$$

$$T_{ij} = f(T_i, T_j, C_{ij}) \tag{12.6b}$$

$$T_{ijm} = f(T_{ij}, C_{ijM}, C_{ijM'}) \tag{12.6c}$$

$$T_{ijMP} = f(T_{ijMP}, C_{ijMP}, C_{ijMP'}) \tag{12.6d}$$

where the prime notation refers to alternative modes (M') or routes (P').

While widely used, the sequential modeling approach has serious limitations. Clearly, the series of calculations required to calibrate this set of equations places tremendous strains on the databases available and, in most studies, large and expensive surveys are needed to gather the necessary information. Also, as pointed out above, it is difficult to incorporate the desirable feedback from assignment and other stages to trip generation so that quality of service variables are adequately and consistently reflected in each submodel of the sequence. Statistically, while it is generally possible to test the significance of the individual models in the sequence, it is not possible to undertake statistical tests of the overall recursive system. The approach is also deficient in that it does not embrace the fundamental tenet of travel demand, namely that it is derived from the desire to participate in some final activity.

One of the reasons why disaggregate economic models have been developed is to avoid some of these problems and to approach more closely to the basic decision-making unit, the household (Ben-Akiva and Lerman, 1985).

12.5   Disaggregate Modeling

The substantial data required to satisfactorily calibrate the submodels, and the difficulty of transferring models once estimated from one data area to another, combined with dissatisfaction with the basically mechanistic and physical nature of the sequential approach, has resulted in alternative mathematical approaches being developed. This second generation of models employing economic-based, disaggregate methods of travel demand forecasting emphasizes the economic–psychological influences on travel behavior at the individual household level.

The idea is that households are utility maximizers who, mainly for mathematical convenience, are considered to make travel decisions in isolation from other activities. The emphasis is on short-run decisions rather than long-run mobility decisions. Small stratified samples of households (about 700 or so) provide the data input into the models, which tend to be probabilistic, rather than deterministic, in nature (that is, they forecast the probability of household travel patterns rather than the average number and type of trips to be undertaken).

A personal disaggregate model of trip-making would be of the general form:

$$P(f,d,h,m,t) = P(f)P(d/f)P(h/f,d)P(rn/f,d,h)P(r/f,d,h,m) \tag{12.7}$$

where $P(f,d,h,m,r)$ is the probability that an individual will undertake a trip with frequency (f) to destination (d) during time of day (h) using mode (m) and via route (r) out of a choice set comprising all possible combinations of frequencies, destinations, times of day, modes, and routes available to the individual. For actual planning or assessment, the forecasts produced from such models must be aggregated up to the level of the geographical zone – it is the inter-zonal level, for example, which determines the level of public transport demand. While there are claims that the approach can be used in comprehensive transport planning, its main role to date has been in policy assessment (for example, looking at carpooling proposals, pollution controls, public transport subsidies, etc.).

Broadly, disaggregate models are characterized by two main features. First, they explicitly recognize that travel decisions emerge out of individuals' optimizing behavior and, if it is pointed out that the final goods consumed as a result of travel are normal, then at the very minimum the demand for travel ought to be related positively to disposable incomes and negatively to the prices of transport services. Second, most have their origins in the 'attribute theory of demand' associated with Kelvin Lancaster (1966). This approach to human behavior assumes that people desire to maximize a utility function that has, as its arguments, commodity attributes rather than the quantities of the actual goods consumed. In other words, if we represent the amounts of attributes by the vector z, the amounts of commodities (in this case, travel alternatives) by the vector x, posit a utility function, $U(z)$, and a production of attribute function, $G(x)$, which reflects the attributes of different travel alternatives, and assume that potential travelers are constrained by income, y, and the price of travel, p, then we can reduce the problem to solving:

$$\text{max } U(z) \tag{12.8}$$

subject to:

$$z = G(x), \; x \geq 0, \; p.x \leq y$$

The selection of the attributes can also be seen diagrammatically in Figure 12.7, which looks at a very simple mode choice situation. Potential travelers have a fixed budget, and a choice of three modes (car, train, and bus) which have different attribute-supply characteristics in terms of speed and economy. With a given budget the traveler can enjoy the combination of attributes seen on the frontier – for example, if all trips were made by train then the bundle of attributes would be S_T and E_T. Of course, combinations of modes may be made for the budget. The final selection will depend on the consumers' preferences for speed and economy and, since the aim is to maximize utility, this will be at the point where the highest possible constrained indifference curve (I_2) is reached. By using a combination of train and car, the traveler will enjoy E of economy and S of speed.

As an example, if one is considering air transport between the United Kingdom and the United States, then the alternative commodities would be the different fare packages offered by the airlines, and the attributes of each would be characteristics such as money costs, speed, period of advance booking, timing, type of aircraft, in-plane service (food, drink, films, etc.), stop-over regulations, required length of stay at destination, etc.

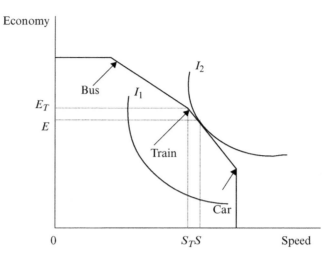

Figure 12.7   *The attribute choices in mode selection*

In terms of application, direct attempts were initially made to apply Lancaster's theory at the aggregate level by Richard Quandt (1976) and associates in the context of abstract mode modeling. At the inter-urban level Quandt and Baumol (1966) developed an abstract mode model for air, bus, and car journeys between 16 city pairs in California using cost and time (both absolute and relative) as the determining attributes, but the results were inferior to those obtained from more conventional trip-distribution models.

Howrey's (1969) early study of air travel out of Cleveland produced an abstract mode model with correct signs, significant coefficients, and a good overall fit to survey data. However, while its explanatory power proved statistically superior to a conventional gravity model it turned out to be inferior in terms of *ex post* forecasting quality. Talvitie (1973) concentrated on developing the framework to handle intra-urban travel, while Baumol and Vinod (1970), by combining the attributed theory of demand with an inventory theory of goods handling, adapted the approach to deal with urban freight transport demand.

While some of the calibration problems that were associated with the early aggregate abstract mode models have been resolved, it has been the introduction of disaggregate approaches that has marked the greatest advances. The major advance in this context was the realization that everyone has a different utility function, partly because of quantifiable differences in their personal characteristics, but also partly because of random factors. While the heterogeneous nature of the population poses serious problems, the work of Domenich and McFadden (1976) in modeling the random factors, and especially their theoretical work on justifying the use of 'multinomial logit models', forms the basis of much modern disaggregate analysis. The forms of disaggregate model that have been developed along these lines, and the range of applications to which they have been applied, are many.

Most of the recent work on disaggregate modeling has centered on mathematical and calibration issues and there is no intention of taking discussion of such matters any further in this book. The mathematical complexity stems from the fact that one is looking at discrete choices – that is, whether a person makes a trip or not – and this involves complications not normally encountered when considering continuous functions.

12.6   Interactive and Stated-preference Modeling

While the sequential and disaggregate approaches to transport demand analysis concentrate on developing sophisticated mathematical simulations, recently there has been a growth of interest in 'behavioral realism', and an emphasis on 'understanding the phenomenon' (Dix, 1977). This is sometimes called the activity-based approach (McNally and Rindt, 2008), because it has sought to embrace a richer, holistic framework in which travel behavior is analysed as a daily or multi-day pattern of behavior related to life-styles and participation in various activities.

The idea is that the demand for travel is derived from the activity patterns of individuals and households. The basic idea has much to do with the concept of time-geography developed by Torsten Hägerstrand (1970). Underlying this, is the idea that an individual's choice of a specific activity pattern is viewed as a solution to an allocation problem involving limited resources of time and space. In this sense actual behavior is not that useful, but rather there is a need to put more emphasis on the constraints that limit people's actions.

These approaches to modeling have also been tied in with the greater use of stated-preference techniques that we have already encountered in Chapter 6 in the context of contingency evaluation procedures. This latter approach, which, to adopt Kroes and Sheldon's (1988) definition, is 'a family of techniques which use individual respondents' statements about their preferences in a set of transport options to estimate utility functions', is often claimed to be helpful when:

- there is insufficient variation in revealed preference data to examine all variables of interest;
- there is a high level of correlation between the explanatory variables in a revealed preference model, making statistical estimation of parameters difficult;
- a radically new technology or policy takes the analysis outside of the realms where current revealed behavior is relevant; and
- variables are not easily expressed in standard units (for example, when the interest is in the effects on demand of less-turbulent travel by air).

The aim of interactive modeling is to develop models that get closer to the essential decision process underlying travel behavior. Rather than simply incorporate variables such as household status in mathematical models because the

statistical 'explanation' of the model appears to be improved, interactive modeling seeks to explain why status affects travel behavior. Theoretically, travel is seen
as one of a whole range of complementary and competitive activities operating
in a sequence of events in time and space. It is seen to represent the method by
which people trade time to move location in order to enjoy successive activities.
Generally, time and space constraints are thought to limit the choices of activities
open to individuals. The technique is still far from fully developed, but it has been
applied only in a relatively limited number of small-scale forecasting studies (for
example, by Peter Jones, 1978 in the United Kingdom to school bus operations;
by Fowkes and Preston, 1991 to new local rail services; and by Phifer et al., 1980
in the United States to energy constraints).

The emphasis of interactive models is upon the household (or individual)
as the decision-making unit. According to Heggie (1978), ideally an interactive
model should exhibit six main properties:

- It should involve the entire household and allow for interaction between its
  members.
- It should make existing constraints on household behavior quite explicit.
- It should start from the household's existing pattern of behavior.
- It should work by confronting the household with realistic changes in its
  travel environment and allowing it to respond realistically.
- It should allow for the influence of long-term adaptation.
- It should be able to tell the investigator something fundamental that he/she
  did not know before.

In general, the approach is typified by a small sample and careful survey techniques, often involving such things as 'board games', such as the 'household activities travel simulator' (HATS) developed by the Oxford University Transport Studies
Unit, or other visual aids, usually computer-based simulations these days, to permit
participants to fully appreciate the implications of changes in transport policy upon
their own behavior. In a sense it represents an attempt to conduct laboratory experiments by eliciting responses in the context of known information and constraints.

The HATS approach, for example, was to confront a household with a
map of the local area together with a 24-hour 'strip representation of colored
pieces' showing how current activities of the household are spread over space and
throughout the day. Changes to the transport system were then postulated (for
example, reduced parking availability in the local urban center) and the effects
on the household's activities throughout the day were simulated by adjustments
to the strip representation. In this way, changes in the transport system could
be seen to influence the entire 24-hour life pattern of the household, and apparently unsuspected changes in 'remote' trip-making behavior can be traced back
to the primary change. It makes clear the constraints and linkages that may affect
activity and transport choices. The emphasis is on the micro unit with the aim of
being able to develop simple models that permit much clearer insights into the
overall effects of transport policy. By asking respondents to trace the effect of

changes in transport provision on the entire set of activities undertaken during a day (or week), information on important travel intentions can be seen and the relationships between travel and non-travel activities become explicit.

More recent studies have adopted more sophisticated experimentation procedures, often involving computers, which provide for greater flexibility and easier interaction with those being 'interviewed'. Examples of programs of this genre include ALBATROS (A Learning-Based Transportation Oriented Simulation System), the first computational process model of the complete activity scheduling process that could be fully estimated from data, and TRANSIMS, an attempt to replace the entire traditional transport paradigm, which has an activity-based front end linked to a population synthesizer and integrated with a micro simulation of modeled travel behavior.

While this aspect of the approach has been refined, important technical issues remain regarding using the information gathered from stated-preference-type experiments for forecasting. There is still, for example, much to be learned about why some households give strategically biased responses; there are difficulties in handling habit, inertia, and hysteresis in an experimental framework. At a more technical level, John Bates (1988) points to our lack of knowledge about the error structures associated with stated-preference data and the problems of pooling data across individuals.

In contrast to the more traditional revealed-preference schools, advocates of this approach, however, point to both the specific recognition that travel is a derived demand and the fact that transport policies have qualitative, as well as quantitative, effects on people's lives. In the longer term, when operational models are more fully developed, the framework may offer the much-sought-after basis for integrating land-use and transport planning assessments. In the short term, the approach has offered useful insights and a method for cross-checking the validity of conventional statistical analysis of behavioral data.

As techniques of data collection and analysis have improved, so more recently hybrid stated-revealed preference techniques have been used to look at such things as multi-modal trip choices in Madrid (Cascajo et al., 2017), choice of mode and route by shippers in the Pacific Northwest, (Train and Wilson, 2007), and local travel behavior (Rudloff and Straub, 2021).

References

Bates, J. (1988) Econometric issues in stated preference analysis, *Journal of Transport Economics and Policy*, 22, 59–70.

Baumol, W.J. and Vinod, H.D. (1970) An inventory theoretic model of freight transport demand, *Management Science*, 16, 413–41.

Ben-Akiva, M. and Lerman, S. (1985) *Discrete Choice Analysis: Theory and Application to Travel Demand*, MIT Press.

Berechman, J. and Gordon, P. (1986) Linked models of land use–transport interactions: a review, in B. Hutchinson and M. Balty (eds), *Advances in Urban Systems Modelling*, North Holland.

Cascajo, R., Garcia-Martinez, A., and Monzo, A. (2017) Stated preference survey for estimating passenger transfer penalties: design and application to Madrid, *European Transport Research Review*, 9, 1–11.

Dix, M.C. (1977) Report on investigations of household travel decision making behaviour, in E.J. Visser (ed.), *Transport Decisions in an Age of Uncertainty*, Martinus Nijhoff.

Domenich, T. and McFadden, D. (1976) *Urban Travel Demand: A Behavioural Analysis*, North Holland.

Flyvbjerg, B. (2007) Cost overruns and demand shortfalls in urban rail and other infrastructure. *Transportation Planning and Technology*, 30, 9–30.

Flyvbjerg, B., Skamris Holm, M.K., and Buhl, S.L. (2002) Underestimating costs in public works projects: error or lie? *Journal of the American Planning Association*, 68, 279–95.

Fowkes, A.S. and Preston, J. (1991) Novel approaches to forecasting the demand for new local rail services, *Transportation Research Part A*, 25, 209–18.

Friedman, M. (1953) The methodology of positive economics, in M. Friedman (ed.), *Essays in Positive Economics*, University of Chicago Press.

Hägerstrand, T. (1970) What about people in regions? *Papers of the Regional Science Association*, 24, 7–21.

Heggie, I. (1978) Putting behaviour into behavioural models of travel choice, *Journal of the Operational Research Society*, 29, 541–50.

Howrey, E.P. (1969) On the choice of forecasting models for air travel, *Journal of Regional Science*, 9, 215–24.

Jones, P.M. (1978) School hour revisions in West Oxfordshire: an exploratory study using HATS, Technical Report, Oxford University Transport Studies Unit.

Kroes, K.P. and Sheldon, R.J. (1988) Stated preference methods: an introduction, *Journal of Transport Economics and Policy*, 22, 11–26.

Lancaster, K.J. (1966) A new approach to consumer theory, *Journal of Political Economy*, 74, 132–57.

Lay, M.G. (2005) The history of transport planning, in K.J. Button and D.A. Hensher (eds), *Handbook of Transport Strategy: Policy Institutions*, Pergamon.

Mackinder, I. and Evans, S. (1981) The predictive accuracies of British transport studies in urban areas, TRRL Report SR 699.

McFadden, D. (2001) Economic choices, *American Economic Review*, 91, 351–78.

McNally, M.G. (2008) The four-step model, in D.A. Hensher and K.J. Button (eds), *Handbook of Transport Modeling*, 2nd edn, Elsevier.

McNally, M.G. and Rindt, C.R. (2008) The activity-based approach, in D.A. Hensher and K.J. Button (eds), *Handbook of Transport Modeling*, 2nd edn, Elsevier.

Phifer, S.P., Neven, A.J., and Hartgen, D.T. (1980) Family reactions to energy constraints, Paper presented at the Transportation Research Board Annual Meeting, Washington DC.

Pickrell, D.H. (1989) Urban rail transit projects: forecast versus actual ridership and costs, Report, US Department of Transportation.

Quandt, R.E. (1976) The theory of travel demand, *Transportation Research*, 10, 411–13.

Quandt, R.E. and Baumol, W.J. (1966) The demand for abstract transport modes: theory and measurement, *Journal of Regional Science*, 6, 13–26.

Rudloff, C. and Straub, M. (2021) Mobility surveys beyond stated preference: introducing MyTrips, an SP-off-RP survey tool, and results of two case studies, *European Transport. Research Review,* 13, https://doi.org/10.1186/s12544-021-00510-5.

Stopher, P.R. (1992) Use of an activity-based diary to collect household travel data, *Transportation*, 19, 159–76.

Stopher, P.R. (2008) Survey and sampling strategies, in D.A. Hensher and K.J. Button (eds), *Handbook of Transport Modeling*, 2nd edn, Elsevier.

Talvitie, A.P. (1973) A direct demand model for downtown work trips, *Transportation*, 2, 121–52.

Train, K. and Wilson, W. (2007) Estimation on stated-preference experiments constructed from revealed-preference choices, *Transportation Research Part B*, 42, 191–203.

UK Department of Transport (1977) Transport policy, Policy Document, DoT.

UK House of Commons Committee of Public Accounts (1988) Road planning, Report, HMSO.

UK Ministry of Transport (1963) Traffic in towns, Report, HMSO.

US Federal Highways Administration (1973) Urban origin–destination surveys, Report, UDDOT.

Webster, F.V., Bly, P.H., and Paulley, N.J. (eds) (1988) *Urban Land-use and Transport Interaction*, Avebury.

Weiner, E. (2008) *Urban Transportation Planning in the United States: History, Policy, and Practice*, Springer.

13   Transport and Economic Development

. . . .

13.1   Transport's Role in Development

Economists have long been concerned with assessing the links between changes in the transport sector and the evolving pattern of economic development within the area that it serves. While the importance of transport in economic growth and development has never seriously been questioned, its exact role and influence have been subjected to periodic reappraisals. The subject is made more difficult because the impacts of transport are not always intended, and thus can have unforeseen consequences. The underlying problem is, however, a more general one, in that our general understanding of what causes economic development is poor. Charles Kindleberger (1958) made the point over 60 years ago:

> We have suggested that there is no agreement on how economic development pro-
> ceeds and have implied that this is because the process is not simple. There are many
> variables involved, and there is a wide range of substitutability among ingredients –
> land, capital, and the quality and quantity of labor, and technology can substitute
> for one another, above certain minima, although there are at the same time certain
> complementary relationships among them. The will to economize and organization
> are probably the only indispensable ingredients. For the rest, none are necessary, and
> none sufficient.

The interest in the topic, though, is not purely an academic matter. There are public concerns regarding regional disparities within countries and with the economic performances and differences between levels of national economic prosperity, and especially so between the 'North' and the 'South'. This has brought forth efforts to stimulate growth in lagging economies by investing in infrastructure, including transport, and in enhancing the performance of existing infrastructure. The creation of the World Bank, various regional development banks, such as the Inter-American Development Bank, and a plethora of other bi-lateral and multi-lateral organizations is a tangible institutional manifestation of these concerns at the macro level. This is setting aside any consideration of the use of transport investment programs as part of a Keynesian-style macro-economic stimulus package; it is about dynamics rather than comparative statics.

The form and scale of the measures that could be taken, and indeed their general desirability, are matters of significant practical interest. In consequence, while Kindleberger is still correct, in that our knowledge is in many ways very limited, efforts to clarify the situation continue. The work on development economics and the role that transport can play in the economic development process is extensive.

To provide some context for our discussions we begin by considering the theories of economic development and how transport fits into them. Without an understanding of how economic development takes place, it is not possible to study transport's contribution. We then move to look at more specific issues, beginning with a long-standing debate in economics about the role that public transport infrastructure can play in stimulating economic productivity. This has largely been an empirical debate that was initiated in the 1980s regarding questions about the role infrastructure policies should play in macroeconomic policy. This leads on to questions regarding the ripple effects on economic performance of individual transport initiatives.

We then move on to consider the more macro problems of stimulating economic growth in the Third World, before proceeding to consider the problems of formulating a common transport policy to foster the economic growth ambitions of the member states of the European Union. At a more micro level there are also questions concerning the ways in which transport provision can stimulate economic growth within certain parts of a country or for a given urban area.

While the discussion of transport and economic development has been sectionalized for expositional convenience, it is important to emphasize that in practice considerable trade-offs may be necessary between, say, devising a transport policy to stimulate national growth and one designed to assist the development of specified under-developed regions. The poorest countries, especially, often feel they must attempt to increase their national income. Indeed, if one were to accept the 'growth pole' approach to economic development, then national growth is generated by concentrating effort in several strong regional centers. Hence, inter-regional inequality of growth is an inevitable concomitant and condition of growth itself. Consequently, although it may be possible to design a national transport strategy or investment program that assists in the maximization of national economic growth, it may need modifying to ensure that an acceptable degree of equity is retained among the different regions of the country.

13.2   Economic Growth Theory and Transport

First, a little background. In the neoclassical economic framework, which we shall consider in more detail below and which largely represents an extension of eighteenth-century trade theory, transport is not really considered at all. The existence of optimal transport services is assumed, and, if they are lacking in the short term, then it is assumed that a perfectly functioning market would soon supply the optimal amount. The more recent endogenous approach to economic development assumes imperfect markets that need not result in socially optimal outcomes. Again, with reference to transport, these imperfections may entail a lack of adequate financial markets to construct appropriate infrastructure and imperfect markets in making use of the roads, ports, etc. that are available, owing to either market or government failures.

Traditionally, it was argued by Adam Smith and others that transport exerted a strong positive influence on economic development, and that increased production could be directly related to improved transport. In the United Kingdom context, for example, over 150 years ago, Robert Baxter (1866) argued that '[r]ailways have been a most powerful agent in the progress of commerce, in improving the conditions of the working classes, and in developing the agricultural and mineral resources of the country'. Perhaps the strongest advocate of the positive role of transport, however, is Walter Rostow (1960) who, in accounting for economic growth, maintains that '[t]he introduction of railroads has historically been the most powerful single indicator to take-offs. It was decisive in the United States, France, Germany, Canada and Russia'.

A broader brush approach is that of Andersson and Stromquist (1988), who claim that all the major transitions in the European economic systems were accompanied (or initiated) by major changes in transport and communications infrastructure. Four main transport and logistics revolutions can be distinguished:

- the period from the thirteenth century, in which water transport emerged as a new logistic system connecting cities along the rivers and coastal areas (the Hansa economy);
- the period from the sixteenth century (the Golden Age), characterized by a dramatic improvement in sailing and sea transport and by the introduction of new banking systems which stimulated trade to the East Indies and West Indies (with Lisbon, Antwerp, and Amsterdam as major centers);
- the middle of the nineteenth century, marked by the Industrial Revolution, in which the invention of the steam engine generated new transport modes, thereby creating new market areas such as North America; and
- from the 1970s, which is marked by increased information and flexibility; just-in-time systems and material requirements planning have evolved within this framework.

Positive linkages between transport provision and economic development can be divided between the direct transport input and indirect, including multiplier, effects. Good transport offers low shipping costs that have permitted wider markets to be served and the exploitation of large-scale production in an extensive range of activities. In the past, for example, Hunter (1965) postulated a causal linkage between low-cost transport and economic growth. The Industrial Revolution was successful because of a prior revolution in transport technology. Similarly, Owen (1964) argued that a widening of domestic markets through improved transport services is a pre-requisite for national economic development. Further, most undeveloped countries are, for a variety of geographical, economic, and historic reasons, dependent upon international trade and an expansion of this trade is an essential pre-requisite for growth. In these circumstances the provision of efficient port facilities will, according to this school of thought, positively assist development.

The indirect effects stem from the employment created in the construction of transport infrastructure and the jobs associated with operating the transport

---

Exhibit   *Employment implications of the United States' federal highway system*

The Interstate highway system was initiated in 1956 with the passage of the Federal Highway Act. The National Highway System (NHS) Designation Act of 1995 added $5.4 billion to the United States' federal-aid highway program targeted to the NHS. This motivated analysis of the economic impacts of the network.

The NHS consists of 260,000 kilometers of roads that serve major population centers, international border crossings, ports, airports, public transportation facilities, and other inter-modal transportation facilities and major transportation destinations; meet national defense requirements; and serve inter-state and inter-regional travel. It constitutes 4 percent of public roads, but carries more than 40 percent of highway traffic and 70 percent of truck traffic.

Assessing its implications in national labor market studies, the US Federal Highways Administration (FHWA) looked at both the direct effects and the indirect. Regarding the former, it estimated that $1 billion (in 1995 prices) of federal-aid highway program spending in 1996 would nationally support about 7,900 full-time, on-site highway construction jobs.

The table provides the aggregate picture derived from the FHWA studies: aggregate employment supported per $1 billion of NHS investment generated approximately 42,100 jobs in the United States. This is with the caveat that the estimates refer to 'gross' job creation, meaning that the employment impacts of alternative investments have not been considered in this broad level of analysis.

Direct, indirect, and induced employment impacts of federal aid

Employment type	Jobs per $1 billion federal spending
Direct	7,900
Indirect	19,700
Induced	14,500
Total	42,100

See also: G. Michaels (2008) The effect of trade on the demand for skill: evidence from the Interstate highway system, *Review of Economics and Statistics*, 90, 683–701.

---

services. Further, there may be multiplier effects stemming from the substantial inputs of iron, timber, coal, etc. required to construct a modern transport system and which, at least in the context of development in the nineteenth century, were supplied by indigenous heavy industries. Transport also often provided some initial experience of business for many industrialists of the period. The potential multiplier effects for Third World countries today are likely to be substantially less given the growth (itself a function of improved transport) of international trade and tied development aid. Additionally, the technical expertise required to engineer and plan modern transport systems is often unavailable in less developed countries and must be bought from more advanced nations.

The broad theories that underlie these views of the role of transport have evolved over time, and can be divided into two broad conceptual approaches, each seeing transport as impacting on development in somewhat different ways.

Neoclassical Economics

Economists have struggled over many years to explain why some regions' econo-mies, or indeed national economies, perform better than others. Traditional neo-classical, long-run macroeconomic growth theory of the type espoused by Robert Solow (1957) and others argues that per capita income in a region or country depends on local factor endowment, the savings rate, and the impact of exog-enously determined 'technical progress'. Transport is seen as one of the inputs in this context, on a par with other industries.

More formally, an exogenous growth model of the Solow type can be formu-lated by taking a simple Cobb–Douglas production function of the form:

$$Y = A(t)K^{1-b}L^b \tag{13.1}$$

where:

Y is net national product;
K is the capital stock;
L is the labor stock; and
A is the level of technology.

The fact that A is a function of time (t) indicates the standard neoclassical assumption that technology only improves over time for reasons external to the model.

Where regional, as opposed to macro, neoclassical growth models differ from this to some extent is that they treat labor and other factor supplies as both dependent upon the internal demographics and an inherent resource base of a region, and dependent upon factor movements between regions. While most national economies experience relatively small flows of factors of production between them, the much laxer border restrictions within a region tend to foster such flows. This makes factor growth within a region more elastic.

Basically, this spatial mobility of factors of production can help to compen-sate for an initial shortage of a factor in a region. Hence a specific region may grow when there is capital abundance by 'importing' labor from other regions. This, combined with the natural growth in labor supply within the region, can lead to growth through more efficient use of the complementary capital stock, although in the long run there will be convergence in per capita income between the regions, albeit at a higher average wage rate. One can consider parallel move-ments of capital, but this is less relevant to air transportation.

Figure 13.1 offers a simple illustration of the larger point. There are two regions, A and B. Region A enjoys high income and low unemployment

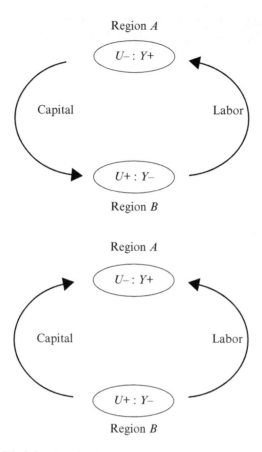

Figure 13.1 *Simplified theories of migration*

(represented as *U–* : *Y+*) whilst region *B* is the mirror image of this. There are decreasing returns to factors of production, including capital. The neoclassical economic model assumes that, with zero costs of migration (including zero transportation costs) and a homogeneous labor force, labor will move from *B* to *A* seeking work and higher pay, whereas, on the assumption of uniform commercial risk across regions, capital will move from *A* to *B* where it can be combined with abundant, cheap labor to maximize returns.

Wages will fall in region *A*, unemployment will increase, and the return on capital will rise as the labor supply grows and capital becomes scarcer. The additional capital and the decreasing size of the labor force in region *B* will push down the marginal return on investment and concurrently push up wages. The process continues until labor costs and unemployment levels are equalized. This equalization is achieved in a world of zero transportation costs and full information about opportunities.

The problem with this way of looking at regional development is that it relies on relatively strong assumptions. Factor movement is not frictionless: there are distance, information, and money costs. Also, factors of production are not homogeneous, and some are more mobile than others. Young, skilled, highly

Exhibit   *Railroads and canals in the United States' economic development*

Robert Fogel won the 1993 Nobel Prize in economics for his work on cliometrics: the use of quantitative methods in history. His early work focused on the role of the railroads in the economic development of the United States. He questioned the established view in the 1960s that the railroads were the main driver of economic growth in the 1800s. His main argument was that, while railways had important implications for the economy, most of the history had been focused on correlations and not on causality. He attacked the 'axiom of indispensability' – the notion that railroads were crucial to the economic growth of the United States in the 1890s – by focusing on two major corollaries: (i) railroads brought great savings in transportation costs; and (ii) their construction generated demands vital for the development of domestic industry. In doing this, he paid attention to the degree to which railways reduced the costs of transporting four agricultural products – wheat, corn, beef, and pork – that made up 80 percent of agricultural shipments. The alternative to rail would at the time have been waterborne transport.

To complete this task, Fogel made several assumptions. The work was aggregate in nature, while there were clear regional variations in the efficiency of the railroad sector and in their strategic importance. The costs of rail transport were also largely embedded in the railroad rates, while those of canals were more complex and some approximations had to be made. The quality of service varied, with railroads having a natural advantage in terms of reliability over canals in the winter when the latter froze, and sometimes in the summer in drought conditions. Canals were simply not a tenable alternative in areas where production was at higher altitudes, due to the necessity to install cost- and time-expensive lock systems in order to reach it. Adjustments for such things as cargo losses in transit and capital costs funded by government, and trans-shipment costs, were added to the canal calculations.

Fogel calculated the costs of both inter-regional and intra-regional distribution and estimated the costs that would have been incurred without the railroads, the difference being the 'social saving'. The main water routes considered were the Great Lakes and Erie Canal route, the Mississippi route, and the inter-coastal route which carried the bulk of traffic. He estimated that savings in transporting these commodities amounted to less than 2 percent of GNP for that year. A hypothetical extension of the formulae to all commodities hauled by rail yielded a saving well below 5 percent of GNP.

The second half of his study concerned measuring the demand represented by railroad construction during the 'take-off' period of 1840 to 1860, the purchase of rails and the impact for the iron industry being his primary focus. The results again countered conventional wisdom. He found that the addition to pig iron production required for rails between 1840 and 1860 only amounted to less than 5 percent of the output of domestic furnaces. Similar findings were discovered for other industries supplying the railroads. His overall estimate was that railroad purchases from the rest of the manufacturing sector accounted for only 3.9 percent of production.

See also: R.W. Fogel (1964) *Railroads and American Economic Growth: Essays in Econometric History*, Johns Hopkins Press.

educated workers, for example, tend to be more mobile than those lacking these characteristics. Investors consider returns on their capital relative to risk incurred; they are not risk-neutral. There is also the issue of technical progress that is simply treated as a sort of residual and uncontrollable factor in the neoclassical framework. This seems excessively fatalistic.

In addition, empirical analysis hardly gives solid support for the neoclassical idea. Testing the validity of the alternative theories, in the absence of easily quantifiable counterfactuals, has frequently involved looking at secondary evidence, and at evidence shedding light on whether there is convergence in the economic growth paths of regions or, at the macro level, nations. The empirical question that is explored becomes one of whether there is convergence in regional economic growth rates in, generally, per capita income or productivity, as is an outcome of the neoclassical model.

The extensive empirical analysis that has emerged has been assisted by the improved data made available in recent years, as well as new models, enhanced econometric techniques, and better understandings of how to measure convergence. There has been the development of the concept of β-convergence measures that has allowed a more rigorous analysis of economic convergence than the more traditional σ-convergence measure that looks for changes in standard statistical indicators of dispersion – normally the variance.

The estimation of possible β-convergence involves a mean-reversion calculation, which occurs if there is a negative relationship between the growth rate of income per capita and the level of initial income. Much of this type of analysis has been carried out at the national level, but it, and the more limited body of analysis that has been conducted at the regional level, does offer some insights into the validity of the idea of endogenous economic growth.

Much of the early work on spatial economic convergence relied upon aggregate, national data sources and focused on σ-convergence measurements. The findings indicated that labor productivity, and per capita income in the world, was converging in the long run and thus provided support to the neoclassical growth theory. The difficulty with this work was that the datasets only contained countries that had already become industrialized, and even for those there were periods of divergence. Improved data subsequently indicated a lack of any general economic convergence.

The more recent work that has made use of β-convergence measures, and embraces a number of subnational studies, tends to find little support for overall convergence, and *ipso facto* the neoclassical model. Robert Barro and Xavier Sala-i-Martin (1991), in several studies that, for example, have examined the economies of American states and European Union regions, find that while there is evidence of convergence in per capita income, it is slow: about 2 percent per annum and well below the 12 percent or so that neoclassical theory would suggest. These are also conditional convergence measures that allow for homogeneity between, for example, the regional economies within a European economy, but diversity between countries that would suggest potential differences in steady-state growth rates for the regions within them.

Hence, there is little support in this body of work for the exogenous growth idea.

'New Economic Growth Theory'

An alternative to the neoclassical model attempts to circumvent some of these intellectual problems. In endogenous growth models, growth over time entails increasing returns to scale for a region. A proportionate increase in labor and capital gives rise to more than proportionate gains in output. This, when embodied into the 'New Growth Theory' or 'New Economic Geography', is consistent with divergence in economic growth along the traditional lines of Gunnar Myrdal's ideas of 'circular-and-cumulative causation', albeit for somewhat different reasons.

The situation can be illustrated by returning to Figure 13.1. Taking the initial starting positions for the two regions, the endogenous growth approach argues that not only will equalization of real wages and employment levels not be attained, but that there may be cases where they diverge further. Labor mobility between regions A and B may be impeded by the various costs of migration (embracing social and search costs as well as simple financial costs) and heterogeneity in the labor market (the jobs available in region A not being compatible with the skills and knowledge of labor in region B).

Equally, capital does not always move from region A to region B because of the higher returns due, not to an actual shortage of capital, but rather to the lesser uncertainty that is to be found in regions that already have a high level of prosperity and a pool of complementary skilled labor. While the earlier regional models focused largely on divergent growth rates in the context of traditional-style industries, the more contemporary form of the theory pays particular attention to the endogenous growth that occurs in regions which have an established highly skilled workforce and the ability to further develop their knowledge-based industries.

The relevance of the emergence of the new thinking, and the empirical analysis that has been found to support at least parts of it, is that it gives a role for government in regional economic policy. If there is circular-and-cumulative causation caused by scale effects of one kind or another, combined with imperfections in the mobility of factors of production, very broadly defined to embrace knowledge, then policies can be devised to compensate. Part of this policy may embrace appropriate transportation elements, and especially those relating to infrastructure provision.

13.3 Transport Infrastructure Investment and Economic Productivity

Large transport infrastructure investments, such as the United States Federal Highway System, have often been credited with having major impacts on the economic efficiency of a country. Fogel's work questioned whether that was always the case, but the issue resurfaced in the late 1980s in the context of the role of public investment, when David Aschauer (1989) produced work suggesting that the return on public infrastructure investment, of which transport works form the largest element, was exceeded by a large margin that found for private investment between 1949 and 1985 in the United States. Analysis by Biehl (1991), relating to European regions, came to the same basic conclusion.

Aschauer's analysis took a simple macro national time-series production function for the United States of the general form:

$$Y = f(L,K,J) \tag{13.2}$$

where:

Y indicates output;
L is labor;
K is the stock of private capital; and
J is the shock of public capital.

Aschauser used a Cobb–Douglas specification to estimate the output elasticity of public sector investment. Later work sometimes modified the production framework by adding additional variables, for example Prud'homme (1996) used a function of the general form $Y = f(L,K,J,F)$, where F reflected employees in the public sector. Other studies have used a cost, rather than a production, function of the form $C = f(IP,Q,PK)$, some have used varying levels of aggregation, and some have taken cross-sections of data, often by region, rather than a single national time series. Table 13.1 provides a listing of the results of the main studies. These do not refer specifically to transport investments, but transport is by far the major component in each.

The early studies indicated that when they were conducted, infrastructure expansion would significantly enhance productivity; a 1 percent increase in the public capital stock would raise total factor productivity by 0.39 percent.

Table 13.1   *Summary of estimated output elasticities of public infrastructure investments*

Study	Level of aggregation	Output elasticity of public capital
Aschauer (1989)	National	0.39
Holtz-Eakin (1988)	National	0.39
Munnell (1990)	National	0.34
Costa et al. (1987)	States	0.20
Eisner (1991)	States	0.17
Munnell (1990)	States	0.15
Mera (1973)	Regions	0.20
Duffy-Deno & Eberts (1989)	Urban areas	0.08
Eberts & Fogarty (1987)	Urban areas	0.03

Source: Button (1998). This paper contains the full references to the studies cited.

Exhibit   *Infrastructure investment and economic productivity*

While its physical form has changed over time, investment in public sector transportation infrastructure has, from the days of Adam Smith, been considered a stimulus to economic development. Defining economic development and agreeing on a common form of quantification, however, is difficult, and economists have deployed a variety of definitions over the years. Finding an acceptable measure of infrastructure is equally difficult.

The neoclassical economic work of David Aschauer, although its findings were subsequently questioned, stimulated serious economic debate on the subject. His empirical work was stimulated by the slow-down of economic productivity growth in many advanced economies in the late 1970s and early 1980s. Simple data plotting in the figure, which relates the amount of national productivity growth to the domestic product devoted to public investment between 1973 and 1985, suggests a strong positive relationship at the national level. And public transportation infrastructure constitutes a significant part of any country's non-military public capital. What Aschauer was interested in was a more detailed examination of the United States, and especially whether over time declining public investment had impacted on the United States' economic productivity.

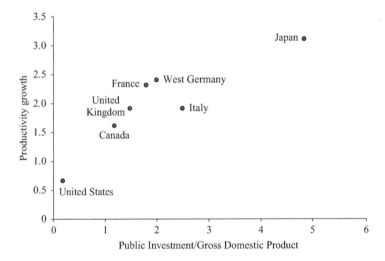

More detailed analysis adjusting for other things that affect economic performance makes use of an aggregate production function. This involves relating a country's real output of goods and services over time to its technical progress, its employment, its stock of non-residential capital, and a measure of public capital stock. Making fairly standard economic assumptions (for example, a Cobb–Douglas production function and allowing for possible economies of scale and congestion effects), and assuming the government provides services directly to the private sector, allows the specific functional form to be specified. This can then be manipulated to see how private sector productivity has changed with respect to public investment.

Estimation of the equations makes use of annual American data for 1949–85, taken from a variety of government sources. As seen in the table, the analysis involves looking at several subperiods. While the average growth in total factor productivity was 1.5 percent from 1950 to 1985, when the capital stock was growing at just over 3.0 percent, there were variations. In the initial period to 1970, factor productivity increased by 2.0 percent, accompanied with capital stock growing by 4.1 percent, but the latter only rose by 0.8 percent in the second part of the period when the public capital stock increased by 1.6 percent, the increase in total factor productivity in the first part of the early 1980s being particularly slow when the public capital stock only increased by 0.7 percent.

Subperiod	Annual growth in total factor productivity (%)	Change in on-military public capital stock (%)
1950–85	1.5	3.0
1950–70	2.0	4.1
1971–85	0.8	1.6
1981–85	0.7	0.7

Aschauer does not claim that public expenditure on infrastructure is the only thing influencing changes in the short-term economic productivity of a country. It is seen in the study as one of several factors, and others may include expenditure on R&D and the costs and availability of various factor inputs, and especially fuel and migrant labor. But it would seem to be an important one.

See also: D.A. Aschauer (1989) Is public infrastructure expenditure productive? *Journal of Monetary Economics*, 23, 177–200.

Later studies, and especially as the level of aggregation moved down from national to state to urban levels, brought this into question. As Ronald Fisher (1997) put it:

> The research is all over the board and somewhat inconsistent in its results as to whether investments in public services can increase levels of economic development. For example, the relationship between transportation investments and development is generally positive (but not overwhelming), and it is statistically significant only half of the time.

Several technical points have also been raised about the way this sort of analysis has been conducted (Gramlich, 1994):

- While the various studies have thrown up positive correlations between economic performance and the quantity of infrastructure, the direction of causality is not immediately clear. Wealthier areas, or times of greater economic growth, may simply provide more resources to be put into public projects. Testing for causality is difficult, and unfortunately the econometric work that has been done is not conclusive. Looking at tourism, a transport-intensive activity, for example, studies of Spain by Balanguer and Cantavella-Jorda (2002) and of Turkey (Gunduz and Hatemi-J., 2005) have suggested that there is a causal link running from tourism to economic development, but contrarily Narayan (2004) finds the linkage to be in the other direction for Fiji.

- The term 'infrastructure' is flexible; there is no agreed definition and taking accountancy data may disguise important measurement, qualitative, and definition factors. In the United States, for example, Aschauer used a four-category core subset of the nine US Bureau of Labor Statistics infrastructure categories, whereas other studies have employed the full set.

- The way that infrastructure is managed, used, and priced may be as important as the level of investment involved. In terms of impact, therefore, account needs to be taken of the short-term levels of utilization, maintenance, and so on, in addition to the stock of, and investment in, capacity.

- While transport is the largest element of most nation's infrastructure, it is not the only one, and ideally one should separate it out from energy, education, health, defense, and so on.

- As Morrison (1993) points out, '[a] clear consensus about the impacts of infrastructure investment has as yet been elusive, at least partly because different methodologies generate varying results and implications'. From an econometric perspective, for example, Sturm and De Haan (1995), looking at American and Dutch data series on the economic effects of public investment, found them to be neither stationary nor co-integrated, suggesting the estimation techniques used in many time series studies are often inappropriate.

- From a purely *a priori* perspective, some of the studies have thrown up rates of return that are outside of normal expectations, and well outside of what have been found in most individual micro projects.

- There are also issues regarding how economic development is to be measured. Gallen and Winston (2021) used 2017 US National Household Travel Survey data to develop a 17-equation general equilibrium model to examine the effects of government increases in publicly funded transportation infrastructure on individuals' accessibility to jobs and firms' accessibility to workers, on the availability, price, quality, and variety of consumer goods and services, on the intensity of competition among firms and their productivity, and on economic growth attributable to agglomeration economies, incorporating effects on households and firms. They focused on permanent changes and economic welfare. By incorporating shopping and commuting time wedges, they examined the costly time to build infrastructure, and efficient government pricing and investment policy, which are important for assessing the effects of infrastructure spending on welfare and GDP. The evidence shows that such spending can result in greater firm productivity and reductions in commuting and shopping–travel time. But they also show that it is important to distinguish an infrastructure spending policy's effect on GDP. Welfare improvements in GDP may overstate the improvements in an economy from increased infrastructure spending. Specifically in the case study, a 5 percent increase in transportation infrastructure financed by tax-payers generated a $79 billion increase in GDP, but a much lower welfare gain of $25 billion. The divergence occurs because GDP may increase without increasing welfare when households are indifferent to a marginal increase in work. Given that transportation infrastructure acts as a complement to labor, it is also possible to increase labor even as welfare decreases because of increased taxation.

13.4   The Multiplier Impacts of a Transport Investment

While at the abstract macro level there seems, from the empirical evidence, to be only a very general link between transport provision and economic development at best, it is at the more meso level that investment decisions are made. Major transport investments are generally neither simple in engineering terms, nor in their economic implications. Chapter 11 dealt with the microeconomic matters of assessing the pros and cons of a transport investment; here we look at transport provision in terms of its implications for stimulating economic activity at a higher level of aggregation.

A new airport, which for specificity is what is considered, goes through several stages from its planning to becoming fully operational and heavily used. Each of these phases generates its own type of income multiplier effect on the region. Figure 13.2 offers a simple diagram tracing out the temporal and spatial impacts together with some indication (the size of the arrows) of their respective magnitudes. It should be noted that the monikers attached to the various levels of multiplier sometimes differ in the literature, as indicated below:

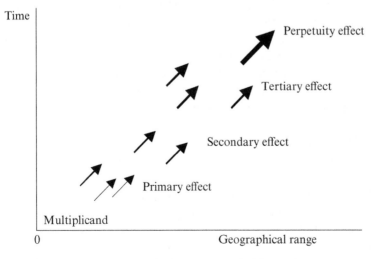

Figure 13.2   *The various economic multipliers associated with an airport investment*

- *Primary (or direct)*. The primary multiplier stems from the income that is associated with the multiplicand inherent in the construction of the facility, and the rounds of expenditure that emanate as part of that money are recycled through the local economy. The size of the local multiplier is often tempered in the case of an airport, if there is a need for significant inflows of labor, raw materials, and equipment to plan and construct the facility. Leakages of this kind are often substantial because new airports or major extensions are rare events in aggregate let alone in a particular region. As a result, there is seldom either adequate local expertise or equipment available. Even when local resources are used, there may be crowding-out effects if these are taken from other sectors of the regional economy and, thereby, reduce the multiplier effects of these sectors. Added to all this are frequent implementation delays due to planning, input shortage, and other factors that can produce small or even negative labor and output responses to increases in government investment in the short run (Leeper et al., 2010).
- *Secondary (or supplier)*. Once an airport is operational, it pumps money into the local economy through the staff that it directly employs and the activities of the airlines that make use of the facility. This income, in turn, has multiplier effects on the regional economy. Airports can be major employers but there is a largely bi-modal distribution in the labor force. While airports do employ many highly skilled and, thus, generally highly paid workers, many jobs are unskilled or semi-skilled (for example, in terms of drivers, aircraft cleaners, workers in concessions, and baggage handlers). Equally, while the airlines using the airport may maintain a staff to handle ticketing and aircraft maintenance, as well as have aircrew stopping overnight at local hotels, the numbers are generally relatively small compared to the land-take and investment in infrastructure and operational equipment.
- *Tertiary (or induced)*. The tertiary multiplier is the one that normally attracts most attention in the economic development literature. It is concerned with the amount of economic activity drawn to the region by the existence of an airport, and with the subsequent ripple effects that result as this pumps income into the area. These regional economic effects can be substantial. For example, Memphis Shelby Airport, the major United States hub for FedEx, is surrounded by warehouse and distribution facilities – one of the largest concentrations in the world. These facilities house products as varied as just-in-time surgery and orthopedic devices, home decor products, and DVDs, all of which are shipped from Memphis to destinations around the world. But elsewhere, and at much smaller facilities, the presence of air services is important for many industries, not only in their cargo needs but more often in terms of allowing their employees and customers easy access to their facilities and markets. High-technology industry makes extensive use of air transport, as do tourists.
- *Perpetuity*. While the tertiary multiplier effect can often be pronounced when an airport is suitably located and an extensive range of destinations

offered, its effect largely stems from a movement up the local production function. The airport itself, or extensions to an existing facility, is justified because there is an existing demand for air transportation services. The perpetuity effect is often, although not always, associated with the development of a large airport that shifts the regional production function upwards. Essentially it changes the structure of the regional economy. For example, many islands in the Caribbean and the Mediterranean have had their entire economies changed, usually from fishing and agriculture to tourism, as the result of the construction of a large airport. Air travel, after the construction of airport infrastructure, is also vital to the growth of tourism in larger regions, such as the coasts of Spain and of Miami. Additionally, as alluded to earlier, high-technology corridors have emerged at locations that had either been farmland before or dependent on more traditional industries.

Some general estimations by the Economic Policy Institute of the multiplier effects associated with an additional $1 million of expenditure on various modes of transport are seen in Table 13.2. These would suggest that, in general, expenditures on transport activities such as transit, trucking, and tourism have the largest multiplier effects.

Looking at less-aggregate cases, however, reveals that empirical evidence has not always been very helpful in sorting out the diverse ideas concerning the links between specific transport initiatives and economic development. This is seen, for example, in the summaries of studies conducted in industrial countries in the 1980s set out in Table 13.3. One of the difficulties is that economic development itself is not easy to define, and as can be seen from the table, several measures can be used in addition to simply the impact on local GDP. Additionally, the nature of the transport investments or other initiatives have implications for its influence on the wider economy. In other words, generalization concerning multiplier effects is highly context-specific.

Table 13.2   *United States employment multipliers per $1 million in final demand, all private sector industries*

	Direct	*Supplier*	*Induced*	*Total indirect*
Air transport	2.50	4.03	2.91	6.93
Rail transport	2.64	4.27	2.64	6.91
Water transport	1.06	5.80	2.43	8.22
Truck transport	5.01	5.42	4.16	9.58
Transit & ground passenger transport	8.04	8.84	4.93	13.77
Pipeline transport	1.46	3.18	1.45	4.63
Scenic & sightseeing transport & support activities for transport	4.99	6.71	4.39	11.11
Couriers & messengers	6.90	5.83	5.01	10.83
Warehousing & storage	9.18	4.88	5.37	10.25

Table 13.3   *Summary of findings looking at transport and development in industrialized countries*

Study	Geographical scale	Infrastructure	Conclusions
Botham (1980)	28 zones (UK)	Changing nature of highways	Small, centralizing on employment
Briggs (1981)	Non-metropolitan counties (US)	Provision of highways	Presence of Interstate highway is no guarantee of county development
Clearly & Thomas (1973)	Regional level (UK)	New estuarial crossing	Little relocation but changes in firms' operations
Dodgson (1974)	Zones in north (UK)	New motorway	Small effect on employment
Eagle et al. (1987)	87 counties (US)	New highway	No increased employment
Evers et al. (1987)	Regional level	High-speed rail	Some effect on (Netherlands) employment
Forrest et al. (1987)	Metropolitan	Light rapid transit	Property blight – good areas (US) for urban renewal
Judge (1983)	Regional level (UK)	New motorway	Small economic impact
Langley (1981)	Highway corridor (US)	Highway	Devalued property in areas
Mackie et al. (1986)	Regional level	New estuarial crossing	Small overall effect
Mills (1981)	Metropolitan areas (US)	Interstate highways	No significant effect on location patterns
Moon (1986)	Metropolitan areas (US)	Highway crossings	Existence of 'interchange villages'
Pickett (1984)	Local districts	Light rapid transit	Properties close to the (UK) line benefitted
Stephandes (1990)	87 counties (US) expenditure	New highway	Could affect employment – depends on county
Stephandes et al. (1986)	87 counties (US)	New highway expenditure	Some positive association with employment
Watterson (1986)	Metropolitan area (UK)	Light rapid transit	Modest growth in land use
Wilson et al. (1982)	Regional level (US)	Existing highways	Transport affects locations decisions but not development

Source: Button et al. (1995). This paper contains the full references to the studies cited.

There are also some serious caveats that can often lead to over-estimations using income or employment multipliers at the regional level. Multipliers were derived as part of demand-side macroeconomics at a time when factor supply constraints were not an issue. In practice, regions, and especially those where the economy has been performing poorly, often have supply constraints that limit the size of multiplier effects. Most empirical work tends to use macro-parameters that may not be relevant for the region under consideration.

While multipliers are often useful for considering the impacts on the region enjoying the new air transportation services, they only consider the gross effects. The initial injection of resources is often from outside the region; the multiplicand has to come from somewhere, and there are opportunity costs associated with resources drawn in during successive multiplier rounds, and this means that there is an opportunity cost involved. In the case of an airport intended to open up a tourist area, for example, this may stimulate more tourism in the aggregate, but some of the visitors will be attracted from alternative destinations. As with any activity that allows trade, airports have both a traffic generation and a traffic diversion effect.

In addition, while there may be positive multiplier effects, the closure of an airport or airline service may produce a downward spiral as income circulation is reduced. This can lead to retention of a facility or service that may not be justified. Investment, therefore, should be viewed over a long horizon, and simply to assess the short-term effects of, say, developing a small airport to stimulate local residential development or tourism may not be enduring and leave the area with significant stranded costs. Reliance on one industry that is in turn dependent on another is also a risky development strategy.

This causal view of transport and economic development has come under question in recent years. The cliometrics (the systematic application of economic theory, econometric techniques, and other mathematical methods to the study of history) work of Fogel (1964) in the United States, for example, offers evidence that American growth in the nineteenth century would have been quite possible without the advent of the railways – waterways supplying a comprehensive transport system at comparable costs. The view that the railways were the motivating force behind American economic development has given way to a weaker position, namely that good transport permits economic expansion.

Economic development is, thus, now generally seen as a complex process with transport permitting the exploitation of the natural resources and talents of a country; it is, therefore, necessary but not sufficient for development. Transport can release working capital from one area that can be used more productively as fixed capital elsewhere, although a necessary prior condition is the existence of suitable productive opportunities in potential markets. Public infrastructure in this sense should be set in the context of the availability of private capital: many parts of the world, for example, would not benefit from more transport infrastructure because of the lack of private resources.

Looked at from a slightly different perspective, improved transport can help overcome bottle-necks in production and thus further foster economic expansion. This is, for example, the underlying position taken by Roger Vickerman (1987) when examining the regional impacts of the Channel Tunnel between the United Kingdom and France. A difficulty, of course, if this is true, is that the bottle-neck may be some distance from the region and superficially appear unconnected with it. Accepting this caveat, the basic view of this school of thought is that transport is seen more as a facilitator than as a generator of development.

In many developing countries the inadequacy of transport facilities is one of the major bottlenecks to socio-economic development and a national integration. Often the lack of transport makes it difficult to introduce other social infrastructure such as education and medical services. The dissemination of the modern techniques and inputs of agricultural production and the linking of agriculture to other sectors of the economy through the market is hampered by the absence or inadequacy of transport facilities. As a result of these and other factors, the productivity of agriculture – the dominant sector in developing economics – is deplorably low. (Ahmed et al., 1976)

While the approaches sketched out above ascribe a positive role to transport in economic development, albeit in different ways, there is a feeling among some economists that an excess of scarce resources sometimes tends to be devoted to transport improvements. As with any scarce input it is possible to define an optimal provision of transport to facilitate development so that resources being drawn from other activities are not wasted. Excess provision can have an economic cost such as reduced or missed opportunities; the aim is thus to optimize 'crowding out'.

At a given point in economic development, a country requires a critical level of transport provision so that its growth potential is maximized – hence there is an optimum transport capacity for any development level. It has been argued, however, that there are economic forces that tend to lead to an excess of transport provision (especially high-cost infrastructure) at the expense of more efficient and productive projects. More specifically, Wilson (1966) pointed to the lumpiness of transport capital that, together with its longevity and associated externalities, makes it particularly difficult to estimate future costs and benefits. Consequently, decisions to devote resources to transport are not easily reversible or readily corrected.

Albert Hirschman (1958) highlighted the political acceptability of transport, arguing that the sector attracts resources simply because it is difficult for mistakes of an economic nature to be proved even after major projects have been completed. Also, development planners tend to be mainly concerned with allocating public investment funds, and it is, therefore, natural that they should claim transport, communications, energy, drainage, etc. as being of over-riding and fundamental importance. Further, given the industrial composition of wealthier developed countries with an established heavy industrial base, tied aid for transport schemes has a firm attraction. Those adopting this rather skeptical approach to the role of transport, therefore, accept that an adequate basic transport system is an obvious *sine qua non* for modern economic development but question whether the opportunity costs involved in further improving transport are necessarily justified.

13.5 Transport Economics in Less Developed Countries

Transport investment forms a major component of the capital formation of less developed countries, and expenditure on transport is usually the largest single item in the national budget. Up to 40 percent of public expenditure is devoted to transport infrastructure investment with substantial supplements coming from outside international agencies such as the World Bank or with direct bi-lateral assistance from individual countries. At one level it is important to know whether this is, in aggregate terms, the most practical and efficient method of assisting the poor countries of the world, while at another level it is necessary to be able to assess the development impact of individual transport schemes.

Broadly, transport may be seen to have four functions in assisting economic development:

- First, it is a factor input into the production process, permitting goods and people to be transferred between and within production and consumption centers. Because much of this movement is between rural and urban areas it permits the extension of the money economy into the agricultural sector.
- Transport improvements can shift production possibility functions by altering factor costs and, especially, reducing the levels of inventory tied up in the production process.
- Third, mobility is increased, permitting factors of production, especially labor, to be transferred to places where they may be employed most productively.
- Transport increases the welfare of individuals, by extending the range of social facilities to them, and provides superior public goods such as greater social cohesion and increased national defense.

Transport economists have made significant contributions in assessing in detail the role that transport may play in assisting economic development in Third World countries. At the microeconomic level they have developed techniques of project appraisal that permit a more scientific assessment of the costs and benefits of individual transport projects to be conducted.

Many of the techniques of investment appraisal employed in the developed parts of the world (see Chapter 11) are applicable in Third World conditions, but local situations often require changes of emphasis. This is not surprising considering these techniques were devised to look at transport systems based almost entirely upon mechanical modes, while head-porterage and canoes still account for the greatest proportion of goods movement in many less developed countries.

Basic data are also often not so readily available or reliable in the Third World as in most developed countries, thus limiting the precision of any analysis. Nevertheless, the development of investment appraisal techniques of the type set out by Ian Little and James Mirrlees (1974) permit consistent analysis across investment alternatives both within the transport sector and between the transport sector and other areas of economic activity. Such techniques emphasize the importance of estimating appropriate shadow prices for both inputs into transport and the benefits derived from it. In particular, the shortage of foreign exchange suffered by many less developed countries is highlighted, while it is recognized that higher levels of under-employment and unemployment require adjustments to the wage costs of labor. (The shadow price of labor, estimated as any lost production by diverting it from elsewhere in the economy, is usually negligible, plus an allowance for the disutility associated with the work in the transport sector.)

At the macroeconomic level economists have pointed to the general influence that appropriate transport planning can have in assisting overall economic development. While it may be argued that ideally one should expand transport provision to balance developments elsewhere in the economy, this is not always possible. The balanced growth approach maintains that if transport services are inadequate, then bottle-necks in the economy will curtail the growth process, but if the services are excessive this is both wasteful, in the sense that idle resources could be earning a positive return elsewhere in the economy, and can become demoralizing if the anticipated demand for transport does not materialize relatively quickly. Hirschman takes a somewhat different view, arguing that the relationship between economic development and the provision of social overhead capital, such as transport, is less flexible than members of the balanced growth school believe.

In Figure 13.3, the horizontal axis shows the provision and cost of social overhead capital (which is normally provided by the public sector and will embrace transport as a major component), while the vertical axis measures the total cost of direct productive activities (which are normally undertaken on purely commercial criteria). The balanced growth approach assumes that *DPA* output and *SOC* activities should grow together (that is, along the growth path represented by the ray from the origin), passing through the various curves from *a* to *d* representing successively higher amounts of *DPA/SOC* output.

Hirschman, however, argues that less developed countries are in practice not in a position to follow such a path – partly because of the lack of necessary expertise to ensure the balance is maintained and partly because of inherent indivisibilities in the social overhead capital schemes available. Consequently, growth is inevitably unbalanced and may follow one of two possible courses:

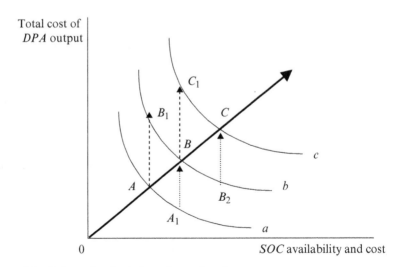

Figure 13.3   *Balanced and unbalanced growth paths*

one based upon excess capacity of SOC (that is, path $A \Rightarrow A_1 \Rightarrow B \Rightarrow B_2 \Rightarrow C$), the other upon a shortage of SOC (that is, path $A \Rightarrow B_1 \Rightarrow B \Rightarrow C_1 \Rightarrow C$). If a strategy of excess SOC capacity is preferred, it is hoped that this will permit DPA to become less expensive and encourage investment in that sector. Alternatively, with the second approach, DPA expansion occurs first and DPA costs will rise substantially. Therefore, considerable economies will be realized through the construction of more extensive SOC facilities. The actual effectiveness of the alternatives depends upon the strength of the profit motive in the DPA sector, and the responsiveness of the public authority in the SOC sector to public demand.

The type of transport provision most suited to developing economies is often of as much importance as the aggregate level of provision. Many developing countries tend to spend scarce development funds on prestige projects to demonstrate visually their capacity to emulate the performance of more developed nations; in other words, X-efficiency is sacrificed for a modern, if superficial, image. More critical is the way in which funds are spent on internal transport provision and whether there are advantages in concentrating limited capital resources in either the road or rail modes.

The appropriateness of different modes often depends upon the geographic–demographic nature of the country. Most less developed countries may be categorized as one of the following:

- densely populated tropical lands;
- tropical lands with low population density;
- mountainous, temperate lands with a low overall density of population but a concentration on a coastal plain or altiplane; or
- thinly populated desert areas with population concentrated along irrigated channels.

The appropriateness of different transport modes changes according to the type of country under consideration, thinly populated, tropical lands having different transport problems to highly urbanized countries with high population densities.

While the railways were important in the development of nineteenth-century economies and characterized colonial development in many countries, the emphasis in recent years has switched to the provision of adequate road infrastructure. This is particularly true in areas where a skeleton of roads already exists and resources can be devoted to improving and extending an established, if rudimentary, network. This approach may be especially fruitful if it links isolated agricultural communities both with each other and with the more advanced areas of the economy. Sixty years ago, Millard (1959) argued that, unlike economically advanced countries, in Third World nations 'the benefits from road construction are almost entirely in the form of new development from traffic which the new road will generate'. The effect is not purely on immediate output but can stimulate a propensity for further development.

Wilson strongly supported road development in Third World countries for this reason, arguing that '[i]nvestment options might usefully be analyzed in terms not only of their direct economic pay-off but also in terms of their influence on attitude' and that '[t]he educational and other spill-over effects of road transportation appear to be greater than those of other modes of transport. This is especially significant at low levels of development'. Having said this, however, there is a danger if integrated planning is not pursued that while improved road facilities may stimulate the agricultural economy, the new links between rural and industrial–urban areas could lead to increased polarization in the spatial economy with an enhanced geographical, as well as sectional, dualism resulting.

In terms of transport, improved port and shipping facilities permit less developed countries to export their products to wider markets and gain foreign exchange, although, as we see later, there are some dangers here. Since the demand for shipping services is derived from that for the final product, the benefits to less economically advanced countries from reducing maritime shipping costs can be illustrated by looking at the quantities of exports from a Third World country and the imports into the market of a higher-income economy.

Figure 13.4 shows a back-to-back diagram where S_i and D_i are the supply and demand schedule for the commodity in the developed country and S_j and D_j are the supply and demand curves in the less economically developed nation. Demand for imports and supply of exports is obtained by subtracting horizontally the domestic supply from demand, the demand for imports (exports) at each

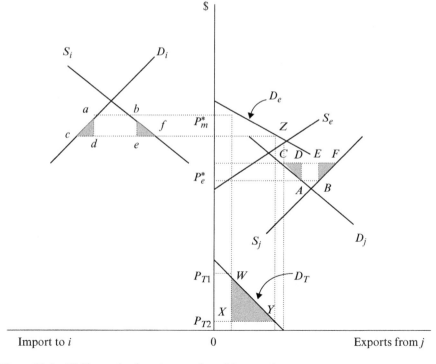

Figure 13.4 *Welfare gains from improved maritime services*

price being the difference between the quantity supplied and demanded assuming domestic and import commodities are perfect substitutes. D_e and S_e in Figure 13.4 are derived in this fashion; the vertical difference between these curves then represents the demand for shipping shown as D_T. (If shipping charges were zero, for example, then the free trade equilibrium would be Z.) Suppose actual shipping rates were P_{T1}, then at that rate the price of imports from country i confronting country j is seen to be P_m^* (the cost, insurance, and freight (CIF) price) while the cost of exports to country j would be seen in country i to be P_e^* (the free on board (FOB) price). Country i would then import an amount ab equal to country j's (the less developed country's) exports of AB.

There is now an improvement in shipping services; this may take the form of better port facilities or more efficient ships or it may be administrative (for example, relaxation of high conference shipping rates). The effect is that shipping costs fall to P_{T2}, resulting in exports from j rising to CF to match the higher imports of cf into the developed country i. Trade has expanded for the less developed country. The net benefit of this trade to the two countries is represented by the shaded areas in the figure. Area adc is the extra consumption enjoyed by the developed, importing country as a result of the fall in the CIF price while bef is a positive production effect resulting from a contraction of i's relatively high-cost industry. The areas ADC and BEF are the symmetrical benefits to the less developed country. (Interestingly the sum of these benefits can be measured directly as the area WXY under the demand curve for shipping services.)

While it can be demonstrated that improved shipping facilities in our example can aid development, it should be noted that the analysis is crucially dependent upon the elasticities of demand for goods in developed and under-developed countries, and the relative costs of supply. This often poses serious problems for less developed countries, as pointed out by the United Nations Conference on Trade and Development (UNCTAD) in 1969, with the less developed nations often paying much of the costs of transport, that is:

> For many of the world's agricultural products, on which developing countries rely for much of their export earnings, supply elasticities are low in the short run ... . Although overall demand elasticities for most of these commodities are also low, the elasticity of demand facing the individual supplier or the whole group of suppliers in a single country is likely to be relatively high, unless that country is the only source of supply, and there is no ready substitute for the commodity ... . The supplier in these cases therefore normally bears the bulk of the transport costs.

In reality, the world is also a little more complicated, with trade involving not simply the production and transport sectors but also various systems of international finance and tariff barriers in effect.

One of the practical problems experienced by many less developed countries has been the fact that shipping lines have combined in conferences to regulate prices and thus have often led to shipping costs, which are often borne by the less developed countries, being higher than in a free market situation. There are also arguments that the existence of non-pricing competition within conferences produces a much higher quality of service (and *ipso facto* cost) than would prevail without collusion and that this is again detrimental to Third World countries. Empirical evidence produced by Devanney et al. (1975), looking at trade between the United States' east coast and Chile, Columbia, Ecuador, and Peru, suggests that the conference system on these routes pushed up shipping rates by about $20 per ton in 1971, most of which would have been borne by the poorer countries.

It may not seem surprising that in these circumstances UNCTAD negotiated a Code of Conduct for Liner Conferences that allocated maritime traffic on a 40:40:20 basis, with 40 percent of the trade allocated to the merchant marine of each of the trading nations and 20 percent to cross-traders. This was intended to give under-developed countries the chance to reap some of the financial rewards from shipping and exert a more immediate influence on their own development. In 1978, for example, Third World countries were in the disadvantaged position of only having 8.6 percent of the world dead-weight tonnage of shipping but generating over 30 percent of the bulk cargoes and over 90 percent of the tanker cargoes.

In the short term, lack of capacity prevented some nations from enacting the full implementation of the Code. Zerby (1979) estimated, for instance, that of the 26 less developed countries he studied, only nine had merchant fleets large enough to handle 40 percent of their exports in 1975 and only 15 had sufficient capacity to handle 40 percent of imports. Attempts to expand the fleets of less developed countries to fulfil 40 percent of the market would, therefore, have resulted in excess capacity in the fleets of the developed countries, but more importantly, given the imbalance in the volume of imports and exports, attempts to meet 40 percent of shipping demand both into and out of Third World nations would lead to a 50 percent excess capacity within their own fleets. Zerby, therefore, felt that a rigid adherence to the 40:40:20 principle was likely to be an extremely costly method of reducing the developing countries' dependence on conference services. In practice it had limited effect, and efforts to reduce the costs of shipping to developing nations moved in other directions (Premti, 2016).

13.6   The Transport Policy of the European Union

Several national groupings have emerged in both the economically developed and the economically less developed world. These entail countries that have come together into loose economic unions with the aim of fostering their common economic interests. The European Union (this term is used throughout for simplicity; the title has changed several times) is one example, and the United States–Mexico–Canada Agreement and the African Continental Free Trade Area are others.

Each grouping has its own priorities and has set about achieving these in its own way. The development of transport policies within the framework of the European Union provides some indication of the importance that is increasingly being attached to transport by these groupings and to some of the problems of creating pan-national transport policies. (Indeed, the challenges are often similar to those when trying to develop a transport strategy in a national federal structure.) The European case also provides a useful illustration of the problems of devising an international transport policy designed primarily to foster economic growth.

The objective of the European Union is 'to promote throughout the Community a harmonious development of economic activities, a continuous and balanced expansion, an increase in stability, an accelerated raising of the standard of living, and closer relations of member states'. A 'Common Transport Policy' (CTP) was important in facilitating the attainment of this aim. The difficulties of agreeing on how to achieve this from a political-economy perspective is illustrated in Figure 13.5. Before integration, there were several access points that allowed interactions between two countries (either side of the dashed line) with internal movements combining to influence location, traffic, and production. Most movement was internal, as seen in the bottom segment of the figure. After integration brought about by the CTP, there was more international trade that affected levels of production, the routes used for transport, and the relative importance of domestic and international markets. The outcome was difficult to foresee, and although aggregate economic welfare would rise, the ultimate distribution of the welfare across locations and industrial sectors was uncertain.

Individual member states also each had their own set of transport objectives. These required modifying to conform with commonly agreed aims and goals with a context of each country having its own sets of institutions and policy tools which would require standardization. Many countries in Europe had traditionally used transport subsidies to protect specific industries or regions, but this may run counter to the Union's objectives of increasing overall economic efficiency or be thought to result in undesirable redistributions of welfare.

Problems with the creation of a transport policy began early. The initial Rome Treaty of 1957 contained an entire chapter on transport, although it limited itself initially to movement of freight by road, rail, and inland waterways. It was not until 1961, however, that a memorandum appeared setting out clear objectives, and not until the following year that an Action Programme was published. The emphasis of these initiatives was on removing obstacles to trade posed by the institutional structures governing transport, and to foster competition once a level playing field of harmonized fiscal, social, and technical conditions had been established. That it took over 40 years to make significant progress towards a substantive policy is in part due to the nature of European geography and the underlying transport market, although continued insistence by nation states on pursuing their individual agendas did not help.

Examination of a map of the European Union provides insights on some of the problems of devising a CTP. Ideally, as we have seen, transport functions most effectively on a hub-and-spoke basis with large concentrations of population and economic activity located at corners and in the center, and with the various transport networks linking them. The central locations act as markets for transport

Before Economic Union

Country A Domestic	International	Country B Domestic
Regulated prices/market access	Few 'gateways'	Regulated prices/market access
National licensing	Document checks	National licensing
National establishment	Bi-lateral license	National establishment
National labor laws	Split tariffs	National labor laws
National technical standards	Different 'gauges'	National technical standards
Split tariffs	Different labor laws	Split tariffs
	Different laws of establishment	

After Economic Union

Country A Domestic	International	Country B Domestic
Competitive markets	Open borders	Competitive markets
National/EU licensing	European licenses	National/EU licensing
EU establishment	Open access to infrastructure	EU establishment
EU/national labor laws	Through tariffs	EU/national labor laws
National/EU technical standards	Different 'gauges'	National/EU technical standards
EU licenses	Coordinated labor laws	EU licenses
EU/national infrastructure policy	EU laws of establishment	EU/national infrastructure policy
	Coordinated EU infrastructure	

Figure 13.5 *Shifts in the European Union's international and domestic transport from 1960*

services in their own rights, but also as interchange and consolidation points for traffic between the corner nodes. In many ways the United States fits this model rather well, but the European Union never has. When there were six members, the bulk of economic activity was at the core, with limited growth at the periphery. The various enlargements over the years have added to the problems of serving peripheral and often sparsely populated areas. The geographical separation of some states and the logical routing of traffic through non-member countries, together with the island nature of others, posed further problems.

The common policy was also not initiated with a clean slate: member states had established transport networks and institutional structures that could not rapidly be changed even if a common set of principles could have been established. At the outset, countries such as France and West Germany carried a significant amount of their freight traffic by rail, whereas others, such as Italy and the Benelux nations, relied more on road transport. The resultant differences were also not simply physical (including variations in railway gauges, vehicle weight limits, and different electricity currents), they also reflected fundamental differences in the ways transport was viewed.

At a macro, political-economy level there are two broad views on the way transport should be treated. Following the Continental philosophy, the objective is to meet wide social goals that require interventions in the market through regulations, public ownership, and direction. This approach particularly dominated much of twentieth-century transport policy thinking in Continental Europe. Its place was taken by a wider, but not complete, acceptance of the Anglo-Saxon approach to transport policy. This treats the sector as little different from other economic activities. Transport provision and use should be efficient in its own right, with efficiency normally best attained by making the maximum use of market forces. Of course, the extremes of either of the approaches never existed; it has been a matter of degree. Even in countries such as the United Kingdom, which was a bastion of the Anglo-Saxon ideology, there existed extensive regimes of regulation and control, and large parts of the transport system were in state or local government ownership.

From a more analytical perspective, the situation may be seen in terms of the ways efficiency is viewed. The approach until the 1970s was to treat transport efficiency largely in terms of maximizing scale efficiency while limiting any dead-weight losses associated with monopoly power. Most transport infrastructure was enjoying economies of scale that could only be exploited by coordinated and, *ipso facto*, regulated, often subsidized, development and in many cases state-owned. Many aspects of operations were also seen as potentially open to monopoly exploitation and hence in need of oversight. This situation changed. From a pragmatic perspective, the high levels of subsidies enjoyed by many elements of the transport sector became politically unsustainable. Economists began to question whether the regulations deployed were achieving their stated aims. Government failures, it was argued, were often larger than the market failures they were trying to correct.

New elements also came into play in the 1970s. Attitudes towards environmental intrusion, for example, changed as part of a wider effort to improve the overall environment and fulfil larger, global commitments on such matters as reducing emissions of global warming gases. Local environmental effects were largely left to individual countries, but as the implications of regional and global environmental intrusions have become more widely appreciated, so the Union's transport policy has become proactive in these areas.

The early thinking regarding a CTP centered on harmonization so that a level playing field could ultimately be created on which competition would be equitable. The European Coal and Steel Community had initiated this approach in the early 1950s and it continued as Union interest moved away from primary products. The Community had removed some artificial tariff barriers relating to rail movements of primary products and the Union's policy initially attempted to expand this idea in the 1960s to cover the general carriage of goods and especially those moved on roads. Road transport was viewed rather differently to railways. It was perceived that the demand and supply features of road haulage markets could lead to excessive competition and supply uncertainties.

Early efforts included seeking to initiate common operating practices (for example, relating to driving hours and vehicle weights) and accounting procedures, and standardizing methods of charging. A forked tariff regime for trucking, with rates only allowed between officially determined maxima and minima, was aimed at meeting the dual problems of possible monopoly exploitation in some circumstances, and of possible inadequate capacity due to excess competition in others. Such rates were stipulated on international movements within the

Union. There were practical problems in setting the cost-based rates, and questions were raised concerning a policy that was aimed at simultaneously tackling monopoly and excess competition. Limitations on the number of international truck movements across borders were marginally reduced by the introduction of a small number of Community quota licenses, authorizing the free movement of holders over the entire European road network.

The 1973 enlargement to nine member states stimulated a renewed interest in transport policy and offered the opportunity to review a whole range of policy areas. The new members – the United Kingdom, Ireland, and Denmark – were more market-oriented in their transport policy objectives. At about the same time, the European Commission raised legal questions concerning the inertia of the Council of Ministers in creating a genuine CTP. It also followed a period of rapid growth in trade within the Union, bringing infrastructure capacity issues to the fore and pressures for more flexible regulation of road freight transport.

The outcome was not dramatic although new sectors entered the debates, most notably maritime transport, and wider objectives concerning environmental protection and energy policy played a role. Overall, the actions in this period were a gentle move to liberalization by making the quota system permanent and expanding the number of licenses increased international intra-Union road freight capacity. The option of using reference tariffs rather than forked tariffs was a reflection of the inherent problems with the latter. A major element of the measures involved improving decision-making regarding the provision of transport infrastructure and about consideration of the way that appropriate charges should be levied for its use. The importance of transport links outside of the EU, but part of a natural European network, also began to play a part in policy formulation, with the Union beginning to develop mechanisms for financing investment in such infrastructure.

The enlargement of the Union, as Greece and then Spain and Portugal joined, had little impact on the CTP. It still essentially remained piecemeal. The only significant change prior to major developments in the early 1990s was the gradual widening of the modes covered. There were, for example, moves to bring maritime and air transport policy in line with Union competition policy.

The accession to membership in the 1970s and early 1980s of countries such as the United Kingdom and Greece with established shipping traditions brought maritime issues to the table and then the Single European Act of 1986 provided a catalyst for initiating a maritime policy. A series of measures were introduced aimed at bringing shipping within the Union's competition policy framework. This came at a time when major changes were beginning to permeate the way in which maritime services were provided. Technical shifts, such as the widespread adoption of containerization, had begun to influence the established cartel arrangements that had characterized scheduled maritime services. (These initial arrangements were 'conferences' that coordinated fares and sailings but later were more integrated 'consortia'.)

The size of the European Union's shipping sector declined significantly in the 1980s in the face of competition from Far East and communist bloc fleets.

The 'First Package' of measures in 1985 sought to improve the competitive structure of European shipping by giving the Commission power to react to predatory behavior by third-party ship owners, and reinterpreted competition policy
to allow block exemptions for shipping conferences, albeit with safeguards. In
1986 a 'Second Package' set out to establish a common registry, although this did
not prove successful. Also, as part of the general effort to liberalize the market,
agreement on cabotage (the provision of a domestic service within a country by
a carrier from another nation) was reached but with exceptions in some markets,
for example the Greek Islands.

Ports policy was largely *ad hoc*. Initial concerns in the early 1990s centered
around modernizing European ports to ensure that they could handle the large
ships that were being introduced. Progress was relatively slow until 2000 when sea
and inland ports were incorporated into the Trans-European Networks (TENs)
initiative with the objective of integrating and prioritizing investment in transport
infrastructure.

The European bi-lateral system of air service agreements covering scheduled air transport between member states was, like those in other parts of the
world, tightly regulated. Typical features of a bi-lateral agreement meant: only
one airline from each country could fly on a particular route with the capacity
offered by each bi-lateral partner also often restricted; revenues were pooled; fares
were approved by the regulatory bodies of the bi-lateral partners; and the designated airlines were substantially state-owned and enjoyed state aid. Domestic air
markets were also highly controlled Air transport in general, however, since the
liberalization of United States domestic markets in the 1970s, was moving away
from a tradition of strict regulation. Until the early 1980s, however, it had been
thought that European aviation policy was outside of the jurisdiction of the
European Commission and a matter for national governments. This changed, following several legal decisions by the European Court of Justice beginning in 1979.

The basic philosophy became that deregulation would take place in stages
(an approach to regulatory reform we shall discuss in more detail in Chapter 14),
with workable competition being the objective and a series of 'packages' being
subsequently enacted. The 1987 package aimed at relaxing existing intra-Union
bi-lateral regimes by, for example, allowing deviations from the traditional air
services agreement that set a 50:50 split of traffic between the two member countries. The decision also required member states to accept multiple designations on
a country-pair basis by another member. It also became easier for countries to
allow more than one of their airlines onto routes. This was extended in the 1989
'Second Package' when all capacity limits between bi-lateral partners were to
disappear, and, further, only if both civil aviation authorities refused to sanction
a fare application could an airline be precluded from offering it to its passengers.
Governments could no longer discriminate against airlines of other member
states provided they met safety criteria, effectively removing national airline iden-
tities within the Union.

The creation of the Single European Market in 1992 and the subsequent
moves towards greater political integration brought important changes to the

CTP and related transport policies. Broadly, the 1987 Single European Act removed institutional barriers to free trade in transport services. At about the same time, efforts at further political integration and economic development led to major new initiatives to provide an integrated European transport infrastructure – for example, the TENs. While there were moves to liberalize industries such as air transport from the late 1980s, the broad basis of European transport policy was established in 'The future development of the Common Transport Policy' (Commission of the European Communities, 1992), which advocated as a guiding principle the need to balance an effective transport system for the Union with a commitment to the protection of the environment.

The changes reflected developments in economic theories that provided new ways of thinking about transport markets. There was also a switch away from concern about problems of optimal scale and monopoly power that had been the intellectual justification for state ownership and regulation of such industries as railways and air transport, to seeking ways of creating conditions favorable to X-efficiency and dynamic efficiency. Technically, this was largely, but not exclusively, a concern with reducing costs replacing that of containing consumer exploitation. There was mounting concern about the costs of regulated transport that had macroeconomic implications for the overall economic development of the Union.

Although terms such as multi-modalism abound in the official literature of the European Union, and, indeed, some initiatives have transcended the conventional bounds of modal-based actions, a useful and pragmatic way of treating these recent developments is by mode.

Road Transport

Road transport is the dominant mode of both freight and passenger transport in Europe; the share of freight going by rail, for example, has fallen from 32 percent in the Union in 1970 to about 18 percent in 2019. Over the period, the freight tonnage in Europe has increased 2.5 times and the share of this going by road has risen from 48 percent to 76 percent. The initial efforts to develop a common policy regarding road transport, however, proved problematic. Technical matters on things like driving hours were more easily solved than those of creating a common economic framework of supply, and economic controls lingered on as countries with less efficient road haulage industries sheltered them from the more competitive fleets. There were also more legitimate efficiency concerns throughout the Union over the wider social costs of road transport, regarding both environmental matters and questions of infrastructure utilization.

The single-market initiative, also later influenced by the potential of new trade with the post-communist states of Eastern and Central Europe, many of which have joined the Union, has resulted in significant reforms to economic regulation in recent years. Earlier measures had helped expand the supply of international trucking permits in Europe and, as part of the 1992 single-market initiative, a phased liberalization was initiated that gradually removed restrictions on trucking movements across national boundaries and phased-in cabotage that had hitherto not been permitted. There was also a considerable reduction in cross-border documentation.

Railways

Rail transport, while largely filling a niche market in many countries, is an important freight mode in much of Continental Europe and provides important passenger services along several major corridors. At the local level, it serves as a key mode for commuter traffic in larger cities. The European Coal and Steel Community undertook considerable economic reform of Europe's freight railways in the 1950s, including the removal of discriminatory freight rates. From the late 1960s and 1970s the emphasis had shifted to the rationalization of the subsidized networks through more effective and transparent cost accountancy. The recent focus has been more on widening access to networks and on technological developments, especially regarding the development of a high-speed rail network as part of the TENs initiative. The Union has also instigated measures aimed at allowing the trains of one member state to use the track of another, with charges based upon economic costs. The implementation of the strategy has been slow and has had limited impact.

The Union has found it difficult to devise practical and economically sound common pricing principles to apply to transport infrastructure despite the proposals of the Oort Report (Oort and Maaskant, 1976). Regarding railways, the gist of the overall proposals is for short-run marginal costs including environmental and congestion costs (as well as wear on the infrastructure) to be recovered. Long-run elements of cost are only to be recovered in narrowly defined circumstances, and in relation only to passenger services. This clearly has implications, especially on the freight side, if genuine full cost-based competition is to be permitted with other transport modes.

Rail transport has also received considerable support as an integral part of making greater use of multi-modal transport systems. Such systems would largely rely upon rail (including piggy-back systems and kangaroo trains) or waterborne modes for trunk haulage, with road transport used as the feeder mode. This is seen as environmentally desirable and as contributing to containing rising levels of road traffic congestion in Europe.

The success of some of the French TGV (*Train à Grande Vitesse*) services, and especially that between Paris and Lyon, where full cost recovery has been attained, has led to a significant interest in this mode. In 1990 the Commission set up a high-level working group to help push forward a common approach to high-speed railway development and a master plan for 2010 was produced. The Union's efforts to harmonize the development of high-speed rail has not been entirely successful and there are significant technical differences, for example between the French and German systems.

In legal terms, between 2001 and 2016, four legislative packages were adopted aimed at gradually opening up rail transport service markets for competition, making national railway systems inter-operable, and defining appropriate framework conditions for the development of a single European railway area. These include charging and capacity allocation rules, common provisions on licensing of railway undertakings and train driver certification, safety requirements, the creation of the European Agency for Railways, and rail regulatory bodies in each member state, as well as rail passenger rights.

The 4th Railway Package adopted in 2016 is designed to complete the Single European Railway Area. Its goal is the revitalization of the sector, making it more competitive *vis-à-vis* other modes of transport. It comprises two 'pillars':

- The 'technical pillar' is designed to boost the competitiveness of the railway sector by significantly reducing costs and administrative burdens for railway undertakings wishing to operate across Europe. It will save firms from having to file multiple applications in the case of operations beyond one single member state. It aims to ensure that European Rail Traffic Management System equipment is inter-operable, and to reduce the multiplicity of remaining national rules.
- The 'market pillar' completes the process of gradual market opening started with the 1st Railway Package. It establishes the general right for railway undertakings established in one member state to operate all types of passenger services everywhere in the EU, lays down rules to improve impartiality in the governance of railway infrastructure and prevent discrimination, and introduces the principle of mandatory tendering for public service contracts in rail. The market pillar is designed to deliver more choice and better quality of rail services for European citizens.

Inland Waterway Transport

Inland waterway transport has been important for the European Union since the beginning. This is mainly because it is a primary concern of the Netherlands and Germany, with France and Belgium also having interests in the mode. Progress in formulating a policy has tended to be slow, in part because of historical agreements covering navigation on the Rhine (for example, the Mannheim Convention), but mainly because the major economic concern has been that of over-capacity, which in 1998 was still estimated at between 20 and 40 percent at the prevailing freight rates. Retraction of supply is almost inevitably difficult to manage, both because few countries are willing to pursue a contraction policy in isolation and because of the resistance of barge owners and labor.

As in other areas of transport, the Union has sought technical standardization, and principles for social harmonization were set out in 1975 and 1979. Economic concerns took over in the 1990s, and in 1990 a system of subsidies designed to stimulate scrappage of vessels was adopted. The introduction of new vessels into the inland fleet is only allowed on a replacement basis. The labor subsidies given in the Netherlands, Belgium, and France (the 'rota system') were phased out by 2000.

These measures were coupled with an initiative in 1995 to coordinate investment in inland waterway infrastructure (the Trans-European Waterway Network), designed to encourage, for environmental reasons, the greater use of waterborne transport. Subsequently, in 'European transport policy for 2010: time to decide' (Commission of the European Communities, 2001), the Commission put emphasis on its Marco Polo Programme on integrating inland waterways transport with rail and maritime transport for the movement of bulk consignments within an inter-modal chain.

Maritime Transport

Much of the emphasis of the European Union's maritime policy in the late 1990s was on the shipping market rather than on protecting the Union's fleet; that is, it is user- rather than supplier-driven. Globally, the sector became increasingly concentrated as, first, consortia grew in importance, mergers took place, and then the resultant large companies formed strategic alliances. An extension of the 1985 rules to cover consortia and other forms of market sharing was initiated in 1992 and subsequently extended as maritime alliances became more complex.

In 1994 the Commission acted to ban the Transatlantic Agreement reached the preceding year by the major shipping companies to gain tighter control over loss-making North Atlantic routes. It did so because the agreement manipulated capacity and rate, and contained articles covering pre- and on-carriage over land. It also fined 14 shipping companies that were members of the Far East Freight Conference for price-fixing because the prices embodied multi-modal carriage and while shipping *per se* enjoyed a block exemption on price agreements, multi-modal services did not.

Ports also attracted attention in the 1990s mainly because advances in technology had led to significant concentrations in activities as shipping companies have moved towards hub-and-spoke operations. The main European ports were working at about 80 percent capacity with many at or near their design capacity. Whether this is a function of a genuine capacity deficiency or reflects inappropriate port pricing charges that do not contain congestion cost elements is debatable. In 2001 the Commission launched an initiative to improve the quality of services offered by ports that involves tightening access standards for pilotage, cargo handling, etc., and to make more transparent the rules of procedure at ports, with the aim of bringing ports more fully into an integrated transport structure.

Air Transport Policy

The final reform of air transport, the 'Third Package', came in 1992 and was phased in from the following year with the aim of having a regulatory structure by 1997 akin to that for US domestic aviation. Since 1997, full cabotage has been permitted, and fares are generally unregulated. Additionally, foreign ownership among Union carriers is permitted, and these carriers have, for Union internal purposes, become European airlines. One result has been an increase in cross-share holdings and a rapidly expanding number of alliances between airlines within the Union. This change did not initially apply to extra-Union agreements where national bi-lateral arrangements still dominate the market.

A ruling by the European Court of Justice in 2002 gave the Commission the authority to negotiate with the United States on liberalizing the transatlantic market. Negotiations subsequently took place but while there was some initial progress through compromise in several technical areas, little substantive agreement emerged for some time regarding the key and fundamental economic issues. The interests of the domestic coalitions of the military and the air labor unions that influence the American stance strongly favor an 'Open Skies' arrangement with free airline access to markets, whilst the Union has favored a much more free market approach that allows for cabotage and flexible movement of capital, via an 'Open Aviation Area'.

The impasse was broken in 2007 with a compromise, short-term agreement that effectively opened the skies over the North Atlantic effective March 30, 2008. This permitted United States airlines to operate intra-European Union flights if this involved an all-cargo flight or a passenger flight as the second leg of a flight started in the States. European airlines are neither permitted to operate intra-United States flights nor to purchase a controlling stake in an American carrier. In November the United Kingdom concluded an individual open-sky agreement with the United States that will supersede the Union agreement post-Brexit.

Overall Impacts

The phased enlargement of the European Union under the Treaties of Nice in 2001 has had implications for transport by affecting the demands placed on the networks of existing member states and those that have acceded. The accession states are reforming their economic structures – important for influencing what is transported and where – and their transport systems. Nevertheless, the difficulties to be overcome are not trivial:

- *Geographical.* Enlargement has had implications for the economics of long-haul transport operations as well as necessitating investment in infrastructure. What the enlargement has not done is to create a 'natural' transport market. The spatial distribution of economic activities still does not have the structure of the United States, where the overall physical market is essentially rectangular with centers of population and economic activities at the corners and in the center, which allow exploitation of efficiency benefits from long-haul carriage and hub-and-spoke structures. In the European Union economic activity is dichotomously distributed and enlargement has added to the central/peripheral nature of the Union.
- *Legal.* There are issues concerning the role of central legal responsibilities and the degree of local national autonomy will inevitably arise. This is shaping the wider legal structure in which macroeconomic policies regarding transport are being formulated, and is influencing the external policies

of the Union – important for transport in a world of global economies and global trade.

- *Economic.* In 2002 the European Union's Commission President raised the issue of the need for a common fiscal policy within Europe, or at least that part of it in the eurozone. Economists have long understood that a common currency requires a common fiscal policy as a concomitant. This involves the Union having responsibility for fiscal transfers above those it now controls. While the exact amount is debated, and depends on the extent to which the center considers distribution as well as macroeconomic stabilization as part of its function, it may well be considerable. This would take away much national autonomy over major transport infrastructure works and influence short-term public expenditure patterns.

These are not trivial changes, and it is impossible to talk about any one in isolation from the others, or without considering the background and the current state of existing Union transport policy. The countries that gained membership in 2004 (Poland, the Czech Republic, Hungary, Slovakia, Lithuania, Latvia, Slovenia, Estonia, Cyprus, and Malta) also offer a variety of different challenges from a transport perspective. Later adding Bulgaria, Romania, and Croatia has compounded the diversity.

The nature of the economies of the post-Soviet transition states, and their relationships to the European Union, has already changed considerably. Nevertheless, there are numerous ways in which their transport systems differ from much of the older Union. They are mostly distant from the core of the Union, making railways a potentially more viable mode for long-distance freight transport. Indeed, the physical area of an enlarged Union offers the prospects of haul lengths comparable with those in the United States, where deregulated railways have at least been maintaining their market share. However, the rail freight networks within transition economies are largely based on dated technologies and are not oriented to meeting transport demands for movements to and from the Union. They have traditionally been excessively labor-intensive and serve as job creators rather than transport suppliers.

Car ownership is considerably lower in the accession countries than in the older ones, but this is changing. This is putting strains on urban infrastructure and poses mounting environmental problems. Smaller states, and some regions within the larger ones, are also themselves subjected to significant transit traffic flows, raising issues of infrastructure capacity and environmental degradation but also matters of charging and pricing – a subject the Union has been singularly poor at addressing. The transition economies also have poorly maintained transport networks largely directed to moving bulk, raw materials to Russia. The road freight sector has begun to develop in response to the needs of modern just-in-time production and some countries are making use of the limited infrastructure links to the West. Transition economies with maritime access and inland waterways make considerable use of them. Enlargement comes at a time of technical change in the sector, with the increasing deployment of a post-Panamax fleet exploiting scale economies and adding pressure for more hub-and-spoke operations and fleet rationalization.

A more recent event has been the departure (Brexit) of the United Kingdom from the European Union in 2020. This re-introduced many of the barriers to free transportation that existed before the United Kingdom joined the Union. While a range of temporary agreements have been put in place, the new situation which came into place in 2021 increases the paperwork required by United Kingdom operators to serve European markets and in many cases removes their automatic rights to enter these markets. British-based transport companies, which were technically European citizens, effectively became simply United Kingdom citizens with limited rights to operate within Union countries.

13.7 Transport Effects on Regional and Urban Development

We now move from macro issues to look at some of the meso-level effects transport may have on economic development. The inter-regional spread of economic activity within a country is of major concern to national governments. Geographical variations in unemployment, income, migration, and industrial structure are of importance because they both result in spatial inequalities in welfare and, in many cases, reduce the overall performance of the national economy. For these reasons, many countries actively pursue policies that attempt to stimulate economic activity in depressed areas and to contain damaging explosive growth in prosperous regions.

The policies, which have varied both in intensity and in form over time, and differ in their nature across countries, have generally concentrated on giving direct financial assistance to industry and on improving the mobility of labor. In addition, there have been attempts at improving the economic infrastructure of what are seen as particularly depressed areas, or in some cases proactive policies where depression is anticipated, with specific emphasis being placed on providing better transport facilities. The policy of biasing transport investment in favor of depressed regions has been subjected to considerable debate over the years.

In the United Kingdom, skepticism about the effectiveness of such a policy as a regional economic development aid was initially expressed by A.J. Brown in a Minority Report of the Hunt Committee Inquiry into the Intermediate Areas as long ago as 1969 and was supported by the findings of the Leitch Committee. A common thread in these studies is that, in a country such as Britain where infrastructure is already relatively comprehensive, transport is seldom an important factor in explaining disparities in regional economic performance. It is now accepted by many developed countries that transport policy motivated by regional policy objectives must be pursued with circumspection and that, in many cases, improved transport facilities may prove counterproductive for development areas.

A simple hypothetical example illustrates the difficulty. We have two regions, *A* and *B*, producing a single homogeneous commodity. The centers of the regions (see Figure 13.6) are *M* miles apart and the commodity can be transported over the area at a constant money cost per mile of $f - t$ per ton. The markets served by the regions differ, however, because it costs $\$C_A$ to produce a ton of the commodity in region A and $\$C_B$ per ton in region B. Consequently, and assuming no production centers exist between the regions, a distribution boundary can be drawn (shown by the dashed line in the figure), which is m_A miles from the center of A and m_B miles from the center of B (where $m_A + m_B = M$). The boundary is determined by the relative production costs of the regions and the costs of transport (that is, $C_A + tm_A = C_B + tm_B$). Basic manipulation of the algebra gives the form:

$$mA = \left(M + \frac{C_B - C_A}{t} \right) \tag{13.3}$$

If, therefore, production is relatively cheap in region A then m_A will increase if infrastructure reduces the cost of transport. Thus, if A is a depressed area then transport improvements could assist in expanding its potential market and, therefore, generate more income and employment, but region A must be a low-cost producer for this to be automatically true. If region B is the depressed one, then quite clearly investment in improved transport will only worsen the regional problem by contracting the market area served by the region. Indeed, at the extreme (where $(C_A - C_B) > M_t$), region B may be forced from the market entirely by the expansion of the low-cost region's market area.

Of course, the model is a considerable simplification. Regions do not normally, for instance, specialize exclusively in the production of a single commodity, but produce a range of goods. Thus, a transport improvement, while damaging certain industries, may increase the competitiveness of others. The final effect of the improved transport facility will then depend upon relative production costs between regions and the importance of transport *vis-à-vis* production costs in the overall cost functions for the various commodities.

Further, costs of production may vary with output and thus (following the 'infant industry argument') it may be beneficial to reduce transport costs if the government's regional policy also involves using grants and subsidies for encouraging the establishment of decreasing cost industry in a depressed area. Supplementary measures of this kind may be necessary if the depressed area is sparsely populated and, to be successful, its industry needs to penetrate the markets of other, more populous, regions to benefit from scale economies. It should be noted, however, that in these circumstances transport improvements must be accompanied by other regional aids if the natural gravitation of decreasing cost industries to centers of population is to be counteracted. Additionally, transport costs tend not to increase linearly with distance because of discontinuities and fixed cost elements in the overall cost function (see Chapter 4). Consequently, the influence of any transport infrastructure improvement is much more difficult to predict than the simple analysis implies.

A good example of misplaced transport investment is Montreal–Mirabel International Airport, near Montreal, which was opened in 1975 as the second-largest airport in the world in terms of surface area that was ever envisaged. It was intended to replace the existing Dorval Airport (now Montreal–Pierre

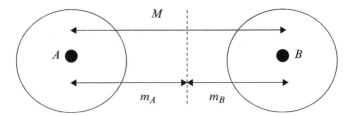

Figure 13.6 *Market areas served by centers A and B*

Elliott Trudeau International Airport) as the eastern air gateway to Canada, and, from 1975 to 1997, all international flights to/from Montreal were required to use Mirabel. However, its distant location and lack of transport links, as well as Montreal's economic decline relative to Toronto, made it unpopular with travelers, so Dorval was not closed as originally planned. Eventually, Mirabel was relegated to the role of a cargo airport.

In summary, there is no general case for thinking that investment in transport infrastructure will automatically improve the economic performance of depressed regions. In a country such as the United Kingdom, where the transport cost differences between the least and the most accessible regions has traditionally only been about 2 percent across industries, the effect of transport investment on regional policy is, in general, unlikely to be substantial. This is particularly true if industrial location is influenced by objectives other than cost minimization (for example, on satisficing principles) or where there is a high degree of X-inefficiency.

Exhibit   *Some macro- and microeconomics of elevator travel*

The density of population and production found in modern city centers would not be possible without the elevator (or 'lift' in English). People are not prepared, and in many cases not able, to climb more than about four or five flights of stairs. Without vertical cable cars, which elevators essentially are, the considerable economies of density that come with efficient urbanization would not be possible.

Something like the modern elevator appeared in 1853 at New York's Exhibition of the Industry of All Nations. Elisha Otis demonstrated the safety catch he had devised to stop an elevator platform from falling. Gaining public confidence and commercializing meant the first steam-powered passenger elevator was installed at 488 Broadway in New York City on March 23, 1857. The first electric elevator was built in Germany by Werner von Siemens in 1880, while Alexander Miles of Duluth, Minnesota patented in 1887 an elevator with automatic doors that closed off the elevator when the car was not being entered or exited. By 1900, completely automated elevators were available.

A real-estate crunch in Manhattan during the 1870s was a catalyst in getting the elevator accepted. At the time there were discussions concerning moving the financial district to uptown New York. Henry Hyde, founder of Equitable Life Assurance Society, argued that by installing a pair of elevators in his headquarters, he could make it the tallest building in the city: seven stories and 130 feet. Between 1910 and 2010, the ratio of the floor space in a building to the area of land taken up doubled in Manhattan. Today, there are roughly 18 million elevators now installed globally.

While beneficial at the macro level, from an individual's perspective elevators can be frustrating. People get annoyed when someone boards an elevator with them only to ride up one floor. There are stairs, could they not just walk up a single flight? But this is not the reaction if someone boards the elevator on the first floor with a third-floor destination, but instead of getting off at the second floor and walking the last flight of stairs, they ride all the way to the third floor.

An intuitive reaction is that in riding to floor N rather than getting off at $N - 1$ is laziness. Such a rider is creating an externality. Getting on the elevator only to ride up one floor delays everybody else. However, the decision to ride to the second floor rather than the third is not the same, because whichever floor the person chooses, the elevator is going to have to stop once. If the person gets on and the floor 2 button is already pushed but 3 is not, then the trade-off is the same because if the person were to get off at the second floor and walk, they would spare everyone else the additional stop at the third floor. So, people get annoyed at a single-floor rider if and only if they get annoyed at this marginal-floor rider.

But there is one more difference. After the person makes the sunk decision to get on the elevator, but before making the marginal decision, the problem changes. In particular, as the person is riding, new information is gained. The person can observe how many other people get on the elevator and are going to be affected by the person's decision.

In social welfare terms this puts the marginal-floor rider in a different position to the single-floor rider, because the single-floor rider's decision whether to board at all is made without knowing how many others will be on the elevator. The marginal-floor rider's decision can, however, be conditioned by the latter. This means there may even be cause to forgive the single-floor rider and be annoyed at the marginal-floor rider. The former may have reasonably expected that few people, if any, were going to be inconvenienced. But if the elevator is nearly full then the total of people's delays due the single-floor rider's decision to board is a sunk cost, but it is an avoidable cost for the marginal-floor rider. If that rider does not get off at the second floor and walk an extra flight, other riders may have cause to be annoyed.

See also: https://cheaptalk.org/2011/05/31/the-welfare-economics-of-elevator-travel/.

While in Table 13.2 several important studies were cited, it is nevertheless true that empirical evidence on the specific regional effect of transport policies is scant, and that which is available is often weakened by the difficulties of isolating transport effects from the effects of other regional policy measures. A counterfactual exercise conducted by Ronald Botham (1980) suggested that road investment in Britain between 1957 and 1972 had little effect, although there was some tendency for it to have a centralizing effect on the distribution of employment in the country. At a more micro level, Linneker and Spence (1991) concluded from their study of the impact of the M25 motorway around London that while it has improved accessibility (and regional market potential) much of this has subsequently been eroded by generated traffic. This study, however, does not allow for the substantial range of other aid measures then operative, nor for intra-regional movements between subregions adjacent to the new facility and those more distant. A study of the high-speed TGV rail system in France by Alain Bonnafous (1987) suggests that, while facilitating development, the overall impact has been small. Studies of airports, for example by Button (2002), have suggested that they may have significant regional impacts that extend beyond the immediate area, but this varies on a case-by-case basis.

Turning to a slightly lower level of spatial aggregation, changes in transport technology have, over time, exerted a strong influence upon the shapes and forms of the urban areas in which we live. The development of steam locomotion in the second half of the nineteenth century substantially improved inter-urban transport and permitted urban growth. Local, distributional services evolved much more slowly, leading, in most cities, to a concentric pattern of development around the main rail (or occasionally port) terminal of the type we saw associated with bid-rent curves in Chapter 3. The wealthy tended, because they could afford transport which was available, to live in the outer rings of housing while industry, being dependent upon good inter-urban transport, and the working-class poor concentrated near the urban core, L_{GT}, the central business district (CBD) – see the upper part of Figure 13.7.

The introduction of motorized local public transport (initially the tramcar and later the omnibus) followed by the motor car encouraged the growth of an axial pattern of urban land use with the former succession of concentric rings of housing being extended (star-like) in ribbon developments along the main road arteries (see the lower part of Figure 13.7). Finally, the widespread adoption of the automobile, combined with improved road systems, limited traffic restraint, and more efficient road freight transport, has led to the growth of multi-nucleus cities where there are numerous subcenters and suburbs – Los Angeles is often cited as the extreme example, as is Phoenix. While this simplified account of urban development misses many important subtleties, it serves to highlight the historical role which transport has had in shaping urban growth.

More recently, the difficulties of most large urban areas in the United States and Europe, unlike rapidly developing countries such as China or India, have not been ones of containing or molding growth but rather of reversing decay. The concern once focused on the role of transport in stimulating urban development has been, since the early 1970s, transformed into concern for inner-city revitalization and redevelopment.

As can be seen from Table 13.4 there were substantial outflows of population from the centers of virtually all major United States cities. For example, between 2000 and 2010, the country's population grew by almost 10 percent, but 35 percent of United States counties, both urban and rural and in all regions, experienced depopulation. Where cities are concerned, 18 percent of those with a population of 100,000 or over in 2010 lost population (Franklin, 2021). This has been accompanied by an even faster exodus of industry. The result of this has been a decay in inner-city public economies (the tax base of such areas has fallen

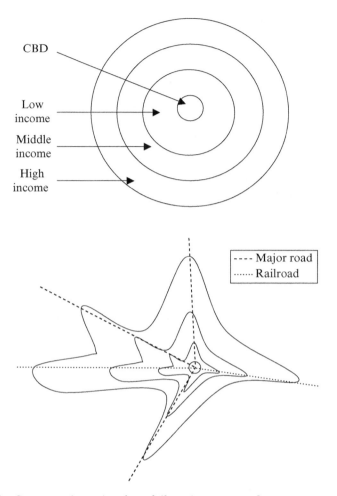

CBD

Low
income

Middle
income

High
income

---- Major road
...... Railroad

Figure 13.7 *Concentric (upper) and axial (lower) city geographies*

while the composition of the population has become increasingly biased towards the old, disabled, and poor) and a rise in unemployment (not only have firms left faster than population, but also it has primarily been manufacturing industry which has been leaving behind large numbers of unemployed, unskilled workers).

The causes of the decline of inner-city areas are complex; regional and urban planning policies are partly responsible, but there have also been changes both in the life-styles aspired to by the population (urban life becoming less attractive as incomes have risen) and in the production functions confronting industry (the land/output ratio has been rising). Improved personal transport, especially higher car ownership levels, has also encouraged more commuting from more distant suburbs.

Official policy to counter the decline of the inner-city areas and to stimulate the redevelopment of urban cores has incorporated a substantial transport component. For example, the UK white paper, 'Policy for the inner cities', made specific reference to the fact that 'Commerce and industry in inner areas needs to be served by transport conveniently and efficiently' and points to the need for

Table 13.4   *Geographical population losses in United States cities (2000–10)*

Geographical unit	Units with loss count (%)	Population loss	Tracts with loss (%)
All tracts	30,269 (41.7)	8,166,465	15,825 (21.8)
Cities of over 100,000 in 2010	49 (17.6)	1,066,549	6,203 (30.1)
Cities of 100,000 plus city CBSAs	10 (6.8)	511,158	10,753 (21.9)
All CBSAs	207 (22.0)	924,707	14,210 (21.4)
Metropolitan areas	42 (11.5)	664,521	12,758 (21.4)
Micropolitan areas	165 (28.7)	260,186	1,452 (19.6)

Note: CBSAs are core-based statistical areas and tracts are census track areas with populations of 1,200–8,000.

Source: US Census Bureau.

local authorities 'to give weight to the implications for local firms when designing traffic management schemes to improve access for central traffic, to ensure efficient loading and to provide adequate and convenient parking'. Additionally, it is argued that movement, notably in terms of journey-to-work trips, needs to be made easier, especially for certain groups of travelers.

At the theoretical level, the bid-rent curve analysis set out in Chapter 3 would seem to imply that cheaper and better public transport would lead to a spread of cities (that is, the residential bid-rent curves would shift up and to the right), while traffic restraint policy would lead to greater concentration of economic activity at the urban core. As Goldstein and Moses (1975) have shown, however, this type of analysis rests upon the assumption of a single CBD with no allowance for possible competing suburban centers. This is unrealistic in the context of most modem conurbations. Figure 13.8 depicts a more typical urban situation with a major urban center – the CBD – serving as the focal employment point dominating the suburban center to which it is linked by road.

The urban core itself is served by good local public transport with people up to B miles away being able to travel in to work by bus. But there are other modes available for workers and they may opt for one of three main employment/ residential location choices. The situation we consider is one of equilibrium, with every household achieving the same utility level:

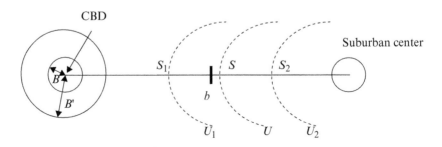

Figure 13.8   *The impact of traffic restraint and public transport subsidies on the urban core*

- Live within the immediate commuting area (radius B) and travel to work at the CBD by bus.
- Live outside the immediate commuting area and travel to work at the CBD by car.
- Commute to the subcenter by car.

In this situation – and excluding residents of the city who elect to take a fourth option, namely working at home – the boundary U will separate those workers employed at the core and those with jobs at the suburban center. This state is one in which no household can improve its utility by changing its place of work, residential location, or mode of transport. The impact of two common alternative strategies on the economy of the central core area are:

1   The generalized cost of car travel in the central city area is increased by either higher parking charges or the imposition of road pricing. This will tend to produce a rapid decline of the urban core in this model. Higher motoring costs will cause the immediate commuting belt to widen out (say to a radius of B' in Figure 13.8) with a reduction in real income for those living $(B' - B)$ miles from the CBD. This will encourage more people either to work at home or to cease to be active in the labor force (if there are other cities in the economy, there may also be some out-migration), leading to a decrease in the labor supply function at the CBD. Also, car travelers confronted by higher costs will seek work at the suburban center, shifting the employment boundary to, say, U_1. The increased competition for jobs at the subcenter will depress real income there, leading, once again, to a general reduction in the overall labor supply in the city. Generally, therefore, traffic restraint in the CBD makes labor conditions less favorable, which will, in the long term, make non-core sites more attractive for industry. The empirical fact that skilled labor tends to be more mobile (both between jobs and locations) is likely to magnify this effect on industrial location.

2   A subsidized express bus service running in bus-only lanes is introduced from a depot at location b to run non-stop into the urban core. This is unlikely to affect those using the existing commuter public transport services around the CBD, although, if fewer car trips and less congestion result, the speed of their journeys may rise – but if the service is, in general cost terms, cheaper than car travel, this will widen the employment market for the urban core. Former car travelers from as far out as S_2 will find that by driving to b and transferring to the express service they reduce the overall cost of traveling to the CBD. Consequently, the boundary marking employee catchment areas will shift to U_2. People living to the left of U_2 will find their real income has risen as a result of lower transport costs (indeed, many people to the left of b may drive out to the depot to catch the bus in to the core) and the labor supply function at the core will have shifted out, making the CBD a more attractive place for industry. People formerly inactive or working at home may also now find it attractive to seek employment at the CBD. The labor

supply for the subcenter has fallen, and wages will have to rise to generate the real-income increase anticipated by employees there. In the long term, the subcenter will become less attractive for employers.

This theoretical analysis suggests that while one common effect of both the traffic restraint policy and the public transport improvement policy is to increase local bus service utilization, the long-run effects on the distribution of population and economic activity are likely to be quite different. Goldstein and Moses (1975) argue, therefore, that even if transport policy cannot cure the malaise of inner-city areas, improved public transport provision can at least slow down the decline.

References

Ahmed, Y., O'Sullivan, P., and Sujono, W.D. (1976) Road investment programming for developing countries: an Indonesian example, Report, Transportation Center, Northwestern University.

Andersson, A. and Stromquist, U. (1988) The emerging C-society, in D.R. Batten and R. Thords (eds), *Transportation for the Future*, Springer.

Aschauer, D.A. (1989) Is public infrastructure expenditure productive? *Journal of Monetary Economics*, 23, 177–200.

Balanguer, J. and Cantavella-Jorda, M. (2002) Tourism as a long-run economic growth factor: the Spanish case, *Applied Economics*, 34, 877–84.

Barro, R.J. and Sala-i-Martin, X. (1991) Convergence across states and regions, *Brookings Papers on Economic Activity*, 1, 107–82.

Baxter, R.D. (1866) Railway extension and its results, *Journal of the Statistical Society*, 29(4), 549–95.

Biehl, D. (1991) The role of infrastructure in regional development, in R.W. Vickerman (ed.), *Infrastructure and Regional Development*, Pion.

Bonnafous, A. (1987) The regional impact of the TGV, *Transportation*, 14, 127–37.

Botham, R.W. (1980) The regional development effects of road investment, *Transportation Planning and Technology*, 6, 97–108.

Button, K.J. (1998) Infrastructure investment, endogenous growth and economic development, *Annals of Regional Science*, 32(1), 145–62.

Button, K.J. (2002) High-technology employment and hub airports: infrastructure's contribution to regional development, in Y. Higano, P. Nijkamp, J. Poot, and V.W. Kobus (eds), *The Region in the New Economy: An International Perspective on Spatial Dynamics in the 21st Century*, Ashgate.

Button, K.J., Leitham, S., McQuaid, R., and Nelson, J.D. (1995) Transport and industrial and commercial location, *Annals of Regional Science*, 29, 189–206.

Commission of the European Communities (1992) The future development of the common transport policy: a global approach to the construction of a community framework for sustainable mobility, Brussels, COM(92) 494 Final.

Commission of the European Communities (2001) European transport policy for 2010: time to decide, CEC.

Devanney, J.W., Livanos, V.M., and Stewart, R.J. (1975) Conference rate-making and the west coast of South America, *Journal of Transport Economics and Policy*, 9(2), 154–77.

Fisher, R.C. (1997) The effects of state and local government public services on economic development, *New England Economic Review*, March/April, 53–82.

Fogel, R. (1964) *Railroads and American Economic Growth: Essays in Econometric History*, John Hopkins Press.

Franklin, R.S. (2021) The demographic burden of population loss in US cities, 2000–2010, *Journal of Geographical Systems*, 23, 209–30.

Gallen, T.S. and Winston, C. (2021) Transportation capital and its effects on the U.S. economy: a general equilibrium approach, *Journal of Macroeconomics*, 69, No 103334.

Goldstein, G.S. and Moses, L.N. (1975) Transport controls and the spatial structure of urban areas, *Papers and Proceedings of the American Economic Association*, 85, 289–94.

Gramlich, E.M. (1994) Infrastructure investment: a review essay, *Journal of Economic Literature*, 32(3), 1176–96.

Gunduz, L. and Hatemi-J., A. (2005) Is the tourism-led growth hypothesis valid for Turkey, *Applied Economics Letters*, 12, 499–504.

Hirschman, A.O. (1958) *The Strategy of Economic Development*, Yale University Press.

Hunter, H. (1965) Transport in Soviet and Chinese development, *Economic Development and Cultural Change*, 14, 71–2.

Kindleberger, C.P. (1958) *Economic Development*, McGraw-Hill.

Leeper, E.M., Walker, T.B., and Yang, S.-C.S. (2010) Government investment and fiscal stimulus, *Journal of Monetary Economics*, 57, 1000–12.

Linneker, B.J. and Spence, N.A. (1991) An accessibility analysis of the impact of the M25 London orbital motorway on Britain, *Regional Studies*, 26, 31–47.

Little, I.M.D. and Mirrlees, J.A. (1974) *Project Appraisal and Planning for Developing Countries*, Heinemann.

Millard, R.S. (1959) Road development in the overseas territories, *Journal of the Royal Society of Arts*, 107, 270–91.

Morrison, J.C. (1993) Macroeconomic relationships between public spending on infrastructure and private sector productivity in the United States, in J.M. Mintz and R.S. Preston (eds), *Infrastructure and Competitiveness,* John Deutsch Institute for the Study of Economic Policy.

Narayan, P.K. (2004) Economic impact of tourism on Fiji's economy: empirical evidence from the computable equilibrium model, *Tourism Economics*, 10, 419–33.

Oort, C.J. and Maaskant, R.H. (1976) Study of the possible solutions for allocating the deficit which may occur in a system of charging for the use of infrastructure aiming at budgetary equilibrium, European Economic Community.

Owen, W. (1964) *Strategy for Mobility*, Brookings Institution.

Premti, A. (2016) Liner shipping: is there a way for more competition? Report, United Nations Conference on Trade and Development.

Prud'homme, R. (1996) Assessing the role of infrastructure in France by means of regionally estimated production functions, in D.F. Batten and C. Karlsson (eds), *Infrastructure and the Complexity of Economic Development*, Springer-Verlag.

Rostow, W.W. (1960) *The Stages of Economic Growth*, Cambridge University Press.

Solow, R.M. (1957) Technical change and the aggregate production function, *Review of Economics and Statistics*, 39, 312–20.

Sturm, J.-E. and De Haan, J. (1995) Is public expenditure really productive? New evidence from the USA and the Netherlands, *Economic Modelling*, 12(1), 60–72.

Vickerman, R.W. (1987) The Channel Tunnel: consequences for regional growth and development, *Regional Studies*, 21, 187–97.

Wilson, G.W. (1966) Towards a theory of transport and development, in G.W. Wilson, B.R. Bergmann, L.V. Hirsch, and M.S. Klein (eds), *The Impact of Highway Investment on Development*, Brookings Institution.

Zerby, J.A. (1979) On the practicality of the UNCTAD 40–40–20 code for liner conferences, *Maritime Policy and Management*, 6, 241–51.

14 Political Economy and Transport Regulation

14.1 Underlying Issues

A considerable amount of economists' efforts on the public sector side are attached to the regulation of transport, and probably an equal amount on the private side to responding to the resultant regulations. A chapter providing an overview of the economic regulation of transport activities must inevitably involve some overlap with other chapters in this volume. This chapter is less than complete in that sense. Economic regulation is also a very large and complex topic and there is no pretense that the coverage here is complete or thorough. It is also one that transcends the transport sector in numerous respects as many nations, for example, modified the ways they looked at economic regulation more generally from the 1970s (Button and Swann, 1992).

Space has already been devoted to policies for containing pollution and for the control of traffic congestion, for instance. We have also implicitly considered the implications of some forms of intervention regarding pricing and market entry. Transport, however, has been a sector that has been subjected to various forms of economic regulation throughout history, and this justifies a more specific examination.

Wider questions concerning such matters as why have regulations been imposed, how have they operated, and how they can be appraised have not been examined in any depth so far. Equally, there are different ways in which transport is supplied with differing degrees of public sector participation in ownership – the ultimate form of regulation – that impact on efficiency and equity implications. Just why this occurs and how it differs between countries raises a further set of economic questions.

Besides the general issues of the various types of regulation and ownership of transport, there have also been significant changes in the way in which many countries approach these regulatory policy issues. We saw, for instance, a considerable relaxation of long-standing entry and price controls in markets as diverse as the United States' domestic aviation and the United Kingdom's bus transport industry in the 1970s and 1980s. This was a trend that has extended into the new market economies of the post-communist states and to many developing nations.

We have also seen extensive privatization of transport infrastructure. This has included airports and air traffic control in the United Kingdom and many other European countries. More build, operate, and transfer public–private partnerships have been formed with the aim of speeding up transport investments.

Many of these initiatives are as focused on the tapping of a wider pool of technical expertise as on exploiting more diverse sources of funding. Private sector involvement at a second tier has also expanded with the franchising-out of operations (for example, of London's bus services and of South American airports) and the greater use of private sector funds in the financing of infrastructure investments (for example, the Channel Tunnel and the French TGV network). The subject, therefore, is an important one and is likely to remain so for some time to come.

What we do not consider here are the generic laws and controls that are imposed in most counties, and thus inevitably affect transport. For example, many countries have generic minimum wage laws, anti-trust and monopoly regulations, social justice constraints, and consumer protection legislation. These apply to all sectors, including transport, although in some cases there are specific exemptions. The implications of such regulations on transport are often far from trivial, but discussion of them is moving us away from the main theme of this book.

While it is often difficult to precisely define the rationale and nature of regulations, a very simple flow chart is seen in Figure 14.1 that gives a broad indication of the types of microeconomic measures involved. In addition, transport is inevitably affected by macroeconomic policies, such as monetary and fiscal policy, and internationally by trade policies. These can influence the aggregate size of the economy and thus the total demand and supply for transport services. But these macro aspects represent wider, cross-sector matters that are outside of the scope of this book.

Also important for the efficiency of transport are the microeconomic regulations that affect the economic and social environments in which transport services are demanded and supplied. Since we have spent some time on the challenges of dealing with areas of social regulation, and especially the environment, the focus here is mainly on the nature of economic regulation in its more traditional sense of seeking to increase the efficiency of transport suppliers. What we do not do, however – although it can be very important – is to offer any overview of generic anti-trust or merger regulations that affect all types of industry or national laws

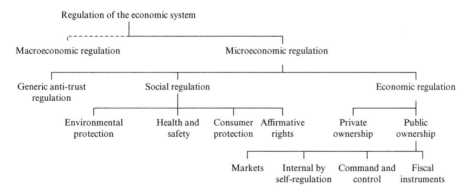

Figure 14.1   *The basic breakdown of types of regulations affecting transport*

governing things such as minimum wages. We essentially push these to one side and attend to areas of economic regulation that are specifically focused on transport matters.

The objective of this chapter is not to describe all the changes in regulation and ownership of transport that have taken place – that would be impossible, although some of the more important developments are reviewed – but rather to explore the economic arguments underlying the various positions taken by policy-makers. Some contextual historical information is helpful in doing this. Initially, however, a little time is spent looking at the various economic theories of regulation and setting trends in transport policy in the context of these theories.

In doing this, we not only look at domestic policies and their affects, but also at international policy, a matter of increasing importance as international trade grows and as globalization takes place. Changes in international transport regulations, which may range from the removal of transport barriers within the European Union to the spread of Open Skies agreements in air transport, have implications for international markets.

In Figure 14.2, for example, if international air services are deregulated then they have direct effects on traffic into and out of the country of interest. But this action also has secondary effects on airlines and other modes within the country that take traffic to and from the international airport. This, in turn, because of economies of scope and density, will lower the costs of some purely domestic services and hence the use made of them. The additional markets that are now opened up will lead to further changes in both domestic and international traffic as industries such as tourism and high-technology companies that use air transport change the scale and nature of the products they supply. In effect, it will have a macro-income effect of increasing national income, inducing a further positive ripple effect on the demand for air transport. Most transport regulation, however,

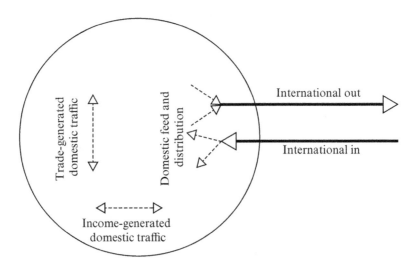

Figure 14.2   *Links between international and domestic transport markets*

focuses on specific elements of the system, for example regional aviation, domestic trunk haul services, or international aviation. Indeed, they are often regulated by different agencies.

14.2   Regulation Theory

Economists have long recognized that markets may, in practice, suffer from serious imperfections, indeed some discussion of this has been set out in previous chapters. Most obviously, these imperfections, or market failures, could adversely affect the users of transport services, perhaps because fares would be suboptimally high or the service offered dangerous. But equally, they may harm third parties through, for example, generating excessive environmental pollution, or the predatory pricing behavior of incumbent operators may reduce the potential viability of other firms wishing to supply transport services and thus deter them from entering the market.

Why Regulate?

A wide range of arguments, some of doubtful economic logic, have been drawn into debates over transport regulation. Broadly, the types of market failure that have attracted most attention embrace:

*   *The containment of monopoly power.* Transport often involves large, indivisible, and specialized infrastructure that lends itself to monopoly provision to maximize scale economies. This has led to long-standing concerns about the potential economic exploitation of monopoly power. This was an issue in the case of the railways, which dominated inland transport for nearly a century from the late 1830s, but while some monopoly power persists in certain areas of transport activity, technical advances across a range of transport modes have reduced the potential for pure monopoly exploitation, at least in most developed countries. More common perhaps is the fear that suppliers of transport services may combine in cartels to limit output and prevent new entrants coming into the market.
*   *The control of excessive competition.* Unregulated competition may limit the quality of service offered to customers and result in instability in the industry – in technical terms there may be no sustainable equilibrium: an empty core may exist. The actual problem is not competition *per se* but rather the possibility that externalities may result or that some sections of the community may not be provided with adequate services. Additionally, in some instances, notably trucking and inter-urban passenger transport, the potential for conditions of monopolistic competition developing also pose problems of possible excess capacity being supplied.
*   *The regulation of externalities.* Imperfections in the market mechanism may result in transport activities imposing costs that are not directly included in

the private sector's decision-making – pollution and congestion being the main causes for concern. This subject has been explored more fully in earlier chapters and we shall not dwell on it here. It is, however, becoming an aspect of regulation that is attracting increasing attention at the global as well as at the national and local levels.

- *The provision of public goods.* Because certain items of infrastructure, such as roads, are thought to exhibit public goods characteristics (that is, non-excludability, whereby use cannot be controlled, and non-rivalness, whereby congestion cannot arise), their provision, it is argued, would be at best inadequate without government intervention. In effect, suppliers could not charge for their use. The fact that one cannot exclude use makes it difficult to price the facilities. The degree to which such infrastructure should be considered as conforming to a public good, however, often depends upon the initial policy in place – for example, it is relatively easy to exclude cars from a road if wished.

- *The provision of high-cost infrastructure.* The sheer cost, long pay-back period, and complexity, combined with possible high levels of risk, make it unlikely that all major pieces of infrastructure would be built or expensive transport engineering research undertaken without some form of government involvement. Adam Smith, as we saw earlier, even conceded that on occasions the government may need to directly provide such facilities, but there are also ways of regulating the private sector to ensure it provides infrastructure.

- *The assistance of groups in 'need' of adequate transport.* As was seen in Chapter 4, the idea of 'need' embraces the notion that, for a variety of reasons, including faults in the existing pattern of income distribution, effective demand is not an adequate guide to transport resource allocation and wider, social criteria should, therefore, be sought. The market thus needs regulations to meet this objective.

- *The existence of high transaction costs.* While free markets may theoretically be capable of optimizing output, this may involve high transaction costs: the costs of 'doing business'. Drivers confronting each other on a road could bargain as to who has the right of way, but a simple rule, say giving priority to the left, is likely to prove more efficient. The problem may also be linked to the difficulties of negotiating for rights of way to construct transport infrastructure.

- *The integration of transport into wider economic policies.* Land use and transport are clearly inter-connected and some degree of coordination may be felt desirable if imperfections exist in either the transport or the land-use markets. Additionally, intervention in the transport sector may form part of a wider government macroeconomic strategy (for example, price controls or investment programs) or industrial policy. The traditional notion of Keynesian fiscal macroeconomic policies of the type adopted in the United States in 2008–2009 to counteract economic recession, for example, often involve significant public investments in transport facilities.

- *The need to reflect the genuine resource costs of transport*. In the case of certain finite, non-renewable resources (for example, mineral fuels), the market mechanism may fail to reflect the full social time preference of society. The government may, therefore, intervene to ensure that the decision-maker is aware of the true shadow price.
- *The improvement of transport coordination*. Because there are numerous suppliers of transport services, inefficient provision may result if their decisions are made independently. There is also the prospect of duplication of transport facilities, and consequential wastage of resources, without some degree of central guidance. This is a topic that we return to in more detail later.
- *To instigate market stability*. Although transport is a derived demand, it can influence the final markets that make use of it. In particular, as seen in Chapter 3, it interacts with land-use patterns. Continual and difficult-to-predict changes in transport services available can negatively affect the confidence of those making locational decisions. Market interventions, such as guaranteeing rail or bus services for a given period of time inject a greater degree of certainty into locational selections (Spiller, 2013). Railroads in the United States, for example, must gain approval from the Surface Transportation Board before railroad lines can be abandoned.

In practice, most official policies claim to cover a range of different problems, although conflicts may and do emerge. For example, policies designed primarily to contain externalities may have adverse effects on income distribution or could run counter to a national economic policy that is pursuing a course of maximizing GNP.

Similarly, measures to ensure that adequate high-cost research is conducted may mean conferring monopoly powers on private suppliers (for example, through the patent system or in terms of government contracts to purchase the fruits of a new technology). Consequently, there is an inevitable blurring across these justifications for government involvement when various policy measures are discussed or introduced. Even more uncertain than the exact justification or objectives underlying some policies is the exact effects the different policy tools employed by policy-makers are likely to exert.

Instruments of Policy

The instruments of transport policy are sometimes broken down into those which, adopting American jargon, are aimed at economic regulation and those which are aimed at social regulation – quantitative and qualitative regulation, in the British vocabulary. The former is concerned with controlling the amount supplied in transport markets, who supplies it, and the price which consumers pay. Social regulation specifies the nature of the transport services provided, relating, for instance, to vehicle design, maximum emissions levels, driving hours, training of personnel, etc. In practice there is an inevitable overlap between the two sets of instruments. Limiting market entry, for example, can contain many adverse environmental effects of transport, while strict quality controls can act to contain competition.

It is perhaps more useful, therefore, simply to provide a listing of the various policy instruments under the following general headings:

- *Taxes and subsidies.* The government may use its fiscal powers either to increase or decrease the costs of various forms of transport or services over different routes – or, indeed, the cost of transport in general. While they may be designed in some cases to consciously affect the costs of transport (for example, subsidies to promote transit use or fuel taxes to finance road construction), in other instances they are pure sumptuary taxes aimed at raising revenue from sources where demand is less price-sensitive. This often involves taxes on transport services used by higher-income groups.
- *Price controls.* Concerns that a monopolist transport service supplier may exploit its ability to price above marginal costs has led to widespread price regulations over the years. These have taken a variety of forms ranging from rate-of-return regulation (which sets prices allowing a profit level to be attained) to price-capping (which allows average prices to rise regularly but at a rate less than general cost levels), each with its particular advantages and challenges.
- *Direct provisions.* Local and central government are direct suppliers, via municipal and nationalized undertakings, of a wide range of transport services. They are also responsible for supplying a substantial amount of transport infrastructure, notably roads, and supplementary services, such as the police. In the context of bodies such as the European Union, the supply may be by pan-national agencies. The link between supply, the infrastructure, and its use may also involve direct public provision of both, as was often the case with airport and state-owned airlines, but this is decreasingly so.
- *Laws and regulations.* Government (and to a lesser extent, local authorities) may legally regulate the transport sector and there has grown up an extensive body of law that, in effect, controls and directs the activities of both transport suppliers and users. Linked with this, there are generic laws that govern financial, labor, and other markets which provide essential inputs into transport industries and thus affect the way in which it functions.
- *Competition policy and consumer protection legislation.* It is useful to distinguish general industrial legislation, governing such things as restrictive practices and mergers, and consumer protection legislation, covering such things as advertising, which embraces all forms of activity in the economy and not just transport. Obviously, as we mentioned earlier, they also apply to transport. In addition, many countries have specific transport-oriented policies aimed at protecting users.
- *Licensing.* The government may regulate either the quality or quantity of transport provision by its ability to grant various forms of licenses to operators, vehicles, or services. The system of driving licenses for cars and

trucks also influences the demand for private transport. A specific form of licensing may be seen in franchising whereby a private sector undertaking may operate a publicly owned transport facility for a designated period. At the much broader level, there have been long-standing policies in international transport that have, *de facto*, imposed a licensing structure to limit the supply of transport services, or to restrict the carriers involved in the trade.

- *The purchase of transport services*. Various non-transport activities of government require the use of transport services – for example, to move military personnel and to supply medical services. Hence, by means of its position as a large consumer, government may exert a degree of countervailing power over transport suppliers. This is often more relevant at the local level of administration, where large fleets of vehicles can be loaned or leased. More indirectly, by purchasing one type of transport service, a government may influence the larger market for these services. For example, the purchase of military transport equipment may allow economies of scale in production that reduces the cost of producing related civilian products. Aircraft engines and frames are often seen in this context.

- *Moral suasion*. In many instances this is of a weak form, usually being educational or the offering of advice on matters such as safety (for example, advertising the advantages of the wearing of seat belts), but it may be stronger when the alternative to accepting advice is the exercise, by government, of others of its powers (for example, the refusal of a license or the withdrawal of a subsidy).

- *Research and development*. Government may influence the long-term development of transport through its own research activities. These are, in part, conducted by its own explicit agents (for example, the Transportation Research Board in the United States) and, in part, through the funding of outside research via contracts. There are also fundamental research initiatives overseen by such bodies as the National Science Foundation in the United States that can impact significantly on transport.

- *Provision of information*. The government, through various agencies, offers certain technical advice to transport users and provides general information to improve the decision-making within transport. Many of these services are specific to transport (for example, weather services for shipping and air transport), while others assist the transport sector less directly (for example, information on trading arrangements overseas). In terms of safety and security, most governments offer warnings of any severe dangers that may exist in other countries.

- *Policies relating to inputs*. Transport is a major user of energy, especially oil, and utilizes a wide range of other raw materials and intermediate products. Government policy relating to the energy and other sectors can therefore have an important indirect bearing on transport. It can, for instance, stipulate the types of fuel that may be sold – lead-free gasoline being required in many countries.

It seems logical, therefore, that if such market imperfections can be identi-
fied, it is in the 'public interest' to intervene and reduce their distortive effects.
This is not a very contentious view. Difficulties arise, however, not from the
notion of public interest but rather from the degree to which intervention can,
in practice, produce public benefit. In the 1970s, as we see below, a growing body
of opinion emerged that regulation had become excessive and no longer served
the public interest. In particular, the ideas of the Chicago School of economists
questioned the motivation underlying the actions of regulators – most notably
that they tend to act as rational economic entities and pursue policies aimed at
furthering their position rather than necessarily that of the public interest (Stigler,
1971). Others considered the power of the regulated industries and argued that,
because of their control of information flows (for example, regarding cost data
which is needed to regulate fares) and their power to lobby, there was a tendency
for them to capture the regulatory process.

Even if regulation is initiated in the public interest, it is not free from
problems. Ideally, policy-makers like to match one policy instrument with one
objective, but this is seldom possible in transport. The problems of interdependence of objectives have already been alluded to, but, in addition, the instruments
themselves frequently have diverse effects. Taxation policies to reduce the use of a
specific mode of transport may prove regressive, while licensing to contain externalities may result in quasi-monopoly powers being given to certain suppliers.

Forecasting, monitoring, and appraising the effects of alternative policy instruments also usually proves difficult. Transport policy is pursued through a package
of instruments and policy changes, usually resulting in several of these instruments
being varied in their intensity at once. The effects of such changes are also only
likely to be fully felt after a lag as agents in the transport market gradually respond
and adjust to the new situation. In the short term, a trucker, for instance, may do
little in response to higher fuel taxation (save pay the additional money), but in the
longer term he or she is likely to modify the method of operation employed and,
in the very long term, may even change the type of vehicle fleet used.

Even if one could isolate occasions when a change is made to a single policy
instrument, it is unlikely that the full effect could be recorded before further
changes take place. Finally, there is the problem of determining the counterfactual – the course of events which would have ensued if policy had not been
changed. Government is frequently reactive in its approach – suggesting that
changing circumstances are already observable by the time policy is enacted – but
on other occasions policy changes represent initiatives and anticipate change.
One can never simply assume that events would have continued the course set
prior to a major policy change.

14.3   Monopoly Power

Although economic regulations have been motivated by a variety of factors,
concern over the exercise of monopoly power has dominated much of the debate

and legislation. The large-scale infrastructure that is needed to support most forms of transport, and the various forms of network economies that can exist in providing transport services, suggest that concentrated supply can minimize cost. Such a concentration, however, allows for the opportunity for suppliers to exploit users by pushing up prices or it can lead to them not having an adequate incentive to manage the system efficiently.

Rate-of-return Regulation

These problems have long been recognized and regulations have been commonplace. State provision has often been used to ensure that users are not exploited by keeping user prices in line with costs. This has widely been used in the provision of physical infrastructure, but also, as we see below, in the provision of services in some countries. The issue of 'government failure', and the capture of systems by politicians and management, has led to other options being pursued in some cases.

Countries such as the United States have sought to control the prices at which the private sector may offer transport services. The traditional methods used, for example by the Civil Aeronautics Board (CAB) and the Interstate Commerce Commission until the 1980s, relied upon rate-of-return regulation. This sets transport prices so that suppliers can earn a 'fair rate of return' on their investments. This allows the transport undertaking to choose its use of inputs, levels of output, and prices when there is no excess above the officially defined fair rate of return. In other words, with only one non-capital input labor, L, the rate-of-return is:

$$(PQ - wL)/K \tag{14.1}$$

where:

P is price;
Q is output;
w is wages; and
K is capital, and this must not exceed the fair rate-of-return:

$$f \geq (PQ - wL)/K \tag{14.2}$$

The main difficulties with this approach involve the incentive structure it offers to over-capitalize – the 'Averch–Johnson effect' (Averch and Johnson, 1962) – and, as discussed in the previous section, the ease with which the system may be captured both by the industry under regulation and the regulators seeking to serve their own ends.

The Averch–Johnson effect is the tendency of companies to engage in excessive amounts of capital accumulation to expand the scale of their profits. If companies' profit/capital ratio is regulated as in equation (14.2), then at a certain percentage there is a strong incentive for them to over-invest to increase profits overall.

Specifically, the main Averch–Johnson result is that the capital/labor ratio selected by a profit-maximizing regulated firm will be greater than that consistent with a cost-minimizing one for any output it chooses to produce. If what is considered by a regulator to be the fair rate of return is greater than the cost of capital, a firm will have an incentive to invest as much as it can, consistent with its production possibilities; the difference between the allowed rate and its actual cost of capital is pure profit. This goes against any optimal efficiency point for capital that the company may have calculated, as higher profit is almost always desired over and above efficiency. This is sometimes called 'gold-plating'.

As an illustration, we assume a railroad uses input labor (L) and capital (K). The production function for the undertaking is therefore $R(K,L)$, with w the cost of labor and r the cost of capital.

The railroad's objective is to maximize profits ($\prod$):

$$\prod = R(K,L) - wL - rK \tag{14.3}$$

Microeconomic theory tells us that this requires that the ratio of the marginal products of the inputs be equal to the ratio of costs:

$$(\delta R/\delta K)/(\delta R/\delta L) = r/w \tag{14.4}$$

The rate-of-return regulator fixes the cost of capital at s – the rate of profit that the utility earns on its rate base. If the regulator sets $s = r$ (the market rate of capital), then there is no problem. But regulators tend to set s larger than r, ($s > r$), to ensure that railroad is able to acquire investment capital, thus:

$$(\delta R/\delta K)/(\delta R/\delta L) = (s/w) > (r/w) \tag{14.5}$$

The railroad will thus tend to use capital and other inputs in inefficient quantities. This can also be seen diagrammatically in Figure 14.3. The isoquant shows a given level of railroad services using various combinations of inputs K and L. With no rate-of-return regulation, the optimal capital–labor substitution rate is $- r/w$ at point E, and using K amount of capital. Introducing rate-return regulation, with 'α' being the amount this is below that prevailing in the market, causes the rate of factor substitution to shift to $-(r - \alpha)/w$. The outcome is an increase of capital use to points $A - J$, and the amount of $K^1 - K$.

Concern with the possible adverse effects of rate-of-return regulations' economic efficiency has been supported by empirical analysis, and with the way it affects American transport provision and prices in the 1960s and 1970s. Table 14.1 provides a brief summary of a series of studies conducted on the rate-of-return regulation of the CAB. In particular, the fact that only inter-state services were regulated, whereas many state systems were not, allowed comparisons to be made.

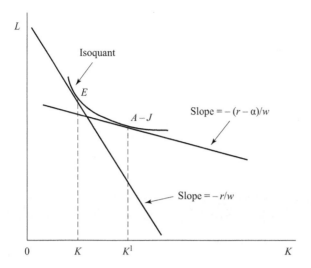

Figure 14.3   *Averch–Johnson effect*

Table 14.1   *Results of United States studies on the implications of airline regulation prior to 1978*

Study	Data	Comparisons	Conclusions
Caves (1962)	CAB routes	Structure, conduct, & performance	Problems with the industry's performance that required changes in the regulatory structure but did not oppose regulation
Levine (1965)	Intra-state & CAB routes	Fares	Regulation caused higher fares & resulted in lower load factors
Jordan (1970)	California & CAB routes	Fares	Regulation caused excess capacity, benefitted aircraft manufacturers, labor unions, & airlines
Keeler (1972)	California & CAB routes	Fares	Regulation caused excess capacity that dissipated any profits from fares set at cartel levels by the CAB
Douglas & Miller (1974)	CAB routes	Fares & flight frequency	Regulation resulted in high fares & suboptimal high qualities of service being offered
DeVany (1975)	California & CAB routes	Fares & flight frequency	Regulation protected the consumer with fares set close to the output-maximizing level
Keeler (1978)	California & CAB routes	Fares	CAB regulation led to excess charges amounting to $2.7 billion per annum

Note: CAB = Civil Aeronautics Board.

Source: Button (1989). This paper contains the full references to the studies cited.

Price-capping

An alternative to rate-of-return regulation developed initially for telecommunications regulation, but subsequently adopted in numerous transport contexts, is 'price-capping'. The aim of this policy of lighted-handed regulation is to squeeze out inefficiencies, and especially *X*-inefficiency, by forcing transport industries to provide their services at increasingly low real prices. It has, for example, been applied to privatized airports in the United Kingdom's National Air Traffic Services (NATS) air traffic control system and its airports.

Exhibit   *Regulated and unregulated airlines*

Prior to deregulation of the United States' domestic inter-state passenger airline market in 1978, fares and airline market entry were federally regulated for cross-state border traffic, but within states the state authority had jurisdiction. While federal regulation was very restrictive, large states such as California were more liberal. Bill Jordan made use of this different structure in 1965 to look at inter-state airline fares in the Northwest Corridor and concluded that they could be 32 to 47 percent lower than they could be if the trunk airlines were relatively unregulated on the Californian model.

Year	Trunk airline load factor (%)	California intra-state load factor (%)
1951	69.6	69.0
1952	67.1	65.9
1953	64.7	67.1
1954	63.4	69.2
1955	64.1	72.2
1956	64.1	75.7
1957	61.5	80.6
1958	60.0	72.4
1959	61.4	71.1
1960	59.5	71.1
1961	56.2	72.1
1962	53.3	75.3
1963	53.8	72.8
1964	55.4	74.9
1965	55.2	63.3
1966	58.5	–
1967	57.2	–
1968	53.0	–
1969	50.3	–
1970	49.3	–

When examining the implications of lower inter-state load factors on the formula-based regulated fares, Keeler constructed a hypothetical optimal cost function for these routes based upon load factors akin to those found in California. This involved developing a long-run cost function embracing such factors as trip length and congestion to provide a counterfactual for comparison with the fares charged. The analysis made use of a long-run cost model, taking account of such things as available ton-miles. A number of adjustments had to be made to allow reasonable comparisons. For example, as can be seen from the table, there were considerable differences in load factors. Keeler assumes that if inter-state routes operated as efficiently as intra-state routes, the former would have a 60 percent load factor.

Keeler found that in 1968 regulated inter-state routes had fares involving 20 to 95 percent over unregulated fares, with the mark-ups tending to rise with distance. Using a slightly different method for 1972, mark-ups were found to range between 48 percent for short and medium routes and 84 percent for long-hauls. These findings support mark-ups of between 47 and 89 percent found by Jordan.

Much of the differential found by Keeler results from the presence of the pioneering low-cost carrier, Pacific Southwest Airlines, in the Californian market. The airline was not only offering lower fares compared to those found on the major inter-state routes, but was also more profitable than a typical trunk carrier. The difference in costs was largely attributed to excess capacity on trunk routes that manifested itself in the very much lower load factors seen in the table.

See also: W.A. Jordan (1970) *Airline Regulation in America*, Johns Hopkins Press; *and* T.E. Keeler (1972) Airline regulation and market performance, *Bell Journal of Economics and Management Science*, 3, 399–424.

In more detail, price-capping regulation adjusts the transport operator's prices according to a price-cap index that reflects the overall rate of inflation in the economy, the ability of the operator to gain efficiencies relative to the average firm in the economy, and the inflation in the operator's input prices relative to the average firm in the economy. The idea is that a technologically dynamic, profit-maximizing supplier will have the incentive and the ability to respond to a price-cap by reducing costs.

Price-capping regulation is sometimes called '*CPI–X*' regulation (known in the United Kingdom as '*RPI–X*'), after the basic formula employed to set price caps. This takes the rate of inflation measured by the consumer (*CPI*) or retail price index (*RPI*) and subtracts an expected annual efficiency saving (*X*). The system provides an incentive for greater efficiency, as any saving above the predicted rate *X* can be passed on to share-holders until the price caps are next reviewed. The rate *X* is based not only on a firm's past performance, but also on the performance of other firms in the industry, and is intended to be a proxy for a competitive market, in industries which are natural monopolies. The problem is that, where there is manifest inefficiency, it is relatively easy to generate a reasonable value for *X*, but as a transport undertaking moves towards a quasi-competitive situation, *X* approaches a normal profit margin. In other words, it converges on rate-of-return regulation.

Contestable Markets

There have been other perspectives on regulating what are seen as natural monop-olies in transport. William Baumol et al.'s (1982) idea of contestable markets, which was touched upon in Chapter 7, for example, argues that with free market entry and exit, effectively the absence of any 'sunk costs', the forces of potential competition temper the monopoly powers of any incumbent transport suppliers. This logically moves to notions of unbundling those elements of transport supply that may be subject to contestable forces and focusing regulation on those that are characterized by elements of sunk costs. This was, for instance, the rationale underlying the deregulation of European airlines and, more generally, modes such as buses and trucking.

Although some studies have supported a weak notion of contestability, the evidence supporting this tends to show that the forces of contestability are weaker than those of actual competition. Scheduled airlines do not seem as affected by potential competition as was initially thought. Moore (1986), for example, found that in the United States fares were lower in markets with more actual carriers, while Steven Morrison (2001) found that actual competition with Southwest Airlines produced aggregate fare savings of $12.9 billion in 1998, whereas poten-tial and adjacent competition produced a saving of only $9.5 billion. As a result, even some of its strongest initial supporters have questioned the limits of its usefulness: 'We now believe that transportation by truck, barges, and even buses may be more contestable than passenger air transportation' (Baumol and Willig, 1986).

Regulating Sunk Costs

Where there are sunk costs, there have been arguments that the monopoly power of transport undertakings may be controlled through initiating 'competition for the market', rather than trying to stimulate competition in the market (Demsetz, 1968). This essentially involves auctioning off the rights to provide the transport service. This may, for example, be used to supply infrastructure such as roads, whereby a concession to build, operate, and toll the facility may be auctioned off with the state taking back the road after some specified period. Basically, the competition is in the rights to have the market for road space rather than in the market for road use.

Several different auctioning methods, with numerous variants, each with their advantages and limitations, are available and have been used in various con-texts in the transport sector:

- *English or ascending-bid auction.* This is the most common form of auction for the sale of goods, with an auctioneer allowing successively higher bids until only a single bidder is left. At each point in the auction, the various potential bidders know the prevailing highest bid. It is simple, but can lead to the winner paying well below the maximum they would have paid.

- *Dutch or descending-bid auction.* In this model, the auctioneer gradually lowers the price until a bidder accepts it. This tends to result in the winner bidding close to the maximum they would be willing to pay because they have no idea of any potential highest offers that may come from competitors.
- *First-price sealed-bid auction.* This approach involves bidders submitting sealed bids, and the 'winner' is the one with the highest bid when they are opened. In this case the bidders have no idea what the competing bids are when they make their offer. This is the most common approach employed in the transport context.
- *Vickrey (1961) or second-price sealed-bid auction.* This variant on the sealed-bid model awards the 'prize' to the highest bidder but the winner only pays the amount of the second-highest bid. This encourages each bidder to make an offer of at least the maximum, but generally more than they would be willing to pay because they realize any penalty of over-bidding will be off-set by only paying the runner-up's bid.

The difficulty with any auction is that it involves game-playing between the auctioneer and those bidding, but with transport there can be specific challenges. In many cases, because transport is essentially a network activity, there are issues of the boundaries of the auction. For example, should it be for a single highway or a set of highways, or one airport or a set of airports? There is also the physical longevity of much transport infrastructure and the problems that may arise if the demand for its use unexpectedly declines significantly during the period of the contract, making it impossible for the company winning the auction to earn a viable return. This may involve the need for renegotiations. In some cases, for example airport slots, the value of one service may be affected by the availability of another. For example, gaining a slot at airport A to offer a service $A => B$ is only useful if a slot at B is also obtained. Secondary trading is common as a way of reconciling this after the initial allocation has been decided.

Despite the challenges of devising these various franchising systems, competition for the market has been widely adopted in many transport contexts, ranging from the auctioning of subsidized bus and rail routes in the United Kingdom (the bid with the lowest subsidy requirement winning), to the awarding of tolled road contracts in the United States, to auctions for airport concessions in many South American countries.

Monopoly Suppliers and the Envelope Theorem

The envelope theorem highlights the differential effects of a price change on a monopoly transport supplier's profit ($\Delta\Pi$ in Figure 14.4) and of social welfare. What it shows is that a relatively large increase in output brought about, for example, by fare or rate controls, can have a large first-order effect on social welfare but limited second-order effects on the supplier's profits.

Assuming for simplicity that the supply and demand functions are linear, the profits curve seen in the figure rises with the quantity sold, is maximized (Q_M), and

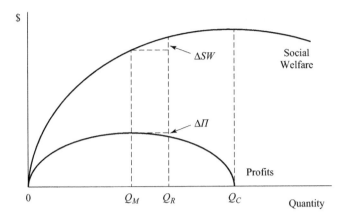

Figure 14.4   *Social welfare and monopoly profit effects of a price reduction*

then declines. In the traditional demand/cost presentation, the zenith is where the supplier's marginal cost is equated with its marginal revenue. Regarding the social welfare function, representing the combination of profits and consumer surplus, this takes a similar path but is maximized when profits fall to zero (Q_C). This is where average costs equal marginal revenue in the standard monopoly model.

If a regulation or a price control is introduced, this will cause the monopolist to increase the quantity of transport services that are sold which in turn will affect both profits and social welfare. Because the profits curve is relatively flat about its zenith, this will mean a small decline in profit ($\Delta\Pi$), but will be accompanied by a larger increase in social welfare (ΔSW). This result obviously only holds locally for arbitrary small changes from the profit-maximizing point.

Additionally, the idea relates to situations where a monopolist transport supplier is charging a single price. It is less valid when the supplier engages in price discrimination, as is common in the scheduled airline market and in many mercantile markets. In these latter cases the profit curve, because it involves charges that extract considerable amounts of consumer surplus, will approach that of the social welfare curve.

While the findings are not universal, substantial gains in social welfare can come from reductions in fares or increases in transport services without a large impact on supplying transport companies' profits.

14.4   Prioritizing Transport Policies

We turn now to examine the various landmarks and phases of transport policy. Recalling Figure 1.1, our attention is largely on the economics of property rights elements of institutions and governance issues involving transaction costs. Social theory is not really a concern, because our attention is largely on the market economies of North America and Europe, and micro issues are market outcomes of the regulatory structures in place and the ways in which they are operationalized.

This section is intended to highlight the way in which transport policy has evolved to match both the changing technical and organizational structure of the sector, and has responded to the differing attitudes of society to transport over the past century and a half. It is in no way intended as a comprehensive piece of economic history. Much of the focus is on the United Kingdom situation because it offers both a more diverse portfolio of regulatory policies and because, unlike countries with federal systems such as the United States, policy is largely controlled by a single authority. But changes elsewhere in the world are also touched upon. The 'story' is slanted in favor of more recent developments.

The Anti-monopoly Phase, Pre-1930

Government has always taken some interest in transport. Traditionally, it had not been the efficiency of the transport market that was the principal concern but rather the insurance that adequate transport was available to fulfil the commitments of defense, administration, and internal stability. The Industrial Revolution placed greater emphasis on the need for an economically efficient transport system which, combined with the rapid technical changes that took place in transport during the later years of the eighteenth century and the early decades of the nineteenth century, resulted in more official intervention. (Indeed, even the Duke of Wellington called for a National Transport Plan for the United Kingdom at one stage.)

While much of the early involvement was to permit canals and railways to be constructed, there was also a political awareness of the potential monopoly powers which such companies could exercise. The 1844 Railway Act in the United Kingdom, for example, gave government the option of purchasing newly formed companies after 21 years (a power never exercised) and maximum rates were normally included in the enabling acts. In all, over 200 regulatory acts were passed before 1930 to appease public concern about the private control exercised over the monopoly of the railway companies.

The Americans followed closely and copied British railroad technology. The Baltimore and Ohio Railroad was the first common carrier and started a passenger train service in May 1830, initially using horses to pull trains. While fostering private ownership and finance, America had passed its first legislation on rate regulation in 1856. Subsequently, Congress passed the Interstate Commerce Act in 1887, creating the Interstate Commerce Commission. The agency's original purpose was to regulate railroads to ensure fair rates, to eliminate rate discrimination, and to regulate other aspects of common carriage.

By the 1920s the British railway companies had to publish their rates, were subject to common carrier obligations, were not allowed to show undue preference, had to present accounts in a prescribed manner, and were subjected to controls over wage bargaining. An element of social service obligation was also apparent in some of this legislation with, initially, railway companies required by law to provide specified cheap services and, subsequently, workmen's tickets.

This type of situation was not unique to the United Kingdom. At the extreme, many Continental European countries, partly for strategic reasons but also in part because of their general approach toward natural monopoly, had developed their rail systems as public enterprises from the outset. Equally, in Canada the inherent advantage of the railways led to concern about the abuse of their powers, including discriminatory practices, and to the passing of the Railway Act of 1903.

The Anti-competition Phase, 1930–45

Advances in trucking and passenger transport in the period after the Second World War substantially eroded the near-monopoly that had been enjoyed by the railways for the previous 80 or so years. The nature of road transport, and especially the relative ease of entry and the low capital requirement necessary, changed the focus towards the regulation of dangerous operating practices and excessive competition. Political pressures from the railway companies, still hampered by numerous restrictions on their commercial freedom, to contain cheap road transport, added emphasis to the debate.

In Britain, besides the financial strains on the regulated railway industry, fears were expressed that excessive competition produces dangerous operating practices and results in inadequate and unreliable services for those situated away from the main transport arteries. The Salter Conference, which reported on trucking in 1932, found that:

> Any individual at present has an unlimited right to enter the haulage industry without any regard to the pressure on the roads or the existing excess of transport facilities .... This unrestricted liberty is fatal to the organization of the industry in a form suitable to a carrier service purported to serve the public.

(It should perhaps be said that the composition of the Salter Conference – it was made up of railwaymen and representatives of established truckers – may have colored its conclusions.)

The legal manifestations of this policy were the passing of the Road Traffic Act, 1930, and of the Road and Rail Traffic Act, 1933, which introduced, respectively, quantity licensing into road passenger transport and trucking. In addition to trying to temper the competitive environment of road transport, the operation of the licensing system for road passenger transport encouraged the provision and cross-subsidization of unprofitable social bus services by virtue of the method of license allocation. Other measures designed to produce greater equality in the operating conditions encountered on the roads and railways included relaxation of certain constraints on railway pricing and the introduction of minimum wage rates and specified employment conditions into the industry.

Elsewhere a plethora of similar regulations were appearing. In the United States, federal legislation was introduced, controlling coastal shipping (1933), inter-urban bus operations (1935), trucking (1935), airlines (1938), inland waterways (1940), and freight forwarders (1942), and many states also tightened their regulatory regimes. Canada initiated regulations over its aviation industry under the 1938 Transport Act, and encouraged coordination, rather than competition, between its main railway operators under the 1933 Canadian National–Canadian Pacific Act.

Central Control and Nationalization in Europe, 1945–51

The years immediately following the end of the Second World War saw in the United Kingdom a period of reconstruction and industrial policies emphasizing the nationalization of industry. The 1947 Transport Act, for the first time outside of war years, brought a substantial part of the British transport system under direct government control. (Although peacetime nationalization was not entirely new, the state-owned British Overseas Airways Corporation was formed in 1939.)

The objectives of the 1947 Act were to secure the provision of an efficient, adequate, economical, and properly integrated system of public inland transport and port facilities. The earlier success of the London Passenger Transport Board gave credence to this view and the British Transport Commission (BTC) was established to emulate. It was given the responsibility of coordinating the newly nationalized railways, long-distance road haulage, sections of public road transport, London Transport, and publicly owned ports and waterways.

It was recognized that for railways to compete efficiently, a much closer price–cost relationship was required. It was impossible, however, for a new set of freight charges to be set before 1955, and meanwhile the BTC was impotent to direct traffic to the mode for which it thought it was best suited. The difficulty was compounded by consignors having a free choice of transport mode, and that own-account trucking vehicles were free from government control. Further, the 1947 Act had little opportunity to work because of, first, the lack of time needed to develop the necessary administration and to reorganize the newly nationalized undertakings, and, second, the inadequate funds available to carry out the necessary investment required in the rail sector.

In the United States, the post-Second World War boom saw many railroads driven out of business due to competition from airlines and the emergent Interstate highways. The rise of the automobile led to the end of passenger train services on most railroads. Trucking businesses had become major competitors by the 1930s and acquired an increased market share of freight business. Railroads continued to carry bulk freight such as coal, steel, and other commodities. Despite the considerably increased competition the railroads encountered, they continued to have their rates and operations regulated, offering them little flexibility in responding to changing market forces. There were no significant moves to nationalize.

A Competitive Framework, 1951–64

The period of successive Conservative administrations between 1951 and 1964 in the United Kingdom witnessed a movement away from a regulatory approach to transport coordination and towards one based upon competition that made use of the natural interplay of economic forces. A policy of decentralized control was pursued and, under the 1953 Transport Act, the railways were freed from many of their long-standing statutory obligations (for example, regarding common carriage and publication of rates and charges). Large sections of nationalized trucking were returned to private ownership. The basic argument for this competitive approach was that even if integration in the fullest sense were practicable, it would result in a large, unwieldy machine, ill-adapted to respond rapidly to the varying demands of industry.

The culmination of these policies was the 1962 Transport Act which freed the railways from most of their remaining legal constraints, regionalized their boards, separated their overall administration from that of trucking, and recognized that commercial viability required some rationalization of the rail network. Nationalized road haulage was given terms of reference requiring it to perform as though it were a 'private enterprise concern'.

The general policy of 'coordination by competition' pursued by the government met with considerable problems after 1962. The railways and public transport in general ran into increasing financial difficulties, while public concern began to grow over both the need to provide additional road space to accommodate growing motor numbers and over the environmental effects of this growth, especially on urban areas. The established method of providing social services by cross-finance from profitable services ceased to be financially viable. Further, there were questions arising concerning the most appropriate ways of exploiting new transport technologies, especially containerization.

Controlled Competition, 1964–74

The Labour administration elected in the United Kingdom in 1964 undertook a series of detailed policy studies that culminated in the 1968 Transport Act. This, in conjunction with the 1968 Town and Country Planning Act, sought to produce a policy based upon 'controlled competition'. It hoped to combine the advantages afforded by the automatic processes of the market mechanism with those of direct control. The policy was comprehensive, setting up passenger transport authorities (PTAs) to control and coordinate urban public transport, devising new systems of quality licensing for trucking, providing specific finance to support socially necessary transport, drawing up a national road-building program, and reconstructing the accounts and activities of the railways. It used all means of policy: market measures such as taxation and subsidy, as well as 'administrative' measures such as licensing and the establishment of new institutions.

The Act was also liberal in the sense that the framework of legislation and licensing that was introduced was intended to provide a basis for 'fair' competition, leaving the coordination of modes, in most sectors, to market forces. The PTAs were introduced in the major conurbations to control urban public transport, but this was in a market where externalities are widespread and competition felt to be unlikely to solve problems of congestion and environmental decay. The inter-urban market was left to competitive forces with intervention limited to preventing excess instability or dangerous practices.

The Conservative government returned to office in 1970 and pledged itself to the repeal of many of the clauses in the 1968 Act, although, in practice, few of the measures they found exceptionable – such as quantity licensing for long-distance trucking – had in fact been implemented. Indeed, the 1972 Local Government Act set up authorities that logically extended the PTA concept and further integrated the long-term planning of overall urban development. The Civil Aviation Authority, which was set up in 1971, rather than reversing the philosophy of the 1968 Act, was designed to control operating practices and improve the stability of the sector. As the Minister for Trade said at the time: 'There are close links between the economics and the financial health of the airlines and the safety of their operations and between operational safety, air worthiness, air traffic control and navigational services'.

The Search for Efficiency, 1974–80

The policy emphasis of the Labour government from 1974 to 1979 was spelt out in the government's document, 'Transport policy':

> First, to contribute to economic growth and higher national prosperity … . Second, to meet social needs by securing a reasonable level of personal mobility … . Third, to minimize the harmful effects, in loss of life and damage to the environment, that are the direct physical results of the transport we use.

In many ways the policies, which reduced government expenditure considerably, moved further towards the free market than the 1968 Transport Act, with greater emphasis now placed on allocative efficiency. Although government expenditure on 'roads and transport' fell from £3,820 million to £3,023 million per annum (at 1978 prices) between 1974 and 1978, this does not mean official intervention was ignored. The 1974 Railway Act, for example, had already introduced the idea of a 'Public Service Obligation', and subsidies were made available to provide services 'comparable' to those existing at the time of the legislation.

Methods of allocating public monies were also modified with the introduction of transport supplementary grants and the need, from 1974, to produce transport policies and programs by local authorities to demonstrate the evolution of coherent local transport policy. This latter idea was later extended in the 1978 Transport Act to embrace public transport services (the Public Transport Plans) at the shire level. But, on the other hand, grand strategies for road building were replaced by piecemeal assessments emphasizing a further shift from the active policy of the Labour administration of the 1960s to rather more reactive policy-making (Gwilliam, 1979).

The emphasis on allocative efficiency and market mechanisms was further strengthened in the 1980 Transport Act introduced by the Conservative government that had been returned the previous year. Quantity licensing in the express coach sector was abolished and free competition (with quality controls) was permitted. Further relaxation of sharing and lift-giving laws also allowed more opportunity for private transport to offer limited forms of public service in rural areas, while policies of denationalization resulted in sales of limited amounts of publicly owned transport assets to private industry. (It is interesting to compare this trend towards both reactive policy-making and a greater reliance on market forces with the developments in the European Community's Common Transport Policy discussed in Chapter 13.)

The Age of Regulatory Reform, 1980 to Late 1990s

The period since the late 1970s has witnessed major reforms in transport regulation. While there are marked national differences in the nature and pace of change, this process has, in the case of public transport modes, been characterized by moves toward more liberal regimes and a withdrawal of government from the ownership of transport operating companies. In contrast, there has been an increasing emphasis on the containment and the management of automobile use both on environmental grounds and because of congestion problems.

The liberalization measures that have been adopted not only represented legal reforms, but also embraced *de facto* changes in interpretation and enforcement of regulations. In addition, they have extended across national boundaries with, for instance, the removal of institutional barriers to free transport operations being an explicit element of the European Community's 1992 initiative. Whereas previously the majority view was that, because of scale economies and the potential for serious market failure, it was in the public interest for government to take an active role in regulating the industry, the prevailing wisdom is now that intervention failures are often potentially more damaging than market imperfections.

The generality of the regulatory trends across industrialized countries raises questions concerning the underlying causes of change. Certainly, in more recent years one can point to the demonstration effects exerted mainly by the deregulation of United States domestic aviation, but there also seem to be more fundamental issues that need addressing.

The first American economists to oppose regulation did so for a straightforward reason. Most subscribed (and still do) to the basic theory that welfare is maximized when the price of each good or service equals its long-run social marginal cost, but evidence mounted in the 1950s, 1960s, and 1970s that regulatory agencies caused prices to diverge from long-run social marginal costs, rather than converge with them. Economic studies of United States aviation provided a cornerstone in this debate. It was the combination of direct evidence that the CAB kept long-haul, high-density fares high and evidence of low fares in the unregulated intra-state markets in California that provided the first evidence that deregulation of inter-city air passenger transportation was justified. Indeed, in the case of airlines, the California markets provided evidence against airline regulation, evidence that could be understood not only by economists, but also by the general traveling public (see again Table 14.1).

By the mid-1960s, a strong case existed for transport deregulation in the United States but there was much research needed to get a full picture; for example, early studies disagreed as to whether the costs of excess rail capacity resulting from closure regulation were high or low. Several subsequent studies considered these issues, as well as the more basic issue regarding how high the social loss from transport regulation was in the United States.

There were also theoretical developments in economics that encouraged deregulation. The Chicago models of regulation made it clear that the public interest is not necessarily served by regulation. However, these models also implied that existing regulations were the result of a rational process, and by the interpretation of some they could be thought to work against deregulation, because they implied that regulation was itself a result of social optimization. Nevertheless, subsequent analyses have extended the analysis to indicate how it could indeed explain regulatory reform. The reason is that changes in technologies, markets, and the balance of political power among different groups can easily stimulate regulatory reform, even in a Chicago-type model. This has been examined in the context of the bus (Button, 1989) and airline industries (Keeler, 1984).

Another theory which supported deregulation was that of contestability, which asserted that, with sufficiently easy entry and exit in a market (there are no sunk costs but there are lags in matching price cuts), even a natural monopoly could have a zero profit, competitive outcome. The model, however, served more as an after-the-fact rationale for deregulation than as a stimulus, because it was only developed after deregulation occurred in most United States industries. Furthermore, as we have seen, subsequent empirical evidence for the United States airline industry has not fully supported the contestability hypothesis.

The resultant changes that have taken place across the world since the mid-1960s have not been uniform either across countries or across modes. Part of this stems from the different starting points that existed in the early 1970s. In very general terms, the United States led the way in legal change with a rush of liberalizing measures during the 1970s and early 1980s, which removed much government control from its domestic transport system – see Table 14.2. Other countries

Table 14.2   *Major legal changes in United States transport regulation (1976–89)*

1976	Railroad Revitalization and Reregulation Reform Act: removed many regulations over rate setting
1977	Air Cargo Deregulation Act: initiated free competition for air cargo services
1978	Airline Deregulation Act: initiated a phased removal of fare setting and market entry controls
1980	Staggers Rail Act: removed many regulations over line abandonments and gave further freedom over rate setting
1980	Motor Carriers Service Act: increased entry and rate setting freedom and reduced the role of rate fixing bureaux
1981	Northeast Rail Reform Act: enabled Conrail to abandon little-used lines
1982	Bus Regulatory Reform Act: eased conditions of market entry and exit and phased in relaxation of rate controls

have followed the trend, in part because of demonstration effects that indicated significant benefits from change but in some cases because of the direct impacts of changes in the United States – Canada, for example, was so affected.

In effect, the systems of Boards and Committees, which regulated the industry, have gradually had their powers curtailed and transport industries are increasingly being treated like other commercial undertakings. Where controls remain, there has been a shift in their emphasis. In inter-state trucking, for example, the 1980 legislation shifted the burden of proof for market entry from the applicant to the protester and this effectively eliminated the major entry barrier. It also created a zone of reasonableness within which rates could vary. Equally, with respect to freight railroads, the reforms gradually removed rate controls, allowed rationalization, and facilitated reorganization, especially mergers.

This quest for efficiency has been emulated in the United Kingdom as, first, the 1980 Transport Act, and then the 1985 Transport Act liberalized bus markets and introduced new financial mechanisms for providing social services. *De facto* reform was brought about in domestic aviation as the Civil Aviation Authority adjusted its position on licensing in 1982. Developments within the European Union meant that there would be further *de jure* changes as cabotage was phased in within the Community by 1997. Indeed, as outlined in Chapter 12, the creation of a Single European Market meant that cabotage rights, albeit initially often in rather limited forms, extend across all transport modes within the European Union.

Similar changes occurred elsewhere with the domestic Canadian trucking market, partly as a result of increased competition from the more efficient American carriers being liberalized in 1987 and its aviation market, after some *de facto* changes in 1984, being legally deregulated in 1988. Reforms of a similar nature ended Australia's 'two airlines' domestic aviation policy in 1990, but liberalization of surface transport has progressed more slowly.

The extensive public ownership of transport that existed in countries such as Canada, Australia, Japan, and most of Europe has meant that reforms there have often also involved elements of privatization. The privatization process, while reducing the direct control of government, has stimulated the creation of new regulations, for example, to limit market power and to meet social objectives. Many of these relate to quality of service, especially safety, and to the nature of ownership (such as governing allowable foreign ownership of shares), but economic regulations have also been imposed.

The sale of transport undertakings through stock market flotation (for instance, British Airways and the British Airports Authority) attracted considerable attention and raised large sums of money for the United Kingdom Exchequer (Table 14.3). Privatization in transport has also taken a diversity of other forms. The former National Bus Company in the United Kingdom, for instance, was broken up and privatized mainly through management buy-outs. In France and Japan private money is increasingly being used to finance railway operations through commercial loans and investments. Open tendering for formerly publicly supplied bus services is now widespread in the United Kingdom, and franchising

Table 14.3   *Transport privatization proceeds in the United Kingdom*

Undertaking	Year	Amount (current prices)
National Freight Corporation	1982	£7 million
British Rail Hotels	1983	£30 million
Associated British Ports	1983–84	£34 million
Sealink	1984	£ 66 million
British Airways	1987	£892 million
British Airports Authority	1987	£1,200 million
National Bus Company	1988	n.a.

Note: n.a. = not available.

systems, albeit on a somewhat different basis, exist in a few Continental European states. In a similar way, Sweden attempted to increase efficiency on parts of its railway network by separating operations from track and allowing private operating companies to tender for services. Actions were also initiated in the United Kingdom although extended, for a period, to embrace privatization of the track with somewhat less success (Bowman, 2015). Overall, the experiences have been mixed.

The regulatory actions in higher-income countries during the 1980s and 1990s had wider knock-on effects. Gradually the effects of reform strategies, especially through the influence and actions of agencies such as the World Bank and regional multi-lateral agencies such as the Asian and Inter-American Development Banks, are also being felt in developing countries. Table 14.4, for example, lists some of the regulatory reforms of local public transport systems that occurred in lower-income countries, including transition economies. There was a general relaxation of economic controls, but these took a diversity of forms, often dependent on the wider responsibilities of the relevant authority and wider national economic and political reforms.

The Notion of 'Sustainable Development', Late 1990s to Date

We saw in previous chapters the impact that transport can inflict on both the built and the natural environments. Regulations of various kinds have long been used to minimize these problems, but the nature of the problems being addressed and the forms of regulation deployed have, as we have seen in Chapter 8, been changing. The use of regulation, and to a lesser extent, fiscal instruments, have reduced, if not necessarily optimized, many of the local and regional adverse external effects. There seems every indication, however, that the political economy of optimizing such things as global warming gas emission will remain challenging.

In broad terms this fits with a wider policy shift that focuses on sustainable development, within which transport policy plays a significant role.

The period since 1980 has witnessed a complete transformation in the way in which policy-makers think about regulating transport markets. The role of government in regulation has moved from directing the operational sides of the

Table 14.4 *Summary of changes in the role of public transport regulatory authorities in developing counties*

Change in role of regulator/transport authority and market structure examples	Examples
Regulation of urban passenger transport introduced or restored	Ghana; Manila (Philippines)
Regulation of passenger transport transferred to the city	Jordan
Regulatory capacity developed within local government	Accra & Kumasi (Ghana); Amman (Jordan); Tbilisi (Georgia); Manila (Philippines)
Changes made to rules for market entry &/or procurement	Accra (Ghana); Lagos (Nigeria); Tbilisi (Georgia)
Regulators develop new models for procurement of services	Recife (Brazil)
Regulators develop new contractual basis for bus services, or amend existing ones	Kaunas (Lithuania); South Africa; Santiago (Chile)
Regulators make direct intervention to restructure private operators	Sri Lanka
Transport authority makes vehicles available to operator	Accra (Ghana); Tbilisi (Georgia); Dhaka (Senegal)
Transport authority provides funding or financial incentives for bus purchases &/or technology upgrades	Kaunas (Lithuania); South Africa; rural areas in Brazil
Transport authority finances transport infrastructure to enhance public transport system quality & level of service & to provide improved operating & maintenance facilities to operators	Accra (Ghana); Amman (Jordan); China; Dar es Salaam (Tanzania); Delhi (India); Mauritius; many other cities

Source: Finn and Mulley (2011).

sector to looking for innovative ways to finance its infrastructure and control its wider impacts on society. Part of this stems from wider developments concerning the perceived role of government *per se*, but the changes in transport have also come about because of specific concerns. The outcome has seldom been as predicted and certainly the more liberal conditions which now exist in most transport markets around the world are not without their problems. In general, however, the changes have afforded the opportunity for users to express their preferences through the market and for regulators to pinpoint specific distortions where intervention can be justified.

In summary, if there is a single conclusion to be drawn from the experience of regulatory reform in transport, it has been that reform has, in general, been an economic success. Though there have been areas in which the policies need improvement (anti-trust, infrastructure, franchise arrangements, etc.), these are small matters of 'fine-tuning' compared with the broad picture of overall success in improving the efficiency of transport provision. What have been lacking are comparable reforms in the regulation of private transport use.

14.5   Paths of Regulatory Reform

Regulations are continually changing as we saw in our discussion of institutions in Chapter 1. This reflects a variety of factors, but here the focus is more on the ways in which the regulatory reforms are enacted. We saw in Chapter 13 that the European Union, for example, staged its reforms of aviation policy over a series of 'Packages'. This was not the way the United States approached the challenge in the case of air transport. This raises issues about the speed at which change in transport regulations is optimal from an economic perspective. Linked to this is the matter of how the transition is best managed, and the role that different incentives and instruments may play in this.

'Big Bang Approach' Versus 'Phased Reform'

There are two basic ways in which regulatory reforms are initiated; they either come in at once as a 'big bang' or they are phased-in in stages. There are economic advantages and disadvantages of each. The big bang approach, typified by the individual modal regulations in the United States in the late 1970s and early 1980s, involves a comprehensive legal change in regulations that comes into effect very rapidly. There are potential costs in this (Figure 14.5).

First, the reforms may leave significant 'stranded costs' in the industry. For example, the infrastructure and hardware of the industry will be designed for the prior regulatory regime and some of it will be redundant under the structures of supply that emerge after reforms, or at least not be ideal in the new situation. Second, the new measures may not themselves be optimal. Changes in regulatory structures impose a wide variety of unforeseen costs on any industry and some of these may be larger than anticipated. Equally, some of the possible benefits of reform may be lost if the reforms are not optimal.

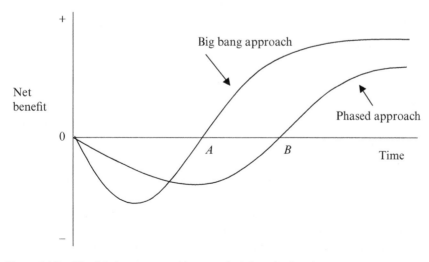

Figure 14.5   *The 'big bang approach' versus the 'phased reform'*

The advantages, on the other hand, are that the big bang change removes considerable uncertainty from the market about the nature of future institutional structures and should, therefore, remove some of the challenges in making investments. It also means that there is less opportunity for those in the industry, or for others with related interests, to manipulate the various stages in the reform process, as may be the case if the changes are phased-in over time. Additionally, there is the expectation of a significant flow of benefits once the reforms have worked their way through the system.

In contrast, a series of smaller changes phased-in allows for stranded costs to be minimized as transport hardware is physically worn out before it needs to be replaced and it allows modification to the new regulatory structure in the light of the experiences gained in the previous phases. But it is prone to capture by vested interests seeking to protect their positions and it takes longer for the benefits of the new regime to work their way through.

In practice, the decisions regarding which approach to adopt are often more to do with political economy than the simple calculation of costs and benefits. Reform generally requires a common perspective of a coalition of interests and this shapes the pattern of change. A relatively strong and established federal structure, such as in the United States, makes it much easier to adopt a big bang approach than in the European Union where basically a strong informal coalition of members is needed to carry through change.

Considerable attention is paid in economics to comparative-static comparisons, normally in terms of efficiency, between the implications of one regulatory regime and another, and to a lesser extent to the merits of the big bang and phased approaches, but there are also more detailed issues of the transition process (Meyer and Tye, 1981). Much depends on the peculiarities of the situation. The matter is seldom purely economic in nature and, for example, there are often long-standing legal contracts that make sudden change difficult, or can only be circumvented by expensive buy-outs. There are also equity considerations. The loss of sunk costs is not just a matter of efficiency but adversely impacts on those who had incurred them under the old regulatory regime, whereas the gains of change are enjoyed by new investors.

United States Versus European Union Transatlantic Aviation Policy

The development of international air transport markets on the North Atlantic offers an example of the ways phasing of regulatory changes may occur and their economic implications. The restrictive bi-lateral air service agreements that typified the institutional structure of international airline markets from the Chicago Convention of 1944 have gradually been eroded by multi-lateral actions of entities such as the European Union and the advent of the Open Skies initiative by the United States (see Table 14.5 for details). This initially involved a loosening up of individual bi-lateral agreements between countries such as Germany and the Netherlands and the United States, but this was done in an *ad hoc* fashion, and agreements with countries such as the United Kingdom remained restrictive.

Table 14.5 *Main features of United States bi-lateral air service agreements*

	Pre-1978 bi-lateral air service agreements	1978–91 open market bi-laterals		Post-1991 Open Skies bi-laterals
		US airlines	*Foreign airlines*	
Market access	Only to specified points	From any point in the US to specified points in foreign countries	Access limited to a number of US points	Unlimited
	Limited 5th freedom rights granted to US carriers	Extensive 5th freedom rights granted		Unlimited 5th freedom rights
	Charter rights not included		Unlimited charter rights	
		7th freedom rights not granted Cabotage not allowed		
Designation	Single – some multiple		Multiple	
	Airlines must be 'substantially and effectively controlled' by nationals of designated state			
Capacity	Capacity agreed or shared 50:50 No capacity/frequency controls under liberal bi-laterals, but subject to review	Break of gauge permitted in some agreements	No frequency or capacity controls	Break-of-gauge rights granted
Tariffs	Approval by both governments (double-approval) or as agreed by IATA	Double-disapproval (filed tariffs operative unless both governments disapproval) or country of origin rules		Free pricing
Code-sharing	Not part of bi-laterals			Code-sharing permitted

Negotiations to reach a more comprehensive structure emerged when the European Commission was given authority to negotiate on behalf of all Union airlines. The effects of such changes have not been easy to isolate, but Figure 14.6 offers a general representation of the issues that are involved in looking at what has happened. It highlights the potential fare and output implications of the various types of transatlantic regulatory regimes that have been considered.

The initial position of the demand curve for transatlantic services under the pre-1980s regulatory regime is assumed linear and shown as D_1 in the figure, and the average cost curve per passenger, which for simplicity is assumed to rise more than linearly with quantity, as C_1. Market forces, however, because of the institutional interventions in place, did not determine fares and capacity across the Atlantic. Capacity under this system was limited (seen as the 'capacity constraint') and fares were regulated. If we assume that the terms reached under the bi-lateral agreement regarding fares allowed for at least cost recovery by the partners' airlines, this implies a fare level up to F_1. The removal of both this capacity constraint and of negotiated pricing, as happens under the Open Skies arrangements, results in competition for air services, and a move toward cost-recovery pricing strategies by the carriers. This would reduce fares to F^*_1.

Open Skies policies that free-up market entry by carriers and the fares they may levy, coupled with the permitting of strategic alliances, not only removes the capacity constraint but also affects both the demand and supply curves for transatlantic air travel. The ability of airlines to more effectively feed their transatlantic routes and coordinate their activities, through the restructuring of their business and networks, will reduce the average cost of carriage to C_2 in the figure. The effect is often reinforced due to downward pressure on costs because, although not strictly part of the Open Skies framework, the wider competitive environment within Europe, and the privatization of many carriers, by heightening commercial pressures, reduces the amount of both static and dynamic X-inefficiency in the

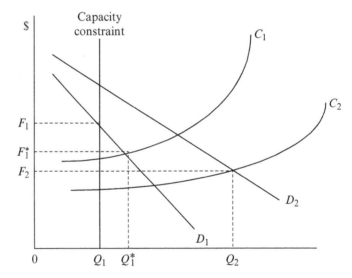

Figure 14.6   *The economics of Open Skies policies*

airline industry. In other words, there is the combined pressure of both free airline markets across the Atlantic and within the two feeder markets at either end.

The Open Skies policy also has stimulation effects on the demand side. By allowing more effective feed to the long-haul stage of transatlantic services through the concentration of traffic at international hub airports, it increases the geographical market being serviced and generates economies of scope and scale. The larger physical market demand, combined usually with the improved quality of the 'product' that accompanies more integrated services, such as code sharing, interchangeable frequent flier programs, common lounges, and through baggage checking, pushes out the demand for international air services to D_2 in the figure.

The outcome of the lowering of costs and the outward shift in demand is that the number of passengers traveling increases to Q_2 and, because Open Skies allows price flexibility, the fare falls to F_2 in the way our example is drawn. It should be noted that fares might not actually fall; indeed, they may rise as the result of the freer market conditions. The reason for this is that the outward shift in demand reflects a better 'quality' of service – for example, more convenient flights, transferability of frequent flier miles, and seamless ticketing – and that, on average, potential travelers are willing to pay more for this than the generic portfolio of features that were found under the old bi-lateral air service structure. (The shift out in demand may counteract the fall in costs resulting in $F^*_1 < F_2$.)

What does become pertinent, however, is the extent to which the fare structure is influenced by the market power of the airlines. The analysis presented in Figure 14.4 assumes that, in the Open Skies environment, fares are set to recover costs; in other words, competition and mergers policy can effectively fulfil the role of regulation. This raises issues as to the nature of a market served by a relatively small number of network carriers. A degree of competition exists between the various alliances for the trunk hauls market, and there is also competition at either end of routes with many other, including low-cost, carriers competing for passengers in overlapping feeder and origin–destination traffic to international hub airports. There are also theoretical reasons derived from game theory suggesting that the outcome in a market with three players approaches that of competition. Nevertheless, each alliance, by dint of product differentiation (for example, they serve different airports), inevitably enjoys some degree of monopoly power. This could lead to fares higher than F_2 and a smaller output than Q_2 with consequential reductions in consumer surplus.

The effects of a full Open Aviation Area – a genuine open market – can be considered an extension of this framework. Free capital markets, together with the ability to have more flexible feeder networks owned by the truck carrier at both ends of transatlantic services, would further lower costs and may generate additional economies of market presence, although this latter effect is unlikely to be large. The ability to invest across national boundaries provides for short-term support in situations of local market fluctuations and more integrated long-term planning of infrastructure; it would in effect produce air networks akin to those enjoyed by United States railroads, which can move investment funds across

states rather than have separate rail companies each limited to intra-state operations. In terms of Figure 14.5, it would mean lower fares and larger air traffic
volumes with concomitant increases in society benefits.

14.6   Studying Regulatory Reform

The impacts of reforms in the economic regulation since the late 1970s have been
extensively researched and debated, but the impossibility of accurately determining counterfactuals – what would have happened in the absence of regulatory
change – leaves much room for debate. Furthermore, many markets have not yet
reached long-run equilibrium. While some sectors such as the United Kingdom's
bus industries and the United States' domestic aviation industries were liberalized
some time ago, many international transport sectors are still in the process of
changing, merging, and shaking out. Infrastructure regulations have also generally been more recent and, because of the physical nature of the assets involved,
take longer to impact.

Experience so far, however, provides some insights on the working of transport markets and the benefits and costs of regulation, but it is not complete,
and infrastructure often remains heavily regulated and some of it is still state-
provided. Also, there have been problems with some of the reforms initially introduced, as for example with rail track in the United Kingdom, and thus there have
been subsequent modifications that make assessment murky.

Overall, however, simply looking at the crude data indicates that regulatory
liberalization during this period conferred significant benefits on the users of
transport services, as efficiency gains from 'deregulation' and privatization were
passed on to consumers in more competitive markets. A simple indication of
this is seen in the pattern of European air transport costs throughout the 1990s,
when reforms were taking place (Figure 14.7); fares and rates fell, to the benefit
of customers.

One important issue in the working of transport markets, as we have seen
in Section 14.3, is that of contestability. Evidence so far indicates strongly that
actual competition is considerably more effective in reducing market power than
is potential competition. But even those skeptical of the contestability of transport markets nevertheless find evidence that the market power of firms in these
markets is nowhere near strong enough to justify regulation. That is, it can be
strongly argued that unregulated markets in transport function quite well by reasonable measures of market performance, compared with other sectors of market
economies, and more efficiently than they did under regulation.

There is, in fact, a strong body of evidence that regulatory reform has
substantially enhanced economic efficiency in the United States, the United
Kingdom, and many other inter-city transport markets, and that the benefits of
that efficiency have been passed on to consumers, as we shall summarize below.
The evidence on more limited experiments in deregulating markets in urban
transport is not so clear, but is still encouraging.

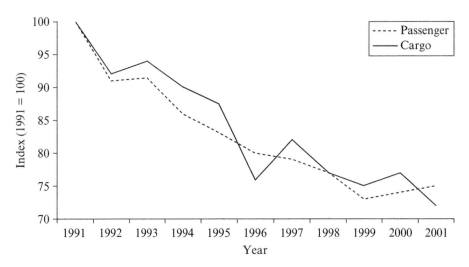

Figure 14.7   *Air fares and cargo rates for European airlines pre and post the enactment of the Third Package*

Although almost all studies trying to analyse the effects of regulatory liberalization for inter-city transport in the United States and the United Kingdom find positive benefits from change, there is nevertheless some controversy around the proper methods for evaluating the costs of excessive regulation. Traditionally, regulation is seen to affect efficiency by imposing static dead-weight loss, encouraging excess capacity, and stifling technological change. The implications of regulation, however, extend beyond these considerations. For example, regulatory change can have a dynamic effect on productivity change, rather than just a one-shot effect on static efficiency. Further, regulatory change will likely redistribute income across different groups and industries, and affect geographical areas differently, as well as changing national productivity.

As regards dynamic shifts in productivity, there have been far fewer studies than of static efficiency. Nevertheless, some studies have been done, including for airlines and for American trucking. In both contexts the studies concluded that deregulation caused accelerated improvement of productivity, at least for a period (Button and Keeler, 1993).

Concerning redistribution, studies clearly indicate that the effects of deregulation in this area are substantial. Early work in the United States, for example, indicated that deregulation of United States aviation benefitted the user by some $6 billion per year (1977 prices) with profits rising to $2.5 billion. Subsequent mergers and structural changes altered these figures, but not significantly (Morrison and Winston, 1995). In the area of freight, American deregulation seems to have had powerful effects on efficiency and distribution. Clifford Winston et al. (1990) found $20 billion (1988 prices) in annual benefit to shippers and their customers. Yet investors in trucking are estimated to have lost over $5 billion per annum, with losses of similar magnitude to labor employed in the industry. On the other hand, investors in railroads appeared to have gained from deregulation. In some cases, such as with the United Kingdom's buses and United States railroads and airlines, there were, however, overall short-term declines in wages from deregulation.

While the privatization of transport supplying industries has been somewhat more recent than many other measures of liberalization, the evidence seems to be that it has enhanced efficiency. In the case of air transport, simple comparisons of productivity between the privately owned major United States carriers in 1987 and the mainly state-owned European carriers indicated the former to be significantly more efficient (Ng and Seabright, 2001). The privatization of British Airways unquestionably improved the company's productivity *vis-à-vis* its nationally owned European rivals. Equally, the privatized United Kingdom bus companies increased productivity. The application of more rigorous analysis to those transport activities still under public ownership tends to indicate that levels of subsidy and intervention in management decision-making leads to technical inefficiency.

In nearly all cases of liberalized regulation, there were concerns on the part of some observers that regulatory change would come at a cost to society in terms of safety and externalities, because the need of firms to minimize costs under a competitive market situation would require them to pay less attention to these considerations. Although it is always difficult to distinguish between long-run trends and short-run fluctuations in transport safety, considerable time has nevertheless now passed since regulatory reform, especially in the United States. Virtually all evidence regarding deregulation and safety in the United States goes in one direction: there has been little change, involving some small improvement.

In the case of airlines, where perhaps the greatest concern of many was safety, not only did deregulation not increase fatalities per passenger-mile, but it saw a continuation of increased safety that was the pattern prior to the Airline Deregulation Act of 1978. Of course, to the extent that deregulation induced inter-modal shifts in traffic, the effects could be complicated. But even here, the most evident effect is positive: low airline fares have induced passengers away from a less-safe mode such as the private car to the safer mode of air transport.

The effects of transport deregulation on the wider environment are, at best, ambiguous. Greater freedom of entry and exit has removed much excess capacity from markets everywhere; this goes for trucking, airlines, and railroads, in the European Union and the United States. Fuller planes, lorries, trains, and railway track should be positive in their effects on the environment. Further, to the extent that freedom of the railroads to compete in the United States takes traffic from roads, that could be thought to be an environmental improvement as well. The major polluter in most contexts is the private car, and little if anything has been done to liberalize the market for car use.

What the phase of liberalization revealed is that, although less regulation may be beneficial, there is still a need for government intervention. A degree of 're-regulation', or modifications to the liberalized structures, has been considered by some, and adopted by a few (Bettini and Oliveira, 2008). In practice, however, the process is one of tidying up, tweaking the various regimes that are in place, and adjusting to new circumstances. Specifically, it is concerned with removing serious market imperfections.

With a few notable exceptions, the liberalization of transport in the twenty-first century has tended to focus on operations. Transport infrastructure investment has in contrast continued to be controlled by, and in many cases owned by, government. How to achieve optimal utilization of this infrastructure and, specifically, the development of appropriate user-charging mechanisms that minimize distortions in liberalized markets has attracted considerable attention. At one level there are matters relating to investment coordination and policy appraisal, especially in the international market, which have attracted little attention from economists.

At another level, there is the matter of efficient use and financing. The separation of infrastructure from operations, as has been the tradition with road and air transport and is being considered by more countries in the context of railways, is seen as one approach to achieving greater efficiency. In North America, recent history has seen monopoly passenger services (such as VIA Rail in Canada as well as Amtrak) hiring track capacity from freight companies. An alternative approach, however, is simply to offer available capacity to the highest bidder along the lines suggested by Harold Demsetz, although this can raise a variety of technical problems. Sweden, nevertheless, went some way in this direction in the early 1980s, and so did the United Kingdom.

An alternative is to develop economic charging regimes. Important in this is the question of cost attribution. In terms of rail transport, for example, considerable advances began to be seen in cost allocation in the United Kingdom during the 1980s. Equally, at airports, our improved understanding now provides a more rational basis for determining landing fees. With respect to road track cost allocation, studies in the United States (Small et al., 1989) and the United Kingdom (Newbery, 1988) provide a similar foundation for more rational user-charging regimes. Indeed, in New Zealand, the Road User Charges system is on a broad user-costs basis. The foundation is, therefore, now laid for more rational charging for infrastructure use.

Anti-trust and mergers have posed serious challenges for regulators both at the domestic and the international level, and have brought forth a significant body of analysis. Where mergers have not been prohibited entirely, *ex post* assessment has often within legal–economic work deployed structure, conduct, and performance measures. This involves analysing the broad structure of the industry (for example, the degree to which it is inherently monopolistic), the ways in which firms behave within it (for example, in terms of fixing prices), and the performance of the industry (for example, in terms of whether consumers benefit from the merger). This is inevitably a rather subjective exercise, but it does allow a multi-dimensional approach to the subject.

Econometric and programming approaches of the type set out in Chapter 5 have been deployed in academic work. Table 14.6 offers a brief summary of some of the analysis on airline alliances under which carriers coordinate some of their activities. This provides a more quantitative assessment of the implications of

Table 14.6   *Studies of the effects of strategic airline alliance*

Study	Alliances	Period	Findings
Gellman Research Associates (1994)	BA/US Air, KLM/NW	1994	Profits increased for all parties with BA and KLM gaining more than their partners
Youssef & Hansen (1994)	Swissair & SAS	1989–91	Increases in flight frequency; variations in fare levels; the strongest service levels had the lowest fare increases
US General Accounting Office (1995)	KLM/NW, USAir/BA, UAL/ Lufthansa, UAL/Ansett, UAL/BMA	1994	All carriers enjoyed increased revenues and traffic gained at competitors' expense, not industry growth
Dresner et al. (1995)	Continental/ SAS, Delta Swissair, KLM/ NW	1987–91	Mixed successes with traffic volumes; in general alliances did not benefit partners
Park (1997)	KLM/NW, Delta/ Swissair/ Sabena	1990–94	Traffic increases at the expense of rivals; complementary alliances lowered fares while parallel alliances increased fares
Oum et al. (2000)	Star Alliance, oneWorld Skyteam, KLM/ NW	1992–94	Increased traffic on alliance routes
Brueckner & Whalen (2000)	US international alliances	1999	Fares are 18–20% lower on international alliance, inter-lining routes

Source: Button (2009). This paper contains the full references to the studies cited.

collusion, although it inevitably misses out some of the less tangible or quantifiable elements of supplying, in this case, air transport services.

In summary, the period since the 1970s has seen considerable change in the way that economic regulations of airlines are viewed and how they are applied, and with this have come innumerable studies analysing what has happened. Given the differences in the timing of changes, the sectors affected, and the nature of the reforms, these studies have often sought to discover the extent to which the experiences in one country, or relating to one mode, are transferable to other counties or modes. For example, the early moves towards lighter regulation in the United States was an opportunity for other countries to learn lessons (Button and Swann, 1992).

The degree to which there has been, or can be, a successful learning experience is not always, however, clear. While it is interesting to speculate over whether, for example, the European Union approach (with its emphasis on gradualism) was optimal, in practice it is very difficult to reach any firm conclusions. Just taking air transport as an example, there was and remain significant differences between the American and European markets (Table 14.7). These differences in the geography, history, structure, and use of the network can make it hard to discern what lessons are relevant, and to decide the extent to which transfers have been successful.

14.7 Disruptive Innovation

As with all sectors of the economy, new technologies and organization practices are continually emerging in transport. Many of these changes act to complement the existing transport services being offered. Intelligent transportation systems, for example, generally complement existing traffic management practices and can often be integrated with existing traffic management technologies. Others disrupt the status quo by rapidly taking up a significant market share and replacing large parts of the market's existing business practices. These interlopers are often described as disruptive technologies or innovations. One can think in terms of Henry Ford's introduction of assembly line techniques of mass production together with a standard, simple-to-use product (the Model T) as an example.

A disruptor may target low-end customers who do not need the full performance valued by customers at the high end of the market, or be a new-market disruptor which targets customers who have needs that were previously unserved by existing incumbents.

When confronted by disruption, incumbent suppliers often call for regulation to protect their position, or to slow down the penetration of the innovative intruder. Transaction costs arguments are often used. Uber, for example, has often appeared in the media, labeled a disruption innovation because of its effects on existing modes of transportation, and most notably on conventional taxi-cabs and public transit. Local transit and taxi-cabs have sought protection by supporting the regulation of Uber, or simply banning Uber from operating. In the 1930s, railroads in many countries called for protection from trucking. In the United States, the 1935 Motor Carrier Act was partly intended to do this.

Offering a precise definition of disruptive innovation is not easy. Christensen et al. (2015) are very clear about what disruptive innovation involves, and '[i]n our experience, too many people who speak of "disruption" have not read a serious book or article on the subject'. They see Uber and other transportation network companies (TNCs) as a special case within the context of the taxi-cab industry, and more of a genuine disruptor to the limousine business with its Uber-SELECT product. This is because disruptive competition involves entry by a small company (which Uber was) into a market where there are established incumbents (which there were) who were focusing on providing products for their most demanding and profitable customers. The disruptive entrant would target neglected customers by offering more suitable functionality and usually lower prices.

Table 14.7   *Differences between the United States and European air transport markets affecting deregulation*

- *Domestic/international traffic split.* Most European carriage and historically its airlines have largely operated in regulated international markets, and the natural inclination for rent-protecting may take longer to erode than occurred in the United States.
- *The non-scheduled market.* European aviation traditionally involved a large non-schedule, component. In 1999, for example, the revenue from passengers by non-scheduled services in the United States was $12 billion out of $772 billion – comparable figures for Europe were $120 billion out of $337 billion. The European charter market has declined significantly since then, mirroring the decline in all-inclusive holidays and the rise of scheduled low-cost carriers such as Ryanair, EasyJet and Norwegian.
- *Market size.* The average route length in Europe is 720 kilometers; in the United States it is 1,220 kilometers. The average number of passengers per scheduled route is about 100,000 in Europe but virtually double that in the United States.
- *Airline size.* The scale of the European market is also reflected in the size of the European Union's airlines. The traditional carriers, such as Lufthansa (with assets of €42.7 billion in 2019), Air France/KLM (€30.7 billion), and British Airways (€24.4 billion) are some of the largest in the world. The largest passenger airlines and cargo carriers as measured by conventional parameters are American-based.
- *Ownership of airlines.* While the United States commercial airline industry has always been in private hands, most major European carriers have traditionally been state-owned and several carriers remain so or have a significant state involvement even after measures of privatization in many countries.
- *Approaches to bankruptcy.* Chapter 11 arrangements in the United States are less stringent than most European bankruptcy regimes and allow for existing management, under supervision, to restructure a company's finances rather than have the assets of the undertaking realized.
- *Subsidies.* America had no tradition of explicitly subsidizing airlines until 2001, except in limited cases of social air services. This situation changed during the Covid-pandemic with short-term assistance provided. There has been a tradition of subsidizing European flag carriers, but Union policy on state subsidies has now been tightened and criteria made explicit under which subsidies may be given.
- *Inter-modal competition.* There is substantial inter-modal competition in Europe, ranging from high-speed train services to good-quality highways. Anything approaching high-speed rails services are extremely limited in the United States.
- *Infrastructure availability.* United States air traffic control is centralized, whereas air traffic control in Europe is a national concern. The EU system comprises a patchwork, while the United States has less than a third the number of en route facilities and standardized mainframe computers. Both markets are moving to satellite control systems – NextGen in the United States and Single European Sky in Europe. Airport capacity in Europe is rapidly being reached at many major terminals, whereas this is a more limited problem in America. More than 50 percent of traffic in Europe passes through 24 airports and, although figures are somewhat subjective on the issue of airport capacity, all of these have reached their technical capacity or are very close to it.
- *Advantage of hindsight.* European policy-makers and airlines have benefitted from the United States' experiences when liberalizing air transport markets, and avoided some of the transition problems.

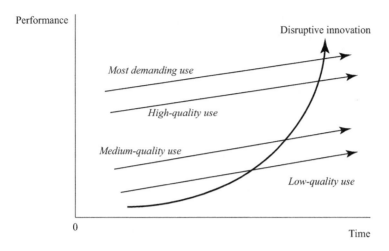

Figure 14.8   *Penetration of a disruptive innovation over time*

Over time, the disrupting innovator takes over increasing amounts of the traditional suppliers' markets. In the example depicted in Figure 14.8, the new disruptive entrant comes in at the lower quality of service which is not being provided
by existing transport suppliers, and then begins taking increasing shares of the
higher-priced, better-quality markets. In practice, a disruptor can enter at any
level of performance that incumbent suppliers are not serving well.

Response from incumbents is initially lax because they are focusing on different markets, and this allows the newcomer to move up the market, taking mainstream business from the incumbents (which Uber, Lyft, and other TNCs have).
However, Uber's ability to take business from taxi-cabs was more to do with
regulations governing price and market entry over the latter's activities, shack-
ling their ability and motivation to innovate, than with being part of consciously
moving into more profitable markets. Uber was initially a rent-seeker circumventing regulation over very similar products, and in particular over taxi drivers.
Further, Uber's approach, once in the market, unlike a disrupter, has been, as we
argue below, that of a sustaining innovator seeking to expand markets and to
improve on traditional taxi services.

Another transport market that has claimed to have experienced disruptive
innovation involves the arrival of low-cost air carriers. The argument is that small
airlines, such as Southwest in the United States, and later Ryanair and EasyJet in
Europe, filled a basic, low-fare, one-class market neglected by full service, incumbent carriers. These carriers subsequently moved successfully into more network-
based services, offering various 'bundles' of services – the so-called 'upmarket
march'. Raynor (2011) puts emphasis on the low-cost airlines' use of standard
aircraft (for example, the Boeing 737 series in the case of Southwest) in neglected
markets, combined with continually updating the series model allowing penetration of mainstream markets.

But, again, while some of the features of disruptive innovation are present,
the incumbent airlines were limited by regulations in virtually all markets from

price discrimination and the networks they could develop. Charter services did offer lower fares but were tied by regulations that in some cases required the combined purchase of an airline ticket and a hotel room, or passengers being members of a 'club' of some kind. Disruptive innovation, as with the TNCs, was of a heavily distorted market and not one where there was a great deal of competition.

14.8   Coordination Via the Market, or by Direction?

Several very important facts emerge from the previous sections. First, government in virtually all countries finds the transport sector extremely difficult to handle; this is perhaps most clearly seen if one reflects on the fact that major pieces of transport legislation appeared on the United Kingdom's statute books every seven or eight years during one half-century period (that is, 1930, 1933, 1947, 1953, 1962, 1968, 1974, 1980, 1985, 2000, 2008, and 2020). These have been supplemented by numerous pieces of minor legislation. There have been substantial shifts both in the way that transport has been viewed and in the type of policy approach pursued.

Second, the changes in policy have exhibited systematic swings between attempts at making greater use of market forces and a more comprehensive level of central control or direction. Intervention has always existed, but the degree and nature of this intervention has differed according to whether confidence was felt in market processes. Recent changes in policy, from the late 1970s, have reflected a greater market orientation while the nationalization of the immediate post-war period followed philosophies of direction. The respective merits of market-orientated policies *vis-à-vis* ones of planned allocation of resources are subjects of considerable debate. While much of the discussion is political (often doctrinal) there is, nevertheless, an important area of economic controversy involved.

It is quite possible that in theory a variety of approaches with quite significant differences in their degree of market orientation could achieve the basic objectives of transport policy, but the standard economic problem of integration or 'coordination' remains difficult in practice. (Coordination is here used in its economic context and is best defined by G.S. Peterson, 1930: 'Coordination is the assignment by whatever means of each facility to those transport tasks which it can perform better than other facilities, under conditions which will ensure its fullest development in the place so found'.) In practice, reliance is never placed entirely on the market mechanism to achieve the desired coordination, or upon direction. The issue is, rather, one of degree and emphasis. It seems useful, however, to look initially at some of the arguments that are advanced for adoption of the extreme position.

The price mechanism is the main instrument of the market and offers an obvious method of coordination, each consumer being able to purchase transport services at the lowest cost. Arguments that transport is a public utility, on a par with street lighting or the police force, are dismissed by advocates of this school, who point out that transport, unlike genuine utilities, would be provided even if government did not exist.

There may be cases (for example, quasi-public goods) where government must act as the supplier, if provision is to be optimal, but providing the rules of marginal cost pricing are pursued, no difficulties arise. If externalities exist, then these can be handled adequately by means of ensuring that property rights are allocated according to accepted rules, while lump-sum transfers could tackle social difficulties associated with hardship. (At the extreme, one may argue that income differences are themselves the result of market forces and should, therefore, be left.)

Insurance markets would handle the longevity of transport infrastructure, and the associated risks. Safety would be ensured by travelers/consignors selecting operators with good safety records, or alternatively they may prefer a higher risk but at a lower charge for the trip. Perfection in the 'safety market' may require government intervention to ensure that users are cognizant of the dangers involved – in this sense information becomes the only 'merit good' to be provided in the transport sector.

Advocates of market approaches to coordination point to the automatic mechanisms involved, and to the freedom of the system from political manipulation. John Hibbs (1982) suggested that the direction of resources by some over-riding body is likely to be less efficient at coordination because '[t]he administrative mind is not likely to possess the qualities of imagination and flair that are necessary if the consumer's interest is to be served'. Cooter and Topakin (1980) produce evidence from the Bay Area Rapid Transit System in the San Francisco Bay Area that provides tentative confirmation of this type of bureaucratic hypothesis; namely, that the technostructure places its interest before that of customers. The validity of this view is, however, debatable, and it has been suggested that the managers of any large undertaking, irrespective of the type of purpose they are charged to pursue, will be motivated by their own self-interest – they will attempt to maximize their power and security. Self-interest at the expense of customer interest, therefore, seems to be a function of the scale of management rather than of ownership or the objectives that are set.

But even if there are potential managerial problems associated with the central direction of resources, these may well be outweighed by the possible benefits. Strictly, planned resource allocation involves the direction of traffic as well as factors of production employed in providing transport services. In general, however, United Kingdom transport policy has seldom attempted to direct traffic, leaving the consumer free to choose his/her mode, route, service, etc. (There are exceptions such as one-way streets, barriers to trucks, etc., but these are rather outside of the main thrust of the debate.)

The most important case, where some degree of direction was intended, concerned the proposed introduction of quantity licensing into long-distance trucking under the Transport Act, 1968. The broad argument here was that it was to the consignor's benefit to be directed to rail in certain instances because of his/her own misperception. ('Inertia and habit will play their part and some consignors may not even be aware of the advantage to them of the new rail services, nor of the true economic cost of their present arrangements', according to early behavioral economics lines of reasoning by the UK Ministry of Transport, 1977). The difficulty with this line of argument, and possibly one of the main reasons the system was never implemented, is that the administrators, in making their allocation, may misperceive the priorities and needs of the consignor.

On the more central issue of service provision, it has been suggested that without directed coordination it is often impossible or prohibitively wasteful for many of the wider goals to be fully achieved. Direct income transfers, for example, may rectify differences in the spending power of households, but it is often a subgroup within a household (for example, housewives) whom one is trying to assist, and direct transfers may not reach them. Further, with so many operators in the transport market, there are suggestions that technical coordination of services would be less efficient (for example, bus services would not act as local distributors to trunk rail services). Private firms may not be willing to undertake substantial capital projects because, unlike government, they cannot spread risk adequately, even where insurance markets do exist. In more simple terms, advocates of direction feel that it is likely to prove overall to be more efficient than an optimally maintained market environment.

Quite clearly, the substance of these lines of argument is likely to vary among transport sectors. It is not surprising, therefore, that in general the allocative mechanism favored for inter-urban transport (especially freight) is that of the market and of price, while intra-urban transport tends to be subjected to considerable planning and control. The widespread occurrence of externalities, the more immediate distribution issues, the interaction of an imperfect transport market with that of an imperfect land market, etc., make it difficult to remove the impedance that exists to the efficient functioning of a pure market for urban transport.

One exception, which should be noted, to the dominance of the market in allocating inter-urban resources is the public provision of roads. Here, as we have seen elsewhere, there are important differences between the way road and rail track costs are passed on to users. Comparable pricing policies are the clear market solution, but increasingly economists have taken the argument further and have suggested that both sets of tracks should be publicly owned and then users should pay on an identical basis for the services rendered – a situation that exists with parts of Sweden's rail network and one that has been actively pursued in the United Kingdom. Open access and economic charging for rail infrastructure is also part of the European Union's transport policy.

Finally, it is becoming increasingly apparent that the tools of direction or control are, in effect, so numerous, sophisticated, and subtle that the distinction between market-oriented policy and control is rapidly ceasing to be a meaningful one. By manipulating price, licensing, operating laws, and work conditions, the government is in effect directing resources and ultimately influencing the traffic patterns that evolve. The tools of policy outlined earlier are all, in effect, tools of direction, but at the same time they may operate as tools to improve the workings of the market. Would road pricing, for example, be extending the market to embrace congestion or would it be a direction of traffic? In this context, the extremes of market versus direction cease to be helpful; one moves to a rather more basic debate concerning the desirability of goals and the relative merits of different policy tools for achieving them.

References

Averch, H. and Johnson, L. (1962) Behavior of the firm under regulatory constraint, *American Economic Review*, 52, 1053–69.

Baumol, W.J. and Willig, R.D. (1986) Contestability: developments since the book, *Oxford Economic Papers*, 38, 9–36.

Baumol, W.J., Panzar, J., and Willig, J. (1982) *Contestable Markets and the Theory of Industry Structure*, Harcourt Brace Jovanovich.

Bettini, H.F.A.J. and Oliveira, A.V.M. (2008) Airline capacity setting after re-regulation: the Brazilian case in the early 2000s, *Journal of Air Transport Management*, 14, 289–92.

Bowman, A. (2015) An illusion of success: the consequences of British rail privatisation, *Accounting Forum*, 39, 51–63.

Button, K.J. (1989) The deregulation of US interstate aviation: an assessment of causes and consequences, Part 2, *Transport Reviews*, 9, 189–215.

Button, K.J. (2009) The impact of EU–US 'Open Skies' agreement on airline market structures and airline networks, *Journal of Air Transport and Management*, 15, 59–71.

Button, K.J. and Keeler, T.E. (1993) The regulation of transport markets, *Economic Journal*, 103, 1017–28.

Button, K.J. and Swann, D. (1992) Transatlantic lessons in aviation deregulation: EEC and US experiences, *Antitrust Bulletin*, 37, 207–55.

Christensen, C.M., Raynor, M.E., and McDonald, R. (2015) What is disruptive innovation? *Harvard Business Review*, December, 44–53.

Cooter, R. and Topakin, G. (1980) Political economy of a public co-operation: pricing objectives of BART, *Journal of Public Economics*, 13, 299–318.

Demsetz, H. (1968) Why regulate utilities? *Journal of Law and Economics*, 11, 55–65.

Finn, B. and Mulley, C. (2011) Urban bus services in developing countries and countries in transition: a framework for regulatory and institutional developments, *Journal of Public Transportation*, 14, 89–107.

Gwilliam, K.M. (1979) Institutions and objectives in transport policy, *Journal of Transport Economics and Policy*, 13, 11–27.

Hibbs, J. (1982) Transport without politics? Hobart Paper 95.

Keeler, T.E. (1984) Theories of regulation and the deregulation movement, *Public Choice*, 44, 103–45.

Meyer, J.R. and Tye, W.B. (1981) The regulatory transition, *American Economic Review, Papers and Proceedings*, 71, 268–72.

Moore, T.G. (1986) US airline deregulation: its effects on passengers, capital and labor, *Journal of Law and Economics*, 29, 1–28.

Morrison, S.A. (2001) Actual, adjacent, and potential competition: estimating the full effects of Southwest Airlines, *Journal of Transport Economics and Policy*, 35, 239–56.

Morrison, S.A. and Winston, C. (1995) *The Evolution of the Airline Industry*, Brookings Institution.

Newbery, D.M. (1988) Road user charges in Britain, *Economic Journal*, 90, 161–76.

Ng, C.K. and Seabright, P. (2001) Competition, privatisation and productive efficiency: Evidence from the airline industry, *Economic Journal*, 111, 591–619.

Peterson, G.S. (1930) Transport Coordination: meaning and purpose, *Journal of Political Economy*, 38, 660–81.

Raynor, M.E. (2011) Disruptive innovation: the Southwest Airlines case revisited, *Strategy and Leadership*, 39, 31–4.

Small, K.A., Winston, C., and Evans, C.A. (1989) *Road Works: A New Highway Pricing and Investment Policy*, Brookings Institution.

Spiller, P.T. (2013) Transaction cost regulation, *Journal of Economic Behavior and Organization*, 89, 232–42.

Stigler, G.J. (1971) The theory of economic regulation, *Bell Journal of Economics and Management Science*, 2, 3–19.

UK Department of Transport (1977) Transport policy, Cmnd 6845, HMSO.

Vickrey, W. (1961) Counter-speculation, auctions, and competitive sealed tenders, *Journal of Finance*, 16, 8–37.

Winston, C., Corsi, T.M., Grimm, C.M., and Evans, C.A. (1990) *The Economic Effects of Surface Freight Deregulation*, Brookings Institution.

Name index

Subject index